OXFORD
G N V Q

Intermediate BUSINESS

DAN MOYNIHAN & BRIAN TITLEY

Oxford University Press 1996

Oxford University Press, Walton Street, Oxford OX2 6DP

Oxford New York
Athens Auckland Bangkok Bombay
Calcutta Cape Town Dar es Salaam Delhi
Florence Hong Kong Istanbul Karachi
Kuala Lumpur Madras Madrid Melbourne
Mexico City Nairobi Paris Singapore
Taipei Tokyo Toronto

and associated companies in
Berlin and Ibadan

Oxford is a trademark of Oxford University Press

© Oxford University Press 1996

First published 1996

ACIP catalogue record for this book is available from the
British Library

ISBN 0 19 833553 9

Produced and Illustrated by Gecko Ltd, Bicester, Oxon

Printed and bound in Great Britain by
Butler & Tanner Ltd, Frome and London

The publishers would like to thank the following for
permission to reproduce photographs:

Ace Photo Agency/J & D Begg: p 361 left; Ace Photo
Agency/Malcolm Birkett: p 209 bottom; Ace Photo Agency/Peter
Hince: p 425; Ace Photo Agency/Mauritius: p 187 bottom; Ace
Photo Agency/Gabe Palmer: p 349; Ace Photo Agency/Eric
Pelham: p15; Birmingham Post & Mail: p 530 bottom left;
Boots The Chemist Ltd: p 292 top right; David Bradford: p 285
middle; British Aircraft Corporation: p 285 middle right; British
Petroleum: p 31 bottom right; British Steel: p 68 bottom
middle, 128 middle left: British Telecom Corporate Pictures: p
378; British Tourist Authority: p 57; Chorley & Handford p 60
bottom; Collections/Tony Myers: p 239; Collections/Anthea
Sieveking: p 368; Colman's of Norwich Archives (now Unilever
Historical Archives): p 80; Jackie Cooper Public Relations: p 86;
Cussons/Sidney Harris: p 326 top; Datawatch Corporation: p
543 top; Philip Davies: p 112 right, 128 bottom right; DHL
Worldwide Express: p 535 bottom left; Environmental Picture
Library/Martin Bond: p 68 top; Environmental Picture
Library/Paul Glendell: p 92 bottom; Environmental Picture
Library/Alan Greig: p 95; Environmental Picture Library/Doug
Perring: p 92 top; Environmental Picture Library/Chris
Westwood: p 128 bottom left; The Financial Times: p 193;
Ford Motor Services: pps 68 bottom left, 74 top left, 161
middle; Format/Brenda Prince: pps 118 left, 209 top;
Format/Mo Wilson: p 22; Greenpeace/ Dorreboon: p 27 top;
Robert Harding Picture Library: pps 100 left, 161 right, 530
top; Hewlett Packard: p 531 bottom right; Holt Studios

International/Jeff Henley: p 76 left; Chris Honeywell: p 83,
291 (milk & hairspray), 331 left, 429 bottom; IBM UK Ltd:
pps 137 left, 152; Imperial War Museum: p 285 top left; Rob
Judges: p 74 bottom right; Ander McIntyre: p 169 left; Marks
& Spencer plc: p 259 bottom; Mark Mason: p 292 top left;
Mattel Consumer Products: p 81; Archie Miles: 517 right;
National Meteorological Office/Crown Copyright: p 59 bottom;
Nissan Motor (GB) Ltd: pps 19 bottom, 33 top left, 130, 137
right, 162; North Western Museum of Science & Industry: p
127 bottom; G O'Brien: pps 410, 535 top; Outward Bound/Duke
of Edinburgh's Award: p 234; Alan Owens: pps 169 right, 242
top, 243 bottom, 311 middle; Parker Knoll: p 161 left; Photo
Reportage: p 229 right; Pictor International: p 352; P & O
Steam Navigation Company: p 89; Pontins Holiday Club: p 112
left; Popperfoto: p 292 bottom right, 313 left; Postman Pat
TM© Woodland Animations Ltd 1995: p 533; Powerstock: p
36 right; PRB/Courier Systems: p 535 bottom right; The Press
Association: p 192; Rex Features: p 313 right; J Sainsbury plc:
p 259 top; Sanyo Uk Sales Ltd: pps 75 bottom, 157 middle, 285
top right, 291 top left; The Science Museum: p 157 top; Shell
Industries: p 32 right; Martin Sookias: pps 25, 27 bottom left &
right; 31 left, 42, 53, 54, 55, 56, 60 top, 68 middle, 73 top &
bottom, 74 bottom left, top middle & middle right, 75 top, 84,
87, 93, 100 right, 114 right, 115 top, 118 right, 127 bottom left
& right, 164, 167, 211 bottom, 229 left, 230 top, 242
bottom, 261, 265, 285 bottom right & top middle, 291 all
except those mentioned elsewhere, 316, 335, 339 bottom,
351, 366, 370, 382, 402, 414, 429 top & middle, 432, 456,
493, 528, 529, 530 bottom right, 531 bottom left & top right,
532, 534 bottom right, 538, 540, 542; Sporting Pictures (UK)
Ltd: pps 231, 324 middle left, 336; ; Tony Stone Images/David
Ash: p 272 left; Tony Stone Images/Bruce Ayres: pps 236 top,
242 middle; Tony Stone Images/Oliver Benn: p 250; Tony Stone
Images/Christopher Bissell: p 292 bottom middle; Tony Stone
Images/Dan Bosler: p 225; Tony Stone Images/Tim Brown: p
272 right; Tony Stone Images/Stuart Cohen: p 292 bottom left;
Tony Stone Images/Frank Herholdt: p 241 bottom; Tony Stone
Images/Walter Hodges: p 517 left; Tony Stone Images/David
Joel: p 211 top; Tony Stone Images/John Lawler: p 236 bottom;
Tony Stone Images/Steven Peters: pps 187 top, 209 middle, 241
top; Tony Stone Images/Michael Rosenfeld: pps 33 top middle,
166; Tony Stone Images/Charles Thatcher: p 240 bottom; Tony
Stone Images/Bill Truslow: p 230 bottom; Tony Stone
Images/Terry Vine: p 361 right; Tony Stone Images/Jeff
Zanuba: p 240 top; Telegraph Colour Library: p 128 top left;
Telegraph Colour Library/ M J Horden: p 68 bottom right;
Telegraph Colour Library/J Young: p 76 right: Tesco Stores Ltd:
p 33 bottom right; Transport Research Laboratory: p 157
bottom; Unilever: p 158; Voluntary Service Overseas: p 257;
Volkswagen/Audi: p 73 middle; Volvo Car Uk Ltd: p 291 top
right; J A Whitaker: p 311 left; C M Whitaker: p 311 right;
Carl Witham: p 74 top right.

The Hairdresser photographs on pages 30 & 285 were provided
by the authors as was the photograph of Stan Laurel & Oliver
Hardy on page 262.

All other photographs courtesy of Oxford University Press

Special thanks to: Anglia Television Ltd; British Standards
Institution; British Telecom; Carlton UK Television; Federation
of Small Businesses; The Forestry Commission; Ford Motor
Services; IKEA; Investors in People; Libearty; McDonald's
Restaurants Ltd; Marks & Spencer plc; Mercedes-Benz AG,
Stuttgart, Germany; Meridian Broadcasting Ltd; Microsoft Ltd;
Puma UK; Radio City Gold; Red Dragon; Rolls Royce plc;
RSPCA; Scottish Television plc; Slazenger; Tate & Lyle; Tyne
Tees Television; Unipart; Virgin Management Ltd; Whale &
Dolphin Conservation Society; World Society for the Protection
of Animals

Contents

Preface

This book aims to provide everything that you need in order to pass the mandatory Intermediate GNVQ Business units offered by BTEC, City and Guilds and the RSA examinations boards. The book has been carefully written to match closely the 1995 GNVQ Business specifications.

The book can be used as a course text to support either a course with a high proportion of teacher/lecturer contact time or one with less contact time and more supported self-study. Students will find a large number of portfolio activities designed to generate evidence for the GNVQ Portfolio as well as numerous test questions to help prepare students for the end of unit tests. All of the activities and questions have been tried and tested by experienced GNVQ teachers and students!

As well as helping students to pass their Intermediate GNVQ with a good grade, the book has been designed to provide a thorough insight into the dynamic and exciting world of business by using a wide range of case studies and real world examples. Each chapter is packed with up to date articles and statistics in order to assist students in carrying out research and in producing coursework using up-to-date research and case studies.

The authors would like to thank the staff at NCVQ without whose consistent and prompt help in providing information this book would not have been possible. Thanks also to Jane, Sarah, Thomas and Julie for their patience and support

Dan Moynihan

Brian Titley

Introduction
for Students

About the Intermediate GNVQ Course in Business

Presenting and Analysing Data

About the Intermediate GNVQ Course in Business

The aim of the Intermediate GNVQ in Business course is to give you a wide knowledge of business, and at the same time to allow you to practise a range of vital skills which you will need for success in the world of business and enterprise. This combination of skills and business knowledge will provide you with a head start when entering employment or further and higher education.

How to demonstrate your business knowledge and skills

The Intermediate GNVQ in Business is very different from any other course you have taken so far. To do well in GNVQ, you will need to solve problems, carry out research, work with others, and show that you can plan what to do on your own when necessary. This has the advantage that your success does not depend on one final exam, but it does mean you need to work steadily throughout the course, and to use your own initiative.

In order to pass your Intermediate GNVQ Business course, you will need to provide **evidence** of the business knowledge and skills you have acquired. This means you must plan your work in order to build up a portfolio of coursework which shows you have understood each part of the course. The quality of your portfolio will determine your final grade, so it is important to:

- Plan what you intend to do in advance
- Collect and use information about business
- Check the quality of your completed work
- Keep a well organized and up-to-date portfolio

Do not expect to produce all of your evidence in the form of written coursework or reports. Some of your evidence will be in the form of records of your contribution to the work of a group of fellow students, or in the form of evidence from a workplace supervisor. Some may be presented in the form of graphs and tables, or video or audio recordings of interviews, discussions and presentations in which you have participated.

Remember that if you lose your work, you lose your evidence, and you may have to do the work all over again. You must store your work securely and safely. If possible, keep back-up copies of computer work on disk. Label your files and disks, and never leave your work in an unlocked file or cabinet.

Business and core skills units

To pass the Intermediate GNVQ in Business, it is necessary to achieve passes in:

- 4 mandatory business units

- 3 core skills units

- 2 optional business units

Some of the business units will require you to pass a test as well as providing coursework evidence in a portfolio.

Each GNVQ unit is divided up into parts called **elements**. Each element sets out the skills, business knowledge, and understanding you will need to pass your Business GNVQ.

The components of an element are:

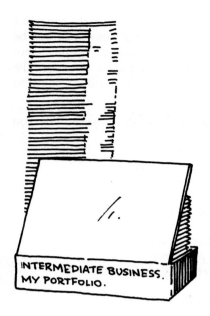

INTERMEDIATE BUSINESS.
MY PORTFOLIO.

- **Performance criteria:** These are the kinds of things that you must demonstrate that you are able to do. They are set out at the end of each chapter. For example, you must be able to describe and give examples of types of employment, explain the purposes of business organizations, and evaluate ways to send and store business documents.

- **Range:** Each unit element has a different **range** of business knowledge and skills that you are expected to learn and use – for example, 'types of employment', 'business organizations', 'purposes', 'evaluate'. You will need to show that you have mastered them in the coursework you produce for the performance criteria.

- **Evidence indicators:** These provide suggestions about the kinds of things you could do to demonstrate your achievement of the performance criteria and range for each unit element. Each chapter in this book provides you with a full range of activities to enable you to produce the right kinds of coursework to pass your Business GNVQ.

Ask your teacher for a copy of the Intermediate Business course specification. This will explain in more detail the meaning of each element and the kinds of things you will need to do in order to produce the necessary evidence. If you are not sure what an element requires you to do, always read the amplification and guidance sections for help. By doing this, you will make sure that the work you produce closely matches the Intermediate GNVQ Business specifications.

Core skills

The aim of the Intermediate GNVQ in Business is to ensure that you can be successful in business. To do this, you not only need knowledge, you also need the right practical skills. For example, you may know about the different types of business organization, but could you advise other people about the best type of business for them to start? Could you make a spoken and visual presentation of your recommendations? You may be able to describe how information technology is used in business, but could you set up and use a spreadsheet? These, and many more, are the practical skills which the Intermediate GNVQ in Business aims to develop.

In your portfolio of coursework you will need to demonstrate that you have mastered the following core skills:

Communication:
Take part in discussions
Produce written materials
Use images
Read and respond to written materials

Application of number:
Collect and record data
Tackle problems
Interpret and present data

Information technology:
Prepare information
Process information
Present information
Evaluate the use of IT

To make sure you are able to cover these core skills you should look carefully at the core skills specifications for your course. Your teacher will be able to provide you with a copy.

The core skill specifications explain exactly what you need to do to demonstrate their achievement. By looking at these before you start a coursework assignment or activity, you can plan to do things in ways that will cover the core skills. For example, in producing a report there may be opportunities to cover information technology core skills by word-processing the report, or by using a spreadsheet to produce graphs.

About this book

This book has been written specially for the new mandatory GNVQ Intermediate Business units launched in September 1995. The book is designed to contain everything that you need in order to achieve a good pass in your Intermediate Business course. It covers the requirements of the mandatory units in Business with BTEC, RSA, and The City & Guilds.

It is designed to be a **comprehensive resource**. That means it will provide you with full explanations of all the things you need to learn about business, including up-to-date business examples, activities, and coursework. The key features of the book are as follows:

✓ **Underpinning knowledge and understanding requirements** of all the mandatory units in Intermediate Business are covered in the text.

✓ **Portfolio Activities,** or coursework tasks, provide everything you need to build a complete portfolio of evidence for assessment. Each

Portfolio Activity indicates the published GNVQ range statements and the main skills you will cover by carrying out the activity.

✓ **Assessment assignments** at the end of each chapter are specially designed to help you produce evidence to demonstrate your achievement of all the performance criteria and range statements in each GNVQ element in the mandatory units. **These are photocopiable.**

✓ **Test questions** at the end of each chapter give you the opportunity to test your understanding of each element and prepare for the mandatory end-of-unit tests. **These are photocopiable.**

✓ **Keywords, wordsearches, or crosswords** at the end of each chapter. **These are photocopiable.**

The book also provides:

✓ **Practical advice** on Application of Number core skills and help in how to present data and work out averages and ranges in data you have collected

✓ Details of useful **publications** to provide you with the information and data you need to complete your studies

✓ Useful **contacts** in the business world, with details of organizations who may be able to provide you with further information and help

We very much hope that you will learn from and enjoy this book and wish you every success with your Intermediate GNVQ qualification in Business.

Dan Moynihan

Brian Titley

Presenting and Analysing Data

Presenting data

The collecting, recording, and presenting of data are important skills you will need to demonstrate in your GNVQ Intermediate business course.

Quantitative and qualitative data

Data simply refers to the information you can collect to help you study business. **Quantitative** data refers to numbers, such as £'s worth of revenues and profits, or numbers of people employed. **Qualitative** data refers to information which cannot be written as a number. For example, a customer might be asked by a business organization to rate their services as either 'very good', 'good,' 'poor,' or 'very poor.' This is useful information about how well the organization is delivering its services to customers, but it can only be written in words and not in numbers.

All the things you can collect data on are called **variables**. For example, if you were to collect figures on the sale of chocolate bars over time, the value of sales can change. They can go up, down, or stay the same: they are variable. Similarly, the number of employees working in a business will also be variable. Numbers employed may rise or fall over time, or simply stay the same. 'Numbers employed' is a variable.

Prices, levels of output, production costs, interest rates – are all variables. There are an endless number of things – or variables – you can collect quantitative data on in business.

Methods of presenting data

This section describes various ways to present quantitative or numerical data on all aspects of business. You must make sure that your portfolio of completed activities and assignments contains evidence that you have used and understood different ways to present data. However, you will not have to produce tables or graphs in your final tests.

Today, there are many computer software programs that help you to produce high-quality tables and graphs easily and quickly. You will demonstrate core skills in information technology if you use a computer to produce tables and graphs. This will include preparing data for input, editing and saving that data, and then printing it out and presenting it.

Tables

One of the easiest ways to present data is in **tables**. They are especially useful if data on a large number of different variables needs to be shown at the same time, or where numbers are needed to make calculations.

Tables are also useful for presenting information expressed in words *and* numbers. For example, Table 1 contains both words and numbers to show the number of people employed in the major industrial sectors in selected countries in 1993. Numbers in the final column for total employment can be found by adding up each row of numbers in columns 2, 3, and 4.

▼ Table 1: Employment by main sectors of business activity, 1992

All tables and graphs should have clear, easy-to-understand titles.

SELECTED COUNTRIES (IN THOUSANDS)

	Agriculture	Industry	Services	Total
United Kingdom	547	6,472	17,311	24,330
France	1,102	6,080	14,541	21,723
Germany	849	10,482	16,923	28,254
Italy	1,508	6,737	11,999	20,244
Canada	550	2,752	9,082	12,384
Japan	3,830	22,110	38,560	64,500
USA	3,257	28,694	87,355	119,306
Belgium	98	1,051	2,587	3,736
Denmark	149	724	1,742	2,615
Finland	174	548	1,309	2,031
Greece	889	1,032	1,799	3,720
Eire	154	322	638	1,114
Luxembourg	6	58	125	189
Netherlands	293	1,645	4,506	6,444
Portugal	482	1,399	2,341	4,222
Spain	1,198	3,632	6,996	11,826
Sweden	137	1,008	2,814	3,959

Always show the source of your data

Employment Gazette (Historical Supplement) October 1994

Charts and graphs

Charts and graphs can be a much better method of displaying numerical information in an easy-to-read way than tables. However, they must be accurately drawn and well presented.

The main ways of presenting data graphically are:

- Pie-charts
- Barcharts
- Scatter plots
- Line graphs

Pie-charts

Pie-charts are a popular method of presentation. They are simply circles divided up into segments to represent proportions.

Any circle (or pie) can be divided into 360 degrees which represents the total amount, or 100%, of your data. Each segment will, therefore, have an angle less than 360°. For example, if one segment is half the total, then the angle of it will be 180° (i.e. 0.5 × 360°). Similarly, a segment which is only 10% of the total will have an angle of 36° (i.e. 0.1 × 360°).

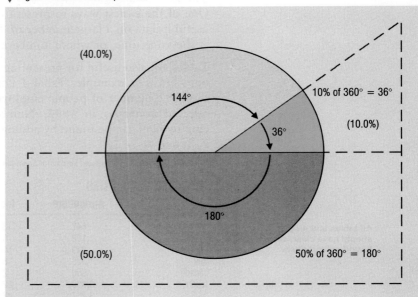

▼ Figure 1: How to draw a piechart

Using Table 1 we can draw a whole pie to represent the total number of people in employment in the UK in 1993. Each segment can then represent the proportion of all those people employed in agriculture, industry, and services. This is shown in Figure 2.

▼ Figure 2: Employment by main sectors of business activity, UK 1993

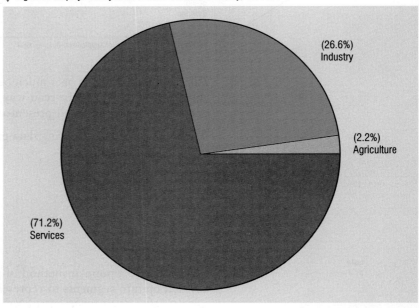

Employment Gazette (Historical Supplement) October 1994

Provide a key. Use colours or shading where possible to distinguish between different components.

Key   Employment in agriculture

       Employment in industry

       Employment in services

To calculate the angle of each segment in Figure 2 you need to use the following equation:

$$\frac{\text{Value of the individual component} \times 360^0}{\text{Total}}$$

The angle, and therefore size of each segment in Figure 2 can be calculated as follows using the figures in Table 1:

For numbers employed in agriculture:

$$\frac{547,000 \times 360^0}{24,330,000} = 8^0$$

For numbers employed in industry:

$$\frac{6,472,000 \times 360^0}{24,330,000} = 96^0$$

For numbers employed in services:

$$\frac{17,311,000 \times 360^0}{24,330,000} = 256^0$$

Bigger piecharts can show bigger totals. One almost five times as large as Figure 2 could represent the 119 million people employed in the USA.

Barcharts

Barcharts are one of the easiest methods of graphical presentation. Bars are drawn along the bottom of a pair of axes to represent the value of different variables. The vertical axis, known as the 'y' axis, gives all the possible values of your chosen variables, usually from zero upwards.

The height of each bar is proportional to the value it represents. For example, Figure 3 uses data from Table 1 to show how many people were employed in agriculture, industry, and services in Germany in 1993, with each business sector represented as a different bar.

▼ Figure 3: Employment by main sector of business activity, Germany 1993

Always label your axes with the names of the variables they show and the units they are measured in.

Keep the scale of axes simple. As far as possible, draw axes with intervals of 1, 10, 100, or 1,000, etc.

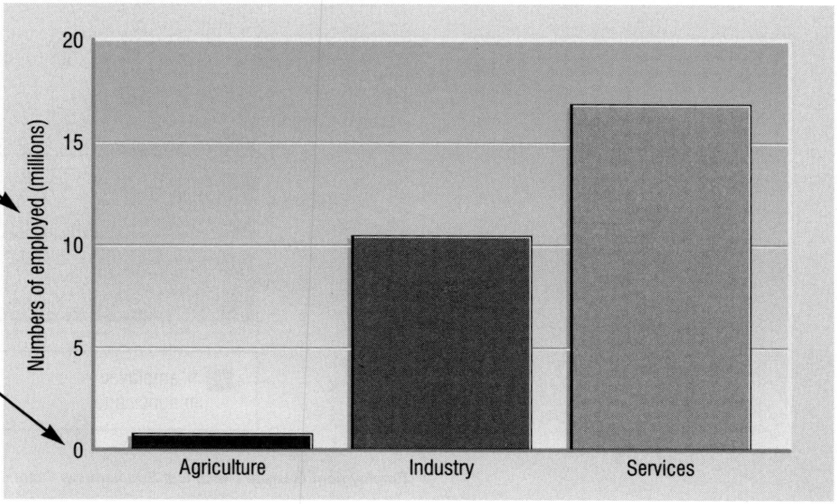

Employment Gazette (Historical Supplement) October 1994

Barcharts are usually presented vertically but can also be displayed horizontally. They can present whole numbers or percentages.

Stacked barcharts

More information can be presented in barcharts by dividing each bar into several parts. For example, Figure 4 uses data from Table 1 on employment in different business sectors for the UK, Germany, and Japan.

▼ *Figure 4: Stacked barchart of employment by main sector of business activity, selected countries 1993*

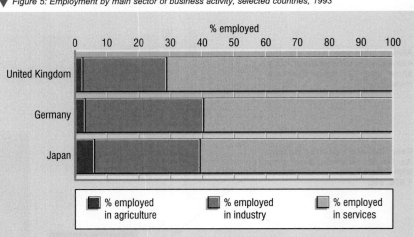

Employment Gazette (Historical Supplement) October 1994

Instead of using numbers employed, we can also use percentages. The total number of people employed in each country is now 100%, so that each parallel bar in Figure 5 is the same length. The graph shows more clearly how important services are in providing employment in Germany, Japan, and especially the UK.

▼ *Figure 5: Employment by main sector of business activity, selected countries, 1993*

Employment Gazette (Historical Supplement) October 1994

Scatter plots

These are plots of data relating one variable to another, for example, height of person by age. However, to make sense, the two variables should be related in some way. For example, it would be silly to draw a scatter plot of the amount of rainfall in different countries by the number of people employed.

In a scatter plot the values of one variable are represented along the vertical (**y**) axis and the value of the other variable along the horizontal (**x**) axis.

In the scatter plot in Figure 6, numbers employed in industry have been plotted against numbers employed in services in 1993 for the G7 countries in Table 1 (the G7 are the seven largest national economies in the developed world). Because all points lie above a 45-degree line drawn out from the origin of the graph, it shows that all these countries have more people employed in services than in manufacturing and construction industries.

▼ *Figure 6: Scatter plot of employment by main sector of business activity, selected countries 1993*

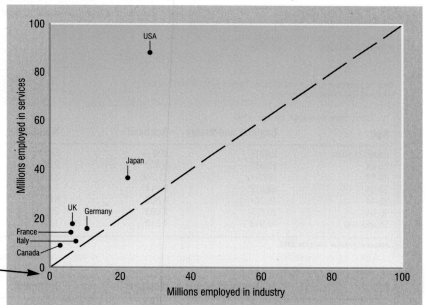

Where the axes join is called the origin.

Employment Gazette (Historical Supplement) October 1994

Line graphs

A mass of points scattered in a graph does not always tell us very much. Sometimes it is more useful to join up the scattered points to form a **line graph**. This can be used to show clearly how two variables are related.

Line graphs are most often used to plot data on the same variables collected over successive time periods – for example, each day, week, month, or year. These time intervals can be plotted along the horizontal axis, and more than one line can be shown on a graph. For example, Figure 7 shows how total UK employment in industry and services changed between 1971 and 1993.

Figure 7: Civilian employment by main sector of business activity, UK 1971-1993

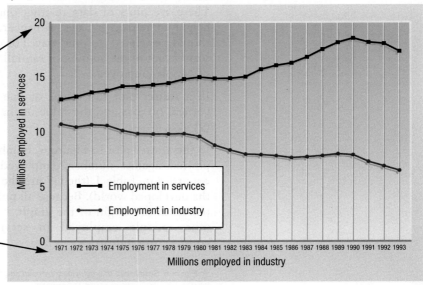

The dependent variable in a graph, for example, sales, output, employment, costs, is normally plotted against the vertical or 'y' axis.

The independent variable, for example, years, quarters, months, is normally plotted against the horizontal or x axis.

Millions employed in industry

Employment Gazette (Historical Supplement) October 1994

Portfolio Activity

Skills: Interpret and present data, Tackle problems, Process information, Present information

▼ *Table: Male marriages, by age, 1993*

Age	England and Wales	Scotland	N Ireland	United Kingdom
Under 21 years	9,471	902	388	11,031
21-24	63,932	6,870	2,568	74,458
25-29	102,942	11,266	3,726	118,255
30-34	55,012	6,214	1,436	62,470
35-44	45,364	4,803	811	51,125
45-54	20,925	2,093	282	23,290
55 and over	13,918	1,218	181	15,384

Annual Abstract of Statistics 1995

▼ *Table: Female marriages, by age 1993*

Age	England and Wales	Scotland	N Ireland	United Kingdom
Under 21 years	28,541	2,461	1,017	32,618
21-24	88,553	9,506	3,438	102,494
25-29	91,735	10,368	3,031	105,223
30-34	42,675	5,002	1,017	48,514
35-44	35,660	3,774	568	40,075
45-54	16,619	1,606	212	18,504
55 and over	7,781	649	109	8,585

Annual Abstract of Statistics 1995

1. If possible, input the data in the two tables above into a computer spreadsheet with graphics functions.

2. Choose appropriate data from the table to present in the form of a pie-chart, barchart, and line graph (use a computer to help you if possible).

3. What business organizations might find the data of use, and why?

Analysing data

Throughout your Intermediate Business course, you will collect and record a large amount of quantitative data on many different variables, such as sales volumes, output, wage levels, employment, prices, etc.

Each item of information you collect on a variable is called an **observation**. The name refers to the fact that you have observed that information. For example, imagine you collect figures on the total number of ice creams sold at a local sweetshop each week. The number sold each week is an observation. After ten weeks you will have ten observations making up your dataset. After one year, your dataset will consist of 52 observations on ice cream sales.

However, lots and lots of numbers will not tell you very much. If a large amount of data is to be of any use to you it must be organized into an easy-to-read format, such as a graph or table. It can also be very useful to summarize your data with one or more single numbers called **summary statistics**. For example, when a large amount of data has been collected, it is very useful to work out an **average value**, such as average monthly sales, the average cost per unit of output, or the average level of spending per person. It may also be useful to show the **range** in your collection of data on a variable, by showing only the highest and lowest values.

Average values

There are three ways an average value can be calculated from a set of data: the arithmetic mean, median, and mode.

The arithmetic mean

The arithmetic mean, or **mean** for short, is the measure most people think of as an average value. It can be calculated very simply by adding together all the individual values in a set of data on one variable, and dividing that sum by the total number of observations on that dataset.

So for example, imagine that you had collected the following data on sales of ice creams at your local sweetshop over the last 10 weeks.

▼ Table 2: Number of ice cream lollies sold per week in local shop

Week	1	2	3	4	5	6	7	8	9	10
Number of ice creams	39	43	38	43	46	43	97	71	52	48

The mean of the number of ice creams sold each week in Table 2 is calculated as:

$$\frac{(39 + 43 + 38 + 43 + 46 + 43 + 97 + 71 + 52 + 48)}{10} = \frac{520}{10} = 52$$

That is, on average, 52 ice creams were sold at the shop each week over the last 10 weeks. This is rather a high figure and suggests that your dataset may not be truly representative of weekly ice cream sales. This is because the mean number of ice creams sold has been affected by the very large number sold in weeks 7 and 8. These were extraordinary weeks caused by a heatwave. The arithmetic mean is, therefore, a very useful measure, but it can be affected by extreme values.

Because the mean has been distorted, it would be wrong for the sweetshop to stock enough ice creams to meet this average level of demand each week. Instead, it would be more sensible to exclude the observations on sales during weeks 7 and 8 and recalculate the mean number of ice creams sold during the other 8 weeks. This gives a figure of 44, a much more sensible figure on which to base a decision on how many ice creams to hold in stock.

The formula for calculating the mean ($\bar{x}$) is given by:

$$\bar{x} = \Sigma \frac{(x_1 + x_2 + x_3 + \dots + x_n)}{n} = \frac{\text{Sum of observations}}{\text{number of observations}}$$

where:

$\bar{x}$ is the symbol used for the mean of dataset

n is the total number of observations in a dataset

x_1, x_2, x_3, etc., are all the individual observation values in a dataset

Σ denotes the sum of all the individual observations

The median

The **median** is the value of the middle observation in a dataset. Unlike the mean, the value of the median does not depend upon the size of any other numbers. Instead the median only depends upon which number is in the middle of a group of numbers. Therefore extremely large or small 'freak' values have no effect on it.

For example, the median of 5, 10, 15, 20, 25 is 15. The median of 1, 2, 3, 4, 5, 6 is 3.5. In the first example there was an odd number of observations so finding the middle value is easy. Where there is an even number of observations, there are two middle values. You will need to add these together and divide by two to get the median value.

Arranging the weekly sales of ice creams from Table 2 in order of magnitude, we can find the median level sold each week as follows:

Weekly sales of ice cream 38   39   43   43   43   46   48   52   71   97

The middle two numbers in the dataset are 43 and 46. The median is therefore (43 + 46) ÷ 2 = 44.5

The main problem with using the median is that it ignores all other observations except those that are in the middle. For example, if the shop only held stocks to meet weekly sales of ice creams of 43, it would be totally unprepared for those periods when demand for ice creams was higher.

The mode

The **mode** is the observation value which occurs the most in a dataset. From Table 2 we can see that sales of 43 ice creams occured in three weeks out of ten. This level of sales is, therefore, called the **modal** value. The shop may use this value to indicate the number of ice creams it must stock each week, given that the chances are that weekly sales will be 43 more often than not.

The range

While it is useful to know the average of a set of data, it can also be very useful to know how the values of all the individual observations are spread around the average. That is, are individual observations widely dispersed or within a narrow range around the average?

Where observation values vary widely, the average value will not be particularly representative of the sample. For example, if a survey revealed that consumers were on average willing to pay £10 for a given product, yet over 50% of those interviewed said they were willing to pay anything up to £5 either side of the average, a firm could not be confident that setting price equal to £10 would maximize sales. If, however, the majority were willing to pay between £9.50 and £10.50 then the price of £10 would be more representative of consumers' willingness to pay.

The range is a simple measure of the spread of observation values in a dataset, calculated by subtracting the difference between the highest value and the lowest value. From Table 2 we can calculate the range in the number of ice creams sold per week by deducting 38 from 97. This gives a range in the number sold of 59.

However, because weeks 7 and 8 are not particularly representative of weekly sales in general, due to the heatwave, we could ignore them. This gives a new range of 14 between weekly sales of 38 and 52 ice creams. Like the mean, therefore, the range can be distorted by very high, or very low, values.

Now try the following activity using a computer spreadsheet to help you. Many computer software packages have functions which allow you to calculate the mean, median, mode, and/or range of a series of numbers.

Portfolio Activity

Skills: Tackle problems

Whitford Stores is a small independent supermarket. It would like to encourage repeat sales by giving regular customers discounts on their shopping bills. However, it first needs to find out how many trips a 'regular' customer makes to their supermarket. To do this it has collected the following information from customers over a one-week period. The data simply lists the number of times each customer used the store that week to make purchases.

2	2	6	1
2	2	1	1
12	3	4	3
3	4	9	2
5	2	5	4
4	4	3	4
5	3	2	3
2	2	4	9
11	5	7	1
2	1	2	1
1	2	1	2
5	1	8	3
3	1	3	10

If possible, input the above data into a spreadsheet, then undertake the following tasks:

1. Calculate the mean number of times a person visits the supermarket each week.

2. Sort the data into order from the least number of visits to the most, and then find the median number of times a person can be expected to shop at the supermarket.

3. What is the modal number of visits per customer?

4. What is the range in the dataset?

5. Use your calculations to advise Whitford Stores on how many visits a 'regular' customer could be expected to make to the store each week. Your advice should include the advantages and disadvantages of using either the mean, median, mode, or range to summarize information about visits to the supermarket.

Business Organizations and Employment

Unit One

unit 1

chapter 1 *Purposes and Types of Business Organizations*

Key ideas

Consumers are people, or other businesses, who demand goods and services to satisfy their needs and wants. **Producers** are people who provide goods and services to satisfy the needs and wants of consumers.

Production is the process of making goods and services, or **products**.

Businesses can have different **purposes**. Some aim to **increase their market share** and **improve customer services** in the hope of making as much **profit** as possible. Other organizations may not seek to make a profit and instead provide a **charitable** or **public service**.

Different types of businesses may be grouped together into **industrial sectors** according to what goods or services they produce.

Primary industries, such as farming and mining, produce natural resources.

Secondary industries, such as manufacturing and construction, use natural resources to produce goods.

Tertiary industries provide personal and commercial services.

The importance of primary industries in terms of employment and output has declined over time. More recently many workers have also lost their jobs in manufacturing industries. Services now employ over 70% of all workers in the UK and account for around 65% of total output.

Business organizations can be distinguished by how they are owned. **Public sector organizations**, such as **nationalized industries**, are owned and controlled by the government. **Private sector organizations** are owned by private individuals. These include **sole traders, partnerships, private limited companies, public limited companies, co-operatives** and **franchises**.

Most sole traders and partnerships are small in terms of the sales revenues they earn and the number of workers they employ. By comparison, public limited companies are often very large.

Owners of sole traders and partnerships have **unlimited liability**. This means they are responsible for all the debts of the business. **Shareholders** in limited companies have **limited liability** and can only lose the amount of money they invested in their firm if it goes bankrupt.

When investigating the **operation** of a particular business, it is useful to look at its location, the products it provides, its links with other organizations, the purpose of the business, its size, and its type of ownership.

Section **1.1**

The purposes of business activity

▼ *Consumers*

▼ *Producers*

What is business?

Evidence of business activity is all around us; the food we eat, the beds we sleep on, the houses we live in, the television we watch, the schools and colleges we attend, the stores we shop at, our doctors and dentists, the cars or trains we travel in – are all examples of goods and services provided by business activity. However, business activity can also create harmful air and noise pollution.

In any society, most people are both consumers and producers. **Consumers** are people, or other businesses, who demand goods and services to satisfy their needs and wants (see 2.2). For example, when we eat meat and vegetables we are satisfying our need for food. When we wear clothes and live in houses we satisfy our needs for warmth and shelter. We visit cinemas and play compact discs and computer games because we want to be entertained. When a business uses up electricity to power equipment, it is satisfying a want to produce other goods and services.

Most people go out to work to earn the money they require to buy the goods and services they and their families need and want. **Producers** are people who work to supply goods and services to satisfy the needs and wants of consumers. **Production** is, therefore, the process of making goods and services, or **products**.

Inputs and outputs

Goods and services are the **outputs** of production by firms. A **firm** is simply a business organization. All businesses are organizations in which people, working together with materials, machines, and other equipment, produce a good and/or service. For example, in the production of bread, a bakery will first need premises in which to operate. It will then require flour, sugar and salt, fridges, ovens, mixers, ladles, spoons and knives, electricity, and bakers, as well as office staff and equipment, and probably some means of transport.

Workers, materials, power supplies, machines, and other equipment are the **inputs** to productive activity. Inputs are likely to have been provided by other firms, known as **suppliers**. Thus, the bakery also consumes goods and services produced by other firms as well as producing goods for other consumers.

▼ *Firms use INPUTS such as natural resources, industrial equipment, and labour to produce OUTPUTS (goods and services)*

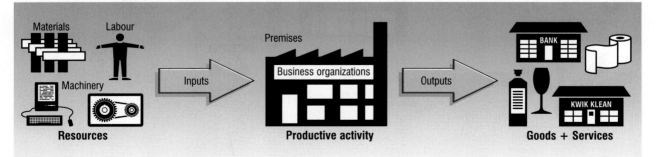

Business refers to the co-operation and organization between people and firms, their materials, buildings and machines, for the purpose of production to satisfy consumer needs and wants. There are a great many different types of business producing many millions of different goods and services for consumers in the UK and all over the world.

Production involves a chain of activity

If the aim of production is to make products to satisfy consumers' needs and wants, the process is not finished until goods and services reach the people who want them.

Production involves a **chain of productive activity** linking a number of business organizations – from those that produce natural resources such as coal, wheat, and oil, to those that use these materials to make finished goods and services, and finally to those who operate warehouses and shops to sell products to the people who want them. Every good or service will have a chain of production linking suppliers with customers.

▼ Figure 1.1: A chain of production for bread

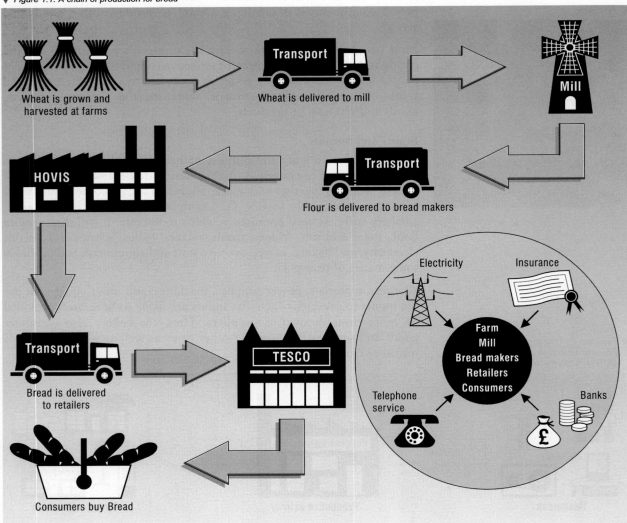

20

Portfolio Activity 1.1

PC: Explain the operation of a business organization

Range: Operation

Skills: Use images, collect and record data

1. Below is a jumble of pictures and descriptions explaining how audio compact discs (CDs) are produced.

   Work in pairs to match each picture to a description. Write down the descriptions to form a chain showing how CDs are produced, from their initial stage to their sale to consumers. Some descriptions can be used more than once.

Descriptions

1. Recording engineers record group in studio

2. Coal and oil are used to generate electricity for use by firms and households

3. Crude oil is refined

4. Shops sell CDs

5. Transport companies deliver goods and materials

6. Consumers buy CDs

7. Coal and oil are dug and drilled from the ground

8. Chemical firms use oil to produce plastics

9. Insurance firm provides insurance to protect firms from risk, damage or theft

10. Discs are pressed

11. Pipeline carries oil to oil refinery

12. Consumers play CDs

13. CDs are packed into CD cases

14. Banks provide finance for firms

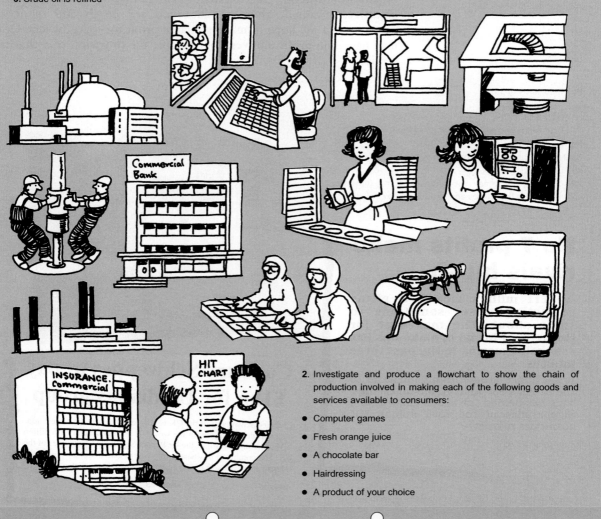

2. Investigate and produce a flowchart to show the chain of production involved in making each of the following goods and services available to consumers:

   - Computer games
   - Fresh orange juice
   - A chocolate bar
   - Hairdressing
   - A product of your choice

Let us consider the chain of production involved in producing compact discs for sale to consumers. In the earliest stages, natural resources such as coal and oil need to be extracted from the ground to power electricity stations. Oil, in turn, is the raw material used to produce plastic for CDs, which are pressed and shaped by machines. Tape recorders and sound engineers are needed to record the music of a pop group for the record. The shop is the final destination of the CD before it is bought. During this process, a great many banks have probably lent money to firms to help them complete their part of the chain. Insurance companies have been involved in case of damage or theft, and transport companies have delivered raw materials and finished goods to those business organizations that require them.

The purposes of business organizations

The main purpose of most business organizations is to produce goods and services to satisfy consumers' needs and wants. However, a business organization will only aim to satisfy needs and wants because it has other objectives in mind. Some produce and sell goods and services to consumers in the hope of making a large **profit** for their owners. Others may have **non-profit motives**, for example the provision of a **charitable service**.

Portfolio Activity 1.2

PC: Explain the purpose of business organizations
Range: Purposes
Skills: Read and respond to written material

What do you think are the purposes of the business organizations in the articles and pictures below?

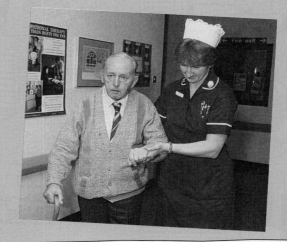

No 7 profits make rivals blush

An £11 million facelift is giving cosmetics bosses something to smile about. The makeover for Boots' No 7 brand of make-ups has sent sales soaring in the past three months.

It has added around £5 million so far to the brand's £50 million annual takings. This has helped the shops giant grab a bigger slice of the £500 million UK cosmetics market.

Daily Mirror 7.4.95

Cadbury Schweppes to pay £1bn for US drinks group

Cadbury Schweppes of the UK is poised to become the largest non-cola soft drink supplier in the world. It has bid around $1.6 billion (£1bn) to buy control of the Dr Pepper/Seven Up Companies of the US. The combined business group would gain about half of all the sales of non-cola soft drinks in the massive US market.

Adapted from The Financial Times 23.1.95

World Society for the Protection of Animals

RSPCA

libearty
The world campaign for bears

WHALE & DOLPHIN
CONSERVATION SOCIETY

British Telecom's regular customer satisfaction surveys show that British phone users have never been happier with the service they are offered, but the company is not resting on its laurels. Constant efforts are being made to improve customer service, and the facilities offered. The research and development department is working as hard as ever to find answers to more of their customers' needs.

Taken from an advertisement for British Telecom Plc

BT

Making a profit

Most firms hope to persuade consumers to buy their goods and services at a price greater than the cost of making them. Selling goods and services generates **revenue** for a business organization. **Profit** is what is left from revenues after all costs have been paid. A firm that is unable to cover its costs with enough sales revenues will make a **loss** and could be forced to close down if losses continue. It is important for a business to make a profit so that it can:

● Pay for wages, materials, rents and other bills, and have enough revenue left over to satisfy the business owners who have invested their money in the business

● Borrow money from banks and other lenders who will want to be sure the business is successful and can afford to repay them

● Use the money to buy new equipment and machinery when it becomes worn out or out-of-date

Business accounts 1996	
	£
Wages	60,000
Rent	10,000
Materials	120,000
Electricity	1,500
Telephone	500
Equipment hire	4,000

Total costs	196,000

Revenue	250,000
	======
Profit	54,000

Business accounts 1995	
	£
Wages	45,000
Rent	8,000
Materials	100,000
Electricity	2,300
Telephone	1,200
Equipment hire	10,000

Total costs	166,500

Revenue	156,000
	======
Loss	−10,500

To help a firm make a good profit from its business activities it may be necessary for it to fulfil certain other objectives.

Increasing market share

If a firm is to make a profit, it will need to persuade consumers to buy its products. The total number of people willing and able to buy a given product is said to form the **market** for that product. For example, the market for cars is made up of all the people who buy cars. Similarly, the market for oranges is made up of all the people who buy oranges. In fact, every product will have a market if consumers want it (see 2.2).

Most firms will compete for consumers with rival firms producing the same or similar goods or services. For example, Coca Cola competes with other cola drinks such as Pepsi, Virgin, and supermarket own brands. Firms will compete to increase their share of the total market.

The size of the market for any particular good or service can be measured by the total value of sales to consumers of that product. Firms, therefore, compete for a share of the total spending by consumers. **Increasing market share** is, therefore, an important objective for many firms.

Making a packet!

In 1993 consumers the world over spent a total of £1.2 billion on crisps. In the UK alone every one of us munches our way through an average of 95 bags per year at a cost of around £16 per person.

Walkers crisps are the market leader, selling around £372 million worth of crisps in 1993 – a market share of 31%. KP crisps are the second biggest selling products in the crisps market with sales of £183 million in 1993 – or 15% of the total market.

Competition between rival crisp producers is fierce. Golden Wonder saw its market share fall by 7% between 1988 and 1993. Supermarkets, on the other hand, have managed to increase their market share to around 19% by offering own label snacks at low prices.

Pringles, made by Procter and Gamble, have also been a success story. Even though they sell at a pricey £1.50, they were the fastest-growing brand in 1993 and captured 4%, or £49 million, of the total market value.

Adapted from the Daily Mirror 21.2.95

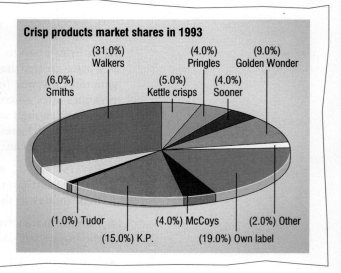

Crisp products market shares in 1993

(31.0%) Walkers
(4.0%) Pringles
(9.0%) Golden Wonder
(6.0%) Smiths
(5.0%) Kettle crisps
(4.0%) Sooner
(1.0%) Tudor
(4.0%) McCoys
(2.0%) Other
(15.0%) K.P.
(19.0%) Own label

Improving customer service

Today, simply producing a good or service to sell to consumers is not enough to persuade them to buy. Suppose you are about to buy a new video recorder costing £400. Would you go ahead if you couldn't exchange it for another one if it was faulty, or couldn't have it repaired if it went wrong?

Consumers need to be confident that, if they change their mind, or if the products they have purchased are not satisfactory or need to be repaired at a later date, the firm will provide refunds, exchange faulty goods, and provide or arrange repairs with the minimum of fuss. These and other customer services are vital to the success of any organization selling goods or services to consumers (see 10.2).

Customer services provided by firms will include:

- Providing information and advice on goods and services
- Giving refunds and replacements
- After-sales care
- Catering for customers with special needs, for example, by providing wheelchair ramps
- Fast and reliable delivery service

Improving these services and persuading customers that they are better than other firms will attract custom, help increase market share, and boost sales revenues and profits.

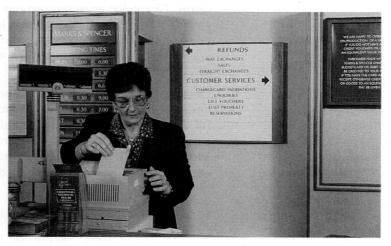

Other business objectives

Other business objectives which may help to increase profits in the long run may include:

- Improving product quality
- Developing new products
- Introducing new technology and production processes
- Expanding the size of the business
- Reducing business costs

Portfolio Activity 1.3

PC: Explain the purpose of business organizations

Range: Purposes

Skills: Tackle problems, interpret and present data, Process information

The soap powder market is dominated by two very large organizations, Procter and Gamble and Unilever. Together their many different brands account for the largest share of a market that was worth £1 billion in 1994.

1. Using the table, calculate the market share of each brand and produce a pie-chart using a computer spreadsheet to show their market shares more clearly.

2. Which soap powder was the market leader and who is it made by?

3. Investigate the various ways in which producers of soap powders can attempt to increase the market share of their products.

Brand	Value of sales in 1994
Daz	£104 million
Fairy	£46 million
Radion	£26 million
Lux	£10 million
Dreft	£11 million
Bold	£86 million
Persil	£273 million
Ariel	£267 million
Surf	£12 million
Supermarket own brands	£149 million
Other	£16 million

Not-for-profit motives

Providing a charitable service

A number of business organizations belong to what is called the **voluntary sector**. Charitable organizations rely on donations of money ('voluntary income') to provide help and care for people and animals in need and other deserving causes. Charities can also raise money by holding special events, such as fêtes and sponsored walks, or even by selling goods, such as T-shirts and Christmas cards.

Organizations like Greenpeace, Libearty, Oxfam, and the British Heart Foundation do not aim to make a profit from their productive activities. All the money received by these and other charities is used to cover the cost of their operations, from day-to-day management and administration, advertising to attract donations, and ultimately – and most importantly – to provide the goods and services to those they aim to help.

▼ Table 1.1: Income of selected charities, UK 1992-93

	TOTAL INCOME	VOLUNTARY INCOME
	£ million	£ million
Save the Children	99.6	70.4
National Trust	132.4	65.2
Oxfam	73.3	53.3
Imperial Cancer Research Fund	53.0	47.5
Barnados	75.5	34.5
Salvation Army	64.5	31.4
Help the Aged	33.2	29.0
British Heart Foundation	42.1	25.7
WWF UK	19.0	15.0

Social Trends 1994

The charitable organization

There are over 170,000 charities in Britain, all of which have **trust status**. This means a person, or group of persons, are appointed as trustees to look after their funds and other assets, such as premises and equipment.

Charities are normally exempt from the payment of tax. The Registrar of Charities therefore exercises careful control on the types of activity that can be registered as charities. This is to prevent corrupt business organizations or individuals from setting up bogus charities in order to avoid paying tax on their incomes.

▼ *Greenpeace – working to protect the environment*

A charitable trust can be set up for the following reasons:

● To help the poor in the UK and overseas, for example, Save the Children and Oxfam

● To advance education, for example, a voluntary aided school or public school

● For religious purposes, for example, to restore or maintain an old church

● To protect and conserve the environment and animals, for example, Greenpeace and the RSPCA

Although charities do not exist to make a profit, they must be organized and run just like any other business organization. They will be interested in generating as much revenue as they can from donations and other sources, to pay for the service they provide to those in need, and they must try to keep their costs as low as possible. They need good managers and workers, and must keep detailed financial records.

Charities can go bankrupt if their income is less than their costs, and they can be closed down if it is found that trustees have misused money – for example, by using it for non-charitable purposes.

Providing a public service

Unlike firms that exist to make a profit, a number of organizations provide goods and services which it is felt everyone should benefit from, regardless of their ability to pay. State education, the National Health Service, the police and fire service, the army and navy, coastguards and street lighting, are all examples of **public services**. Instead of being paid for directly by consumers, these public services are paid for by money raised by the government in taxes (see 1.4).

▼ *Street lights and schools provide a public service*

Mission statements

Most business organizations have a **mission statement** which summarizes their main aims in business. Some examples of mission statements from well known organizations are:

The Boots Company Plc

'Our objective is to maximize the value of the company for the benefit of its shareholders. While vigorously pursuing our commercial interests we will, at all times, seek to enhance our reputation as a well managed, ethical and socially responsible company.'

The Honda Motor Car Company

'We are dedicated to supplying products of the highest efficiency at a reasonable price for worldwide customer satisfaction.'

British Airways Plc

'To be the best and most successful company in the airline industry.'

Business operations

The purpose of any course in business is to study and understand business operations. It is useful to look at and compare different business organizations in terms of:

- **The goods and services they provide:** Some firms provide goods and services for other firms, such as industrial machines or advertising services, while others provide goods and services for ordinary consumers, for example, chocolates and hairdressing (see 2.2).

- **Their size:** Business size can be measured in many different ways. For example, by how many people a firm employs, by how much revenue they earn from sales, or the total value of the buildings, machinery, and other equipment they use (i.e. the value of their capital employed). Table 1.2 lists the top five firms in the UK in 1993 in order of how much revenue they earned. It also gives information on their main products, capital employed, profits, and number of employees.

▼ *Table 1.2: Top 5 firms in the UK by revenue, 1993*

Company name	Main products	Revenue	Capital employed	Profit	No. of employees
		(£ billion)	(£ billion)	(£ billion)	
British Petroleum Plc	Oil & Gas	43.31	22.41	0.78	105,750
'Shell' Transport & Trading Company Plc	Oil & Gas	22.01	13.67	not available	not available
BAT Industries Plc	Tobacco	18.69	29.07	1.89	92,829
British Telecommunications Plc	Telecommunications	13.24	16.87	2.48	183,100
Imperial Chemical Industries Plc	Chemicals & pharmaceuticals	12.06	8.24	-0.10	117,500

From 'The Times 1000' 1994

Small, medium or large?

A firm that employs less than 30 people is usually considered small. However, a firm may be relatively small in terms of how many people it employs but still earn a lot of revenue each year.

Most small organizations in the UK have only one or relatively few owners. They are **sole traders and partnerships** (see 1.3). They tend to provide local personal services, or goods tailored to customer requirements that cannot be mass-produced.

Medium-sized organizations employ between 30-200 employees. They tend to be **private limited companies** that are able to raise money to expand their business operations by selling shares (see 1.3).

Large organizations with over 200 employees will usually be **public limited companies (Plcs)** if they are UK-based (see 1.3). However, many of the very largest organizations in the UK are foreign-owned **multinationals** operating in more than one country. They mass-produce the same products, or offer the same service to customers all over the world (see 2.1). Those based in the USA will usually have 'Corp' or 'Inc' after their names.

- **Their purpose for being in business:** Some organizations are in business to make profit. Others may provide a charitable or public service, for example, the Comic Relief charity and the National Health Service.

- **Where they are located:** Some firms will locate near to the source of their supplies. For example, a colliery will locate over coal deposits in the earth. Firms that import materials from overseas may locate near to ports with good access by road and rail. Other firms may choose to locate near to a supply of skilled labour, or to be close to their customers. For example, banks and building societies are usually found in large towns near to where people live and shop (see 2.1).

- **Their links with other organizations:** Most business organizations tend to specialize in the production of one or a handful of different goods and/or services. Most will, therefore, rely on other firms to provide the other goods and services they need to carry out their business, such as power supplies, office stationery, computer equipment, lighting, transport, banking, insurance, and much more.

Many firms also rely on other firms to be their customers. For example, producers of chocolate bars will rely on wholesalers and shops to buy their products, which they in turn sell on to their customers.

- **How they are owned:** Most business organizations are owned and managed by private individuals. These organizations are said to belong to the **private sector** of the UK and include sole traders, partnerships, limited companies and co-operatives (see 1.3). Most business organizations in the private sector aim to make a profit for their owners, although, as we have seen, a number exist to provide a charitable service.

State-owned organizations are owned and controlled by the government and belong to the **public sector** of the UK. Some public sector organizations operate for profit, but most aim to provide a cost-effective public service (see 1.4).

Because the UK has both private and public sector organizations, it is said to have a **mixed economy**. In fact, most countries have mixed economies although some, like China, have more public sector ownership than others.

Business operations – an example

Business name:	Stefan Alexander
Ownership:	Private sector partnership owned by Mario and Linda D'Andrea
	(Business start-up was funded from family savings. Salon is named after Mario and Linda's two children)
Products:	Haircutting and styling service
Purpose:	To make a profit by providing a friendly and good quality service
Size:	5 full-time employees (including Mario and Linda)
	1 part-time employee
	1 apprentice hairdresser
Annual revenue 1994:	= £60,000 approximately
Location:	Motspur Park, Surrey
	Reasons for choice of location include:
	Near large residential area
	Premises were affordable
	Only one other hairdresser close by
	Owner was familiar with area
	Good schools in area for Mario and Linda's children
Links with other organizations:	Commercial estate agent helped to find suitable premises
	Brother's building firm decorated and fitted out the premises
	Shampoos and other haircare products supplied by Goldwell Ltd and Capital Hair and Beauty Trade Warehouse
	Electricity from South Eastern Electricity Plc
	Telephone service from British Telecom Plc
	End of year accounts prepared by local self-employed accountant
	Government-sponsored apprentice trainee hairdresser supplied by Pruners College
	Council Tax paid to Royal Borough of Kingston-Upon-Thames
	Water supplied by Thames Water
	Income tax paid to Inland Revenue
	Customs and Excise department collects VAT receipts

Portfolio Activity 1.4

PC: Explain the operation of business organizations

Range: Operation

Skills: Collect and record data, Produce written material

Investigate a local business organization of your choice and, with the co-operation of the owner(s) or manager(s), produce a written record of the business operations, similar to that for 'Stefan Alexander' above.

Section **1.2** **Types of business activity**

What is an industry?

Business activities are often classified by grouping together firms producing the same goods or services into industries. An **industry** consists of all those firms producing the same good or service. For example, the construction industry consists of all those firms engaged in building homes, offices, shops, factories, roads, hospitals, or even small garages or patios. The oil and gas industry consists of firms like Esso, BP, and British Gas that extract and sell fossil fuels. The retailing industry consists of firms that operate shops, mail order catalogues, home shopping channels on TV, and outlets through which consumers can buy products.

UK Industries

The **British Standard Industrial Classification (SIC)** groups industries into 17 groups based on broadly common business activities.

Broad structure of SIC (1992)

Section	Description
A	Agriculture, hunting, and forestry
B	Fishing
C	Mining and quarrying
D	Manufacturing
E	Electricity, gas, and water supply
F	Construction
G	Wholesale and retail trade; motor vehicle repair, motorcycles, personal and household goods
H	Hotels and restaurants
I	Transport, storage, and communication
J	Financial intermediation
K	Real estate, renting, and business activities
L	Public administration and defence; compulsory social security
M	Education
N	Health and social work
O	Other community, social, and personal service activities
P	Private households with employed persons
Q	Extra-territorial organizations and bodies

Industrial sectors

Because there are so many different types of industry it is often useful to divide them up into three broad **industrial sectors**, or groupings.

The primary sector

The primary sector consists of firms which produce natural resources by growing plants, like wheat and barley, digging for minerals like coal or copper, or breeding animals. Primary firms are grouped into **primary industries**.

Primary means these industries are the first stage in most production chains, as many of the raw materials grown or dug out of the ground are used to produce something else. Primary industries are sometimes called **extractive industries**, because they extract natural resources from the earth.

Some primary industries
Farming
Fishing
Mining
Quarrying
Oil and gas extraction
Forestry

The secondary sector

Secondary firms use natural resources provided by primary industries to make other goods. For example, a dairy will take milk provided by a farm and turn it into cheese and yoghurt. Iron ore is turned into iron and steel. Oil is refined into petrol and other fuels, and is also used in paints and plastics. Oil, coal, and gas are used to produce electricity.

Using raw materials to make other goods is known as **manufacturing**. Firms involved in manufacturing, and those engaged in construction, are known as **secondary industries**.

Some secondary industries

Clothing
Vehicles
Steel
Electricity
Computers
Processed foods
Furniture
Construction
Metal goods

The tertiary sector (or service sector)
A great many firms do not produce physical products but provide services instead. Firms in the service sector are grouped together as **tertiary industries**.

It is usual to divide tertiary activities into two groups:

- Firms that produce **personal services**, such as doctors, hairdressers, window cleaners, tailors, teachers, and gardeners.

- Firms that produce **commercial services** for other business organizations, such as selling goods in their shops, transporting them, business banking, finance and insurance, advertising services, and communications

Some tertiary industries

Education
Banking
Insurance
Retailing (Shops etc)
Public Administration
Leisure
Health
Distribution
Advertising
Transport

Because retailing – selling goods and services to final consumers – is such an important commercial service on which other firms rely, people often make the mistake of thinking that tertiary industries provide the final link in the chain of production for most goods and services. In fact, retailing is only one of many tertiary industries. Without a great many other commercial services like banking and insurance, transport or advertising, many primary, secondary, and other tertiary firms would find it very difficult to produce anything at all.

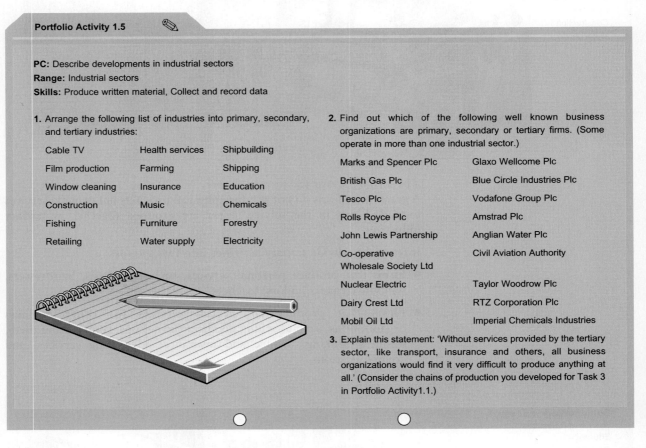

Portfolio Activity 1.5

PC: Describe developments in industrial sectors
Range: Industrial sectors
Skills: Produce written material, Collect and record data

1. Arrange the following list of industries into primary, secondary, and tertiary industries:

Cable TV	Health services	Shipbuilding
Film production	Farming	Shipping
Window cleaning	Insurance	Education
Construction	Music	Chemicals
Fishing	Furniture	Forestry
Retailing	Water supply	Electricity

2. Find out which of the following well known business organizations are primary, secondary or tertiary firms. (Some operate in more than one industrial sector.)

Marks and Spencer Plc	Glaxo Wellcome Plc
British Gas Plc	Blue Circle Industries Plc
Tesco Plc	Vodafone Group Plc
Rolls Royce Plc	Amstrad Plc
John Lewis Partnership	Anglian Water Plc
Co-operative Wholesale Society Ltd	Civil Aviation Authority
Nuclear Electric	Taylor Woodrow Plc
Dairy Crest Ltd	RTZ Corporation Plc
Mobil Oil Ltd	Imperial Chemicals Industries

3. Explain this statement: 'Without services provided by the tertiary sector, like transport, insurance and others, all business organizations would find it very difficult to produce anything at all.' (Consider the chains of production you developed for Task 3 in Portfolio Activity 1.1.)

Developments in industrial sectors

Significant changes have taken place in the industrial make-up of the UK over time. We can examine these changes in terms of the number of people employed and the amount of output from each of the major industrial sectors.

Figures 1.2 and 1.3 show how the proportion of total employment and total output accounted for by each sector has changed since 1971.

The decline of the primary sector

Many years ago, most people in the UK relied on farming and other primary industries, such as coal and tin mining, for jobs and incomes. Today, the picture is very different.

▼ Figure 1.2: Employment by main sector of business activity 1971-1993

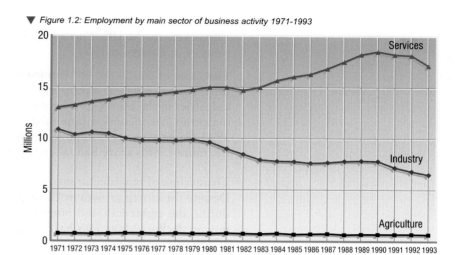

Employment Gazette (Historical Supplement) October 1994

▼ Figure 1.3: Value of output in manufacturing, as a % of total UK output 1982-1993

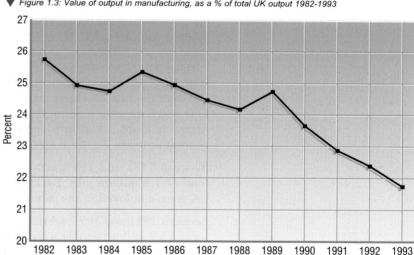

Annual Abstract of Statistics 1995

During the Industrial Revolution in the UK, which is thought to have started in 1760, millions of workers left farming and mining to get jobs in the new factories producing textiles and clothing, rolling stock for the new railways, ships, and industrial machinery.

The new manufacturing industries consumed large amounts of raw materials such as coal for power, iron and steel, wood, and rubber. An increasing amount of these raw materials were imported from cheap sources overseas.

Because an increasing number of people no longer worked the land to provide their own supply of food, there was an increase in the demand for food from workers employed in factories. Despite the falling number of farm workers, new farming technology and cheap food imports from overseas ensured that an ever-increasing supply of food could be provided for the growing number of manufacturing workers in towns and cities.

By 1994 primary industries employed just 407,000 workers – just 2% of all workers in the UK. This compares to 3.8% of workers employed in primary industries in 1971.

The value of goods and services from the primary sector has grown over time, but has fallen as a proportion of the total value of output from all industries in the UK . This is because the output of secondary and tertiary industries has increased faster than output from primary industries. In 1971 primary sector output accounted for just 4% of the value of total UK output. This share had fallen slightly by 1994.

The decline of manufacturing

Despite the strong growth in UK manufacturing employment and output during the eighteenth and nineteenth centuries, this industrial sector is now in decline. Many jobs have been lost from manufacturing industries and their contribution to the total UK output of goods and services has fallen.

Between 1971 and 1994, over 4 million jobs were lost from manufacturing and construction industries in the UK (see also 3.1). Over the same period the proportion of the total value of UK output provided by these industries fell, from 41% in 1971 to 28% in 1994.

The growth of services

With the rapid growth in the incomes and wealth of many workers in the UK over the last 70 years, many people have been taking more leisure time and have used more of their money to spend on consumer services. Many millions of people now work in shops, offices, transport, communications, financial services, and other tertiary sector jobs.

Between 1971 and 1981, services like banking and insurance created a total of 1.8 million jobs. By 1981, around 61% of all employees in the UK were employed in the service sector.

Between 1981 and 1994, services created another 2 million jobs. By 1994, some 15.7 million people were employed by the service sector – around 73% of all UK employees (see 3.2). The service sector now produces around 68% of the total value of UK output, up from 55% in 1971.

▼ *Declining*

▼ *Growing*

Portfolio Activity 1.6

PC: Describe developments in industrial sectors
Range: Developments
Skills: Read and respond to written material

1. Below is a jumbled group of reasons for the rapid increase in the importance of the tertiary sector in the UK and other developed countries. Match up each reason for growth with its possible effect on the service sector in the economy.

Reasons for growth

- Rise in consumers' incomes, allowing them to spend more on luxury goods, e.g. TVs, videos, cars

- Increase in peoples' savings as incomes have risen

- Increase in number of tourists, as people can afford to travel more

- Increase in number of people wanting to own their own home

- Reduction in the number of hours many people work each week (the average working week of full-time employees in the UK in 1994 was 36.4 hours)

Impacts on service sector

- More solicitors, building societies, estate agents, and insurance services

- Increase in demand for leisure activities and leisure centres

- Increase in number of large shops and shopping centres

- More holiday shops, restaurants, and hotels

- Increase in banking and financial services

2. What evidence is there of growth in the service sector in your local town? Conduct a local business survey using business telephone directories, and from your own observations. Your local authority, Chamber of Commerce, and Training and Enterprise Council (TEC, or LEC in Scotland) may also provide useful information.

Deindustrialization

The shift experienced in the UK and many other developed countries, away from manufacturing and towards the service sector for jobs and output, is called **deindustrialization**.

Primary	Secondary	Tertiary
Declining:	**Declining:**	**Growing:**
Agriculture	Iron and steel	Financial and business services
Coal mining	Shipbuilding	Education
Fishing	Motor vehicles	Medical services
Water supply	Machine tools	Communications
Quarrying	Textiles Construction	Catering

Deindustrialization in the UK has meant:

- The number of jobs in manufacturing has fallen steadily through time

- The output of manufactured goods has fallen compared to the total output of all goods and services produced in the UK

- The UK share in the output of manufactured goods from all over the world has fallen

- The UK now spends more on foreign manufactured goods **(imports)** than it earns from selling its own manufactured goods to foreign countries **(exports)**

What has caused deindustrialization in the UK?

A number of reasons have been suggested for the decline of manufacturing industry in the UK and many other developed countries:

- The biggest decline in manufacturing has been in old traditional industries such as textiles, shipbuilding, and motor vehicles. Rising incomes have allowed consumers to spend an increasing amount of money on leisure and other services.

- Old traditional industries have suffered increased competition from business organizations in newly industrialized countries overseas, such as Japan, and now China, Malaysia, and Taiwan, where wages, and therefore product prices, tend to be lower.

- A number of UK firms have closed down and moved their operations to newly industrialized countries, like China and Malaysia in South East Asia, because wages there are so much cheaper there yet the quality of work is good.

- As people have become wealthier, they have demanded more personal services such as banking, property and car insurance, financial and legal advice, and improved communications.

What does the future hold?

It is difficult to predict what will happen to the industrial sectors of the UK in the future, but a number of trends seem likely:

● Continued growth in services

● Technological advance in services and manufacturing, which will make production rely more on machinery and equipment and less on workers

● Workers will need to update and change their work skills to keep pace with the new technology

● High unemployment, especially among older manufacturing workers

Between 1984 and 1994, the total number of people in work or looking for work (i.e. the total workforce) in the UK increased from 27.3 million to 27.9 million (see Table 3.1). Although the number of jobs in services increased at the same time, there were not enough jobs for everyone looking for work, including those people who had lost their jobs from manufacturing industry. As a result, the number of people unemployed in the UK increased.

▼ Figure 1.4: Unemployment in the UK

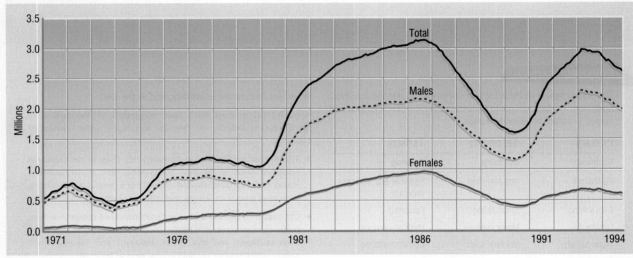

Social Trends 1995

The total number of people in the UK registered as unemployed increased from 693,000 in 1971 to over 3 million in 1985 (see Figure 1.4). Despite falling back to around 1.7 million in 1990, unemployment increased again to nearly 3 million people by 1992. That meant around 1 in every 10 workers in the UK was unemployed.

High levels of unemployment may continue as technological advance means more and more workers' jobs are replaced by machines and the skills they have become out of date. Service industries rely heavily on the use of computers and other office equipment, and do not require large numbers of employees. Just look at how workers' trades have changed over time and how they may continue to change in the future:

Prominent trades in 1900	Declining trades in the 1990s (why?...)	Growth areas in the 1990s (why?...)
Ash collectors	Air couriers (electronic mail)	Advertising (TV and Internet)
Starchers	Insurance claims assessors (computers)	Security devices and services (rising crime)
Blood driers	Bailiffs (electronic credit freezes)	Sports equipment (more leisure time)
Mourning hat band makers	Checkout staff (image recognition software)	Cable manufacturers (more TV and computer networks)
Lamp black makers	Cash register suppliers (computers)	Computer programmers
Lamplighters	Coal merchants (electricity)	Recycling (tighter controls on waste)
Ice merchants	Secretarial services (voice recognition software)	Career consultants (rising unemployment)
Soot merchants	Layout artists (computer templates)	Dating agencies (less time for personal contact)
Whale oil refiners	Factory cleaning (intelligent robots)	Telemarketing (wider access to consumers)
Saddlers	Typewriter manufacturers (word processors)	Stress managers (pressures of everyday life and work)
Livery stable keepers	Draughting equipment makers (computer aided design)	Cruise companies (rising incomes, business travel)
Soap makers	Notaries and commissioners of oaths in courts (video recordings)	
	Film processors (video and digital technology)	

Adapted from the New Scientist 16.4.94

UK industry and jobs are also facing increasing competition from firms overseas, especially from developing countries like China, Malaysia, and Taiwan, where output is high but wages remain very low. Firms in these countries are, therefore, able to produce similar goods and services to UK firms but at a much lower cost and final price to consumers.

A number of people have argued that the only way for UK manufacturing to recover is to concentrate on making high-quality products which many foreign countries are unable to produce. Successful UK examples of using this strategy include Rolls Royce cars and some of the silverware firms in the Midlands producing high-quality cutlery.

Portfolio Activity 1.7

PC: Describe developments in industrial sectors

Range: Developments

Skills: Read and respond to written material, Produce written material

1. What does the article suggest is happening to employment in car manufacturing?

2. What are the causes of these changes in employment?

3. What kind of industrial sectors might these unemployed workers look at when searching for new jobs? What problems might they find when looking for jobs in other sectors?

4. What evidence is there of the decline of manufacturing industries in your area? (For example, how many manufacturing firms are located in your area? How many people do they employ? How many have closed down recently? How many job vacancies exist in local newspapers and job centres for manufacturing firms?)

The Throwaway Workforce

You could call it 'junk labour'. This seems a good description for what could develop into one of the most important changes at work since Ford started the moving production line 80 years ago.

For the first time, large firms are saying that their workers should not expect to have a job past middle age. This is because when technology and new ways of doing things are developed, older workers may be too difficult to train and so will need to be replaced. Well educated young people, straight from school are easier to train for high technology production lines. Young workers are also cheap.

The Chairman of Fiat Cars says he 'fears' for the future of any car worker aged over 40. Fiat is opening a new car factory in Italy. The factory will cost £1.5 billion and will be built using the latest technology. The average age for all the Fiat workforce is 45. The average age for workers in the new factory will be just 26. The firm is taking on workers with no previous experience in car production. Some experts say that these workers will have a short working life, being replaced by other young workers when more new technology is introduced in the future.

Some experts say that in future, there may be no factory workers at all. This is because of the introduction of robot-based car plants around the world. These are cutting employment opportunities for both managers and workers.

London Evening Standard 11.10.93

Section **1.3** ## Private sector business organizations

Starting a business

People who start up and run business organizations are known as **entrepreneurs**. They are the people who take the risks and decisions necessary to organize production and make a firm run successfully.

Within each industrial sector in the UK there are a wide range of different types of business organization that can be started by private individuals, from small one-person businesses to huge multinational firms. Walk down your local high street or browse through a local business phone directory and you will see many examples of each type of business.

▼ Figure 1.5: Types of private sector business organization

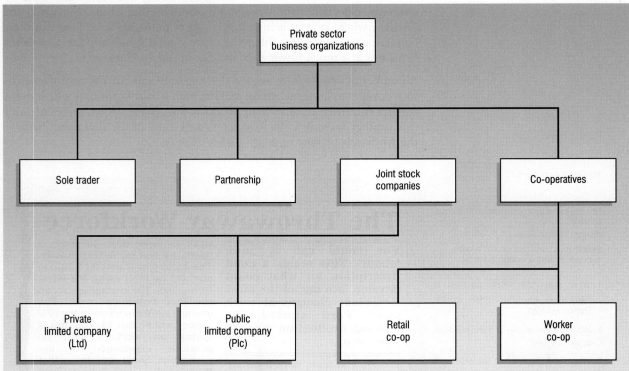

Each type of business organization can be distinguished from other types by considering:

- Who owns it
- Whether owners will have to repay any business debts
- Who controls the organization from day to day
- How the business is financed
- Who gets the profits

▼ *Paula Smith wants to start her own business*

Some key considerations

To find out about different types of business organization and ownership, we shall follow the fortunes of a young entrepreneur called Paula Smith.

Paula is an unemployed school leaver. She is good at cooking and so she decides to set up her own catering business providing sandwiches and snacks to nearby office workers. However, before she starts up her business venture, Paula, like all entrepreneurs, must ask herself three vital questions. The answers to these questions will help her to decide which type of business is best for her.

Question 1: Will I have enough money?

To start a business an entrepreneur will need **capital**. This is the money used to finance a business. Money used to pay for premises, machinery, and other equipment is known as **fixed capital**. Money used to pay for bills, such as electricity, purchases of materials, wages, the telephone, etc., is known as **working capital**.

Some businesses will need more capital than others. If Paula cannot raise enough money herself to equip her business she may need to find other people, or **partners**, who would like to help finance her business and share in its ownership. This type of business is known as a **partnership**. If yet more money is needed, Paula might consider forming a **limited company** and selling shares in the ownership of her business to other people.

Once the business is established, it could become self-financing if Paula is able to earn enough revenue from the sale of her catering services to more than cover the cost of providing them. Paula can draw on her profits to give herself a weekly or monthly wage to live on. Any profit left over can be used to invest in her business, for example, to buy new equipment or move into larger premises. So-called **retained profits** provide a major source of finance for established firms of all types and sizes, reducing their need to take on expensive bank loans to pay for business expansion.

Small firms are the business!

Britain's 5-million-strong army of small business owners are clocking up long hours to help lift the country out of recession. A survey by Lloyds Bank reveals that 55% put in more than 50 hours a week, while almost all – 95% – worked more than the national employee average of 38 hours a week. Some 7% worked more than 70 hours each week, while over a third worked every weekend. Only one in ten never worked on Saturdays.

The findings come from the Lloyds Bank/Small Business Research Trust Small Business Management report. It shows that 39% of their time is spent producing goods or serving customers, 21% on paperwork, 15% on the phone, 11% at meetings, 8% travelling, and 6% dealing with the taxman.

Daily Mirror 9.6.93

Question 2: Can I manage the business alone?

All budding entrepreneurs, including Paula, must decide whether or not they can manage alone before choosing the type of business organization they wish to form. Running a business on your own will often require working long hours and being a 'jack of all trades'. Paula must not only be a skilled caterer, but will also need to manage the business, do the accounts, advertise, employ staff if necessary, be familiar with employment laws, pay the bills, negotiate with suppliers – and much more. Setting up in business with other people can spread the load and allow more work to be done.

Question 3: Will I risk everything I own?

As the owner of her own business, Paula is entitled to any profits she makes. However, she also has the responsibility of finding money to pay for the firm's debts if the business should fail. This financial responsibility is called the **owner's liability**.

Before starting up her business, Paula must decide if she is willing to risk all her savings and possessions if the business were to fail. The answer to this question will influence the type of business organization she chooses, because some businesses are more risky than others.

Some business owners have **unlimited liability**. This means that they are liable to pay all business debts and may have to sell their personal possessions – house, car, furniture, jewellery – to do so. Business owners will be taken to court and declared bankrupt if debts are not repaid.

However, some business owners enjoy **limited liability**. This means that they will only lose the amount of money they invested in the business if it fails. They will not have to sell personal possessions to raise money to clear business debts. This reduces the risks involved.

Types of business ownership

The sole trader

A **sole trader** is a business owned and controlled by one person. It is the oldest and most popular type of business in the UK, because it is easy to set up. Many of the largest and most successful businesses in the world started life many years ago as sole traders.

Most sole traders are small organizations in the tertiary sector selling personal services such as hairdressing, carpet cleaning, aromatherapy, painting and decorating, plumbing, and running small local shops.

Sole traders will usually dip into their own savings to start their business, or will borrow from family, friends, or a high street bank. Some may grow to employ several people or have a number of branches, but so long as there is only one owner, the business will remain a sole trader. Most sole traders employ few if any staff, and many work from home in order to save the expense of paying for premises.

▼ *A sole trader*

Sole traders can trade under their own name or a suitable trading name. The name of the business does not have to be registered, but care must be taken not to use the name of another business or one that would imply a connection with royalty or government. For example, if you were to set up a small record shop, you could not call it 'Our Price Records' or 'Royal Records'.

Portfolio Activity 1.8

PC: Explain the differences between types of business ownership

Range: Types of business ownership

Skills: Read and respond to written material

Read the article and list the advantages and disadvantages of being a sole trader:

THE LOCAL INFORMER

Serving Up SNAX!

Paula Smith is now the proud owner of 'SNAX' sandwich and coffee shop in the High Street. Paula was busy serving home-made takeaway rolls, pasta dishes and salad snacks to hungry office and shop workers from nearby when we popped in to sample her lunchtime menu. We asked her why she decided to open her own shop.

'I was unemployed for a long time,' explained Paula. 'By running my own business I am ensured a job and I get any profits – not that I've made any yet. I have to work every hour I can and run the business on my own; buying food, making sandwiches, cooking, serving, cleaning, doing the accounts. You name it, I do it.'

Starting your own business is expensive, as Paula soon discovered. 'I used most of my savings to get the business off the ground, and my bank manager supplied me with a small loan. What with the rent of the shop space, hire of machinery, insurance payments, heating and lighting bills, I have to make at least

£600 a month from the shop before I can break even. And of course if I can't, I am out of work again and left holding the debts!'

Customers can look forward to a personal and friendly atmosphere in the shop and, with a prime location near to offices in the town centre, Paula may be able to look forward to better times ahead. 'I certainly hope so,' she agreed. 'I might even be able to give other people jobs, but I will still be the boss. My own boss! I don't have to answer to anyone. Not bad, is it?'

SNAX also provides sandwiches and snacks for business functions and parties.

The advantages of a sole trader

- **The sole trader business is a very personal one.** The owner of the business will have personal contact with customers and staff. S/he will be able to find out quickly what people want and then change what the business produces to suit what customers wish to buy. Furthermore, because anybody dealing with the firm deals with the owner personally, this can encourage customers to be loyal to the business.

- **The sole trader is his/her own boss.** Because s/he is the only owner of the business, the sole trader does not have to consult anyone else before making a decision. This means that they can make decisions quickly. They can decide whether or not to expand the business, what jobs to do and when, who to employ, etc.

- **The sole trader receives all the profit.** Being your own boss means not having to share profits with anyone. This is an important advantage to most people and it explains in part why the sole trader type of business is so popular.

- **It is easy to set up a sole trader business.** Sole traders need very little capital to start up with, so it is fairly easy for one person to set up a business alone. There are also very few legal formalities to complete before starting to trade.

Disadvantages of the sole trader

- **The sole trader has unlimited liability.** Unlimited liability means that the sole trader could lose his or her possessions to pay off debts in the event of bankruptcy. Unlimited liability exists because, in the eyes of the law, the sole trader business and its owner are one and the same. So if the business owes money, its owner must pay up.

- **The sole trader has full responsibility for the business.** As the sole owner of a business, the sole trader must take all of the decisions. Most people are not good at everything, but sole traders still need to be able to manage the business, do the bookkeeping, advertising, buying and selling, and many other things. This means that the sole trader may have to work long hours and if they are ill, or go on holiday, there is no one to take over the running of the business.

- **Sole traders lack capital.** Sole traders like Paula often have to rely on using their own savings or loans from family and friends to start up their businesses. Banks are often unwilling to lend money to new small businesses, especially if the owner has little experience of business and there is a risk of failure. Banks loans are also expensive to repay once interest is added.

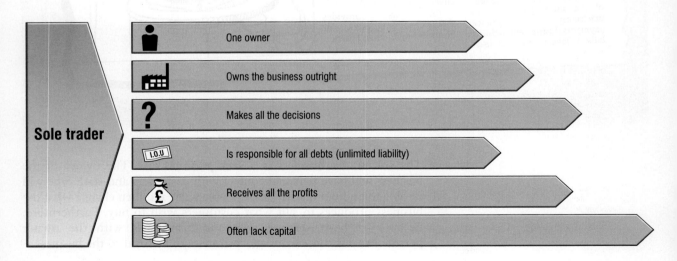

Sole trader

- One owner
- Owns the business outright
- Makes all the decisions
- Is responsible for all debts (unlimited liability)
- Receives all the profits
- Often lack capital

Partnerships

A sole trader may find it difficult to manage a business alone or raise enough money to expand. A partnership can help overcome this problem, and can be set up quite easily.

A **partnership** is a business agreement, normally between 2 to 20 people, to finance and work together in a business with the aim of making a profit. Partnerships are common in professions such as doctors, insurance brokers, and vets, although they can also be found in other occupations such as builders, garages, and in small factories. Firms of accountants, solicitors, and members of the Stock Exchange are allowed to have more than 20 partners.

Most partnerships will draw up a **deed of partnership**. This will usually contain the following information:

- How much capital each partner invested in the business
- How profits (and losses) are shared among the partners
- Rules for accepting new partners and expelling existing ones
- Rules for ending the partnership

Terms and conditions like these help partners to avoid disagreements.

Let us assume Paula Smith's business is doing well and she decides to expand SNAX. She takes on two partners, Tom and Sarah. They now own the business with Paula, help to manage it, and share in any profits. The reasons why Paula has decided to share her business are explained by the advantages of forming a partnership.

Portfolio Activity 1.9

PC: Explain the differences between types of business ownership

Range: Types of business ownership

Skills: Read and respond to written material

Read the article below and identify the advantages and disadvantages of forming a partnership.

THE LOCAL INFORMER

SNAX Bites Newtown!

Today Paula Smith, owner of SNAX, celebrates over one year's successful trading with the opening of another new shop, this time in Newtown. So what is the secret of Paula's success?

'There is clearly a market for high-quality competitively priced sandwiches and snacks for business functions and for people to take away to eat for breakfast or lunch. People seem to come back again and again. They like the variety we offer.'

Using her own money, Paula Smith acquired the premises and equipped her shop. Banks were unwilling to lend her money to expand because of the obvious risks such as an outlet faces from increasing competition from fast food chains. With giants such as McDonalds, Pizzaland and Burger King in nearly every high street, the threat of competition has become stronger. 'Luckily I have made contacts in my business dealings and have two partners now to help run and finance the business,' Paula

explained. 'Not only have they put up a large amount of money, but they will also be able to relieve me of some of the responsibilities I've carried for over a year now. For example, Tom is a qualified Chef and Sarah is an accountant by profession.'

Tom Blunt and Sarah Foster are the two new partners in the SNAX enterprise. Running a business poses many risks and the collapse of the firm could mean all those personally involved losing their possessions to repay debts. So why did Sarah take the risk ? 'It's a challenge,' she said. 'I was an accountant, but now I'm a full-time housewife and I wanted something else to keep me occupied.'

What problems, if any, do the partners think may occur? They told us that finding

the money to decorate and refit the shops is their biggest problem. 'And we all had disagreements about how to layout the two stores. But we're all friends, really,' they laughed.

Advantages of a partnership

- **Partners bring new skills and ideas to the business.** Paula has taken on Sarah and Tom as partners because they have skills which her business needs. This means that the partners can carry out a wider range of jobs than a sole trader could alone, and they can provide cover when one partner is ill or on holiday.

- **More partners means more money for the business.** If other people want to share in the ownership and control of a business then they must pay money to do so. This money can then be used to expand the business.

- **Partners can help in decision-making.** A sole trader has full responsibility for making decisions in a business, whereas in a partnership all decisions are shared.

- **Setting up a partnership is easy.** There are few legal requirements involved in setting up a partnership, although it is advisable to use a solicitor to draw up a partnership agreement.

Disadvantages of a partnership

- **Partners can disagree.** The more partners there are, the more likely are disagreements. If Paula, Sarah, and Tom find they cannot agree on important decisions affecting the company, the business will suffer.

- **Partnerships have unlimited liability.** Just like a sole trader, in an ordinary partnership, partners stand to lose everything they have if the business goes bankrupt. Furthermore, each partner is held responsible for the actions of the other partners.

It is, however, possible to have a **limited partnership** where some partners have limited liability. They are called **limited partners** or sleeping partners. Like ordinary partners, they pay money into the business in return for a share in the ownership and profits. However, they do not play a part in the day-to-day running of the business.

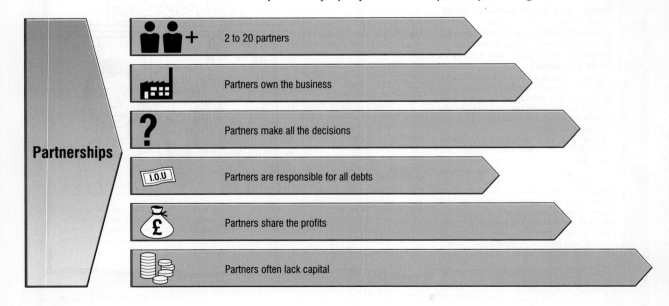

Partnerships

- 2 to 20 partners
- Partners own the business
- Partners make all the decisions
- Partners are responsible for all debts
- Partners share the profits
- Partners often lack capital

● **Partnerships lack capital.** Because there are more people in a partnership, the business will have more money than a sole trader, but it is still difficult for a partnership to have more than 20 partners (except for firms of solicitors, accountants and stockbrokers). This puts a limit on the amount of money that may be brought into the business.

None of the very large businesses in the UK, or indeed in the world, are partnerships. This is simply because no partnership could raise enough money to expand into a large enterprise. Other types of business are needed to do this. These other forms of business enterprise are known as **joint stock companies.**

Joint stock companies

Joint stock companies are also known as **limited companies.** These are companies that sell shares to investors in order to raise money.

There are two main types of limited company:

● The **private limited company** (Ltd)

● The **public limited company** (Plc)

Most of the smaller joint stock companies are private limited companies, and there are about half a million in existence in the UK at present. Public limited companies tend to be much larger in size, but fewer in number.

In order to set up a limited company the law requires that two legal documents are drawn up. These are;

● A **memorandum of association**

● The **articles of association**

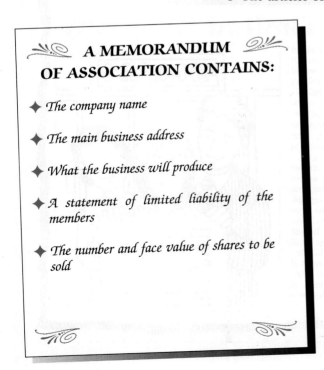

A MEMORANDUM OF ASSOCIATION CONTAINS:

✦ The company name

✦ The main business address

✦ What the business will produce

✦ A statement of limited liability of the members

✦ The number and face value of shares to be sold

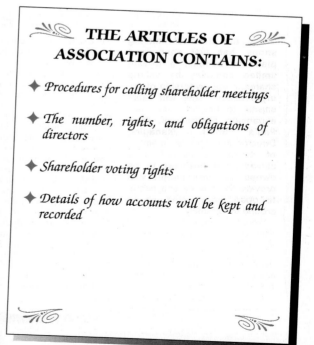

THE ARTICLES OF ASSOCIATION CONTAINS:

✦ Procedures for calling shareholder meetings

✦ The number, rights, and obligations of directors

✦ Shareholder voting rights

✦ Details of how accounts will be kept and recorded

Once these two documents have been agreed they are sent to **Companies House** – a government body that watches over limited companies. If everything is in order, the Registrar of Companies issues a **Certificate of Incorporation** which allows the company to start trading.

The private limited company

After several years of trading, the SNAX Partnership has become very successful. To build upon this success, the partnership now wants to open up a chain of shops around the country, but to do this they need a lot more money.

To raise the capital they need to expand the business, they can form a private limited company. These companies can be recognized by the letters 'Ltd' after their names, i.e. SNAX Ltd. However, forming a limited company means changing the form of ownership and control of the business, and how profits are used.

Portfolio Activity 1.10

PC: Explain the differences between types of business ownership

Range: Types of business ownership

Skills: Read and respond to written material

Read the article below;

1. How do private limited companies like SNAX raise the money they need to expand?

2. What does the word 'limited' stand for in 'private limited company'?

3. What is the name given to the people who are elected to run a private limited company?

4. Paula Smith suggests in the article that she would like to remain 'at the head of the company' and run the business from day to day. Who will decide if Paula can remain in this position, and how is this done?

5. Draw up a list of advantages and disadvantages of forming a private limited company.

THE LOCAL INFORMER

SNAX to become a Limited Company

SNAX, the chain of catering shops, has just announced plans to become a private limited company by selling shares in the ownership of the organization. This will raise capital to finance their new expansion programme. Miss Paula Smith, Managing Director and founder member of SNAX, explained how allowing the business to be owned by more people can provide the money she needs to open more SNAX shops around the country.

'We simply invite people to buy share certificates in the company,' she said, 'and this allows them to become owners of the business and share in its profits.' Shares will normally be sold to family, friends and workers in the company.

As a shareholder of SNAX, a person will also be allowed to have a say in how the company should be run. 'Of course,' Paula continued, 'I would like to remain as a director of SNAX but if all the other shareholders decide they don't want me at the head of the company, they can vote me out and elect other directors to run the business.' Each year shareholders can vote for directors at a special shareholders' meeting.

We asked Paula Smith why people would want to buy shares in her company. 'We are a growing and profitable company,' she replied. 'The more profit we make, the more shareholders receive in dividends. Also, as we are a private limited company, all shareholders will benefit from having limited liability, and so in the very unlikely event of SNAX closing down due to bad debts, shareholders would only lose, at most, the money they paid for their shares.'

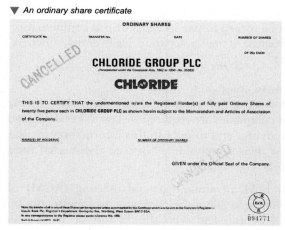

▼ *An ordinary share certificate*

ORDINARY SHARES

CERTIFICATE No.   TRANSFER No.   DATE   NUMBER OF SHARES

OF 25p EACH

CANCELLED

CHLORIDE GROUP PLC
(Incorporated under the Companies Acts, 1862 to 1890 - No. 25389)

CHLORIDE

THIS IS TO CERTIFY THAT the undermentioned is/are the Registered Holder(s) of fully paid Ordinary Shares of twenty five pence each in **CHLORIDE GROUP PLC** as shown herein subject to the Memorandum and Articles of Association of the Company.

NAME(S) OF HOLDER(S)   NUMBER OF ORDINARY SHARES

GIVEN under the Official Seal of the Company.

094771

How a private limited company raises money

Private limited companies can raise money for expansion by selling shares to people. A **share** is simply a piece of paper which states that the person who holds it has paid for part of the company and now has a share in its ownership. The value printed on a share, or its **face value**, is the price at which the company first sold the share.

If SNAX Ltd sells 10,000 shares at £1 each, then the company will receive £10,000. The people who buy these shares are called **shareholders**. The more shares a person holds, the more of the company they own, and the bigger their share of profits. The profit paid out on a share is known as a **dividend**. For example, SNAX Ltd may pay out 10 pence of their profits for every share held. Therefore, a person who owns 1,000 shares will receive total dividends worth £100 (1,000 × 10 pence).

Ownership and control

Most shareholders do not wish to become involved as owners in the daily running of their company. Instead they appoint a board of directors to run the company on a daily basis (see 6.1). This is done by voting at the shareholders' meeting.

Every company must hold an **annual general meeting (AGM)** every year. At this meeting the board of directors report on company performance during the year and the shareholders then vote on whether they wish the existing board to continue to run the business. Each shareholder gets one vote for every share they own. Shareholders with a large number of shares can vote for themselves to be a company director if they wish.

In the case of SNAX, Paula, Tom, and Sarah will only stay in charge if the other shareholders remain happy with their performance, or if they together hold 51% or more of the shares. Any person, or group of persons acting together, holding over 51% of the shares in a company is said to have a **controlling interest**. That is, they can outvote all of the other shareholders if they wish.

Advantages of a private limited company

- **Shareholders have limited liability**. A person who owns part of a limited company is only responsible for the repayment of any debts up to the value of the shares they hold. Without limited liability, people would be unwilling to buy shares, because if the company went bankrupt they would end up losing a lot of money – and even their personal possessions – to repay debts.

- **Shareholders have no management worries**. If shareholders in a company had to run the business, they would have to take on all the worries and responsibilities themselves. However, they can choose to pass on this responsibility to company directors to manage the business on their behalf.

- **The company is a separate legal entity**. In the eyes of the law, a limited company is not the same as its owners. As a result, if the company owes money, the company can be sued and taken to court, but the owners cannot. The company can be forced to pay its debts or pay compensation out of company funds because it has a separate legal entity. Owners' funds are entirely separate.

Disadvantages of private limited companies

- **Limited companies must disclose information about themselves to the general public.** All limited companies are required by law to keep detailed records of their trading activities and to publish this information in a set of **annual accounts** so that their shareholders can read about what their company is doing (see 12.1).

- **Limited companies must hold an annual general meeting (AGM) of shareholders each year.** This is to allow the company owners to vote on how the company should be run and who should run it. This is an advantage to the shareholders as it gives them a say in the running of the company, but it also means that the original owners of the company could lose control.

- **Private limited companies cannot sell their shares to the general public.** Private limited companies have to sell their shares privately to people they know, like family, friends, and employees. This is a big disadvantage because it is possible to sell many more shares, and raise far more money by advertising shares for sale to anyone who wants to buy them. This means that private limited companies are confined to being small to medium-sized firms, unable to raise vast amounts of money to expand.

Private Limited Company

- Minimum of 2 shareholders
- Shareholders own the business
- Shareholders have limited liability
- Shareholders share the profits
- Shares are sold privately
- Companies must publish accounts and hold AGMs
- Directors are elected to run the company

The public limited company

Imagine now that SNAX has become so successful that it develops plans to expand overseas into major cities around the world. To do this, Paula Smith and the other shareholders decide to form a **public limited company**. This will allow them to raise capital from the sale of shares to the general public and other business organizations in the UK and abroad.

Public limited companies are among the largest and most successful firms in the UK. Examples include such well known names as Marks and Spencers Plc, British Telecom Plc, and National Westminster Bank Plc.

Portfolio Activity 1.11

PC: Explain the differences between types of business ownership

Range: Types of business ownership

Skills: Read and respond to written material

Read the article below;

1. How do public limited companies like SNAX Plc raise finance for expansion?

2. How much money will the SNAX share issue raise?

3. Why is it easier for a Plc to raise capital than a private limited company?

4. Why are the original owners of the Plc more likely to lose their control of the company than if they were in a smaller company?

5. Draw up a list of advantages and disadvantages of forming a public limited company.

THE CITY TIMES

SNAX Attacks the Stock Market

SNAX, one of the country's leading private catering firms, has announced plans to sell shares through the Stock Exchange. The Council of the Stock Exchange revealed yesterday that the company has received a full listing which will allow it to float shares on the full stock market and become a public limited company (Plc).

'Our plans are to open a number of SNAX outlets overseas in major business capitals such as Paris, Brussels, Madrid, Frankfurt, Tokyo, and New York,' explained Tom Blunt, one of the original partners in the SNAX organization. 'This of course requires a substantial injection of cash into the company, but we feel confident that sales and profits will be extremely good.'

SNAX was formed nine years ago by Miss Paula Smith, an unemployed cook from London. The company first sold shares privately to friends and workers four years ago and has gone from strength to strength, with a sales turnover for last year topping £10 million and profits after tax of £940,000.

The new issue of two million shares at 120 pence each will be available from next month and, with dividend forecasts looking good, it is likely that the shares will be snapped up quickly by many thousands of investors.

Going public by selling shares to the general public can be expensive, but the financial rewards can be great. A major

advertising campaign in national newspapers will prepare prospective shareholders for the launch of the company onto the full stock market.

The issue of who controls the company will be discussed and subject to vote at the next AGM, where existing shareholders will be joined by many of the new shareholders. Ms Paula Smith, Ms Sarah Foster, and Mr Tom Blunt – the three original partners – are confident, however, that with their controlling interest in share ownership they can

retain their positions as company directors.

'My only fear is that the management may find it difficult to cope if the company grows too quickly or gets too big,' explained Miss Smith. 'Good managers who can run the various outlets in the company and who can work as part of a team are hard to find.'

The application list for the purchase of the shares will open on Thursday June 21st. Dealings in shares are expected to start a week later.

▼ *An advertisement for the sale of shares in McBride Plc.*

McBride plc

Share Offer

McBride is the largest manufacturer of private label household and personal care products in Europe. Private label household and personal care products are sold by retailers as an alternative to branded products. The Group's principal customers comprise many of the major European grocery retailers which sell its products under their own labels or as minor brands, including Asda, Safeway, J Sainsbury and Tesco in the U.K. and Intermarché, Leclerc and Promodes in France. Typical household products include textile washing powders, dishwash products, fabric conditioners and other cleaning products. Personal care products include shampoos, foam baths, deodorants, toothpastes and mouthwashes.

For further information on how to apply for shares in the McBride Share Offer, please call your stockbroker or one of the Share Shops listed below:

City Deal Services Limited 01708 738887	Skipton Building Society 0113 245 2888
Hargreaves Lansdown 0117 988 9977	The Share Centre Ltd 0800 800008
ShareLink Limited 0345 665665	YorkSHARE/Yorkshire Building Society 0800 736736

Sponsored by S.G.Warburg & Co. Ltd.

Advantages of a public limited company

- **Public limited companies can sell shares on the Stock Exchange.** The UK Stock Exchange is one of the largest markets in the world for the purchase and sale of shares. A Plc is able to raise money from the sale of its shares on the stock market to people all over the world.

- **A Plc can advertise the sale of shares.** The Plc can attract shareholders by placing advertisements in newspapers and on television. Private limited companies are not allowed to do this.

Disadvantages of a public limited company

- **Forming and launching a Plc is an expensive business.** Many legal documents are required. Advertisements in newspapers are needed, and a prospectus needs to be published as a pamphlet or as a spread in a newspaper.

- **The original owners of the company may lose control.** This is especially a risk where there are many shareholders. They have the right to attend annual general meetings (AGMs), to vote on company policy, and on who should be a director to manage the company from day to day.

Many Plcs have thousands of shareholders, many of whom do not have the time to attend such meetings. This is especially true of the small shareholder who has only a limited number of shares, and therefore limited voting power. Only a handful of shareholders actually use their vote, and so directors, once elected, act very much on their own. In this way, the majority of owners may lose control over their business. This is known as the **divorce of ownership from control**.

Another problem for small shareholders is the tendency for large financial institutions like pension funds and insurance companies to buy up large quantities of shares (most shares in the UK are owned by these institutions). As there is only one vote per share, small shareholders can be regularly outvoted by the large financial institutions.

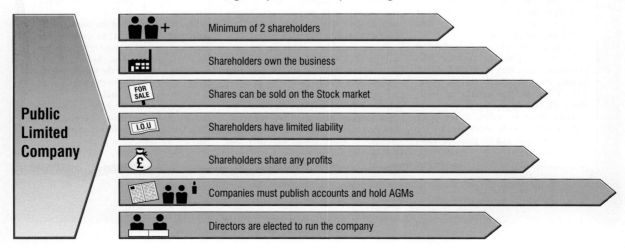

Public Limited Company

- Minimum of 2 shareholders
- Shareholders own the business
- Shares can be sold on the Stock market
- Shareholders have limited liability
- Shareholders share any profits
- Companies must publish accounts and hold AGMs
- Directors are elected to run the company

- **Some Plcs may have management problems.** Some companies may grow so large that it becomes difficult for the senior managers to control all aspects of the business effectively. The more people there are in a business, the more people there are to consult when decisions are taken. This can make decision-making slow and disagreements can occur.

Co-operatives

A **co-operative** is an organization formed by people joining together to organize production, make decisions, and share profits. All members have an equal say in running the business and share equally in the profits.

There are two main types of co-operative enterprise:

- **Worker co-operatives** are organizations which are owned by their workers, as in a farming co-operative. They pool their money to buy equipment and share equally in decision-making and any business profits. The number of worker co-operatives grew rapidly during the 1970s when many firms were closing down and making their workers unemployed. The UK government set up the **Co-operative Development Agency (CDA)** to provide advice and financial assistance to help employees to buy the firms they worked for.

There are very few worker co-operatives in the UK compared to countries like France, Spain, and Italy, where this type of business ownership is very popular.

- **Retail co-operatives** are shops run for the benefit of their customers. The first retail co-operative society was formed in 1844 when a group of workers who could not afford to pay high food prices joined together to buy food direct from wholesalers. Because they were able to buy food in bulk, suppliers would often give them discounts.

The principles of modern retail co-operatives are much the same:

- Modern co-operatives are owned by their members

- Any person can become a member by buying a share – often for as little as £1

- Members elect a board of directors to run the co-operative

- Each member is allowed one vote regardless of the number of shares they hold

- Profits are shared between members and customers

Today many of the smaller retail co-operative shops have closed because of competition with large supermarkets. To compete, a number of co-operatives have formed into larger superstores selling a wide variety of goods and services, normally located on large out-of-town sites.

The co-operative movement has also successfully expanded into other activities such as banking, insurance, travel agents, funeral services, and bakeries. The largest single retailing co-operative is the Co-operative Retail Society based in Manchester.

▼ *Retail Co-operatives*

In Time
of Need

Funeral
Pre-payment
Plan

Co-operative Funeral
Service
A Division of
Oxford & Swindon Co-operative Society

Worker co-operatives	Retail co-operatives
Workers own all the shares	Owned by its members
Managed by its workers	Managers run the organization
Workers have limited liability	Owners have limited liability
Workers share the profits	Customers and shareholders receive profits

Franchises

This form of business ownership was first introduced in the USA but is fast growing in popularity in the UK. A franchise is an agreement between two parties:

- The **franchiser** – an existing, usually well known company with an established market for its product

- The **franchisee** – a person, or group of people, who buy the right to use the business name of the franchiser and make or sell its product in a particular location. Well known examples of franchise operations include McDonalds, Sock Shop, Wimpy, Prontaprint and Pizza Hut. It is also increasingly common for smaller organizations to franchise parts of their operations. For example, your local milkman may have franchised his round from the dairy. Department stores will also franchise space within their stores to other retailers.

To buy a franchise a person, or group of entrepreneurs, will have to pay a large fee plus a percentage of their sales revenue to the parent company. In return, the parent company will often provide training, equipment, materials, advertising, and help finding premises.

Advantages of buying a franchise
- Product likely to be well known
- Franchiser will often advertise and promote the product
- Banks may be more willing to lend money to a well known franchise
- Risk of business failure is low

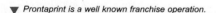
▼ *Prontaprint is a well known franchise operation.*

Disadvantages of buying a franchise
- Cost of buying franchise could be high
- A proportion of business profits are paid to the franchiser
- Franchise agreement can be withdrawn
- Role of business owners reduced to 'branch managers'. Most aspects of business will be decided by the parent company

Portfolio Activity 1.12

PC: Explain the differences between types of business ownership
Range: Types of business ownership
Skills: Produce written material

A friend has asked for your advice on buying into the franchise advertised opposite.

Write a short report using a word processor offering the following advice to your friend:

● What is a franchise?

● How a franchise works

● The advantages of buying a franchise rather than setting up a sole trader organization or partnership

● The disadvantages of buying a franchise

You can find out more about this fast growing business sector from the British Franchise Association and from *Business Franchise* magazine.

Interested in running a business with a difference, something with a massive industry and demand?
Well, Auto Aid has the answer.

We have developed and helped design a major breakthrough in repair technology and have turned a good idea into a massive money making business for the nineties, with **earnings that you would not believe.**

Our repair and renovation service is being demanded by vehicle owners, operators and insurers as well as hotels, restaurants, pubs, clubs, airlines, car hire, car leasing, in fact anyone who has any plastic or fabric — We need repair distributors to join our fast growing business in the UK

We offer the most comprehensive Mobile Repair Service available, and can supply repair systems that will repair things that you would never believe possible, they include car carpets, car dashboards, car door lining, car bumpers, car seats, three piece suites, chesterfields, leather top desks, bar counters, chairs, settees and any kind of carpet Priced at £2,350 + VAT

Call for more information 01908 217818

Portfolio Activity 1.13

PC: Explain the differences between types of business ownership
Range: Types of business ownership, differences
Skills: Produce written material

1. Below is a table listing how different types of business are owned, controlled, pay debts, raise finance, and use their profits. Copy out and complete the table by filling in the blank spaces.

2. Look around your local area and try to identify businesses that are:
   a sole traders
   b partnerships
   c private limited companies
   d public limited companies
   e co-operatives
   f franchises
   For each business try to explain why you think the type of business, and what it produces, is suited to that particular form of organization. A local phone directory would be a useful source of information.

Business Feature	Sole trader	Partnership	Private Limited Company	Public Limited Company	Worker co-operative	Retail co-operative	Franchise
Ownership				Shareholders			
Control	Run by owner						
Main source(s) of finance	Own savings/ bank loans		Selling shares to family and friends				
Liability							
Who gets profits?				Shareholders		Given to customers as stamps or lower prices	

Section **1.4**

Public sector organizations

Central and local government

The **public sector** in the UK is made up of organizations which are funded by, and responsible to, local and central government. These organizations affect our daily lives by the way in which they raise money and through the services they provide and the rules they make.

Some examples of central government services	Some examples of local government services
Major road building and maintenance	Street lighting
Tax assessment and collection	Parking enforcement
National Health Service	Refuse collection
Armed services	Libraries
Social security payments	Parks
Collection of economic and social statistics	Schools
Consumer protection	Cutting grass verges
Immigration services	Local road building and maintenance
Air traffic control	Council housing
Law and order	Housing benefits
Post office	Fire service

Local government
Local government includes:

- District councils

- County councils (regional councils in Scotland)

- London borough councils

Local voters elect council representatives to make decisions that affect their communities. Each representative is known as a **councillor** and usually represents one of the main political parties. If voters are unhappy, they will choose another set of councillors to represent them at council elections which are held every four years.

The decisions of local councils and the day-to-day running of their offices are carried out by paid employees known as **local government officers**.

Expenditure and finance
Local authorities provide public services to local businesses and communities such as education, leisure facilities, refuse collection, housing, the maintenance of local roads, and parking enforcement.

Councils raise money in a number of ways:

- Most of their money is provided by grants from central government

- Council Tax

- Charges for services, such as the use of swimming pools or leisure centres

- Rents from council houses

▼ *Town Halls are the offices of Local government*

- Proceeds from the sale of council houses and council land
- Loans

The Council Tax

The **Council Tax** was introduced on 1 April 1993 to replace the Community Charge (or 'Poll Tax'). The Council Tax is a local tax set by individual councils.

Each household receives a tax bill each year based on the value of their property. Each house or flat will have been placed in one of eight Council Tax valuation bands. Charges for each band are set each year by local councils and may differ between different areas.

In general, the higher the value of the property, the more Council Tax the household will pay. People living on their own qualify for a 25%

discount. Those on low incomes and the disabled can also claim reductions. It is usual for people to pay the tax in ten monthly instalments.

Business rates

Businesses do not pay Council Tax. Instead, they pay a tax called the **Business Rate** based on the value of business property. Business rates are collected by local authorities but paid to the central government. The central government then shares out the revenue among councils, based on the size of their local population.

Central government

Voters elect **Members of Parliament (MPs)** to form the central government to be responsible for mainly national issues. The political party with the most MPs forms the government. The Conservative Party formed the central government in the UK between 1979 and 1996. If voters are unhappy with their MP, or the government as a whole, they can vote for another representative every four to five years.

The main central government decision-making body is the **Cabinet** which normally consists of around 21 ministers headed by the Prime Minister. Each minister is appointed by the Prime Minister to be responsible for the activities of a government department.

There are around 20 central government departments, including the Department of Transport, the Department of Trade and Industry (DTi), the Treasury, and the Ministry of Defence. Each department has its own budget to spend on the provision of a range of services and has to submit these spending plans to the Treasury each year for approval.

Civil servants are employed by the central government in departments to develop and control economic, social, environmental, and foreign policies.

▼ Central government in the UK is based at the Houses of Parliament

Expenditure and finance
Central government raises money mainly from taxes. There are two main types of tax:

- **Direct taxes** on incomes and business profits
- **Indirect taxes** on goods and services, such as Value Added Tax (VAT) and customs and excise duties

Central government also raises some money from interest charged on loans, dividends on shares it owns in some public limited companies, and charges for some public services, such as post office deliveries.

The government uses the money it raises to pay for the provision of public services such as the NHS, social security, and major road-building schemes. If government spending in one year is greater than the amount raised in taxes and other revenues, the government will borrow the difference.

In 1993-94, the UK government raised £230.8 billion from taxes and other receipts, and spent a total of £283 billion (see Figure 1.6).

▼ *Figure 1.6: General government expenditure and receipts 1993-94*

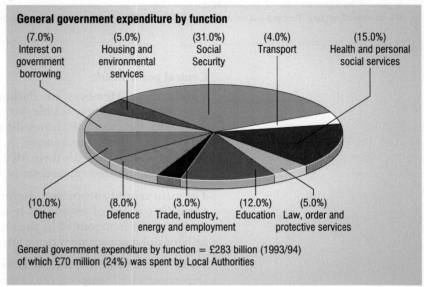

General government expenditure by function

(7.0%) Interest on government borrowing

(5.0%) Housing and environmental services

(31.0%) Social Security

(4.0%) Transport

(15.0%) Health and personal social services

(10.0%) Other

(8.0%) Defence

(3.0%) Trade, industry, energy and employment

(12.0%) Education

(5.0%) Law, order and protective services

General government expenditure by function = £283 billion (1993/94) of which £70 million (24%) was spent by Local Authorities

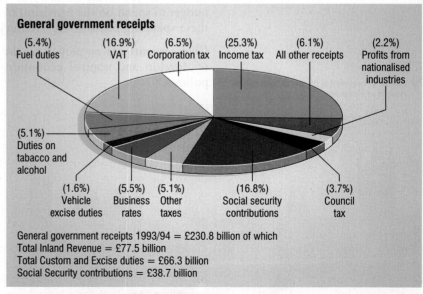

General government receipts

(5.4%) Fuel duties

(16.9%) VAT

(6.5%) Corporation tax

(25.3%) Income tax

(6.1%) All other receipts

(2.2%) Profits from nationalised industries

(5.1%) Duties on tabacco and alcohol

(1.6%) Vehicle excise duties

(5.5%) Business rates

(5.1%) Other taxes

(16.8%) Social security contributions

(3.7%) Council tax

General government receipts 1993/94 = £230.8 billion of which
Total Inland Revenue = £77.5 billion
Total Custom and Excise duties = £66.3 billion
Social Security contributions = £38.7 billion

Financial Statement and Budget Report 1994-95

PC: Explain the differences between types of business ownership
Range: Business organizations, differences
Skills: Interpret and present data

1. Look at Figure 1.6. How much did the government need to borrow in 1993-94?

2. From Figure 1.6 make a list of the sources of government revenue in order of size. Which is the most important source of revenue to the government?

3. Every year in late November the government sets out its plans for spending and raising revenue. This is known as the **Budget**. Make sure you watch or listen to the next Budget to find out about the government's plans and the reasons for them. National newspapers carry full reports of the Budget announcements the following day. Use these to write a short report explaining what taxes have gone up/down and why, how spending plans have changed, and why. Produce pie charts like those in Figure 1.6, using a computer spreadsheet for the new revenue and spending plans.

A number of organizations are under central government control. These are:

● Executive agencies

● QUANGOs

● Public corporations

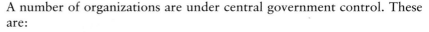

▼ *The Meteorological Office and Forestry Commission are both run by executive agencies.*

Forestry Commission

Executive agencies

A number of public services, such as the Royal Mint, prisons, the provision of statistics, passports, and benefit payments are run by **executive agencies**. These organizations are run in a business-like way with independent control over how they spend the money allocated to them each year from central government. However, agencies remain accountable to government ministers.

QUANGOS ('quasi-autonomous non-government organizations')

These are unelected government bodies run by boards of directors to manage a particular government initiative. They include regional health authorities, research councils, industrial tribunals, and Training and Enterprise Councils (TECs – see 7.3). The number of QUANGOs has increased in recent years. Being 'quasi-autonomous' means they can be run from day to day rather like a private sector business without the direct control of government officials.

Public corporations

Most **public corporations** are responsible for the day-to-day running of industries owned and controlled by central government which sell goods or services directly to consumers. These are called **nationalized industries**. Examples include the Post Office and Nuclear Electricity generation.

However, public corporations also run the Bank of England and the Civil Aviation Authority, which are not involved in trading activities, and the British Broadcasting Authority (BBC), which is neither owned by the government nor the private sector.

▼ *The Post Office and the Civil Aviation Authority are run by public corporations.*

Public corporations have a number of features in common:

- Each is controlled by a government minister. For example, the BBC is accountable to the Home Office minister, the Post Office to the President of the Board of Trade and Industry, and the Bank of England to the Chancellor of the Exchequer at the Treasury.

- Each has a board of directors who are responsible for the organization. These are appointed by the government minister responsible for the industry.

- Each has a separate legal identity from the government. This means that legal action can only be taken against a corporation and not the government.

- Each must publish an annual report and financial accounts.

- Each is financed by revenues from the sale of its services to consumers and by central government grant. (The BBC is financed by the TV licence fee set by the government each year and by revenues from the sale of programmes.)

- Public corporations do not have to make an overall profit, although they are expected to earn at least an 8% profit on the value of any new investments (this is known as the **required rate of return**). For example, if the Post Office invested £100,000 in a new post office shop, it would be required to earn at least £108,000 in revenue from it.

- Public corporations may be allowed by central government to retain all or some of any profits made to plough back into improving their services. However, the government may instead decide to use these profits to finance other public services and help reduce taxes.

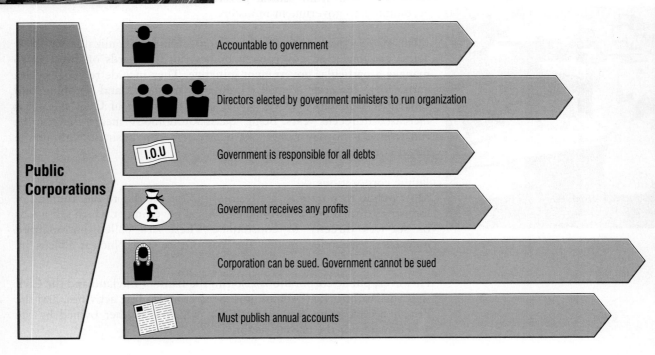

Public Corporations

- Accountable to government
- Directors elected by government ministers to run organization
- I.O.U — Government is responsible for all debts
- £ — Government receives any profits
- Corporation can be sued. Government cannot be sued
- Must publish annual accounts

Nationalization or privatization?

Nationalization refers to the transfer of an industry from private to public ownership by the passing of an Act of Parliament forcing private owners to sell their shares to the government. Between the end of the Second World War and the late 1970s, successive UK governments took over the ownership of whole industries such as coal, electricity, gas, and the railways. Each nationalized industry was run by a public corporation.

Nationalized industries 1982

British Coal	National Girobank
Electricity (England and Wales)	British Airways
N of Scotland Hydro Electric	British Airports Authority
S of Scotland Electricity	British Rail
British Gas	British Waterways
British Steel	National Bus Company
British Telecom	Scottish Transport Group
Post Office	British Shipbuilders
London Transport	Civil Aviation Authority

Why were industries nationalized?

UK governments have in the past taken entire industries into public sector ownership for the following reasons:

- **To control natural monopolies:** Some industries need to be very large in order to take full advantage of the cost savings large-scale production can bring. Sometimes this can mean that they become the only supplier of a product to a market and can take advantage of their position to charge high prices to consumers. Such **monopolies** are best controlled by government.

- **For safety:** Some industries, such as nuclear energy, are thought to be too dangerous to be controlled by private entrepreneurs.

- **To protect employment:** Some firms were nationalized because they faced closure as private sector loss-making organizations. For example, in 1975 central government rescued British Leyland to protect the jobs of car workers.

- **To maintain a public service:** Nationalized industries can provide services even if they make a loss, such as postal deliveries and rail services in rural areas. Private firms seeking to make profit would not operate these services.

Since 1979 many nationalized industries like gas, steel, electricity, and water have been returned to private sector ownership. **Privatization** refers to the sale of shares in government-owned nationalized industries to the general public and to private sector firms. The first and most significant sale was in 1984 when British Telecom was sold.

By 1995 about two-thirds of the nationalized industries of the early 1980s and more than 920,000 jobs had been transferred to the private sector. Only the following industries remained state-owned with plans to sell off parts of the railways and the nuclear electricity industry well advanced by 1995.

Nationalized industries 1995

Post Office	British Rail (passenger services)
Nuclear Electric	British shipbuilders
London Transport	Railtrack (track & signalling authority)
National Girobank	Scottish Water
Scottish Nuclear	

Those in support of privatization argue that:

- If these industries are forced to compete for profit they will become more competitive, improve their product quality and reduce prices

- Consumers will be able to choose from a wide variety of goods and services from different producers instead of just one

- The sale of shares in these industries raises revenue for the government which can be used to lower taxes

- Private individuals can own shares in these organizations and vote on how they should be run

Those against privatization argue that:

- Many privatized industries still dominate the markets they supply and have been able to raise their prices and cut services

- Private sector organizations will not protect public services. For example, it is argued by some people that the sale of franchises to private sector firms to run railway services will result in fewer services and higher fares

- Most of the shares in privatized organizations have been bought by large financial organizations such as banks and insurance companies who are only interested in making big profits

Privatization also involves allowing private sector firms to compete with public sector organizations to supply a product, or even take over the activity completely. For example, local councils now pay private sector organizations to collect rubbish rather than employing their own refuse collectors. It is likely that many executive agencies will eventually be sold off to private sector firms.

Portfolio Activity 1.15

PC: Explain the differences between types of business ownership
Range: Types of business ownership, Differences
Skills: Produce written material, Collect and record data

When a nationalized industry is privatized it becomes a public limited company. Prepare a short report to discuss how a nationalized industry differs from a Plc in terms of:

- Purposes
- Ownership
- Control

- Finance
- Use of profits
- Liability

Wherever possible use examples of real industries, such as steel, electricity, gas, telecommunications, and others which have been privatized in the UK.

Key words

In your own words, write down explanations and definitions of the following key words and terms from this chapter:

Consumers	Fixed capital	Voluntary sector	AGM
Producers	Working capital	Charity	Controlling interest
Production	Retained profits	Public service	Stock Exchange
Inputs and Outputs	Unlimited liability	Private sector	Co-operative
Products	Limited liability	Public sector	Franchise
Firms	Sole trader	Industry	Local government
Suppliers	Partnership	Primary sector/industries	Central government
Business	Sleeping partner	Secondary sector/industries	Direct taxes
Chain of production	Joint stock companies	Manufacturing	Indirect taxes
Revenue	Private limited company	Tertiary sector/industries	Public corporations
Profit/loss	Public limited company	Personal services	Nationalized industries
Market	Shareholders	Commercial services	Privatization
Market share	Dividend	Deindustrialization	Entrepreneurs
Customer services	Board of directors		

Tests and Assignment

You must demonstrate that you are able to:

1. Describe developments in industrial sectors
2. Explain the purposes of business organizations
3. Explain differences between types of business ownership
4. Explain the operation of one business organization

1 Which of the following is an example of a secondary industry?

A farming

B mining

C car manufacture

D oil drilling

2 Which of the following is an example of a tertiary industry?

A house building

B fishing

C banking

D farming

3 British Telecom is an example of:

A a public limited company

B a public corporation

C a primary sector industry

D a nationalized industry

4 What is the most likely main purpose of a sole trader grocery?

A to get well known among customers

B to sell the best quality groceries

C to make a profit for its owner

D to sell as many groceries as possible

5 What is the main purpose of a government-owned organization?

A to provide a service to the public

B to grow as quickly as possible

C to provide competition for private firms

D to make as much profit as possible

6 In which type of organization does the owner (or owners) have unlimited liability?

A sole trader

B private limited company

C public limited company

D franchise

7 A limited company is owned by:

A directors

B a public corporation

C the government

D shareholders

8 The maximum number of partners there can be in an ordinary partnership is:

A 2

B 11

C unlimited

D 20

9 Which organization is in the secondary sector of the economy?

A Midland Bank

B British Coal

C The Samaritans

D Ford Motors

10 A business where a member of the public can buy the right to use another firm's name and products is known as a:

A charity

B co-operative

C sole trader

D franchise

11 Services like the fire service, police, and ambulance service are provided for everyone. These are paid for by:

A sales revenues

B sponsorship by industry

C charitable donations

D government

12 A primary industry:

   A is the most important

   B produces natural resources

   C maximizes profit

   D uses raw materials to manufacture

13 Which of the following organizations is NOT likely to be in the public sector?

   A a sixth-form college

   B a hospital

   C a supermarket

   D a JobCentre

14 Which occupation is most likely to be in a secondary industry?

   A coal miner

   B farm labourer

   C accountant

   D chemical engineer

15 A US-owned supermarket discount store has recently opened in the UK. In the first year of operation its main business objective is likely to be:

   A gain market share

   B reduce costs

   C improve product quality

   D maximize profits

16 **a.** Explain what the following industries produce and give two examples of each type:

   ● primary industries

   ● secondary industries

   ● tertiary industries

b. Tertiary industry employment and output in most developed countries has expanded significantly over time while manufacturing industry has been in decline. Suggest and explain two possible reasons for this.

17 In 1990 Ken Webster opened a shop, 'Games, Games, Games', selling computer games and machines. By 1992 business was so good that he decided to open another shop. He asked his sister if she would invest her savings in his business and run the new shop as his partner.

   A What is a sole trader?

   B What were the advantages of forming the partnership for Ken?

In 1993, Ken and his sister decided to expand further by opening a chain of new shops in different towns. To raise the money, they formed a private limited company and sold shares in their business to family and friends. By 1994 Games, Games, Games Ltd had 15 shops.

   C What does the word 'limited' refer to in the company name?

   D What percentage of shares should Ken and his sister hold if they want to keep overall control of the company?

In 1995 Ken decided to franchise their business idea rather than forming a Plc in order to expand.

   E What is a Plc?

   F What is a franchise?

   G Suggest and explain two possible reasons why Ken chose to franchise rather than to form a Plc.

assessment assignment

The following assignment meets all the evidence requirements needed to fulfil all the performance criteria in element 1.1. In addition, it covers the following range points and core skills:

Range: Developments
Industrial sectors
Purposes
Business organizations
Types of business ownership
Differences
Operation

Skills: **Communication**
Produce written material
Use images
Application of number
Collect and record data
Interpret and present data
Information technology
Prepare, process and present information

Tasks

1. Write a summary describing developments in the primary, secondary, and tertiary sectors in the UK. This should include:

- Examples of typical business activities in each sector

- An explanation of the recent growth or decline in each sector

- A graph showing changes in the number of people employed in each sector over time

If possible, produce your summary using a word processor.

2. Identify **seven** business organizations, each one representing a different form of business ownership. Your chosen organizations should include at least:

- One public sector organization

- One small private sector organization

- One medium-sized private sector organization

- One large private sector organization

For each business organization you have chosen, write a brief summary covering the following information:

- The name of the organization

- Where it is located

- Public or private sector?

- The type of goods or services it provides

- The main purposes of the organization

- The type of ownership

- Who controls the organization

- Usual sources of finance

- Use of profits, if any

3. Prepare and produce a detailed written report on the operations of a business organization you are familiar with, for example, through family or friends, from a saturday or part-time job, or work experience.

Your report should discuss in detail the following information about your chosen business:

- Business name

- Types of goods and/or services it provides

- Industrial sector

- Main purposes of the organization

- Location, and reasons for the choice of location

- Size (employment, turnover, etc.)

- Type of ownership

- Usual sources of finance

- Use of profits, if any

- Links with other businesses as a supplier and a customer

Use a word processor or desktop publishing package to prepare your report. Include a title page showing the title of the project, your name, and the date the project was completed, and a contents page listing the titles and page numbers of different sections. Where appropriate, use any data collected on sales, employment levels, etc., over time to plot graphs to include in your report. Photographs of your business and products would also be useful.

chapter 2

The Location, Markets, Products, and Environment of Business

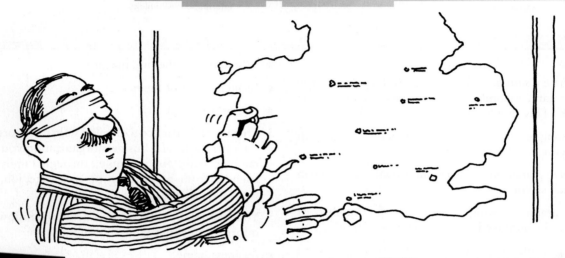

Key ideas

Businesses will seek least-cost locations for their offices, shops, or factories. They will consider how near they need to be to supplies of their **natural resources**, to their **customers**, to a supply of **labour**, to **other businesses** that may be suppliers or competitors, to good **transport services**, and whether any UK or European Union **government incentives** are available.

The location of **footloose** organizations is not greatly influenced by factors such as closeness to materials or markets. **Multinational** organizations locate their operations in many different countries.

Business organizations make **products** – goods and services – to satisfy **consumer needs and wants**. Many different products are available in modern countries for individual consumers, government, and other businesses to use.

Consumers are able to **demand** products if they are willing and able to pay for them.

Durable goods are those which last a long time, such as cars, video recorders, lawn mowers, and jewellery. **Consumable goods** tend to be used up quickly, such as foods, drinks, paper, and washing powders.

Firms also provide **services**, such as banking, insurance, cleaning, hairdressing, nursing, advertising, and many more.

All goods and services are sold in **markets**. The market for a good or service is made up of all the producers who supply the products and all the people and other organizations that buy it.

If a good or service has a **domestic market**, its sale is limited to just one country, for example, a national newspaper. However, many goods and services are produced and sold all over the world in large **international markets**.

In an **expanding market**, consumer demand and product sales will be increasing. In a **contracting market** consumer demand and sales will be falling.

To find out what consumers want, business organizations use **market research**. This involves gathering and analysing information about markets for goods and services, often through the use of **questionnaires** to interview consumers.

On the basis of market research information, firms may change their existing products, prices, and promotions, or produce new products to meet changing consumer demands. **Product design** and **production** are important business activities.

Firms will use **marketing communications** such as advertising, sales literature, and sponsorship to promote their goods and services to potential consumers.

Selling products is vital to the success of most organizations. Firms who want to make a profit will need to make **sales**. Providing **after-sales services**, such as giving refunds, exchanges, or repairs, can encourage consumers to buy.

Businesses can be influenced by a number of factors beyond their control. These can include the **legal** system, which seeks to protect consumers, workers, and the environment; changes in consumer attitudes and buying habits; the actions of rival firms; and changes in the weather and other aspects of the natural environment.

Section **2.1**   **Business location**

▼ *Advertising to attract business*

SO MANY COMPANIES FIND WALES HAS SUCCESS WRITTEN ALL OVER IT.

The same thing seems to happen to companies who move to Wales.

They grow.

Multinationals like Sony, Pilkington, British Airways, Bosch, Toyota and a host of smaller companies are all now bigger companies.

It happens for a combination of reasons.

The development opportunities in Wales, the first class communications, the skilled, adaptable workforce, and the advice and assistance of the

THE WELSH ADVANTAGE

Welsh Development Agency.

Move to Wales and we'll do everything to help your company grow.

To find out how we can help your business grow in Wales, post or fax your business card to us on 01222 345615 at the International Division, Welsh Development Agency, Pearl House, Greyfriars Road, Cardiff, CF1 3XX, UK.

Alternatively you can telephone our Customer Services Team on 01222 828820.

Choosing the right location for a business can mean the difference between success or failure. There is no such thing as a perfect site for a factory, office, or shop, but some locations are clearly better than others.

Sometimes firms have only a limited amount of choice about where to locate. For example, establishing a shipbuilders inland and many miles from the sea is not a good idea. A coal mine can only locate where there are coal deposits. An international airport will need a lot of land and should be away from residential areas, although not so far away that people are unwilling to travel to it.

However, for most business organizations the major concern is cost. The cost of establishing a new business, either by moving into existing premises or building new ones, can be very high. In general, any firm will attempt to choose a location that offers the least disadvantages and the most advantages at the lowest possible cost.

▼ *Some businesses have to be located in particular places.*

Business location – the deciding factors

More than 300 international companies were asked to give their priorities when choosing locations for their business operations. The results, on a scale from 0 to 10, were:

Availability and quality of telephone and fax lines	8.5
A stable political situation	7.9
Cheap labour costs	7.8
Reliable power supply	7.5
Closeness to market	7.3
Healthy economy	7.2
A stable social climate	7.2
Availability of skilled workers	7.0

Financial Times 11.10.93

Portfolio Activity 2.1

PC: Explain the reasons for location of businesses
Range: Reasons for location
Skill: Take part in discussions, Produce written material

In groups, consider the following plans for four new firms. Make a list of the factors that each firm should take into account before deciding upon a final location.

The supermarket

A new supermarket requires a 20-acre site with ample parking space. A wide variety of goods and services will be sold by a staff of 150 people. Restaurants and customer facilities will also be offered.

The steel plant

A large plant will occupy over 75 acres and many of the new materials will be imported from overseas. For every ton of steel produced, 4 tonnes of coal, limestone, and iron ore are required. A workforce of 300 people is required.

The motor car company

A 250-acre site of flat land is needed to accommodate a new automated car assembly plant with a proposed workforce of 450 people. Car parts will be received from other plants around the country and brought to this plant for assembly.

Cable TV station

A new cable TV company wants to find an existing office block to house its equipment and a workforce of some 150 technicians. It will need space outside the building to place satellite dishes to receive satellite TV stations, and parking space for 50 cars. The company aims to have at least 1 million households connected to the cable TV system within 3 years.

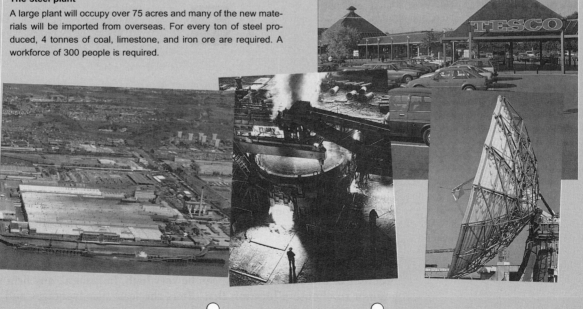

There are a large number of factors which affect the location decision of a firm. These include:

● **Taking advantage of natural factors.** Some firms may want to take advantage of natural factors such as the weather or soil conditions. For example, many fruit and vegetable producers have located in the Scilly Isles because of the early Spring. Similarly, a major port was located at Southampton on the south coast of Britain because of the size of the natural harbour and because there are four high tides each day.

● **Being near to raw materials.** Many years ago, whole industries grew up around deposits of the raw materials they used for power and to produce other goods. For example, Sheffield become an important

Market or materials?

Wherever a firm locates, it will have to pay transport costs for bringing raw materials to it or for delivering the finished products to customers. All firms must take these costs into account when choosing a location.

A firm that is **bulk reducing** may find it cheaper to locate near to suppliers of raw materials or components. This is because the raw materials or components used by a firm are bulkier and/or weigh more than the finished products. A good example of bulk-reducing production is the making of steel from iron ore. Four tonnes of iron ore, coal, and limestone rock are used to produce just one ton of steel in a blast furnace.

A firm that is **bulk increasing** may find it cheaper to locate nearer to its customers than to a source of supply. Bulk-increasing production

involves either using smaller components to assemble larger products – for example, making cars, video recorders, or furniture – or adding weight to raw materials used. For example, beer making involves adding a lot of water to hops and barley. The beer then has to be transported in bottles or barrels.

For some industries, however, transport costs are not a significant factor in their choice of location. These are called **footloose** industries. The production of new communications and computer equipment tends to be footloose because materials, components, and finished products tend to be light and easy to transport. However, many of these footloose firms have tended to locate together near to major motorways and airports, especially in the South East of England. This gives them easy access to London and international markets, and to a large supply of skilled workers.

▼ *Bulk reducing*

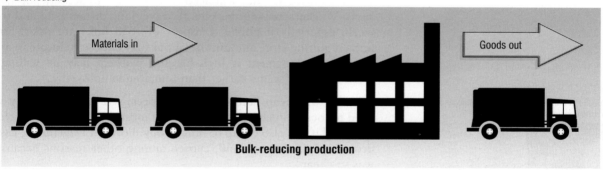

Bulk-reducing production

▼ *Bulk increasing*

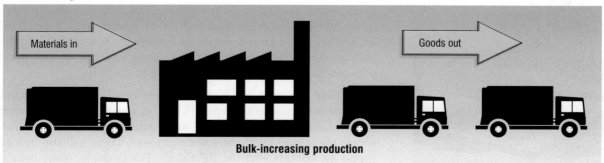

Bulk-increasing production

centre in the UK for steel production because of nearby deposits of coal, iron ore, and limestone. Old heavy industries, such as ship and locomotive engine building, also located near to coal deposits and producers of iron and steel, primarily in northern England. These materials were bulky and expensive to transport over long distances.

Today, many raw materials such as coal, iron ore, and wood are bought from overseas, and so a large number of firms are located near to major ports. The biggest port is at Rotterdam in the Netherlands. The port has giant terminals in which it stores iron ore, oil, grain, and many other commodities which are then distributed to the vast mainland European market.

- **Being near to the market.** Any firm that makes and sells goods or services will want to be within easy reach of its customers. A shop may wish to locate in or near to the shopping centre of a town. A factory may also wish to be near its point of sale because the goods made may be heavy and expensive to deliver. For example, many firms producing electrical and other parts for cars are located near the large car producers in the Midlands area of the UK.

- **Being near to transport facilities.** Transport is an important consideration for any firm. Raw materials and finished goods need to be transported cheaply and easily to wholesalers and retailers. Customers also need to be able to reach shops easily and workers need to get to their place of work. Good road and rail links can reduce the costs and time it takes to travel and to transport goods.

- **Being near to a supply of labour.** Many firms require a large and skilled workforce. They will need to locate near to densely populated areas. Workers may not be keen to travel long distances to and from work, especially if public transport or road links are poor. Some firms requiring large amounts of labour may choose to locate in areas where unemployment is high because workers may be willing to work for lower wages rather than remain unemployed.

- **Locating on cheap land or in cheap premises.** A large factory will need to locate on cheap land. Not only must this land be available, it is helpful if it is also cheap to rent or buy. Fords at Dagenham, Essex, occupies 500 acres of land, chosen among other reasons because it was so cheap.

A growing number of people are operating small businesses from home, often because it is the cheapest and most convenient option. Most home-based businesses will either manufacture products that do not require a large amount of machinery and other equipment, such as stuffed toys or dried flower arrangements, or will provide personal services such as child-minding or cleaning.

- **Being near to rival firms.** Sometimes it is an advantage for a business to locate near competing firms. This is because there are likely to be a range of suppliers, or **ancillary firms** nearby which will be able to supply the business with the parts it requires. There will also be a good supply of workers with the right skills. For example, many computer hardware and software firms in Britain locate in and around the so-called 'Silicon valley' area of Cambridge because of these advantages.

▼ Working at home is becoming increasingly popular for small business owners.

● **Government incentives.** Firms may be offered financial and other incentives, both by local and central government, to locate in areas of high unemployment in order to create jobs and incomes for local people. For example, local authorities may provide rent-free premises or reduce the business rates a firm would have to pay for a period of time. Central government also offers a range of incentives, from special grants to pay for new machinery and to help pay for worker training, to contracts to carry out government work.

Regional policy

Both the European Union and UK governments have operated a regional policy for a number of years to encourage firms to locate in areas which suffer from high unemployment and industrial decline.

Two types of **assisted area** have been identified by the UK government. These are:

● **Development Areas (DAs)**

● **Intermediate Areas (IAs)**

▼ *Figure 2.1: The Assisted Areas*

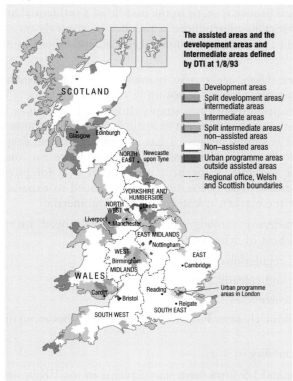

The assisted areas and the developement areas and Intermediate areas defined by DTI at 1/8/93

  Development areas
  Split development areas/ intermediate areas
  Intermediate areas
  Split intermediate areas/ non–assisted areas
  Non–assisted areas
  Urban programme areas outside assisted areas
---- Regional office, Welsh and Scottish boundaries

From 'The Enterprise Initiative' DTi, September 1993

Three forms of financial assistance are available to new and existing firms in these areas:

● **Regional Selective Assistance** consists of grants for companies of any size, primarily in manufacturing, to help pay for business expansion that will create or safeguard employment and earn a profit.

● **Regional Enterprise Grants** are for small firms of less than 25 employees. Grants will cover 15% of the cost of new plant and machinery up to a maximum of £15,000. 'Innovation' grants of 50% of the cost of new product and process development up to a maximum of £25,000, are also available.

● The **Consultancy Initiative** allows firms with less than 500 employees to claim two-thirds of the cost of hiring business consultants to provide advice on marketing, planning, finance, design, and other aspects of their business.

In addition, the government has recognized that even in regions where unemployment is low there can still be smaller areas in decline, particularly in inner cities. To help inner-city areas the government has created:

● **Inner City Task Force Areas** – Inner City Task Forces operate in around 16 run-down areas in major conurbations such as Edinburgh, Leeds, and London. They are able to provide grants and loans through **Task Force Development Funds (TFDFs)** to some small businesses.

● **Enterprise Zones** – There are around 26 of these zones earmarked for major office, factory, housing and leisure development, for example, Docklands to the east of London, Telford, and the Swansea Valley. New business locations in these zones will not have to pay business rates and will be almost free of planning controls; 100% tax allowances are also available on the construction of property within these areas.

The European Union has six main objectives for its regional policy. Areas within Europe have been identified as in need of assistance as follows;

Objective	Types of area
1	Assisting areas lagging behind, e.g. Northern Ireland, Merseyside
2	Assisting areas of industrial decline
3	Combatting long-term unemployment
4	Assisting workers to adapt to industrial change
5a	Assisting the adjustment of agricultural structures
5b	Rural development

The EU will spend £120 billion to be spent on these six areas between 1994 and 1999. Just over half will be spent in the four poorest member states: Spain, Portugal, Greece, and Ireland. The UK's allocation will total some £9.5 billion – around £3.6 billion of which will be spent on objectives 1, 2, and 5b in areas such as Northern Ireland, Merseyside, and the North East.

Tesco puts 69p wine at the end of the Chunnel

WINE was selling for almost a quarter of its British supermarket price yesterday when Tesco opened its massive cut-price liquor store in Calais, France.

The food giant, which says it lost £46 million to the cross-Channel drinks trade last year, has joined the retail exodus to France with its own range of 1,500 wines, spirits and beers.

'Customers have been coming to us to buy food and going across the Channel to buy drink since European trade barriers came down in 1993. We needed to open a store where they were going to buy the drink,' explained Tesco spokesman Steve Clarke.

Daily Mail 23.3.95

A dangerous world for business

According to a survey of international security risks, Algeria is the most dangerous place in the world in which to do business, while Syria, Botswana, Malaysia, Singapore, and Switzerland are among the safest.

Algeria, where extremists are carrying out a campaign of sabotage against foreign businesses, particularly oil and gas installations, is rated as 'high risk.' Colombia, where drug trafficking and guerrilla violence is commonplace, also ranks among the high risk countries.

The UK, where bombs have exploded in the City of London, is rated as 'medium risk' – on a level with Bangladesh, North Korea, and the Philippines. France, Germany, Poland and Hungary are considered low risk.

The Times 25.8.94

The government of the European Union (EU) operates a similar **regional policy** to encourage firms to locate and expand in deprived areas of Europe, including in the UK.

● **Planning controls.** For environmental and social reasons, firms are not allowed to locate anywhere they want. For example, it would not be particularly pleasant if a huge power station was built on a local beauty spot, or in the middle of a residential area. The government has introduced a number of controls on new development to protect environmental, social, and other business interests.

● **Other factors.** There are a great many other factors a firm will take into account when choosing a suitable location. For example, a business owner may simply choose to locate his or her business in an area they like. An existing business may choose to stay where it is simply because it has always been there, despite the fact that the original reason for locating there no longer applies – for example, to be near a source of coal for power. Staying put rather than re-locating despite a need to expand or move nearer the market, is known as **industrial inertia**.

A firm considering moving overseas will also need to take account of a host of other factors:

– Rules and regulations in foreign countries

– Language and cultural barriers

– Different currencies

– The economic climate. For example, is business booming or in a slump?

– Political stability

Many Japanese and US firms have set up plants in the UK in order to be inside the European Union (EU) area (see 7.1). The EU adds a large tax (known as a **tariff**) onto the price of goods imported from non-EU member countries. This makes imported goods expensive, so that European consumers do not buy so many of them. By producing and selling goods inside the EU, foreign firms can avoid this tariff.

Businesses that have operations located in more than one country are known as **multinationals**. These will often employ many thousands of employees and raise many billions of pounds in revenue from the sale of their goods and services. Imperial Chemicals Industries Plc (ICI) is a British-owned multinational company with business operations in more than 50 countries.

Portfolio Activity 2.3

PC: Explain the reasons for location of businesses

Range: Reasons for location

Skills: Collect and record data, Use images, Produce written materials

You and a partner want to open a small restaurant in your local area serving different dishes from around the world.

Obtain a detailed ordnance survey map and street map of your local area. On the map identify as far as possible the location of your possible suppliers, rival restaurants, and the area from which you are likely to attract customers.

Use the maps and your local knowledge to pick **three** possible sites for your new business venture. Make a list of the advantages and disadvantages of each site, and then select the 'winning' site. Write down the reasons for your final choice of location.

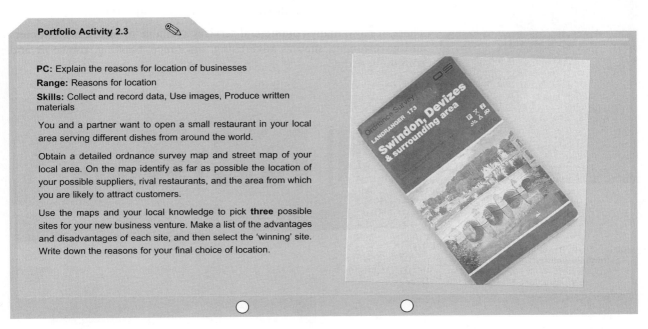

Section	2.2

Business products and markets

Once a business has moved to its chosen location, it can set about the task of organizing production. Raw materials, labour, machinery, and other equipment can be organized to produce all manner of different items in modern industrial countries. The products (goods and services) of business activity can be classified under two main headings:

Consumer goods and services

A **consumer good** is any good that satisfies consumers' wants. **Consumer durables** are goods that last a long time, for example, cars, videos, washing machines, furniture. **Non-durable goods** (sometimes called **consumables**) are goods that are used up quickly or have a relatively short life, for example, food, drink, petrol, washing powder.

Ordinary consumers also want services such as banking, insurance, hairdressing, teaching, dry-cleaning, to satisfy their many wants. These are called **consumer services**.

▼ *Consumer durables*

▼ *Industrial products*

Industrial goods and services

Some firms do not produce goods or services for ordinary consumers. Instead, they provide goods and services for other businesses and for central and local government. Ploughs, robots, power stations, computers, factory buildings, power stations, roads, juggernauts – these are all examples of industrial goods used by business organizations to help them produce and distribute other goods and services.

There are also many **commercial services** available to business consumers and government, such as advertising, insurance, banking, transport and communications.

Portfolio Activity 2.4

PC: Identify products provided by business organizations
Range: Products
Skills: Collect and record data, Produce written material

1. Look at the 3 photographs. Which retail outlet sells:

   a non-durable consumer goods

   b durable consumer goods

   c personal services ?

2. Visit examples of the types of business organizations shown in the photographs and make a list of the industrial goods they use, and what they are used for.

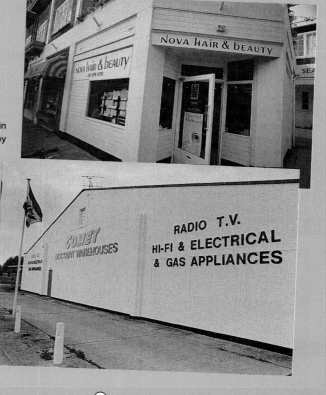

▼ *National lottery instant cards have a domestic UK market*

▼ *Compact disc players have an international market*

What is a market?

All goods or services produced by business organizations are sold in markets. A **market** is defined as consisting of all those people willing and able to buy goods and services and all those willing and able to supply them (see 1.1). For example, the market for televisions will consist of the producers of televisions and the people who buy them. Similarly, there will be a market for cars, hairdressing, video recorders, window cleaning, and all other goods and services.

For a market to exist, consumers must need or want the product that producers are willing and able to supply. If a producer makes a product nobody wants, then there is no market for that product. But if consumers want something that producers have not yet provided, then there is a clear market opportunity (see 8.1).

Types of market

Markets for most products today are made up of consumers and producers spread across very large areas. For example, the market for recorded music is international, because both consumers and producers of recorded music live and operate in many countries. Similarly, products like oil, sugar, video recorders, and insurance are sold all over the world. These goods and services have huge **international markets**.

Other markets may be in one particular country only and are called **domestic markets**. For example, the market for a local newspaper in Manchester will be confined to the immediate surrounding area. Similarly, national newspapers like the *Daily Mirror* or *The Times* are unlikely to sell very well abroad.

Sometimes the market for a product such as toothpaste is made up of many millions of individual consumers buying from just a few producers like Unilever and Procter and Gamble who together sell most brands of toothpaste. Other markets are made up of firms buying components and finished products from each other such as computer hardware components and software in order to make other products. Some markets can be very specialized – for example, the market for weapons is made up of just a small number of firms selling to governments.

Consumer needs and wants

Everyone needs a minimum of food, drink, and clothing or shelter to protect them from the elements. However, our **needs** are few compared to our **wants**. People want cars, video recorders, designer clothes, pop concerts, foreign holidays, and much more, for the pleasure they give, not because they are necessary to maintain life and ensure survival.

Business organizations can help to create wants for their products today by **advertising** (see 9.1). Advertisements use clever slogans and catch-phrases to try to persuade people to want particular goods and services.

▼ *Needs?*

▼ *Wants?*

Portfolio Activity 2.5

PC: Describe markets for businesses' products based on demand
Range: Demand
Skills: Produce written material, Present information, Collect and record data

Choose a product that most people buy, and investigate how advertising is used to create a want for it. Using a word processor, write a short report of your findings to answer the following questions:

● What forms of advertising are used?

● What messages do the advertisements use to create wants?
● What evidence is there of an increased want for the product?

To answer the last question, you may be able to obtain past sales figures from the producers of your chosen product, or perhaps from a local shop that sells it. Or simply use your own observations of the purchases made by your friends and family, or how often people repeat any slogans or jingles that may have been used in the adverts.

Demand

Businesses do not produce goods and services just to satisfy needs or wants. Their primary aim is to make a profit (see 1.1). This means they will only be willing to provide goods and services to consumers who are willing and able to pay for them.

Consumers are said to **demand** goods and services when they are willing and able to buy them. When someone wants a good or service but cannot pay for them, they are unable to demand them. Therefore, if profit-seeking producers are to supply the products that consumers demand, consumers must be able to pay for their products at a price which exceeds their costs.

Today, most people earn money to buy the things they need and want by working in one particular occupation, such as nursing, accountancy, bricklaying, company management. Very few people attempt to satisfy their own needs and wants by their own work. That is, in a modern society, most people rely on business organizations to satisfy their needs and wants.

Portfolio Activity 2.6

PC: Describe markets for businesses' products based on demand
Range: Demand
Skills: Produce written material

1. Write down what you understand to be the difference between needs and wants.

2. Now make a list of products which satisfy your needs, and products which you want. Which is the longer list?

3. How many of the goods and services you **want** are you able to **demand**?

Consumer or customer?

From the point of view of businesses which produce goods or services, there is an important difference between a consumer and a customer. Consumers are *potential* customers for a business. For example, you may be willing and able to buy Pepsi Cola at a Sainsbury's supermarket. This makes you a **consumer** in the markets for cola drinks and supermarket retail services. Cola producers and supermarkets will be competing for your custom. However, the fact that you choose to buy Coca Cola at a Tesco store means you are neither a customer of Pepsi or Sainsburys, but a paying **customer** for Coca Cola and Tesco.

Firms can lose customers to rival firms. However, they can also lose customers if there is a general fall in demand for their product – perhaps because of a change in consumer tastes. Without enough demand for their products, firms soon run into difficulties, as the article below about the Disney theme park in Paris shows.

24% Off
Euro Disney slash prices

Troubled Euro Disney slashed admission prices by 24% yesterday in a bid to save its crumbling Magic Kingdom. The French fun centre – still struggling to match the worldwide appeal of the American original – saw attendances fall by a million in the past 12 months. And although spending curbs have helped check huge losses, the pleasure park outside Paris needs bigger crowds to make it profitable.

Yesterday's cuts mean that high season prices for adults, starting next April, will now drop from £30 to £23. And the low-season figure, which takes effect in October, will be reduced from about £27.50 to £18.00. The food between rides will also be cheaper as restaurant charges come down again.

The price cuts were revealed by the Chairman of Disney who said that the cuts would help the park to break even by 1996. He is convinced that lower prices will lead to an increase in the number of visitors. If that does not happen, the park will be hit by further talk of closure. It has suffered massive losses since opening with a spectacular fanfare in April 1992.

Daily Mirror 15.12.94

Contracting and expanding markets

Consumer wants are always changing because of factors such as fashion, social and cultural change, growing incomes, new legal requirements, and many more (see 8.1). It is important that firms keep pace with changing consumer wants and develop existing or new products that people will continue to buy.

If consumer demand for a particular good or service is falling over time, the market for that product is said to be **shrinking** or **contracting**. Firms making that good or service will suffer declining sales and profits. Some may even be forced to close down.

Contracting markets

▼ *Typewriters*

▼ *Vinyl LPs*

Expanding markets

▼ *Multimedia personal computers*

▼ *Mobile phones*

If, on the other hand, consumer demand for a particular good or service is rising over time, the market is said to be **expanding**. Those firms already producing the good or service will experience rising sales and profits. They may have to expand production to meet demand, and it is likely that other firms will be attracted to the market too. New firms will also want to produce the same good or service because of the opportunity to earn sales revenues and profits. Some examples of contracting and expanding markets in the mid-1990s are shown in the pictures on this page.

▼ *DIY – an expanding market*

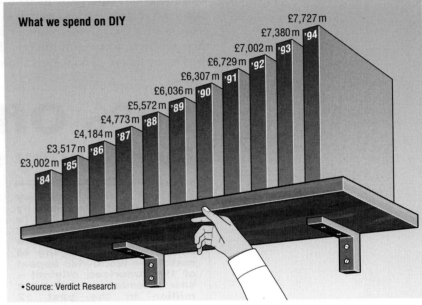

What we spend on DIY

£3,002 m '84
£3,517 m '85
£4,184 m '86
£4,773 m '87
£5,572 m '88
£6,036 m '89
£6,307 m '90
£6,729 m '91
£7,002 m '92
£7,380 m '93
£7,727 m '94

• Source: Verdict Research

Daily Mirror 26.1.95

Portfolio Activity 2.7

PC: Describe markets for businesses' products based on demand, Identify products provided by business organizations

Range: Markets, Demand, Products

Skills: Read and respond to written material, Collect and record data, Present information

Read the article on page 79;

1. Is consumer demand for garden products fulfilling a need or a want?

2. Is the market for garden products expanding or contracting?

3. Undertake your own research into this market. Based on your research, would you say that wants for garden products are mainly created by consumer demand? Or are they created by firms advertising heavily? Use a word processor to write up your findings in a short report.

PLANTS, BULBS AND SHRUBS	£1.09 billion
PONDS AND BARBECUES	£425 million
GARDEN BUILDINGS	£360 million
CHEMICALS	£275 million
TOOLS	£250 million
GARDEN FURNITURE	£205 million
TOTAL	**£2.6 billion**

Graphic : DAVID ACE

4. How would you classify the following garden products – as consumables or durables?

Seeds

Conifers and shrubs

Flower pots

Fertilisers and weedkillers

Patio furniture

Rocks for rockeries

Lawn mowers

The growth industry that's worth £2.6 billion a year

Britain has grown into a gardener's world and that is good news for the economy as we spend record amounts on our favourite hobby. The green-fingered nation bought plants and equipment worth £2.6 billion last year, according to a report out today which claims that specialist garden centres have been one of the fastest growing retail sectors over the last five years.

The survey by market researchers Mintel shows that money spent on gardens dwarfed the £227 million spent on visits to cinemas and is close to the £2.8 billion spent on records, tapes and CDs. Spending on growing stock, such as plants, shrubs and bulbs has shot up in value by 40% per cent since 1988. The report questioned more than 1,000 people nationwide and found

that men are still more likely to be the main gardeners in a household – 41% compared to 31% of women.

Mintel spokesman Helen Doherty said "There are three factors which determine spending on gardening – wealth, climate and the growth in home ownership."

Daily Mail 20.4.94

Choosing the right product for a new business

Imagine you want to start up your own business. What do you want to produce? Is it a good or a service? Is the product something people will buy on a regular basis, such as food, or something that they are likely to want only now and again, such as expensive jewellery or a carpet cleaning service?

It is not necessary to be innovative and make an entirely new product. But it will be necessary to offer consumers something new or different compared to your rivals.

Developing an existing product

It is important to pick a good or service for which the market is expanding. More opportunities for new business organizations exist in markets which are expanding. Market research can help to identify which these are (see 2.3). An expanding market will not make your business a success, but you will have a better chance of doing well if demand for your chosen good or service is growing.

Once you have a good or service to produce, you must then decide how you will improve on what is already on offer, so that you can attract customers away from rival firms. Factors which will influence consumers to buy include:

● Product quality

● Product appearance (size, shape, colour, texture, taste, smell, labelling, incorporated technology, etc.)

▼ *Developing existing products to keep up with changing consumer wants can give old products a new lease of life and increase their sales*

- Product image (often created by advertising)
- Price
- Where the product is sold
- Delivery times
- After-sales service

Remember that rival firms are also likely to be re-designing their goods or services as materials improve, technology advances, and consumers' tastes change. Old products may even be given a new lease of life in the market simply by designing new packaging and advertisements.

Producing a new product

Alternatively you might think of an entirely new good or service that no other firm makes, for which there is a **gap in the market**.

Many of the products we take for granted today started as the innovations of private individuals. For example, Percy Shaw became a multi-millionaire after inventing 'cats eyes' for roads. The idea came to him after seeing his car headlights reflected in broken glass. Swedish brothers Gad and Hans Rausing made £5.2 billion from their simple invention, the TetraPak Milk Carton.

As long as consumers want or need your new product, you could make a success of your business by being the first producer in the new market. You might even advertise heavily to create an attractive image for the product so that consumers will want it.

▼ *Can you improve on existing products, or produce an entirely new good or service?*

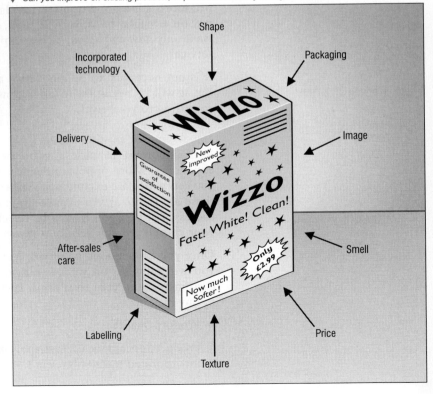

Some recent product developments

- Unpacking your shopping trolley at a supermarket checkout could soon become a thing of the past thanks to the new Supertag technology developed by the British-based computer firm ICL. Simply wheel your shopping trolley through an electronic arch and it will automatically add up your bill from barcodes printed on packaging.

- Video phones allow telephone users to see each other as they speak. Sound and pictures from a tiny camera in the video phone are converted into signals which can be sent in an instant over telephone lines to another video phone which then displays the video picture. Just don't use it in the bath!

- Microsurgery using optical fibre and laser technology is now possible. Large incisions into people's bodies are no longer necessary for many operations. Doctors are able to look inside people's bodies using fibre optic cables linked to monitor screens and use lasers to cut instead of scalpels and knives.

- Car buyers could soon be putting on space-style virtual reality headsets to test-drive new computerized images of cars in car showrooms. Ford developed the system in partnership with IBM and the Virtuality Group to launch the Ford Galaxy in Autumn 1995. Virtual reality is also being used to design everything from supermarkets to petrol refineries without having to build 3D prototype models.

- The UK could have up to 100 TV channels early next century without the need for cable or satellite, using digital technology. Digital television will also produce high quality pictures and sound in wide screen format.

- An American company has developed an 'intelligent' dustbin called Can Scan that is able to read barcodes on packets, tins, and bottles you throw away. It then uses a built-in cellular radio modem link to a computer to order replacements from a supermarket.

Portfolio Activity 2.8

PC: Explain activities undertaken by businesses to improve their market position

Range: Markets, Demand, Products

Skills: Read and respond to written material, Produce written material

1. How has Mattel developed the Barbie product in order to make more sales and reflect the changing tastes of consumers?

2. Can you think of any other products which have been 'kept alive' by regular changes in their design or advertising? In groups, discuss and make a list describing how each product and/or its advertising has changed over time.

All dolled up

Toys are a changing business in which last year's hit often becomes this year's turkey. All the more remarkable that a doll created in the 1950s should remain one of the toy industry's hottest properties.

Barbie, the world's best-selling doll, celebrates her 35th birthday at this month's New York toy fair, having sold 775 million of herself worldwide. There are few signs that she has reached maturity. Sales of Barbie and her accessories have more than doubled in the past five years, to more than $1 billion in 1993. Barbie has helped to make her owner Mattel, into America's biggest toy maker.

Barbie's secret according to John Amerman, Chairman of Mattel is that 'the product is regularly changed and freshened.' Barbie has been kitted out as a teacher, a doctor, a horsewoman, even a Presidential candidate. Barbie accessories include Ken, Barbie's partner, and a growing number of friends of different races. The latest success is a Barbie with floor-length hair that turns pink when sprayed with water.

These spin-offs mean that the average American girl owns eight Barbie dolls and buys two or three new ones every year.

The Economist 15.2.94

Getting a share of the market

Competition for consumers between rival firms is rather like fighting over slices of a cake. Most firms will want to get a bigger slice than their rivals.

The cake represents all the spending of consumers on a particular product. The size of the cake, therefore, reflects the size of the market for a good or service, measured by the total amount spent on that product by consumers in any one period of time – usually one year (see 1.1). The **market share** of a business is, therefore, its share of total sales.

If you decide to produce a good or service that is in competition with those provided by existing firms, your first objective will be to make sales and obtain a share of the market.

For example, suppose you want to make and sell dried flower arrangements. Imagine that consumers spent £900,000 on them last year and are expected to spend £1 million in the current year. If you make and sell £50,000-worth of dried flower arrangements this year, you will have captured 5% of the value of the market (£50,000/£1,000,000 × 100 = 5%). However, because you are a new firm supplying the market for dried flower arrangements, your market share of 5% must mean that existing firms have lost 5% of the value of total sales to you. It is unlikely you will be able to do this without making flower arrangements that are much better than existing products, selling them at a lower price, and using a lot of advertising to create consumer wants for them.

Portfolio Activity 2.9

PC: Propose products which would meet market demand
Range: Markets, Demand, Propose products
Skills: Collect and record data, Produce written material, Use images

1. From your own knowledge and further research, identify and list at least three markets that are currently expanding and three which are contracting.

2. For the goods and/or services you have identified in Task 1, list and explain possible reasons for the growth or decline in sales. Useful sources of data will include newspapers and magazines, discussions with shop sales staff and business owners/managers.

3. Propose a new or existing good or service which you would like to produce if your ran your own business. Give reasons for your choice based on your knowledge of consumer wants and needs, the growth in consumer demand for it, and the amount of competition from existing firms.

4. To find out more about the market for your product, design a short questionnaire to use on a group of people. Try to establish how much people might be willing to pay for your product, how often they are likely to buy it, what the main rival products are and who provides them, and the particular design features consumers would like to see.

5. Make a sketch of the good or service you chose in Task 3. Show and describe features it will have, including size, shape, colour, texture, weight, materials used (and a list of possible suppliers), labelling, and packaging.

6. Write up your proposal and research findings in a word-processed report, including diagrams.

7. Ask your class group to act as joint owners of your new business venture and present your proposals to them. Your research findings and written proposals should be no longer than a one-page summary. Hand out copies of this at the beginning of your presentation. The presentation itself should last no more than 10 minutes. Make good use of any diagrams or models you have constructed to illustrate your product.

Section **2.3**

Business activities

Simply choosing the best location and the right good or service for your business is not enough to ensure that it is a success. There are a number of activities the business must perform, and perform well. These are:

- **Market research** – the gathering and analysis of information on markets for goods and services
- **Product design** – planning, designing and testing products and packaging
- **Production** – organizing labour, materials, and machines to make new goods or services
- **Marketing communications** – giving information about products to potential consumers and persuading them to buy
- **Sales** – distributing and selling products to customers
- **After-sales service** – allowing customers to exchange products, giving refunds, dealing with complaints, making repairs, etc.

Market research

Why do firms need market research? A business will only be successful if it produces what consumers want both now and in the future, and does so better than rival firms. In order to find out what consumers want and what rival firms are up to, business organizations will use **market research** (see 11.2). This involves gathering and analysing information about markets for goods and services.

Market research can provide information to help answer many important questions about product design and marketing. With the help of this information a firm can:

- Design products at prices that will appeal to consumers
- Develop advertising that encourages people to buy their products
- Make sure their products are readily available at places where consumers are most likely to buy them
- Provide the after-sales care that customers want

All these activities will help a firm to establish a customer base, increase their market share, and generate sales and profits.

Sources of market research information

There are two main sources of information a firm can use to gather information about its market:

- **Customers and potential customers** can be asked questions about goods and services they buy or may like to buy. Pre-designed questionnaires can be used to interview people face-to-face or over the telephone. Questionnaires can also be sent through the post for people to fill in and return. Simply observing consumer buying habits over time can also provide useful information.

- **Published information** is available in newspapers and magazines, government statistical journals, annual reports of rival companies, and many other sources. Information can also come from the organization's internal records, such as details of production costs, consumer complaints, and sales over time.

Portfolio Activity 2.10

PC: Explain activities undertaken by businesses to improve their market position

Range: Activities undertaken by business

Skills: Read and respond to written material, Collect and record data, Produce written material

1. What sort of market research information is being collected in the article and how is it being collected?

2. Why and how are the firms in the article making use of the market research information?

3. Visit a business organization that you know:

   a List the types of information you think the organization will need to know about its market and briefly explain why each is important.

   b Investigate how the business finds out about its market. Explain each method and the reasons it is used.

4. A friend plans to open a shop selling high quality chocolates. She wants to find out more about the retail chocolate market and, in particular, if there is a consumer want for her shop in your local area. Write a short report for her to explain the type of information she will need and the most appropriate method(s) she could use to obtain the information.

5. What other activities will she need to undertake in her business to help expand her share of the market?

Eyes on buyers

It is called retail surveillance and it is the latest weapon in the armoury of stores who want their customers to keep shopping until they drop.

By using tiny cameras to watch shoppers move up and down the aisles, a store can see how well the layout of goods suits shoppers and then change it if necessary. For example, it has been traditional to put meat in the middle of stores, with vegetables housed near the entrance. But actual video footage of shoppers moving backwards and forwards between the two has persuaded a number of stores to rethink their layout policy.

For an increasing number of stores, including Dixons and Curry's, capturing shoppers on video can also unravel the mystery of what makes us buy. Hidden cameras can pinpoint the products we linger over and those we ignore; they can record our reaction to new products and can tell a retailer how much attention we pay to price or to product labels.

By studying tapes of several thousands of customers, electrical group Curry's discovered that 'potentially disruptive influences' such as bored children and partners were hampering sales of large electrical items such as fridges. The installation of 'listening posts' for CDs near the fridges and freezers now helps keep partners occupied while the purchasers get on with the business of choosing household appliances. A pile of newspapers near the changing rooms in a clothes shop can have the same effect.

A team from National Opinion Polls, a specialist market research agency, spent three days watching people buy baby products at a Bedfordshire branch of Somerfield. After watching over 30 hours of film, the team discovered that 'people pay great attention to labels on babyfood wrappers, and in many cases, after reading the ingredients, put the foods back on the shelf.'

NOP also found out that a 'high proportion of people who buy baby products are in their sixties – possibly grandparents, but hardly those consumers (parents) who babyfoods advertising is aimed at.'

Adapted from the Financial Times 23.3.95

Product design

In order for a firm to be able to make what customers want, it must have a group of people who design the goods and services to meet consumer demands. In many organizations this is done by departments known variously as **research and development (R&D)**, **design**, or **product planning** (see 4.2).

The work of designers concerns two main areas:

● The appearance of the product and how people will use it

● How well the product performs or how long it lasts

The objective of the R&D department will be to produce a design for a product that satisfies consumer wants at a price consumers will be willing to pay. It must also meet continual demands to make products which are better quality, safer, and quicker, easier, and cheaper to make. The R&D department in most organizations will therefore consider not just the design of new products or modifications to existing products, but also new methods of making them.

For example, the R&D department in a pottery-making firm would be concerned with developing new plate designs, testing clays, paints, and glazes, testing finished plates for durability and heat resistance in microwave ovens and dishwashers, designing packaging, and finally introducing them into production. Similarly, a car manufacturer would design new models showing not just their appearance, but also detailed engineering solutions concerning in-car safety, aerodynamics, engine fuel economy, and performance.

Design must consider the best materials to use (and how much they will cost), size, durability, smell, taste, texture, colour, packaging, incorporated technology, and many other features of goods and services. The first step is usually to make a small number of products from technical drawings and use these 'prototypes' to test consumer reaction. Similarly, a service can be tried out on a small number of consumers first, before making it generally available.

Production

The main purpose of production is to turn **inputs** into **outputs** (see 1.1). The inputs are materials and the efforts of workers and machinery, while the outputs are the goods and services that match agreed designs.

In most organizations people concerned with production will have a number of functions (see 4.2). These are:

● To set targets for the number of products to make per period and agree production schedules to meet them

● To plan for the amount of labour, materials and equipment needed

● To ensure that product quality is maintained

● To minimize cost and waste

● To keep machinery and equipment in good working order

● To install new equipment when necessary

Marketing communications

Starting the production of a new product from the beginning can be very expensive in terms of time, equipment, and money, so firms often aim to expand sales as quickly as possible after launching the product onto the market. The best way to ensure that sales grow quickly is to create a **marketing campaign** or **strategy** to inform consumers about the product and to persuade them to buy it.

A firm's communications with the market are called **marketing communications**. They include:

- Advertising
- Sales promotions
- Sales literature
- Product sponsorship

'Mind the gap'

This Wonderbra advert is one of a number created by Susanna Hailstone of the TBWA advertising agency. Weekly sales soared by 7,000 after the striking poster campaign was launched.

Advertising

The most popular way of communicating information and messages about products to potential consumers is through advertising, either in newspapers or magazines, on television or radio, at the cinema, on posters, T- shirts, or through a variety of other media (see 9.1).

Sales promotions

Once advertising has gained the interest and attention of the consumer, **sales promotions** are designed to make them want to buy and keep on buying the same product (see 9.1). Sales promotions include competitions with big prizes, free gifts, money-off coupons in magazines and on product packaging, point of sale displays, and showing off products at exhibitions and trade fairs.

Sales literature

Handouts, leaflets, promotional booklets, and catalogues are all useful ways of providing information about products and prices, and also presenting products attractively to create a consumer want. Some leaflets may be posted direct to people's homes. This is called **direct mail**.

▼ *Sales literature; Mail order catologues and Product Leaflets*

Product sponsorship

Increasingly firms seek endorsements for their products by paying celebrities, particularly pop stars or sports personalities, to use them (see 9.1). Many consumers will want to buy the same products as their pop or sporting heroes.

Portfolio Activity 2.11

PC: Explain activities undertaken by businesses to improve their market position

Range: Activities undertaken by businesses

Skills: Collect and record data, Produce written material

1. Investigate the marketing communications used to promote these products. What images are created for these products through advertising?

   Write up your findings in a short word-processed report. Include in your report:

   • Examples of marketing communications used

   • An explanation of why firms are often willing to spend many millions of pounds on marketing communications

2. Investigate the marketing communications used by one business organization you are familiar with. Find out why they use some forms of marketing communications and not others. How much do they spend on marketing communications?

▼ Selling

Sales

Selling is a personal communication between a business organization and a customer with the aim of making a sale. This personal communication may be between a customer ordering goods or services over the phone or by mail order, or face-to-face with a sales assistant in a shop.

Selling is vital for the success of most business organizations. Market research, product development, production, and marketing will all have been wasted if an organization cannot sell its products.

Advertising and other marketing communications may persuade a consumer to buy a certain product. However, if the sales staff a customer deals with are unhelpful or disorganized, it can put the customer off buying that product, and discourage them from returning to the same supplier in the future to buy more.

After-sales service

When you buy a good or service there is always a risk that you will change your mind or it will go wrong or fail to please in some way. If you are unable to get a refund, replacement, or repair, you may think twice about ever buying that good or service again, especially if it is an expensive item like a television, video recorder, or car. Businesses that are able to offer customers the chance to return, exchange, or repair items that are unsatisfactory are more likely to attract custom than firms that do not provide such after-sales care.

▼ Dealing with customer complaints

▼ Carrying out repairs

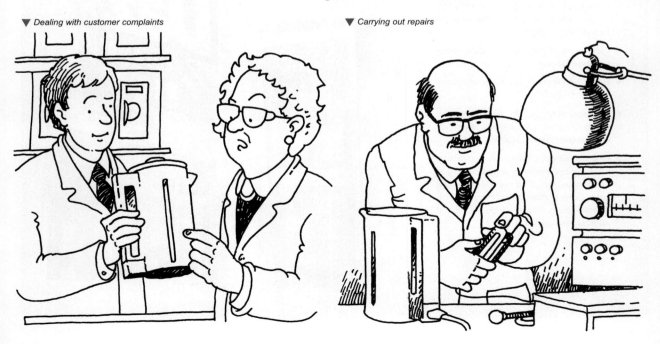

▼ *Giving refunds*

Most business organizations provide after-sales services to meet the needs of their customers, to persuade consumers to buy, and to gain their loyalty to the product and the organization, so that they return to make **repeat purchases** time and time again. After-sales services include:

- Arranging replacements
- Giving refunds
- Providing technical advice and spare parts
- Undertaking or arranging repairs
- Dealing with customer complaints
- Follow-up phone calls or letters to customers

Section **2.4**   **The business environment**

Portfolio Activity 2.12

PC: Explain influences of the business environment on business organizations

Range: Influences of the business environment

Skills: Read and respond to written material, Collect and record data

1. Read the articles below then write a few brief sentences to explain how the activities and decisions of each business are being influenced by forces beyond their control.

Plans for 400 out-of town stores beat Government plan

Last month the Environment Secretary announced a virtual end to the building of out-of-town shopping, business parks and housing, which could only be reached by car, in order to protect shops in towns. While in response some grocery chains have cut their building programme, Sainsbury still aims to open 20 new stores a year for the next four years. Safeway has cut its target from 25 new stores but is still aiming for 21 to 23 new superstores a year.

Mr Richard Hyman, Chairman of Verdict, an independent retail consultancy, doubted whether limits on out-of-town shopping by government would be acceptable. The fact is that a very large slice of British retailing has grown up because of the convenience of people being able to use their cars when shopping.

The Daily Telegraph 4.4.94

Ferry firm's live aid

The P&O ferry firm threatened yesterday to stop carrying live animals across the Channel for slaughter. Chairman Lord Sterling said the warning followed a review of the opinions of passengers, members of the public and members of staff.

They were all clearly worried about conditions for animals while they were being moved long distances on the continent after leaving the ferries. Under current rules, live animals can be carried for up to 24 hours without a break including for water and this limit is often broken on the continent according to the RSPCA.

The RSPCA and other animal welfare groups have been waging campaigns to highlight alleged cruelty in the live animals export trade. Britain exported 2 million last year.

Daily Mail 30.7.94

2. Collect further evidence of influences on business activities from newspapers, magazines, and TV programmes.

3. Using the articles and others you have collected, sort the different types of influences into the following categories:

- Actions of rival firms
- Actions of consumers
- Changes in laws
- Changes in nature

Assemble the articles and your comments into a folder.

Coca-Cola market share falls below 50%

Coca-Cola's share of the £670 million UK cola market has fallen below 50% for the first time, say figures from Taylor Nelson AGB, the market research group. This was shortly after the arrival of new colas from Mr Richard Branson's Virgin group and supermarket chain Safeway, and six months after Classic Cola was launched by J Sainsbury, the UK's biggest food retailer. These figures highlight the threat posed to Coca-Cola, which has dominated the market since its UK launch in 1921 by this year's new products.

Financial Times 19.12.94

Sunday working rights for shop staff

NEW RIGHTS for shop workers to protect them from being compelled to work on Sundays are contained in the new Sunday Trading Act. It gives shop workers the right not be dismissed, made redundant, or subjected to any other detriment for refusing to work on Sundays.

Employment Gazette 5.94

Divorce rate sparks surge in toy market

Britain's toy market is booming thanks to the soaring divorce rate. As one in three parents split, the number of 'guilt gifts' given by estranged mums and dads is growing. According to Mintel, the divorce generation's 'portable kids' are being lavished with new portable toys. Sales of small cheap toys like Polly Pocket, Mighty Max, Trolls, and Monster in my Pocket boosted toy sales in Britain to £1.57 billion last year.

Daily Mail 30.6.94

Brussels finally goes bananas

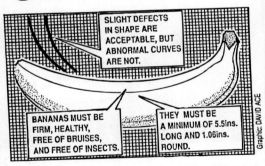

SLIGHT DEFECTS IN SHAPE ARE ACCEPTABLE, BUT ABNORMAL CURVES ARE NOT.

BANANAS MUST BE FIRM, HEALTHY, FREE OF BRUISES, AND FREE OF INSECTS.

THEY MUST BE A MINIMUM OF 5.5ins. LONG AND 1.06ins. ROUND.

Graphic: DAVID ACE

THE ruling from Brussels was straight to the point – bananas should not bend. Or to be precise, they must not bend 'abnormally'. If they do they will be banned from sale from next year.

The latest decree of the European Union (EU) also insists that they must be a minimum of 5.5 inches long and 1.06 inches round. They have to be firm, healthy, practically free of bruises, and as free from insects as possible, they say.

EU-wide standards were needed, it has been argued, to improve the quality of bananas on sale in the shops, and to help traders who order their fruit by telephone.

Daily Mail 21.9.94

Coffee price soars after new frosts

SHOPPERS may have to fork out 20 per cent more for their jars of Gold Blend and other brands over the next few months after more disastrous frosts overnight in Brazil, the world's biggest coffee producer. The price of coffee on the London Commodities Exchange soared from $3076 a tonne to $3950 a tonne as reports reached the City that up to half of next year's Brazilian crop may have been destroyed.

Evening Standard 11.7.94

What is the business environment?

It has been said that 'business is war'. This means that being in business involves competing with other firms to win a share of their sales and profits, while at the same time trying to stop other firms taking away your own customers and profits. As in a real war, the battlefield is always changing, as armies advance or retreat and new tactics and offensives are planned and carried out. The side that is best able to plan for and cope with all these changes will win.

In business, the enemies are rival firms, and the battlefield is the environment in which businesses operate. The decisions and activities carried out within a business will be influenced by changes taking place in this 'business environment'. A business that ignores these changes will not be successful and in some cases could be breaking the law and be forced to close down.

▼ *The business environment*

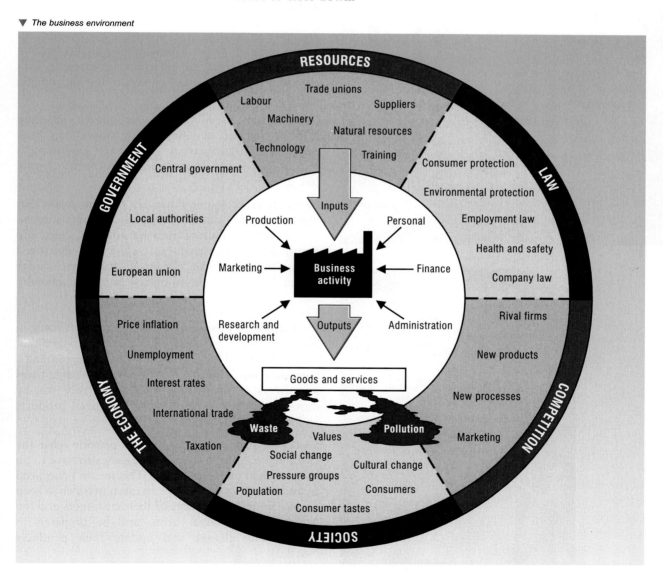

The business environment is influenced by:

● Changes in the weather and the natural environment

● The actions of rival firms introducing new products, prices and advertising campaigns

● Changes in laws and other controls by central and local government

● Changes in the attitudes, tastes, and spending patterns of consumers

Each of these influences is considered in detail below.

▼ *The natural environment affects business activity.*

The natural environment

The physical or natural environment will always have a great impact on the way in which businesses operate. Changes in the weather can affect crops, which will affect the price of the raw materials for a great many food manufacturers. For example, a drought can result in a poor harvest which will force up the price of wheat. The weather can also have an affect on consumers' buying habits, for example, with spending on clothes and holidays following changes in the seasons.

Fierce storms, flooding, and earthquakes can cause a lot of damage, and firms must ensure they have adequate insurance cover. The natural environment will also affect where some businesses locate (see 2.1).

In recent years people have also become aware that business activity can affect the natural environment. Atmospheric pollution from burning oil, coal, and petrol has caused acid rain which has destroyed forests and killed fish. Chemicals and other sewage dumped at sea has caused disease in marine animals.

The competitive environment

It would be easy to create a successful firm if being in business simply involved supplying a product that people want and are willing to pay for. But running a business is much harder than this, because other firms are always trying to take sales away from you by introducing their own new and improved products and marketing strategies.

Successful firms not only have to provide what the customer wants and will pay for, they also have to do it better than the competition. This means firms need to undertake regular market research in order to keep up to date with the wants of their customers and the actions of their rival firms, and be prepared to continuously change and update their products (see 2.2).

Portfolio Activity 2.13

PC: Explain influences of the business environment on business organizations

Range: Influences of the business environment

Skills: Read and respond to written material, Collect and record data, Use images

Pools firm Vernons prepares to write off £100m

THE NATIONAL Lottery has given football pools firms a £100-million kicking.

Ladbroke boss Peter George now accepts that the once-prized Vernons name could now be worthless and is writing off its £100 million value.

Ladbroke reckons Vernons' takings could be down by as much as £30 million from last year's £174 million. It is already saving cash by cutting 95 jobs at the firm's Liverpool HQ. And it hopes that bigger prizes and TV ads will help pull in more punters.

Daily Mirror 9.3.95

1. What does the article suggest has happened to the market share of football pools companies in the market for betting and gambling, and why this has happened?

2. Suggest how the owners of Vernons pools plan to compete with the National Lottery. What other marketing communication methods and product developments could they use? Give reasons for your recommendations.

3. Investigate competition in a market for a good or service of your choice. Write a report which describes:

- The major firms in the market
- How they compete on prices
- How they compete by other means, for example, on packaging, brand image, quality, etc.
- How effective their means of competing are
- Other strategies firms might use to try to expand their market shares and the total size of the market

Include in your report any examples of marketing materials used by the firms to promote their products.

▼ *Price competition*

▼ *Non-price competition*

Competition between rival firms for the purchases of consumers can take many forms. **Price competition** involves competing to offer the consumer the best price for a product. This can include cutting prices, holding sales, offering discounts, and other special offers such as 'two for the price of one' promotions.

Firms can also compete on aspects other than price, for example, by trying to outdo each other on product quality and special product features, and also through advertising and other promotional strategies (see 9.1). These are all forms of **non-price competition**.

The social environment

The social environment is people. People are consumers, and through their spending decisions they will determine the success or failure of many business organizations. Apart from their level of income, the spending decisions of individuals will be determined by their values, beliefs, and attitudes (see 8.2).

By making choices on which products to buy, people have a major influence on what firms produce. In the end, firms must listen to what their customers want, or they will be replaced by other firms who do.

In recent years consumers have become more health-conscious, and more concerned about the environment and animal rights. For example, many people now prefer to buy from firms that promote a more caring image towards the environment and animals rights, like The Body Shop and the Co-operative Bank.

Consumers' views can be influenced by pressure groups who are themselves just groups of concerned consumers. These can be groups fighting local issues such as the building of a new road through woodland, or international groups such as Greenpeace fighting global issues such as cruelty to animals and pollution.

The legal environment

Both local and central government have passed a number of laws and regulations which aim to protect consumers, workers, and the environment from abuse and malpractice by businesses. The owners of firms found to be breaking these laws can be fined heavily or even imprisoned.

These laws and regulations relate to:

- **Consumer protection.** Laws have been passed which are designed to protect consumers from businesses who may mislead the consumer or put their safety at risk. For example, the **Trade Descriptions Act** makes it illegal to make false or misleading claims about the contents, effects, or prices of products (see 9.2). Firms are also required to make sure that their products meet government and European Union regulations on health and safety, for example in standards for electrical appliances, food, and children's toys.

- **Health and safety.** A number of laws have been in existence for many years to protect employees and members of the public from health and safety hazards at their place of work (see 5.3). Positive steps to prevent accidents and to promote health and safety must be taken by all organizations. Employees are also obliged to take reasonable care and to co-operate with their employers on safety matters.

- **Employment.** The relationship between employers and their employees is regulated by a number of laws in the UK (see 5.3) Together, these acts give workers:

  - guaranteed payment of wages

  - statutory sick pay

  - redundancy payments

  - maternity leave for female employees and the right to return to the same job afterwards

  - the right not to be discriminated against on grounds of sex, race, marital status, religion, or trade union membership

  - the right not to be unfairly dismissed

▼ *Environmental protection laws are supposed to stop this happening. Some businesses continue to break the law.*

● **Environmental Protection.** The Environment Act 1990 and a growing body of European laws on the environment regulate the behaviour of firms in the UK, and these are supported by the Inspectorate of Pollution in Britain. Taken together, these laws control many thousands of different industrial processes, which might, if uncontrolled, cause noise or chemical pollution in the air, land, or water. Local authorities are also required by government to monitor some 30,000 industrial processes for unacceptable levels of pollution.

● **Competition.** A number of laws seek to protect the public against business practices which may reduce competition and force product prices to rise and quality to suffer. For example, it is illegal for firms supplying the same type of product to agree to fix their prices at a high level rather than compete.

Key words

Write definitions and explanations for the following key words and terms that have appeared in this chapter:

bulk-reducing production	expanding market	industrial goods	price competition
bulk-increasing production	market research	services	non-price competition
footloose industries	sample	durable goods	the business environment
ancillary firms	marketing communications	non-durable goods	consumer protection laws
regional policy	sales promotions	domestic market	health and safety laws
assisted areas	sales literature	international market	employment laws
multinationals	selling	needs and wants	environmental protection laws
consumer goods	after-sales service	demand	health and safety laws
		contracting market	

You must demonstrate that you are able to:

1. Explain the reasons for the location of businesses

2. Explain influences of the business environment on business organizations

3. Describe markets for businesses' products based on demand

4. Identify products provided by business organizations

5. Explain activities undertaken by business to improve their market position

6. Propose products which would meet market demand

1 Gregson Arts Ltd sells paintings and art materials. Which of the following would be the most suitable place to locate?

A near a small village

B in a seaside town

C in the countryside

D near a densely populated city

2 A business has an idea for a new product. How could it find out if consumers will buy it?

A produce it and see how well it does

B advertise

C give away free samples

D carry out market research

3 The owner of a computer games shop finds that she is selling more games on CD than on cassette. What is the main reason for this?

A the market for games is expanding

B CDs take up less storage space

C CDs are cheaper than tapes

D the market for games is contracting

4 A sponsor will support a sporting event in order to:

A reduce the price of products

B increase spending on advertising

C promote goods and services

D encourage competitors

5 A toy manufacturer wants to introduce a new board game. What should the company do to ensure the design will be successful?

A launch the first idea it has as quickly as possible

B copy an existing board game

C carry out market research

D produce a TV or radio advert

6 A business might use competitions to promote goods in order to:

A increase sales

B reduce profits

C increase costs

D improve product quality

7 Which type of business is best located near to natural resources?

A a cinema

B a bank

C a coal-fired power station

D a take-away restaurant

8 A firm's market share is measured by:

A the amount of product that it makes

B the sales of its product compound to total market sales

C product quality

D the cost of its product

9 Which of the following is a consumable product?

A computer

B office stationery

C fax machine

D telephone answering machine

10 Which of these is a durable product?

A motorcycle

B a newspaper

C food

D soap

11 Which of these is a service?

   A car manufacturing

   B farming

   C pre-packed food production

   D banking

12 A document used to find out about consumers' opinions of a new product is:

   A a sales leaflet

   B a questionnaire

   C direct mail

   D a product catalogue

13 A supermarket chain wants to build a new superstore. Which of the following information would be most useful when choosing between two areas?

   A population

   B numbers of males and females

   C cost of living

   D road and rail links?

14 The UK firm XYZ Ltd has just opened new factories in Malaysia and China. What does this suggest about the type of market the business is in?

   A it is a local market

   B it is a domestic market

   C it is a European market

   D it is an international market

Questions 15-17 share the following answer options:

   A near a large residential area

   B near a supply of skilled labour

   C near a source of raw materials

   D near good transport links

What is likely to be the best location for the following businesses?

15 A supermarket

16 An international business management consultancy

17 A television parts manufacturer

18 In providing after-sales service, a business is likely to:

   A increase its sales

   B improve product quality

   C lower its costs

   D receive more complaints

19 In a time of rising unemployment, a firm is likely to experience:

   A rising wage costs

   B falling sales

   C rising sales

   D rising profits

20 All of the following are outside influences on business except:

   A government economic policy

   B new laws regulating advertising

   C better management of sales staff

   D more competitors entering the market

21 **a.** Suggest three factors that might influence the choice of location for a small bakery.

b. What type of market will the bakery serve?

c. i What is the difference between a consumable and durable good?

   ii What type of goods does a bakery produce?

   iii Do the type of goods a bakery provides serve a need or a want, or both? Explain your answer carefully, using examples.

d. Explain three activities the bakery will need to undertake if it is to expand its share of the market.

e. Explain two influences on the bakery which are likely to be beyond the control of the organization.

22 **a.** What is market research, and why is it important for business?

b. Suggest two ways a new soft drinks maker could collect information about the market.

c. 'The international market for soft drinks is expanding.' Explain what this statement means.

d. Suggest three marketing communications the new soft drinks manufacturer could use to promote its products.

(**assessment assignment**)

The following assignment meets the evidence requirements needed to fulfil all the performance criteria in element 1.2. In addition it covers the following range points and core skills:

Range: Reasons for location	**Skills: Communication**
Influences of the business environment	Take part in discussions
Markets	Produce written material
Demand	Use images
Products provided	**Application of number**
Activities undertaken by businesses	Collect and record data
Propose products	**Information technology**
	Prepare information
	Process information
	Present information

This assignment requires you to produce two reports using a word processor.

Report 1

1. Conduct a survey of businesses in your area, using your own observations and knowledge, and interviews with business owners and managers. Investigate the locations chosen by different kinds of business organization. For example, you might like to look at the location of a small retail firm, a garage, a larger retail supermarket, a hairdresser, a building society, a school or college, and a factory.

2. Make brief summary notes on how good you think each location is for that kind of business and say why you think this.

3. Focus on one of your organizations in particular and draw a map to show its location.

4. On your map, highlight the location of any natural resources (unlikely for most kinds of organization), where other firms are, where competitors are, and transport facilities for workers and customers.

5. Produce a report on whether the location of this particular firm is a good one. Carefully explain your points referring to the location criteria in this chapter and any that you can add to them.

Report 2

6. For the same organization as Task 3 above, or another that you have looked at, report on the market for its goods and services and how the business has marketed itself and its products. Include a description of:

- The business and its operations (see 1.1)
- The types of goods and services it produces
- The total size of the market (i.e. amount of money spent on the product each year)
- The market share of your chosen organization
- Whether the market is expanding or contracting
- The marketing communications the organization uses, and why it uses them

You may wish to comment on how successful their marketing communications have been, from evidence of growth in sales, or your observations of people's interest in the products.

7. On the basis of your findings in Task 6, propose a new or changed product which you think might be more successful. Give reasons for your proposal. This should include a diagram or model of your new or modified product.

8. For the organization you have chosen in Task 6, report on the kind of business environment it faces. How do legal, environmental, and public influences affect the business?

chapter *3* *Investigating Employment*

Key ideas

The UK **workforce** is made up of all those people willing and able to work: employees in employment, the self-employed, HM forces personnel, and those on work-related government training schemes.

Increasing numbers of females are joining the workforce, many as part-time workers.

Most people in the UK and other countries in the European Union (EU) are employed in service industries. The number employed in manufacturing industries has been falling.

Regional patterns of employment differ. The South East of England has a higher proportion of workers in services than northern England, Wales, and Scotland, where more workers tend to work in manufacturing industries. This is partly because in the past manufacturing industries located in these areas to be near raw material supplies. Regional grants from the UK and EU governments may attract firms to areas of high unemployment.

Different **types of employment** exist. People can be employed on a **full-time** or **part-time** basis, on either a **permanent** or **temporary contract**, or be **self-employed**.

The numbers of part-time, temporary, and self-employed workers has increased over time, to replace full-time permanent jobs.

Manual occupations, such as bricklaying or lorry driving, involve a large element of physical work. **Non-manual occupations** are those which require their employees to use their mental abilities more, such as many office-based jobs.

Employers increasingly want workers who are **skilled** in particular trades and tasks.

Some jobs have better **working conditions** than others. They include levels of **wages, salaries** and other payments, **hours of work, holiday entitlement, job security, opportunities for training** and **career progression**, and the **physical conditions** of the workplace.

On-the-job training involves teaching work skills while employees carry out their normal duties. For **off-the-job training,** employees will be released from their work to attend courses.

Workers will choose between the jobs they would like to do, according to the working conditions they offer, and the time and cost of travel to and from work.

New technology has affected working conditions in many jobs. Robots, computers, and other forms of technology have taken over some tasks previously carried out by workers. Many workers have become **de-skilled** or have even lost their jobs altogether. New technology is used in many jobs today to increase productivity, and workers have been expected to learn new skills.

There are many factors which influence the **level of employment** in the UK. Falling consumer demand during an economic recession and increasing competition from overseas can mean jobs are lost. Some UK firms have even located overseas because wage levels in some countries are much lower than in the UK. As wages rise, firms tend to employ less workers.

Section **3.1**   # What is employment?

The changing nature of employment

▼ *Then*

'I started work at 15 years of age in 1934. A local printers took me on as an apprentice compositor [typesetter] to learn how to set up pages of type for printing. After five years I completed my training but was then called up to fight in the war. I returned to the same printing firm in 1945 after the end of the war and stayed with them for 20 years until they closed down because of a lack of work. I then found a job at another printing company for the next 16 years. I was still a compositor but was promoted to supervisor of the typesetting room after five years. In 1981 at the age of 62 I was made redundant. The firm had installed new computer technology that made my skills obsolete.'

▼ *Now*

'After leaving school at 18 with an A level in English and Business Studies, I went to work as a filing clerk in a big insurance company. After three years I was really bored, so I went to night school to train as a secretary. I then got a job as secretary in a small solicitors' office for a couple of years before I decided to pack it in for a job with British Airways as ground staff. I would have liked to become air crew, but after four years BA had still not offered the position to me. So I went back to doing secretarial work, this time for a TV production company. The production company wanted me to work full-time on a popular programme they made about holidays. I did that for five years before I was promoted to the programme researcher on a two year contract.'

The two case studies above show just how different the world of work is today compared to the past. Many years ago people leaving school to look for work would join a firm as an apprentice and learn a particular trade, such as carpentry, car maintenance, or engineering. Once skilled in these trades, they were likely to work full-time in the same profession, and often with the same organization, for the rest of their life. A privileged few went on to universities to get degrees, while others inherited family businesses or took the risk of starting their own.

Today, the picture is very different. Few jobs are for life. Jobs in many occupations and business organizations are less secure than they have been in the past. Demands on workers, for new skills and greater effort, are changing all the time. Unemployment is high.

On average, most people today spend about five years in the same job before moving on. Many are likely to change career and undertake completely different work. Only around 30% of those currently in work have been in the same job for 10 years or more. Also, fewer jobs are full-time.

The nature of work is changing all the time. Some of biggest changes that have occurred recently, and seem likely to continue into the future, are:

● More women are going out to work

● More and more jobs are in service industries and less and less in manufacturing industries

● A growing number of jobs are part-time

● An increasing number of jobs employ people only for short periods of time

● Unemployment is rising

● Demand for skilled labour is increasing

This chapter examines these changes in the pattern of employment in the UK; why they have occurred, and what impact they have had on people in work.

The UK workforce

In 1994 25.2 million people 'went to' work in the UK. At the same time, 2.6 million people were officially looking for work or on work-related government training programmes preparing for work, according to government figures. In total, therefore, almost 28 million people in the UK were in work or seeking work. Of these, 3.3 million people were self-employed, while 21.7 million worked for an employer, including the armed forces. All those people in work or unemployed make up the **total workforce** in the UK.

▼ *Table 3.1: Distribution of the UK workforce (millions)*

	1984	1994
Employees in employment	**21.2**	**21.4**
Male	11.9	10.8
Female	9.3	10.6
Self-employed	**2.7**	**3.3**
Male	2.1	2.5
Female	0.6	0.8
HM forces	**0.33**	**0.25**
Male	0.31	0.23
Female	0.02	0.02
Unemployed	**2.9**	**2.6**
Male	2.0	2.0
Female	0.9	0.6
Work-related government training programmes (WRGTP)	**0.18**	**0.32**
Male	0.10	0.20
Female	0.08	0.12
Total workforce	**27.3**	**27.9**
Male	16.4	15.7
Female	10.9	12.2

Annual Abstract of Statistics 1995

Why are more women going to work?

One of the most significant changes in the UK workforce over time has been the increasing participation of women. In 1994 the number of women in work or looking for work was 12.2 million, or 44% of the total workforce. In 1984, 10.9 million women were in the workforce, or just under 40% (see Table 3.1). Go back further and the numbers were even less.

There are a number of reasons why more women are now in work or seeking work than ever before. These include:

- Attitudes towards working women have changed

- Many women are getting married and starting families later in life so that they can have a career

- Increasing availability of part-time jobs has encouraged more women to join the workforce

- Equal opportunities legislation has helped to improve the pay and conditions of women at work (see 5.3).

Figure 3.1 shows the increase in the number of women in the UK workforce in each region between 1971 and 1993. It also shows that in most regions the number of males in the workforce has fallen significantly over the same period.

▼ Figure 3.1: Percentage changes in the UK workforce 1971-1993

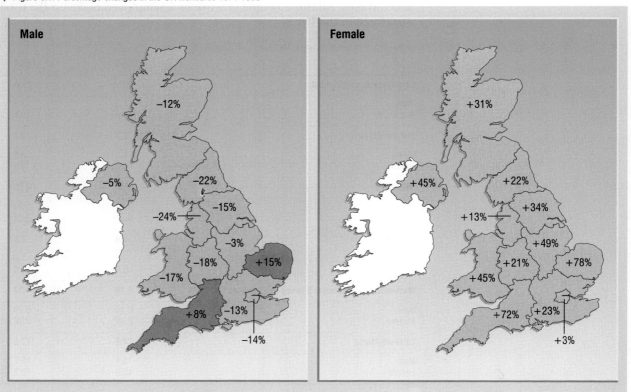

Employment Gazette (Historical Supplement) October 1994

102

Where do people work?

Industrial sectors in the UK and European Union

Most people in the UK and other European Union countries work in the service sector (see 1.2). Industries such as transport and communications, distribution, banking, insurance, and public administration, health and education, employ almost 70% of all workers in the UK. As you can see from Figure 3.2 on page 104, only the Netherlands appears to employ a larger proportion of all its workers in services.

In contrast, secondary industries in the UK – manufacturing and construction – only employ around 30% of workers, with fewer than 2% employed in agriculture. With very few exceptions, most other countries in the EU display the same pattern. Only Greece employs nearly as many people in agriculture as it does in secondary industries. Spain, Portugal, and Eire also employ 10% or more of their workers in farming. In these countries, agriculture, including the sale of fruits, vegetables, and other farm produce exported overseas, remains an important provider of incomes.

Many years ago all these countries would have employed far more people in agriculture and manufacturing industries. However, the fall in employment in these industries and the significant growth in service sector employment has occurred in every developed country. This has been called **deindustrialization** (see 1.2).

Table 3.2 shows that more UK male employees work in manufacturing industries than females. However, whereas 41% of all male employees worked in these industries in 1971, only 28% of male employees did so in 1994. In contrast, most females are employed in service industries, with the vast majority in distribution, hotels and catering, and other services such as public administration, health, and education. Only 15% of females worked in primary or secondary industries in the UK in 1994 compared to 32% in 1971.

▼ Figure 3.2: Civilian employment by industrial sector, European Union* 1993

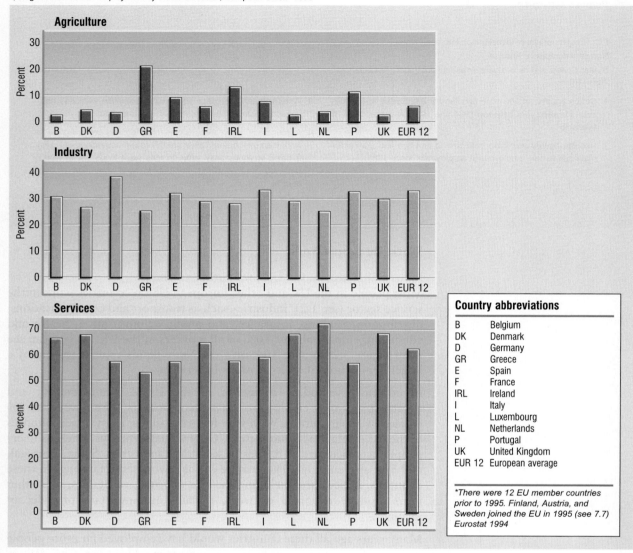

Country abbreviations

B	Belgium
DK	Denmark
D	Germany
GR	Greece
E	Spain
F	France
IRL	Ireland
I	Italy
L	Luxembourg
NL	Netherlands
P	Portugal
UK	United Kingdom
EUR 12	European average

*There were 12 EU member countries prior to 1995. Finland, Austria, and Sweden joined the EU in 1995 (see 7.7) Eurostat 1994

▼ Table 3.2: UK employees by industry and gender

	Males		(Per cent)		Females		(Per cent)	
	1971	1981	1991	1994	1971	1981	1991	1994
Agriculture	2	2	2	2	1	1	1	1
Energy and water supply	5	5	3	2	1	1	1	1
Manufacturing	41	35	29	28	29	19	13	12
Construction	8	8	7	6	1	1	1	1
Distribution, hotels, catering and repairs	13	15	19	20	23	24	25	24
Transport and communication	10	9	9	9	3	3	3	3
Financial and business services	5	7	11	13	7	9	13	13
Other services	15	18	20	21	35	41	44	45
All employees (=100%)(thousands)	13,425	12,277	11,254	10,539	8,224	9,107	10,467	10,363

Social Trends 1995

Occupations

So what jobs do people do in the UK? Just because someone works in a manufacturing plant, it does not mean they are a machinery operator. Similarly, not everyone who works in an office is a secretary or manager. People can have very different occupations within the same industries.

Figure 3.3 shows the distribution of male and female employees in the UK between different occupational groups. Most male employees are either plant or machine operators, managers, and administrators, or in craft or related occupations, such as painters and decorators. In contrast, most women are either clerical or secretarial staff. Over 15% of female employees also provide personal and protective services, such as hairdressing and nursing, while just over 10% are involved in sales as assistants in shops. Far fewer women are managers or administrators or operate machinery, than men.

Occupations in which most women work also tend to be those containing the greatest numbers of part-time workers: clerical and secretarial, childcare and catering, personal services, and sales.

▼ Figure 3.3: Employees and self-employed by gender and occupation, Spring 1994

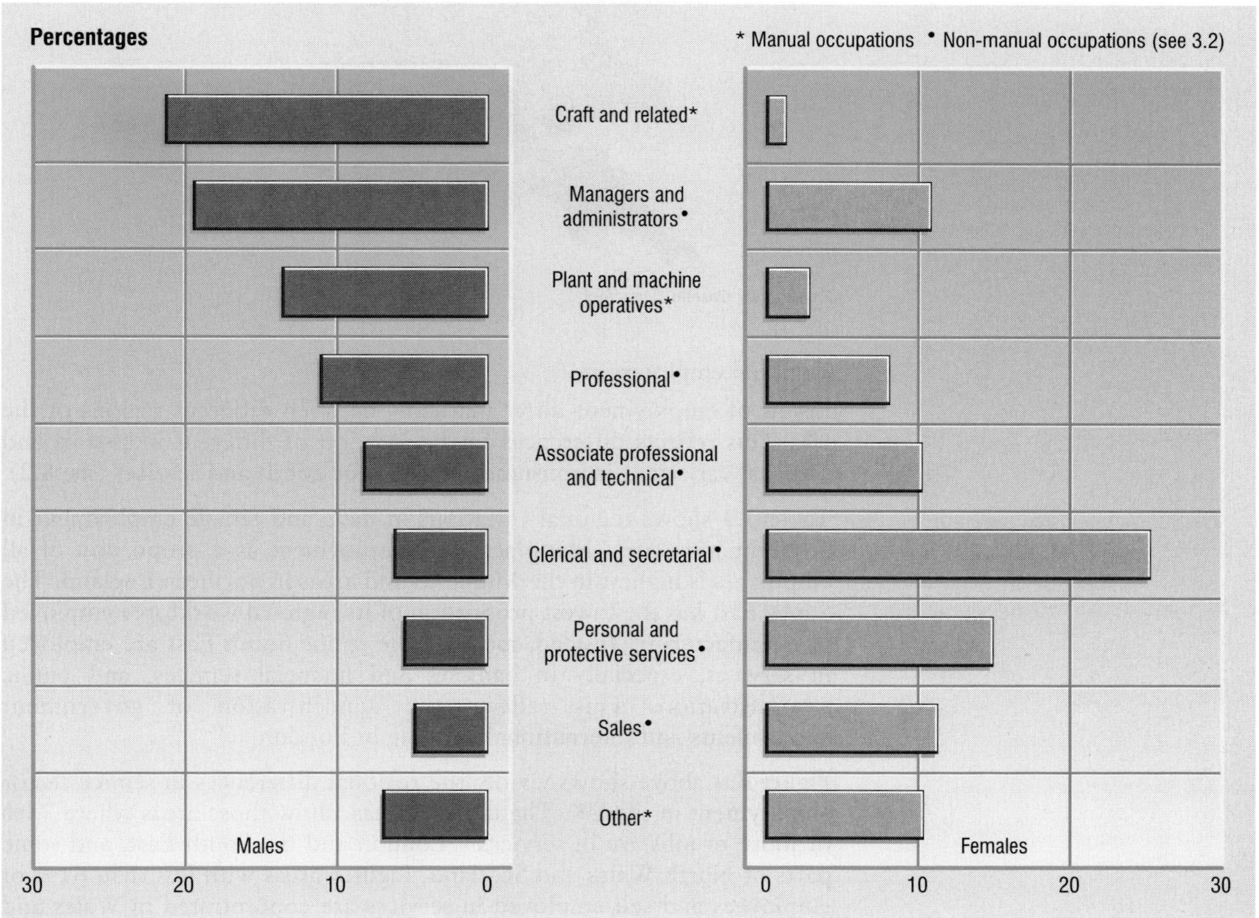

Social Trends 1995

▼ *Figure 3.4: Percentage of employees and self-employed in service industries by area, Autumn 1993*

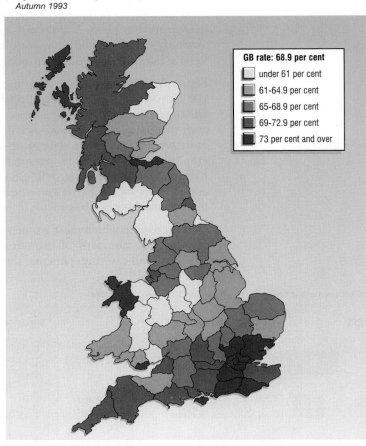

Employment Gazette June 1994

Regional employment

Levels of employment differ markedly between different regions of the UK. This reflects differences in the location of different industries and regional variations in consumer demand for goods and services (see 8.2).

Table 3.3 shows regional variations in male and female employment in different industries. Manufacturing employment as a proportion of all employees is highest in the Midlands and areas in northern England. The South East has the lowest proportion of its regional workforce employed in manufacturing. Instead, most people in the South East are employed in services, especially in banking and financial services, and public administration. This reflects the concentration of government departments and international banking in London.

Figure 3.4 above shows vividly the regional differences in service sector employment in the UK. The darkest areas show those areas where 73% or more of jobs are in services – London and the South East, and some parts of North Wales and Scotland. Lighter areas with less than 61% of employees and self-employed in services are concentrated in Wales and the Midlands, and the North West of England.

▼ Table 3.3: Employees in employment; by industry and gender 1994

	Agriculture, forestry, fishing	Energy and water supply	Manufacturing	Construction, hotels, catering, and repairs	Distribution and commun- ications	Transport	Banking, finance, and insurance services	Public Administration and other services	All industries and services (= 100%) thousands
MALES (Per cent)									
UK	1.9	2.5	27.9	6.4	19.1	8.8	12.1	21.3	10,929
North	1.6	3.8	32.2	8.9	15.7	7.7	8.2	21.8	550
Yorkshire & Humberside	1.8	3.2	33.2	7.0	18.9	7.9	9.0	19.0	923
East Midlands	2.4	3.0	37.8	5.6	18.6	7.2	7.6	17.8	759
East Anglia	4.4	2.6	28.3	5.7	18.8	10.5	10.0	19.8	406
South East	0.9	1.9	19.9	5.3	20.7	10.6	18.0	22.7	3,525
South West	3.3	2.0	27.0	5.3	21.4	7.7	11.3	22.0	843
West Midlands	1.7	1.8	39.6	6.1	18.2	6.8	9.1	16.7	1,022
North West	1.0	2.1	32.4	6.4	18.7	8.4	10.4	20.5	1,153
England	1.6	2.3	28.3	6.0	19.5	8.9	12.7	20.7	9,181
Wales	3.1	3.2	30.7	7.0	16.9	7.4	8.8	23.0	481
Scotland	2.2	4.5	24.6	9.5	17.7	8.6	9.7	23.1	993
N Ireland	6.1	2.1	23.7	7.2	17.0	6.0	7.0	30.9	274
FEMALES (Per cent)									
UK	0.7	0.7	12.4	1.3	23.7	2.9	13.0	45.3	10,622
North	0.4	0.9	12.9	1.2	25.4	2.0	8.1	49.0	528
Yorkshire & Humberside	0.6	0.7	14.2	1.5	24.8	2.3	11.0	44.8	908
East Midlands	1.0	0.5	20.6	1.3	22.9	2.3	8.8	42.5	741
East Anglia	2.2	0.7	12.6	1.2	25.0	3.1	12.6	42.6	381
South East	0.5	0.7	9.4	1.4	22.1	3.8	17.9	44.2	3,375
South West	1.1	0.7	9.4	1.2	27.5	2.1	12.5	45.4	841
West Midlands	0.8	0.7	16.2	1.4	23.0	2.6	11.6	43.8	952
North West	0.4	0.8	13.3	1.1	25.1	2.8	11.2	45.4	1,159
England	0.7	0.7	12.4	1.3	24.6	3.0	13.6	44.5	8,885
Wales	0.7	0.8	13.2	1.1	24.0	1.9	8.7	49.1	476
Scotland	0.5	0.8	12.0	1.4	24.0	2.5	10.9	47.8	991
N Ireland	0.9	0.4	12.6	0.8	20.7	1.6	7.6	55.5	270

Regional Trends 1995

Portfolio Activity 3.2

PC: Collect, analyse and explain information about employment in different regions

Range: Information

Skills: Collect and record data, Interpret and present data, Process and present information

1. Ask your teacher for a copy of the latest issue of the annual government publication *Regional Trends*. Alternatively arrange to borrow it from your local library.

2. Use the latest copy of *Regional Trends* to update the figures on regional employment in Table 3.3 above. Examine both sets of figures and write a brief commentary on how patterns of male and female employment in different industries in different regions have changed over time.

3. In groups, use Table 3.3 or your more up-to-date figures on regional employment to produce 8 UK maps similar to that in Figure 3.4, for the first 4 industry groupings. One member of each group can produce one or two of the maps. First you must each decide on a suitable key and colour coding for each map.

For example, the person producing a map for male employment in 'agriculture, forestry, and fishing' might choose the following keys and colours:

under 1%	white
1% – 2%	yellow
2% – 3%	orange
over 3%	red

4. The easiest way to produce maps is to use a computer graphics package that allows you to shade areas in different colours. Ask a computer teacher for advice. Failing this, photocopy a map of the UK with regional boundaries twelve times for your group, and use colour pencils.

5. Write a few brief sentences to describe the regional patterns of employment shown by each map your group has produced. Remember to photocopy a full set of maps and commentaries for each member of your group to include in all your individual portfolios.

Section **3.2**   Types of employment

Working solution to part-time future

If you are one of the lucky ones driving to a full-time job this morning with its promise of security, retirement, and a pension, here's something that might make you a little less complacent.

Full-time employment is on the way out. Already employers, both private and Government, are contracting out the services they need to outside firms.

Permanent staff are being replaced by part-timers, by people on short-term contracts which may or may not be renewed, or by calling workers in only when they are needed.

In ten years' time far fewer of us will have actual jobs, according to US business consultant William Bridges in his book Jobshift.

Instead you may find yourself with a patchwork of part-time jobs and selling your particular skill to several employers for so many days or weeks a month.

Daily Mirror 21.2.95

The nature of employment is changing. Full-time jobs are slowly disappearing and being replaced by part-time and temporary jobs. Increasing numbers of people unable to find work or fed up with working for somebody else are becoming self-employed. In this section we will examine these different types of employment.

Self-employment

People who start and run their own businesses are **self-employed**. But many self-employed people may still work for someone else. They will often be employed for short periods of time, usually to complete special projects and can be either full-time or part-time. However, self-employed employees will have very different rights and responsibilities to other employees in the same organizations. Self-employed workers will have to pay their own expenses incurred during working, for example, business travel and equipment, from their income. They will also have to make provision for their own pensions, and are unlikely to receive sick or holiday pay (see 7.2).

Only around 1 million people in the UK were self-employed during the 1950s and 1960s. By 1994 over 3 million people were registered as self-employed. Many people became self-employed during the mid-1980s when unemployment in the UK rose to over 3 million people (see Figure 3.5). Many workers found it difficult to get new jobs and so decided to start up their own businesses instead. Self-employment had the added attraction of allowing them to be their own boss. However, many small businesses fail each year. Also, being self-employed often means working long hours and doing all the paperwork yourself (see 7.2).

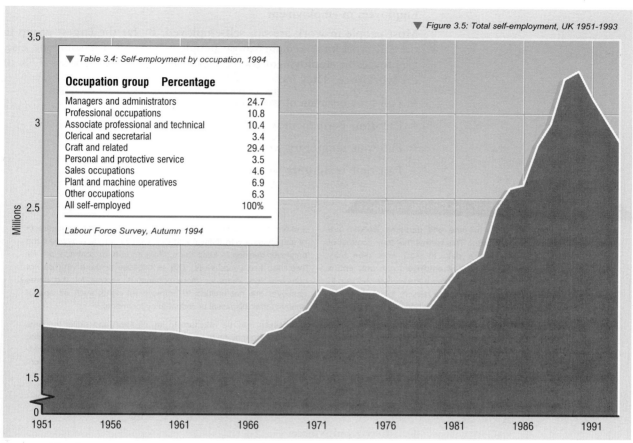

▼ Figure 3.5: Total self-employment, UK 1951-1993

▼ Table 3.4: Self-employment by occupation, 1994

Occupation group	Percentage
Managers and administrators	24.7
Professional occupations	10.8
Associate professional and technical	10.4
Clerical and secretarial	3.4
Craft and related	29.4
Personal and protective service	3.5
Sales occupations	4.6
Plant and machine operatives	6.9
Other occupations	6.3
All self-employed	100%

Labour Force Survey, Autumn 1994

Employment Gazette

The most popular occupations for the self-employed are either as managers and administrators of businesses, or in craft and related occupations, such as artists, designers, gardeners, painters, decorators, and carpenters. Most self-employed people are male (see Table 3.5 below).

▼ Table 3.5: Distribution of UK employees (1993)

	Men		Women		All	
	(000s)	Per cent	(000s)	Per cent	(000s)	Per cent
All in employment	13,934	100	11,446	100	25,381	100
Traditional workforce						
Full-time permanent employees	10,204	61.8	5,480	47.9	15,685	61.8
Flexible workforce						
Full-time temporary employees	393	2.8	266	2.3	659	2.6
Part-time permanent employees	513	3.7	4,204	36.7	4,718	18.6
Part-time temporary employees	174	1.2	451	3.9	624	2.5
Full-time self-employed	2,171	15.6	419	3.7	2,590	10.2
Part-time self-employed	199	1.4	390	3.4	589	2.3
Government training schemes	236	1.7	123	1.1	359	1.4
Unpaid family workers	43	0.3	111	1.0	154	0.6

Employment Gazette July 1994

Employees in employment

Most people in work are not self-employed. By far the largest group in the UK workforce remains those people who work for someone else. **Employees in employment** totalled 21.4 million in 1994, some 77% of the workforce. They include:

- Full-time permanent workers
- Part-time permanent workers
- Full-time temporary workers
- Part-time temporary workers

The traditional workforce v. the flexible workforce

Table 3.5 shows that most full-time and part-time workers are employed on a **permanent** basis. This means that their contract of employment will only specify a date to start work (see 5.3). **Permanent employment** means that employers can only end a contract of employment with an employee if the worker chooses to leave, or if s/he has to be fired for good reason, for example, for stealing, or if s/he has to be made redundant because their job is no longer needed.

People in full-time permanent jobs are often called the **traditional workforce**. It is these jobs which are slowly being replaced by part-time and temporary jobs. Part-timers and temporary workers are being called the **flexible workforce** because employers can hire and fire them more easily. Many will have only short-term contracts of employment with definite end-dates which can be renewed if the employer decides to keep them. Most short-term contracts are for less than two years' work. This is because workers who do not complete two years or more continuous service for the same employer are not entitled to employment rights such as appeal against unfair dismissal or redundancy payments.

Businesses may be reluctant to lay off loyal and skilled full-time workers, who may have received expensive training, when demand for their products falls. Instead they are increasingly taking on part-time and temporary workers for busy periods, and then laying them off when demand is slack.

Full-time employment

Most employees are employed on a **full-time** basis, but an increasing number of jobs are either part-time or temporary. There has also been an increase in the numbers of workers employed on short-term contracts for short periods of time, after which contracts may or may not be renewed.

Part-time employment

A **part-time employee** is officially defined as a person who normally works less than 30 hours a week excluding lunch breaks and overtime work. Some part-time employment may be the result of **job sharing** whereby two or more workers are employed to carry out one full-time job between them (see 4.3).

In 1971 around 3.4 million people were part-timers. By 1994 almost 6 million people worked part-time compared to around 19 million full-time jobs. Figure 3.6 shows that the number of part-time jobs has increased significantly over time. Most part-time workers are women.

There are a number of reasons why firms want to employ part-time workers:

- **Some jobs only take a few hours each day to complete:** Classic examples are cleaners, who are typically employed for a few hours before or after normal working hours, and catering employees commonly working mid-morning to mid-afternoon.

▼ *Figure 3.6: Number of part-time jobs, June of each year, Great Britain 1971-1994*

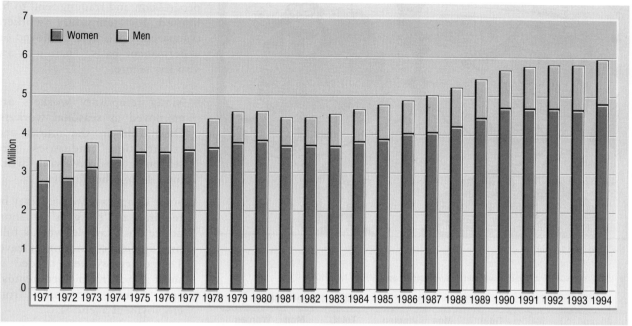

Employment Gazette December 1994

● **To match employment levels to peaks in consumer demand:** Part-time workers can be used to work extra hours when a firm is busy or wants to open longer, for example for late-night or Sunday shopping. Part-timers are particularly attractive to employers in these situations because they rarely qualify for overtime rates of pay beyond the standard working day. For example, the Burton retailing group now employs only part-time staff.

● **Staffing levels can be adjusted easily:** Part-time workers tend to change their jobs more often than full-time workers. This means firms are more able to cut their workforce on a voluntary basis, without the need for redundancies.

● **Part-time workers may be cheaper to employ than full-time workers:** Employers must pay national insurance contributions (NICs) to the government for every worker they employ earning over a certain amount each week. In 1994-95 this lower limit was £56. Because many part-timers do not work enough hours each week to reach this level of pay, employers save paying NICs. Also, until 1994 many part-time workers in the UK did not qualify for the same employment rights as their full-time colleagues, such as redundancy compensation or maternity leave (see 5.3).

Temporary employment

Temporary workers are used by firms to provide extra help during busy times or to cover for employees who are absent. Unlike many other employees, temporary workers will not have a permanent contract of employment with their employer. They are usually only employed for short periods of time, either on a full-time or part-time basis.

The Economist 22.5.93

▼ Table 3.6: Number of full-time and part-time workers by age, GB Winter 1993-94

	All Full-time[a] (000s)			All Part-time[ab] (000s)		
	Total	Men	Women	Total	Men	Women
All 16+	18,432	12,455	5,977	5,893	906	4,988
16-19	546	308	237	574	247	326
20-24	2,215	1,252	964	353	108	245
25-34	5,342	3,612	1,730	1,192	91	1,101
35-49	6,778	4,686	2,092	2,147	112	2,035
50-59(f) 64(m)	3,339	2,509	830	1,115	198	917
60+(f) 65+(m)	212	88	124	512	149	363

a Not including persons on government employment and training programmes or unpaid family workers.
b Include students, particularly in the 16-19 age groups.

Employment Gazette September 1994

Opportunities for career progression and training tend to be limited for temporary workers compared to workers employed on a permanent basis. Their jobs are also less secure.

- Many temporary workers are employed as **seasonal** workers. Often jobs in the tourist and construction industries are seasonal jobs involving work only during the summer.

- Some temporary workers may be required to 'fill gaps' at short notice, for example, when a full-time employee is sick or on leave. Temporary workers needed at short notice (nicknamed 'temps') are often recruited from employment agencies.

- Some workers may be employed for one-off projects on short-term contracts because they have specialist skills required by a business. Workers may also be hired on short-term contracts to provide support services to an organization, such as catering, cleaning, and equipment maintenance.

▼ Seasonal workers

▼ Temps

▼ Casual workers

- **Casual workers** may be employed on a day-to-day basis, usually with no formal contract of employment. They may be required to help out in a shop, office, or on a building site, and will usually receive 'cash in hand' for their efforts. Because casual workers are paid in cash only when they are needed this type of work is often called **unofficial employment**. Casual workers do not qualify for any of the benefits available to officially employed people, such as holidays, sick pay, pensions, or redundancy payments.

In the Summer of 1994, 1.45 million employees worked in temporary jobs: 676,000 men and 776,000 women – around 7% of the total UK workforce.

▼ Figure 3.7: Percentage of employees in temporary employment by region, GB, Winter 1993-94

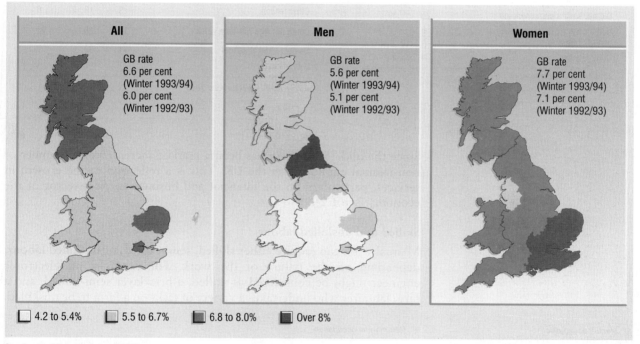

All	Men	Women
GB rate 6.6 per cent (Winter 1993/94) 6.0 per cent (Winter 1992/93)	GB rate 5.6 per cent (Winter 1993/94) 5.1 per cent (Winter 1992/93)	GB rate 7.7 per cent (Winter 1993/94) 7.1 per cent (Winter 1992/93)

☐ 4.2 to 5.4% ☐ 5.5 to 6.7% ▨ 6.8 to 8.0% ■ Over 8%

Employment Gazette August 1994

Manual and non-manual employment

Some jobs are considered **manual occupations** and others are thought of as **non-manual** (turn back to figure 3.3 on page 105).

Manual occupations, such as construction work and operating machinery, involve a large amount of physical work 'by hand' or with the aid of machinery. Non-manual occupations are those which involve more work 'with the mind', for example, most office work. These are also sometimes called **white collar occupations** because people who work in offices tend to wear shirts and ties.

However, most manual workers will also need to complete some administrative or 'white collar' tasks in their jobs, for example, making calculations, solving problems, filling out forms, etc. Similarly, many non-manual workers may be required to use equipment and undertake some repetitive manual tasks.

Why do people want part-time or temporary work?

People work part-time and in temporary jobs for a number of reasons. Some people do so simply because they do not need a full-time wage or because they want to spend more time with their family. However, some people argue they have been forced to take part-time or temporary work because there are simply not enough vacant full-time jobs on offer.

▼ Temporary employees by reason for taking temporary main job (Great Britain, Autumn 1994)

Main Reasons for working in a temporary job (Per cent)	All	Men	Women
Could not find a permanent job	45	53	38
Did not want a permanent job	25	17	32
Had a contract which included a period of training	6	7	5
Other reasons	24	23	25

Employment Gazette April 1995

▼ Part-time workers by reason for taking a part-time job (Great Britain, Autumn 1994)

Reasons for taking part-time work (Per cent)	All	Men	Women
Did not want full-time work	74	38	81
because:			
Financially secure but want to work part-time	12	14	12
Earn enough money working part-time	7	5	7
Want to spend more time with family	22	1	26
Domestic commitments	21	2	25
Other reason	9	13	8
Could not find full-time work	14	29	11
Student / still at school	11	30	7
Ill or disabled	1	3	1

Employment Gazette April 1995

Since the mid-1980s there has been a marked increase in the number of non-manual employees in the UK. This is a reflection of the growth in services, particularly in the financial and business services sector of the economy (see 1.2).

Skilled and unskilled labour

Manual work can require either **skilled, semi-skilled, or unskilled labour**, depending on the nature of the work. For example, an electronic engineer might be considered as skilled, a bricklayer semi-skilled, and a farm labourer who undertakes a variety of tasks on a farm to be unskilled.

▼ Manual occupation

▼ Non-manual occupation

▼ *Skilled, semi-skilled, or unskilled labour?*

Similarly non-manual work can be either skilled – for example, a computer programmer – or unskilled, such as an office messenger. However, it is difficult to draw a hard-and-fast line. Doctors, nurses, teachers, accountants, lawyers, and computer programmers are clearly highly skilled people. But a farm labourer will also need skills to operate farm machinery and drive tractors. Secretaries must be able to use computers and have good communication skills.

In general, a worker is considered skilled if s/he needs to undergo intensive education and/or training in order to carry out his or her job.

The demand for skilled workers is increasing all the time. Firms want people who are able to do their jobs well and can also adapt their skills to a variety of tasks. Technological change also means that the demand for skills by business is always changing. For example, the introduction of computers created a demand for workers with skills in programming. Workers must continually update their skills through education and training if they want to keep their jobs.

Skill needs in Britain

A survey of employers' needs for workers with different skills is carried out each year by the Department of Employment. In 1994, 1 in 5 employers interviewed said they were having problems recruiting new employees with the right skills. The hardest-to-fill vacancies were in:

- Health and social work
- Machine operations in manufacturing
- Finance
- Hotels and restaurants
- Education

Portfolio Activity 3.3

PC: Describe and give examples of types of employment, Compare working conditions for employees in different organizations
Range: Types of employment, Compare working conditions
Skills: Collect and record data, Produce written material

1. Draw up a table with the following column headings:

   – Job advertised
   – Type of employment (full-time or part-time)
   – Type of contract (permanent or temporary)
   – Manual or non-manual
   – Skilled, semi-skilled, or unskilled
   – Skills, qualifications required
   – Hours of work
   – Wages/salary
   – Other benefits (e.g. holidays, free medical insurance, pension, etc.)

Now in groups, select at least 20 different job adverts from local papers and complete your table with brief details about each job. Also consider how far the wages or salary for each job reflects other aspects such as skills and qualifications needed, level of responsibility, hours of work, etc.

2. Find out how many different types of employment exist in a medium-sized organization of your choice, and in comparison with your school. For each organization draw a pie-chart to show percentages employed in each of the following categories:

   – full-time permanent employees
   – full-time temporary employees
   – part-time temporary employees
   – part-time permanent employees
   – others

3. Write to or visit your nearest Training and Enterprise Council (TEC) to find out about the skills employers in your area want their workers to have.

Section **3.3** **Working conditions**

Why do people want to work?

Most people go to work or seek work to earn money to pay for the goods and services they need and want (see 2.1). People will supply their labour in return for wages or salaries.

However, other aspects of working are also important to people. Many people want the opportunity to mix with other people, be creative, and have responsibility over an area of work, or for caring for others – for example, nurses and charity workers. Others such as directors of large companies, or politicians want the **status** certain jobs give them. Often workers are attracted to different jobs by other benefits such as free medical insurance or a company car.

All of the above factors give people **satisfaction** in their jobs. When choosing between different jobs, people will naturally take into account how much they pay and the amount of job satisfaction they think they will get from them.

What makes a job satisfying?

- Good wages and other benefits, e.g. pension, company car
- Generous holiday entitlement
- Pleasant working environment
- Challenging and interesting tasks
- Variety in the working day
- Opportunities to learn and try new ideas
- Availability of training
- Working as part of a team

- Job security
- Being consulted on management decisions
- Having responsibility
- Regular feedback on performance
- Recognition for good work through pay bonuses or promotion
- Good social relationships inside and outside of work with work colleagues

---

Portfolio Activity 3.4

PC: Present results of a comparison of working conditions
Range: Compare working conditions
Skills: Take part in discussions, Collect and record data

Conduct a survey of at least five employees you know. Prepare a short questionnaire in order to find out what they like and what they dislike about their work and the organizations they work for.

Write up a short report of the findings from your survey. Conclude your report by suggesting what you think are the main factors that give workers job satisfaction.

In choosing between different jobs, people will also consider how long it takes them to travel to and from work to home and the cost of travelling. For example, it would not be sensible to spend over two hours travelling each day at a cost of over £10 if the job is for three hours each evening part-time at £5 an hour! Some firms may help their employees with the cost of their travel by giving them allowances or interest-free loans to buy season tickets.

However, in some cases the work itself may involve travelling long distances. For example, sales representatives will often have to travel around the country or even abroad to promote their products. Couriers and hauliers often carry goods for delivery over long distances. Business managers may have to attend meetings with other organizations at home and abroad. Some people are attracted to particular jobs because of the prospects of travel and are usually able to claim travelling expenses from their employers.

The journey to work

Greater London residents in full-time employment made 1.7 million trips from home to work during a typical weekday in 1991, according to the 1991 London Area Transport Survey.

Sixty-three per cent of trips from home to work in London were less than 5 miles. Of these, 45% were by car, 31% by public transport, and 17% on foot. Less than 1% of trips from home to work were over 30 miles long.

What are working conditions?

When people go to work they will expect to receive a number of benefits from their employers and to work in environments that are both pleasant and safe.

The main **working conditions** of any type of employment are:

- The hours of work, including any overtime
- Level and method of payment, and other benefits
- Entitlements to holidays
- Job security
- Opportunities for career progression
- Training opportunities
- The physical conditions of the workplace, which should be both healthy and safe to work in

If working conditions are unreasonable, the job satisfaction of workers will suffer. The firms responsible will find it difficult to keep existing staff and to recruit new workers.

Portfolio Activity 3.5

PC: Compare working conditions for employees in different organizations

Range: Compare working conditions

Skills: Read and respond to written material, Collect and record data, Produce written material

1. Consider the two employees in the pictures below. How do you think their working conditions might compare?

▼ *Full-time permanent construction site supervisor. Studies engineering at college for three years. Currently on day release to study management skills with a view to possible promotion to site manager. Starts work at 7.30 am every day, sometimes including Saturday and Sunday. Current salary around £1,500 per month including overtime. Five weeks holiday each year.*

▼ *Full-time administration assistant in a government department on short-term contract. Hoping to have contract extended or made permanent. Able to work flexitime as long he is in before 10 am and doesn't leave until after 4.30 pm. Any additional hours worked can be totalled and added to basic leave of 22 days per year. Salary currently £10,000 per year. Has received some computer training.*

2. Collect information on the jobs of two people you know. One should be a permanent full-time employee and the other either part-time, temporary, self-employed, or employed on a short-term contract. From interviews and your own observations and knowledge of the work they do, compare their working conditions and write up your findings in a short word-processed report.

Hours of work

All employees will have agreed hours they are expected to work each day, week, month or year, depending on the precise form of agreement. The basic working week in the UK is 37.5 to 40 hours each week for manual workers and 35-38 hours for non-manual workers. However, due to overtime, many workers work longer than the basic week, especially in manual occupations.

Actual hours and days worked will vary between jobs. Some employees – for example, staff in shops – may have to arrive and leave work at the same time every day to coincide with opening and closing times. Many shop workers are also obliged to work some Saturdays and Sundays in return for days off during the week. Most office staff work what is considered the 'normal' working week from 9 am to 5.30 pm Monday to Friday each week. **Shiftwork** and **flexitime** also mean hours of work can vary widely between industries and occupations (see 4.3).

▼ Table 3.7: Average hours per week worked by employment status, 1994

All employees	32.4
Full-time	38.2
Part-time	15.5
Self-employed	**39.4**
Full-time	45.6
Part-time	12.7
Total employees and self-employed	**33.3**

Employment Gazette May 1995

In 1994, the self-employed and all employees – full-time, part-time, permanent, and temporary – worked an average of 33.3 hours each week in their main jobs. Full-time employees worked an average of 38.2 hours each week, compared to 15.5 hours for part-time workers, while full-time self-employed people averaged 45.6 hours each week.

People working in service industries tended to work 30.8 hours each week, compared to manufacturing workers who averaged 34.9 hours. Because more women work part-time than men, the average number of hours worked by females in work was 25.5 compared to 37.7 hours worked each week by men.

Pay

Wages and salaries
Wages and salaries are payments made to workers.

● Workers who receive a **salary** normally receive the same amount of money each month, regardless of the number of hours they work each day, week, or month. Monthly payments will simply be calculated as 1/12th of an agreed annual salary. The amount received by a worker is only likely to change if they are promoted, demoted, or receive a pay rise. Workers in clerical, managerial, and professional occupations tend to be paid salaries.

● Workers who receive **wages** are normally paid by the hour at the end of each week or month. The more hours they work per day, week, or month, the more pay they will receive. Often, work outside of normal hours, for example, early in the morning, late in the evening, or at weekends, will be paid at **overtime** rates which are 1.5 times or twice the normal hourly wage rate. Manual workers are usually paid an hourly **wage rate** and are required to 'clock on and off' as proof of the number of hours they have worked.

Other payments

In addition to wages and salaries, workers may receive additional payments that make up their earnings:

Performance-related pay (PRP) describes systems that link the pay of workers to some measure of individual, group, or organizational effort. These can include:

● **Piecework** payments, normally expressed as a rate per unit of output. The more an individual or group of workers produces, the more they are paid. The wages of factory workers will often be topped up by these payments to give them an incentive to work harder and produce more.

● **Bonuses**, for good work or meeting a tight deadline. Many workers get a pay bonus at Christmas from their employers as a gesture of goodwill.

● **Merit pay**, where the employee receives a level of bonus or basic pay linked to an assessment and appraisal of their performance by their superiors. This system is popular in office-based occupations.

● **Profit-sharing** and **share option schemes**, whereby individual employees receive a reward in terms of cash or company shares. The size of reward will normally depend on company profits over a given period.

Commission is often paid to workers involved in sales, such as insurance and double-glazing salespeople, financial advisers, and travel agents, according to the value of sales they achieve.

Non-monetary rewards are 'payments' in a form other than money, for example, free medical insurance, subsidized meals, and company cars. They make a job more attractive, but do not add to employees' earnings.

Gross and net earnings

The total earnings of an employee each week or month will consist of wages plus any overtime and other payments such as bonuses. It is usual for an employer to deduct income tax and national insurance contributions from the gross earnings of their employees before they are paid (see 5.4). Payments after these deductions have been made are known as **net earnings**. Self-employed workers are responsible for paying their own taxes direct to the government tax authority, the Inland Revenue.

▼ Figure 3.8: Some typical occupations in each range of the distribution of gross weekly earnings

Wage differentials

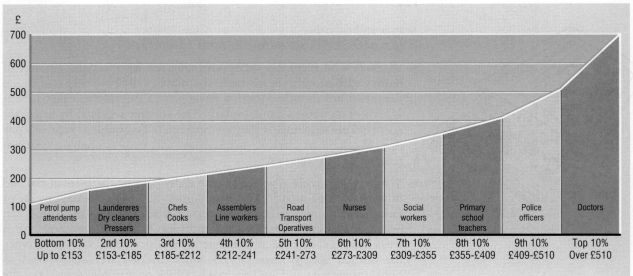

	Bottom 10% Up to £153	2nd 10% £153-£185	3rd 10% £185-£212	4th 10% £212-241	5th 10% £241-273	6th 10% £273-£309	7th 10% £309-£355	8th 10% £355-£409	9th 10% £409-£510	Top 10% Over £510
	Petrol pump attendents	Laundereres Dry cleaners Pressers	Chefs Cooks	Assemblers Line workers	Road Transport Operatives	Nurses	Social workers	Primary school teachers	Police officers	Doctors

Employment Gazette November 1993

The differences in wages paid to people doing different jobs are known as **wage differentials** (see Figure 3.8). Clearly, some people earn more than others simply because they work longer hours. But there are a number of other reasons why wage differentials exist:

- Workers with skills in high demand by firms will tend to receive higher wages than those with old or unwanted skills, especially if the skilled workers are in short supply.

- Workers who are willing to work unsociable hours or do dangerous jobs will also be paid more – for example, coal miners and the police. Unless organizations offer these workers good wages, they will find it difficult to recruit and retain them.

- Some jobs require long periods of education and training. People might be discouraged from studying to become doctors, lawyers, or other professionals if they did not have the incentive of high wages or salaries after qualifying.

- If consumer demand for a particular good or service is high, the firm making or providing it may want to take on more employees to increase production. This will tend to push up the wages of those workers in demand.

- In some areas of the UK, high levels of unemployment have tended to depress wage and salary levels offered by firms because unemployed workers are often willing to accept lower pay in order to get work. This has resulted in **regional wage differentials** – different wage rates for the same job but in different areas.

▼ *Figure 3.9: Average gross weekly earnings by age and sex, full-time workers, April 1994*

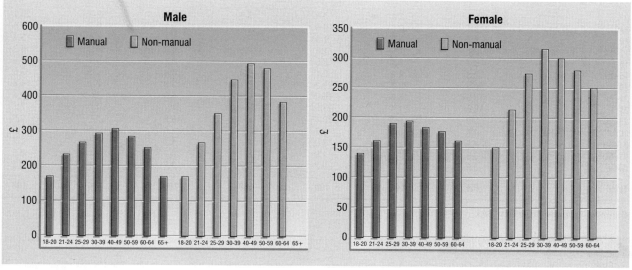

*Employment Gazette April 1995
(New Earnings Survey 1994)*

The spread of average weekly earnings among full-time male and female manual and non-manual employees by age and sex are shown in Figure 3.9. Two facts are immediately obvious: non-manual employees tend to be paid more than manual workers, and male employees tend to earn more than females. Earnings of male workers tend to peak when they are in their forties, while female earnings tend to peak in their thirties.

Holiday entitlement

There is no law in the UK that states how much holiday workers should be entitled to. Employers are able to decide how much or how little holiday they are prepared to give and pay for. However, employers that are reluctant to give their employees much holiday will find that their workers will lack motivation and may look for jobs elsewhere. Table 3.8 on page 122 shows that most UK employees receive four to five weeks' paid leave each year. On average, full-time employees receive 24 days paid annual holiday (men 23 days and women 25 days).

However, the table also shows that in 1992, 3.1 per cent of full-time employees and 32.7 per cent of part-timers received no paid holiday (10.1 per cent of all employees). Around 15 per cent of full-time employees received less than four weeks' holiday and 7 per cent received less than three.

The vast majority of workers receiving no paid holiday either worked only a small number of hours each week in part-time employment, were employed on a temporary contract, or had worked for their employer for less than a year.

▼ Table 3.8: Employees' paid annual holiday entitlement (days)

	Full-time			Part-time		
	All employees	All	Male	Female	All	Male	Female
All employees (000s)	21,351	16,222	10,558	5,664	5,129	622	4,507
Days holiday							**Per cent**
0	10.1	3.1	3.0	3.2	32.7	59.3	29.1
1–9	2.4	0.7	0.6	0.7	8.1	9.7	7.9
10	2.7	1.8	1.9	1.6	5.3	4.4	5.4
11–14	2.7	1.5	1.5	1.6	6.6	4.2	6.9
15	6.4	6.4	6.5	6.4	6.2	4.1	6.5
16–19	2.3	2.0	2.1	1.9	3.4	*	3.6
20	20.9	23.1	23.2	23.1	13.9	7.2	14.8
21–24	13.9	16.0	15.9	16.3	6.9	3.8	7.4
25	18.0	21.4	21.5	21.4	7.1	2.1	7.7
26–29	8.2	9.7	10.1	9.0	3.2	*	3.5
30	4.8	5.9	6.7	4.2	1.5	*	1.5
31–40	2.9	3.5	3.9	2.8	1.1	*	1.2
41–50	0.9	1.0	1.0	1.1	0.7	*	0.8
50+	3.6	3.8	2.2	6.7	3.2	*	3.5
Total	**100**	**100**	**100**	**100**	**100**	**100**	**100**

Employment Gazette, September 1993

The European Union Working Time Directive

The UK has few legal restrictions on hours of work, except for those jobs which involve driving goods and public service vehicles, where laws have been introduced for reasons of public safety. However, the UK has been resisting a 1993 European Union (EU) Directive which sets an upper limit of 48 hours per week, including overtime, for all employees. The EU directive also states that all workers should be entitled to a minimum of four weeks' paid holiday each year and minimum rest periods each day. The UK has argued that these restrictions on hours would introduce unnecessary bureaucracy and impose significant costs on UK industry. Many firms, especially in agriculture, construction, and manufacturing, rely on employees working up to and over 48 hours each week, rather than having to take on extra staff. Many workers also rely on overtime working to boost their pay packets.

Career progression

Defining what we mean by a 'career' is difficult. Simply working in the same job or a number of different jobs during your working life would not normally be thought of as a career, especially if those jobs involve mundane, repetitive work.

A career normally means working your way up an organization, gaining more experience, and taking on more responsibility in return for more pay. However, not everybody wants to progress in this way. Some people prefer to try out new things, and move from one department to another within the same organization – for example, from production to marketing to finance – broadening their experience as they go. Sometimes, a person's career prospects can be limited by the number of jobs available, or because they are not thought to be suitable for promotion. In other cases career moves may be ruled out because the job involves too much travelling, or because the employee is not able or willing to relocate.

Because of the falling number of full-time permanent jobs, many career opportunities are disappearing. Part-time and temporary jobs present fewer career opportunities to workers, because so many tend to be low-paid and low-skilled.

Careers in banking – an example

Management Grades

After Grade 5, the next step is a managerial position, either in a branch, starting with a small one and working your way up, or as a manager of a department undertaking a specialist role, such as personnel, marketing and sales, business finance, auditing and credit control, international, or IT.

Grades 4–5

By this stage, an employee will be working closely with the management team and probably supervising a small team of people. Dealings with customers will become more complex and could involve analysing balance sheets and lending propositions, and preparing reports.

Grade 3

When an employee reaches this grade, they will take on supervisory duties and support more junior members of staff. An employee might be responsible for buying and selling foreign currency and travellers' cheques, assisting customers, and even granting some loans.

Grade 2

Most jobs at this level involve meeting customers – perhaps as a cashier or receptionist – maintaining cash-dispenser machines, processing standing orders, issuing cash cards, and closing accounts.

Grade 1

In this trainee grade you will be expected to undertake basic clerical duties such as inputting records onto computers, filing, faxing, photocopying, and handling routine customer enquiries.

Jobs in banking are graded according to how difficult they are, how much responsibility they carry, and how much experience they require.

Portfolio Activity 3.6

PC: Present results of a comparison of working conditions

Range: Compare working conditions

Skills: Collect and record data, Produce written material

Investigate and report on career opportunities in a business sector of your choice, such as catering, construction, manufacturing, insurance, or retailing.

As a guide, here are some questions you might need to research if you choose health care provision as your business sector:

- What types of jobs are available?

- How can people apply to be a hospital porter or ambulance driver?

- How can people become nurses?

- What qualifications and experience will they need to be promoted to a sister or matron?

- What qualifications and training do people need to become doctors?

- What areas can doctors and nurses specialize in – for example, radiology, physiotherapy, maternity?

- How can doctors become consultants and surgeons?

- What are the main responsibilities of each job?

Opportunities for training

Training workers to improve their existing skills and learn new ones can be very important to a business. Training workers can improve the amount and quality of work they do.

Often training is linked to new developments to give workers the skills to operate new production processes and equipment. A worker may also undergo training – for example, in keeping business accounts – in order to take on a new role in the firm. Training, therefore, is especially important in career development and can increase the satisfaction workers get from their jobs.

However, training can be expensive. Firms will tend to restrict training to what is entirely necessary and will often only train employees who are likely to stay with the firm for a long time. Permanent full-time workers will, therefore, tend to receive more training than their temporary and part-time colleagues. Training for these workers will tend to be short lived and 'on the job'. It will also focus only on the skills they need to carry out their immediate tasks, such as operating an electronic cash register, and on essential health and safety matters.

Types of training

New employees are often introduced to their organization through a programme of **induction training**. This involves learning about the way the business works and what other staff do. For example, it may contain information about:

- The history and development of the business
- On-site facilities, such as canteens and toilets
- Rules and safety procedures
- Relationships between different jobs
- Employee benefits and services

Once in a job, an employee may receive training to develop their work skills. This can be **on-the-job** or **off-the-job** training.

When training is on-the-job, employees are trained while they are carrying out their normal duties at their place of work. This can take a number of forms:

- **Shadowing** – when a new worker is shown what to do by an experienced worker. It can vary from simply sitting next to a machine operator or attending meetings with another office employee.

- **Job rotation** – involves a employee training to do different jobs over short periods of time, either to become multi-skilled or simply to gain knowledge of the way in which the whole company functions. This is often an important element in the training of management trainees.

- **Apprenticeships** – here, the training is normally sufficiently long and thorough to ensure that very little extra training will ever be necessary, apart from some occasional updating of worker skills and knowledge.

Off-the-job training will involve employees attending courses and training programmes away from their normal jobs:

- **In-house courses** are run by firms for their own employees. Some large organizations, like banks and building societies, even have their own residential training centres or colleges offering a variety of courses run by specialist training officers.

- **External courses** may be run by another employer or at a specialist training centre, or with a supplier of new equipment who is willing to train workers how to use it.

- **Vocational and professional courses** are provided by colleges, universities, and increasingly schools, as a means of supporting what is learnt in the workplace. Vocational courses, such as NVQs, provide training in competencies or job-related skills. Professional courses, for example, in accountancy, engineering, or law, are normally completed by university graduates entering these professions in order to develop their careers.

Training in London

A survey of employers by the London Training and Enterprise Councils (TECs) in 1994-95, showed that over 60% of firms in London provided induction training for new employees. Training in information technology was also very important. Relatively few firms provided training in manual skills.

Employers identified the major areas of training growth as:

- Customer care
- Quality awareness
- Information technology
- Training related to environmental legislation
- Health and safety

Leading themes in training (% of all firms providing training in the previous 12 months)

Portfolio Activity 3.7

PC: Present results of a comparison of working conditions

Range: Compare working conditions

Skills: Collect and record data, Take part in discussions, Produce written material, Present information

Look at the pictures below.

1. For each one suggest:

   i   What knowledge or skills are being taught?

   ii What kinds of training methods are being used?

   iii What types of business organization would you expect to use these training methods?

   iv What other forms of training could be used to train the workers in each case?

2. Investigate the training available to two employees you know, preferably in different occupations and industrial sectors. What methods are used to train them? What skills are they trained in? What are the benefits of training to the trainee and to their employers?

Job security

Most employees today want to work in a secure job where they can plan ahead knowing they are unlikely to be made redundant. But in practice this is becoming increasingly rare.

▼ *UK coal mines were once thought to offer their employees jobs for life. Few mines are still working in the UK today.*

Temporary employment is perhaps the least secure form of employment. But even permanent jobs cannot be entirely safe in an ever-changing business environment. For example, many years ago, people living and working in coalmining towns and villages in the UK thought they had jobs for life. Fathers, sons, and even grandsons worked in the local pits. Today, few coal mines exist and most mining jobs have disappeared due to advances in mining technology, competition from cheaper coal imports from overseas, and a switch in household demand towards cleaner sources of fuel, namely electricity and gas.

Changes in technology, competition from rival firms at home and overseas, changes in consumer demand – can all lead to changes in numbers employed in different industries and occupations (see 3.4). However, some jobs are less affected by these changes than others. For example, traditionally secure jobs include:

- **Teaching** – because there will always be schoolchildren and students who need to be taught
- **Doctors** – because people will always get ill
- **Emergency services** – such as the police and fire brigade

In the past, office jobs in the public sector were often considered to be among the most secure. Civil servants in government departments provide advice to whichever political party forms the UK government. They do not have to make a profit, nor are they affected by competition or consumer demand. However, more recently jobs in the civil service have become less secure as the UK government has cut staff numbers in a bid to reduce costs. Personal computers have also done away with a number of tasks which in the past were carried out by office workers.

▼ *Secure jobs?*

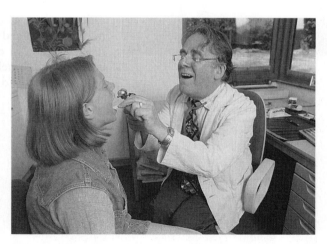

The working environment
Working conditions vary greatly from industry to industry and from organization to organization. For example, consider the physical aspects of an office compared to a large iron and steel foundry. The office is probably air-conditioned, carpeted, attractively decorated, and quiet. The steel plant is likely to be hot, dirty, smelly, noisy, and potentially hazardous to workers' health.

▼ *Pleasant working environment?*

▼ *Unpleasant working environment?*

Even within the same industry working conditions can vary widely. For example, contrast the worker on an outside market stall with the assistant in a plush department store, or the policeman on the beat with an inspector in an office, or machine operators in a large modern computer-aided manufacturing plant with those in an old run-down factory.

In a typical week in the UK, around 9 workers are killed as a result of accidents in the workplace. Many more receive injury or suffer health problems related to working, from stress to breathing disorders. It is not surprising that firms are required by law to provide, as far as possible, a healthy and safe environment for their workers and customers (see 5.3). A firm that fails to take into account the health and safety of its workers will not only find it difficult to recruit and retain its staff, but will fail to meet targets for output, sales, and profits.

Measures that can make a workplace safer, healthier, and more pleasant to work in include:

- Providing protective clothing, goggles, breathing masks if appropriate
- Providing ear protectors against excessive noise
- Training staff in health and safety matters
- Maintaining safety equipment and clothing
- Allowing breaks for lunch and tea so that workers do not become tired
- Providing First Aid kits and medical officers
- Controlling workplace temperatures
- Installing filters to reduce air pollution
- Refurbishing offices and canteens

How necessary these measures are will depend on the materials and processes being used and the nature of the environment. For example, office workers will need to be aware of fire drills and precautions relating to the prolonged use of computer screens, the movement of office furniture, etc. In contrast, many manufacturing plants are by their very nature noisy, smelly and potentially hazardous places to work in, and stricter health and safety measures will be needed.

▼ *Health and safety at work*

Portfolio Activity 3.8

PC: Present results of a comparison of working conditions

Range: Compare working conditions

Skills: Read and respond to written material, Produce written material, Use images

Office workers face a harsh new world

Executives working for International Business Machines (IBM) in the USA have seen the future and it looks like a warehouse. Gone is the polished nameplate and the family photograph on their own desk. Their new district office is as impersonal as a left luggage locker.

When Debbie Zilai, a 40-year-old manager, arrives for work she is assigned an empty cubicle in a vast steel fortress, once used as an iron box warehouse.

The warehouse in Cranford, New Jersey, is divided into 350 bare work stations with just a telephone, a computer and a black plastic tray. Nothing can be left overnight because somebody new will be assigned to each desk the next day. IBM has provided only 350 desks between 800 employees. This is because it wants to make sure its executives are out on the road meeting clients and pushing for new business.

Employees cannot afford to argue with these changes when they know that IBM is planning to cut 60,000 jobs worldwide by the end of 1994 and is taking radical steps to reduce its manufacturing and office space to reduce costs.

Adapted from The Sunday Times 3.4.94

1. How has the introduction of new technology affected the working conditions of employees at IBM?

2. Why has IBM introduced new technology and working conditions for many of its employees?

3. What do you think the physical working conditions of the following jobs are like?

 – farmer
 – doctor
 – hairdresser
 – shop assistant
 – builder
 – secretary
 – fireman
 – soldier
 – steel foundry worker
 – bus driver
 – TV newsreader
 – laboratory assistant

4. Investigate and report on the working environments in two workplaces of your choice. They should be sufficiently different to allow you to make a good comparison.

Write up a short report, using photographs or drawings of your two workplaces to illustrate points you make. Your report should describe:

• The characteristics of each environment in terms of place (i.e. indoors or outdoors), lighting, smell, noise, temperature, potential hazards, cleanliness, etc.

• Measures that have been used to improve each working environment

• Any additional measures that you think could be taken to improve each environment further

The impact and use of technology

The nature and working conditions of many jobs have changed dramatically over the last ten years or more due to technological advance. Technology has had the following impact on jobs:

• It has created new jobs and a demand for workers with new skills

• It has replaced workers and made them redundant

• It has affected the tasks workers carry out

• It has influenced the location of jobs

All of these changes will continue as technology advances. What is new and in demand one year will be obsolete the next.

Computers are at the heart of many technological developments in manufacturing and service industries. Computers can be used to design goods, factory, office, and shop layouts, control whole assembly lines, and to communicate information accurately and quickly over long distances, allowing firms to contact their suppliers and customers quickly and easily (see 14.5).

Technology in the office

Here are just some of the devices modern office workers are expected to use. Office workers make great use of computers to help them produce documents, make complex calculations, and prepare graphs – all in a fraction of the time it would have taken using typewriters or calculators. Computers can also store vast amounts of data rather than using up space to store files in endless rows of filing cabinets.

As office systems have become computerized, less administrative staff have been required.

TELEX

COMPUTER NETWORKS

INTERNET

TELEPHONE ANSWERING MACHINES

FAX MACHINE

Electronic mail

PAGER

VIDEOPHONES

Mobile phones

Videoconferencing facilities

Technology in the factory

In many industries robots are now used to perform dangerous, repetitive, or very intricate jobs faster and more accurately than human labour. This has improved the working conditions of many workers no longer required to do these tasks, but it has also meant that many manufacturing jobs have simply disappeared.

Most robots are simply 'intelligent arms' which can be programmed and controlled by computers to carry out assembly work, paint spraying, packing, welding and other tasks. This is known as **computer-aided manufacture (CAM)**.

Computer-aided design (CAD) is capable of generating, storing, and using geometric graphics. CAD is used by design engineers in many industries to solve design problems, from modelling new products and packaging to designing a new office layout.

The newspaper and magazine printing and publishing industry has been also revolutionized by the introduction of personal computers and desktop publishing software. Journalists are now able to write and design the layout of their articles on computers directly linked to the printing presses. The craft skills of typesetters are now no longer wanted.

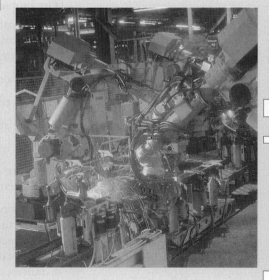

Technology in shops

ISBN 0-19-832751-X

9 780198 327516

Technological change has had a great impact on retailing. Computers can be used for automated stock control. For example, a central computer in a supermarket can be hooked up to cash registers to monitor sales. When sales of certain items have reduced stocks to a pre-set level, the computer can automatically send out electronic orders for more to the computers of suppliers.

Self-service in shops is now commonplace thanks to **barcodes** on products. Each barcode contains information about a product, such as brand name and price, which can be read by electronic cash registers. Automated tills can also add up accurately, print cheques, process credit and debit card purchases, and work out any change that needs to be paid. No longer do shop assistants have to punch in prices to a till or even add up prices in their heads.

In the future people may simply order goods and services via computers in their own homes linked to shops and warehouses. Satellite TV has also created home shopping channels such as QVC.

Technology and the number of jobs

Technology has created many new jobs in the electronics and computer industries. These jobs have not just been for workers who manufacture and assemble consumer electronic goods, such as video recorders, CD players, computers, and telecommunications equipment, such as mobile phones. Many more jobs have also been created for people who research, develop, market, distribute, and sell these advanced products.

Most medium-sized and large organizations can afford to employ their own in-house computer specialists to advise on their use, develop programs, and maintain equipment. However, technological change has also made many workers redundant. People have lost their jobs because:

- New machinery and equipment, such as robots and automated manufacturing processes, can do the work instead

- Fewer supervisors and managers are needed to control machinery

- Firms have been able to increase output without the need for additional workers and in some cases with far fewer employees. Because new machinery is often faster than human labour, production costs can be much lower.

- Firms which have been unable to keep up with, or afford, technological developments in production have been forced to close down. This is because their costs were so much higher than those firms who were able to use the new technology.

However, there has been a lot of scaremongering about technology taking over people's jobs. Some jobs, such as hairdressing, nursing, teaching, and acting, can never be replaced by machinery because they are based on human contact. These and many other jobs can only be helped by new technology, not replaced by it.

Technology and productivity

The amount of output produced per period by the human, natural and man-made resources employed in an organization is known as their **productivity**. If more output can be produced using the same or less labour, materials, and machinery, then their productivity will have increased.

131

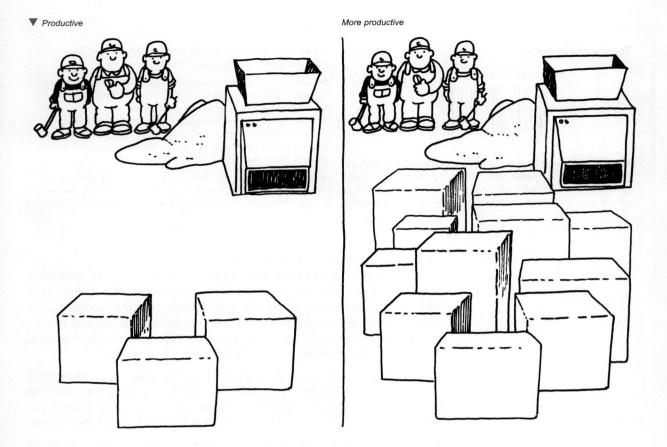

▼ *Productive*

More productive

Introducing new equipment in the factory, shop, or office has enabled many organizations to become more productive without having to employ more workers. New equipment can help workers complete tasks faster and with less waste than before, and even replace those workers altogether. The result is that more output can be produced with less labour input.

Technology and skills
The tasks undertaken by some workers have been greatly affected by new technology.

- **De-skilling:** De-skilling has affected many occupations. For example, sales assistants no longer need to type in prices to a cash register or add up rows of figures – barcodes containing this information are now simply read by electronic scanners. Many consumer electronic goods can now be repaired simply by replacing their printed circuits. This means that firms no longer need skilled workers to diagnose faults and make repairs.

Because a number of jobs have been de-skilled, employers have been able to replace their skilled workers with semi- or unskilled labour on lower wages.

▼ *De-skilling*

Before

After

- **Multi-skilling:** Workers whose tasks are now carried out by machines are often expected to take on other tasks. This means they must broaden their skills, usually through training, and be flexible enough to take on a variety of different tasks. This is known as **multi-skilling**. Taking on more responsibilities can help to make jobs more varied and interesting.

- **Up-skilling:** As computer equipment has been introduced to workplaces, workers are expected to be able to use them to good effect. As a result some workers have had to become more skilled than they were before. This is known as **up-skilling**. For example, a typist formerly producing letters with a typewriter may now be required to design and produce a vast array of different documents using a computer and supporting word processing, graphics, and desktop publishing packages. However, prolonged use of computers can cause eye strain and **RSI (repetitive strain injury)** to people's hands and wrists from overuse of keyboards.

Technology and the location of industry

New technology has also affected where jobs are. The electronics industry does not have to be close to a source of raw materials or power like many old manufacturing industries. But it does need to have good transport links so that products can reach a large international market easily. For example, many hi-tech electronics companies have located in towns along the M4 motorway near to other good motorway links, Heathrow airport and London. This area has been called 'Silicon Valley' (see 2.1).

Being near to a supply of skilled labour is another factor that many firms take into consideration when deciding where to locate. Many large offices locate in and around London for this reason. However, improvements in telecommunications could make this a thing of the past. Mobile phones, fax machines, and the ability of computers to send and retrieve information over phonelines have meant that people out at meetings or working elsewhere can still keep in touch with the organization they work for.

Teleworking involves employees working at home or in special **tele-cottages** linked to their employing organization by computer networks (see 4.3).

Portfolio Activity 3.9

PC: Present results of a comparison of working conditions, Analyse skills for employment and self-employment (element 2.4)

Range: Compare working conditions

Skills: Collect and record data, Take part in discussions, Produce written material

1. Suggest how technology may have affected the work of people in the following occupations:

   - sales staff
   - journalists
   - secretaries
   - welders
   - draughtsmen
   - nurses
   - assembly line workers
   - bank staff

2. Choose **one** occupation from the list to investigate in more detail. From your own observations and from discussions you have had with people in your chosen occupation, write a short report on the impact of new technology on their work.

   Your report should consider and try to answer the following questions:

   - What equipment do they now need to use?

   - What skills do they need to use the equipment?

   - Have they become de-skilled, multi-skilled, or up-skilled?

   - Has the technology made their jobs easier/harder, more or less stressful, more interesting or more boring?

   - Has the technology they use created jobs or destroyed jobs?

Section **3.4** **What determines employment?**

Portfolio Activity 3.10

PC: Analyse and explain differences about employment in different regions

Range: Analyse

Skills: Read and respond to written materials

Read the articles below. For each article write a short note to explain what is happening to the level of employment, and why.

Samsung to invest £450m in UK

Samsung of South Korea, the world's 14th largest industrial group, is to invest £450m to build a manufacturing plant at Wynyard, Cleveland, in the north-east of England.

The factory which will produce consumer goods ranging from microwave ovens to computer monitors will eventually create 3,000 jobs in an area of high unemployment.

The UK government offered Samsung £58m in regional grants and loans to secure the project. Mr Chan Bea, managing director of Samsung, said the move was part of Samsung's globalization strategy and a move against European Union trade restrictions on non-EU goods and services.

Financial Times 18.10.94

New plant puts GM in the fast lane

IN EISENACH, where once 10,000 East Germans laboured to build 100,000 rattle-trap Wartburg cars a year, Adam Opel is just three months away from its target of producing 125,000 vehicles with less than 20% of the old workforce.

Patrolling the walkway above the newly robotized welding line in the bodyshop, where human beings do just 2% of the work, he tots up the advantages of Opel's showpiece works. According to the measuring standards set by the Massachusetts Institute of Technology, it takes just 18.3 hours to build a car in Eisenach, compared to around 25 at GM's British subsidiary, Vauxhall.

Financial Times 9.8.93

Services hit as recovery slows

Britain's recovery is slowing, particularly in the service sector which is highly sensitive to consumer demand. Recent gains in employment may be reversed, the British Chamber of Commerce warned.

The chambers said their latest survey of 8,015 companies in manufacturing and services showed that sales and orders fell in the last quarter and remain below pre-recession levels.

Financial Times 20.1.94

Great Call of China

A British firm is to axe one of its factories and switch production to China to cut costs. For every ten pounds paid in wages to its UK workforce, British Polythene Industries will pay out just £1 in China.

The firm said that the move was the only way it could beat cheap imports from the Far East. Around 150 jobs will be lost when it closes its factory at Telford, Shropshire, which makes thin carrier bags for supermarkets.

Daily Mail 7.2.95

Sales revival is just the ticket for bus builders

BRITAIN'S bus builders are enjoying a sharp sales recovery after almost a decade of weak demand.

The introduction of mini- and midi-buses, operating with greater frequency than traditional double-deck vehicles, has started to win increases in the number of travellers. The increase in demand for bus travel is now feeding through to new orders for manufacturers.

Dennis, the leading bus chassis manufacturer has reported that its sales in the eight months to August were 32.5 per cent up on last year. Overall, Dennis expects to build 1,100 chassis this year at its Guildford works, where recruitment has lifted numbers employed to about 460.

The Times 6.10.94

What determines the level of employment in the UK?

There are two main factors that determine the overall level of employment in the UK:

1 The level of demand for all goods and services
During an economic recession, unemployment will tend to rise as many firms cut back production and reduce the number of workers they employ. Economic recession means that the demand for most goods and services will be falling or low because consumers are neither willing or able to spend as much on goods and services as they did in the past. During the economic recession in the UK in the early 1990s, unemployment increased to almost 3 million workers in 1993 as consumers bought over 3% less goods and services in 1992 than they did in 1990.

It follows that during periods of economic recovery and boom, when total spending on goods and services tends to increase rapidly, firms in many industries will want to increase their output to match consumer demand and will hire more workers as a result.

Because government economic policy is able to influence demand for goods and services in the UK, it can also affect the level of employment.

For example, when demand for UK goods and services is low, the government may cut taxes to give people more money to spend and/or raise government spending (see 1.4).

2 Competition from overseas

UK firms not only compete with each other to sell their goods and services to consumers at home and overseas, but also compete with foreign firms selling their goods and services in the UK. If overseas firms are able to offer better-quality products at lower prices than UK firms, consumers will buy from them. Demand for UK goods and services will fall, and some firms may be forced to cut production and make workers redundant.

Whole industries in the UK such as shipbuilding, motorcycle manufacturing, and coal mining have almost disappeared because of competition from cheaper suppliers overseas.

What determines the level of employment in particular areas?

In Chapter 2 we learnt that the physical environment was a very important factor influencing the location of a number of organizations. In the past, iron and steel-making plants located near to coal mines and limestone deposits in order to have access to raw materials and power. Many of the old UK industries such as ship and locomotive engine-building located near to these steelworks. Similarly, farms need good fertile soil or open grazing land. Many of these industries were big employers in the past.

▼ *Important farming areas*

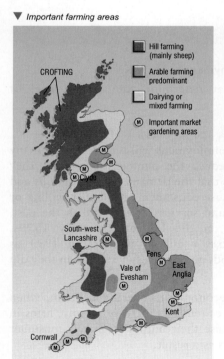

▼ *Coal deposits (1987)*

▼ *Oil fields (1994)*

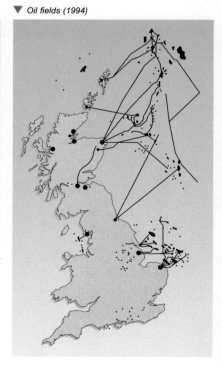

The location of, and employment in, primary industries is highly dependent on physical factors such as the quality and geography of land, and availability of mineral and oil deposits.

Today, geography is a less important factor in location than it was many years ago, although the oil industry remains a big employer in Scotland and the Shetland Isles, because they are near to the North Sea oil fields. Many of the old manufacturing industries that once located near coal fields and other mineral deposits have declined, due to changing consumer wants and overseas competition (see 1.2). As a result many people have been left unemployed in the regions where they were located, especially in northern England, Scotland, and Wales.

The government has for some time been willing to give grants to encourage firms to start up in areas of high unemployment as part of its **regional policy** (see 2.1). Grants are also available to firms already in these assisted areas to help them to keep going and continue to employ local workers.

Availability of cheap land and grants from the UK government were important factors for many of the hi-tech electronics companies now located in Scotland's 'Silicon Glen.'

Inward investment

Inward investment refers to the location of foreign-owned business organizations setting up operations in the UK. There are now over 4,000 US and 210 Japanese manufacturing companies in the UK. Together they employ nearly 20% of UK manufacturing employees. There are also many foreign-owned organizations providing services in the UK.

Many foreign-owned firms have been attracted to the UK because they are able to gain access to the large European market, the availability of skilled workers, and because grants are available to them to set up in areas of high unemployment.

▼ *The UK is more successful at attracting US and Japanese firms than any other European country.*

What determines the level of employment in particular industries?

At any given time some firms in some industries will be recruiting more workers, while others will be making workers redundant. This is because the changes that are always happening in the business environment affect some firms and not others (see 2.4).

Some of the main factors that determine how many people are employed in a particular industry are:

- **The level and strength of demand for individual goods and services:** Consumer wants are always changing. Over a given time, consumer demand for some goods and services will be rising, while demand for others will be falling. Firms whose products are in demand are likely to expand production. This will mean they will need to take on more workers – or they could ask their existing employees to work overtime, and/or invest in more machinery.

  Employment will tend to fall in markets that are contracting and increase in markets which are expanding (see 2.2). Expanding markets in the mid-1990s include personal computers and DIY. Contracting markets include tobacco and typewriters.

- **Wage levels:** The more money a firm has to pay in wages or salaries, the fewer workers it will tend to employ. As wages rise, using more machinery instead may be a cheaper option to produce goods and services. On the other hand, if wages are low, a firm may be tempted to employ more workers, especially if they work hard and earn the firm more profit.

  Wages tend to be lower in areas of high unemployment because unemployed workers may be willing to accept lower wages in order to get jobs. On the other hand, workers with skills that are in short supply may be able to demand higher wages than workers with skills that are generally available. The firms that offer the highest wages will find it easier to recruit workers with much-needed skills (see 3.3).

  Because wages are so much lower in developing countries such as China, Malaysia, and the Philippines, an increasing number of UK businesses have been closing down their operations here and moving them overseas.

- **New technology:** New technology has destroyed jobs as well as creating new ones. Some industrial processes have become automated and now need fewer workers than before (see 3.3). For example, assembly lines in car manufacturing and food processing employ computer-controlled robots to carry out many of the tasks once completed by human effort. On the other hand, many thousands of jobs have been created in the computer industry, and the demand for workers with skills in computing has risen.

Key wordsearch

Hidden in the box of jumbled letters below are some key words and terms from this chapter. Use the definitions below to help you find them.

S	W	O	R	K	I	N	G	C	O	N	D	I	T	I	O	N	S	R
E	A	Q	T	E	M	P	O	R	A	R	Y	U	C	W	F	K	U	E
L	G	E	R	T	Y	B	C	V	Q	S	L	N	W	O	X	G	W	G
F	L	E	X	I	T	I	M	E	S	F	A	E	D	R	H	P	E	I
E	O	E	Y	X	Q	W	E	R	M	T	Y	M	U	K	I	E	U	O
M	C	A	S	R	J	H	G	F	A	D	S	P	A	F	O	R	K	N
P	A	R	T	T	I	M	E	J	N	K	Z	L	X	O	C	M	O	A
L	J	N	R	A	Q	W	E	R	U	T	Y	O	T	R	V	A	R	L
O	A	I	Z	R	S	L	P	O	A	I	U	Y	Z	C	B	N	I	P
Y	C	N	U	W	J	K	Y	N	L	V	A	M	U	E	N	E	W	O
M	K	G	P	D	H	A	I	H	G	F	S	E	W	I	M	N	P	L
E	I	S	U	N	S	K	I	L	L	E	D	N	O	A	P	T	Q	I
N	E	T	Y	O	Q	R	Z	G	L	H	I	T	R	U	G	Z	N	C
T	O	E	F	U	L	L	T	I	M	E	C	K	W	I	M	E	V	Y
X	O	N	T	H	E	J	O	B	V	K	D	O	P	E	T	D	S	L
D	E	I	N	D	U	S	T	R	I	A	L	I	S	A	T	I	O	N

Key words

Definitions

- All those people in work or seeking work
- The decline in manufacturing industry
- Working for yourself
- Work involving less than 30 hours per week
- Work involving more than 30 hours each week
- An employment contract that can only be ended if the employee leaves, is fired, or made redundant
- An employment contract that is time-limited
- Work requiring a large amount of physical effort
- Payments made to workers according to the number of hours they work
- Willing to work but without paid employment
- Government policy to encourage new business start-ups in areas of high unemployment
- Manual work requiring no specific skills
- Workers who have achieved a high level of proficiency in a number of work tasks or trades
- Payments made to workers which are fixed and do not vary with the number of hours worked
- Working outside of 'usual' hours
- A system which allows a workers to choose when to start and when to finish work each day within agreed limits
- Training that takes place at work as normal duties are carried out
- The total amount received by an employee in pay
- The physical and non-physical characteristics of different types of employment and jobs

The following key words and terms are **not** included in the wordsearch above. Use some or all of them to make up a second wordsearch. Add definitions of your own like those above, and try out your wordsearch on a classmate.

flexible workforce	seasonal workers
temps	white-collar occupations
job sharing	casual workers
shiftwork	performance-related pay
wage differentials	induction training
off-the-job training	computer-aided manufacture
computer-aided design	productivity
de-skilling	multi-skilling
inward investment	teleworking

Test and Assignment

You must demonstrate that you are able to:

1. Describe and give examples of types of employment

2. Collect, analyse and explain information about employment in different regions

3. Compare working conditions for employees in different organizations

4. Present results of investigation into employment, or comparison of working conditions

1 Which of the following are most likely to be self-employed?

A pilots

B nurses

C builders

D traffic wardens

2 Employers may prefer to employ part-time staff because:

A they work longer hours

B they are more flexible

C they need less training

D they tend to be women

3 A person who is employed at a holiday camp during the summer is best described as:

A a full-time worker

B a part-time worker

C a casual worker

D a temporary worker

4 Which of the following statements is true of part-time employees?

A only work at weekends

B employed during peaks in consumer demand

C always cheaper to employ

D work harder

5 A particular feature of casual working is:

A hours of work will vary according to demand

B workers will receive holiday pay

C workers will receive compensation if they are made redundant

D workers will always pay income tax and national insurance

Questions 6-8 share the following answer options:

A salary

B overtime

C piece rates

D commission

Which of the above methods is most likely to be used to pay the following employees?

6 A manager in a large bank

7 Factory workers paid according to how much they produce

8 A person selling holiday timeshares

9 When John joined a large insurance company he was introduced to the firm in a specially designed training programme. This is known as:

A on-the-job training

B vocational training

C induction training

D off-the-job training

10 A manufacturing plant has decided to automate production using computer-controlled robots. What is likely to happen to the workforce?

A it will be cut

B it will be paid less wages

C it will be increased

D it will be up-skilled

11 Which of the following member countries of the European Union has the highest proportion of workers employed in agriculture?

A United Kingdom

B Germany

C Italy

D Greece

12 What is de-skilling?

   A training a worker to carry out more tasks

   B a fall in skill shortages

   C reductions in skill needs and employment caused by new technology

   D contracting out to self-employed people with specialist skills

Questions 13-16 share the following answer options:

   A falling consumer demand during an economic recession

   B more people visiting tourist attractions during the summer

   C an increase in government grants available in assisted areas

   D increasing use of easy-to-use computer word processors

Which of the above factors are likely to cause the following changes in employment?

13 Increased employment in areas of high unemployment

14 A fall in the employment of secretarial and clerical staff

15 Increased employment of temporary workers

16 Rising general unemployment

17 **a.** What are the main features of the following types of employment?

- full-time permanent employment

- part-time permanent employment

- temporary employment

- self-employment

b. Suggest two reasons why the number of people employed part-time has increased.

18 **a.** Suggest two factors that may explain the level of employment in your local area.

b. Explain two ways new technology has affected jobs in manufacturing industries.

19 **a.** What are working conditions?

b. Suggest at least four conditions that could be compared in different jobs.

c. Compare the likely working conditions of a full-time permanent machine operator in a large manufacturing plant with a part-time temporary office worker.

assessment assignment

The following assignment meets the evidence requirements needed to fulfil all the performance criteria in element 1.3. In addition it covers the following range points and core skills:

Range: Types of employment
Analyse Information
Compare working conditions

Skills: **Communication**
Take part in discussions
Use images
Produce written material
Application of number
Interpret and present data
Information technology
Prepare information
Present information

Tasks

1. a Find seven examples of the following types of employee:

- Full-time worker
- Part-time worker
- An employee with a permanent contract of employment
- Temporary worker
- A skilled worker
- An unskilled worker
- A self-employed worker

The employees you identify in each category can be family members, friends, or people in business organizations you work in or are familiar with.

b Interview each employee to find out:

- Their name and job title
- Their main duties and responsibilities at work
- Why they chose the particular type of employment they are engaged in

c Write a summary for each employee describing their type of employment and using information you collected from your interviews.

2 Investigate the working conditions of two people working for different organizations in your area. Ideally one should be a permanent full-time employee and the other a part-time or temporary employee. From your investigations write a report to compare their jobs in terms of:

- Hours of work, including days they work and any overtime
- Pay and other benefits
- The skill(s) they need to do their jobs
- The amount and type of technology they use
- Career/promotion opportunities
- Training opportunities
- Job security
- Physical conditions
- Health and safety in the workplace
- Their travel to work times and cost of travel

3. a Give a 5-10 minute presentation to your class on the main findings from your report on working conditions in Task 2. These could be summarized on a handout to give to each member of your class. You should also use visual aids to illustrate what you are talking about. These could include photos of people at work, and overhead projector slides listing your main points.

b Keep a record of how you prepared, organized, and conducted the presentation. This should include notes on:

(Before the presentation)

- How you gathered evidence about the working conditions of two employees

- Deadlines you set yourself to produce your script, handouts, and visual aids for the presentation
- How you collected/prepared the visual aids
- What you had to do to book a room and equipment, such as an overhead slide projector, for the presentation

(After the presentation)

- How long the presentation lasted
- Any problems that arose during the presentation (e.g. slides in wrong order)
- How you attempted to solve any problems
- Any questions asked by your audience and your answers
- Whether you thought the presentation went well
- What you might do to improve the presentation if you had a second chance

4. a Choose **one** area in the UK and **one** area in the rest of the European Union (EU). Collect information about employment for both areas as follows:

- The number and percentage of people employed
- Numbers and percentages of males and females employed by age
- The numbers and percentages of people employed in the primary, secondary, and tertiary industrial sectors

Useful sources of information will include:

- Statistical publications such as Social Trends, (see chapter 8), Regional Trends and Labour market trends (formerly The Employment Gazette).
- Department for Education and Employment
- Training and Enterprise Councils
- Local Authorities (Local Economic Development Department)
- Local Chambers of Commerce
- Local libraries

b Produce a short report using a word processor to compare and contrast the information you have collected on employment in your two areas. This should include:

- An explanation of the differences in the number of people employed in each area
- A description of growth or decline in one manufacturing industry or one service industry in each area
- Relevant tables and graphs to show percentages of males and females employed in different industries, and how levels of employment in primary, secondary, and tertiary industries have changed over time.

Some useful publications;

Labour Market Trends
A highly recommended monthly journal by the Office for National Statistics containing a wealth of data on the UK labour market–employment, average earnings, and hours, productivity, unemployment, training and international comparisons. Particular features and surveys of the labour market are reported in depth with supporting graphs, tables and charts often in colour. New employment and training initiatives, policies and parliamentary questions feature as news items in the magazine.

Regional Trends
This annual publication provides a detailed description of all the regions of the UK covering a wide range of social, vital, demographic, industrial and economic statistics, such as population and households, employment and output, housing and living conditions, income and spending, and much more.

Ask your tutor or your local library for copies of the latest editions of these publications. The Annual Abstract of Statistics and Regional Trends can also be purchased from any HMSO bookshop or through other well known bookshops.

People in Business Organizations

Unit Two

unit **2**

chapter 4 Organizational Structures and Working Arrangements

Key ideas

Organizational structure refers to the relationships between employees in an organization: what they do, who is in charge, and who they report to.

The structure of an organization can be shown on an **organization chart**. This is a diagram that shows how activities are arranged in an organization, who employees report to, and the **span of control** of each manager.

Most organizations group employees who do the same or similar work into **departments**. Each department will perform a different role in the organization.

Departments will carry out the following roles: **research and development, production, purchasing, accounting, human resources, marketing, sales, administration, customer services, computer services** and **distribution**.

All departments in an organization rely on each other to carry out their functions. That is, departments are **interdependent**.

The structure of most business organizations is like a pyramid, with a few senior managers at the top and a large number of less senior employees at the base. This is called a **hierarchical organization**.

The hierarchy in a business refers to the layers of management from the most senior managers down to junior managers or supervisors of the lowest rank. This is called the **chain of command**.

The hierarchy (or number of layers of management in an organization) may be **flat** or **tall**. In a **tall organizational structure** there are many layers of management. **Flat organizational structures** are those which have few or even just one level of management.

In a **centralized organization** senior managers have the most authority and responsibility and make the most important decisions. In a **decentralized organization** authority and responsibility are delegated to lower levels of management.

In a **matrix organization** special projects are carried out by teams from different departments. Each team member is likely to have two bosses, the project leader and their usual department manager.

Different organizations may have different **working arrangements** for their employees, including different types of **employment contracts, hours of work, workplaces**, and **teamwork** arrangements.

An employee's **workbase** may be outdoors or indoors, in a shop, office, factory, or even at home. Some employees may have to be mobile and travel between different places of work.

Organizations are introducing more flexible working arrangements for their employees, including **team working, Flexitime, shiftwork, job sharing, teleworking**, and **part-time** and **fixed term contracts**.

Reasons for changes to working arrangements include the need to improve productivity and quality assurance, introduction of new technology, and improving competitiveness.

Section **4.1**   ## Organizational structures

Organizational structure refers to the way in which a firm organizes its business activities.

Any business organization, whatever its size, whether in the public or private sector, will need to organize its business activities and the employees who carry them out. Without a clear organizational structure, employees will not know what jobs to do, or what their responsibilities are. It would also be unclear who they should get their orders from, or give orders to.

It is vitally important that everyone in an organization knows exactly what they should be doing and what everybody else does. Unless this is the case, people can waste time trying to find out who can mend their machine, check the accounts, order materials, advertise new products, recruit new staff, and so on. Worse still, if individual employees cannot find the right person to perform a particular task, they may try to do something they are not qualified to do. An organizational structure makes all of these things clear. It will show:

- Who does what job
- Who is in charge
- Who makes the decisions
- Who carries out decisions
- How decisions and other information are communicated between employees

How to organize business activities

In any organization it makes sense to group people who do similar tasks together. For example, it would not be sensible for employees in selling and marketing to work with production workers operating noisy machinery. If people are grouped according to the jobs they do, it makes it easier for them to talk to each other about their work, decide who does what and how work should be done, and solve work-related problems. Groups of people organized together to carry out particular business functions, such as production, sales, personnel, and accounts, are known as **departments** (see 4.2).

In small organizations, everyone tends to 'muck in', doing whatever is necessary to keep the business running. However, some people in the business will spend more of their time doing some things rather than others, depending on their skills and qualifications. For example, a person with skills in bookkeeping is an obvious choice to keep accounting records. Others may be better employed in production or in selling the firm's products. That is, it makes sense if people in an organization **specialize** in the tasks or jobs they are best able to do. This is called **labour specialization**.

In larger organizations it is even more important that people specialize in particular jobs. With large numbers of staff it is important that there are some people who can take decisions on who should do what. That is, organizations require **management**. Managers will need to identify the skills of different workers and give them tasks that are suited to them. Managers will also need to check with their staff to make sure tasks are being carried out to the right standard. In very large organizations there may be many different layers of management, each with different degrees of seniority.

Organization charts

The way in which activities and employees are organized in a business can be shown on an **organization chart**. This will show the relationships between different employees in an organization using lines and arrows. These are the **lines of authority**. Employees at the same level in a chart have the same amount of authority and responsibility over employees placed below them in the chart.

▼ Figure 4.1: An example of an organization chart for a small business

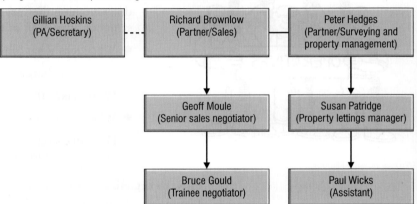

Figure 4.1 shows the organization chart for Brownlow Commercial, a small commercial property sales and management business. Richard Brownlow and Peter Hedges are the partners and senior managers of the business. They both have more authority and responsibility than any employee below them in the chart. They will pass instructions down to employees below them. That is, they will give employees under their command instructions on what jobs they should carry out. This is called **delegation**.

Line managers have the authority to delegate work tasks to the employees under their command. For example, Geoff Moule, the Senior Sales Negotiator in Brownlow Commercial, can delegate work tasks to his assistant. Geoff has the same level of authority as Susan Partridge, the Property Lettings Manager, and therefore appears at the same level in the chart, but he cannot delegate work tasks directly to her assistant, Paul Wicks.

In turn, employees are **accountable** to their line managers. Not only must they report back to them on work completed or any work-related problems, but they must also get their agreement to change their work tasks, take annual leave, etc. From Figure 4.1 it is clear that Bruce Gould is accountable to Geoff Moule who is, in turn, accountable to Richard Brownlow.

Gillian Hoskins is the personal assistant of Richard Brownlow. She is shown as being linked to him by a dotted line. This tells us she only ever reports to Richard Brownlow, but does not have the same level of authority as him despite appearing at the same level.

Portfolio Activity 4.1

PC: Produce organizational charts showing departments

Range: Organizational structures, Functions

Skills: Use images, Collect and record data, Produce written material

1. Draw an organization chart for your school/college.

2. What departments can you identify in the structure?

3. Which employees in the structure have management responsibilities?

4. How many different layers of management are there?

5. Repeat Tasks 1-4 for a small business organization of your choice.

Choosing an organizational structure

Different organizations will be structured in different ways. There is no single 'correct' way to structure an organization. Each organization will choose a structure according to its objectives, and how it proposes to meet them.

Hierarchical organizations

The organizational **hierarchy** refers to the layers of management in an organization, from the most senior managers down to supervisors.

In any organizational hierarchy there will be:

- **A clearly defined management structure.** Everyone will have an official job title and know their precise responsibilities. Each employee only has one immediate line manager to take orders from and report back to.

- **A clearly defined salary scale.** The amount an employee is paid will tend to rise, the higher up the hierarchy they are.

- **Standard rules and procedures** on hours of work, arranging annual leave, job appraisal, promotions, discipline, etc.

- **Agreed rules and guidelines** on dress, arranging business meetings, the layout of business documents such as letters and memos (see 14.2), etc.

- **Agreed policy** on health and safety, equal opportunities, training, etc.

- **Common standards** of internal customer services (i.e. providing help and support to other parts of the same organization) and external customer services (i.e. to individuals and businesses who buy the goods and services of the organization)

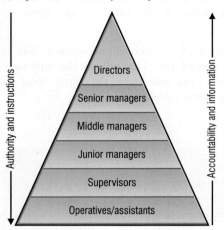

▼ Figure 4.2: The hierarchy in an organization

Authority and instructions →

- Directors
- Senior managers
- Middle managers
- Junior managers
- Supervisors
- Operatives/assistants

Accountability and information →

The structure of a **hierarchical organization** looks like a pyramid, as shown in Figure 4.2. It is narrow at the top with a small number of senior managers, wider in the middle to represent a larger number of middle managers, and widest at the bottom, showing a large number of employees who have little or no management responsibilities. These employees are called **operatives** or **assistants**, or are simply known as 'shop floor' workers (see 6.1).

In a large business there may be many management levels. Top management – directors or chief executives – are normally concerned with long-term plans for their business, and seeing that these are carried out (see 6.1). A senior manager will usually be placed in charge of each department, and will take decisions that affect the running of their department. Middle and more junior managers will be expected to put their decisions into practice, organize the day-to-day activities of shop floor workers, and report back on progress.

A clear **chain of command** runs in a line from the top layers of management down through each department in the organization to the 'shop floor'. The higher up a hierarchy, the more authority a manager will have over other employees. Orders are passed down the chain of command while information on which further decisions are based – for example, sales figures, revenues, output, staff turnover, etc. – is passed up the organization to senior managers.

In a small business there are unlikely to be many layers of management. For example, in a small one-person enterprise – a sole trader – the business owner is likely to be both manager and worker, making all the decisions and carrying them out.

The main advantages and disadvantages of having a hierarchical structure in a business organization are:

Advantages

+ Everyone knows what their job role is, who to accept work tasks from, and who to report to.

+ The authority and responsibilities of different employees are clear to all staff.

+ Senior managers are able to make all the decisions and control the whole organization.

Disadvantages

– Because there may be many layers of management, passing information up the hierarchy to inform senior managers can take a long time and slow down business decisions.

– Senior managers cannot possibly know enough about each department in a large organization to make the best decisions.

– If senior managers make all the decisions, it can discourage less senior managers and other employees from proposing new ideas and using their own initiative to solve business problems.

– There tends to be a lot of bureaucracy, i.e. too much paperwork and too many rules and regulations designed to make everybody work the same way. This can waste time and effort.

Flat or tall organizational structures?

Some businesses have many layers of management, each with a different level of seniority. This is called a **tall structure**. Organizations which have relatively few layers of management are said to have a **flat structure**.

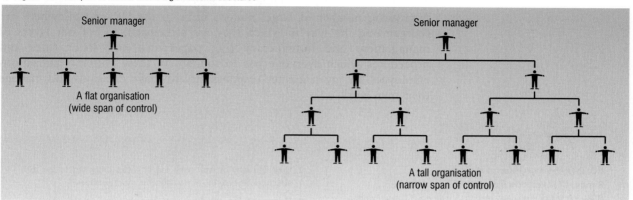

In a tall organization the chain of command is long, but the **span of control** of each manager in the hierarchy will tend to be narrow. This means that each manager will have relatively few employees to command. For example, if 3 middle managers report to a senior manager, the span of control of the senior manager is 3. If each middle manager has 5 junior managers or supervisors reporting to them, then each middle manager would have a span of control of 5.

In a flat organization the chain of command is short, with perhaps only one or two management levels. This helps communication between top managers and 'shop floor' workers. However, each manager may have responsibility over a relatively large number of staff. That is, their span of control is wide. For example, in a large supermarket the store manager may have control over 50 employees or more.

Figure 4.3 shows two simple charts for a tall organization and a flat organization. Each has the same number of employees. In the tall organization in the diagram, the span of control of each manager is 2 employees. In the flat organization the span of control is 5 employees.

The advantages and disadvantages of having a tall organizational structure with a narrow span of control include:

Advantages:

+ It enables managers to supervise their employees closely

+ Managers have fewer staff to communicate with, and so are able to communicate more easily with those they have under their command

+ It allows people to specialize in the tasks they are best at

Disadvantages:

− Because there are more managers, management costs are high

− Senior managers may find it difficult to manage large numbers of more junior managers

− Too much supervision in an organization may prevent staff taking the initiative and reduce their motivation to work hard

The advantages and disadvantages of having a flat organizational structure with a wide span of control will include:

Advantages:

+ Senior management decisions can be taken and implemented more quickly because fewer layers of management are involved

+ Because there are fewer managers, the cost of supervising staff is lower

+ Staff have greater freedom to make their own decisions and may work harder

Disadvantages:

− Staff may find that they have more than one boss to take orders from and report back to

− Senior managers will have less say in the control and future direction of their business

− Because each manager has more staff to deal with it becomes more difficult to get to know them all and supervise their work

Why are more firms becoming flat organizations?

A growing number of large modern firms in the UK and elsewhere are reorganizing the way in which they are structured, to cut out layers of management and bureaucracy (i.e. paperwork and strict rules and procedures which everyone has to follow). In these flatter organizations employees are given greater responsibility to make decisions and manage their own work.

Portfolio Activity 4.2

PC: Describe organizational structures

Range: Organizational structures

Skills: Read and respond to written material, Produce written material

1. Why might a tall organizational structure be a problem for a firm working in a quickly changing consumer market?

2. How and why do you think the changes proposed to the IBM structure will help the firm to become more profitable?

3. Investigate the structure of a local business organization, for example, a supermarket, bank, or small factory. Draw an organization chart for the business and comment on whether you think the organization has a tall or flat structure, and the possible advantages and disadvantages of the chosen structure for that organization.

The shake up of Big Blues' army

IBM was once the largest and most successful computer firm in the world. Today the company faces falling sales and losses. Competition in the UK computer market is the fiercest in the world and IBM has been forced to change to survive.

The structure of the company has changed a great deal. Eight layers of management have been cut down to four. Early retirement and redundancy have reduced staff numbers from 18,600 in 1985 to 11,000 in 1993. 80% of the workforce now come face to face with their customers, compared with only 45% two years ago.

The firm is being split down into a number of smaller departments and the departments at headquarters will have to sell their services to the rest of the company. For example, if a part of the company does not wish to buy pension services from the head office finance department, they may buy these from any outside supplier.

▼ IBM's U.K. headquarters

In markets such as consumer electronics, where consumer wants change very rapidly, and new versions of products like camcorders and TVs are produced every few months, organizations need to keep in close touch with their customers. They cannot afford to wait until information has passed through many layers of management before developing new products. In these conditions a flat structure is better.

Quick decisions on new products, prices, and promotions are needed to attract customers away from rival firms. In a flat structure, these important decisions can be taken quickly by managers. Staff also tend to have more freedom to work without guidance or interference from managers. Many creative and innovative firms such as advertising agencies have flat structures in order to enable them to react quickly to changes.

Portfolio Activity 4.3

PC: Describe organizational structures

Range: Organizational structures

Skills: Read and respond to written material, Produce written material

1. Look at the organization chart below for an organization that imports wines from all over the world to sell to UK retailers.

- How many layers of management are there?
- What is the average span of control of all the managers?
- Who is Sharon Slater's line manager?
- Can Raj De Souza give Sharon orders?
- Who should Sharon report to if a problem arises when her line manager is away?
- Has Sharon got more or less authority than Kiran Sojimi, Paul Raha, and Clive Young?

2. The organization is restructured as follows:

- Karina Plummer leaves to have a baby

- Paul Raha leaves to set up his own small business
- The white and red wine divisions in the sales department are merged
- Sue Bullen is appointed the sales department manager
- Raj De Souza retires
- Alison Frost becomes head of purchasing
- Andrew McKewan and Ken Jones leave for other jobs
- Customer accounts and wages staff now report directly to the manager of finance and accounts, Michael Anthony

Re-draw the chart to show these changes. Is the new structure taller or flatter than the original structure? Now answer the same questions as in Task 1 for the new organizational structure.

3. Do you think the re-organized structure meets the needs of the business better than the structure it had initially? In groups discuss the possible advantages and disadvantages of each structure to the organization. Make a note of your discussions to place in your file of work.

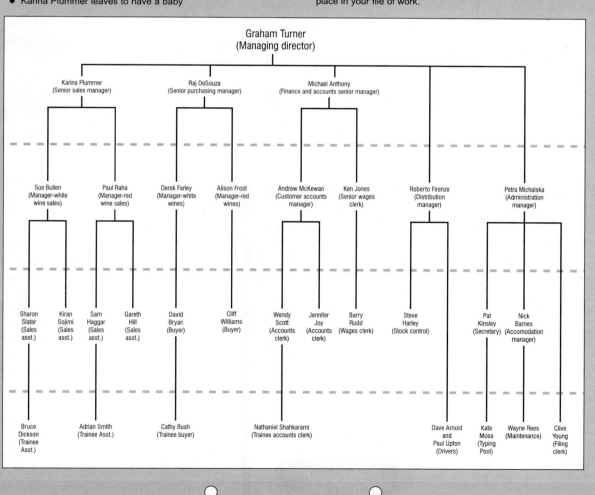

The matrix structure

In a **matrix structure,** employees with different skills will be borrowed from different departments within the organization to form project teams – for example, to create and launch a new product, or to install new computer equipment.

A matrix structure is different to the more usual hierarchical structure because members of staff can belong to a department, for example, marketing, and also to a project team working together to carry out a specific task.

▼ *Figure 4.4: An example of a matrix organization structure*

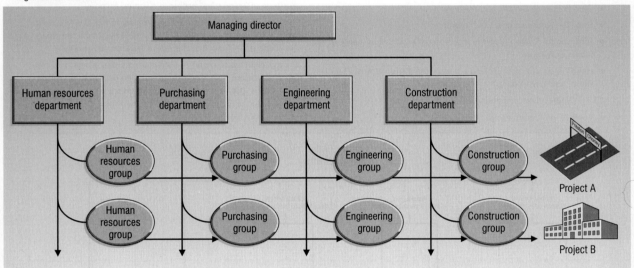

Ford maps out a global ambition

Ford, the world's second largest vehicle maker, is putting into place the biggest shake-up in its 92-year history. Under the title of Ford 2000, the group is trying to change itself from a multinational company organized into separate countries into a global car manufacturing business organized by the products it makes.

Ford aims to create a global company which will be the world's leading car company. But it has a long way to go. Ford is well behind General Motors, with sales of 6.64 million vehicles to GM's 8.33 million. In terms of quality, customers thought Ford were less than average in the USA last year.

In response to this, Ford has decided to redesign its organization to make more cars at a lower cost. The aim is to join up the companies operating in different countries around the world to form a global organization. The Chairman of Ford says, 'We cannot afford to waste time and money on making different car parts and engines all around the world to meet nearly identical customers' demands.'

Ford will create five vehicle centres around the world and each will be totally responsible for the world-wide development of particular cars and trucks. Ford will produce a new family car for sales all around the world using identical parts wherever it is sold.

Ford is creating a matrix structure. Instead of staff just belonging to a department like accounting or sales, they will be part of a team responsible for producing an entire car. The first loyalty of staff will be to their 'car team' rather than to their department. 'It's like a Formula One team: if a problem comes up, everyone will work on it. You always race to win, and it's no use saying afterwards that the chassis worked well, but it was a shame about the engine. If one part fails, the race is lost and the whole team fails.'

Ford has cut its layers of management from 14 down to just 7.

Figure 4.4 presents one way of changing the organizational structure of a large construction firm into a matrix organization. The organization has two special projects: project A, to widen a motorway for the UK government; and project B, to build a new office block in Hong Kong. A project manager is appointed to each project and is allocated staff with appropriate skills from all the other departments in the organization to complete the project. After the projects are completed the organization could change back to its original structure.

Matrix structures are becoming increasingly popular among large modern organizations. This is because by creating project teams, employees can concentrate their efforts on making, promoting, and selling one particular product. This may help a firm to increase the output, quality, and sales of that product.

Section **4.2** **Departments in organizations**

What is a department?

Every organization must perform a number of functions if it is to be successful. Important business functions include:

- Research and development of new products and production processes
- Purchasing materials and equipment
- Producing goods and services
- Marketing
- Selling
- Distribution of goods
- Customer services
- Accounting
- Managing human resources (personnel)
- Administration
- Computer services

In medium-sized and large organizations employees will often be organized together into groups, so that each group can specialize in carrying out one of the functions above. Each group of employees carrying out one particular function is called a **department**.

Figure 4.5 shows all the main business departments you are likely to find in any large private sector organization. The number and size of individual departments will, of course, vary between different organizations. In small firms there are too few employees to divide up into specialized departments.

▼ Figure 4.5: Business departments

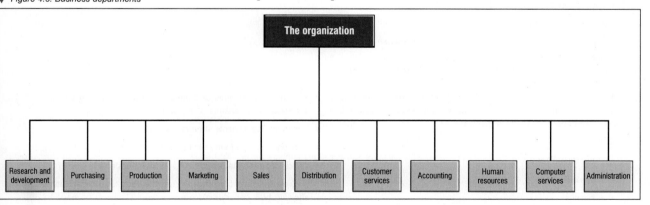

Production, sales, and marketing are usually considered to be the key operations in business. All the other departments, such as purchasing, human resources, accounts, and administration, provide **support services** for the production, sales and marketing departments. In practice, every department in a business organization will depend on work carried out by every other department. That is, they are **functionally interdependent**.

Other ways to form departments

Grouping workers into departments according to the business function they perform is just one way of organizing the structure of a business. Workers may also be grouped together according to the product they provide (such as in a matrix structure), the type of customers they deal with, or according to the region they serve or where they are located.

For example, consider the diagrams below which show the various ways departments in a large consumer electronics manufacturer might be organized:

- **Departments for different products/services:** An organization that produces many different products or brands may find it difficult to manage with each department working on all of them at once. Organizing staff into groups or departments working on one product each allows managers to group the resources needed to produce each product.

- **Departments for different customer groups:** Departments can be organized according to a firm's main customers. For example, most banks have specialized mortgage, foreign exchange, and small business departments.

- **Departments for different regions:** Departments can be created according to the place in which work is done, or by market areas. Most large organizations operate on a regional basis. Multinational organizations will have offices, factories, and often shops in different countries.

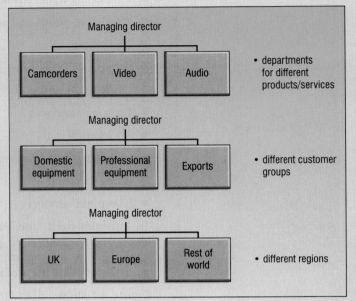

- departments for different products/services

- different customer groups

- different regions

Portfolio Activity 4.4

PC: Produce organizational charts showing departments

Range: Departments

Skills: Use images, Produce written material, Collect and record data

1. For the types of organizations listed below, discuss in groups the main business functions employees will need to perform, and how departments could be organized:

- An international bank
- A department store
- A school/college
- A hospital
- An insurance company
- A hotel

2. a Choose three types of organization from the above list and investigate local examples. Try to find out:

- The main departments in each organization
- The main jobs performed in each department
- Which departments provide support for other departments

b Draw a simple organization chart for each local organization showing how departments are arranged. (There is no need to show individual employees in each department.)

c Write a short note explaining why each local organization has chosen to organize departments in the way shown in your chart.

▼ Meeting consumer wants for improved styling and better picture and sound quality of television sets has been made possible by research and development.

▼ Engineers at the Transport Research Laboratory conduct a motorcycle impact test with a prototype airbag.

The research and development (R&D) department

In a highly competitive business environment, research and development (R&D) is increasingly important to the success of business organizations. Each year, businesses spend many billions of pounds developing new products and methods of producing them. However successful a product is now, one day it will be replaced by a new or better product. For this reason, the future success of most businesses depends upon the work of the research and development department in coming up with new ideas and products which can be developed and sold in the future.

New products are being introduced all the time, especially in the highly competitive consumer electronics market. Every few months manufacturers of audio and visual consumer electronics equipment bring out new models with different features. Consider the development of television sets over the last few years. They have become slimmer, they can produce stereo sound, surround sound, and Dolby pro-logic sound from no less than 5 speakers. Screen size has increased, and widescreen TVs have now been introduced. The next generation of TV sets will be able to produce high-definition TV pictures (HDTV) as well as digital broadcast images. Each new development tempts the consumer to replace their old TV set with a new one.

Industrial and engineering design

Most firms work hard to stay ahead of competition from rival products and firms. This means finding out what consumers want, what they are likely to want in the near future, and developing ways to produce the products that are needed. The marketing department can advise R&D on the results of market research on consumer opinions about products and consumer wants.

Designing new products or improving existing products is called **industrial design**. People who work in R&D on industrial design matters will consider many features of different products including:

- Image
- Durability
- Smell
- Taste
- Texture
- Colours

- User friendliness
- Packaging
- How easy it is to maintain/repair
- Safety
- Incorporated technology
- Shape

Product performance will also be very important. **Engineering design** considers how well a product does the job it is supposed to do. For example, does a washing powder work in low temperatures? Does it remove grease stains? Does it soften clothes and towels? Similarly, it will consider how many miles a car travels on each gallon of petrol, how it holds the road in wet conditions, and how many seconds it takes to accelerate from 0 to 60 miles per hour.

Industrial and engineering design are needed, whether the product in question is a highly technical personal computer, a new medicine, an industrial laser, or just a simple cake, children's toy, or choc ice.

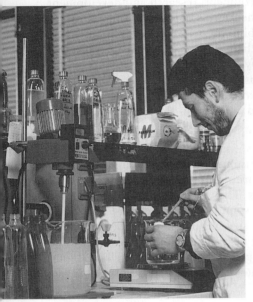

▼ Scientists at Unilever Plc test the performance of a new cleaning liquid.

The R&D department not only designs new products and re-designs old ones, but also advises the production department on the best way to produce them.

What is CAD?

Computer-aided design (CAD) refers to the use of interactive computer programs to generate, store, and use geometric graphics. CAD is used by design engineers in many industries to solve design problems ranging from the creation of new product packaging to the design of a new office block. The benefits of using CAD are:

- Reduction in lead times between product design and production
- A wide range of designs can be examined and evaluated without the need for building 3D prototypes
- Modifications and changes are easily made

An extremely important consideration in product design is cost. That is, can the product be produced in the right quantities at a price the consumer is willing to pay? There is no point producing a good or service that consumers cannot afford or are unwilling to pay for. It is the job of research and development staff to work out if the product can be produced at a price consumers can afford.

Many new products can initially be sold at high prices because they are new, and because consumers who buy them can boast of being the first to own them. For example, the first home video recorders that became widely available in the early 1970s were priced at £700 or more. These early video systems are no longer available. New designs like VHS and Super VHS were introduced and now dominate the home video market. In 1995, a basic VHS machine could be purchased for as little as £150, while £700 would buy a top-of-the-range super VHS machine with a host of features not available on the basic early systems, such as Nicam digital stereo sound, widescreen playback, editing facilities, etc.

The prices of many consumer electronic products have fallen significantly over time because of technological advances developed by R&D departments in large electronics manufacturers.

Portfolio Activity 4.5

PC: Describe the work and explain the interdependence of departments within business organizations

Range: Departments

Skills: Produce written material, Collect and record data, Take part in discussions

1. Make a list of all the features of the following goods and services which designers could change/improve so that they appeal more to consumers:

- Chocolate bars
- Motor cars
- Washing powders
- Computer game consoles
- Cough mixture
- A car wash
- Public transport
- Bank services

2. Using words and pictures, write a short report charting the development of any product or service of your choice over time.

For example, you might like to consider the development of computer game consoles, from the very earliest machines which contained simple tennis games, through to the Sega Megadrive and Nintendo SNES that use cartridges, and finally to the new 32-bit and 64-bit machines that play games CDs. Alternatively, you could choose something completely different, like toothpaste, oven-ready meals, medicines, or a make of motor car.

3. As a class, invite a industrial designer to give a short talk about his or her work. If the talk is able to go ahead:

a Agree a list of questions you would like to ask beforehand

b Take notes during the talk

c After the talk, write a short paper on why research and development is so important in modern business, and the role of the industrial designer

4. As a class group, discuss how you think the work of the research and development department will depend on work carried out by the following departments:

• Marketing

• Human resources

• Finance

• Computer services

Keep a note of the discussions for your portfolio.

Purchasing department

The purchasing department will specialize in buying in the goods and services that the firm needs in order to operate. Items purchased will include the raw materials used in production, paper and computer supplies used by office staff, new furniture, and any other items the organization needs. Services bought in from outside the firm may include cleaning, painting and decorating, and computer maintenance.

Purchasing staff need to carry out the following jobs:

• Advising other departments about the kinds of goods and services available, and how well these might meet their needs

• Finding and negotiating with suppliers

• Buying raw materials, components, and machinery for the production department

• Ordering other goods and services for the whole organization

• Taking delivery of goods

• Checking goods and services received against orders (see 12.4)

• Arranging payment of invoices through the accounting department

Purchasing, therefore, involves buying materials and other goods and services of the right quality, in the right quantities, and at the right price. People who buy supplies will usually become specialists in the particular goods they buy. For example, Nescafé employs people who specialize in securing supplies of high quality coffee beans to make coffee. Marks & Spencer employs specialists to buy fashion ideas and clothing.

Large firms can often buy in bulk and obtain discounts from suppliers (see 12.3). However, this can take up valuable storage space. Because of this, many large modern organizations now use a purchasing system known as **Just In Time (JIT)** production. Under this system materials and components used in production are ordered and then delivered 'just in time' to be processed. This allows the purchasing organization to keep stocks to a minimum. For this system to work efficiently, suppliers must be reliable in terms of delivery times and product quality. If either is at fault, production will be held up.

Today many functions in purchasing are computerized. For example, computers can send and receive orders and invoices without the need for paper documents. This is called **Electronic Data Interchange** (see 12.2).

Production department

Production departments are a feature of manufacturing firms (see 1.2). The role of the production department is to make goods of the right quality, in the right quantity, and at the least cost. To do this requires careful planning, monitoring, and control.

Production planning

It is essential that a business can supply enough goods to meet consumer demand. This requires careful planning of the whole production process, namely:

- How much should be produced and by when
- The method of production to use
- What raw materials or components are needed and in what quantities
- What machinery and other equipment is needed
- How many workers are required and what skills they need
- The level of automation in production
- How the product will be packaged and packed for shipment

Production managers must work closely with staff from the research and development department, and sales and marketing departments. They will need to know what customers want, and how products can be made as attractive as possible to consumers. In addition, the sales department will advise production on how much of the goods or services should be produced to meet consumer demand; the purchasing department will buy the necessary materials and equipment to make the goods; and the human resources department will recruit production workers with the right skills.

Cost is an important consideration in production planning. The cost of materials, equipment, and labour will largely determine the cost of each product and, therefore, the price at which it can be sold to make a profit. Resources must therefore be combined in the most efficient way, so as to keep the cost of producing each unit of output as low as possible. For example, employing ten people to operate only five sewing machines is clearly not the most efficient way of producing clothes. The cost of each garment would be less if the firm employed more machines and less labour.

Methods of production

In general, there are three main ways production can be organized in a firm. These are:

1. Job production

This method is used for producing single or one-off orders where each order is custom built. For example, designer clothes, custom-built furniture, flower arrangements for weddings, even the building of ships and space rockets are all examples of job production.

2. Flow production

This method involves the manufacture of a product in a continuously moving process. Flow production is used to mass-produce identical products such as video recorders and cars on an assembly line.

3. Batch production

This method is used for producing a limited number of identical products to meet a specific order, for example, 1,000 calling cards, or 50,000 pre-recorded video cassettes of a particular film.

The precise method of production chosen will depend on the type of product, the level of consumer demand, and the size of the firm. For example, ships are built to individual specifications. They cannot be mass-produced like video recorders or toothpaste. Small firms will not have the capacity to mass-produce items, while clearly the market for designer jewellery is too small to make mass production worthwhile.

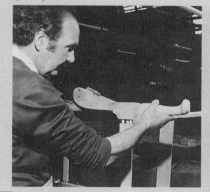
▼ Job production

▼ Flow production

▼ Batch production

Monitoring and controlling production

It is important to monitor and control production to make sure there are no problems and that production targets and schedules are met. Production control will involve:

- **Scheduling** – working out the sequence, and time, in which jobs have to be performed

- **Monitoring** – checking that work is progressing on schedule and that production targets will be met. If any problems arise and slow down production, such as machine breakdowns or late delivery of materials, schedules will need to be rearranged. In addition, it is important to make sure that machines are not over- or underused and receive regular maintenance.

- **Cost control** – Information provided to the accounting department will allow production costs to be monitored.

- **Stock control** – Production will be interrupted if stocks of materials or components run out. The purpose of stock control is to make sure this does not happen.

- **Quality control** – This involves ensuring that the final product and its features entirely satisfy the consumer. It can be done by inspecting quality at every stage in the production process, including the quality of materials and components, work in progress, packaging, and the work of individual employees, even those in other departments such as sales, customer services, marketing, etc. This is called **Total Quality Management** or **TQM** (see 4.4).

A number of these controls can be computerized. For example, orders for more materials can be sent automatically by a computer when stocks fall to a pre-determined level; equipment can be used to check the size, weight, and ripeness of different fruits and vegetables; progress can be monitored from data automatically fed into a computer every time products move onto another part of an automated production line.

What is CAM?

Increasingly computers are being used to automate and control manufacturing processes. Machines such as industrial robots can receive instructions from information entered into a computer. The use of computers in manufacturing is known as **computer-aided manufacture (CAM)**.

In some industries CAM can be directly linked to computer-aided design (CAD) packages. For example, knitting machines can produce jumper designs planned on a computer. Similarly, industrial robots can learn the shape of cars they are required to paint from computerized images developed using CAD.

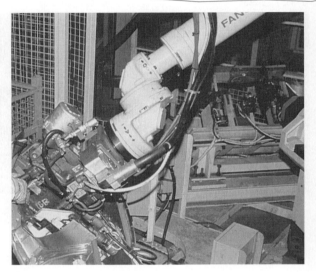

Portfolio Activity 4.6

PC: Describe the work and explain the interdependence of departments within business organizations

Range: Departments

Skills: Produce written material, Collect and record data, Present information

Arrange a class visit to a manufacturing plant. Take notes during your visit and gather enough information to produce a short report to discuss the following:

- The main functions of the production department
- The number of employees in the production department
- Examples of job titles in the production department
- The type of products made

- How much is produced each day, week, or month on average
- The method of production
- How quality is controlled in production
- The type of materials and components used in production
- The type of machinery used
- The level of automation in production
- The layout of the factory floor (include a diagram in your report to show where machinery, stores, etc., are located)
- How production depends on the work of other departments, especially R&D, purchasing, sales, and human resources. Use a word processor to write up your report.

Marketing department

The main role of the marketing department is to identify what customers will be willing to buy and then to encourage them to buy the product at a price that will earn the organization a profit.

There are four main functions of a marketing department in a firm:

- **Market research** – This involves finding out what different consumers want in terms of products and product features, what prices they are willing to pay, where they like to buy products, and how they respond to advertising. It can involve holding personal interviews, sending questionnaires through the post, telephone surveys, and consumer opinion panels (see 11.2).

- **Advertising** – This aims to raise consumer awareness of the firm's products. Firms can choose to advertise their goods and services through a variety of media, including newspapers, radio, TV, posters, and cinema (see 9.1).

- **Promotion** – This includes marketing methods such as exhibitions and trade fairs, competitions, money-off coupons, sponsorship or celebrity endorsement, special packaging, logos, etc. (see 9.1).

- **Public relations** – This involves maintaining good relations with other organizations and the general public in order to give the firm a good, and high-profile, image. For example, organizations can sponsor local events and give donations to charities.

Many organizations pay outside firms that specialize in marketing to provide marketing services. These specialist agencies can plan and run public relations, advertising, and promotional campaigns, and carry out market research.

The marketing department will work closely with the R&D and sales departments in identifying what customers want and then developing attractive products that will encourage consumers to spend their money.

Sales department

In many organizations sales and marketing functions will be carried out by one department. However, selling is such an important activity that larger firms will normally have a separate sales department.

The role of the sales department is to create orders for goods and services. The sales department may control a salesforce whose job is to visit customers and persuade them to buy.

The sales department will be expected to carry out a number of functions fast and effectively. These include:

- Responding to requests for information on products, prices, delivery times, methods of payment, etc.

- Responding to customers' orders for goods or services (see 12.3)

- Organizing deliveries with the distribution department

- Receiving payments by various methods, including cash, credit card, and hire purchase (see 12.3) An organization will risk annoying their customers and losing their custom to rival firms if any of the above tasks are mismanaged or take too long. Good sales staff are essential to any organization engaged in selling.

▼ *Distribution*

The sales department will work closely with marketing in designing advertising material, and also with production in order to ensure that the right goods are available in the right quantities to meet customers' orders.

Distribution department

The role of distribution is to ensure that goods and services are available to customers when they want them. The distribution department must therefore ensure that the right goods are delivered in the right quantities at the time agreed with the customer, for the minimum cost. This is often called **logistics** – the science of storing and moving goods efficiently. Achieving this may involve the following tasks:

- Delivering supplies to other organizations
- Choosing delivery methods, e.g. by road, rail, air
- Vehicle maintenance
- Distribution of finished products to wholesalers, retail outlets, or direct to consumers
- Checking in goods received
- Storage
- Checking goods out
- Monitoring the movement of goods and work in progress within a factory
- Monitoring the movement of goods within a retail outlet (i.e. from the stockroom)
- Control of stock to ensure goods are available when they are required

Some firms run their own transport fleet to distribute goods, while others hire outside contractors to deliver for them. Distribution is an essential department, because no matter what the other departments do, if distribution does not get the right goods to the customer in time, then there will be no sale.

Distribution functions have been greatly helped by new technology. The use of barcodes on products and barcode readers means that stock records can be updated regularly and quickly.

Many large transport firms use 'routemaster' computer programs which produce a map for drivers showing the quickest route to a delivery address, taking into account the time of day and likely road conditions.

Customer services department

In addition to sales and marketing departments, many large organizations have a customer services department which specializes in assisting the public with enquiries about the firm's products and other matters.

Staff in customer services need to know a great deal about their firm and must also have good communications skills. They will also arrange after sales care for customers, such as repairs and refunds. Customer services are discussed in detail in section 11.1.

Accounts department

The key business activities of controlling finance and keeping accounts are usually carried out by the accounting department.

Finance

It is the job of the accounts manager to make sure the organization has enough capital, either from its own funds and/or from borrowing, to finance its operations. This will include obtaining money to pay for new projects, such as buying new premises, investing in new machinery or a computer system. The accounts manager will calculate if the new project is worth undertaking by comparing the predicted revenues (or cost savings) from the investment with the cost of the project.

In addition, wages and salaries will often be paid from the financial division of the accounting department.

Accounts

Accounts staff are responsible for recording and analysing all the different financial transactions in the firm (see 12.1). They will keep track of all of the cash entering and leaving the business, as well as the amount of credit given to customers and amounts owed by the firm to suppliers. Information about these day-to-day financial activities is recorded in a financial accounting system, which is usually held on computer.

- **Financial accountants** use accounting records to prepare business accounts. These will include the end-of-year accounts which summarize how much the business is worth and how much profit it made (see 13.1). These accounts will be made available to the tax authorities and business owners.

- **Cost accountants** will monitor business costs, including those directly related to production, such as materials and machine hire, and costs which arise due to activities such as sales, marketing, human resource management and even the accounting department itself.

- **Management accountants** are expected to provide the managers of the firm with up-to-date financial information to show how well the firm is doing at any moment in time, and to predict how well it is likely to do in the future.

Small organizations may buy in the services of a self-employed accountant or an accountancy firm. Large firms can often afford to employ their own full-time accountants.

The accounting department will work with every other department in the organization. It will need information from sales on the amount of money coming into the business, and from purchasing and production on how much they are spending. The accounting department will also set budgets for each department, and will monitor how actual business performance compares to financial plans (see 13.1).

Human resources department

The most valuable resource in any business organization is its people, or **human resources**. The success of a business will depend on the quality of it's workforce.

The size of the human resources (or personnel) department will vary according to the number of people employed in the firm – and often with the importance a firm attaches to keeping its staff happy. The larger the firm, the larger the department tends to be, and the more specialists it can afford to employ with skills in human resource management.

All departments in an organization will rely on the human resource department to carry out the following functions:

- The recruitment and selection of staff with the skills and experience the organization needs
- Providing employment advice and information
- Providing terms and conditions of employment to new employees
- Managing changes in working arrangements, for example, due to the introduction of new technology, changes in organizational structure, etc. (see 4.3).
- Developing and promoting induction courses and training for employees
- Handling staff promotions and transfers
- Developing and handling staff appraisal procedures
- Developing and handling grievance procedures and complaints by staff
- Handling employee discipline and dismissal
- Dealing with redundancies and redundancy pay
- Administering pay and conditions of service, such as holiday entitlements and maternity pay
- Taking part in negotiations with trade unions and employee representatives on pay and conditions
- Looking after staff welfare, which can include (particularly in larger organizations) employing a staff nurse, and supervising canteen and sports facilities
- Ensuring health and safety at work guidelines are followed
- Keeping staff records on every employee

The functions of a human resources department are considered in detail in Chapter 5, when we shall examine the rights and responsibilities of employees and their employers.

Administration department

It is the job of the administration department to support all the other departments in a business by providing a range of services for the whole organization. These can include:

- Staffing a reception
- Operating the switchboard
- Providing typing/word processing services
- Photocopying
- Data processing
- Filing

▼ A company canteen

- Running the mailroom
- Internal deliveries and collections of post
- Arranging security and cleaning services
- Planning and managing relocations
- Providing staff telephone and office number directories
- Maintaining the premises (i.e. furniture, air conditioning systems, decorations, etc.)

The size and importance of the administration department in an organization will vary considerably. Most departments in modern organizations employ their own clerical and administration staff to provide a number of the above services, such as photocopying and filing, rather than having these jobs done centrally.

Members of the administration department will include clerical, office and secretarial staff, messengers, cleaners, and the office manager. In a limited company, the company secretary may oversee the work of the administration department. S/he will also have responsibility for making sure the company meets legal requirements, arranging board of directors' meetings, and communicating with shareholders (see 6.1).

Computer services department

Modern organizations use computers to help carry out tasks in every department of the business. Most office administration is computerized: wages and salaries, purchases and sales, accounts, filing, routine administration – all these tasks and more will involve the use of computers. Modern production processes also use computer-aided design and manufacturing.

Making sure computers function reliably, and helping users is, therefore, an important service. A small firm may rely on help from outside computer specialists and telephone support lines. Large organizations may employ teams of full-time computer specialists to provide these services.

Computing staff will be expected to provide the following support services to every department:

- Advising on new equipment and software
- Testing and installing new equipment and software
- Giving advice to users
- Organizing 'hands on' training programmes (with the human resources department)
- Repairing faults

Departments in public sector organizations

Public sector organizations will also be organized into departments based on the very different functions they perform compared to many private sector organizations. Departments will differ because most public sector organizations:

- Provide a service

▼ Reception services are usually provided by the administration department in an organization

- Do not aim to make sales revenues or profit
- Are responsible for advising on, implementing, and managing government policies

For example:

- Central government is divided into around 20 different departments, including Transport, Health, Education and Employment, Trade and Industry, etc (see 1.4). Each central government department is an entire organization in itself. For example, the Department of Transport (DoT) is an organization with some 12,000 employees in England and Wales. In turn the DoT is divided up into many different departments with different responsibilities for roads, railways, buses, shipping, aviation, London, research, road safety, plus more familiar ones for human resources, purchasing, and finance.

- Local authorities may have separate departments for housing, economic development, parks and leisure, environmental health, legal advice, finance, and administration.

- Schools and universities have departments based on the subjects they teach and research, including business, economics, chemistry, engineering, biology, mathematics, computing, etc.

- Hospitals may be organized into departments for different medical conditions and types of treatment, such as physiotherapy, maternity, cardiology, audiology, paediatric, geriatric, etc.

Many public sector organizations tend to have tall structures in which decision-making is centralized. This is because many of the decisions made will involve spending taxpayers' money and can affect individuals and businesses in the local and national economy.

Portfolio Activity 4.7

PC: Describe the work and explain the interdependence of departments within business organizations
Range: Departments
Skills: Read and respond to written material, Produce written material, Collect and record data

1. In which departments are you likely to find the following jobs?

Data processor	Secretary
Engineer	Cleaner
Technician	Welfare officer
Scientist	Despatch clerk
Training officer	Machine operative
Accountant	Clerical assistant
Quality controller	Public relations manager
Mechanic	Credit controller

Buyer	Warehouse supervisor
Receptionist	Designer
Personnel manager	Chief cashier
Security guard	Production planner
Shipping clerk	Advertising executive
Wages clerk	Messenger
WP operator	Maintenance engineer
Draughtsman	Ledger clerk
Sales assistant	Statistician
Purchasing clerk	Customer liaison officer
Recruitment consultant	Management accountant

2. Produce a short report using a word processor describing the main functions performed by each department in a business organization of your choice. Also include a list of at least three examples of different jobs in each department.

Section **4.3**   # Working arrangements

PC: Identify and explain differences in working arrangements

Range: Differences in working arrangements

Skills: Read and respond to written material

Study the two case studies below. How do the working arrangements of the two employees differ?

Case Study 1

Natasha Sehli is a clerical officer employed by Dack Limited, a firm producing office equipment. Natasha has been employed on a six-month contract to transfer sales records from a paper-based system to a new computer.

Natasha works for much of her time as part of a team of six people, all working on the same project. Her contract requires her to work for 37 hours per week. She can start work each day at any time between 7 am and 10 am and finish at any time between 4 pm and 6 pm as long as she works 37 hours per week and is available between 10 am and 4 pm every weekday in the office. Natasha may sometimes be asked to work extra time. If she does, she is paid overtime.

If Natasha is off sick she will not be paid. She is also not entitled to any holiday during her six-month contract.

Case Study 2

Alok Basu is senior manager of the finance department in Dack Limited. Alok is on a permanent contract, which includes performance-related pay worth up to 15% of total salary if he meets his targets. Alok's contract specifies his job role and the kinds of things he must achieve, such as controlling budgets and ensuring accurate financial records. Alok's contract does not state the length of the working week. He is expected to achieve his job targets and it is up to him how long he works in order to do this.

As Alok's work involves visiting other branches of the company, he finds that his work time is split between the head office and travelling around the UK. While on the road, he makes use of a portable laptop computer, with built-in fax machine and modem provided by the firm to enable speedy communication with head office. Alok is paid an allowance for each night he is away from home, and this is in addition to the cost of the accommodation.

His contract includes 6 weeks' holiday a year and free private health insurance for himself and his family. Alok is provided with a free company car and a mileage allowance of 40 pence per mile.

What are working arrangements ?

Just as firms must choose an organizational structure to suit their needs, they must also choose the working arrangements of their employees to meet their business requirements. Employees will be expected to conform to these arrangements. Working arrangements will be agreed for:

- The type of employment contract
- Hours of work
- Places of work
- Working with others

Flexible working arrangements

Working arrangements will vary from one organization to another. Many organizations have introduced more flexible working arrangements which allow them to match staffing levels more easily to changes in the workload. For example, a growing number of firms are :

- Employing more people on part-time and fixed term contracts, instead of permanent full-time employment contracts

- Replacing fixed hours of work by shiftwork and Flexitime

- Making workplaces more flexible, as information technology enables more people to work from home using computer and telephone links

- Grouping workers into teams and giving them the responsibility of deciding how their work should be organized

The reasons for these major changes will be explored in Section 4.4.

▼ Table 4.1: Employees with flexible working patterns, by gender, Spring 1994

UNITED KINGDOM			PERCENTAGES
	Male	Female	All persons
Full-time			
Flexible working hours	9.7	15.4	11.7
Annualized working hours	5.6	6.4	5.8
Term-time working	1.1	4.7	2.4
Job sharing	-	0.2	0.1
Nine day fortnight	0.7	0.4	0.6
Four and a half day week	3.2	3.1	3.1
All full-time employees (=100%)(thousands)	10,573	5,681	16,254
Part-time			
Flexible working hours	7.3	9.1	8.8
Annualized working hours	3.1	5.3	5.0
Term-time working	4.9	10.3	9.6
Job sharing	1.8	2.5	2.4
Nine day fortnight	-	-	-
Four and a half day week	-	0.3	0.3
All part-time employees(=100%)(thousands)	745	4,760	5,506

1 It is possible for respondents to appear in more than one category.
Social Trends 1995

Types of employment contract

It is a legal requirement for an employer to provide each employee with a written contract of employment setting out the terms and conditions of their job (see 5.3). Terms and conditions in contracts will vary. Increasingly, workers are being offered part-time and temporary contracts rather than full-time permanent contracts (see 3.2).

Permanent full-time employment

Employees who work under contract for an unspecified period of time for 30 or more hours each week are full-time workers who have a **permanent contract** of employment. Their contract to work for an employer will only end when they leave, retire, are sacked, or made redundant.

In 1995 around 15 million workers in the UK had permanent full-time contracts.

Permanent part-time employment

A growing number of workers are employed to work fewer than 30 hours each week. These people are defined as **part-time employees.** Many have permanent contracts which specify a date to begin work in an organization but will give no date when employment might end.

Some part-time contracts are for term-time working only. These allow working parents to spend the school holidays at home looking after their children.

In 1995 there were over 6 million part-time employees in the UK, mostly on permanent contracts. Over 80% of these workers were female.

Fixed term employment

Fixed term contracts can involve full-time or part-time work, but will only last for a fixed period of time, typically from 6 months to two years. Fixed term contracts will specify a start date and an end date for the employment.

A growing number of workers are employed on fixed term contracts in order to carry out a particular task for an employer. This gives employers the advantage of being able to change the number of workers they employ to suit their needs by simply hiring more staff for short periods of time or by not renewing the contracts of existing staff. Workers on short fixed term contracts are often not entitled to sick or holiday leave and pay, and are unlikely to receive overtime pay for weekend or late-night working.

Fixed-term contracts are increasingly being offered to what are called 'external workers'. These are people who provide support services and advice to business organizations. They will include agency 'temps', the self-employed, and workers sub-contracted from other firms. External workers will tend to carry out jobs such as catering, cleaning, computer maintenance, public relations, etc. Consultants may also be employed for special one-off projects, such as designing and installing new office equipment, or advising on a new factory location.

Job sharing

As the name suggests, job sharing involves dividing up a full-time job between two or more part-time workers. The main problem is that each of those undertaking the job must be aware of the tasks undertaken by the other person.

For an employer, job sharing means that there is cover when one of the employees is off sick or on holiday. For the employee, job sharing can provide the flexibility of not having to go to work every day. This can be especially useful to parents with young children, or people running their own small business in their spare time.

Hours of work

In the past, contracts of employment required workers to work a fixed number of hours, usually around 38 per week, between set times – for example, 9 am to 5 pm. However, a growing number of workers are now working to different patterns:

- **Shiftwork** involves working blocks of hours each day in order to keep a firm in production 24 hours each day. It can often involve working at night.

- **Annualized hours systems** allow the employer to vary the time the worker has to come in to work and leave each day

- **Flexitime** enables the employee to choose what time to start and leave work each day, within agreed limits

Shiftwork

Firms that want to keep production lines running or remain open for trade for more than 8 or 9 hours each day will require their employees to work in **shifts**.

Shiftwork involves using different groups of workers in rotation. For example, a manufacturer who wants to keep running 24 hours a day may employ workers on three shifts: 12 pm to 8 am, 8 am to 4 pm, and 4 pm to 12 pm. In the same way, shops which open from 8 am to 9 pm may use two or three overlapping shifts, plus part-time and Saturday workers. Workers on night time shifts will often be paid an additional shift allowance.

Annualized hours systems

Under this system workers are contracted to work a given number of hours over a 12-month period rather than a specified number of hours each week. This means that a business can choose to vary the number of hours worked from week to week or seasonally to meet its requirements – for example, to match changes in consumer demand.

Flexitime

Unlike the annualized hours system, Flexitime gives the employee the ability to choose, within limits, when to start and finish work as long as they are in work for a set period each day, known as **core time**. For example, an employee may be able to come into work at any time between 7 am and 10 pm in the morning, and leave at any time between 4 pm and 6 pm at night. This period is **Flexitime**. Core time is, therefore, between 10 am and 4 pm, and the employee must be in work during this period.

However, Flexitime does not mean an employee can come into work at 9.55 am every day and leave at 4.05 pm. They must work an agreed number of hours – usually around 37.5 – each week. Any time spent at work over and above these agreed hours can normally be built up and taken as extra holiday entitlement.

Because some people like to start early and some prefer to start later each morning, a business organization will benefit from an extended period of staff cover, allowing it to stay open or in production longer each day.

Flexitime tends to be a feature of office-based jobs: it is not very practical for shops or manufacturing plants to allow workers to turn up for work when they choose.

▼ *Table 4.2: People usually engaged in weekend working, shiftwork and night work, Spring 1994*

UNITED KINGDOM

	Total (thousands)	As a percentage of all in employment
Saturday working	6,289	24.6
Shiftwork	4,138	16.2
Sunday working	3,110	12.2
Night work	1,577	6.2

Social Trends 1995

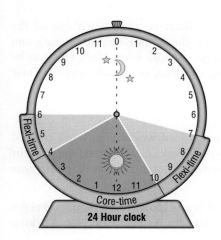

Portfolio Activity 4.9

PC: Identify and explain difference in working arrangements

Range: Differences in working arrangements

Skills: Read and respond to written material, Produce written material

Read the follow statements by employees and employers.

'I often take a quick walk around the offices early in the morning. Some days there is no one in before 10 am!'

'If I am tired I can have an extra hour in bed in the morning and just work later that night. If I had to go in early, I would just be tired all day and wouldn't get much done.'

'I like to come in a bit later each morning to avoid the crowds on the trains during the peak.'

'Staff morale has improved since they have been allowed to choose what hours to work.'

'I remember when everybody used to come in at 9 am and left at 5.30. Now the office is usually manned between 8 am to 6.30 pm every day.'

'I seem to be spending more of my time each day now checking through all the Flexitime sheets of all my staff to make sure they are working all the hours they are supposed to!'

'Since they introduced Flexitime it is impossible to get everyone in to attend a business meeting before 10.30 in the morning.'

'Because staff cover is often available into the early evening now, there is no need to pay workers to work as much overtime as before'.

'I drive to work every day. On a bad day it can take up to an hour. However, if I leave home before 7.30 in the morning I can avoid the traffic and get to work by 8 am. I can then leave at 4 pm and avoid the traffic coming home.'

1. From the statements, list the advantages and disadvantages to an employee and an employer of using Flexitime, compared to starting and finishing work at times set by the employer.

2. You are the manager of a large department store with the following opening times:

Monday to Friday	8 am to 9 pm
Saturday	8 am to 6 pm
Sunday	10 am to 4 pm

Write a short paper to explain how using different contracts and working arrangements for different employees will help you ensure that there is staff cover all the time the store is open.

Place of work

One important working arrangement is where workers are based during working hours. **Workbases** can be indoors, such as in an office, factory, or shop, or outdoors, for example, on a farm, building site, or fishing boat. Some workers may also be expected to be mobile – for example, sales representatives visiting wholesalers and retailers all over the country. Increasingly, workers are also able to work from home and keep in touch with their headquarters using modern communications equipment.

▼ *Workbases*

ORGANIZATIONAL WORKBASES

OFFICES · FACTORY · SHOP · HOME · MOBILE · OUTDOORS

▼ *Occupations of teleworkers*

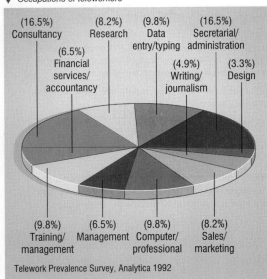

(16.5%) Consultancy
(8.2%) Research
(9.8%) Data entry/typing
(16.5%) Secretarial/administration
(6.5%) Financial services/accountancy
(4.9%) Writing/journalism
(3.3%) Design
(9.8%) Training/management
(6.5%) Management
(9.8%) Computer/professional
(8.2%) Sales/marketing

Telework Prevalence Survey, Analytica 1992

Mobile work

A large number of workers spend very little time at one particular workbase. Instead, they are mobile and carry out their work at different locations. Some mobile workers may even be expected to travel overseas to carry out work or attend meetings.

Sales representatives, plumbers, electricians, double-glazing fitters, painters and decorators, and ambulance drivers are all examples of jobs which are mobile. Can you think of any more?

Teleworking

Teleworking is a growing feature of employment in the UK. It has become possible because of advances in technology.

Teleworking involves employees working away from the main location of their employing organization and keeping in touch via electronic mail, fax machines, and even by new videophones.

Teleworking can involve working in special telecottages equipped with sophisticated computer and communications equipment. Employees may be able to drive to a telecottage near their home, rather than commuting long distances by car, bus, or train into town and city centres. A growing number of people are also able to telework from home.

The number of workers in the UK who are teleworking is still quite small, but growing – around 650,000 in 1993.

THE ADVANTAGES OF TELEWORKING

+ With more of its staff teleworking, a firm can reduce floorspace in its headquarters and save rent

+ Firms can motivate staff to work harder by reducing stress associated with travel and the workbase environment

+ Workers may demand lower wage rises because the cost of their travel, including public transport fares, petrol prices, and parking charges, will be less

THE DISADVANTAGES OF TELEWORKING

− Staff working at home may not spend all the time that they should working

− The cost of equipment for teleworkers can be high

− It can be difficult to get staff together for meetings at short notice

− Teleworking makes on-the-job training difficult

Portfolio Activity 4.10

PC: Identify and explain differences in working arrangements
Range: Differences in working arrangements
Skills: Take part in discussions

In small groups discuss the following problems. (Do not forget to take notes and write up the main points arising from your discussions to file in your portfolio).

1. Which of the following groups of workers do you think could carry out their normal working duties by teleworking?

● Secretary

● Nurse

● Accountant

● Builder

● Data processor

● Teacher

● Journalist

● Electrician

2. You are the manager of a marketing office in a medium-sized organization. Three of your staff have asked if they can work from home three days each week. What problems might this cause you in trying to run the department? What are the advantages? Do you support their request or not?

Teamworking

All jobs require some teamwork. Even if you work most of the time in an office on your own, you will probably be part of a team. One person will do the filing, another will perform secretarial duties, while a manager will make decisions on what jobs need to be done, and by when. Many organizations want their workers to feel they are part of one big team, all working towards the same objectives and sharing in the success of the business.

However, organizations are also encouraging employees to work together in small teams, rather than on their own. Often this involves dividing the workforce into small groups, usually of around 6-12 employees, with each group being responsible for organizing and carrying out their work as they think best. Teams can combine workers with different skills and experience to work on different projects. In this way, the idea is that team members will be motivated by each other to work harder, solve work-related problems, and improve the quality of their work (see 6.2).

The scope for teamwork in an organization will depend on the jobs people do. For example, doctors, plumbers, and hairdressers will tend to spend most of their time working individually, whereas car assembly workers or people who plan and design advertising campaigns will tend to work closely with colleagues.

Decentralized and centralized decision-making

Firms using lots of teams of workers are said to have a **decentralized** decision-making structure. That is, more decisions are made by workers rather than by senior managers at head office.

Other firms may prefer senior managers to take all of the decisions and then tell staff what to do. In this case, decision-making is said to be **centralized**. The main advantage of centralization is the ability of senior managers to make decisions quickly, especially when the business environment is changing rapidly (see 2.4).

In general, the larger the organization, the more decentralized it is likely to be. This is because it is impossible for senior management to maintain direct control over all business activities. For example, large retail organizations with a number of branches at different locations, like Tesco and B&Q, tend to have flat, decentralized organizational structures. Each store will have a manager able to take decisions on staff requirements, store layout, stock control, etc.

However, certain functions within a business will always be controlled from 'the centre'. For example, decisions about budget allocations between different departments, new products, and advertising campaigns are likely to be centralized, because they affect the whole organization. Support services such as preparing customer accounts, purchasing, and wages are also likely to provided centrally, and are therefore called **centralized services**.

Empowerment

Empowerment has become a popular term in business in the 1990s. It means motivating staff in lower grades in an organization, by allowing them to contribute to decision-making. This can be as simple as sales staff in McDonalds being allowed to greet and thank customers in their own way, rather than having to use standard phrases recommended by senior managers.

In other firms, teams have been empowered with the responsibility to organize their own work. Worker representatives may even be allowed to attend board meetings to discuss company plans and policies with all the other directors.

Portfolio Activity 4.11

PC: Identify and explain differences in working arrangements
Range: Differences in working arrangements
Skills: Produce written material, Collect and record data, Take part in discussions

1. Draw a table with at least 10 rows like the one started below.

2. Complete the table in Task 1, using information on the working arrangements of each job advertised below. Details about one job have already been provided for you.

3. Collect information from at least another 5 job advertisements from your local newspapers, and use it to complete and extend your table on working arrangements.

4. Interview at least two employees with different working arrangements. Try to find out what they like about their working arrangements and what they dislike about them.

5. Interview at least two employers in different organizations that use different working arrangements. Try to find out why each organization has chosen to use its particular working arrangements, i.e. how do they benefit the firm and its staff?

6. Write a short report on the findings from your interviews in Tasks 4 and 5.

7. What type of working arrangements would you prefer if you were:

   a an employee

   b an employer

   In each case explain your choice of working arrangements.

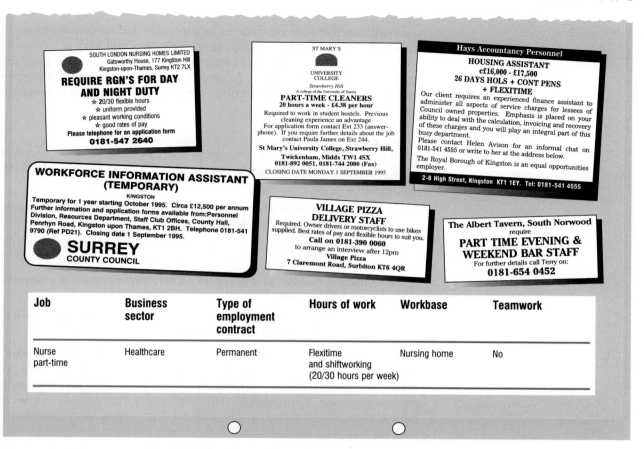

Job	Business sector	Type of employment contract	Hours of work	Workbase	Teamwork
Nurse part-time	Healthcare	Permanent	Flexitime and shiftworking (20/30 hours per week)	Nursing home	No

Section **4.4**

Why working arrangements are changing

There are a number of reasons why firms are introducing different and more flexible working arrangements for their employees. These include:

- To become more competitive
- To increase productivity
- To improve the quality of goods and services
- To introduce new technology

In practice, all these reasons are related. A firm that fails to increase productivity, improve product quality, and introduce modern technology will fail to compete with rival firms that do make these changes.

Competition

Competition between firms and rival products is increasing in many markets. Not only can consumers choose between the same or similar goods and services provided by different organizations, but they can also choose to spend their money on an increasing array of different goods and services. For example, firms that produce and sell computer games consoles not only compete against each other, but also compete against firms selling other electronic goods such as videos and CD players, and even holidays, furniture, or jewellery.

If an organization is to continue to be profitable and remain in business, it will need to fight off this competition. That is, it will have to persuade consumers that their product is better than the same or another product provided by their competitors. Advertising can help, but the main way to become more competitive is to offer consumers a better quality good or service at a lower price.

Changing working arrangements to be more competitive

Introducing new working arrangements can help a firm become more competitive, by reducing costs and improving quality. Methods can include:

- Introducing Flexitime and shiftworking, so that the organization can remain in production longer or stay open later to serve customers
- Reducing floorspace and saving rent by allowing more staff to telework
- Reducing the number of employees on full-time permanent contracts to reduce labour costs
- Decentralizing decision-making, so that managers in the organization can respond more quickly to changes in consumer demand

By creating flexible workforces and employing more temporary and part-time workers, firms can change their levels of staffing more easily to match changes in consumer demand. If all employees were on permanent contracts, cutting the number of staff employed during periods of low or falling consumer demand would lead to high redundancy payments, whereas staff who are employed on short-term contracts for less than two years are not entitled to any redundancy payments from their employers.

Productivity

Cutting production costs in order to offer consumers lower prices is all about increasing productivity, i.e. increasing output without increasing costs by the same amount. If more can be produced with the same inputs for the same, or a lower, total cost, then the cost of each unit produced will be lower. This will allow a firm to set their price below that of their less productive competitors, and sell more goods or services.

Measuring productivity

If more output can be produced by using the same or less labour, materials, and machinery, then productivity will be increased.

It is relatively easy to measure productivity in a manufacturing plant because there is a physical product. For example, if car workers produce 50 cars a day one week and 60 cars in the following week using the same amount of machinery, then their productivity will have increased.

Productivity in organizations that provide services can be measured by the work flow – for example, number of windows cleaned per hour, number of haircuts given, number of patients seen, etc. Alternatively, it can be measured by sales revenue per employee. If a firm increases sales revenues without having to employ extra staff or equipment, or raising prices, then clearly employees must be working harder.

Changing working arrangements to increase productivity

Modern organizations are always looking for ways to improve productivity. One way to do this is by introducing new working arrangements. For example:

- Flexitime, teleworking, and teamworking may give workers more job satisfaction, which will motivate them to work harder and produce more

- Organizing employees in teams can encourage increased group effort and output

- Shiftworking will allow a firm to carry on producing goods 24 hours a day

- Investing in new machinery and equipment can replace human effort. This will allow a firm to cut the numbers of permanent staff it employs and thus reduce wage costs.

Quality assurance

Increasingly customers today are demanding higher quality goods and services. This means that brands which have a reputation for being unreliable or for regularly breaking down will be avoided by customers in favour of higher quality products.

In Britain firms can win awards for providing a high quality good or service. The **British Standards Institution (BSI)** sets quality and safety standards for a wide range of products. Products meeting the BSI standards are awarded a kitemark to indicate that they have reached the necessary standards. Products awarded the kitemark will have a competitive advantage over products which fail to display the symbol to the consumer. In addition, firms can earn the **ISO 9000** award by achieving a set of quality standards agreed across the European Union.

Changing working arrangements to improve quality

Some of the most successful organizations today have achieved their dominant position by concentrating on product quality. Introducing teamworking has often been the key to successful quality management programmes.

Grouping employees in teams and giving them responsibility for organizing their work can improve their sense of pride in the goods and services they produce. Team members will work together to improve their work and may often compete against other teams to be the best.

Teamworking has also allowed many organizations to implement **Total Quality Management (TQM)**. The aim of TQM is to focus the attention of all staff on the quality of what they do at every stage in the production process. This is achieved by encouraging staff to believe that they are all working for the customer, even staff who provide other employees with services. So for example, an office engineer providing a service to a worker in the same company would treat him as a valued customer, even though they both work for the same firm.

Portfolio Activity 4.12

PC: Explain and give examples of reasons for change in working arrangements in one business organization

Range: Reasons for change

Skills: Read and respond to written material

1. Suggest how you might measure productivity in the customer payments department at Barclaycard.

2. Suggest how competition with other credit card companies has forced Barclaycard to consider the quality of service provided by its customer payments department.

3. What were the main steps the department took in order to improve the quality of its service?

4. What evidence is there that quality management had a beneficial impact on the department?

5. Suggest any other ways Barclaycard could change working arrangements in customer payments to improve productivity and quality of service.

ISO 9000 at Barclaycard

At Barclaycard, the customer payments department processes payments from cardholders. The work is routine and repetitive, with incoming mail varying between 40,000 and 200,000 items a day. Staff were queuing up to transfer, and absenteeism was a problem. For all that, the department was picked as a pilot for the ISO 9000 quality standard.

Jenny Harris, manager of the department, explained that the first step was to explain that a large part of quality management is about taking responsibility for tasks and finding answers to problems. 'It is a question of working smarter, not harder,' says Harris. She told her staff: 'You are the experts and must decide as a team the best way to handle the job.' Staff started to regularly discuss how they did their jobs and ways to improve them with each other, and management began to listen.

It was a big change, but it worked. Before, the department was unable to cope with flows of mail at certain times. This meant that Barclaycard lost money because uncashed cheques don't earn interest and customers grumbled when letters were not answered quickly. Now, same-day processing of letters is guaranteed and sickness levels among staff have dropped by half.

'Now we are confident about the way in which we do our jobs, there are fewer checks and controls, leaving us with more time to spend on improving what we are doing,' says Harris.

Evening Standard 20.2.95

Industrial robots replacing manufacturing workers

The world's industrial robot population is forecast to soar by more than a third over the four years to 1997, according to a report published by the International Federation of Robotics. Japan accounts for more than half the world's robot stock, equivalent to 325 robots for every 10,000 manufacturing workers. It is followed by Singapore, Sweden, Italy, and Germany. Use of robots is widespread in the motor vehicle industry. Here robots are used most often for welding and paint spraying.

Financial Times 7.10.94

The impact of new technology

Introducing new technology can significantly improve productivity in a firm. Machines and equipment used in factories, offices, and shops are getting faster and more accurate all the time (see 3.3).

In some cases, new technology has replaced human skills and efforts. For example, industrial robots are now able to assemble and paint cars and have replaced many tasks once done by humans. In other cases, it has increased the range of skills workers must have. Not only must they do the job they have always done, but they must also know how to use computers. Technology has also created a demand for new skills such as data processing, programming, and computer maintenance.

The impact of new technology on working arrangements

New technology has affected working arrangements in many organizations. In most cases it has allowed firms to be more flexible in their employment practices:

- New machines can be introduced which allow firms to cut the number of staff employed on permanent contracts without reducing the amount of production

- It has encouraged teleworking

- Organizations have tended to decentralize decision-making because employees are now able to keep in regular contact with senior managers using new telecommunications equipment

- People who can provide specialist skills in computer programming and maintenance can be hired on fixed term contracts

Businesses are sometimes forced to introduce new ways of working because of competition from other firms. For example, Japanese cars are made largely by robots and tend to be cheaper and of higher quality than European cars. Because sales of Japanese cars have been rising in Europe, European car producers have been forced to adopt Japanese working practices, including using new technology, faster design and development of new cars, and better training for workers. Unless firms adopt work practices to match the best in the market, they will find sales falling and may eventually go out of business.

Portfolio Activity 4.13

PC: Explain and give examples of reasons for change in working arrangements in one business organization

Range: Reasons for change

Skills: Read and respond to written material

1. What might the advantages of this new technology be to a business organization?

2. How might this technology change working arrangements:

   a in a typical office?

   b for a mobile sales representative?

The Office Walker

London solicitor Ronnie Fox is a man on the move, and his office moves with him. Ronnie's got what all businessmen and women may soon be carrying – the office on an arm.

He's test driving the complete communications console designed to keep people in touch wherever they are. The design concept was built by technologists at BT's laboratories and is a demonstration of how the telephone, videophone, fax, and computer can all come together in a single package.

Fax messages appear as data on the screen of the wrist-worn device which weighs just two pounds. BT has planned a prototype and is talking to computer and mobile communications equipment-makers.

Daily Mirror 11.1.95

Key crossword

Across

1. Term used to describe layers of management in an organization being arranged like a pyramid with the most senior managers at the top (9).

2. Groups of employees carrying out the same or similar business functions are arranged into these (11).

4. In this type of organizational structure employees from different departments are arranged into project teams (6).

6. An organization is described as this if it has few layers of management (4).

10. Contracts of employment which specify a date for an employee to start work but no end date (9).

11. Using workers in rotation so that a firm has staff cover 24 hours a day (9).

15. A contract of employment that specifies a date for the employee to start work and a definite date to finish work (5,4).

16. The department that attempts to identify what customers want and encourages them to buy (9).

17. The person who has the authority to delegate work tasks to an employee (4,7).

18. This department provides support to all the other departments in an organization by providing filing, secretarial, mail and data processing services (14).

19. Organizing employees into small groups (8).

20. The ratio of outputs to inputs in a firm (12).

Down

1. This department is responsible for recruiting, selecting, and looking after the welfare of employees (5, 9).

2. This department arranges deliveries to customers (12).

3. The way in which firms organize their business activities is called this (9).

5. Describes the structure of an organization that has many layers of management (4).

7. Short for computer systems that can be used to control the production process (1,1,1).

8. Place of work, whether a shop, office, factory or the home (8).

9. Giving instructions to employees under your command (10).

12. An arrangement whereby workers can choose, within reason, what times to start and finish work each day (9).

13. The role of this department is to create orders for goods and services (5).

14. Short for computer programs that allow the user to create complex 3D designs (1,1,1).

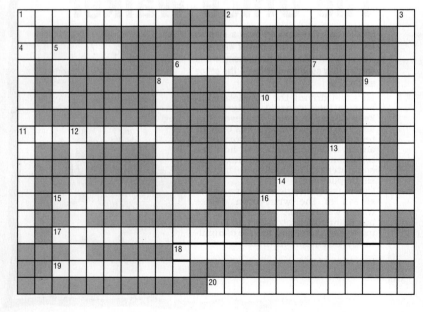

The following key words and terms are not included in the crossword. Refer back to the chapter if necessary to write explanations for each one:

Organization chart
Chain of command
Span of control
Research and development
Industrial design
Engineering design
Production
Purchasing
Accounting
Logistics
Customer Services
Working arrangements
Annualized hours
Core time systems
Job sharing
Centralized services
Empowerment
Productivity
Quality assurance

You must demonstrate that you are able to:

1. Describe organizational structures

2. Produce organizational charts showing departments

3. Describe the work and explain the interdependence of departments within business organizations

4. Identify and explain differences in working arrangements

5. Explain and give examples of reasons for changes in working arrangements

1 What kind of organizational structure has only a few layers of management?

A hierarchical

B tall

C matrix

D flat

2 Which of the following is an advantage of a flat organizational structure?

A employees feel that their managers are a long way away in the organization

B communications are fast between the top and bottom of the firm

C there is a need for a great deal of paperwork

D managers have less control over their staff

3 A production department makes finished products. Which department delivers the goods to the customer?

A human resources

B distribution

C finance

D marketing

4 What is the role of the human resources department?

A payment of bills

B delivery of goods

C market research

D recruitment and selection of staff

5 The role of the accounting department is to:

A keep records of financial transactions and manage payments and receipts

B choose raw materials for the production department

C design new products

D look after staff

6 All of the following are working arrangements set by an employer except:

A the number of hours an employee works

B working in a team

C how an employee travels to work

D the workbase of an employee

7 From the diagrams below, which organization has a structure which could be described as matrix?

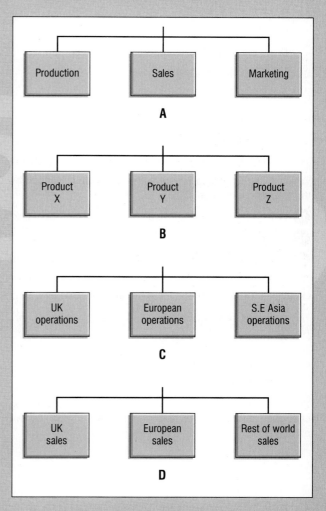

A

Production | Sales | Marketing

B

Product X | Product Y | Product Z

C

UK operations | European operations | S.E Asia operations

D

UK sales | European sales | Rest of world sales

8 The organizational structure of a company shows:

   A the layout of offices and factory floors

   B who people report to

   C working arrangements

   D the number of people employed

9 In a matrix organization structure:

   A employees work in separate departments

   B employees work on their own

   C employees work as members of project teams as well as members of departments

   D employees work from home

10 In a hierarchical organization structure, each employee has:

   A one line manager

   B no line managers

   C no clear job role

   D no other employees reporting to him/her

Questions 11-13 share the following answer options:

   A shiftwork

   B teleworking

   C fixed term contract

   D permanent contract

Which of the working arrangements above are described by the following statements?

11 Working from home using a computer and modem link

12 Being employed for a fixed period of time

13 A firm which uses employees in rotation to provide staff cover 24 hours a day.

Questions 14-16 share the following answer options:

   A to use new technology

   B to increase productivity

   C to be more competitive

   D to improve product quality

Which of the above reasons best explains why the following changes to working arrangements were made by an employer?

14 More part-time workers being employed to reduce the total wage bill

15 Using shiftwork to keep a firm in production 24 hours a day

16 Organizing employees into small teams able to work together to solve production problems and control the tasks they do

Questions 17-19 share the following answer options:

   A office

   B shop

   C outdoors

   D factory

In which of the above workbases are you likely to find the following workers?

17 A sales assistant

18 An accountant

19 A national parks ranger

20 a. What is an organizational structure?

   b. Draw two simple organization charts to shows layers of management in a tall hierarchical structure and a flatter organization.

   c. Make a list of the main departments you are likely to find in a large organization that makes video recorders and sells them all over the world.

   d. Explain how the work of the production department in an organization that manufactures cars will depend on the work carried out by purchasing, human resources, and accounting departments in the same firm.

21 a. Explain the difference between shiftwork and Flexitime working.

   b. What is teleworking?

   c. Explain the difference between a permanent contract of employment and a fixed term contract.

   d. Explain why a firm producing computer games systems for a large international market may introduce shiftwork in its factories.

(**assessment assignment**)—

The following assignment meets the evidence requirements needed to fulfil all the performance criteria in element 2.1. In addition it covers the following range points and core skills:

Range: Organizational structures
Departments
Differences in working arrangements
Reasons for change

Skills: **Communication**
Produce written material
Use images
Application of number
Collect and record data
Information technology
Prepare, process, and present information

Tasks

1. a Choose two local business organizations with which you are familiar. One should have a hierarchical structure and the other a flatter or matrix structure.

b For each organization investigate and make brief notes on the following:

- How each organization is structured

- Their different departments/divisions

- The main functions of each department/division

- How each department depends on the work of other departments

- The number of layers of management

- The number of managers

- The average span of control of a manager

- The number of non-managerial employees

- The different working arrangements of employees

- Evidence of teamworking

- Why teamworking was introduced

- Factors that have caused changes to working arrangements

From your investigations complete Tasks 2-5. Once you have finished them, file all your work, including your notes from Task 1, in a folder marked 'Organization structures and working arrangements'.

2. a Draw a carefully labelled organization chart for each organization.

b Write a short note to explain the structure of each organization and how they differ from each other.

3. Write a short report to explain:

a The work carried out by each department in your two organizations

b How the work of any one department links to the work of another department in the same organization. For example, how does the work of the production department rely on the work of sales, purchasing, or human resources?

4. Write a short report to compare working arrangements used in your chosen organizations. Particular reference should be given to teamwork. This should cover why teamworking was introduced and, if applicable, how teamworking operates to the benefit of an organization. (See also section 6.2 for help).

If neither firm uses teamworking, explain how one of your chosen organizations could use teamwork, and what the advantages of this approach to work might be.

5. Write a summary to explain how at least one of the following factors – productivity, technology, quality assurance, or competition – has caused one of your chosen organizations to change working arrangements for its employees.

chapter 5

chapter 5

Investigating Employee and Employer Responsibilities and Rights

Key ideas

When employees and employers cooperate with each other, businesses are more likely to survive. Good **industrial relations** will improve employees' commitment to their business and help them to work more efficiently.

There are many different ways of settling disagreements between employees and employers. These include **negotiations with trade unions**, seeking the help of the **Advisory, Conciliation, and Arbitration Service (ACAS)**, taking a case to an **Industrial Tribunal** and the **European Court of Justice**.

Many organizations have a formal **grievance procedure** to deal with complaints from, and disagreements with, individual employees.

A **trade union** is an organization of workers whose main purpose is to represent the interests of its members (workers) in the workplace. Unions play an important part in protecting employees' rights and negotiating with employers over terms and conditions of employment. This is often called **collective bargaining**.

Employees and employers have certain legal **rights and responsibilities** at work.

Employers have the right to expect employees to carry out the terms and conditions of employment as set out in their **contract of employment** and to **discipline** employees that do not. Employees must also comply with **health and safety regulations**.

Employees' rights include the **right to remuneration**, good levels of **health and safety at work**, and employers' compliance with the **terms and conditions of employment** as laid down in contracts of employment. Employees also have the right **not to be discriminated against** at work due to their sex, race, religion, or disability.

Both employers and employees have the right to **legal representation** in an industrial tribunal, a civil law court, and the European Court of Social Justice.

Employers' responsibilities towards their employees include **explaining their business objectives, offering and facilitating training, complying with health and safety regulations, and implementing equal opportunities legislation** at work.

Employers will also be expected to calculate the pay of their employees correctly and deduct **national insurance** contributions and **income tax**.

Employees' responsibilities include meeting the **terms and conditions in their contract of employment, meeting health and safety regulations**, and **working towards business objectives**. They will also be expected to **meet customers' needs** and **maintain quality standards**.

Section **5.1**

Employer and employee cooperation

▼ *Them and Us?*

Industrial relations

The term **industrial relations** covers every aspect of the relationship between employers and their employees. Good relations will help to prevent disagreements over pay and conditions of service and motivate employees to higher levels of productivity.

Good relations can be developed through regular meetings and consultation between employers and their employees or their representatives. These meetings allow workers to discuss grievances and proposals for pay increases, changes in working practices, and job cuts. Employers' proposals are much more likely to be accepted and successful if workers are consulted and involved in the decision-making process.

The benefits of employer and employee cooperation

The most profitable businesses in Britain are successful because they make what the customer wants, at the right price and quality, and can deliver the product when and where consumers want it. In order to do these things, employees and employers need to work together, to get along well, and to want their business to succeed. People in successful firms spend their time thinking about how to work better and beat competition from rival firms.

In business, therefore, there are a number of important benefits to be gained from maintaining good relations and cooperation between employers and employees. These are:

● **The survival of the business:** The most valuable resource in any business organization are its employees. There is a direct relationship between the quality and attitudes of the workforce and business success.

If employees and employers do not trust each other; if they fail to talk regularly about their concerns, or fail to listen to what others have to say, then relations between them will be poor. In this situation, both employers and employees will be putting their energy into trying to beat each other, instead of trying to beat the competition.

Workers and managers may become demoralized if they fail to cooperate. The firm may start to produce poorer quality products as a result and let their customers down by failing to deliver the right goods and services at the right time. When this happens, the survival of the firm may be threatened by rival firms who are better able to serve their customers, and the jobs of workers and managers may be lost.

● **Improved employee commitment to their business:** A dissatisfied worker is a worker who lacks commitment to the job and the organization. Workers who are demoralized are unlikely to work hard and produce their best work. They will be disruptive, and output, sales, and profits will suffer.

Employees will be dissatisfied with their work if they feel they are not being rewarded for their efforts, if they are treated badly, given unreasonable targets to meet, or if their views and concerns are not listened to. After all, why should they devote more of their time and effort to an organization that does not seem to care about them?

● **Improved efficiency:** Employees who are consulted about management decisions, treated fairly by their employer, and praised for their efforts are more likely to feel good about the business, work harder, and improve the quality of their work. This means there will be gains in efficiency. That is, more can be produced in the same amount of time with the same number of employees and machines.

Portfolio Activity 5.1

PC: Explain the benefits of employer and employee cooperation

Range: Benefits of employer and employee cooperation

Skills: Read and respond to written material

Case Study 1

On arriving at work, Michelle York is told that her boss wants to see her. Michelle is told off for being poor at her job, which involves keeping computerized records of sales. She is told that her work is too slow and contains too many mistakes. Her boss informs her that she is being formally warned, and that the warning is going on her record. Michelle explains that she has received no training in using the computer, and that a new computer program was introduced last month, also without any training in how to use it.

Case Study 2

Robert works in the reprographics section of a large firm. His job is to organize the desktop publishing of publicity materials and to supervise staff operating the photocopiers. Robert reports to Janice, the head of department, who has overall responsibility for managing the work.

One morning while Janice is out of the office, the main photocopier breaks down. The sales director urgently needs some new publicity materials copied for a meeting with his sales teams. Robert calls in the copier engineer, who reports that the copier motor has blown, and that it will be expensive to replace. Robert agrees to have the work done.

On her return to work, Janice is angry that the decision to replace the motor was taken without her approval. Robert explains that the motor would have had to be replaced anyway, because the machine would not work without it and the sales director needed copies made urgently. Robert felt he was using his initiative to help the firm. Janice angrily replies that Robert is paid to photocopy and not use his initiative.

Case Study 3

The Rocket Car Company produces hand-made sports cars. Much of the work is done by workers using welding equipment. The firm regularly reminds its staff that for their own health and safety they should wear protective goggles and clothing. The management have also pinned notices all around the factory floor.

Bob Piggott, who has been working at the plant for 15 years, refuses to wear the goggles. Two new staff have been employed and are being trained by Bob. He insists that they will do their jobs better if protective goggles are not worn. Management are very concerned about the safety of the men's eyes.

Case Study 4

Jim Aldhouse has worked at Isaac Printing Enterprises for five years. Paul Isaac, the Managing Director, has sunk a great deal of his own money into the firm to ensure that it has the most up-to-date printing equipment. However, Jim is a troublemaker and is spreading rumours that Paul is taking money from the firm by employing his family and friends as advisors and consultants rather than giving the workers a pay rise. Workers are angry and intend to strike.

Paul explains to his workforce that family and friends are only used when they have particular skills that are needed. For example, his uncle is a qualified accountant. It is cheaper to use the services of family and friends, and the firm must keep costs down in order to offer customers lower prices. This also means keeping wage costs down. If his workforce refuses to do overtime or goes on strike, the firm will lose custom and will ultimately have to cut staff numbers.

For each of the situations above suggest:

● Why staff have failed to cooperate and disagreements have occurred

● What problems have been caused by the lack of cooperation and disagreements between staff

● The likely impact on business costs

● How staff should have behaved instead

Section **5.2**   ## Ways to resolve disagreements

Portfolio Activity 5.2

PC: Describe ways to resolve disagreements
Range: Ways to resolve disagreements, Benefits of employer and employee cooperation
Skills: Read and respond to written materials

Read the articles below and suggest in each case:

- Why the disagreement between employees and employers has occurred
- How the two sides in the dispute could attempt to settle their disagreements
- The consequences for employees and employer if they fail to reach an agreement

---

Gas workers face 16% pay cut

British Gas management were slammed last night for planning to cut their workers' salaries just weeks after their chief executive won a massive 75% rise.

Top union chiefs attacked the 'kick in the teeth' for low paid showroom workers, while Cedric Brown now earns £475,000 a year.

A leaked letter claimed that pay cuts of up to 16 per cent were on the cards, with holiday entitlements also slashed from 33 to 27 days a year. A company spokesman denied that morale was at an all-time low since the chief executive's massive pay rise.

Daily Mirror 15.12.94

Car firm for 'women only' guilty of bias

A firm which sacked its salesmen to create an all-women team was found guilty yesterday of 'blatant sex discrimination.'

Car dealers Swithland Motors said it had tried to remove the 'Arthur Daley image' by employing female staff. It felt women were more sincere and could relate better to customers. But Michael Smith, 34, of Solihull, West Midlands, won his claim that he had been discriminated against on the grounds of sex. Mr Smith was among those who lost their jobs at the Colmore Depot, Birmingham, when it was taken over by Swithland Motors in 1991. The jobs, he claimed, were filled by women. The firm, which operates a string of car showrooms throughout the Midlands had boasted about its policy in a sales advert. The girls, it said, are polite, friendly, bubbly, and reliable. The firm denied discrimination.

Daily Mail 21.6.94

Dispute-hit Timex plant will close, unions fear

The Timex plant in Dundee, scene of Britain's ugliest industrial dispute of recent years, is likely to close by Christmas, union officials said last night.

The dispute began in February after 340 workers were locked out and sacked after going on strike. The strike was in response to management attempts to cut the numbers of staff due to falling watch sales. The sacked workers, replaced by raw recruits hired locally, recently rejected an offer of their jobs back on the condition that they accepted a 27% pay cut.

Independent 15.6.93

Why do disagreements between employers and employees occur?

Sometimes relations and cooperation between employers and their staff can break down. There can be many reasons.

Individual grievances

Individual employees may feel they have been unfairly treated by their employer or a more senior member of staff, for example, due to sexual

▼ *Poor facilities?*

▼ *Harassment?*

or racial harassment. However, the most common grievance against employers is unfair dismissal. Dismissal of an employee under the following circumstances is illegal in the UK:

- Failing to give the required period of notice as set out in the contract of employment in the case of redundancy
- For going on strike, when others who have done the same have not been dismissed
- For joining or refusing to leave a trade union
- On grounds of sex, race, or religion
- Due to illness or pregnancy

Employee grievances may also arise due to:

- Incorrect calculation of pay
- Being overlooked for promotion
- Unfair allocation of overtime
- Poor physical working conditions
- Not being allowed time off
- Sexual or racial harassment
- A line manager being rude or unreasonable

Many organizations have a formal **grievance procedure** to deal with complaints from individual employees. A typical grievance procedure will allow both sides in a dispute to present their case to their department manager. The manager will examine the facts and then present his or her decision on what action should be taken, if any. If the employee is not satisfied with the decision they can take their case to more senior managers, or in some cases even a joint consultative committee of unions and management representatives. If the employee is still not satisfied with the outcome, they can apply to have the case examined by an industrial tribunal.

Industrial disputes

Sometimes disagreements can arise between an organization and its entire workforce. Such large-scale disputes can occur for a number of reasons:

- **Pay:** Employees will often demand higher wages if the cost of living is rising or if other groups of workers are getting larger pay rises. Employees may also demand higher pay if their firm is making large profits, or if management are giving themselves large pay rises. A business may be reluctant to pay higher wages if output and sales have not increased, because it will reduce profits.

- **Changes in hours and conditions of work:** Employees will also tend to push for a shorter working week and longer holidays. This again will reduce output and raise costs for an employer, and may be resisted.

- **Redundancies:** Sometimes employers will cut the size of their workforce in an attempt to reduce their costs. New technology may be introduced which requires less labour input. Employees who risk being made redundant may fight to keep their jobs.

- **Changes in working practices:** Disputes may occur if employers attempt to change the way in which work is done without consulting employees, or if workers feel that the new arrangements are not as good as before (see 4.3). For example, an employer may introduce shiftwork in an attempt to reduce overtime working. Employees may try to resist these changes.

The largest industrial disputes, 1978-1994

1978 **A strike in the motor industry** for a pay increase outside government guidelines accounted for 2.5 million (27 per cent) for the 9.4 million days lost in 1978.

1979 A strike by **engineering workers** accounted for 16.0 million (54 per cent) of the total of 29.5 million working days lost in that year.

1980 The **national steel strike** accounted for 8.8 million (74 per cent) of the total of 12.0 million working days lost.

1984 The days lost in the **miners' strike** in protest against pit closures accounted for 22.4 million (83 per cent) of the total of 27.1 million working days lost.

1985 The continuing **miners' strike** accounted for 4.0 million (63 per cent) of the 6.4 million days lost.

1987 A strike in the **telecommunications industry** accounted for 1.5 million (41 per cent) of the 3.5 million days lost.

1988 A **postal workers'** strike accounted for 1.0 million (28 per cent) of the 3.7 milllion days lost.

1989 A strike by **council workers** accounted for 2.0 million (49 per cent) of the 4.1 million days lost.

1990 The campaign for a 35 hour week by **engineering unions** accounted for 327,000 working days lost in five separate disputes. The majority were in one dispute that involved the loss of 301,000 days (16 per cent) out of the annual total.

1991 A strike by **council workers** over redundancy matters accounted for the loss of 102,000 working days (13 per cent) of the annual total.

1992 A strike by **council workers** over redundancies accounted for 81,000 working days lost (15 per cent) of the 0.5 million days total.

1993 A strike by **civil servants** over market testing, privatisation and cuts in service accounted for 162,000 working days lost (25 per cent) out of the 0.6 million days total. The workers involved in this one-day strike accounted for 42 per cent of all workers on strike in 1993.

1994 A strike by **college lecturers** accounted for 63,000 (22 per cent) of the 0.28 million days lost, and a strike by signalling grades accounted for 54,000 (19 per cent) of the annual total.

Employment Gazette July 1995

Resolving disputes

There are a number of ways employers and employees can attempt to settle their disagreements. These include:

- Negotiation between employers and trade unions
- Seeking the help of the **Advisory, Conciliation, and Arbitration Service (ACAS)**
- Taking the dispute to an **industrial tribunal**
- Seeking **civil legal action**
- Appealing to the **European Court of Justice**

We will now consider these options in more detail.

Trade union negotiation

A **trade union** is an organization of workers whose main purpose is to represent the interests of its members (workers) in the workplace. Unions play a key role in resolving disputes between employers and individual employees and with their entire workforce.

Employees in many organizations, whether production operatives or managers, can belong to a trade union. Many trades unions for professional and managerial workers prefer to call themselves **staff associations**.

Several unions or staff associations can represent the interests of workers in the same workplace. For example, teachers and other staff in schools or colleges may belong to the National Union of Teachers (NUT), the Professional Association of Teachers (PAT), or the National Union of Public Employees (NUPE), among others.

Employees who belong to a trade union can seek the help and advice of union officials if they feel they have been unfairly treated or harassed by their employer or by another member of staff. The union official will be able to present the views and rights of the aggrieved employee to representatives of the employer.

Collective bargaining

The process of negotiating over pay and working conditions between trade union and employer representatives is called **collective bargaining**.

Collective bargaining may be organized so that a negotiated settlement determines pay and conditions for all firms in a particular industry, or in local agreements between particular companies and their own workers.

In addition to bargaining on wages and conditions, unions and employers will also negotiate about redundancies and the introduction of new technology.

What happens if negotiations fail?

If a union and an employer fail to reach agreement, they may enlist the help of the **Advisory, Conciliation, and Arbitration Service (ACAS)** to resolve the dispute.

If these further negotiations with unions and ACAS fail, and if one side feels that the other has broken the law, the dispute may be taken to a court of law or to an informal type of court for settling employment disputes called an **industrial tribunal**.

Finally, both parties can appeal to the highest court in Europe for a decision, the **European Court of Justice**.

Industrial action

When negotiations fail, trade unions may resort to the following types of industrial action to put pressure on their employers:

- **Overtime ban** – when workers refuse to work more than their normal hours. Many firms rely on overtime to meet production targets and deadlines.

- **Work-to-rule** – when workers comply with every rule and regulation at work in order to slow down production

- **Go slow** – working deliberately slowly

- **Sit-in** – when workers refuse to leave their place of work, often in an attempt to stop their firm from being closed down

- **Strikes** – when negotiations between unions and employers fail, a trade union may recommend that their members withdraw their labour and refuse to work. A strike can be **official**, if it has the backing of the union, or **unofficial** if it is called by workers without the support of their union.

Workers on strike may **picket** their firms by standing outside trying to persuade other people – fellow workers or members of other unions not involved in the dispute – not to enter the premises. However, going on strike will mean a loss of wages for workers, and can result in them losing their jobs if the firm is forced to reduce production as a result of lost customers and profits.

In extreme cases, an employer may retaliate by locking workers out of the firm with no pay.

▼ *Striking workers picketing their place of work*

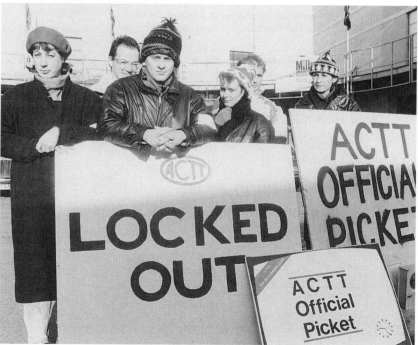

About trade unions

Trade union membership

The trade union movement started many years ago in the last century. Workers, dissatisfied with poor pay and often hazardous working conditions, organized themselves into groups in order to negotiate as one voice with powerful employers.

Total union membership in 1993 was around 9 million. Most unions are quite small with memberships of less than 1,000. Around 80% of current union members belong to the largest 20 unions. However, union membership has been in decline since the early 1980s. Rising unemployment, the increased participation of women in the labour force, and the growth of part-time employment have all tended to reduce trade union membership.

The aims of trade unions

The main functions of trade unions are:

- To defend employee rights
- To secure improvements in working conditions, including holiday entitlements, hours of work, and health and safety
- To secure adequate pay for their members
- To secure improvements in sick pay, pensions, and industrial injury benefits
- To provide education, training, and recreational and social amenities for members
- To encourage firms to increase worker participation in business decision-making

Types of trade union

There a number of different types of trade union:

Craft unions: These are the oldest form of union and are made up of workers skilled in particular crafts. Craft unions usually include workers with the same skill across several industries, for example, the Electrical, Electronic, Telecommunications, and Plumbing Union (EETPU)

General unions: These unions are for semi- and unskilled workers not covered by craft unions. General unions do not restrict membership to workers with specific skills. The Transport and General Workers Union (TGWU) and National Union of Public Employees (NUPE) are general unions.

Industrial unions: These unions cover all workers in a particular industry, regardless of status. The National Union of Mineworkers (NUM) is an example.

White-collar unions or staff associations: These unions restrict membership to professional, administrative, and clerical employees. They have expanded since 1950 due to the growth of services in the UK economy. This category of unions include the National and Local Government Officers Association (NALGO) and the Association of Scientific, Technical, and Managerial Staffs (ASTMS).

The structure of a trade union

Every union in the UK is entirely independent and self-governing, but many are affiliated to the Trade Union Congress (TUC), which provides coordination and national representation for the entire union movement.

The TUC is headed by the general council, which is the TUC's executive decision-making body. It meets every year to discuss and establish policy. Each union can send delegates to the meeting, debate, and vote on policy.

The internal structure of trade unions varies widely, but there is a typical pattern extending from full-time union officials in the union headquarters, to union members in factories, shops, and offices.

The typical structure of a trade union:

General secretary – head of a union

National executive – policy-making group. An important role of the executive is to negotiate pay and conditions with employers

Full-time officials – union members at headquarters who assist local branches

Union branches – these coordinate the affairs of union members at a local level

Shop stewards – conduct day-to-day business of the union in their place of work, as well as carrying out the job they are employed to do

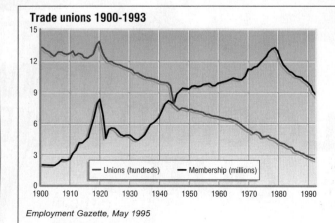

Trade unions 1900-1993

— Unions (hundreds)   — Membership (millions)

Employment Gazette, May 1995

1993 TOP TEN UNIONS	MEMBERSHIP (THOUSANDS)
Unison	1,465
Transport and General Workers Union	949
Amalgamated Engineering and Electrical Union	835
General Municipal Boilermakers and Allied Trade Unions	809
Manufacturing Science & Finance Union	516
Royal College of Nursing of the UK	303
Union of Shop Distributive and Allied Workers	299
Graphical Paper and Media Union	250
National Union of Teachers	232
National Association of School Masters and Union of Women Teachers	207

Employment Gazette May 1995

PC: Describe ways to resolve disagreements
Range: Ways to resolve disagreements
Skills: Take part in discussions, Produce written materials

In groups of four, act out the following roles in an industrial dispute between an employer and a trade union. Your job is to try to find a settlement both sides in the dispute are willing to accept.

Characters in the dispute

Union representatives

1. The shop steward
2. A machine operator

Management representatives

1. The managing director
2. The work study engineer

UNION THREATENS ACTION OVER NEW MACHINERY

The Association of Metalworkers are today threatening to undertake industrial action if the decision to install new computer-assisted metal shaping and grinding machinery in AK Metals Plc Sunderland plant is taken without assurance on pay and redundancies. The local branch of the union has asked for a 5% wage increase to operate the new machinery.

'Any strike could damage the company considerably,' explained Mr Graham Stone, managing director of AK Metals (North). A large overseas order has boosted the company's prospects recently and they are keen to fulfil it. Any disruption could threaten their international reputation. The management are also keen to avoid any increase in wage costs.

Workers are claiming that the new technology requires a higher level of skill and concentration and compensation is sought. They are also seeking management assurances that there will be no redundancies as a result of the new machines.

The two sides in the dispute have agreed to meet and negotiate today.

The union brief

The machine operators want a pay rise for operating more complex and demanding machinery. You also want to set an example for the future. You do not want the management to think that every time it introduces new ways of working it can overlook its workforce. What you want is a share in the increased profits that will come from the new machines.

You also fear that redundancies may follow as machines replace workers, and you want to limit the number of jobs lost.

You both know that the firm has recently received a large order from abroad, so you need to be careful that you do not cause the firm to lose the business. Losing the order could mean losing jobs.

Your tasks before negotiations

Before you enter negotiations, write a brief report for all your union members to read, pointing out your demands and the management's position. This should include answers to questions like:

● What is your pay claim?
● Why have you made this pay claim?
● What has been the management response?
● What forms of action could the union take, if necessary?
● Why are both you and the management keen to avoid a strike?

Your tasks after negotiations

Write a report highlighting the results of negotiations, that is, what agreements were reached, if any?

If no firm agreement was reached, do you advise your members to accept or reject the management's offer? What will the union do next?

The management brief

The work study engineer has concluded that the machines require no more effort to operate than the old ones. In fact, you feel that they ease pressure on the skilled operator. No pay rise is necessary to compensate.

As the managing director, you fear that any cost reductions from the increased output from specialist machinery may be lost if workers push for higher wages. It may even allow lower-cost competitors to undercut your prices. Also, if you are unable to cut the number of jobs, your plant will be overmanned and wage costs will be much higher than they need to be. However, you do not want to lose the goodwill of the workforce at a critical time, with an overseas order to fulfil.

Your tasks before negotiations

Write an information sheet for the other management staff, including answers to such questions as:

- What wage claim has the union asked for?
- Why are you keen to meet this claim?
- Why are you keen to avoid a strike?
- What will be discussed with the union?

Task after negotiations

Prepare another management document to report on agreements reached and their effects on the company. Outline the action that will be taken if negotiations break down and no firm agreement is reached.

The negotiations

The four people taking part in the roleplay should try to negotiate an agreement acceptable to both sides. If you cannot reach an agreement perhaps your tutor can join in to act as an independent commentator, or ask for the meeting to take a short break while you work out what to do next.

The Advisory, Conciliation, and Arbitration Service (ACAS)

If negotiations between employer and employee representatives fail to reach a settlement that is acceptable to both sides, they may ask for the help of the **Advisory, Conciliation, and Arbitration Service (ACAS)**.

ACAS is an independent organization set up by the government in 1975 to help settle disputes between employers and unions. It publishes a code of good practice which employers may wish to follow when dealing with their employees.

The main aim of ACAS is to improve relations between employers and employees by bringing opposing parties together and attempting to find solutions to disputes.

When employers and employees are unable to agree, they may wish to talk with an independent organization like ACAS. In its conciliation role, ACAS will listen to both sides in a dispute and look for possible common ground. When asked to arbitrate, ACAS will listen to all the people involved in a dispute and make a decision for both sides on what to do. Sometimes both sides in a dispute may agree in advance to accept whatever ACAS decides.

ACAS in Northern Ireland is known as the **Labour Relations Agency**.

Industrial tribunal

If an employee, or group of employees, feels that an employer has treated them unfairly and broken employment law, they can take their case to an **industrial tribunal**.

An industrial tribunal is rather like a court of law. It is less formal than the type of court you often see on television, but it has the authority to settle cases under a range of employment laws, such as wrongful or unfair dismissal or discrimination.

Each tribunal is made up of three people – a legally trained chairperson, plus one employer and one employee representative. They will listen to each side in the dispute and then make their recommendations. They can either reject the claim or make one of three decisions in favour of the employee, which the employer is legally bound to abide by. These are that:

● The employee is to be given back their old job
● The employee is to be given another job
● The employee is to be compensated

Both employer and employee have the right to appeal against a decision by the industrial tribunal.

▼ Figure 5.1: Applications to industrial tribunals, by jurisdiction, 1993-94

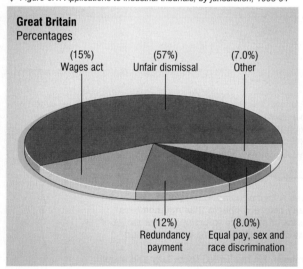

Great Britain
Percentages

(15%) Wages act
(57%) Unfair dismissal
(7.0%) Other
(12%) Redundancy payment
(8.0%) Equal pay, sex and race discrimination

Social Trends 1995

Officers bullied pregnant PC

A policewoman won a sexism battle yesterday against bosses who blocked her promotion to sergeant.

PC Suzanne Box claimed that senior officers intimidated and bullied her in her struggle to climb through the ranks. Her commander apologized to her for their behaviour, but admits there was nothing he could do to help, she said. She applied for promotion in 1993 while six months pregnant, but felt totally intimidated during an assessment hearing with a chief inspector. 'He was abrupt and I realized that I wasn't getting a fair hearing,' she said in a statement. She had already been told that she was not suitable for promotion by a detective chief inspector because she was pregnant. Yesterday an industrial tribunal awarded her an undisclosed sum after the Metropolitan Police admitted sexual discrimination.

Daily Mail 7.2.95

Civil legal action

Instead of going to an industrial tribunal, an employee may decide to seek compensation for unfair dismissal by taking their employer to court. However, this can be expensive because it involves employing a solicitor, and sometimes a barrister as well. If the employer wins the case, then the employee may have to pay both sets of legal costs.

Because court cases can involve bad publicity, employers may sometimes wish to make an out-of-court settlement with a former employee, or suggest that both parties go to arbitration with an independent body deciding the outcome of the case.

The European Court of Justice

The **European Court of Justice** is run by judges from the member countries of the European Union (see 7.1). The role of the court is to settle cases where European Union laws or directives are concerned.

An employee, or employer, can appeal to the European Court if they believe that British courts have failed to apply European laws correctly.

The European Court is often used as a last resort to settle a disagreement between employees and firms if they have failed to reach a satisfactory settlement in a UK court.

EU directives

The European Union has passed a number of directives which aim to give workers in member countries the same basic employment rights. These include:

- A maximum working week of 48 hours
- Freedom to join unions and take strike action
- Equal treatment for part-time and full-time workers
- Access to appropriate training and re-training opportunities
- Equal treatment for men and women
- The right to be consulted on changes in organization, new working methods, mergers, and redundancies

- Protection of rights of pregnant women, with working hours and conditions to be adapted if the job endangers health
- Freedom to move between EU member states for work and to enjoy the same terms and conditions of employment, such as pay and holidays, as native workers, and have equal recognition of qualifications

Individual EU member countries can choose when and how to introduce these directives. The UK government has decided not to introduce some of them on the grounds that they would raise business costs and reduce employment opportunities.

Portfolio Activity 5.4

PC: Describe ways to resolve disagreements
Range: Ways to resolve disagreements
Skills: Take Part in discussions, Produce written materials

You are the head of the production department in a large manufacturing plant making electric irons. Paul Downie, a union shop steward, has been asked by a team of workers to make an official complaint about their treatment by a production supervisor, Mr. Frampton

'I have been asked by the members of my union to make a formal complaint against Mr Martin Frampton, one of the production supervisors. Let me say before we begin that my members understand perfectly well that the company is under a lot of pressure to bring its new range of products to the market. We understand that this means that staff will be under stress and pressurized.

'However, Mr Frampton has been abusive to my members. He has called them lazy and stupid when they have failed to meet targets. One worker was told off publicly in front of his workmates and shouted at as if he were a child. Mr Frampton expects us to produce twice as much as we did before, in under half the time. It cannot be done – these targets are unreasonable. We cannot work in the way demanded by Mr Frampton. I am sure that if this treatment continues, some of my members will become so stressed that it will affect their health and work attendance. If this happens we will fall behind even further.

'We all want the firm to be a success, but it takes time to learn to produce a new range of goods, and staff must be treated like adults.'

You listen carefully to Paul's views and agree to follow up the complaint by talking to the supervisor. A short while later, Mr Frampton comes to your office…

'Perhaps I have been pushing too hard, but we all know that if we don't get the new range out by the end of the month, we'll lose our customers – and they may never come back. What with the redundancies last year and the financial mess the firm's in, I've tried to ensure that we all keep our jobs by pushing the men to get the job done by the deadline.

'Management have said we need to get the goods in the shops in the next four weeks. The production manager said we'd be able to produce the first batches in two weeks' time. At present we're at least a week behind target. The men are working too slowly, and taking too long to learn how to produce the new range. I shouldn't have shouted in public, and I will apologize, but we must keep the pressure up. We can't have staff threatening to go off sick if they are asked to meet reasonable deadlines.'

1. **a** You have now heard both sides of the disagreement and must come to a decision. Do you agree with Paul or his supervisor? Or do you think a compromise is better? What are the reasons for your decision?

   b What further action could Paul take if he is not satisfied with your decision?

   c What could be the effect of the dispute on the organization?

2. **a** Find out about the grievance procedure of your school/college and one other organization of your choice.

   b What trade unions, if any, represent the interests of employees in your school/college and other organization?

3. Using desktop publishing software, prepare a fact sheet advising employees what to do if they feel they have been unfairly treated. To do this, you will need to investigate:

   ● The grounds on which employees can claim unfair treatment in terms of, for example, discrimination, harassment, dismissal, redundancy, and unequal pay

   ● The role of industrial tribunals, ACAS, civil courts, and the EU Court of Social Justice, and how to apply to them.

Section **5.3**

The rights of employees and employers

Legal obligations

If employees and employers are to cooperate with each other, it is important that both parties live up to what is expected of them. When you start work you will expect your employer to pay you correctly, to make sure your workplace is clean and not hazardous to your health, and to treat you fairly.

Your employer will also have expectations of you. You will be expected to turn up for work on time, follow the rules and regulations of the organization, cooperate with your colleagues, make good use of your skills, and be honest and trustworthy.

Many of the expectations of employees and employers are influenced by laws passed in the UK. Employment law and health and safety regulations give employers and their employees certain legal rights and obligations which must be observed.

Employers' rights

An employer has the following main legal rights in the UK:

● Employees are expected to comply with the terms and conditions of their employment contract

- Employees are expected to comply with health and safety regulations

- Employers may take appropriate disciplinary action against an employee who does not comply with the terms of their contract or health and safety regulations, or who commits an offence against fellow workers or their organization (for example, stealing)

- Employers have the right to defend their actions at ACAS, an industrial tribunal, and the European Court of Justice (see 5.2)

Employees' rights

An employee has the following main legal rights in the UK:

- An employer is expected to comply with the terms and conditions of their contract with an employee

- An employee has certain rights relating to remuneration for their work, including the calculation and payment of wages and salaries, deductions of income tax and national insurance, sick pay and maternity pay, and compensation for industrial injury or redundancy

- Employees have the right not to be discriminated against in any way because of their sex, marital status, race, religion, disability, or membership of a trade union

- Employees have the right to legal representation against an employer at ACAS, an industrial tribunal, and the European Court of Justice (see 5.2)

Let us now examine the rights of employers and employees in more detail.

More employee rights

In addition to the main legal rights opposite, employment laws also give employees the following rights immediately they start work:

* The right not to suffer unlawful deductions from pay
* The right to work in a safe and healthy environment
* The right to receive statutory sick pay (SSP) during illness
* The right to itemized pay statements
* The right to return to work after illness
* The right to time off work for public duties, for example, jury service
* The right not to be dismissed, made redundant or subjected to any other detriment for refusing to work on Sundays
* The right of women to receive equal pay as men for work of equal value
* The right of women to maternity leave and reasonable time off for ante-natal care
* The right of women to return to work after maternity leave

After two years of continuous employment for the same employer, employees also qualify for the following rights:

* The right of women to receive maternity pay
* The right not to be unfairly dismissed
* The right to redundancy payment
* The right to time off to look for work or arrange training in a redundancy situation

The contract of employment

When you are offered a job, the offer will be subject to certain **terms and conditions**. These may be explained to you at an interview and will usually be set out in a letter confirming your appointment. Figure 5.2 shows an example of a letter confirming the appointment of a new employee.

Employers are required to provide both full-time and part-time workers with a written statement of their terms and conditions of employment within 13 weeks of their starting a job.

▼ Figure 5.2: A letter confirming employment

Leigh Limited
12-18 Green Street
Newtown
Newshire NX4 7YY

Ms K Jennings
34 Saunders Close
Newtown
Newshire NX7 8RG

14 May 199X

Dear Karen

Appointment as Receptionist

We are pleased to confirm your appointment for the above post. The terms and conditions of your appointment are given below.

1. The job will start on 1 June 199X.
2. You will be paid a salary of £15,000 per year, payable monthly in arrears into your bank account.
3. Your work performance against targets set by your manager will be reviewed every six months. Salary will also be reviewed at the same time.
4. Hours of work are from 8.15 am to 5.30 pm from Monday to Thursday and from 8.15 am to 4 pm on Friday. You will also be required to attend a special sales evening for our customers at the factory every two months. Hours will include attendance at this evening between 6 pm and 10 pm. The date of each sales evening will be given one month in advance and will be paid at a rate of £8 per hour as overtime. This sum may be reviewed at the six-monthly salary review.
5. The appointment is subject to two weeks' notice in writing.
6. Your line manager will be the head of administration.
7. This appointment is subject to a 1-month probationary period. If performance is satisfactory after this period, the probationary period will end. If performance is unsatisfactory, the probationary period may be extended or the employment may be terminated at the discretion of your line manager.
8. Sickness must be notified as early as possible, ideally at least one hour before start of work. Sickness of up to five working days requires a self-certification form. A longer period of sickness requires a doctor's certificate. Statutory Sick Pay (SSP) will be paid where appropriate for a period up to 20 weeks in a year. After that period, any entitlement to SSP will be paid by the Department of Health and Social Security.
9. Holiday entitlement accrues at one day per month in the first year of employment and one and a half day's per month thereafter. Holiday entitlement may be taken after three months' employment and notice of at least three weeks is required.
10. At all times, conduct befitting a representative of our firm when dealing with the public will be expected.

Any grievances relating to this employment should follow the company grievance procedure. Grievances in the first instance should be referred to your line manager, thereafter to the managing director in writing.

Please sign and return the enclosed copy indicating your acceptance of these terms and conditions.

Yours sincerely

Allan Salt

Allan Salt
Administration Manager

Terms and conditions

A contract of employment is drawn up by the employer and signed by the employee. It is a legally binding agreement and can be enforced in law. A contract can contain any details, but as a minimum it must contain the following:

* Name of employer and employee
* Date on which employment started
* Date on which employment will end if the contract is for fixed term only
* Job title
* Rates of pay, payment intervals, and method of payment
* Normal hours of work and related conditions, such as meal breaks
* Holiday entitlement, holiday pay, and public holidays
* Conditions relating to sickness, injury, and maternity pay
* Pension arrangements
* Length of notice to quit to and from employee
* Disciplinary rules and procedures
* Arrangements for handling employee grievances

Other conditions may cover topics such as trade union membership, dress codes, the need for confidentiality, work locations, etc.

All of the above are called the **expressed terms** – that is, terms which are openly agreed between employer and employee. Because the range of expressed terms can be enormous, some organizations will not provide full written details in a contract, but will instead direct employees to company handbooks, where the rules of the company and other matters are set in out in more detail.

In addition, there will be unwritten **implied terms** which are assumed to be part of a contract. For example, employees will be expected to work towards the achievement of organizational goals, obey reasonable orders from their managers, wear suitable and acceptable clothing, and produce good quality work. Both employer and employee are expected to be trustworthy, act in good faith, and exercise due care to ensure health and safety in the workplace.

Health and safety at work

Employees have a legal right to expect their employers to provide a healthy and safe working environment. In return, employers have a legal right to expect employees to comply with health and safety regulations in an organization.

Portfolio Activity 5.5

PC: Explain employee rights and responsibilities, Explain employer rights and responsibilities
Range: Employer rights, Employee rights
Skills: Read and respond to written materials, Produce written material

1. Study the letter in Figure 5.2 on page 201.

   a What are the expressed terms in the offer of employment?

   b What implied terms do you think Karen will be expected to work to in her job?

2. In the first few months of her appointment Karen is asked to do the following:

- Wear more business-like clothes in reception instead of jeans and tee-shirts. Karen has agreed in order to pass her probationary period, but intends to wear what she likes once this period is over.

- Pop out to the local Chinese takeaway to get the managing director some lunch because he is too busy to do it himself. Karen refuses because she is meeting someone for lunch.

- Wash the senior sales manager's car during a quiet period when she has little to do. Karen refuses point blank.

- Attend a sales evening in four weeks' time. Karen has already booked to go to a concert that night and refuses to attend. The company has offered to reimburse her ticket if she is unable to sell it to someone else.

- Attend a three-day training course in customer care. Karen does not want to go because the training centre is 50 miles away and would involve a long train journey. Her employer will pay the cost of the travel.

- After two months' employment, Karen has asked to take two days' holiday in three weeks' time. It is a busy period for the firm and her request is refused. Karen feels this is an injustice and intends to discuss the matter with the senior human resources manager.

Discuss whether the organization was right to ask Karen to do these things, and if Karen was right to refuse or feel aggrieved.

There are a numbers of laws relating to health and safety in all workplaces, including factories, offices, shops, and railway stations. These are mainly contained in the 1974 **Health and Safety at Work Act,** which requires employers to 'ensure as far as is reasonably practicable, the health, safety, and welfare at work of all staff.' The Act requires:

- Firms to provide all necessary safety equipment and clothing free of charge

- Employers to provide a safe working environment

- Union-appointed representatives to have the right to inspect the workplace and investigate the causes of any accident

The Act also requires employees to take reasonable care to avoid injury to themselves or to others by their work activities, and to cooperate with employers and others in meeting statutory requirements. Employees must not interfere with or avoid anything provided to protect their health, safety, or welfare.

There are also a number of European Union regulations on health and safety at work. These cover the provision and use of work equipment, including the use of computer keyboards and screens, the provision and availability of protective clothing, manual handling operations, and workplace conditions.

The Health and Safety Executive

Health and safety laws are enforced by the **Health and Safety Executive (HSE)** set up by the government. Inspectors appointed by the HSE have the power to enter and inspect workplaces. Legally binding improvement orders can be issued, and in some cases prohibition orders which require an immediate end of an unsafe practice or process. The HSE also issues codes of good practice to employers.

Disciplinary action

Employers are entitled to discipline and to sack workers if necessary. To do so, they must draw up a **disciplinary procedure**, and employees must be made aware of it.

A disciplinary procedure usually involves a series of steps including verbal warnings, a written warning, and, if the offence persists, a final written warning. Dismissal will follow if the final written warning is made within twelve months of the first. Alternatively, if an employee is involved in a serious breach of company rules (such as theft or a deliberate and dangerous action which breaks health and safety rules) s/he may be suspended (with or without pay), or dismissed immediately. The employee should be given the right to appeal and independent assessment at any stage throughout this procedure.

Figure 5.3 shows a typical disciplinary procedure used in organizations.

▼ *Figure 5.3: A typical disciplinary and dismissal procedure*

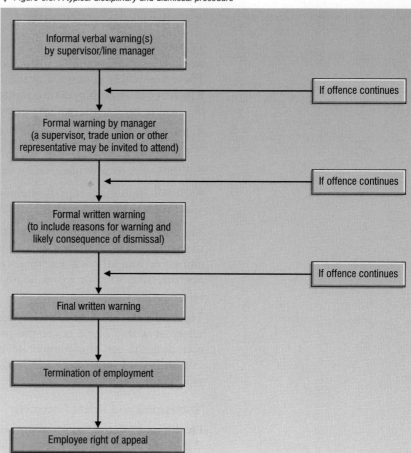

'Fair and legal' dismissal

In law there are only five main reasons for dismissing or sacking an employee which are considered 'fair and legal'. These are:

● **Redundancy** – when employees are no longer needed, perhaps due to a decline in business, the introduction of new technology, or a business reorganization. Employees who have worked for the same organization for more than two years have a right to receive compensation for the loss of their job. This is called a **redundancy payment,** and its size will usually depend on the length of their service and how much the employee earned each month or year.

Portfolio Activity 5.6

PC: Explain employee rights and responsibilities, Explain employer rights and responsibilities

Range: Employer rights, Employee rights

Skills: Read and respond to written materials, Produce written material

1. In small groups: You are a group of senior managers in a large organization. Below is an assortment of offences committed by employees. In each case discuss whether the employee needs to be disciplined and if you decide disciplinary action is necessary, which of the following actions you will take:

A an informal verbal warning

B a formal verbal warning

C a formal written warning

D a final written warning

E instant dismissal

If you choose C or D as the appropriate action, then you must warn your employee of one of the following punishments:

● Suspension with pay pending a disciplinary investigation

● Suspension without pay

● Transfer to another job in the organization

● Demotion to a more junior position

● Dismissal

Which punishment do you think is appropriate in each case? Give reasons for your decisions.

	An office worker has left confidential papers about future product developments on her desk overnight. They should have been locked away in a secure filing cabinet.	An employee is found drunk at work. His wife has recently died and he is of previous good record.
A production worker is caught stealing computer parts.	A supervisor who has already received a verbal warning and a written one for continual lateness is late again without a reasonable excuse.	A sales manager is accused of sexually harassing his secretary. She has reliable witnesses within the firm to confirm the harassment.
The police inform the organization that they have detained one of their van drivers for drink driving while making deliveries.	An employee who has been verbally warned for incompetence at his job has recently failed to meet his work targets and has caused a whole section of staff to underperform.	A newly promoted manager clearly cannot cope with the demands of his new job and has lost the respect of his staff.

- **Gross misconduct** – drunkenness, theft, fraud, disobedience, frequent lateness or absence, giving out confidential information, sexual harassment or negligence which involves a breach of contract

- **Incompetence** – when the worker is clearly not able to do their job and produces sub-standard work

- **If continued employment breaks laws** – for example, if a heavy goods vehicle driver has been banned for drink driving

- **Important other reasons** – such as an employee or group of employees refusing to accept changes in working practices

Remuneration

Employees have a legal right to expect their employers to pay them according to terms set out in their contract of employment.

Wage protection is provided by the **Wages Act 1986**. This sets out conditions for payments to workers, excluding redundancy payments, expenses or loans, and deductions.

Wage protection is also covered by the **Equal Pay Acts of 1970/1983**. These state that an employee doing the same or broadly similar work to a member of the opposite sex in the same organization is entitled to the same rate of pay and conditions, for example, relating to duties, holidays, overtime, and hours.

A 1983 amendment to the Equal Pay Act allowed female employees to claim equal pay for work of 'equal value' to that done by a man, in terms of effort, skills, and type of decision-making required. So for example, a female sales manager could not be paid significantly less or more than a male sales manager in the same organization. If their wages did differ, it would have to be for reasons such as differences in level of responsibility, length of service bonuses, performance-related payments, etc.

Equal opportunities at work

Employees have a legal right not to be discriminated against on grounds of sex, race, religion, marital status, disability, or trade union affiliation. This applies to job adverts, interviews, selection, training, promotion, dismissal, and terms of employment.

If employees feel that they have been discriminated against, they can take their case to an industrial tribunal (see 5.2). They can also ask for the help of the **Equal Opportunities Commission (EOC)**, a government body set up in 1975 to:

- Promote equal opportunities through codes of good practice

- Investigate complaints of discrimination

- Provide legal advice and financial help when a case goes to court or industrial tribunal

- Monitor the pay gap between men and women

- Review the Equal Pay Act

- Issue notices preventing an organization from discriminating

Anti-discrimination legislation

A number of laws have been passed by the UK government to protect workers from discrimination. The main laws are:

Disabled Persons (Employment) Acts 1944/1958

These require employers with 20 or more full-time employees to employ sufficient registered disabled people to make up 3% of their total workforce. In addition, certain jobs, such as car park attendants, should be reserved for disabled people.

Race Relations Act 1976

This states that it is illegal for an employer to discriminate on grounds of colour, race, or ethnic origin in employment, education, training, and the provision of housing and other services.

Sex Discrimination Acts 1975/1986

This makes it illegal to discriminate against a person on grounds of sex or marital status, whether in job adverts, interviews, selection, training, promotion, dismissal, and terms of employment. The 1986 Act removed restrictions on the hours women could work each week.

The **Fair Employment (NI) Act** in Northern Ireland contains much of the same legislation.

The right to legal representation

Both employers and employees have the same legal right to approach the Advisory, Conciliation, and Arbitration Service (ACAS) and to take their case to an industrial tribunal in the event of disputes (see 5.2).

Section **5.4**

Employee and employer responsibilities

Employment laws and health and safety regulations not only give employers and employees certain rights, but also make them responsible for observing the rights of each other.

Employer responsibilities

Employers have the following responsibilities to look after their employees:

- To explain business objectives
- To offer and facilitate training
- To implement equal opportunities at work
- To comply with health and safety regulations
- To calculate their pay and any deductions (remuneration)

Employee responsibilities

Employers can expect their employees to have the following responsibilities:

- To comply with the terms and conditions in their contract of employment
- To meet health and safety regulations
- To meet the objectives of the business
- To meet customers' needs
- To maintain quality standards

We will now consider the responsibilities of both employers and employees in more detail.

Explaining business objectives

In order to be successful, everybody in a firm has to know the objectives of their organization – output, sales, profits, market share – and how to achieve them (see 1.1).

Many firms provide information about their objectives in the form of a **mission statement**. A mission statement states in simple terms what the organization hopes to achieve (see 1.1).

However, if employees are to work towards the achievement of objectives they will need much more precise information on objectives and targets – for example, to increase sales by 10% over the next 12 months, to reduce costs by 20%, and/or to raise profits by 5%.

Some firms set objectives for individual departments to work towards. For example, the production department may be set output and quality targets, while the human resources department may have an objective to develop staff training programmes. All departments will be expected to be run efficiently and not to spend more than they have been allocated in their budget (see 13.1).

Offering and facilitating training

An important function of the human resources department is to make sure that the organization has a workforce with the necessary skills to achieve its objectives. A good employer will recognize that it is in their own best interests to provide induction training for new staff, as well as regular training for employees throughout their careers.

Training to develop work skills is most often divided into:

- **On-the-job training** – where employees learn skills while they are carrying out their job, for example, how to operate new machinery (see 3.3)
- **Off-the-job training** – where employees learn skills on courses, for example, studying for professional qualifications

In both cases, instruction in matters of health and safety at work can be an important part of job-related training.

The need for training

Well planned training, matched to the needs of the firm, is of as much benefit to the business as it is to individual employees. In general, the following training needs will arise within an organization over time:

- Induction courses to introduce new employees to the objectives and workings of the organization, and their particular jobs
- To improve the skills of existing workers, so as to achieve higher levels of productivity and reduce production costs
- To facilitate the successful introduction of new equipment, products, and processes
- To reorganize job roles and tasks within the organization
- To prepare an individual employee for promotion
- To make employees aware of health and safety measures
- To create new skills in existing workers
- To teach employees a wider variety of skills (**multi-skilling**)

Investors in People

The **Investors in People (IiP)** award is a new national training standard set up by the government to help British business get the most from its employees. Firms may apply to their local Training and Enterprise Council (TEC) to gain IiP status. In order to qualify for the award a firm must:

- Make a public commitment to develop all employees to achieve its business objectives
- Regularly review the training and development needs of all of its employees
- Take action to train and develop staff on recruitment and throughout their employment

- Regularly check training to assess achievement and make improvements

INVESTORS IN PEOPLE

▼ *Equal opportunities at work*

For the employee, training may lead to improved motivation simply because it allows staff to do their jobs better and because it raises confidence and improves promotion prospects.

For the employer, training can improve the productivity of employees and bring new ideas and working methods to a firm. Training can also improve health and safety procedures and so reduce accidents in the workplace.

Implementing equal opportunities at work

All employees have a right not to be discriminated against at their place of work. It is the responsibility of an employer to make sure that equal opportunities laws are observed in all aspects of their relationship with employees (see 5.3). This means that the wording of job adverts, the selection of new employees, wage and salary levels, attendance on training programmes, selection of employees for promotion, dismissal, must all be free from discrimination on grounds of sex, marital status, race, religion, or disability.

Types of unlawful discrimination

Discrimination at work can take a number of forms. Few are legal:

- **Direct discrimination** occurs when a person is treated less favourably than another because of their sex, race, religion, disability, etc. For example, this may occur when a pregnant woman is selected for redundancy, or a West Indian person is overlooked for promotion or paid less simply because of the colour of his or her skin.

- **Indirect discrimination** occurs when certain people would find it hard to meet a specific requirement. For example, advertising a job for people who are over six feet tall or who have red hair.

- **Victimization** occurs when a person is treated less favourably after claiming they have been discriminated against repeatedly. For example, a female worker could claim she has been victimized if she is made redundant or moved to a less well paid job because she had complained that her boss was sexually harassing her.

Male claims of discrimination in jobs increase sharply

Sex discrimination complaints at work soared by nearly 66% last year. For the first time, men formed a large proportion of those claiming that companies were discriminating against them because of their sex.

Ms Valerie Amos, Chief Executive of the Equal Opportunities Commission, said that the recession had made men much more aware of their rights. Many of the men complaining about being turned down for jobs were aged between 55 and 60 and had been made redundant. Higher numbers of unemployed men and more jobs in service industries have driven men to look for work in jobs in what have been traditionally female areas of work.

The commission warned companies not to discriminate against men applying for traditionally 'women's' jobs after a 50-year-old man was turned down for a post in a children's nursery last year. He later won £600 at an industrial tribunal.

Financial Times 16.6.93

Legal discrimination

Discrimination is only legal where it involves a 'genuine occupational qualification'. This means it is possible to advertise, recruit, train, promote, and dismiss employees on grounds of their different skills, performance, and behaviour at work.

Discrimination on grounds of age is not illegal in the UK, although it is considered to be unfair by many people. If elected to government, the Labour Party intends to introduce legislation to make age discrimination illegal.

Job advertising

It is legal for an employer to express a preference for one type of person over another in a job advert if there is a genuine occupational qualification for the job concerned. For example, advertising for the following is legal:

- For a coloured actor to appear in a TV programme
- For a female housemistress to work in a girls' boarding school
- For a male attendant for a male toilet
- For male applicants for jobs in countries overseas which may have laws or customs that prevent women doing some types of work
- For a West Indian person to communicate with, and understand the needs of West Indian people in a community project

Equal opportunities at the BBC

'The BBC is committed to equal opportunities for all, irrespective of race, colour, creed, ethnic or national origins, gender, marital status, sexuality, disability, or age.

'We are committed to taking positive action to promote such equality of opportunity, and our recruitment, training, and promotion procedures are based on the requirements of the job.'

Equal opportunities policy

Although not required to do so by law, many firms have written their own equal opportunities policies which attempt to remove discrimination in the selection, payment, training, and promotion of their workers. Leading public and private sector organizations, such as Rank Xerox, Shell UK, British Airways, the BBC, and government departments have all adopted these type of policies.

PC: Explain employer rights and responsibilities
Range: Employer responsibilities
Skills: Produce written material

Obtain a copy of the equal opportunities policy statement for an organization with which you are familiar. Identify ways in which the organization has implemented its policy. Consider the advantages and disadvantages of the policy and how it might be improved if necessary. Ask staff what they think of the policy.

Alternatively, if your chosen organization does not have an equal opportunities policy, find out if they have plans to introduce one, and why. Prepare your own draft policy statement for the organization to discuss with personnel staff, and suggest ways in which they might implement the policy in terms of staff recruitment, pay, training, promotion, etc.

Compliance with health and safety regulations

The statistics on work-related accidents in Britain are grim. In a typical week:

- 9 workers are killed
- 1 child, 1 adult, and 1 elderly person are killed
- 400 people suffer major injuries

– all as a result of work-related accidents.

It is not surprising, therefore, that firms are required by law to provide a healthy and safe environment for their workers and customers (see 5.3). Implementing health and safety measures will increase business costs in the short run. However, a firm that does not consider the interests of its employees is unlikely to achieve its business goals. A healthier workforce, and one that has fewer accidents, is more productive and will reduce costs in the long run.

Health and safety measures in the workplace can include:

- Promoting hygienic conditions
- Protection from hazardous substances
- Training staff in health and safety matters
- Providing ear protectors against noise
- Maintaining safety equipment and clothing
- Breaks for lunch and tea so that workers do not become tired
- Providing First Aid kits and trained medical officers
- Controlling workplace temperature
- Reducing workplace air and noise pollution

Clearly, the need for many of these measures will depend precisely on the nature of the product and production processes in the workplace. For example, office workers may need only to be aware of fire drills and precautions relating to the prolonged use of computer screens or movement of office furniture. In contrast, many industrial workers operate potentially dangerous machinery and handle hazardous substances, and many more safety measures will be needed.

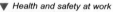
▼ *Health and safety at work*

Sick as a building

BLOCKED OR stuffy nose, dry eyes, dry throat, headaches, and lethargy are some of symptoms of Sick Building Syndrome.

How to Deal with Sick Building Syndrome: Guidance for Employers, Building Owners and Building Managers is the first published HSE guidance on the subject.

Solutions can be simple and cheap and employers are advised to do the simplest things first. For example:

- look for the obvious such as a breakdown in the air-conditioning system;
- check the symptoms, to see how widespread they really are, or whether they are confined to a particular group or area;
- ask staff if they know of any problem or likely causes; and.

- if this doesn't solve the problem, the building services and the maintenance and cleaning procedures should be checked

Employment Gazette April 1995

Health and safety policy

Every employer should produce a written statement of their policy on health and safety, including details of how the policy should be carried out. This will include details of safe working practices, how accidents should be reported, First Aid representatives, etc. All employees should be made familiar with these details and are expected to comply with them.

Large organizations can also set up **safety committees** to discuss health and safety issues and how improvements can be made. Senior and junior staff are usually represented on these committees, including any trade union safety representatives who are able to check on the day-to-day operation of the policy. This will include inspecting safety equipment and other possible hazards, investigating accidents and employee complaints, and talking with Health and Safety Executive inspectors (see 5.3).

Portfolio Activity 5.8

PC: Explain employer rights and responsibilities

Range: Employer responsibilities

Skills: Read and respond to written materials, Collect and record data, Produce written material

1. From the article, suggest why it is so important for employers to develop and promote health and safety measures in their workplace.

2. What does the article suggest an employer should do to reduce the risk of accidents and ill health at work?

Daily Mirror 2.8.95

£12bn lost by accident

POOR SAFETY COSTS FIRMS £50 A SECOND

ACCIDENTS and work-linked ill health are costing British industry a fortune.

Around 30 million working days are lost through illness and injury, costing £12 billion a year – £50 a second.

The cost of incidents is reflected in the level of claims paid by employers' liability insurers.

Latest figures show that about £3 billion was paid out in claims over the past four years because employers failed to provide a safe, healthy workplace.

As well as these claims, businesses also face hidden costs, says the Association of British Insurers.

These include retraining, the costs of any investigation and clearing up environmental damage. And machines may also have to be shut down, hitting production.

Not all accidents are avoidable, but most firms could do more to minimise the risk.

Doubt

Nearly a quarter of accidents are caused by falls from a height, and about one-third involve being struck by a moving vehicle or moving or falling object.

By IAN MILLER

By law, most employers must insure for a minimum of £2 million for claims arising from any one incident.

Firms should check with their insurers if they are in doubt over their cover. The following five-point checklist should help firms avoid disaster:

- LOOK for hazards and ask employees for their views on dangers.
- DECIDE who might be harmed and how. Don't forget about cleaners, contractors and visitors who are not there all the time.

- EVALUATE the risks. Where a hazard is spotted, assess whether the risk is high, medium or low and ensure that you stay within the law.
- RECORD the findings – businesses with more than five employees must record significant findings to show proper checks are made.
- REVIEW the assessment regularly. As your business grows or work practices change, further changes may be needed if new hazards develop.

3. Investigate the health and safety policy and procedures of your school/college. What improvements would you recommend, if any? To help develop your own ideas it might be useful to collect statistics on past accidents and their causes, if available, to see where improvements might be made. Check with your main school/college office if this information is available.

4. Devise a health and safety 'fun' quiz for your tutors. Use the quiz to find out much they know about the health and safety

procedures of your school/college. This could also help you with the second part of Task 3 above.

5. Compare the health and safety measures in your school/college with those in another business organization with which you are familiar. Do they differ and if so, why?

Remuneration

Most people go to work to earn money. Employers have a responsibility to their employees to calculate their pay and any deductions correctly.

Payments

Some workers are paid **wages**, calculated by multiplying the number of hours they work each week by an appropriate hourly wage rate. Higher overtime rates may apply if an employee works more hours than they have to according to their employment contract. Wages are normally paid weekly or monthly (see 3.3).

Some employees receive **salaries**. A salary is the total amount a worker will be paid a year. Salaried workers will receive one-twelfth of their annual salary each month, and do not usually get overtime payments for working longer than they have to.

Additional payments

Some workers on a basic wage or salary may also receive additional payments. For example:

- **Piece rates** are paid per unit of output produced. The more an employee makes, the more money s/he will be paid.

- **Commission** is often paid to employees involved in sales, such as insurance and double-glazing salespeople, financial advisers, and travel agents. Commission is based on a percentage of the value of sales they achieve.

- **Bonuses** may include one-off bonuses paid at Christmas as a token of goodwill or profit-sharing schemes which pay employees bonuses when profits are good

- **Performance-related pay (PRP)** rewards an employee for good work. Some organizations hold staff appraisal interviews each year with all their employees. An employee who is thought to have performed well will receive a high appraisal mark and PRP.

- **Fringe benefits** are 'payments' to employees in a form other than money, for example:

  – An **occupational pension scheme** allows the employer to make pension contributions on behalf of an employee. This is paid in addition to the state retirement pension.

  – **Occupational sick pay** is paid in addition to statutory sick pay, so that employees do not suffer any loss of earnings while they are off sick

  – **Holiday pay** ensures that employees do not lose earnings while they are taking time off. Most employees receive between 4-6 annual leave weeks depending on their job, length of service, and level of seniority.

Other fringe benefits include **company cars, subsidized meals, and free private health insurance.**

Deductions from pay

By law, employers are only allowed to make the following deductions from an employee's wage or salary:

- Statutory deductions required by law, i.e. national insurance and income tax

- Voluntary contributions agreed in writing by an employee, e.g. trade union subscriptions, give-as-you-earn donations to charities, subscriptions to clubs and societies, additional pension contributions, etc.

National insurance contributions (NICs): All employees, unless they are on very low wages, have to pay NICs. These allow them to claim government benefits such as:

- Jobseeker's allowance (unemployment benefit)

- Retirement pension

- Child benefit

- Statutory sick pay (SSP)

- Statutory maternity pay

- Widow's benefit

- Industrial disability benefit

To make sure people only claim what they are entitled to, everyone is issued with their own national insurance number by the Department of Social Security (DSS).

Unless a worker is self-employed, the employer will calculate and deduct NICs from the employee's weekly or monthly pay, details of which will be recorded on their pay slip (see 13.3). Self-employed people pay NICs direct to the DSS, usually every three months.

Income tax: Income tax is paid by both employed and self-employed people, the amount depending on how much they earn in a tax year (from 6 April one year to 5 April the next). Employers are responsible for calculating the amount of income tax each employee is liable for and then deducting this amount from their weekly or monthly pay. This is known as the **Pay-As-You-Earn (PAYE)** scheme (see 13.3). The employer will then pay all the income tax they have collected to the Inland Revenue.

Self-employed people will fill in a tax return each year giving details of their income and expenses. The Inland Revenue will then calculate the amount of tax they owe, which is normally payable in two equal lump sums – one in January and a second the following July. From 1996/97, self-employed people will be assessed over a two-year period and have their earnings averaged out over that period.

Meeting customer needs

The main objective of private sector businesses is to make a profit. In order to make a profit, firms must provide goods and services which meet customers' wants at a price they will pay. A vital role for employees is to

meet customers' needs by providing a product and level of service that they want and will pay for.

For example, most of us can think of occasions when we have been in to a shop and have been unhappy with the kind of service provided. Perhaps the sales assistants have been slow to serve us or they have lacked manners, or been rude, or ignorant about the products they were trying to sell.

Today, customers demand good service from businesses and will go elsewhere if they do not get it. Good service means not just the right product at the right price; it also means dealing with staff who are helpful and who put the customer first (see 10.2).

Meeting quality standards

Employers expect their employees to produce work of an agreed quality. Poor quality work increases business costs through wastage, and can mean a loss of sales from dissatisfied customers.

Successful firms are always trying to improve the quality of the service they provide. Some businesses use a technique know as **Total Quality Management (TQM)** to improve the way they do things (see 5.4). This method encourages all workers to think carefully about what they can do to improve the quality of their work.

Key words

Write explanations and definitions for the following key words and terms in this chapter:

National insurance contributions	Performance-related pay	Overtime ban	TUC
Health and Safety at Work Act	Direct discrimination	Industrial relations	ACAS
Equal Opportunities Commission	Equal opportunities	Industrial disputes	HSE
European Court of Justice	Off-the-job training	Unfair dismissal	Multiskilling
Disciplinary procedure	Investors in People	Redundancy	Wages
Indirect discrimination	Contract of employment	Trade union	Salary
Grievance procedure	Collective bargaining	Work to rule	Piece rates
Direct discrimination	Industrial tribunal	Strike	Commission
Direct discrimination	Fringe benefits	Redundancy	Income tax

Test Questions and Assessment Assignment

You must demonstrate that you are able to:

1. Explain the benefits of employer and employee cooperation

2. Describe ways to resolve disagreements

3. Explain employer rights and responsibilities

4. Explain employee rights and responsibilities

Questions 1-3 share the following answer options:

A Equal Pay Act

B Health and Safety at Work Act

C Race Relations Act

D Sex Discrimination Act

Which of the above laws would an organization be breaking if it:

1 Failed to give workmen working with chemicals protective clothing?

2 Sacked a woman because she was pregnant?

3 Advertised a job for 'English male drivers only'?

4 The role of ACAS is to:

A help employers in settling disputes with trade unions

B help trade unions in settling disputes with employers

C make decisions which are legally binding on employers and employees

D from an independent standpoint, assist employers and employees to reach agreement

5 Which of the following reasons for dismissing an employee would be unfair?

A for joining a trade union

B for redundancy due to a fall in sales of the product

C for very poor time-keeping

D for sexual harassment

6 Two people, a man and a woman, are both interviewed for the same job. The employer lets slip that the successful candidate got the job because he is a man. Which law is broken?

A Race Relations Act

B Equal Pay Act

C Sex Discrimination Act

D Health and Safety at Work Act

7 What is the main advantage to employees of having a contract of employment?

A it guarantees that you can never be sacked

B it guarantees that you will be promoted

C it explains how to behave at work

D it clearly states your rights and responsibilities as a worker

8 Callum is in dispute with his manager about how much holiday he can have. Where should this be written down?

A equal opportunities law

B job description

C contract of employment

D employment law

9 Which of the following is the most likely reason for instant dismissal?

A illness for a few days confirmed by a medical note

B serious theft

C being late back from lunch

D attending a union meeting after work

10 Which of the following is a legal responsibility of an employer?

A to ensure that health and safety standards at work are met

B to give staff regular training

C to provide a quiet place to rest during breaks

D to ensure that food can be bought on the premises for staff

11 An organization may lawfully alter employees' working conditions if:

A it needs to raise profits

B it feels it would be better for the firm

C it needs to cut back on staff

D it has the agreement of the employee

12 Under health and safety legislation, who has a legal responsibility to report any health and safety hazards?

A both employers and employees

B employees only

C company owners

D customers

13 Which of the following does an employer have a legal responsibility to deduct from an employee's wages?

A union membership fees

B income tax

C season ticket loan repayments

D subscriptions to a social club

14 About which of the following matters do employers have the right to be consulted by employees?

A if they want to join a trade union

B if they want to join a social club

C if they want to take evening classes

D when they want to take annual leave

15 One of the main reasons why an employee might join a trade union is:

A to benefit from collective bargaining

B to get more overtime

C to improve their chances of promotion

D to go on strike

16 Which of the following details are given in the remuneration section of a contract of employment?

A holiday entitlements

B main duties

C trade union membership

D pay

17 A friend of yours claims she has been unfairly dismissed by her employer because she is pregnant. What would you advise her to do?

A take her case to the European Court of Social Justice

B nothing

C write to her employer demanding redundancy pay

D take her case to an industrial tribunal

18 **a.** Describe three benefits to a firm from cooperation between the employer and employees.

b. Suggest three reasons why a dispute between an employer and an employee may occur.

c. What is an industrial tribunal and why may an employer or employee use one?

19 **a.** Explain how the following legislation affects the rights and responsibilities of both employer and employees at work:

- equal opportunity laws
- health and safety law

b. An employee has a right to receive a contract of employment. Describe five terms and conditions that are likely to appear in a contract of employment.

20 **a.** What is a trade union? Give an example of a union.

b. Suggest four main aims of a trade union.

c. Suggest three types of industrial action a union could take during a dispute with an employer.

d. What role can ACAS play in an industrial dispute?

assessment assignment

Assessment Assignment

The following assignment meets all the evidence requirements needed to fulfil all the performance criteria in element 2.2. In addition it covers the following range points and core skills:

Range: Benefits of employer and employee cooperation
Ways to resolve disagreements
Employer rights
Employer responsibilities
Employee rights
Employee responsibilities

Skills: **Communication**
Prepare written material
Take part in discussions
Information technology
Prepare information
Present information

Tasks

You work for Monster Discs, a small but quickly growing mail order company that sells 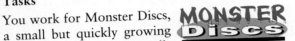 audio and video compact discs. The owner of the organization is an ex-musician who knows little about organizing a business, but a lot about popular music. At the moment, you are in charge of CD stock, but would like to take responsibility for human resources when the organization grows. You are very interested in setting things up in the new firm so that any future disagreements with employees can be settled. Monster Discs currently has 22 members of staff.

1. **Produce a report on the benefits of employer and employee cooperation and how disagreements may be resolved.**

   Janet Lake is the managing director of Monster Discs. She would like you to advise her whether it is worthwhile setting up ways of solving disputes between the organization and employees.

   You should write a brief report explaining how another business organization has gained from good relationships between the employer and employees, and how Monster Discs could learn from this example. The report should give examples of disagreements between employers and employees and explain how these were resolved, including internal grievance procedures and trade union negotiation, and describing the role of external bodies such as ACAS, industrial tribunals, and the European Court of Social Justice.

To write your report you will need to investigate the benefits of good employer and employee relations in a business organization of your choice by completing the following tasks:

a Arrange to visit and interview the human resources manager at your chosen organization. (Alternatively, invite the human resources manager to your school/college to give a presentation to your class group.)

b Prepare a list of questions to ask at the interview. These should attempt to find out:

- The benefits of cooperation between the employing organization and employees

- The objectives of the business and how they are explained to employees

- The health and safety policy of the business and how employees are made aware of it

- The equal opportunities policy of the organization

- Grievance and disciplinary procedures used in the organization

- Examples of past disagreements between the business and individual employees or groups of employees

- Examples of how different disagreements were resolved

c Conduct the interview with the human resources manager at the agreed time and venue. Take notes during the interview.

d Find newspaper examples of disputes between employer and employees which have involved trade union negotiation or the use of external courts to resolve them.

e Use a word processor to write the report of your findings and recommendations to the managing director of Monster Discs.

2. **Prepare a pamphlet to explain employer and employee rights and responsibilities.**

After reading your report Janet Lake has agreed that setting up procedures to resolve disagreements in the workplace is a good idea. She also thinks it would be worthwhile making sure both senior managers and more junior staff are aware of their legal rights and responsibilities. She is keen to avoid situations in which disagreements may arise because employees have not been informed of what is expected of them, or what they should expect from their employer.

Janet Lake has asked you to produce an attractive, easy to read pamphlet for all members of Monster Discs staff which explains employee and employers rights and responsibilities.

Your pamphlet should:

- Summarize the main legal rights and responsibilities of employers and employees
- Explain at least two rights and responsibilities in detail
- Explain how employer and employee responsibilities are affected by legislation, especially laws on equal opportunities at work
- Describe the procedures (grievance, trades union negotiation, industrial tribunals, courts, etc.) which might be available if legal rights and responsibilities are not upheld.

Use a desktop publishing package or word processor to produce your pamphlet.

3. File all your work in a folder titled 'Employee and Employer Rights and Responsibilities'.

 chapter 6

chapter 6 *Present Results of Investigations into Job Roles*

Key ideas

A number of job roles can be identified within a company. These are: **director, manager, supervisor, production operative,** and **support staff.**

There are three main **levels** of responsibility within any organizational hierarchy. Directors and department heads at the **senior level** have the most responsibility. Middle managers and supervisors are at the **middle level** of an organization. **Junior-level staff** include junior support staff and production operatives who operate machinery and other equipment to provide goods and services.

Workers at all levels in an organization often work in **teams**. A team approach to work often improves commitment to job roles and helps workers to achieve work objectives and targets. Team approaches therefore not only help individual workers, they also help the whole organization.

Job roles tend to be grouped according to business activities, such as **human resourcing, producing, accounting, administration, selling, distributing, providing customer service, cleaning,** and **security**. Workers that perform similar activities tend to be grouped together in departments.

In carrying out their jobs, workers must perform a series of tasks. **Routine tasks** include **planning, decision-making, problem-solving,** and the **setting** and **achievement of targets**.

Sometimes unexpected or **non-routine tasks** arise, such as dealing with an emergency or accident. Workers need to be prepared for both routine and non-routine events. Organizations will often develop contingency plans in case of emergency – for example, procedures for evacuating business premises in case of fire.

Section **6.1**

Job roles in organizations

When you start work, or go on work experience, you will notice that even in the smallest business, workers have different jobs to do. That is, workers specialize in particular jobs in order to make the best use of their individual talents and abilities (see 4.1).

By specializing in particular jobs, workers not only use their existing skills, but they can get better through practice. You may also notice that in all but the smallest of organizations, different workers have different levels of responsibility and authority, from the most junior staff, to middle managers, and finally to senior managers. Typical job roles at different levels in an organization are shown in Figure 6.1. You will remember from Section 4.1 that organizations with a pyramid-like structure are called hierarchical organizations. The pyramid-like structure tells us that the organization has more staff at lower levels than it does at senior management levels.

▼ *Figure 6.1: Typical job roles at different levels in an organization*

Levels of responsibility in an organization

Most jobs in business can be grouped into one of three levels. These are:

- Senior-level jobs
- Middle-level jobs
- Junior-level jobs

Staff at senior levels will have more responsibility than employees at lower levels in an organization. Senior staff will also have more authority than employees at lower levels. They will have the authority to tell staff below them what tasks they need to carry out, and the targets they will have to meet.

How many people there are working at each level depends upon the structure of the particular organization (see 4.1). Organizations with flat structures tend to have fewer middle and senior staff than tall structures. A worker cooperative is a totally flat organization in which all the workers will have the same level of responsibility (see 1.3).

Staff at senior levels

The **managing director** or **MD** is normally the most senior member of staff in a limited company, followed by the board of directors.

In public sector organizations, the most senior member of staff is usually called the **chief executive**. In a central government department the most senior post is called the **permanent under-secretary of state** (see 1.4).

Senior managers tend to focus on setting policy and on the overall direction of the firm rather than on the day-to-day details.

Depending on the firm and their exact job role, managers can be senior or middle-ranking staff. Managers running large departments like finance, production, and marketing are generally thought of as senior managers. A manager running a section within a department – for example, an invoicing section within a finance department – is most likely to be a middle manager, or in a supervisory role.

Staff at the middle level

Middle managers and supervisors are considered to be at the middle level in an organization. They both have management responsibilities over more junior staff. As such, they are considered to be the 'first line' of management in an organization. Middle managers tend to work closely with supervisors, production operatives, and junior staff. The main role of middle managers is to carry out the instructions of more senior management, to pass them down to more junior staff, and relay information up to senior managers. Giving instructions to junior staff requires good management and communication skills. A middle manager is unlikely to earn the respect of his or her junior staff, or get them to work willingly, if s/he talks down to them or simply blames them if anything goes wrong or if targets are not met.

Because information technology enables information to be communicated quickly and effectively, many middle management posts in large organizations have disappeared in recent years. This has led to flatter organizations with fewer layers of management.

Staff at the junior level

Junior staff include production operatives and some support staff, including administrative and filing clerks, cleaners, security guards, drivers, sales assistants, etc. Any staff below the level of supervisor are considered to be junior staff.

Junior staff work on the 'shop floor', which means they are the people who actually produce goods and services and are often the people seen by the public at the point of sale (see 10.1). The 'shop floor' simply refers to anywhere junior staff carry out their work tasks – in a factory, office or shop.

Junior staff receive instructions from middle and senior managers and in turn provide them with production, sales, cost, and other information about the performance of the business. Their chief responsibility is to organize and carry out their own allocated tasks well.

Portfolio Activity 6.1

PC: Identify and describe individuals' job roles at different levels in an organization

Range: Levels, Job roles

Skills: Read and respond to written material

Read the articles and discuss the following questions in your class group with your tutor. Take notes of the discussion to include in your portfolio.

1. Why do you think middle managers have been removed from some organizations?

2. What has changed in the years between the writing of the two articles?

3. What might the value of middle managers be?

4. Can, and should, a firm have self-managing teams *and* middle managers as well?

Management experts see middle managers, the product managers and department heads as being people who separate the boardroom from the shop floor. At first sight, middle managers seem to be in the way of everything to do with progress. Successful companies seem to want to give responsibility to self-managing teams, but middle managers make their living by controlling the flow of information up and down in the firm.

Yet suddenly, experts are having second thoughts. There is growing evidence that when middle managers are cut and the size of organizations is reduced, firms lose important expertise and experience. Many firms who slashed layers of middle managers now find that they have no real gain in performance.

Middle managers, it now appears, bring what might be called a 'middle level perspective' to a company's work. Top managers think big strategic thoughts, but have only a vague idea of what is happening on the ground. Frontline workers know their own jobs but have no idea of how they fit into long-term company plans. Middle managers act as go-betweens: they know enough about both the shop floor and their customers to see how a strategy can be turned into new products.

The Economist 4.2.95

'The Death of Loyalty'

The job losses among the world's largest companies continue to grow. Recent job cuts have been at firms earning good profits. Jobs are going not just on the factory floor, but among the middle managers and professionals who usually manage to keep their jobs. Because of foreign competition and new technology, many firms are removing layers of middle managers and giving more responsibility to self-managing staff teams further down in the organization. The idea is that by giving workers lower down in the firm more responsibility, it will cut out the need for middle managers, and so be cheaper. The theory is that workers will be better motivated and so will work harder.

The Economist 3.4.93

Job levels in departments

Most medium-to-large organizations are organized into departments in which staff carry out a narrow range of specialist roles – for example, managing human resources, accounting, sales and marketing, production, etc. (see 4.2).

Each department within an organization will have its own hierarchy. For example, the sales department in an organization is likely to have a sales director and/or senior sales manager in charge. Middle managers and supervisors in sales may have particular responsibility for given areas of sales, for example, UK sales, European sales, and sales to the rest of the world. They will pass on instructions to junior sales representatives. Similarly, all other departments will tend to have their own senior, middle, and junior levels.

Career progression

Jobs at different levels will be graded according to the experience and qualifications needed to do them. Extra allowances are often paid for seniority, length of service, and performance. In different departments, jobs at junior, middle, and senior levels are likely to be graded in the same way. In this way, the different levels in an organization are said to provide a career path, or ladder, for competent employees to climb up.

Career progression involves working your way up through the different levels within an organization to reach more senior positions which have more responsibility and attract a higher level of pay. The level at which a new entrant joins an organization will depend upon their previous experience and qualifications. Generally, the better qualified an applicant, the higher up the career ladder they will start.

Age is not necessarily a good guide to seniority in an organization. You might think that most young people would be lower down the career ladder. But not everyone wants to rise to the top of an organization and have all the responsibility of a senior position. Also, younger people with drive and ambition may progress up the different levels in an organization quite quickly.

Job levels in the Civil Service

People who work in government departments are called **civil servants**. It is their job to provide support and advice to government ministers and to put their policies into practice.

Each government department is headed by a senior civil servant called the **permanent secretary** – a grade 1 post in the civil service career structure. A permanent secretary in the civil service is broadly equivalent to being the managing director of a large company.

As you can see in the diagram, below grade 1 in the Civil Service is a clear hierarchy of less senior posts. Most people with management potential enter the civil service at **executive officer** or **higher executive officer** level. Some may even progress to become a permanent secretary one day.

Civil Service posts...	and their company equivalents:
Permanent secretary (Grade 1)	Managing director
Deputy secretary (Grade 2)	Directors
Under secretary (Grade 3) Senior principal officer (Grade 5)	Senior managers
Principal (Grade 7) Senior executive officer (SEO) Higher executive officer (HEO)	Middle managers
Executive officer (EO) Administrative officer (AO) Administrative assistant (AA)	Junior staff

PC: Identify and describe individuals' job roles at different levels in an organization

Range: Levels, Job roles

Skills: Read and respond to written material

1. Investigate job roles at different levels:

- in your school/college

- within an organization of your choice.

2. Draw a diagram for each organization in Task 1 to show typical career paths for their staff.

Job roles

We will now consider in more detail the different tasks and responsibilities of the main job roles you can expect to find at different levels in a typical medium-to-large company.

▼ *A board meeting*

Directors

Directors are chosen or elected by shareholders – the people and/or firms who own the company. All limited companies must have at least one director.

Most companies have more than one director. Individual directors are often in charge of particular departments in the firm, for example, the sales director or human resources director. They are responsible for setting the long-term targets for their departments and ensuring that these targets are met.

All the directors of a company form the **board of directors**, which is collectively responsible for the long-term planning and the overall strategy of the firm.

The board of directors has a number of responsibilities, some of them laid down in law. These are:

- Setting business objectives

- Deciding long-term policies and plans to achieve set objectives

- Monitoring business performance

- Controlling company activities

- Making important financial decisions

- Safeguarding funds invested by shareholders

- Determining the distribution of profits

- Preparing and publishing an annual report

- Protecting the company against fraud and inefficiency

The board of directors of a company will meet regularly in a boardroom. Two types of director will be present at these meetings:

- **Executive directors** are employees of the company who are full-time members of the board of directors.

- **Non-executive directors** are not employees of the company. It is their job to provide the benefit of their experience and specialist knowledge to the business. Being non-executive, these directors have no management responsibility for particular parts of the business. They may provide useful links with other organizations because of directorships they hold in other companies.

The directors are responsible for the overall running of the company. They must ensure that it is well managed. All directors are accountable to their shareholders – the people who own the company. Every year, directors must report on the progress of the firm to the shareholders at the **annual general meeting (AGM)**. If shareholders are dissatisfied with the performance of directors, they can vote to replace them. This means that a major job role of directors is to ensure that shareholders are kept happy. Some directors may be also be owners, or shareholders, of the company as well.

In large companies, directors tend to leave the day-to-day running of the business and decision-making to the managing director. The **managing director (MD)** is responsible for ensuring that decisions made by the full board of directors are carried out. That is, the managing director is both a director and a senior manager. The MD is usually seen by the workers in the firm as 'the Boss'. In some organizations the MD is known as the chief executive.

Specific duties and responsibilities of a managing director will include:

- Appointing senior managers

- Implementing company policies designed to achieve business goals

- Supervising and coordinating day-to-day activities within the company

- Meeting, and taking part in negotiations on major issues with, important trade union and government officials, key suppliers, and customers

▼ *Inside a boardroom*

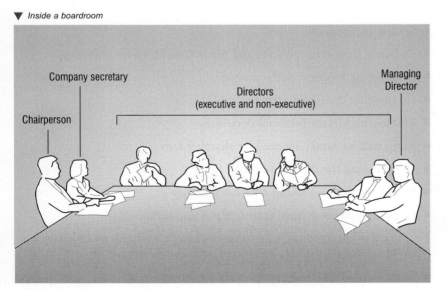

Company secretary

Chairperson

Directors
(executive and non-executive)

Managing
Director

Managers

A manager is not a director. His or her main responsibilities will be to carry out the plans made by the directors and take care of the day-to-day running of the organization. For example, the directors might decide that an electronics firm should make CD players and aim to have a 25% market share at the luxury end of the market by the end of the year. But the managers will decide how to organize the staff, materials, and machines to produce and promote CD players in order to achieve that target.

Managers influence all aspects of modern organizations. Production managers run manufacturing operations that produce goods to satisfy customer wants and needs. Sales managers organize sales teams to sell goods and services. Human resources managers recruit staff.

Senior managers may be heads of department, supported by middle managers and supervisors who look after individual sections within a department.

Managers have the following responsibilities:

- Carry out the instructions of their directors
- Allocate work tasks to staff
- Motivate staff to increase work effort
- Make sure staff are doing their work properly and are meeting targets and deadlines
- Sort out day-to-day problems
- Staff appraisal
- Identify staff training needs
- Keep directors informed of progress and any major problems
- Inform staff of directors' decisions on long-term plans for the organization (if they are not confidential)
- Administrative duties

All organizations – businesses, government departments, charities, even sports teams – need good managers to achieve their objectives. Whether or not an organization meets its objectives in terms of output, sales, profit, and/or costs largely depends on the quality of its management.

Portfolio Activity 6.3

PC: Identify and describe individuals' job roles at different levels within organizations

Range: Job roles

Skills: Produce written material, Read and respond to written material

Make a list of all the different tasks managers must perform in an organization and the qualities you think they need to carry out their tasks successfully. To help you, use these job adverts for managers and your own observations of managers in organizations you are familiar with, either in your school/college, place of work experience, etc.

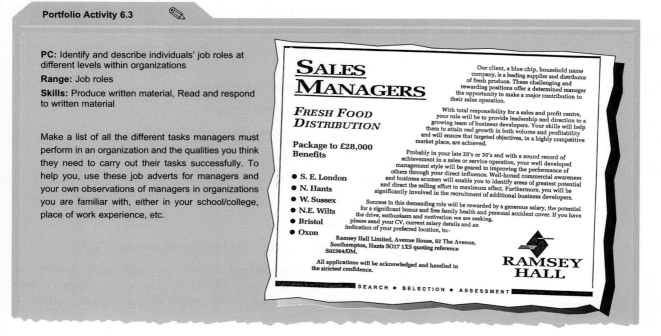

Supervisors

Supervisors are sometimes known as **first line managers**. They are often employees who are able to lead a team because of their long experience in the job. However, some supervisors may be new recruits to an organization who have a degree or other useful qualification and have been identified as likely future managers.

The responsibilities of a supervisor are similar in many ways to those of managers. However, supervisors will tend to be far more involved with day-to-day operations and shop floor workers than their line managers.

Supervisors are rarely involved in decision-making about long-term planning or strategy.

For example, supervisors will be expected to:

- Make sure their staff get things done

- Sort out any mechanical problems or other hold-ups

- Make sure the working area of their staff is kept clean and tidy

- Make sure supplies of materials are readily available for their staff

- Look after staff welfare and morale

- Enforce discipline

- Organize overtime working and leave arrangements

Increasingly, firms are replacing supervisors with team leaders or self-managing teams. The aim of this is to give workers more power over the organization of their work and so improve their motivation and efficiency.

Portfolio Activity 6.4

PC: Identify and describe individuals' job roles at different levels within organizations

Range: Job roles

Skills: Read and respond to written materials, Produce written material

Using the two job adverts for supervisors in different organizations below, make a list of the tasks a supervisor could be expected to perform, and the qualities they should possess. Also draw on any personal experience you have of supervisors, or junior managers, in organizations you are familiar with.

SCAFFOLDING SUPERVISOR/ESTIMATOR

MG Scaffolding is a well established scaffolding contractor, and we wish to continue our expansion in the Cambridge area by appointing an experienced Scaffolding/Estimator to join our management team.

To be considered for this position you must be able to demonstrate the following attributes:-

★ Minimum of 5 years experience in the Scaffolding Industry.
★ Proven skills in the planning, motivation and control of labour, and materials planning.
★ The ability to achieve demanding operational and financial targets.
★ Flexible and enthusiastic approach to work.

We offer an attractive remuneration package, including competitive salary, performance related bonus scheme, and Company car.

Please apply in writing enclosing a C.V. to:

The Operations Director
MG Scaffold Limited, Industrial Estate
Stanton Harcourt, Oxford OX8 1SL

Croner Publications Ltd, the country's leading publisher in business information is seeking a

SUPERVISOR

to join our Electronic Product Help Desk to promote quality customer care in the developing field of electronic publishing.

As Supervisor, you will be responsible for providing front-line support to subscribers over the telephone, supporting a team of executives and producing a variety of management information and statistics.

A sound educational background to GCSE level (or equivalent) is necessary, together with a working knowledge of PCs, ideally Wordperfect and Lotus spreadsheet packages.

Previous supervisory experience, preferably with a telephone/customer service environment, is essential, together with a mature and flexible approach to work.

As a progressive company, Croner Publications Ltd offers a competitive salary and an attractive benefits package including life assurance, a pension scheme (subject to qualifying conditions), 28 days' holiday and medical cover. Hours of work are normally 35 per week as appropriate, within an 8am - 6pm framework.

Applicants should write, with a CV and details of current salary, to Moira Jevons at:-

Croner Publications Ltd
Croner House, London Road,
Kingston-Upon-Thames, Surrey KT2 6SR

Tel: 081-547 3333
Fax: 081-541 1733

Closing date: Friday 7 October 1994

NON-SMOKERS PREFERRED

▼ *Production operatives at work*

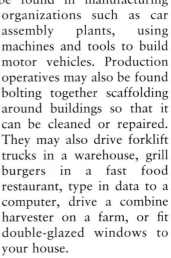

Production operatives

A production operative is a worker who operates machinery and equipment to make or assemble goods, or to supply a service. For example, production operatives can be found in manufacturing organizations such as car assembly plants, using machines and tools to build motor vehicles. Production operatives may also be found bolting together scaffolding around buildings so that it can be cleaned or repaired. They may also drive forklift trucks in a warehouse, grill burgers in a fast food restaurant, type in data to a computer, drive a combine harvester on a farm, or fit double-glazed windows to your house.

▼ *Support staff provide a variety of useful functions in an organization from cleaning (above) to highly trained advisors and consultants (below).*

Production operatives may be skilled or semi-skilled, and will usually have no responsibilities for managing other people. They are expected only to make day-to-day decisions concerning their particular job. If they work in teams, they will be involved in group discussions but are unlikely to be team leaders (see 6.2).

Support staff

If staff do not work in the production department of an organization, they are likely to be providing a support function to those who do. Employees in other departments, such as accounts, human resources, sales or marketing provide a wide range of services, both to employees within the organization and to external customers. All these employees, whether senior managers or junior staff, are known as **support staff**.

Support staff services are designed to ensure that the organization runs smoothly. Services provided internally might include administration, purchasing materials, advertising, staff recruitment, caretaking, security, computer maintenance, cleaning, canteen services, etc. (see 4.2). Services provided to customers might include dealing with customer enquiries and after-sales service (see 10.1).

Support staff may be very junior or very senior. Senior support staff may include highly trained legal executives providing advice on the law, or computer systems analysts writing computer programs.

Portfolio Activity 6.5

PC: Identify and describe individuals' job roles at different levels within organizations

Range: Job roles

Skills: Read and respond to written material, Produce written material

In small groups, discuss and list the production operatives and support staff you might expect to find in the following organizations:

- A large construction company
- A coal mine
- A leisure centre
- A supermarket
- A hospital
- Your school/college

Is there any similarity between the lists for the different organizations? If so, why do you think this is?

Section **6.2**   ## Team working

Working as a team is not only good in rugby or football but it can also be good for business.

Proctor and Gamble report that productivity is up to 40% higher in plants that use team-based production. The company argues that teams eliminate waste by reducing the number of managers and reduce errors by keeping people interested in their work.

Teamwork has also paid off at Rover Group Plc. A team of site maintenance engineers noticed that deliveries of parts were being delayed, and production held up, because drivers were getting lost in their huge industrial complex. The team conducted a survey to find out the main road junctions where drivers were making wrong turns, and designed a series of colour-coded signs to point them towards the right buildings. Deliveries now arrive on time to use in production, thanks to a team that was allowed to solve problems and organize its work without having to agree every decision with management.

Being at work means being with people. In order to do well at work, it is necessary to be able to get along with other people and to be able to work as part of a **team** (see 4.3).

A team of people is not the same thing as a group of people. A team is a group with a purpose. That is, a team is a group working together to achieve shared aims and objectives. These objectives might be to increase output or sales by 10%, or to deal with customer enquiries quickly – or any other business objective (see 1.1).

For example, workers in car assembly plants often work in teams to produce cars. Typically, a team of 10-25 production operatives will now build a car from start to finish. Many years ago, few workers in car plants ever saw the final product because each worker would specialize in one particular task on a continuously moving production line – for example, bolting on wheels or bonnets, or fitting seats and upholstery. Today, car workers are expected to carry out a wider variety of tasks in their teams in order to assemble a complete car.

Teams working together on an assembly line, like production operatives in car plants, will tend to work closely together. However, other teams – for example, sales teams covering a wide area – may meet infrequently and will spend most of their time working alone.

Most junior staff tend to work in teams reporting to a supervisor or manager. Middle and senior staff also often work as members of teams, but are also more likely to have individual job roles which only they and one or two others can perform. For example, there may be 100 production operatives working on a production line, many of whom may do similar jobs, but there are only likely to be a few production managers.

Portfolio Activity 6.6

PC: Explain the benefits of team membership in performing job roles

Range: Benefits of team membership

Skills: Take part in discussions

The 'Odds and Ends Container Game'

Imagine that your class group works in a manufacturing plant which supplies handy-sized containers for odds and ends such as paperclips, drawing pins, and elastic bands.

Your class has been divided into work teams of 4-5 students each. However, your class tutor has also selected around 3 students who must work on their own.

Individually, or in your work teams, you must organize your time (around 30-45 minutes), labour, materials, and equipment, to produce containers of the highest quality with as little waste as possible.

Each team or individual will need these materials and equipment:

Materials and equipment required

- Up to 30 sheets A4 white paper
- 1 pair of scissors
- 1 stick of glue
- 1 pencil
- 1 ruler

Organizing production

Each team or individual can decide how to organize the different tasks. Each container is worth £5 to your firm. But any finished or partially finished container that does not meet quality standards agreed with your tutor is a loss of £8 to your firm.

The group or individual that has produced (without cheating!) the highest value of output at the end of the game, wins.

After the game, discuss as a class group:

1. How well each team performed compared to each other teams and individual production workers.

2. Different roles played by different members in each team. Who were good team members, who were not, and why? Did a natural team leader emerge? Who had the best ideas?

3. How the performance of each team could have been improved.

4. What you think the benefits of working in a team are over individual working:

   a for individual team members?

   b for a business organization?

Record your class discussion using an audio tape recorder. After the discussion listen to the tape and take notes to include in your portfolio.

Container design

Each container should be made to these specifications:

Stage 1 Cut a perfect square from a sheet of A4 paper.

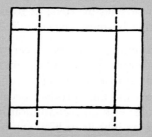

Stage 2 Draw markings as shown. Folds (———) and cuts (– – –).

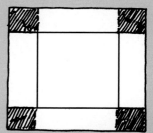

Stage 3 Apply glue to shaded area.

Stage 4 Secure sides of paper.

Stage 5 Check quality of container.

Stage 6 Collect up all end paper pieces from your work team and hand them to your tutor at the end of the game. These can be stapled together to make rough notepads on which to write key words and other information.

The benefits of team membership

Increasing numbers of firms are dividing up their workforce into small teams. Each group is given the responsibility for organizing its day-to-day work tasks, arranging the layout of equipment and furniture, meeting agreed output and quality targets, and solving problems. A team leader may be appointed to supervise a team, take on some managerial responsibilities over the team, and report back to more senior managers on progress.

The formation of work teams is thought to have the following benefits:

- Teams are more likely to achieve their objectives and targets

- Teams can develop a 'team spirit' of cooperation, and a greater awareness of the needs of individual members

- Teams display more commitment to their job roles because they are motivated by their increased responsibility

The achievement of objectives and targets

A well balanced and well managed team of people can draw upon the knowledge, skills, and experience of its different members to solve a greater variety of problems than a single worker. Because workers have different skills and abilities, a team of workers is likely to be able to cope with much more than a group of individuals.

Cooperation between workers in teams and the increased responsibility they have over their own work can motivate workers to greater effort and quality in their work. Teams of production workers can improve their productivity. Support staff can improve their level of service. Teams may also compete with each other to be the best team in terms of output, sales, or service levels.

The perfect team?

How well a team works depends very much upon the people in the team and the jobs they have to do. Research by management experts suggests that people tend to perform different roles when placed in teams, and that a successful team needs one of each of the following kinds of person:

The team leader

This is the person who coordinates the work of the team. The team leader needs to be strong enough to keep the team focused on its work tasks and prevent members becoming distracted by other things.

The shaper

The shaper is highly strung, outgoing, and dominant. The shaper has lots of energy and drive to get things done. S/he can be over-sensitive and impatient.

The plant

The plant is clever and thinks up new and original ideas. The plant can be careless about details and may need to be encouraged to contribute.

The monitor

The monitor is intelligent but not particularly creative. S/he is less involved than the others and can be aloof. The monitor checks the work of the group and is dependable, but can be blunt and cold.

The resource-gatherer

The resource-gatherer is a popular team member, sociable and relaxed. S/he brings in new contacts, ideas, and developments to the group. S/he is a salesperson.

The company worker

The company worker is an organizer. S/he makes ideas actually work. The company worker is most at home with charts and plans. S/he can be unexciting, is not a good leader, but is a good administrator.

The supporter

The supporter holds the team together by being supportive to others, by listening, and encouraging. S/he is the sort of person you do not notice when s/he's there but miss when s/he is not.

The finisher

Without the finisher, the team might never meet its deadlines. S/he is the one who checks the details, worries about deadlines, and pushes others along. S/he always follows tasks through and this can make her/him unpopular.

From Belbin, RM, Management Teams, 1981

Awareness of the needs of team members

In successful teams, members help each other and share their problems and successes. Some people are naturally good team members, while others need to learn to become good team members. Good team members are prepared to listen to each other, to encourage each other in their work, and to express their views and opinions. In this way, workers become happier about their work and more productive.

People who are unwilling to accept the views and opinions of others make poor team members and can upset the whole team, causing their output and service levels to fall. A good manager will combine workers into teams s/he thinks will work well together.

Anyone can learn to become a good team member if they are willing to try. Many businesses spend large sums of money on activities designed to improve team spirit and cooperation. Often these are outdoor activities such as orienteering, rock climbing, and karting. The idea is that these activities will help teams to 'bond' together.

Improving commitment

Once a good team spirit has been created, employees are more likely to like each other and to like their work. It is much harder for a negative person to criticize and disturb the working of others if they are part of a good team. Happier workers are more likely to be better motivated and harder working.

▼ Team building through mutual support and cooperation on an outward bound course

---

What can go wrong with team working?

Despite the benefits claimed for dividing a workforce into teams, it can also create problems which managers need to be aware of. For example:

- Team discussions may involve 'too much talk and not enough action'.

- Some members may be put off by dominant personalities within the team and fail to make what could have been good suggestions.

- Some teams may develop attitudes which are at odds with the organization. For example, team members may be told by their colleagues, 'Don't work too hard – they won't thank you for it!'

In order to keep team workers motivated and interested in their jobs, some firms practise **job rotation**. This involves swapping jobs around between staff in order to give them variety and an understanding of the kind of work done by other employees.

Section 6.3

Activities and tasks performed by people at work

In all but the smallest organizations, workers will tend to specialize in carrying out a limited number of activities. Workers who undertake similar activities, whether they are senior managers or junior staff, will be grouped together in departments.

You will recall from Section 4.2 that some of the main activities performed by workers in different departments in an organization include:

- Human resourcing

- Producing goods and services

- Selling
- Marketing
- Distribution
- Providing customer services
- Providing support services such as cleaning and security

So for example, workers involved in producing goods will tend to work together in the production department. Staff who are engaged in selling will work together in the sales department. Employees who recruit staff and manage their welfare will be employed in the human resources department, and so on.

You should now re-read Section 4.2 to refresh your knowledge of activities undertaken by staff in different departments.

Tasks involved in job roles

Specific work tasks vary widely between different job roles. For example, you would not expect a director to carry out the task of driving a forklift truck or taking orders for goods from customers. The director will be more concerned with long-term planning, managing the finance of the business, and taking strategic decisions on products, prices, and promotions.

However, certain tasks are common to all job roles at all levels in an organization, whatever the business activity workers are engaged in. These tasks can be:

- **Routine tasks:** planning, decision-making, problem-solving, setting targets, achieving targets

- **Non-routine tasks:** dealing with emergencies or accidents

It is generally true to say that the more junior a worker is in the organization, the more routine tasks they will have to do. Those higher up the organization are likely to encounter many more non-routine, problem-solving-type tasks.

Routine tasks

In all job roles, people need to be able to plan, make decisions, and solve problems. The kind of decisions to be made and the type of planning and problem-solving that needs to be done by an employee will depend upon his or her level of responsibility in a firm.

For example, senior managers will spend more of their time planning and decision-making than middle managers and junior staff. More junior staff will tend to spend more of their time trying to achieve targets agreed with middle managers.

Some decisions and problems occur regularly, and workers become so familiar with them that they become easy to carry out. These are known as **routine tasks**. For example, it is routine for an administrative assistant to get involved in filing and photocopying, or for a telesales assistant to take orders from customers over the phone.

▼ *Some routine tasks: planning ...*

▼ *...and problem-solving*

Planning

Nearly all workers have to plan their work in some way. They will plan what they want to achieve, how they will achieve it, by when, and what resources they will need. Directors will discuss and make important long-term plans for the entire organization. Middle managers and supervisors will have to plan their own work and how they will allocate job tasks to the staff below them. Many production operatives will have to plan and organize their work tasks from day to day.

Plans are made for different periods of time and at different levels in an organization:

● **Strategic or long-term planning**, typically over 1-5 years, is usually undertaken by directors at the most senior levels in the organization. For example, they will plan the introduction of new equipment and new products. They will consider business expansion plans and ways to raise long-term finance. They will discuss and approve budget plans in order to control the spending of their individual departments over the next 12 months or more (see 13.1).

● **Tactical or medium-term planning**, typically over 6 months to 1 or 2 years, is usually undertaken by senior departmental and middle managers to make sure the business will achieve its overall objectives. For example, they will plan how to re-organize their departments, introduce new working arrangements, set stock levels, and provide for manpower needs.

● **Operational or short-term planning**, typically up to 6 months into the future, is carried out by almost everyone in an organization. It can include scheduling meetings, organizing leave arrangements for staff to ensure there is adequate cover when people are away on holiday, and on-the-job training. Production operatives will plan their day-to-day activities in order to meet agreed targets, which may include short-term targets, such as increasing output or sales by 10% in the two months leading up Christmas.

Decision-making

Everyone in life has to make decisions and choose between alternative courses of action. In a small organization the owner will tend to make all the decisions – high-risk ones that could affect the long-term success of

---

The business plan

It has been said that a business that fails to plan is 'a business that plans to fail.' If you decide to set up your own business it is useful to set out your plans in a business plan. A good business plan will set out the following details:

● Your business objectives, in terms of sales, profit, customer service, etc.

● What you hope to achieve in the short, medium, and long term

● How the business/product will be marketed

● How production will be organized, and the methods to be used

● The resources you will need: labour, materials, premises, equipment, etc.

● How much money you will need to start your business, and possible methods of finance

A bank will insist on seeing your business plan before agreeing to lend you money. Your business plan will identify the key factors that will determine the success of your business and how much money of your own you are willing to invest in the venture. It will also show the bank manager and other potential lenders of money for your business that you have 'done your homework' by investigating different courses of action for your new business.

the business, and low-risk decisions – for example, whether or not to buy a new fax machine.

In a large organization, senior managers tend to make the most important decisions that will affect the business as a whole. These **strategic or managerial decisions** may involve:

- Future plans, including business location, expansion, and products
- Alternative sources of finance
- Different promotional strategies, including company image
- Staffing levels and the total wage bill
- Organizational structures
- Budgets – and much more…

Senior staff may give more junior staff the power to make some important decisions. This is known as **delegation**. However, the senior member of staff remains responsible for any decisions made by their staff. When unexpected or non-routine events occur, junior staff may refer the matter to their immediate managers for decision.

Operational or short-term decisions are those which affect the day-to-day running of an organization and tend to be made by middle and junior-level staff. For example, the administration manager may decide to reorganize the filing system to make it easier to use (see 14.5). A production supervisor may have to decide between different production schedules. Production operatives working in teams will decide together how best to organize their work tasks and areas on a day-to-day basis.

Problem-solving

Problems will arise in every business, and when they do, decisions have to be made on the best way to solve them. Problem-solving is an everyday task in almost any job.

▼ *Oops! Another problem to solve!*

Problems can be major – for example, a leak in a nuclear power station – or minor, such as losing the key to a filing cabinet. Some problems are easily solved, while others take a lot of time, money, and effort to solve. But whatever the problem, it should be solved quickly, or it can mean higher costs and lower output, sales, and profits for the business. For example, a problem with machinery will slow down production. A problem with a computer can slow down the speed at which customer orders are processed, and this could lead to loss of business. A member of staff could cause problems by being disruptive or always being late for work.

The key to effective problem-solving is to think each problem through carefully, consider alternative solutions, and learn from past mistakes.

Setting and achieving targets

Setting and working towards targets is a normal part of working for staff in sales, production, and finance departments. Sales staff usually have sales targets to meet, and salaries and bonuses are often based upon these. Production staff are also required to meet production targets and to ensure that quality is maintained. Finance department staff often set targets for other departments by giving them budgets for spending which they must not exceed (see 13.1). Working towards these targets, whether for sales, production, or spending, is a routine and accepted part of day-to-day life for staff in a wide range of jobs.

Overall business targets, such as annual output, sales, profit, and total spending, are usually agreed by senior managers. It is then up to middle managers, supervisors, and team leaders to devise plans for meeting these targets. This will often involve setting daily, weekly, or monthly targets for their staff to achieve for output, sales, and spending, and then monitoring progress to make sure targets are being met.

Setting realistic targets is important. Setting targets too high may place too much strain on workers and machines. Targets that are too low will mean the organization is working below capacity. In order to set realistic targets, managers will need information on what is achievable. This can be done by consulting staff who operate machinery, make sales, and organize spending.

Portfolio Activity 6.6

PC: Identify tasks in job roles

Range: Tasks

Skills: Read and respond to written materials, Produce written material

Which departments in an organization are likely to set the following targets?

- Reduce customer complaints by 20%

- Increase sales by 15% in the run-up to Christmas

- Reduce equipment costs by 15% over the next 12 months

- Process any customer order within 2 working days

- Deliver customer orders within 5 working days

- Install a new computer network in all offices within 6 months

- Ensure all production staff are trained in the use of new equipment within 3 months

- Reduce waste by 10% below last year's levels

- Negotiate a maximum 2-day lead time between orders and deliveries with all main suppliers by June

- Reduce staff turnover and absenteeism by 20%
- Cut the number of faulty and sub-standard products by 80% by 1998
- Raise £500,000 additional finance for business expansion from a new share issue

- Complete market research analysis of customer shopping habits by mid-October
- Reduce machine downtime by 25% per shift
- Answer every telephone call within 6 rings

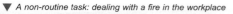
▼ *A non-routine task: dealing with a fire in the workplace*

Non-routine tasks

From time to time, things happen at work which are 'out of the ordinary'. Dealing with these unexpected or 'out of the ordinary' events involves **non-routine tasks**. For example, the human resources manager may have to deal with a sudden industrial dispute or a strike by workers over pay and conditions. Similarly, workers in an administration department may arrive at work to find that their computer network and records have been stolen, or production staff may have to manage after one of their colleagues is seriously injured at work, or when their machines are faulty and break down.

Non-routine accidents and emergencies happen, and workers need to be able to cope with them. Organizations often have **contingency plans** which can be put into action immediately when something goes wrong. In general, the higher up an individual is in an organization, the more often he or she will be expected to cope with non-routine events.

Portfolio Activity 6.7

PC: Identify tasks in job roles
Range: Tasks
Skills: Read and respond to written materials, Produce written material

You work as the customer service manager in a large department store. You are the most senior member of staff on your floor. How would you deal with the following emergencies?

- You observe a customer who is getting very angry about having to wait for service and is waving his hands and pointing aggressively close to the face of a junior sales assistant.
- There is a bomb scare, and it is Saturday morning and the store is full.
- A customer faints in front of you, and her young child starts to cry.

- A customer has been caught by a sales assistant stealing an item of clothing. Her family have appeared and are starting to get very agitated.

In each case, are there any contingency plans or procedures you could devise in order to be better prepared for these events in future?

Discuss your answers as a class group with your tutor.

Section **6.4**

Investigating job roles, activities and tasks

Lightning Computers Plc – a case study

This section presents case studies on different people with different job roles at different levels in an organization called Lightning Computers Plc – a manufacturer and supplier of personal computers. Read them and learn about the different activities and tasks they carry out and the skills they need to do them successfully. Then answer the questions that follow in Portfolio Activity 6.8 on page 244.

Case Study 1

Jack Douglas, Managing Director

'I am responsible for running the whole business. With the board of directors, I make decisions about long-term policy for the firm, and it is my job to see that these policies are carried out. In the end, the shareholders will judge how well I run the company, and if they do not like what I do, they can fire me.

'An important part of my job is knowing what is going on in the business. I keep in contact with employees at all levels in the firm so that I know their concerns and worries. It is also important that staff feel able to contribute ideas and suggestions about how best to improve the working of the firm. I try to be approachable and interested in my workers.'

A typical day for Jack

8.30 am: Jack starts the day with a meeting with the marketing director in order to discuss the latest sales figures and the plans for launching a new and improved Pentium multimedia computer.

11 am: Jack meets with the director of human resources in order to see how recent discussions with the trades union shop steward over pay bargaining went. The human resources director warns that the union may threaten a strike if planned

redundancies go ahead. Jack suggests the company offers an extra 2% in pay this year in order to avoid problems with strikes and lost production.

2 pm: The early afternoon is spent with a group of major shareholders explaining plans for building a new computer assembly plant, and the ways in which it might be financed. Jack gives the shareholders a tour of the existing plant, explaining the problems caused by lack of space and storage areas.

5 pm: In the late afternoon Jack tours the assembly plant, chatting with workers, and then spends ten minutes talking with customer services staff finding out about the kinds of complaints received recently.

7.30 pm: Jack attends a local business function organized by the Chamber of Commerce.

Case Study 2

Callum McFarlane, Director of Human Resources

'I am in charge of recruiting, training, and disciplining staff at all levels in the firm. I report directly to the managing director. I work closely with all of the other managers on staff matters.

'My job is to ensure that we have the right people, with the right skills for the jobs that need to be done. I get involved in organizing training, interviewing for promotions, and also in disciplinary procedures when these arise. I have to be approachable by staff and sensitive to their needs and the needs of the company.'

A typical day for Callum

8.45 am: Callum starts his day with a meeting with the production manager to review health and safety matters on the factory shop floor. It was agreed that the firm needs to increase the number of trained First Aiders on the production line, and that Callum would select staff to attend training.

10.30 am: A meeting with departmental heads to plan the recruitment needs of the firm over the next six months. This is followed by a meeting with the two human resources assistant managers in order to brief them on the kinds of posts that the firm needs to fill and the terms and conditions that the firm wishes to offer these new staff.

1.30 pm: Callum meets with the training manager to review plans to train production staff in the operation of new computer assembly methods.

3.45 pm: A meeting with two staff who have recently passed their NVQ qualifications in electronics. Callum praises them for their efforts. Photographs are taken for the in-house company magazine.

Case Study 3

Helen Vining, Production Manager

'It is my job to ensure that the computers are produced in the right numbers, to the right quality, and at the right time. I supervise all of the production workers and junior managers. My boss is the production director, and I work closely with the sales manager, who keeps me informed about what customers want and what they think about the quality of our products. I also work closely with the purchasing manager. Together we agree the best materials, and the prices at which we would like to buy, in order to produce the computers.

'If there are any problems with the speed or quality of production, it is my job to sort them out. Like all of the managers in this firm, I try to ensure that the views of production workers are listened to and that their ideas to improve the working of the firm are taken seriously.'

A typical day for Helen

6 am: Helen arrives at work with the first shift of production workers. There is a problem on the production line because they are running out of disk drives to install in the new computers, and the supplier has failed to deliver on time. Helen talks to the production director at home who telephones the supplier to threaten that all future business will go elsewhere if supplies are not delivered today.

11 am: Helen meets with a group of production supervisors to hear their ideas for improving the way work is done on the production line. They request more training for certain staff, and Helen agrees to put this to the human resources department.

2.45 pm: Helen attends a meeting with the human resources director to consider what to do about an employee accused of producing poor quality work. It was agreed to issue a formal warning and also to arrange a two-day retraining course.

4 pm: The managing director talks to Helen about why production figures for new computers were below the target set for the month.

Case Study 4

Linda Potts, Marketing Manager

'My job is to ensure that the public find out about our products and then to persuade them to buy. There is a lot of competition in the computer industry and so marketing is very important in making our products stand out in the mind of the customer. I report to the marketing director who, together with the board of directors, sets our overall marketing policy. My job is to manage the marketing department to carry this out.

'My team is made up of 30 staff. Some are responsible for placing advertisements in national computer magazines. Others are responsible for working with advertising agencies to come up with new adverts and promotional methods. The remainder take customer orders and answer queries from the public.'

A typical day for Linda

9.15 am: Linda starts the day with a meeting with Paul Isaacs, the in-house artist. Paul has designed a new range of logos and ideas for posters to advertise computers. Linda likes the advertisement designs but is a little worried that they may be expensive. She arranges a meeting between Paul, herself, and the finance director for later in the week to discuss budgets.

11 am: Linda attends a meeting with the managing director and production manager to discuss why sales of new computers are below target. She explains that the market is very competitive at present and she recommends that prices are cut and advertising spending increased. The managing director agrees to this and Linda immediately arranges a sales team meeting to work out a strategy to relaunch the products at a lower price using double the amount of advertising.

2.30 pm: Linda meets with the editor of a new computer magazine who is keen for Linda to place adverts for Lightning PCs in the magazine. Linda pushes hard to arrange a discount and succeeds in getting a four-page advert at 60% of the usual price as an introductory offer.

Case Study 5

David Osgood, Central Services Manager in Administration Department

'Central services provide a wide range of background services which are needed by other departments so that they can get their own work done. We provide some of these services "in-house", for example, computer maintenance, security, and cleaning. Other services, such as catering, we buy in from private contractors. In a company like this, which produces a large number of valuable computers, it is essential that we have tight security.

Central services ensures that security guards are on duty 24 hours a day and that the site is patrolled at night. Cleaning is also important because dust and dirt damage delicate computer components and can also be dangerous in the workplace. We employ our teams of cleaners who work in shifts every six hours to keep the site clean and tidy. We prefer to employ our own staff rather than hire an agency to do it because that way we can train them ourselves and have more control over who we get.

'I have to work closely with all of the other departmental managers to ensure that I know what kind of services they need and how happy they are with existing provision. My line manager is head of the administration department, which also provides office services, such as filing and photocopying to all other departments.'

A typical day for David

9 am: David starts the day by walking around the factory and checking that it is clean and well maintained. He finds some areas that have not been cleaned and contacts the cleaning supervisor and demands that the early morning cleaning team is sent back to the areas that need further work.

10.45 am: Later in the morning Helen, the production manager, calls and is angry because burglars have broken in and stolen computer parts from the stores. She wants to know why this was not picked up by the security staff. David suspects that the guards were watching TV in another part of the building. He demands that the head of security meet with him immediately.

2.40 pm: In the afternoon the catering company sends in a representative to talk about renewing their contract and David pushes very hard to keep the cost low.

Case Study 6

Trudi Lawrence, Telesales Operative

'My job is to take enquiries from customers over the telephone. We advertise our computers in national magazines and most of our sales are made by phone. I help customers to choose the right kind of machine for their needs, so I have to keep up to date with all of the details about our products.

'When customers telephone through with complaints, I have to deal with them as quickly as possible and try and keep the customer happy. It can be a difficult and demanding job, but I enjoy talking with the public. I also earn commission on every sale made.'

A typical day for Trudi

10.30 am: Trudi works Flexitime and so arrives for work at 10.30. Immediately she sets about taking calls from customers to answer their enquiries and entering details about their orders for computers and accessories into her computer.

2.30 pm: After lunch the telesales team leader asks Trudi to follow up some of the customer complaints received that day with the production department. This takes Trudi until 6 pm when she leaves to go home.

Case Study 7

Robert Kemp, Administration Assistant

'I left school last year and this is my first job. I work with 20 other staff, around half of whom are recent school leavers. My job is to do clerical work around the office. Sometimes I am asked to file copies of invoices or customer orders. Sometimes I am required to word-process letters or type sales figures into a spreadsheet. My work is quite varied, and the human resources manager has arranged for me to take an NVQ in business on a part-time day-release basis when I finish my probation.'

A typical day for Robert

8.30 am: On arrival at work Robert is given a large amount of urgent photocopying to do.

9.45 am: The machine breaks down and Robert is authorized by his supervisor to go the printers in the High Street to finish his photocopying.

11 am: Robert is asked to complete the filing of copy invoices sent out the previous day. This takes until lunchtime.

2 pm: Robert does some word processing and entry of sales figures into a spreadsheet.

4.30 pm: Robert leaves work to enrol at his college for an evening class.

Case Study 8

Derrick Brown, Shipping Clerk

'I work in the distribution department. My job is to keep careful records of the computer parts and finished computers that we hold in stock. If we run low on any components I inform the distribution manager, who will work with the purchasing department to re-order the components.

'I also work with other warehouse staff in despatching computers to customers. Our job is to ensure that finished computers are carefully packaged and despatched by courier as quickly as possible to the customer. If we do not do our job properly, we will let down all of the other departments. Customers are rightly upset if they are sent the wrong machine, or if it is damaged, or late arriving.'

A typical day for Derrick

7.30 am: Derrick starts work and checks the consignments ready to go out that morning. He makes sure that the private courier signs for them before leaving the depot.

9 am: The rest of the morning is spent ensuring that the right machines are packaged and despatched to the correct customers.

11 am: The telesales team pass on some complaints from customers who say they have not received their machines, and Derrick spends most of the afternoon tracing the paperwork to go with these orders, in order to establish what has happened to the computers.

Case Study 9

Akhtar Khan, Production Operative

'I work in a team with 5 other people. There are about 15 teams on the factory floor. It is our job to assemble computer parts and test the final products before they are sent off to be packed.

'My team has been allocated its own work area, and we have been able to lay out our work benches and equipment in a way that best suits us. We have a target number of different computers to assemble and test each week. We have not missed a target yet, although some weeks we have just scraped through.

'We work well as a team. We help each other in our work and try to solve any production problems together.'

A typical day for Akhtar

4 pm: Akhtar clocks on for his evening shift from 4 pm through to 12 pm. Some weeks he will be on an early shift and others the nightshift. After having a chat with some members of another work team, he starts work with his own group.

6.30 pm: Akhtar's welding gun has burnt out and will not work. Output will be down if he cannot get it fixed. He telephones the maintenance crew for help. They are busy and cannot send someone to look at the welding gun until 8 pm at the earliest. To get around the problem until then, the team reorganizes their assembly line so that Akhtar can share a welding gun.

9.40 pm: A new batch of 50 monitor casings that have been delivered to their work area display hairline cracks. Team members discuss whether they can still be used. They agree that there is a risk that in use heat given off by the monitor could expand these tiny cracks into major faults. They discuss the flaw with their supervisor who agrees to take it up with Helen Vining, the production manager.

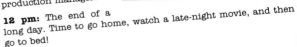

12 pm: The end of a long day. Time to go home, watch a late-night movie, and then go to bed!

Portfolio Activity 6.8

PC: Identify activities performed by individuals at different levels within organizations, Identify tasks in job roles

Range: Activities, Tasks

Skills: Read and respond to written materials, Produce written material

Now that you have read about some of the different people who work for Lightning Computers Plc, complete the following exercise:

1. For each employee, suggest what level their job role is in the organization – senior, middle, or junior?

2. What is the main business activity each employee is involved in?

3. For each employee try to find examples where they:

- Have planned ahead
- Made a decision
- Tried to solve a problem
- Were involved in setting or achieving targets

- Provided a supporting role to other staff
- Undertook non-routine tasks

Where you are unable to find examples of these tasks from the case studies, try to think of other examples of tasks they are likely to carry out in a 'typical day'.

4. What would you say are the main differences between the job roles of directors and less senior staff in Lightning Computers Plc?

5. Which levels of staff are most likely to deal with customers? What skills in communication will these members of staff need?

6. Why do you think Lightning Computers Plc employs so many young staff in its administration department? What kind of skills might be useful for a young school leaver to have who wished to work in administration?

Key words

Write explanations and definitions of the following key words and terms from this chapter:

Job roles	Board of directors	Production operative	Operational/short-term planning
Senior staff	Executive director	Support staff	Managerial decisions
Middle managers	Non-executive director	Teamwork	Delegation
First line managers	Managing director	Routine tasks	Operational decisions
Junior staff	Manager	Strategic/long-term planning	Non-routine tasks
Director	Supervisor	Tactical/medium-term planning	Contingency plans

You must demonstrate that you are able to:

1. Identify and describe individuals' job roles at different levels within organizations

2. Explain the benefits of team membership in performing job roles

3. Identify activities performed by individuals at different levels within organizations

4. Identify tasks in job roles

5. Present results of investigation into job roles

1 What is the main role of the managing director of a company?

A managing a particular department

B marketing products and winning sales

C long-term planning

D controlling budgets for all departments

2 A company which makes furniture has set targets for performance. Which target could be set for the sales team?

A to increase production by 20%

B to reduce faulty items produced by 10%

C to introduce tighter security

D to improve sales by 5%

3 What is the main job role of a departmental manager?

A deciding on long-term policy for a company

B controlling the work of staff in a particular department

C managing the work of other departmental managers

D sitting with the board of directors

4 A main responsibility of the distribution manager in a firm is to ensure that:

A production targets are met on time

B customers want what the firm produces

C customers receive the right goods at the right time

D sales targets are met

5 A possible benefit of team membership in an organization is:

A improved commitment of team members to their job roles

B being able to blame others when things go wrong

C not having a particular job role

D not having to report to anyone

6 The first line manager of a production team is:

A a production operative

B a member of support staff

C a company director

D a production supervisor

Questions 7-9 share the following answer options:

A managing director

B human resources manager

C purchasing manager

D customer services manager

Which of the above will take responsibility for:

7 Overall control of the company?

8 Meeting target reductions in the number of customer complaints?

9 Organizing staff training?

10 A director of a company wants a report on production techniques because output targets are not being met. Who will s/he be most likely to ask to prepare the report?

A a production operative

B a production team leader

C a production supervisor

D the production manager

11 Who has the responsibility for getting customers to buy a company's products?

A the marketing director

B an administration assistant

C a production team supervisor

D a sales manager

12 Which manager is responsible for advertising job vacancies?

A the production manager

B the distribution manager

C the human resources manager

D the purchasing manager

13 Which of the following is a non-routine task in business?

A setting departmental budgets

B dealing with a power failure

C planning future staffing needs

D decision-making

Questions 14 and 15 share the following answer options:

A finance director

B sportswear department supervisor

C sales assistant

D customer services manager

Which of the above job roles in a large department store is a:

14 Senior-level post?

15 Junior-level post?

16 a. Give three examples of routine tasks carried out by staff in a business organization.

b. Give two examples of non-routine tasks in business.

c. What are the main differences between the role of managers and directors in a company?

d. Suggest two targets a production department may have to achieve.

e. Suggest two targets a sales department may have to achieve.

17 Write a short paragraph to explain the main responsibilities of each of the following job roles:

• managing director

• manager

• supervisor

• production operative

• support staff

assessment assignment

The following assignment covers all the evidence requirements needed to fulfil all the performance criteria in element 2.3. In addition, it covers the following range points and core skills:

Range: Job roles
    Levels
    Benefits of team membership
    Activities
    Tasks

Skills: Communication
    Take part in discussions
    Produce written material
    Use images
    Information technology
    Process information
    Present information

Tasks

1. a Choose a business organization where you will be able to investigate different job roles and get permission from the owner or a senior manager to carry out your research.

b Research the job roles of three employees of the organization. One should be at a senior level, the other a middle manager, and the third a junior staff member.

Your research should include observing the employees at work and conducting interviews with them. For each employee try to find out:

- What is their job title?
- What are their main business activities?
- How many staff members do they have authority over?
- Who do they report to?
- Do they plan their work, and if so, what do they plan, and over what time periods?
- Does their job involve making decisions? If so, what sort of decisions do they make? Are they high, medium or low-risk decisions?
- Do they have to solve problems? If so, what sort of problems?
- Are they involved in setting targets? If so, what sort of targets?

- Are they expected to achieve targets? If so, what sort of targets?
- Do they ever have to deal with accidents, emergencies, or any other non-routine tasks? Does the organization have any contingency plans for dealing with emergencies? Give one example.
- Ask each employee to give you an example of a non-routine task, and how they dealt with it.
- Do they provide a support function for any other members of staff?
- Do they work as part of a team? If so, how often does their team meet? What do they think are the benefits of their team membership personally and for their employer?

c Use a word processor to prepare a short report on each job role, describing their main day-to-day activities and tasks. Your report should also say to what extent these staff work as part of a team and explain how this helps team members to perform better in their job roles.

2. Make a 5-10 minute presentation to your tutor and class group describing one job role in some detail.

a Choose one job role from the three you investigated in Task 1.

b Prepare notes or a script for your presentation. This should describe the title and level of the job in the organization, the main activities the job holder carries out, and how the following are dealt with:

- One routine problem-solving task

- One non-routine task (and any contingency plans used, for example, procedures for evacuating the premises)

c Prepare some posters or slides for your talk, listing and describing some of the key activities and tasks performed by the employee in your chosen job role. Also prepare posters or slides to show any contingency plans and procedures for dealing with an emergency.

d Arrange a time and venue for your presentation. Make sure your class and tutor are informed of these details and that any equipment you need, for example, an overhead slide projector, is available.

e Make your presentation. Allow some time to answer questions at the end.

You may record your presentation on video or audio tape to include in your portfolio, along with your written notes and visual materials.

chapter 7

chapter 7 Prepare for Employment or Self-employment

Key ideas

It is possible to be **self-employed** or to work in full-time, part-time, or temporary **paid employment**. Employment may be in **private sector** organizations or in **public sector** organizations which are owned and controlled by the government. People who work for the **voluntary sector** provide their employment for free.

A person can become self-employed by setting up their own business or by buying an existing business. Business start-ups can take a variety of forms, including an **enterprise scheme, partnership,** as a shareholder in a **limited company**, or a **franchise**.

Local **Training and Enterprise Councils** are able to offer advice, training, and financial help to new business owners.

Opportunities for employment and self-employment may present themselves locally, nationally, in the European Union, or elsewhere in the world.

Information and advice about opportunities for employment or self-employment are available from a wide range of sources, including local **Jobcentres**, the **media, careers offices, employment agencies**, the **Federation of Small Businesses**, local **Training and Enterprise Councils (TECs)**, and **charitable organizations**, such as the Prince's Youth Business Trust.

To create opportunities for employment or self-employment, people need to have certain **skills.** Workers must be able to: work independently and with others, manage their time, make decisions, solve problems, plan ahead, seek information, evaluate the impact of decisions and changes on business, communicate effectively, use numbers, and make use of information technology.

In addition, people in employment or self-employment must have **occupational skills** which are specific to their individual jobs or the businesses they run.

In order to succeed in business, it is important to analyse your own skills and identify areas in which you need to develop or improve your skills through further education and training.

▼ *Going to work*

Employment

There are many opportunities in the UK for employment for people who want to work. These include a vast range of jobs and careers working for others, as well as opportunities for self-employment. In 1995 nearly 21 million people in the UK were employed by others and over 3 million were self-employed (see 3.1).

However, unemployment in the UK remains high – around 2.7 million people in 1995 – and many thousands of businesses fail each year. This means competition for jobs is fierce. Many self-employed people are also unable to find work. Getting and keeping a job, or becoming self-employed can, therefore, be very difficult. All the more reason why it is important to prepare now for employment or self-employment. In this chapter we will consider how you can do this.

Portfolio Activity 7.1

PC: Identify types of employment and self-employment
Range: Types of employment and self employment
Skills: Read and respond to written material

Below is an extract from an interview with three working people. Which of the three people do you think is:

- In paid employment?
- Self-employed?
- A voluntary worker?

Question: **How many hours do you work each day?**

John: On average, between 7 and 9. It depends on what I have to get done and how urgent it is.

Angie: Oh, too many! I often work late into the night, tidying up, doing the accounts, and preparing orders for more stock.

Paul: I work about two days each week. Probably for no more than 4 to 5 hours each day. It depends how I'm feeling.

Question: **What sort of things do you do in your work?**

John: I'm an assistant in the marketing department. Basically, I help prepare adverts and buy space for them in magazines.

Angie: It would be easier to say what I don't do! I am the purchasing manager, the accountant, the production planner, and the sales and marketing manager. Does that give you a good idea?

Paul: I usually help out with a number of routine, but very necessary, administrative tasks, such as opening and filing incoming mail, counting donations, and sending out publicity leaflets.

Question: **What do you like about your work?**

John: Oh, the usual. The money, the people I work with – and going home at half-past five!

Angie: Being your own boss!

Paul: Knowing that, in some small way, I am helping to save wildlife and animals around the world from exploitation and suffering.

Going to work

Employment can be divided into:

- **Paid employment**, either in the private sector or public sector
- Unpaid or **voluntary work**, mainly in charitable organizations

Most people want paid employment unless they have enough money already, have retired from work, or simply do not want to work.

Employment: why work for someone else?

Working for someone else can provide a secure job with regular payments. As an employee, you will also be entitled to paid holiday, sick pay, and maternity leave. However, it also means someone else telling you what to do, and there are few very wealthy employees. A fall in demand for the good or service you provide, or the introduction of new equipment that can do your job for you, may also mean that your employer no longer needs to employ you, and makes you redundant.

Being self-employed and running your own business may earn you more money, but it also involves more risk. Your business may fail and you could lose all the money you put into it. Being self-employed also means having to make all of the decisions in the business. You may work long hours and find little time to go away on holiday. Even if you do find the time, who is going to run your business when you are away, ill, or pregnant? Working for someone else can remove many of these worries.

Where can I work?

In the UK it is possible to work in the **private** or **public sector**. The private sector consists of private individuals, the business organizations they own and control, and the **voluntary** sector. Private sector business organizations are either:

- Sole traders
- Partnerships
- Limited companies
- Cooperatives
- Franchises
- Charities

Each of these types of organization were examined in detail in Section 1.3.

The public sector in the UK consists of organizations accountable to central and local government. These are:

- **Central government departments**, e.g. Transport, Environment, Health, National Heritage, etc. Most of the people who are employed in government departments are called **civil servants**.

- **Local authorities**, i.e. regional, county, district, and London borough councils.

- **Public corporations** – organizations which run the day-to-day operations of industries which are accountable to central government and sell goods or services directly to consumers, e.g. the Post Office, the BBC.

- **Executive agencies** – bodies run like businesses to provide a number of public services, e.g. the Highways Agency, Meteorological Office, Royal Mint, Benefits Agency.

- **QUANGOs (Quasi-Autonomous Non-Government Organizations)** – unelected government bodies run by boards of directors to manage particular government services, e.g. regional health authorities, research councils, industrial tribunals, and Training and Enterprise Councils (see 7.2).

Public sector organizations were discussed in detail in Section 1.4.

In 1994 there were 6 million employees in the public sector in the UK, and over 15 million employees in the private sector.

▼ Figure 7.1: Employees in the private and public sectors by occupation, Great Britain, Winter 1993-94

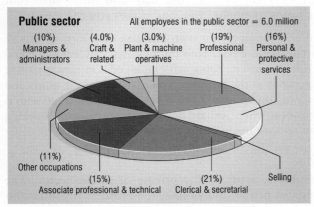

Public sector   All employees in the public sector = 6.0 million

(10%) Managers & administrators
(4.0%) Craft & related
(3.0%) Plant & machine operatives
(19%) Professional
(16%) Personal & protective services
(11%) Other occupations
(15%) Associate professional & technical
(21%) Clerical & secretarial
Selling

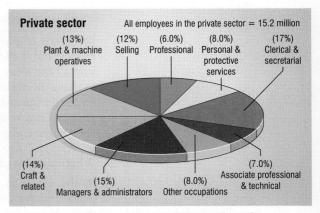

Private sector   All employees in the private sector = 15.2 million

(13%) Plant & machine operatives
(12%) Selling
(6.0%) Professional
(8.0%) Personal & protective services
(17%) Clerical & secretarial
(14%) Craft & related
(15%) Managers & administrators
(8.0%) Other occupations
(7.0%) Associate professional & technical

Note: The number of employees in the public plus private sector does not equal the total number of employees as some respondents did not answer the question.

Opportunities for paid employment

Opportunities for paid employment can be found in your local area, other areas of the UK, or even overseas. However, before you decide where you would like to work, it is best to consider what jobs you would like to do.

In Chapter 3 we considered the growth of employment in services, particularly in financial and business services, and the decline of traditional manufacturing industries such as shipbuilding and boiler-making. Manufacturing firms that remain are becoming increasingly automated, reducing the need for workers while at the same time expanding the demand for workers who are skilled computer programmers and technicians. The growth in personal and leisure services has created more opportunities for part-time and temporary work at the expense of full-time permanent employment, and there are increasing opportunities for women to go to work (see 3.1).

Opportunities for work are changing all the time as consumer demand expands for some goods and services and decreases for others. By making careful choices in education and training and choosing an expanding industry to work in, it is possible for a worker to learn skills that will improve his or her chances of getting a job and staying in employment. The more skills you have and the more flexible you are, then the more job opportunities will be open to you.

The mobility of labour

The **mobility of labour** refers to how easy or difficult it is for people to change jobs.

People who are unable to move easily between different occupations are said to be **occupationally immobile**. This is usually because they do not have the necessary skills, experience, and training to carry out other jobs. For example, it would be difficult for a shop assistant to get a job as a doctor without first being trained for many years. Similarly, an accountant could not become a computer programmer overnight. However, accountants could be considered for a wide range of professional and managerial jobs in different organizations if they had good skills in management, communication, numeracy, and IT. The more skills a person has, the more mobile they are, and the greater are their opportunities for employment.

Geographic immobility refers to people being unable to move to find work in other areas. For example, people may not want to move away from family and friends, or to unsettle their children by moving them to another school. Others simply cannot afford to move.

Local opportunities

The first place to consider looking for a job is locally. You will need to consider if you want any of the jobs that are available and whether you have the right skills to do them. Jobs available in your local area will depend on the type of business organizations that have located there.

You can look at advertisements for jobs in local newspapers and in your local Jobcentre. Other organizations in your area, or nearby, may also be able to help you find a suitable job (see 7.3).

National opportunities

Most people in paid employment in the UK work in services. Figure 7.2 shows that in mid-1995, around 73% of UK employees were employed in service industries. However, the availability and range of jobs varies significantly between different areas in the UK. More employees in Greater London work in services than in any other part of the UK, whereas the highest proportion of employees employed in manufacturing industries (around 29%) live in the East Midlands (see 3.1).

▼ Figure 7.2: Employees by industry, UK 1995

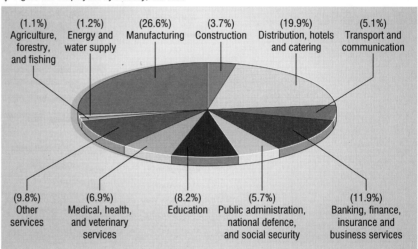

(1.1%) Agriculture, forestry, and fishing
(1.2%) Energy and water supply
(26.6%) Manufacturing
(3.7%) Construction
(19.9%) Distribution, hotels and catering
(5.1%) Transport and communication
(9.8%) Other services
(6.9%) Medical, health, and veterinary services
(8.2%) Education
(5.7%) Public administration, national defence, and social security
(11.9%) Banking, finance, insurance and business services

Portfolio Activity 7.2

PC: Identify opportunities for employment or self-employment
Range: Opportunities for employment and self employment
Skills: Interpret and present data, Prepare written material

1. Refer back to Table 3.3 on page 93

  a Using Table 3.3, suggest where the following people are most likely to find the jobs they are looking for:

● Karen wants a job in the headquarters of an international bank

● James wants to be a construction site engineer

● Thomas wants to work in catering

● Tokiko wants to work as a petrochemist in the oil and gas industry

● Hasha wants to work in forestry

● Clare wants to work in telecommunications

● Petra wants to work in government administration

  b Produce a pie chart for the region in which you live, to show the percentage of workers employed in the major industries. How does your region compare to the pattern of employment in different industries in the UK as a whole, as shown in Figure 7.2?

2. The graphs below show predictions for employment in London and the UK up to the year 2005, for different categories of workers. The changes are shown as percentages.

a What do the graphs suggest may happen to opportunities for employment in the future?

b What do they suggest about the skills you might need to get a job in the future? How you could try to develop these skills through education, training, and work experience?

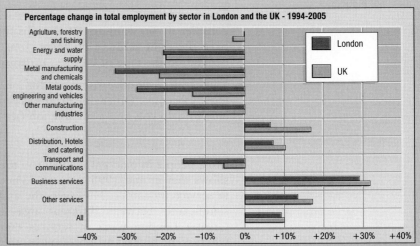

Percentage change in total employment by sector in London and the UK - 1994-2005

Cambridge Econometrics, June 1994

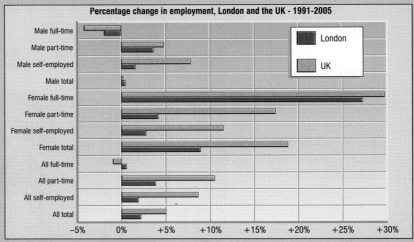

Percentage change in employment, London and the UK - 1991-2005

Cambridge Econometrics, June 1994

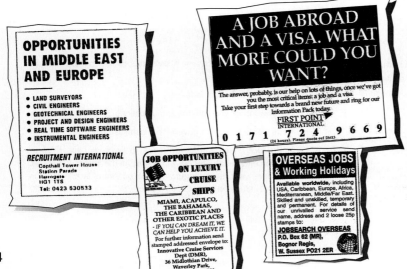

International opportunities

People who go abroad for a summer holiday often return saying they would like to live in the place they have visited. But few consider what it would actually be like to live and work abroad. It is not like being on holiday. Imagine travelling to work every day in Greece or Italy during the long hot summers. And it it is not always sunny. Most countries have their share of rain and cold weather, like the UK. You will also need to learn a new language, customs, and laws if you live and work abroad.

However, some people do go abroad to work. Some may do temporary work during the summer in hotels or bars. Others may work abroad for several years, or even stay there for their entire career.

One way of finding out whether you would like to work abroad is to go on a working holiday first. Many university students do this during their long summer vacations, because it is a relatively cheap way to see foreign countries. For example, working holidays can include picking fruit in France, supervising children in summer camps in the USA, digging wells in Africa, working in holiday camps in Spain, etc. There are a number of organizations which can arrange working holidays. 'Survival guides' to living and working overseas are also available in most good bookshops.

Opportunities for work overseas vary from country to country. In underdeveloped countries, opportunities for jobs in manufacturing and service industries are likely to be very limited. Those that do exist may involve long hours of work and be very poorly paid.

On the other hand, many developed countries have high levels of unemployment. Table 7.1 shows the number of people out of work as a percentage of the total workforce in a number of countries in mid-1995. At this time, 1 in 8.5 workers were without a job in the UK. For this reason, a number of countries limit the number of people from other countries who can work there by issuing visas or work permits. These are strictly limited in number and are usually only valid for a fixed period of time, after which the holder has to return to his or her own country. However, these restrictions do not apply to UK citizens applying for work in European Union (EU) member countries. As a UK citizen, you are entitled to work anywhere in the EU.

▼ Table 7.1: Unemployment as a percentage of total labour force, selected countries, 1995

COUNTRY	UNEMPLOYMENT RATE (%)	COUNTRY	UNEMPLOYMENT RATE (%)
United Kingdom	8.5	Italy	11.6
Australia	8.5	Japan	3.1
Austria	5.3	Luxembourg	2.8
Belgium	9.8	Netherlands	6.9
Canada	9.5	Norway	5.4
Denmark	11.3	Portugal	7.2
Finland	17.6	Spain	22.8
France	12.2	Sweden	9.6
Germany	6.8	Switzerland	3.8
Greece	11.2	USA	5.6
Irish Republic	14.4		

Employment Gazette, August 1995, and OECD World Economic Outlook

Opportunities in the European Union

The European Union (EU) began in 1958 when six countries – West Germany, Italy, France, Belgium, the Netherlands, and Luxembourg – signed the Treaty of Rome agreement. The aim of the treaty was to develop closer trading, economic, and political ties between the member countries.

By 1993 the UK, Spain, Portugal, Greece, Eire, and Denmark had also joined, making a total of 12 member states (the 'EU12'), and forming a market of over 350 million people. They were joined by Austria, Finland, and Sweden in January 1995, to make up the current 15 members (the 'EU15').

▼ *The European Community in 1995*

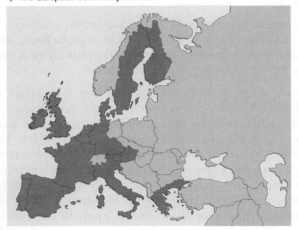

Turkey and Cyprus have also applied for membership, with many more considering joining, such as the former communist countries of Poland and Hungary.

Opportunities for employment in Europe have increased since the introduction of the Single European Market on 1 January 1993. The single market is designed to allow the free movement of goods, services, and people between European Union (EU) member countries.

With the opening of European markets, EU citizens can now travel freely and live and work in any EU country. This means that there will be more and more opportunities to live and work abroad in future. Because European unemployment is relatively high, the job opportunities that do exist are usually for highly qualified, professional people with some command of a foreign language. However, it remains difficult to compare the educational and training qualifications of a UK worker with those required of workers abroad. Language barriers are becoming less of a problem as most Europeans are now taught to speak English.

The **Commission of the European Communities** makes proposals on policy and legislation in the EU. It is a useful source of information on member countries and on EU policy on employment. It has UK regional offices at the following addresses:

England: 8 Storeys Gate, London SW1P 3AT

Wales: 4 Cathedral Street, Cardiff CF1 1SG

Scotland: 9 Alva Street, Edinburgh EH2 4PH

N Ireland: 9/15 Bedford Street, Belfast BT2 7EG

Portfolio Activity 7.3

PC: Identify opportunities for employment or self-employment
Range: Opportunities for employment and self-employment
Skills: Interpret and present data, Tackle problems, Present information

1. Enter the figures in Table 7.1 into a computer spreadsheet (use more up-to-date figures if they are available). Use spreadsheet functions to produce a barchart comparing unemployment rates in the different countries. Do not forget to label each bar appropriately, and provide titles for the vertical axis and for the entire barchart.

2. Use the spreadsheet to work out the average rate of unemployment in the 15 member countries of the European Union.

3. Print out a copy of your spreadsheet and barchart to file in your portfolio.

4. List the capital cities in each EU member country.

5. Choose one EU member country to investigate in more detail. Try to find out as much as you can about the following in your chosen country:

- Population
- Number of people employed in different industrial sectors
- Number of people unemployed
- Main exports to the UK (including tourism)
- Main imports from the UK
- Employment opportunities

From your research produce a short 'Country Report' covering the above items. Use a word processor to prepare your report and include any graphs you have drawn or produced with a spreadsheet from data you have collected.

Useful sources of information will include:

- The Commission of the European Communities
- Your local Jobcentre (see 7.3)
- Your local library
- Newspapers and business magazines
- Publications and 'survival guides' on working overseas

The Fundraising Group

We are a small active group looking for ways to raise funds for Oxford MIND. Meetings of the group take place the last Thursday of each month at 12.15 p.m.

If you think you can spare even two hours a month, please join us. For details of the next meeting please contact Nicky Clargo on (01865) 511702.

The MIND Shop

If you are interested in working among a friendly group of people in the MIND Shop, please call Lyn Blizzard on (01865) 510668. Donations of clothes, stamps and bric-a-brac are always appreciated.

Oxford Befriending Scheme

The Oxford Befriending Scheme is looking for volunteers who are willing to spend some regular time with someone who has become lonely as a result of long term mental health problem. Anyone can apply. Your friendship might make a difference to someone who is isolated or lonely.

For further details please contact Veronica Young on (01865) 311252.

Voluntary work: why work for free?

A growing number of people are using their skills to help those who are less fortunate than themselves. Voluntary work is unpaid and can be full or part-time – perhaps only a few hours here and there. Many organizations rely on the unpaid skills and help of volunteers.

Opportunities for voluntary work

There are many opportunities for voluntary work, both locally, nationally, and even internationally. For example, your local hospital may require people to greet patients and visitors, drivers to take elderly and disabled people on excursions, or disc jockeys to run a hospital radio station. Junior and infant schools will often rely on the help of parents and guardians to supervise fêtes and sports days. Local environmental groups may need help to clean up rivers and areas of wasteland.

Many national and international charities are pleased to accept the help of people who can simply hand out leaflets and collect donations, as well as those who are able to advise on accounts, using computers, construction, veterinary care, etc. Some people also volunteer to risk their lives for others by manning lifeboats or rescuing people trapped on mountains or in caves.

Opportunities also exist for voluntary work overseas. The **Voluntary Service Overseas (VSO)** organization recruits people to work in developing countries all over the world, normally for a two-year period. People with skills in medicine, teaching, building, and farming are much in demand. VSO organizes contracts which pay living expenses or a small income to cover essentials only.

Why they queue up for a new life as a volunteer

Voluntary Service Overseas does not agree with claims that we are living in a less caring world. According to VSO, the largest agency of its kind in the world, more people than ever want to help people in developing countries and in Eastern Europe.

It handled 67,000 inquiries last year, received 7,500 firm applications, and at any time has around 1,700 workers in 55 countries.

'There has been a steady increase in people applying to do VSO in the past five years, and statistics show that numbers have kept rising since we launched in 1958,' said Frances Tuke of VSO.

Volunteers want to go abroad for various reasons – following redundancy, as a career break, a change of direction in lifestyle, or simply to make a contribution to another society. At least one in ten applicants is aged over 50. VSO is frequently asked for accountants, craft business advisers, legal specialists, managers, and teachers, and midwives are always in short supply.

VSO is based at 317 Putney Bridge Road, London SW15 2PN.

Daily Mail 10.2.94

Section **7.2**

Self-employment

Not everyone wants to work for someone else. More and more people in the UK are becoming self-employed. In 1981, around 2 million people were self-employed. By mid-1995 this had risen to over 3.3 million, or nearly 12% of the total UK working population (see 3.1). Many people became self-employed after they had been made redundant from paid employment.

Some self-employed people run their own business. The number of businesses in the UK increased from 2 million in 1980 to around 3 million in 1994. The vast majority of these firms are small, employing fewer than 20 employees.

▼ Figure 7.3: Number of firms in the UK

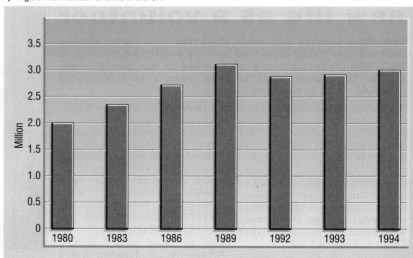

Adapted from 'Competitiveness: Helping Smaller Firms', Department of Trade and Industry (DTi), May 1995

Some self-employed workers sell their skills to other firms and therefore continue to be employed by someone else. However, here the employer is a customer buying in the skills of the self-employed worker, who will usually be employed on a fixed term contract and, unlike other employees, will be paid their income before the deduction of income tax and national insurance contributions (see 5.4). It is then up to the self-employed worker to add up how much income they have received in a year, how much they have paid out in work-related expenses, and then to inform the tax authorities.

'Giants grow from small beginnings'

Every business started small – even today's High Street giants. Just look at Sainsbury, which this year celebrates its 125th anniversary. Set up by humble Londoner John Sainsbury, its first store in Drury Lane was a dairy. Competition was fierce, but by the late 1880s he had established five stores and the first own-brand products had been launched.

The number of shops had reached nearly 50 by 1900. Now the company has more than 300 supermarkets and last year recorded a £6.3 billion turnover and a £460 million profit.

Michael Marks is another rags-to-riches story. He arrived at 19 and couldn't speak English. But it didn't stop him setting up what is today a High Street institution – Marks & Spencer. He started out as a travelling salesman selling needles and thread around Yorkshire mining villages. It was

Daily Mirror 7.3.95

back-breaking work, but the money paid for a little stall in Leeds market.

Within a few years, Marks and his new partner Thomas Spencer had 50 stalls. After Marks' death his successors moved the stores upmarket. Now Marks & Spencer sells one in three pairs of knickers, one in four suits, employs 52,000 people in the UK and has more than 600 stores worldwide. In 1994-5, turnover was £6.5 billion and it made £850 million profit.

Becoming self-employed can be very satisfying and financially rewarding. You can decide how many hours to work and when to work, and you will be completely responsible for organizing your own time. You are able to keep any profit you make after tax. However, you will also be liable to pay off any debts if you make a loss. There is no guarantee of success in business. It may involve long hours of work, more worry, and a big financial risk.

PC: Identify types of employment and self-employment

Range: Skills for employment and self-employment

Skills: Take part in discussions, Read and respond to written material

1. From the case study below, list the possible advantages and disadvantages of being self-employed and running your own business.

2. Do you know anyone who is self-employed? If so, interview them to find out the type of work they do, and why they chose to become self-employed. What skills do they need to be self-employed? What are the advantages and disadvantages of 'being your own boss'?

3. Identify at least three other people who are self-employed. What work do they do?

Case Study

J V Motors is a family-owned garage and car repair business in Park Royal, London. Antonio Vollo, his brother and father came to England from Italy in 1972 and opened their garage. They are now looking for larger premises.

'Since we opened the garage the number of cars we take in for repair has grown enormously,' explained Antonio. 'We have managed to win several contracts to repair and maintain the car fleets of a number of well known car hire companies. This has been good for business, but sometimes they are very slow to pay their bills, and this can cause us cashflow problems. We have often had to draw heavily on family savings to pay garage bills and pay our workers. Sometimes there is not even enough money left for me to draw a wage from the business!' In addition to cashflow problems, Antonio and his family have found it difficult to persuade banks to lend money to their business. 'They seem to think small family-run businesses are too risky,' Antonio sighed.

We asked Antonio what it is like running his own business. 'I don't really like being told what to do,' he replied, 'so for me the biggest advantage is being your own boss. However, that does not mean I have the choice when to get up and go to work and when to leave. Sometimes I work such long hours I don't even get to see my family until weekends!'

He continued, 'I suppose another advantage is that I can indulge in my hobby of doing up old classic cars. That's the bit I enjoy the most!'

So what are Antonio's responsibilities? 'Well, apart from fixing some cars myself, I also have to prepare insurance quotes, order spare parts and paints, do the accounts, make up wage packets, and make sure the right amount of tax has been deducted from each, make certain the premises meet safety standards, recruit and train new staff. You name it, I do it!' We asked Antonio about holidays. 'Not this year,' he laughed. 'Most of our staff want the whole of August off, and I can't afford to close the garage and lose business. Maybe nearer Christmas I'll have a few days off.'

But surely being your own boss means you get to keep any profits after tax? 'That's true,' said Antonio, 'when there are some to keep! Some years are better than others. But in general, as we have expanded our business we have ploughed a lot of our profits back into new machinery, improving the premises and so on. But hopefully it's a case of bread today, jam tomorrow...'

The family business

In 1994 almost two-thirds of the 370,000 new business start-ups in the UK had no full-time workers apart from the immediate family of the owners.

Most family-run businesses are small organizations, owned and managed by members of the same family. Ownership of family businesses is often passed down through generations. Perhaps you know someone who works in their parents' shop or small business? Some family businesses advertise the fact by including the words '& Sons' in their trading name.

Many of today's large companies, like Marks & Spencer and the John Lewis Partnership, started life many years ago as small sole traders – organizations owned and controlled by one person. Many relatives of their founders still own parts of these companies and take an active interest in their running.

▼ Family business

Starting your own business

If working in a family business is not possible for you, then it is possible to become self-employed by starting up your own small business. Finding enough money for a new business start-up is usually the main problem.

If you are considering starting a new business, there are several possible sources of finance worth exploring:

- Personal savings topped up by money from family and/or friends

- Asking your bank manager for a bank loan or overdraft

- Applying to the Economic Development Department of your local authority for a grant

- Applying to your local Training and Enterprise Council for a business start-up scheme grant

- Visiting your local Jobcentre to find out about other sources of finance available to a new business

In addition to financial help you will need legal and other advice on how to start and run a successful business. This is available from a variety of different organizations. We will look at these in detail in Section 7.3.

Enterprise schemes

Financial help for new businesses is available from government organizations called **Training and Enterprise Councils (TECs)**.

TECs have been set up all over the UK to help local businesses. Local TECs are working with banks, enterprise agencies, and other partners to offer support schemes to meet local needs. All these schemes offer advice and training to new business owners and access to financial assistance. A total of £10 million is being made available by the government over the period 1995-1998 to support over 5,000 new businesses. To help them get started, new business owners can receive weekly payments from their local TECs. The amount paid varies by area but can be between £30 to £90 per week for up to six months. To be selected for these schemes, you will need to convince your local TEC that you have the skills and experience to make the business a success, and that you have drawn up detailed plans of action on all aspects of running your business.

In addition, UK businesses can use services provided by local **Business Links** 'shops'. These are run jointly by TECs, Chambers of Commerce,

Enterprise Agencies, local authorities, the Department of Trade and Industry (DTi), and other providers of business support. As well as providing business advice, Business Links can put small businesses looking for finance in touch with business 'angels' – people and organizations who want to invest money in new businesses in return for a share in their profits.

Financial help is also available to new businesses from the UK and European Union governments, through a number of schemes aimed at promoting employment in areas of high employment. These regional policies are discussed in detail in Section 2.1.

Portfolio Activity 7.6

PC: Select information from relevant sources which applies to identified employment opportunities

Range: Information sources

Skills: Collect and record data, Produce written material

1. Find out where your nearest TEC and Business Link centre are located.

2. Some of you may already be running your own small business venture as part of the Young Enterprise Scheme at your local school or college. If not, try and think of a business you would like to start. Be realistic in your choice. For example, you could not expect to start a car assembly plant or a bank. Running a

mobile disco for hire, catering for parties, making soft toys, painting and decorating, are all examples of business enterprise you could start up easily.

3. Write to your nearest TEC and Business Link asking for information on the help they could provide to start the business you have chosen in Task 2.

4. Write a short note summarizing:

- **All** the possible sources of finance for your chosen business venture in Task 2

- Any non-financial help available from TECs and Business Links

---

Partnership

You will remember from Section 1.3 that it is possible to start up in business with other people to form a **partnership**. Being in a partnership means that there are others to finance it and share in decision-making.

Don't let your partner get you in a fine mess

Going into business with a friend sounds like an ideal way to make a living, but it can be a recipe for disaster. Take Oliver Hardy, whose life was thrown into turmoil when he tried to set up a fishing business with Stan Laurel in the comedy classic 'Towed In a Hole'. The outcome was a disaster, but while their screen capers were funny, a real-life partnership failure is no laughing matter.

Thousands of bright-eyed people with a bit of get up and go start a business with a friend and are blind to the dangers.

'Partnerships are like marriages,' says Stephen Alambritis. 'A partnership is just as likely to break up when it's successful because one half might want to plough back profits into the business, whereas the other wants to take the money and run.'

So to ensure success, it is essential to follow a few basic steps. If it's a modest venture, get a solicitor to draw up a partnership agreement outlining where the profits will go and saying what will happen if one half of the partnership dies or wants to leave. Most lawyers will charge no more than £200 to draw this up. If both partners plan to invest a big stake in the business, form a limited company – although this will cost more.

Daily Mirror 28.2.95

To create a partnership, it is advisable to have a solicitor draw up a partnership agreement between the partners. This sets out details such as how much capital each partner is to invest in the business, how profits (and losses) are to be shared among the partners, and procedures for accepting new partners.

Portfolio Activity 7.7

PC: Identify opportunities for employment or self-employment
Range: Opportunities for self-employment
Skills: Collect and record data, Produce written material

1. Find examples of employment as a partner in a business. For example, look in your local shopping centre or high street at signs for different business names with the words '& Partners' in the title. Also look at business names in a business telephone directory.

2. Divide up a sheet of A4 paper into three columns. In your first column, list all the examples of partnerships you have discovered. In the second column, list the types of goods or services each one provides. In your third column list the type of jobs you would expect to find in each partnership.

Little big hit

Franchising has almost been a licence to print money for husband and wife team Bob and Christine Little. They are one of the star businesses in KallKwik's nationwide network of 200 printing centres. The couple now in their fifties set up in 1984 with a £20,000 bank loan.

Turnover has escalated to more than £600,000 a year and now they employ more than 14 people at their Peterborough shop. Bob Little said, 'The beauty of franchising was that we were buying into a successful business. It has been hard work, but very rewarding.'

Daily Mirror 7.3.95

Franchise

An increasingly popular way of becoming a new business owner is by buying a **franchise** (see 1.3). If you become a franchisee, it means you have bought the right to open a business trading under the same name and making and/or selling the same products as the franchise organization. In effect, this allows you to buy into an established product and brand name.

Buying into the franchise can be expensive and will usually involve paying a share of the profits to the parent company. But the risk of the business failing can be much less if you buy into an already successful firm.

The Body Shop, The British School of Motoring, Pizza Hut, Benetton, McDonalds, and Kentucky Fried Chicken are just some examples of popular and successful franchise organizations.

Private limited company

It is also possible to become a business owner by buying into an existing private limited company or setting up a new one. You will recall from Section 1.3 that in a private limited company, the owners are shareholders. The more shares you hold, the more power you have, and the bigger your slice of any profits.

Setting up a new limited company could not be easier today. It is possible to form single-member companies in which you are the only shareholder. New companies can also be bought 'off the shelf'. This means that someone else has thought up a business name, registered that name with the Registrar of Companies, and completed all the necessary paperwork and legal documents. All you have to do is pick the name of a company you like from a list, pay an agreed fee, sign relevant papers to prove ownership, and then start trading.

Opportunities for self-employment

If you cannot raise enough money to start your own business, your opportunities for self-employment will be limited. However, becoming self-employed need not be expensive. For example, there are few start-up costs involved if you suddenly decide to become a self-employed aerobics instructor or financial advisor.

Most of the costs involved in starting a new business are for buying machinery, equipment, and premises. Hiring equipment and renting premises can reduce business costs and spread them out over monthly payments. Increasing numbers of small businesses and self-employed people are also working from home to reduce their business costs (see 4.3). They can keep in touch with customers and suppliers by phone or fax or computer, all of which are relatively inexpensive to buy nowadays.

Just as those who want to work for someone else are most likely to find paid employment in growing industrial sectors, so are the self-employed. There are an increasing number of opportunities for self-employment in growing service areas such as accountancy, law, financial services, and many others. There is also a growing demand for those with the ability to use information technology or a foreign language in the workplace.

Opportunities for self-employment may be found locally, nationally, or even abroad. Your chances of making a new business venture a success are higher if the market for the good or service you decide to provide is expanding (see 2.2) – i.e. consumer demand for the product is rising. Of course, business success is never assured. You will need to persuade consumers your good or service is better in terms of quality and price than rival businesses. But your chances of success are much lower in a market which is contracting and where consumers are buying less and less of a good or service.

Section **7.3** ## Sources of information for employment and self-employment

A wide variety of private and public sector organizations exist to help people wishing to become employed or self-employed in the UK. These can provide information on employment and business opportunities, as well as advice, guidance, training, and in some cases, capital and grants.

Portfolio Activity 7.9

PC: Select information from relevant sources which applies to identified employment opportunities

Range: Information sources

Skills: Collect and record data, Produce written material

The pictures above represent some of the main sources of information about opportunities for employment and self-employment in the UK. For each picture, investigate how the organization or item shown can help with finding a job or with business start-up, and write a brief summary of your findings.

Jobcentres

Most large towns have a **Jobcentre** provided by the government's Employment Service. In your local Jobcentre you will find noticeboards containing information on job vacancies available locally, nationally, and even overseas. Specialist advisers are on hand to provide help and advice.

The Employment Service runs a number of workshops and 'Job Clubs' which unemployed people can attend to discuss the problems they are having finding paid employment. These workshops also provide intensive help on how to look for jobs, writing letters of application, and job interview techniques.

Special job-search workshops run by trained advisers are available for people who have lost professional and managerial jobs, the long-term unemployed, and the disabled. Your local Jobcentre can also put you in touch with the **Overseas Placing Unit** of the Employment Service for specialist help finding work abroad.

The media

Radio, TV, and newspapers are important sources of information. Not only do they advertise job vacancies, they can also give useful advice on how to apply for jobs, and ideas about self-employment. They can provide stories about how others have achieved success or failure in business, and tell you about expanding markets for different goods and services.

There are an increasing number of local radio and TV stations, due primarily to the widespread introduction of cable television networks. Even national radio and TV stations transmit job information and business programmes. Some programmes are produced specially for students on business courses in schools and colleges, but you may need to use your video recorder to tape them, because they are often shown during the day when many people are out.

Local and national newspapers carry job adverts as well as business information and stories. In some newspapers, different types of job vacancies are advertised on different days of the week. So, for example, if you are interested in public sector appointments you should look in *The Guardian* newspaper every Wednesday. If you are looking for a job in computers, you should look in the same paper on Thursdays.

Magazines and journals are another source of information. There are job magazines that simply advertise job vacancies, or specialist magazines, such as *Nursing Times, Construction News, The Economist*, and many more, that will advertise jobs available in their particular subject areas.

Portfolio Activity 7.10

PC: Select information from relevant sources which applies to identified employment opportunities
Range: Information sources
Skills: Collect and record data, Produce written material

1. As a group, collect a sample of local and national newspapers and specialist business magazines.

2. Analyse each publication in terms of:

- The types of jobs they advertise
- The amount of space devoted to job adverts
- What other information they contain that may be useful to someone seeking employment or self-employment

3. Write up your findings in a short one-page summary.

Careers Service

Every area has a free **careers service** to advise students on the kinds of career opportunities available and how to take advantage of them. Careers counsellors are available to provide detailed help and guidance for young people seeking to enter the world of work.

In your local careers office you should find lots of leaflets and brochures of useful information on finding, preparing, and training for employment. Files will contain details of every college and university education and training course available in the UK.

Careers officers will be able to refer to a database of occupations to tell you about all the different types of jobs you could do in a particular business area of your choice – for example, healthcare, leisure and entertainment, or finance. The database will tell you about the qualifications and experience you will need for each job, the pay and conditions you could expect, opportunities and prospects, training, and where to find out more information.

Employment agencies

You will find many examples of **employment agencies** in your local business telephone directory. They are commercial organizations which specialize in recruiting and selecting staff for employers – for example, Alfred Marks, Reed Employment, Kelly Temporary Services. An employer will inform an agency of a job vacancy. The agency will then try to find a suitable candidate to fill the post in return for a fee. Some agencies specialize in certain occupations – for example, secretarial and clerical jobs, computing jobs, accountancy, or managerial positions.

You can register with an agency who will then try to find you a job. A member of staff from the agency will interview you to find out:

● The type of job you want

● If you are looking for permanent or temporary work

● If you want to work full-time or part-time

● What skills and qualifications you have

● Previous working experience

If the agency is notified of a job for which you might be suited, they will contact you and arrange an interview with the employer. However, there is no guarantee that they will be able to find you the job you want.

The Federation of Small Businesses

The **Federation of Small Businesses (FSB)** has a membership of around 70,000 people who are self-employed or who own, or are directors of, small businesses. It aims to ensure that the UK and European Union governments, opposition parties, and civil servants are aware of the problems and needs of small businesses, and their potential to provide jobs and incomes.

Some of the benefits of membership of the FSB include:

- Legal advice, available every hour of every day
- Specialist advice on tax, VAT, health and safety, and employment law
- Legal and professional expenses insurance

FSB staff and members can also provide helpful advice on business start-up.

Commercial banks

Local branches of all the major high street banks – Midland, Barclays, Lloyds, and National Westminster – offer many services for the small business owner. Many have small business advisors who can provide help and advice on how to start up a new business, and how to prepare business plans and obtain financial assistance.

Many of the banks provide free booklets, brochures, and information packs to people who want to set up their own business. They may also be willing to lend money to people who have a good business idea and have developed a detailed plan of action on how to make their business a success.

Information from banks

Factsheets and brochures produced by banks can advise on every aspect of starting and running a business, including:

- Market research
- Finding premises
- Writing a business plan
- Marketing
- Understanding business accounts
- Preparing budgets
- Tax and national insurance
- Business rates
- Obtaining finance
- Planning production

- Managing quality
- Employing staff
- Employee rights
- Health and safety matters
- Understanding legal requirements
- Using information technology
- Finding suppliers
- Costing and pricing
- Waste and recycling

The main high street banks also produce reports on different industry sectors, as well as reports on business conditions in particular countries.

Training and Enterprise Councils

You will remember from Section 7.2 that TECs are government- and business-sponsored organizations with over 80 local offices across England and Wales and over 20 in Scotland (where they are known as

Local Enterprise Councils). They provide a range of services for businesses, including:

- Identifying skills needed by local business and developing appropriate training courses
- Helping employers to develop and improve their own training courses
- Encouraging close cooperation between local schools/colleges and business
- Helping to finance business start-up through enterprise schemes
- Offering free advice and counselling on business matters

Charitable organizations

People looking for voluntary work can get in touch with a large number of charitable organizations who will be only too pleased to hear from them and benefit from their work. Some may even have paid vacancies which they may want to fill.

However, there are also a number of charitable organizations that provide training and advice for young people who want to start up in business. One of the best known is the **Prince's Youth Business Trust,** based at 5 Cleveland Place, London SW1Y 6JJ.

The Prince's Youth Business Trust helps 18 to 29-year-olds who are out of work, or finding it hard to get started, by backing them with cash. The trust gives grants of up to £1,500 to individuals, or £3,000 for groups setting up in business, and up to £5,000 for expanding businesses. Loans are also made available on easy repayment terms and special help is available for the disabled.

Portfolio Activity 7.11

PC: Select information from relevant sources which applies to identified employment opportunities

Range: Information sources

Skills: Collect and record data, Produce written material

1. As a class group, investigate the following sources of information on employment and self-employment:

- Your local Jobcentre
- Your local careers office
- Local employment agencies
- The Federation of Small Businesses
- Local banks
- Your local TEC
- The Prince's Youth Business Trust
- Voluntary Service Overseas

Each class member should be responsible for visiting or contacting one of the organizations listed above to find out more about the services they offer.

2. Sort out all the information gathered from Task 1 into a carefully indexed file so that every member of your class is able to make use of it.

3. (This task should be completed on your own.) From the information gathered by your class, produce two information leaflets using desktop publishing or word processing software.

Your first leaflet should explain sources of information for people who want to find out more about getting employment. The second leaflet should be about sources of information and help available to people who want to start up their own business.

Both leaflets should contain useful information in an attractive layout.

Section **7.4**

Skills for employment and self-employment

Your opportunities for employment or self-employment will very much depend on the skills you have. For example, if you cannot speak a foreign language, the opportunity to work as an interpreter will not be open to you.

Transferable skills

Many of the skills needed for success in self-employment are also required for success in employment. Whether a worker is employed by someone else or is self-employed, s/he will need to be able to communicate, work with others, complete tasks to an acceptable level of quality, and work to time deadlines. These kinds of skills are called **transferable skills**. That is, they are general skills which workers need in all kinds of jobs, whether employed or self-employed.

Useful transferable skills include:

- The ability to work independently and with others
- Managing time
- Decision-making
- Problem-solving
- Planning ahead
- Finding and evaluating information
- Effective written and oral communication
- Using numbers
- Using information technology

Occupational skills

Other skills are **job-specific** or **occupational skills**. For example: a motor mechanic needs car repair skills to mend a car, a hairdresser needs to be skilled in cutting and styling hair, an accountant needs skills in bookkeeping, a person running their own pottery-making business needs to be skilled in pottery. Both employed and self-employed people will need specific skills to do their jobs effectively.

Working independently or with others

Unless you own and run a business on your own, it is more than likely that you will have to work with other people. In self-employment you may work in a partnership or private limited company and will have to work with the other owners to run the business. Some jobs may involve more contact with other workers than others. For example, if you work in a large manufacturing firm, you may be part of a production or sales team (see 6.2).

However, many employers are also looking for employees who are **self-starters**, that is, staff they can rely upon to organize their own work tasks, take decisions, and carry them out without the need for supervision.

Portfolio Activity 7.12

PC: Analyse skills for employment or self-employment
Range: Skills
Skills: Use images, Produce written material

Klaus Schenker, Nicola Newman, and Robert Marriott run a vehicle repair business. The photographs below show a number of the tasks they have to carry out each day.

1. For each task shown make a list of:

- The **job-specific** skills needed to complete the task
- The **transferable** skills needed to complete the task

2. If you were a mechanic employed in the organization, which of the tasks shown do you think you might be asked to carry out? What skills would you need, and how are they likely to differ from the partners who own and run the business?

ESTIMATING REPAIR COSTS

PURCHASING SPARES

MOT TESTS

ADMINISTRATION

INTERVIEWING NEW STAFF

GOING TO THE BANK

CAR SPRAYING

DISCUSSING INSURANCE CLAIMS

RECEIVING PAYMENTS

DOING THE ACCOUNTS

MAKING REPAIRS

▼ *Being able to work on your own and with others are important skills.*

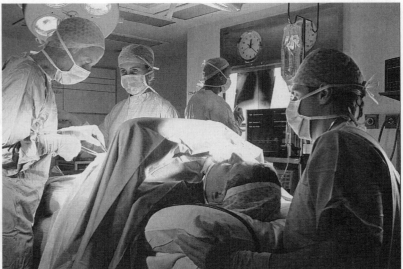

Firms that buy in self-employed people on fixed term contracts will also be relying on them to carry out specialized tasks independently.

The ability to work independently and as part of a team are, therefore, very important skills for both employment and self-employment.

▼ *'I'm late, I'm late, for a very important date'*

Time management

'Time is money' is an expression frequently used in business. Wasting time means less work is done, less is produced, and less revenue. If you are an employee, you may not care about wasting time, because it is your employer not you that loses. However, time-wasters are not tolerated, and you could find yourself out of a job. If you are self-employed, any time you waste means less money for you.

It is important to organize your time in employment or self-employment. For example, turning up late for a meeting can look very bad for you as an employee, and could mean losing a customer if you were self-employed. However, having too many meetings, or letting them run on, can also be a great waste of productive time.

Good time management involves:

- **Planning ahead:** to make sure you have the information, materials and equipment you need to carry out each particular task
- **Setting targets** for the amount of work you can reasonably expect to do in a given period of time
- **Setting realistic deadline**s for yourself to complete work tasks
- **Monitoring your progress** against targets and deadlines

Decision-making

Deciding whether you want to be self-employed or employed, and the type of job you want to do is difficult enough. However, it is likely that you will need to make different decisions almost every day throughout your working life. Having the confidence and ability to take decisions is an important skill. It is especially important if you are a small business owner and have no one else to make decisions for you. But even in employment, you will need to take decisions – whether you are a manager or a shop-floor worker, whether it is about long- term business plans, or how to organize your work each day (see 6.3). Employers will want to know that they have employees who have the ability to make the right decisions to improve their own performance and the performance of the organization.

Problem-solving

Decision-making and problem-solving are closely related (see 6.3). Thinking about a problem often involves making a decision about how best to correct it. Problems can arise in every department in a business. For example, machines can continually break down in production. The problem could be that they are overloaded or simply worn out. It would be up to the machine operators to identify the problem and offer solutions. Managers may then need to decide between cutting output or getting new machines. If managers opt for new machines, then they must decide between buying or hiring. A source of finance then has to be decided too.

Planning

In order to be successful in employment or self-employment, it is necessary to plan in advance.

In setting up a new business or attempting to find employment, it is a good idea to create an **action plan**. The plan should list the key things that need to be done, in order, and also give the timescales by which they will take place, and the sources of information, advice, and support to be used along the way. This plan can then provide a very useful framework for running your business to achieve your goals.

Planning for business

The business

- Have you chosen a business idea that will suit your strong points?
- Have you thought about and taken into account your strengths and weaknesses in running a business on a day-by-day basis?
- Have you thought about plans for running the business if you should become ill or have an accident?
- Have you considered your immediate, short-term (1-12 months), and long-term (1-5 years) business goals?

Production

- What materials will you need?
- Who will supply them?
- What skills do you need?
- What method of production will you use?
- What level of output do you want?

Sales and marketing

- Have you worked out what your main selling points will be?
- Have you identified your target market (who you will sell to) and any important features about your customers that would help you to sell to them more easily?
- Have you estimated your likely share in the market and future growth of sales?
- Have you produced projected sales figures for your first year of trading?
- Have you decided on how you will get your product to shops and customers?
- Have you decided on how to promote your goods?

Planning for business...continued

Costs

- Have you worked out your likely business costs?
- Do you know when you will have to pay the costs?
- Have you worked out how many items you need to sell in order to break even?

Accounting and finance

- How much money will your business require on a day-to-day basis in order to survive?
- Have you worked out how much you will need and for what?
- Do you need to borrow money in the first year, and have you spoken to the bank about this?
- Have you identified grants and other sources of finance which can be used?

Fixed assets

- Do you know what kind of assets (premises, machinery, equipment, etc.) you need?
- Have you worked out where to get them and on what terms?
- Have you decided between renting, hiring, and buying?

Location

- Have you identified a location for the business?
- Have you identified potential competition in the area?
- How will customers get to the business?
- Is there room for expansion?

Planning for employment

A plan for paid employment (or voluntary work) might include:

- An investigation of the types of work available
- Considering the advantages and disadvantages of different jobs
- Considering the experience and skills required for a particular job
- How and when you will gain these skills
- How you will go about finding jobs

- Preparing a summary of your educational qualifications, work experience, positions of responsibility held, and interests. (This is called a **curriculum vitae** or **CV**)
- Preparing for any job interviews you are invited to attend
- Thinking about the skills you want to have in 12 months' time/5 years' time
- Thinking about the position you want to reach in 12 months' time/5 years' time

Planning ahead should continue throughout your employment or self-employment – for example, developing a long-term plan for growth in your business, planning the work of other employees, planning your own work. Without a plan to work to you will waste time every day thinking what to do next, and may lose sight of the goals you are working towards.

Information-seeking

Finding opportunities for employment and self-employment involves a great deal of information-seeking, from newspapers, TV, Jobcentres, employment agencies, and so on (see 7.3). However, throughout your working life you will need to gather information on an almost daily basis in order to carry out your work. Information can be in the form of numbers, charts and graphs, text, audiovisual material, or can simply be passed on by speaking to other people.

Some jobs involve nothing but finding out information, such as news reporting or researching. As a self-employed person you will want to find out about rival firms, prices, materials to use, production processes, new equipment, suppliers, costs, outputs, and revenues. As an employee, you may have to gather some of the same information to do your job properly.

Information is needed for planning and to inform decision-making. A skilled information-seeker will know exactly what they are looking for, why the information is needed, possible sources, and be able to sort out what is relevant and irrelevant.

Evaluating

In employment or self-employment, it is important to **evaluate** the impact of your decisions, and those taken by others, on business costs and revenues.

Evaluating involves estimating, surveying, and measuring the impact of various changes on business performance. For example, as an employee or someone who is self-employed, you may want to evaluate:

- How well a work task was carried out by yourself or your fellow-workers
- Your own performance, and that of your fellow-workers and suppliers.
- Information, in terms of how up-to-date, accurate, and relevant it is to your needs
- The impact of a change in organizational structure
- The benefit of installing new computer and communications equipment
- The effectiveness of a new marketing campaign
- The safety and performance of a new product
- Changes in working arrangements
- The installation of new security equipment and procedures – and much more...

Communication

Communication involves:

- Talking to customers
- Taking part in discussions
- Negotiating with employees and suppliers
- Writing letters, memos, notices, and reports (see 14.2)
- Reading and responding to written information and requests
- Giving presentations
- Listening to others

However, for communication to be effective, the right information must get to the right people at the right time. If you fail to communicate effectively with work colleagues, suppliers, and customers, you will not be very successful in either employment or self-employment.

The way you think about yourself and communicate with others is vital for success at work. Junior staff are rarely given advice about how to communicate and present themselves to others. With this in mind, consultant Meribeth Bunch has produced a tape designed to help people to do better at work. Here are her top ten tips:

1. You have to want to be there, even if you don't like your job. Others can tell if you are not interested. Look for parts of your work that you do enjoy and make the most of those.

2. Be curious about your work and about customers and other people you work with. Find out more about the goods or services sold by your firm and learn from the ways other people do things.

3. When you don't understand, ask. It's better to be clear than to base your actions on assumptions. Check you understand by saying: 'Let me see if I've got this right' and summarize what you think you've been told.

4. Learn to listen. Concentrate on what others have to say without interrupting. Don't form questions in your mind when they are talking – this stops you from listening and you might hear something that helps you to understand things differently.

5. Take criticism. If a boss doesn't like the way you do something, ask how you can do it differently.

6. When you are in charge, lead by example.

7. Keep fit. This will help you appear to be dynamic rather than sleepy at work.

8. Acknowledge other people. Always let others know that you have seen them, even if you are just passing. Being acknowledged makes people feel respected and makes them feel more positive towards you.

9. Use your eyes effectively. Look at people when they are talking to you, but try not to stare.

10. Be aware. Be sensitive to how others are feeling, and take this into account in the way you behave towards them.

Application of number

A lot of useful business information is in number form, presented either in tables or graphs and charts. Being able to understand and prepare tables, graphs, and charts, to estimate and measure things, and use maths and statistical techniques are all very important numerical skills.

Access to most further education courses and many jobs is difficult unless you have proven numerical skills. Many employers want new staff to have at least a GCSE in mathematics. Of course, some jobs involve using numbers far more than others. For example, mathematics teachers, accountants, economists, and engineers use numbers and graphs almost all the time. However, most jobs involve at least some work with numbers.

If you are self-employed you will need to work out your costs, set prices to earn a profit, keep business accounts, and give details of your earnings to the tax authorities. You may also wish to identify how your costs and revenues have changed over time – for example, is there a seasonal pattern in sales? Has there been an upward trend in sales?

Portfolio Activity 7.13

PC: Analyse skills for employment or self-employment
Range: Skills
Skills: Take part in discussions

All the jobs listed opposite involve using numbers. In groups, discuss and list as many of the ways numbers are used in each job as you can.

- Sales assistant
- Financial accountant
- Sales manager
- Production planner
- Farm owner
- Pilot
- Bricklayer

Information technology

The use of IT is becoming widespread in business. Whether you are an employee or self-employed, skills in the use of IT equipment are increasingly important, from simply processing and presenting information using a computer word processor or spreadsheet package, to programming and using specialized equipment and machinery in the production of goods and services.

(If you have not done so already, you may want to complete Portfolio Activity 3.9 on page 118 at this point. It asks you to consider how IT has affected skills in a number of jobs.)

Portfolio Activity 7.14

PC: Analyse skills for employment or self-employment
Range: Analyse
Skills: Read and respond to written material

Using the questions given opposite, and your knowledge of yourself and how you perform in different situations, analyse whether you could run your own business or are better suited to finding employment.

Analysing your skills

Not everybody is suited to self-employment. Being self-employed means being able to manage yourself and others. It also means being able to organize your own time and being able to decide what to do without anyone telling you. Some people enjoy managing themselves, while others prefer to work for someone else and have their work organized for them. Not everyone wants to be in a position of being responsible for their own hours of work, their own earnings, and their own success or failure.

One of the first things you should ask yourself, therefore, is whether you have the personal skills you need to become self-employed, or if you are better suited to being an employee. Consider the questionnaire opposite:

So you think you can run your own business?

A questionnaire

An entrepreneur needs certain skills to allow him or her to run a successful business. The following questions will help you find out if you are the type to start up and run your own successful business. For each question, tick the answer you think describes yourself the best – and try to be honest!

1. Are you good at getting things going by yourself?

a I do things on my own initiative. I don't need anyone to tell me what to do.

b Once someone's explained what to do, I get on with it.

c I bide my time. I won't put myself out till I have to.

2. How do you get on with people?

a I like people. I get on with just about anybody.

b I have my close circle of friends – I don't really need anyone else.

c I'm never at ease with other people, most people irritate me.

d I'm always uncomfortable with strangers.

So you think you can run your own business?...continued

3. Can you lead and motivate others?

a I can get most people to go along with me when I start something.

b I'm very good at giving orders once I know what to do.

c Once something is moving, I'll probably join in.

4. Can you take responsibility?

a I like to take charge and see things through.

b I'll take over if I have to, but I'd prefer someone else to be responsible.

c There's always an eager beaver around waiting to show off. I leave it all to them.

d 'Never volunteer' – that's my motto.

5. Are you a good organizer?

a I like to have a plan to work to. Most of my friends leave it to me to get things organized.

b As long as I can keep to a plan it's plain sailing. When unexpected problems arise, I get confused.

c You can get everything carefully prepared, then something comes along to upset the applecart. So I just take things as they come.

6. How good a worker are you?

a I know what it means to work long hours. I'm quite willing to work hard for something I want.

b I'll work hard for a while, but when I've had enough that's it.

c I can't see that working hard is that important. Look at all the people who take it easy and still have a good life.

7. Can you make decisions?

a I often make snap decisions. They usually work out well.

b Yes, if I have time to think about them. If I don't have much time, I often make decisions I regret.

c I prefer to leave the decisions to others.

8. Can people trust what you say?

a I'm as straight as a die. I don't say things I don't mean.

b I sometimes bend the truth a little to avoid hurting people's feelings..

c I change what I say to suit the person I'm talking to.

9. Can you stay the course?

a If I decide to do something nothing will stop me.

b I usually finish what I start – if it goes well.

c If it doesn't go right the first time I lose interest and do something else.

10. How good is your health?

a I can keep going from dawn to dusk, no problem.

b I have enough energy to do most of the things I want to do.

c I seem to run out of energy before most of my friends.

Own skills achievement

As we have seen, improving your existing skills and developing new skills will widen your opportunities for employment or self-employment. But in order to improve your skills and develop new ones, you first need to identify your own strengths and weaknesses.

The following activity is designed to make you think about the skills you have, and how good you are in each skill.

Portfolio Activity 7.15

PC: Discuss own strengths and weaknesses in relation to skills for employment and self-employment

Range: Analyse

Skills: Read and respond to written material

Make four photocopies of the questionnaire opposite, and then complete the following tasks in pairs.

1. The questionnaire lists a number of useful skills needed in employment or self-employment. Mark with a cross how competent you are in each skill, ranging from 'very good' to 'very poor' (your partner should also complete a questionnaire). If you answer mostly 'good' and 'very good' for all the skills listed you are probably not being truthful.

2. Now complete the same questionnaire, but this time mark how competent you think your partner is in the various skills listed. (Your partner should complete a questionnaire based on their assessment of your skills.)

3. Now swap the questionnaire you completed about each other in Task 2. How does the view of your partner compare with your assessment of your own skills? Discuss with your partner why their view of your skills may differ from your own. Make notes from your discussion.

4. Write up your discussion notes into a summary covering:
- Your view of your own strengths and weaknesses in skills for employment or self-employment
- Your partner's view of your strengths and weaknesses
- Where your views differ and where they agree
- How you could attempt to develop and improve your skills

Skills	Very good	Good	Satisfactory	Poor	Very poor
Personal skills Working on your own Working with others Knowing your own strengths and weaknesses Drive and determination Working under pressure Coping with stress Acceptance of responsibility					
Organizational skills Planning ahead Setting targets Managing time and people Checking on performance Problem-solving Finding and using information Storing and referencing information					
Communication skills Reading Spelling Grammar Writing letters Taking notes Speaking to people Speaking in public Negotiating Listening to others					
Numeracy Finding and using data Recording data Making sense of statistics Mathematics Drawing tables and charts Doing the accounts Completing financial documents Handling cash					
Using information technology Operating machines Using communications equipment Typing/word processing Using spreadsheets Installing computer software Solving problems with equipment Repairing machines					

Ways to improve and develop your skills

Your education does not finish when you leave school, college, or university. Throughout your life you will learn new things and new ways of doing things. In employment or self-employment, constant change in the business environment means it is even more important to continue to learn new skills and improve your old ones. Many people are unemployed today simply because their old skills are no longer wanted.

Both the government and employers encourage 'lifetime learning'. This means the continued participation of employees and people in self-employment in education and training throughout their working lives. Only by keeping the skills of business owners, managers, and employees up-to-date can UK businesses remain competitive.

- **Further education:** Most schools and colleges run part-time evening courses specially designed for people who work during the day. You can study for a range of different qualifications in many different subject areas:

  – academic qualifications include GCSEs, A/s and A Levels, and university degrees

  – vocational qualifications are a work-related alternative to academic qualifications and include GNVQs, BTEC First, BTEC National, and Higher National Diplomas (HNDs) and Certificates (HNCs)

  – National Vocational Qualifications (NVQs) are based partly on how well you perform in your job compared to standards agreed by employers in the industry in which you work.

- **On-the-job training:** This involves learning skills while you are at work, for example, how to use a particular machine, and will normally involve working alongside more experienced people (see 3.3).

- **Off-the-job training:** This involves attending training courses in work-related skills, in time management, communication, using IT, and occupation-specific skills.

Portfolio Activity 7.16

PC: Analyse skills for employment or self-employment
Range: Analyse
Skills: Collect and record data, Produce written material

1. From the questionnaire you completed in Portfolio Activity 7.15, choose two skills in which your performance is only satisfactory, poor, or very poor.

2. Investigate all the ways you could develop and improve these skills. Useful sources of information will include local schools and colleges, training centres, specialized training organizations, and your local Training and Enterprise Council.

3. Write up the findings from your investigations into a short report using a word processor.

Key words

In your own words, write down explanations and definitions of the following key words and terms from this chapter:

Paid employment	European Union	Business angels	Commercial banks
Voluntary work	Voluntary Service Overseas	Partnership	Prince's Youth Business Trust
Private sector	Self-employment	Franchise	Transferable skills
Public sector	Family business	Jobcentre	Occupational skills
Commission of the European Communities	Training and Enterprise Council	Employment agencies	Careers Service
	Business Links	Federation of Small Businesses	

Test and Assignment

You must demonstrate that you are able to:

1. Identify types of employment and self-employment
2. Identify opportunities for employment and self-employment
3. Select information from relevant sources which applies to identified employment opportunities
4. Analyse skills for employment or self-employment
5. Discuss own strengths and weaknesses in relation to skills for employment or self-employment

Questions 1-4 share the following answer options:

A Training and Enterprise Council

B local newspaper

C Jobcentre

D careers office

Which of the above is best placed to offer the following information?

1 Information about local job opportunities

2 Advice on types of employment available and skills required

3 Advice and counselling for new business owners

4 Financial assistance for new business start-ups

Questions 5-7 share the following answer options:

A enterprise scheme

B family business

C partnership

D franchise

Which ways of owning your own business do the following describe?

5 Business start-up helped financially by a local Training and Enterprise Council

6 Buying the right to trade under the same name as an established organization and to make and sell an established product

7 An organization with two or more owners who participate in the running of the business

Questions 8-11 share the following answer options:

A planning

B time management

C evaluating

D application of number

Which of the above skills would be useful in the following situations?

8 You work in a large advertising agency. Your boss has asked you to make arrangements for a presentation of ideas on a new advertising campaign to an important business customer.

9 You are a mobile self-employed hairdresser who visits customers in their own homes. On a busy day you can have up to 20 appointments within a 30-mile radius.

10 You have been asked by your line manager to consider the advantages and disadvantages of developing a new filing system.

11 You are the senior manager of the accounts department in large public limited company. The board of directors has asked you to produce a report on business performance over the last six months.

12 Which of the following skills would you class as an occupational skill?

A working with others

B problem-solving

C bookkeeping

D information-seeking

Questions 13-15 share the following answer options:

A enrol on an evening course to study GCSE mathematics

B ask your line manager if you can attend a daytime course on using spreadsheets

C contact your local Training and Enterprise Council

D ask the help of an experienced work colleague

Which of the above methods would you choose if you were trying to develop and improve your skills in:

13 Running a small business?

14 Application of number?

15 Information technology?

16 a. Suggest three sources of information a person could use to help them find opportunities for employment overseas.

b. Suggest and describe three sources of information and help available to small business owners in the UK.

c. Describe the main differences between employment, voluntary work, and self-employment.

17 List five skills that are required for success in employment or self-employment, and explain why each one is so important. If possible, use examples of business situations in which each skill would be useful.

assessment assignment 281

Assessment Assignment

The following assignment covers all the evidence requirements needed to fulfil all the performance criteria in element 2.4 In addition, it covers the following range points and core skills:

Range: Types of employment and self-employment
Opportunities
Information sources
Analyse
Skills

Skills: Communication
Take part in discussions
Produce written material
Information technology
Present information

Tasks

1. Interview three people who engage in the following types of employment:

- Paid employment

- Voluntary employment

- Self-employment

  The people you choose can be friends, family, or people you know through work experience.

  With the permission of the person you are interviewing, you may record or video the interview. If this is not possible, take notes. Each interviewee should be asked:

- Their name

- How they came to be in their current employment

- What personal and occupational skills and qualifications they need to do their job

  Write a summary of each interview using a word processor. Audio and videotapes of interviews can also be submitted as evidence.

2. Collect three examples of local, national, and international opportunities for employment or self-employment. Sources of information can include:

- Job advertisements in local and national newspapers and magazines

- Articles in newspapers and magazines

- Taped broadcasts from TV and radio

- Careers offices and Jobcentres

- Employment agencies

- Training and Enterprise Councils

Use a word processor to summarize your findings, giving details of where you found the information. Carefully file the information you have found along with your summary in a folder marked 'Opportunities for employment and self-employment: information'.

3. Prepare a chart showing:

- The skills you will need in employment and self-employment

- An analysis of what skills you have achieved

- How you intend to improve and develop each one of your skills

- How you intend to learn skills you have yet to achieve

4. In pairs, discuss your strengths and weaknesses, and those of your partner, in relation to the skills for employment and self-employment you listed in Task 3. What skills do you have or not have? Does your partner agree with your assessment of your own skills? Do you agree with their assessment of their own skills?

   a Record or videotape your discussion as evidence of completion of this task. At the beginning of the discussion, state your name and the name of your partner, and the time and place the discussion took place.

   b At the end of the discussion, write a short note to include with your audio or videotape summarizing the content of your discussion.

5. Prepare a file of your evidence from Tasks 1, 3, and 4 to include in your portfolio. Your file should have a suitable filename and a typed contents page summarizing all the material included in it.

chapter 8

Consumers and Customers

Unit Three

unit **3**

chapter 8 The Importance of Consumers and Customers

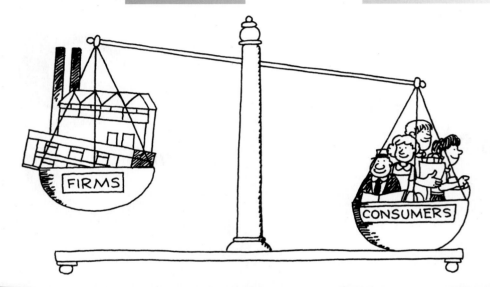

Key ideas

Consumers create demand for goods and services to satisfy their needs and wants. This **stimulates the supply of goods and services** from producers, provided these can be produced at a profit.

Firms will often target their products and promotions at different **market segments**. Each market segment is made up of consumers with similar **characteristics**, in terms of their **age, gender, location,** and **lifestyle**.

Consumers with different characteristics tend to have different **buying habits** in terms of the **type of goods and services** they buy, their **level of buying,** and **frequency of buying**.

Trends in consumer demand can be long-term or short-term. A long-term upward trend in sales means sales have been rising for 2-3 years or more. A long-term downward trend in sales means they have been falling over time.

Trends in sales can also be short-lived, for example, increased sales of toys before Christmas. Successful firms are those that are able to use information on past trends in sales to predict consumer demand in the future.

An **increase in consumer demand** for a good or service may occur because consumers have more **money to spend**, more **confidence to spend**, because their **needs and wants** have changed, and/or due to **successful advertising**.

A **fall in consumer demand** for a good or service may occur because consumers have less money to spend, less confidence to spend, or their needs and wants have changed in favour of other items.

Price inflation can reduce the purchasing power of consumers. If **earnings** increase more slowly than prices, the amount of goods and services consumers can afford will fall over time.

Customers are essential for **business survival**. They provide income, repeat business, and contribute to profit.

In addition, customers provide a valuable source of **market research information** for businesses, giving them information on what consumers want to buy, how often they will buy, and the product features they desire.

Section **8.1**   **Consumers and business**

Portfolio Activity 8.1

PC: Identify and explain the buying habits of consumers with different characteristics

Range: Buying habits of consumers

Skills: Use images, Produce written material

1. Which of the goods and services in the pictures do you think are purchased by the following:

- Private individuals
- Firms
- Government

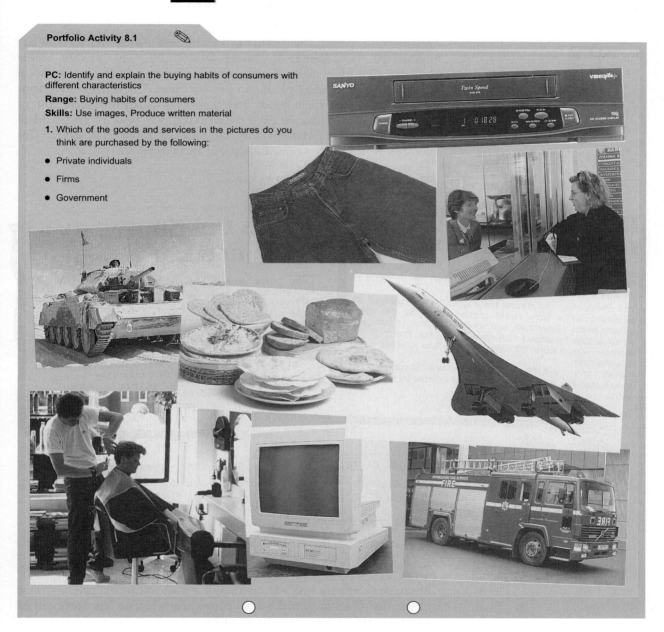

Who are consumers?

People who want and use goods and services are called **consumers** (see 1.1). Consumers can be individuals, other firms, or even the government.

For example, individuals are likely to want bread, video recorders, clothes, haircuts, and other personal goods and services. Firms will want machinery and materials to be able to produce goods and services. Local and central government will also want to use machinery such as

In 1994 consumers spent a total of £850 billion on goods and services in the UK, including those sold overseas.

computers, fire engines, and tanks to provide their public services (see 1.4). Many goods and services produced in the UK are also sold to individual consumers, governments, and firms overseas as exports.

All over the world a vast amount of different goods and services are purchased by different consumers every day. The private sector organizations that make these goods and services will only do so if consumers are willing and able to pay for them. The revenue that firms earn from selling their goods and services will pay for their cost of production. Any sales revenue over and above costs is profit. Most private sector organizations will not produce goods and services for consumers unless they can earn a profit from doing so.

The effect of consumers on business

Quick-shop drivers fuel garage boom

BRITISH shoppers now spend £31 billion a year in 'convenience shopping' in what is seen as a dramatic change in shopping habits.

The corner shop still attracts the majority of the business, 38 per cent, while high street grocers have 32 per cent, supermarkets 19 per cent, and specialist chains 11 per cent. Petrol station forecourts now have 6 per cent. The forecourt business – now worth £2 billion a year – has doubled in the last two years.

Shell is investing £350 million in convenience shopping on its forecourts, with facilities in a quarter of its sites by the end of 1994.

Daily Mail 15.11.94

Now's the time to pick up a new car bargain

The sorry state of Britain's recession-hit motor trade is bad news for dealers – but it means you could pick up a real bargain. The slump in sales has forced many car makers to cut production. While thousands of vehicles remain unsold, the manufacturer's plight can be turned to the buyer's advantage. For cut-throat competition means there has probably never been a better time to buy a new car. With the new registrations only months away, dealers are falling over themselves to shift older stock. This means there could be tasty deals to be had for the determined bargain hunter.

Daily Mirror 23.5.95

The articles above show just how important consumers are to the success of a business. Consumer demand is able to influence the following business decisions:

- The type of goods and services produced
- The quantities produced
- The price at which goods and services are sold

Businesses compete with one another to attract consumer spending. This means that firms must make what consumers want, or risk going out of business. This competition between firms leads to the production of a wide variety of different goods and services designed to suit many different tastes and levels of spending.

Consumers also influence the quantity of goods and services produced and their price through the amount they spend. If spending is low, firms will produce fewer goods and services, and the price of these is likely to be low. If consumers want to buy more of a particular product than firms can supply, the price of that product may have to rise to ration the available supply before firms can expand their production to meet the surge in demand.

Let us now consider these impacts in some more detail.

Consumers create demand

Consumers create demand for goods and services. **Consumer demand** refers to the willingness of consumers to buy goods and services. However, firms must be sure that consumers have the money to pay for their products. That is, consumers must have **purchasing power**.

Consumers with enough money to buy the goods and services they want have **effective consumer demand**. This means that firms are likely to meet their demands for goods and services. Without effective consumer demand, firms would be unable to sell goods and services to make a profit. Workers would not be required to make goods and services, and many people would be unemployed.

Strong or weak demand?

If sales for a particular good or service are rising and remain high, this indicates that consumer demand is strong. When demand is strong, consumers may be willing to pay a higher price to obtain the goods and services they want. Firms will also want to expand production to meet the demand, because they are likely to earn more sales revenue and profit. Because of the potential for profit, new firms may start up to produce the goods and services that are in strong demand.

If, however, consumer demand for a good or service is weak, sales will be low and probably falling. Prices may have to fall to tempt consumers to buy up stocks of finished goods and to use services. When demand for a good or service is low, there is only room for a few firms to produce all that consumers want. Some firms may be forced to cut production. Others may close down or switch to the production of goods and services for which demand is rising or strong.

Strong demand

Weak demand

Consumers stimulate the supply of goods and services

Effective demand encourages firms to produce goods and services in the hope of earning a profit. Video recorders are only produced by firms because consumers want them and are willing to pay a price that yields a profit for the manufacturers. Similarly, chickens are farmed to produce eggs because people want to eat them and are willing and able to pay for them at a price that gives farmers a profit.

The government is the largest single consumer in the UK, spending over £160 billion in 1994 alone on everything from supplies of paper to the building of new hospitals and motorways. Private sector firms are willing to supply anything from supplies of paper to major construction services because the UK government is willing and able to pay for them.

Changes in consumer demand

Because consumers stimulate a supply of goods and services through their spending decisions, it follows that changes in demand can affect the production decisions of firms.

- An **increase in demand** for a particular good will provide firms with an incentive to increase their production. If more people want a product, firms can sell more and earn more profit. For example, there has recently been an increase in demand for herbal drinks. Consider the impact this has on business:

  - Firms that produce herbal drinks experience an increase in their sales revenues

  - Stocks of herbal drinks fall as demand increases

  - Producers of herbal drinks expand their output. To do this, they need more herbs and other ingredients, plus more cans, bottles, and paper for labels. They may also need to buy more machinery and hire more workers

  - Firms that supply the herbs and other materials experience an increase in orders. At first they supply these orders from stock, but as stocks run out, they too must expand their output to meet the increased demand.

- A **fall in demand** means consumers buy less goods and services. As firms' sales revenues fall, stocks build up and production has to be cut. For example, many smaller video rental shops have closed down in recent years because more people are now going to the cinema, buying films on video, or paying for film channels on cable TV. The video rental market is now dominated by Blockbuster, which has had to expand into video sales and computer game rentals in order to keep attracting consumers.

Changes in demand for goods and services occur for many reasons. The main ones are changes in the amount of money people have available to spend, and changes in consumer needs and wants. As incomes rise, people have more money to spend on all goods and services. However, peoples' wants also change over time. For example, consumers are buying more wine; demand for beef has fallen following concern over 'mad cow' disease; attendances at the opera are up; attendances at football matches are down – and so on.

We will consider causes of change in consumer demand in detail in Section 8.4.

Portfolio Activity 8.2

PC: Describe the effect of consumers on sales of goods and services

Range: Effect of consumers

Skills: Read and respond to written materials, Produce written material

1. Look at the table below, headed 'The battle for your business'. Explain why you think Rumbelows was eventually forced to close down while Dixons and Comet continued in business.

2. In what ways would you say consumer demand changed over time to make Rumbelows unprofitable?

3. Suggest measures Rumbelows could have taken to stay in business.

4. Collect other examples from the local and national press, showing how changes in consumer demand have affected sales of goods and services, and how different firms have adapted.

5. Using the example of Rumbelows and any others you have collected, write a summary to explain the impact of changes in consumer demand for different goods and services on firms and their workers.

How You killed off

SHOWROOM SHOWDOWN

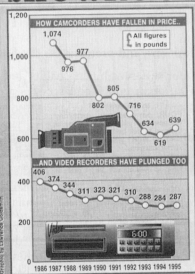

THE BATTLE FOR YOUR BUSINESS				
COMPANY	STAFF	STORES	SALES	PROFIT
COMET	4,920	225	£500m	£17.7
DIXONS	10,000	756	£1,500m	£73m
RUMBELOWS	2,900	285	£200m	(-£12m)

Another famous name is to disappear from the High Street with the news that the electrical retailer, Rumbelows, is to close after running up losses of £50 million. The decision to pull the plug is a tragedy for the 2,900 staff who will lose their jobs.

It is a harsh reality of today's consumer society in which the customer calls the shots. For the savage recession has given birth to a new breed of supershopper, who will travel far and wide for a bargain – and who is not afraid to haggle in the high street.

Rumbelows' management blames the collapse on fierce competition sparked by rivals such as Dixons and Comet. Rumbelows was still stuck in the high street when Dixons was spending £100 million in a ten-year programme moving its Currys chain out of town. Five years ago, Currys had just 20 out-of-town superstores and 550 high street shops. Today there are 200 of each. Dixons believes that out-of-town stores are profitable because their size enables them to offer the variety that the customer wants.

Daily Mirror 8.2.95

The buying habits of consumers

Dividing up the market

Information about the buying habits of different types of consumers is extremely valuable to business organizations. They need to know about the types of consumers who want to buy their products so that they can develop new products and promotions that will appeal to them.

In order to make decisions about the type of products to make, packaging, prices, advertising, and other promotions, business organizations will want to know about the following:

- The types of goods and services consumers buy
- How much they buy
- How often they buy

These **buying habits** will tend to vary between different groups of consumers depending on:

- Their age
- Their gender
- Where they live
- Their lifestyle, tastes, fashions, and preferences

It is precisely because of our different buying habits and characteristics that such a vast array of different goods and services are produced by business organizations to satisfy our wants.

Market segments

In order to plan products and promotions, firms divide up the people who are likely to buy their product into different groups known as **market segments**. Each market segment consists of consumers with similar characteristics, such as age, sex, location, and/or lifestyle.

Buying habits will differ between different market segments. For example, the type of clothes and cars bought by young people on high earnings will be very different to those bought by families. However, the buying habits of consumers in the same market segment are likely to be broadly similar. For example, most young parents will buy disposable nappies and baby foods frequently.

Target audiences

Firms can use information on the buying habits of different market segments to design products, advertising, and other promotions that will appeal to them. A market segment that has a particular product aimed at it – for example, teenage pop magazines or holidays for the over-50s – is known as a **target audience**.

▼ Products and promotions aimed at particular target audiences

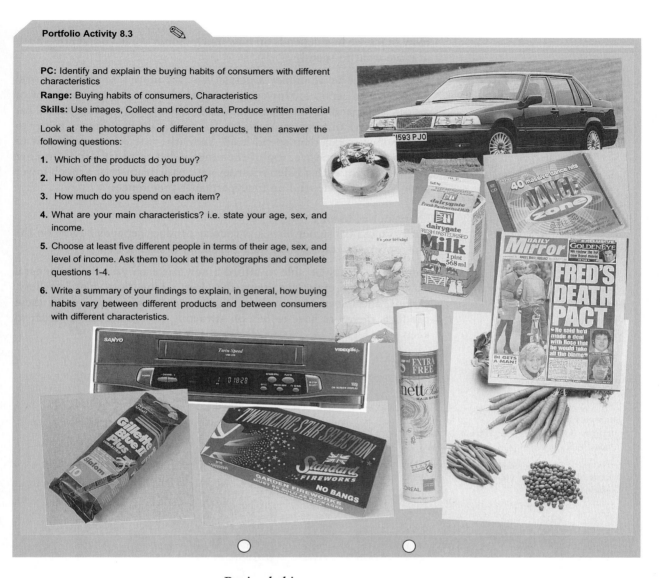

PC: Identify and explain the buying habits of consumers with different characteristics

Range: Buying habits of consumers, Characteristics

Skills: Use images, Collect and record data, Produce written material

Look at the photographs of different products, then answer the following questions:

1. Which of the products do you buy?

2. How often do you buy each product?

3. How much do you spend on each item?

4. What are your main characteristics? i.e. state your age, sex, and income.

5. Choose at least five different people in terms of their age, sex, and level of income. Ask them to look at the photographs and complete questions 1-4.

6. Write a summary of your findings to explain, in general, how buying habits vary between different products and between consumers with different characteristics.

Buying habits

The type of goods and services we buy depends on our needs and wants. Most people regardless of their age, sex, income, or location, have the same basic needs for food, clothing, and shelter. However, the type of food, clothes, houses or flats, and other goods and services we buy will differ because we have different tastes and levels of income.

Needs also vary because of our health and age. Disabled and elderly people tend to have different needs to other people and therefore buy different goods and services.

Our wants as consumers are vast and differ between people. However, some general patterns emerge. For example, young people are more interested in pop music and street fashions than middle-aged people or pensioners. People on high incomes are more likely to use the services of financial advisors and banks.

Level of buying

How much we buy depends on how much money we have and how much of it we want to spend.

In general, the more money a person has, the more s/he tends to spend on goods and services. However, even people with the same amount of money will spend different amounts on different goods and services. That is, people have different propensities to spend. One person may prefer to save money rather than spend it all. Similarly, one person will want to buy the most expensive, top-of-the-range video recorder, while another may be content with a video recorder with basic features at a much lower price. Much will depend on their particular preferences.

Frequency of buying

How often a consumer buys a particular product depends largely on the type of product rather than their particular preferences.

Some people may be able to afford a new car each year, but in general cars and other expensive items that last a long time, like jewellery, carpets, and televisions, are bought infrequently. Firms that make these products therefore have to rely on attracting new customers in order to keep sales high.

Portfolio Activity 8.4

PC: Identify and explain the buying habits of consumers with different characteristics

Range: Buying habits of consumers, Characteristics

Skills: Use images, Produce written material

Working in groups, suggest how the characteristics and buying habits of the consumers in the pictures may differ, and give your reasons.

Some goods and services, such as bread, meat, washing powders, and newspapers are bought regularly by nearly everyone. These products are used up quickly, and repeat purchases have to be made every day, week, or month. Banks are used frequently by people to pay in and withdraw money. Some people may visit a hairdressers on a regular basis, while others prefer to grow their hair long and will only pop in for a trim now and again. Consumer demand for some goods and services is seasonal. For example, Easter eggs at Easter, suntan lotions during the summer, fireworks for 5th November, and cards, trees, and decorations in the run-up to Christmas.

Consumer characteristics

Age
Our needs, wants, and buying habits tend to change as we grow older. Consumers can therefore be divided up into market segments separated by age. For example, the package holiday industry has designed special holidays and selling strategies aimed at the 18-30 age group, parents with young children, and the over-50s.

Businesses which depend heavily on selling products aimed at particular age groups will be very interested in government population forecasts. For example, producers of baby clothes and foods will be especially keen to know if birth rates are likely to rise or fall.

Birth and death rates in the UK are quite low. Fewer babies are being born, and more people are living longer. In 1993 there were just under 12 million people aged under 16 in the UK, compared to over 14 million in 1971. On the other hand, there were around 9 million people over 65 years of age in 1993 compared to just over 7 million in 1971. The number of people over 65 in the UK is forecast to increase to over 15 million by 2041 (see Portfolio Activity 8.12). These changes in the age structure of the UK population will affect the pattern of consumer demand.

Gender
Men and women have different buying habits and tend to be attracted by different kinds of promotions and marketing activities. For example, a recent study found that when shopping, men were more likely to pick up and look at products coloured either blue or green, while women are more likely to look at products packaged in lighter shades.

In the UK at present, women live on average nearly seven years longer than men. Therefore, goods and services aimed at the elderly are more likely to be bought by women, and so advertising needs to be designed with this in mind.

Firms and advertising agencies study the different buying habits of men and women, and design products and advertising for them accordingly. However, they have to be careful, because in many cases products used by one sex are bought as gifts by the other. For example, men buy their wives and girlfriends perfume and lingerie, and women buy their boyfriends and husbands aftershave and boxer shorts.

▼ *Targeting holidays at different age groups*

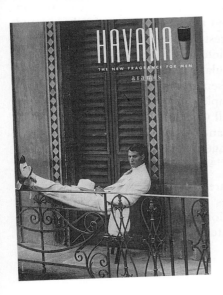

▼ *Figure 8.1: Average weekly earnings before tax, by area, April 1994*

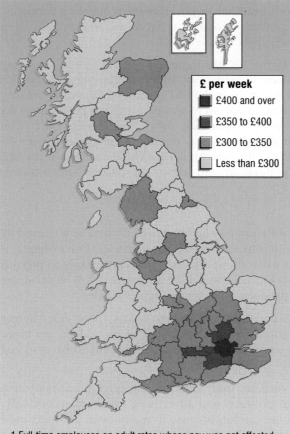

£ per week
■ £400 and over
■ £350 to £400
■ £300 to £350
□ Less than £300

1 Full-time employees on adult rates whose pay was not affected for the survey period by absence.

Social Trends 1995

The characteristics of consumers in different geographic regions

Incomes and buying habits differ between regions of the country. This is shown by the map in Figure 8.1, which gives details of average gross weekly earnings per person in April 1994 in the different regions in the UK. The highest earnings were in the South East, in particular in Greater London, where average weekly earnings were £415. Cornwall had the lowest average weekly earnings at £265. Firms can use this geographical information to divide consumers into groups by region in order to target their products and advertising.

Not only are there regional differences in incomes, but lifestyles also differ according to the region, leading to different spending patterns and different opportunities to sell products. For example, research shows that in Scotland people tend to consume more fried food and cigarettes than the rest of the country. This information will be of special interest to firms attempting to sell health foods. Particular features of different parts of the country also present opportunities for targeting products. For example, can you think of any products that are likely to sell well at seaside resorts in England, ski resorts in Scotland, or at major tourist attractions such as Stonehenge, the Tower of London, or Edinburgh Castle?

Television regions are often used as a way of identifying regional boundaries and of creating regional market segments. Television advertisements can then be designed to appeal to consumers in particular regions.

PC: Identify and explain the buying habits of consumers with different characteristics

Range: Buying habits of consumers, Characteristics

Skills: Tackle problems, Interpret and present data

HOUSEHOLD EXPENDITURE: BY REGION, 1993

United Kingdom — **Percentages**

	Housing	Fuel light, and power	Food	Alcohol and tobacco	Clothing and footwear	Household goods and services	Motoring and fares	Leisure goods and services	Other goods and services	Average expenditure (=100%) (£per week)
United Kingdom	16.2	4.8	18.1	6.3	6.3	13.9	15.6	14.0	4.8	276.68
North	15.0	5.3	19.1	8.0	6.5	14.7	14.2	12.5	4.6	245.94
Yorkshire & Humberside	14.7	5.0	18.2	8.0	6.7	12.6	16.6	13.4	4.9	263.06
East Midlands	16.1	5.2	18.8	6.6	5.8	13.9	15.2	13.8	4.8	262.15
East Anglia	16.9	4.8	18.5	4.6	6.1	13.8	17.7	13.0	4.5	260.46
South East	18.2	4.1	16.8	5.2	5.9	14.8	15.2	15.0	4.8	321.10
South West	16.1	4.8	18.3	5.8	5.5	13.7	17.4	13.3	5.1	268.14
West Midlands	15.3	5.3	18.8	6.2	5.9	13.5	16.4	13.9	4.7	238.19
North West	15.7	5.0	18.0	7.4	7.0	13.6	14.7	14.3	4.3	261.81
England	16.7	4.7	17.8	6.2	6.1	14.0	15.7	14.2	4.7	280.09
Wales	15.7	5.6	19.5	7.2	7.1	13.6	15.1	12.3	3.9	249.45
Scotland	13.4	5.1	18.8	7.5	7.2	12.8	15.6	14.4	5.3	264.84
Northern Ireland	9.4	6.6	22.9	6.4	7.6	14.0	16.5	12.1	4.3	255.32

Source: Central Statistical Office

1. Input the data from the table above into a computer spreadsheet.

2. Use your spreadsheet to convert all the percentage figures into cash amounts (£). For example, if we know that the average household in the UK spends 16.2% of their average weekly expenditure on housing, then we can calculate that this is the equivalent of £44.82 (= 0.162 x £276.68) in cash.

3. Now use your spreadsheet to produce a barchart showing average weekly household expenditure in £ (on the vertical axis) by each region (on the horizontal axis). Check and print out your graph, then write a short summary to describe the pattern of expenditure across different regions in the UK, and to explain why the average household in some areas spends more than others.

4. Now produce individual barcharts for spending on each category of goods and services. There are nine in total. Each barchart should show average weekly expenditure in £ on each category of goods and services (on the vertical axes) by each region (on the horizontal axes). Check and print out your graphs.

5. Now use your graphs to answer the following questions:

- On which categories of goods and services is household spending broadly similar in every region? Can you explain why this should be?

- On which categories of goods and services does spending by households differ markedly between different regions? Can you suggest why this is so?

6. Identify the region you live in. Use the graphs you have produced to describe how average household expenditure on the different goods and services in your region differs from (a) one other region at the other end of the country; and (b) the UK as a whole.

Consumers in different countries
Did you know that there are more cars and television sets per 1,000 people living in the USA than in any other country? Consumer demand varies not only by region within a country, but it also varies across different countries.

Differences in consumer buying habits in different countries can be caused by differences in income and standards of living, lifestyle, culture, and beliefs. As an example, you only have to think of the different foods eaten by people in different countries.

But did you also know that Marks & Spencers opened its first store in China in 1995? The markets for many goods and services are expanding internationally as people in different countries discover more about products sold overseas. This has been helped by increasing travel and tourism between countries and the globalization of western television via satellite. For example, most countries now receive the music channel MTV. As a result, music, films, and fashion advertised on MTV can reach consumers spread over a very wide geographical area.

Examples of products sold globally include Coca Cola, Levi jeans, and McDonalds hamburgers. These products are identical wherever they are sold, and advertising and selling methods can be the same in all countries.

Would you work two days for a burger?

The next time you chomp through a Big Mac, spare a thought for the customer in Nigeria who has to work nearly two days to earn the money for the same burger.
A survey this week of world prices and earnings using the Big Mac and a large portion of fries as the currency unit, revealed that the hungry British have to work for only 36 minutes to earn enough dough for their juicy treat. Times are harder in South America, where workers take 107 minutes and 243 minutes in Caracas to find the cash. But that's hardly a crumb of comfort for the worker in the Nigerian capital Lagos who has to toll for more than 11 working hours – well into a second working day to buy a bumper burger.

The survey shows that despite being sold in 72 countries, from 14,000 retail outlets, the Big Mac is still a luxury for many people.

Adapted from the Daily Mirror 13.9.94

AMOUNT OF WORKING TIME NEEDED TO BUY A BIG MAC

CHICAGO	14 mins
HOUSTON	17 mins
LOS ANGELES	19 mins
MEXICO CITY	90 mins
LAGOS	683 mins
CARACAS	243 mins
RIO DE JANEIRO	107 mins
BUENOS AIRES	66 mins
JOHANNESBURG	45 mins
NAIROBI	177 mins
LONDON	36 mins
PRAGUE	141 mins
BUDAPEST	128 mins
BOMBAY	92 mins
MANILA	126 mins
SYDNEY	26 mins

Graphic by Lawrence Goldsmith

Consumer lifestyle

Firms will often target their products and promotions at consumers with different lifestyles. **Lifestyle** describes the way we live and how we spend our time. The lifestyle a person has will depend on a number of factors, including their social class, tastes, preferences, fashions, religious beliefs, and culture.

Because many people want their lifestyles to be more glamorous and exciting, products are often advertised in a way that suggests that buying those products will allow them to lead the lifestyle they want.

- **Socio-economic group (SEG):** Firms will often divide up potential consumers into different socio-economic groups which rank people by their occupations, which in turn are often closely related to levels of education and income. People within each SEG tend to have similar lifestyles and buying habits.

Table 8.1 shows how people in the UK are classified into six SEGs.

▼ *Table 8.1: Socio-economic groups, UK 1993*

Socio-economic group	Occupations	% of population
A Upper/Upper middle class	Higher managerial, administrative, or professional	3%
B Middle class	Intermediate managerial, administrative, or professional	13%
C1 Lower middle class	Supervisory or clerical and junior managerial, administrative, or professional	23%
C2 Skilled working class	Skilled manual workers	32%
D Working class	Semi-skilled and unskilled manual workers	19%
E Very low income earners	Unemployed, state pensioners, disabled, and casual workers	10%

Joint Industry Committee for National Readership Surveys, JICNARS

Research shows that people in groups D and E spend more time watching TV than other groups, with around 30% of them preferring to read the *Sun* newspaper. Consumers in groups A and B spend more

For richer... for poorer

THE scandalous gap in living standards between Britain's highest and lowest earners is exposed today. The bottom 10 per cent earn below £74 a week while the top 10 per cent rake in £718 or more. And the poor can only wince and tighten their belts as the fat-cats lap up the luxuries of life.

A damning government survey of nearly 7,000 households has shown that the rich spend:

- EIGHT times as much on housing as the poor – £98 per week against £12.
- SIXTEEN times as much on motoring and travel – £105 against £6.70.
- TEN times as much on clothes – £29 against £3.
- FOUR times as much on food – £88.79 against £20.23.

The bare necessities of life cost the poor a greater part of their income – those on less than £74 spend £9.30 a week on lighting and fuel, compared with £18.99 by those on more than £718.

Daily Mirror 5.8.94

WHERE THE MONEY GOES

	Bottom 10%	Top 10%		Bottom 10%	Top 10%
Food			**Travel**		
Bread, rolls	£1.08	£2.48	Motoring & costs	£4.12	£84.05
biscuits, cakes	£1.15	£3.81	Bus & coach fares	81p	£1.32
Poultry etc	£1.83	£5.37	total fares and travel	£1.77	£19.72
Milk	£1.07	£1.72	**Household goods**		
Milk products, inc cream	81p	£3.53	Furniture	£1.30	£16.18
Cheese	51p	£2.09	matches, soaps, cleaning	£1.01	£2.85
			loo paper	32p	66p
Alcohol			gas and electric appliances including repairs	97p	£7.23
Beer, cider	£1.72	£10.55			
Wines, spirits	99p	£11.39	**Leisure goods**		
others	17p	£3.73	TV, video and audio	93p	£9.35
			books, papers, magazines	£1.71	£8.09
Clothes			TV & video rental, TV licence	£1.72	£3.01
women's outer	£1.31	£16.22			
undies and hosiery	49p	£2.51	**Tobacco**		
children and infants	52p	£3.59	cigarettes	£2.89	£4.29
footwear	82p	£6.60	pipe & cigars	nil	58p

time reading books than other groups, and prefer newspapers such as the *Daily Mail* and *The Times*. This is useful information for firms designing advertising campaigns to target their products at consumers.

- **Tastes and preferences:** Everyone has different likes and dislikes. That is, our tastes vary, although firms clearly rely on enough people having broadly similar tastes in order to mass-produce many items.

Our tastes are influenced by a variety of factors, including what is pleasing to the eye as well as pleasing to the tastebuds. Not everyone likes eating hot, spicy Indian or Thai food, whether they are rich or poor. However, rich people may prefer to eat such food in exclusive restaurants, while people on lower incomes may get theirs from a local takeaway.

Tastes are also likely to be influenced by those around us – family, friends, and acquaintances. For example, you may choose to listen to certain types of music or play particular sports to fit in with your friends. Similarly, people may buy cars, take holidays, and wear clothes that are associated with particular socio-economic groups. For example, high-income groups may prefer to spend their money on BMW or Mercedes cars, Caribbean cruises, winter ski-ing holidays, and designer clothes.

Preferences are similar to tastes in many ways. For example, we all have our preferences in music, clothes, food, drinks, etc. Many consumers like to eat cereal in the morning, but some will prefer to buy Sugar Puffs rather than other brands, while others may prefer Harvest Crunch to Cornflakes.

Both our tastes and preferences, and therefore our buying habits, can change with age, fashion, and moral views. For example, increasing numbers of consumers now prefer to buy products which have not been tested on animals or which harm the environment.

- **Fashion:** Changes in fashion affect the buying habits of consumers. Most fashionable goods have a relatively short product lifecycle. This means that new products experience rapid sales growth, a peak in sales, and then start to decline in popularity – all in a relatively short space of time. For example, toys, games, and T-shirts introduced to tie in with the release of a big Hollywood film, such as *The Lion King* or *Jurassic Park*, have lifecycles of only a few months while the film is popular.

Changes in fashion are particularly evident in the clothing industry. For example, after the 1960s and 1970s it was no longer fashionable to wear flared trousers. Each season, clothes designers release their new collections which eventually influence colours and styles many people will wear. Producers of clothes tend to target their new products and adverts at younger people because they tend to follow fashion more closely than other groups of consumers.

Portfolio Activity 8.7

PCe: Identify and explain the buying habits of consumers with different characteristics

Range: Buying habits of consumers, Characteristics

Skills: Interpret and present data, Produce written material

HOUSEHOLD EXPENDITURE, BY SOCIO-ECONOMIC GROUP OF HEAD OF HOUSEHOLD, 1993
United Kingdom   Percentages

	Housing	Fuel, light, and power	Food	Alcohol and tobacco	Clothing and footwear	Household goods and services	Motoring and fares	Leisure goods and services	Other goods and services	Average expenditure (=100%) (£ per week)
Professional	17.6	3.3	15.4	4.1	6.2	14.3	17.7	16.9	4.6	457.38
Employers and managers	18.5	3.6	15.8	5.4	6.6	13.7	14.8	16.5	5.1	445.54
Intermediate non-manual	17.7	3.6	15.3	5.2	6.4	13.9	17.1	14.6	6.3	366.33
Junior non-manual	17.6	4.3	16.7	5.6	6.7	13.9	18.4	12.4	4.5	291.34
Skilled manual	16.1	4.5	19.0	7.8	6.3	13.9	15.7	11.9	4.8	297.94
Semi-skilled manual	15.8	5.1	19.5	8.5	6.7	12.0	17.3	10.6	4.4	245.88
Unskilled manual	14.5	6.1	21.4	10.8	6.2	12.7	12.3	11.5	4.5	210.14
Retired and unoccupied	13.4	6.9	20.8	6.4	5.7	14.9	13.1	14.3	4.6	175.64
All households	17.2	4.1	17.1	6.3	6.5	13.6	16.3	14.0	5.0	335.73

Social Trends 1995

1. Input the above table into a computer spreadsheet.

2. Use the spreadsheet to produce (and print out) a series of barcharts to show how average weekly expenditure, in total and on different categories of goods and services, differs by SEG. For each graph, remember to plot expenditure, or percentages, on the vertical axis and SEG along the horizontal axis.

3. Write a short summary to describe how spending on different categories of goods and services varies by socio-economic group, as shown in your charts.

4. Obtain a sample of different national newspapers. Investigate the types of goods and services advertised in each paper. Are there any similarities or differences in the type and style of adverts between different newspapers?

5. From your research, suggest which socio-economic group(s) you think is/are most likely to read each national newspaper.

6. Obtain the latest copy of the government publication *Social Trends* from your tutor or local library. In the chapter on 'Leisure' you should find a table showing readership of national newspapers by SEG. Check your answers to Task 5 above against this table. How good were your guesses?

7. Use *Social Trends* to find out more about the characteristics of consumers in different socio-economic groups. Look in the chapters on

- Education
- Income and wealth
- Expenditure
- Health
- Housing
- Leisure

Write a short report on your findings to describe the main differences between consumers in different SEGs and why this information may be useful to business organizations.

Section **8.3**   ## Trends in consumer demand

Consumer demand is always changing. Over time, the demand for some goods may fall, while demand for others rises. Products that were popular ten years ago, or even just last year, may no longer be wanted by today's consumers. Business organizations must try to predict what consumers will want next, and produce it before their competitors do, otherwise they risk failure. A firm that does not produce what consumers want, or produces it too late, will not be successful. A **trend** in consumer demand refers to the general direction of change over time. Trends can operate in both directions. If sales are rising, this suggests an upward trend in demand. If sales are falling there is a downward trend.

▼ Figure 8.2: How to recognize a trend in consumer demand

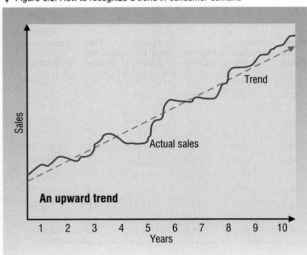

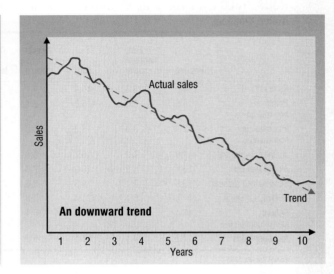

Long-term trends

Some trends may be established over a period of many years. For example, there are now around 23 million cars and light vans in the UK, compared to just over 6 million 30 years ago. The trend towards greater car ownership is likely to continue into the future as our incomes increase. On the other hand, sales of cigarettes in the UK have declined consistently over the last 20 years.

▼ Figure 8.3: Long-term growth in car ownership in the UK

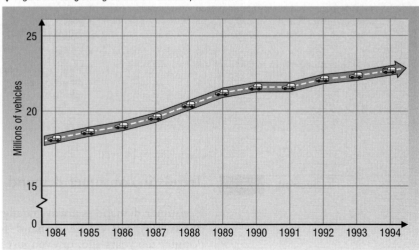

Transport Statistics 1995

Changes in consumer demand which continue in the same general direction for two to three years or more are usually considered to show a long-term trend. A long-term downward trend in consumer demand for particular goods and services can spell trouble for those firms that produce them. Firms may be tempted to switch production to those goods and services which show a continuing upward trend.

Short-term trends

Other changes in demand can be very short-lived, some lasting for as little as a few days, such as the increase in demand for flowers on Mothers' day each year, or tickets for a pop concert. Other short-term changes in demand may be seasonal – for example, the rise in demand for suntan lotion for three to four months each summer, or the increase in demand for toys before Christmas each year. All are examples of short-term trends in consumer demand.

Other short-term trends in demand for particular goods or services may be observed for a year or two before the general direction of demand changes. Many will be to do with changes in tastes and fashion. For example, the craze for Ninja Mutant Turtle toys was relatively short-lived. By the time you read this book, it is likely that the more recent, but similar craze for Power Ranger toys will be over, and demand for them will be falling.

Some short-term trends in consumer demand

You will be able to think of many different examples of short-term trends in consumer demand for different goods and services. Here are just a few:

- Sales of tickets to a pop concert
- Sales of Christmas cards
- Sales of special editions of newspapers and magazines
- Sales of foreign holidays during the summer
- Sales or rentals of a new video film release
- The surge in demand for electricity at around 6-7 pm when people get home from work

Square eyes

The graph below shows the percentage of the population who watch television at various times during the day. There is a rising trend in viewing numbers from 6 pm to 8 pm. After this, numbers of viewers start to fall away again. This two-hour growth period in viewing figures is a short-term trend.

▼ *Radio and television audiences throughout the day, 1992*

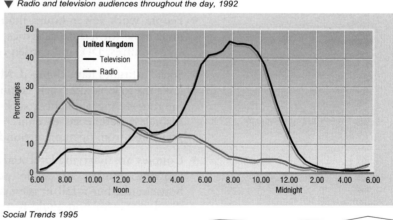

Social Trends 1995

Short- and long-term trends

Long-term trends in demand usually occur for all the products in the same market. For example, there has been a steady growth in the number of compact discs purchased over time, while the demand for vinyl LPs has fallen so markedly that many record companies no longer make them. Similarly, the trend decline in demand for all cigarettes is long-established.

On the other hand, short-term changes in demand often relate to a particular good or service, rather than the entire market. So, for example, pop groups may decline in popularity through time and sell less CDs, despite the growth in sales of CDs in general. Similarly, despite the long-term decline in demand for cigarettes, sales of a brand called 'Death' cigarettes increased after they were launched.

Short-term trends in consumer demand may move in a different direction to the long-term trend. For example, more and more tourists are visiting the UK each year. However, during the Gulf War in Kuwait in 1990, the number of tourists visiting the UK fell sharply – a short-term downward trend – because of the fear of terrorist attacks on American planes. Similarly, tourist numbers tend to fall during the winter compared to the summer.

Past trends

Some trends in consumer demand have developed over many years. For example, in the UK over the last hundred years, there has been a steady trend towards more home ownership and less private renting of accommodation. At the same time, there have been trends towards increased car ownership and more holidays abroad. Most homes now have a television, refrigerator, and telephone. Thirty years ago, very few homes had these items. The reasons for these observed long-term trends in consumer demand are many. Some of the most important are:

- **Most people in the UK now have more money to spend.** This has enabled them to spend more of their incomes meeting their wants, for example, video recorders, jewellery, holidays. The increased use of credit cards to boost our spending also reflects a change in people's attitude towards debt.

- **People work fewer hours than many years ago.** This has given them more time for leisure activities, and has increased demand for holidays, sport centres, DIY and garden centres, restaurants, and pubs.

- **Social attitudes have changed.** More women now go out to work and have less time to look after their families. This has caused an increase in demand for time-saving appliances such as microwave cookers and dishwashers. Also, less people go to church today. Until recently, shops have been prevented from opening on Sunday because of pressure from churchgoers.

- **Couples are marrying later and having fewer children.** This has meant a growing number of single people, an increase in the number of households, but a fall in their average size. This has helped to increase the demand for household furnishings and appliances.

- **People have become more health-conscious.** We now take more exercise, smoke fewer cigarettes, eat less fatty foods, and drink more fruit and herbal drinks.

- **There is growing concern for the environment** – so-called 'green consumerism'. This has affected the way many goods and services are produced. It has increased the demand for products which are not tested on animals and do not release harmful pollutants into the air.

- **Technology has advanced rapidly.** This has meant that once high-cost products such as televisions, CDs, computers, and video recorders have come down in price and can now be afforded by many more people.

Portfolio Activity 8.8

PC: Identify trends in consumer demand
Range: Trends in consumer demand
Skills: Use images, Produce written material

1. Look at the graphs and tables. What past trends in consumer demand can you identify?

2. Suggest possible reasons for the trends in consumer demand you have identified above.

3. Give examples of the kinds of firms that might use this information on trends in consumer demand, and explain how they would do so.

4. Choose one particular product from those shown, and suggest whether you think the past trend in demand will continue into the future or is likely to change direction. Give reasons for your answer.

AVERAGE ATTENDANCES AT FOOTBALL AND RUGBY LEAGUE MATCHES

Great Britain   **Numbers**

	Football Association[1] Premier League[2]	Football League[1] Division One[3]	Scottish Football League Premier Division[4]	Rugby Football League Premier Division
1971/72	31,352	14,652	5,228	
1976/77	29,540	13,529	11,844	
1981/82	22,556	10,282	9,467	
1986/87	19,800	9,000	11,720	4,844
1989/90	20,800	12,500	15,576	6,450
1990/91	22,681	11,457	14,424	6,420
1991/92	21,622	10,525	11,970	6,511
1992/93	21,125	10,641	11,520	6,170
1993/94	23,040	11,752	12,351	5,683

1 League matches only until 1985/86. From 1986/87, Football League attendances include promotion and relegation play-off matches.
2 Prior to 1992/93, Football League Division One.
3 Prior to 1992/93, Football League Division Two.
4 Prior to 1976/77, Scottish League Division One.
Social Trends 1995

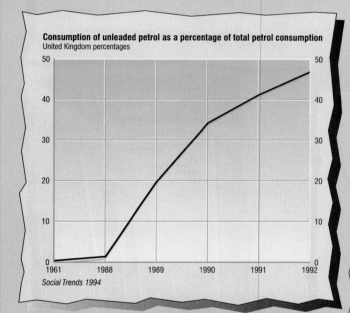

Consumption of unleaded petrol as a percentage of total petrol consumption
United Kingdom percentages
Social Trends 1994

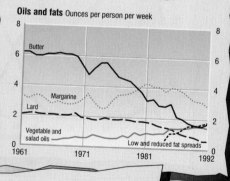

Oils and fats Ounces per person per week

Butter
Margarine
Lard
Vegetable and salad oils
Low and reduced fat spreads

Milks Pints per person per week

Whole milk
Skimmed milk

CINEMA ATTENDANCE[1]:BY AGE

Great Britain   **Percentages**

	1984	1986	1991	1993
7-14	73	87	80	93
15-24	59	82	88	90
25-34	49	65	70	82
35-44	45	60	70	73
45 and over	13	25	39	46
All aged 7 and over	38	53	61	69

1 Percentage claiming to 'ever go' to the cinema
Social Trends 1995

Portfolio Activity 8.8..cont'd ✎

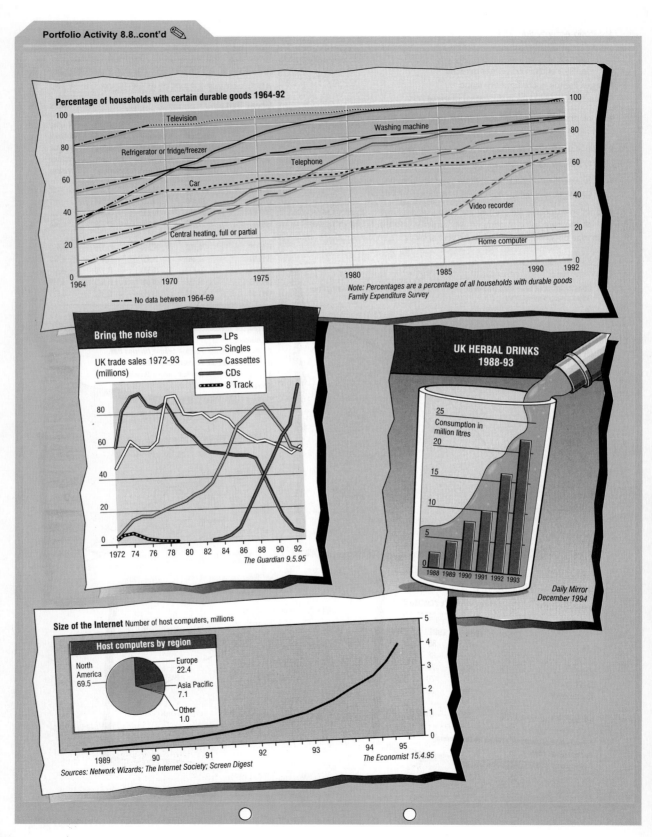

Percentage of households with certain durable goods 1964-92

Television

Washing machine

Refrigerator or fridge/freezer

Telephone

Car

Central heating, full or partial

Video recorder

Home computer

-·-· No data between 1964-69

Note: Percentages are a percentage of all households with durable goods
Family Expenditure Survey

Bring the noise

LPs
Singles
Cassettes
CDs
8 Track

UK trade sales 1972-93
(millions)

The Guardian 9.5.95

UK HERBAL DRINKS 1988-93

Consumption in million litres

Daily Mirror December 1994

Size of the Internet Number of host computers, millions

Host computers by region

North America 69.5

Europe 22.4

Asia Pacific 7.1

Other 1.0

The Economist 15.4.95

Sources: Network Wizards; The Internet Society; Screen Digest

Future trends

Firms investigate past trends in demand in order to predict what might happen in the future. For example, sales of tobacco in Western countries have been falling for many years, and it is likely this long-term trend will continue. Tobacco firms have responded by trying to sell more cigarettes in Third World countries.

Sales of computer CD-ROM drives have been growing steadily in recent years, and again it seems reasonable to guess that this trend will continue (see 14.5). However, guessing at the future using the past can be dangerous, because the future may be completely different. Some experts suggest that the Internet will make text, sound, and video available to all homes on demand in the near future, and that this will make CD-ROM redundant. If this were to happen in the future, demand for CD-ROM would quickly fall.

It is possible to identify a number of current trends in consumer demand which are likely to continue into the future. For example, the growth of the 'green consumer', healthy diets and eating, more computers, and increased cinema attendance are sales trends which have all been growing in recent years. However, technology, fashions, and tastes are changing all the time, and this can lead to new and unexpected changes in demand in the future (see 8.4).

Portfolio Activity 8.9

PC: Identify trends in consumer demand, Produce graphics to illustrate trends

Range: Trends in consumer demand

Skills: Tackle problems, Interpret and present data, Present information

The table below shows how much UK households spent on different kinds of goods and services in the UK between 1971 and 1993. For example, in 1971, UK households spent £7.2 billion on food. By 1993 this had risen to £46.3 billion

▼ *Household expenditure, UK (£ billions)*

	1971	1981	1991	1993	% change 1971-81	% change 1981-91
Food	7.2	25.5	45.2	46.3		
Alcoholic drink	2.6	11.3	24.3	24.4		
Tobacco	1.7	5.6	9.9	10.8		
Clothing and footwear	3.1	10.4	21.7	23.3		
Housing	4.5	23.2	53.7	62.3		
Fuel and power	1.6	7.9	14.7	14.7		
Household goods and services	2.8	10.7	23.9	26.3		
Transport and communication	5.1	26.7	63.6	69.6	523%	238%
Recreation, entertainment, and education	3.2	14.6	36.8	40.6		
Other goods and services	4.1	19.4	73.6	79.6		
Total household expenditure	36.0	155.4	367.4	397.8	432%	236%

1. Input data from the table into a computer spreadsheet.

2. Use your spreadsheet to draw a graph with a vertical axis from £0 to £80 billion, rising in intervals of £10 billion, and a horizontal axis from 1971 to 2001, rising in ten-yearly intervals.

3. Choose five categories of household expenditure from the above table. Plot the figures for total spending on each category for 1971, 1981, and 1991, and join them up to form five line graphs. Remember to label each line appropriately.

4. For each category of expenditure you have plotted, what does the long-term trend change look like over the period 1971-1991? (*Hint:* has household spending risen fast or slowly, fallen fast or slowly, or stayed broadly the same?)

5. Imagine that, for each category of spending, the long-term trend between 1971 and 1991 continues to 2001. Draw a line to show each trend continuing to 2001.

6. Now look at household spending in 1993 for each of the types of spending you have decided to plot. Mark each of the 1993 figures with an X on your graph. For each category, does the 1993 figure appear above or below the long-term trend? Write down and explain your answers. Can you suggest any reasons why spending in 1993 may have differed from the long term trends you have plotted?

7. Use your spreadsheet to calculate the percentage changes in spending for each category between 1971-81 and 1981-91 to complete the last two columns in the table.

8. Use the information on percentage changes in spending between 1971-81 and 1981-91 to examine whether spending on some goods and services has risen faster than others compared to spending as a whole. Write down your findings.

For example, the last row of the table shows that between 1971 and 1981 total household spending on all goods and services expanded by 432%. Much of this increase was due to rising prices. However, the table also shows that over the same period, spending on transport and communications increased by 523% – much faster than spending on all goods and services. This tells us that households were spending a growing proportion of their income on goods and services like cars, air travel, and telephones. This would be useful information for firms to know when planning products for the future.

9. Within each category of spending, suggest some individual products for which demand is likely to have increased over time (for example, within the category food, spending on health food has grown significantly).

Section **8.4** Causes of change in consumer demand

Portfolio Activity 8.10

PC: Explain the causes of change in consumer demand for consumer goods and services

Range: Causes of change in demand

Skills: Read and respond to written material

How times have changed

In 1947 the typical working man took home around £2 a week, but his hours were longer and he usually worked six days so it would take him around half a day to earn half a crown (25p) to pay for a basket of groceries.

Nowadays the average working man's wages are £14,000 a year – around £270 a week – so it would take less than half an hour to earn enough to pay for the same amount of groceries today, even at their higher prices.

Daily Mirror 28.4.94

Divorce rate sparks surge in toy market

Britain's toy market is booming thanks to the soaring divorce rate. As one in three parents split, the number of 'guilt gifts' given by separated mums and dads is growing.

Despite the growth of video and computer games, sales of small, portable toys which can be taken by children from one parent's home to another are increasing. According to market researchers Mintel, the divorce generation's 'portable kids' are being lavished with new portable toys. Mintel say sales of small cheap toys like Polly Pockets, Mighty Max, Trolls, and Monster In my Pocket boosted toy sales in Britain by £1.57 billion last year.

The Independent 30.6.94

Read all the newspaper articles. For each one write down:

- What has caused consumer demand to change
- Which goods and/or services the change in demand has affected
- How the change in demand is likely to affect those firms that produce the goods and services

Consumer spending forecast to rise 17%

Consumer spending is forecast to rise by 17% over and above inflation during the next five years, according to Mintel, the market research organization.

Mintel says the largest spending growth sectors are likely to be household and garden products

medical and school fees and insurance and pensions.

Falls in unemployment will boost consumer confidence, while lower interest rates and price inflation should lead to higher disposable incomes, with spending on homes and security taking priority as the recession ends.

Financial Times 1.2.94

Festive spirit surge

SHOPPERS stocking up on festive spirit stripped supermarket shelves bare as booze sales surged, according to drinks bosses.

Spirits sales more than doubled in the week before Christmas, drinks giant Allied-Domecq revealed last night.

Price-cutting and an advertising push provided a boost, but a rush to beat Budget tax rises also helped.

Daily Mirror 5.1.95

It's a £1.6bn cracker

Biscuit firms will make £1.6 billion this year as sales boom.

Britons eat their way through a staggering 25 pounds of biscuits each year. That works out at £1.36 per person a week on biscuits.

But bosses are spending £18.5 million on TV ads to get people eating even more. 'The only way to grow is to get more people to eat more biscuits,' says McVitie's marketing director, Andy Rush.

Daily Mirror 18.5.95

Changes in demand

Business organizations have little control over the factors that cause short-term or long-term changes in consumer demand for their goods and services. We can divide up the factors that influence consumer demand into two main categories:

- Price
- Non-price factors

Price

As the price of a good or service rises, consumers will tend to buy less of it, simply because they cannot afford to buy so much at higher prices and because cheaper alternatives may be available.

As prices fall, consumers can afford to buy more of a product and may switch from more expensive alternatives.

Technological advance in electronics has reduced the cost of producing high-technology products such as video recorders, compact disc players, camcorders, and computers. Falling production costs have allowed manufacturers to lower their prices without cutting their profits. As the price of these products has tumbled, sales have increased.

Non-price factors

These are factors that cause consumer demand for a good or service to change regardless of the price charged. These factors are considered in detail below.

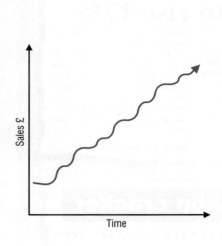

- **An increase in consumer demand:** If demand is rising, consumers will be buying more products. Sales revenues and potential profits will increase. Firms will expand their production to meet demand, especially if the increase in demand is long-lived.

  An increase in demand for a particular good or service may occur because:

  – Consumers have more money to spend

  – The price of other goods and services has increased

  – Consumers have more confidence to spend

  – Consumer needs and wants have changed in favour of the product

  – Advertising has persuaded them to buy

- **A fall in consumer demand:** Falling demand for a good or service, if prolonged, may spell trouble for a business. Stocks of finished goods will build up and may have to be sold off at a lower price. Production may have to be cut, otherwise stocks of unsold goods will build up again. Workers may lose their jobs. Suppliers of machinery and materials will also suffer a cut in their orders.

  A fall in demand for a particular good or service may occur because:

  – Consumers have less money to spend

  – The price of other goods and services has fallen

  – Consumers have less confidence to spend

  – Consumer needs and wants have changed in favour of other products

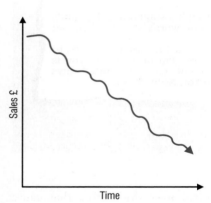

What causes demand to change for goods and services?

'Changes in income'

Both long-term and short-term changes in demand can occur if people have more or less money to spend. The amount of money people have to spend is called their **disposable income**. This is the amount of money they can spend and/or save after they have paid income tax and national insurance contributions (see 5.4).

In general, the more disposable income people have, the more they spend and the stronger is the demand for certain goods. Increases in income tax and national insurance can, therefore, reduce disposable income and cut consumer demand.

One of the main reasons for the long-term growth in the demand for products such as homes, cars, electrical appliances, overseas holidays, financial services, and many more, is the growth in disposable income over time. Between 1950 and 1995 the total disposable income in the UK increased from £9.7 billion to over £110 billion.

However, not all goods and services have experienced an increase in demand as disposable incomes have risen. For example, we do not buy more salt or newspapers simply because our incomes have gone up.

Some products are called **inferior goods,** because as our incomes increase, we tend to buy less of them in favour of more expensive, but still affordable products. For example, more people have bought cars as incomes have increased instead of using public transport. Bus and train passenger numbers have fallen over time. Similarly, our demand for overseas holidays has increased at the expense of holidays in the UK. Other factors affecting demand for goods and services include:

● **Unemployment:** During periods when unemployment is rising, disposable income and consumer demand will tend to fall because less people are at work earning money.

The cost of living

Between 1950 and 1995, UK total disposable income increased from around £10 billion to over £110 billion. But this does not mean we are over 11 times better off now than we were in 1950. At the same time the prices of the goods and services we buy have increased. That is, the **cost of living** has gone up.

Prices tend to rise for two main reasons:

i   People demand more goods and services than firms can supply. This will tend to force up the prices at which firms can sell their products.

ii As the cost of wages, machinery, and/or materials increases, firms' profits will be squeezed unless they can pass on these costs to consumers as higher prices.

Measuring inflation

Between 1950 and 1995 the cost of living in the UK, as measured by the **Retail Prices Index (RPI)**, increased by 17 fold! This suggests that the prices of all goods and services increased on average by around 6.5% per year over this period, so something that may have cost £1 in 1950 may now cost £17. A sustained increase in prices is called **inflation**.

Figure 8.4 below shows how the rate of price inflation in the UK, as measured by the RPI, has changed each year since 1950. It shows that the largest annual increase in prices was in 1975, at over 25%. The lowest rate of increase in prices was recorded in 1993 when prices increased, on average, by less than 2%.

The RPI is calculated by working out the average price of some 600 different goods and services each month. It is, therefore, not a true cost of living measure, because it does not include all the things we spend money on, nor does it tell us the change in the quality of the items we buy over time. However, as new products such as camcorders and computer games are developed, these are added to the 'basket of goods' measured by the RPI.

Purchasing power and inflation

Inflation reduces the purchasing power of the money we spend. For example, if you spend £100 each week you could buy 10 items at £10 each. If prices were to double, your £100 would buy only 5 items at £20 each. Because of inflation, £1 in 1950 is now worth the equivalent of around 6 pence in purchasing power.

As long as our incomes increase faster than prices, we can afford to buy more goods and services. Between 1990 and 1995, prices increased on average by around 4.1% per year. Over the same period, average weekly earnings, including any overtime and bonus payments, increased by almost 5% each year. This means that, in general, people in work have managed to increase the amount of money they have to spend faster than prices have increased.

However, inflation hits people on low or fixed incomes the hardest. People who are unemployed or old age pensioners find it hard to keep up with rising prices.

▼ Figure 8.4: Retail Prices Index, percentage change over 12 months

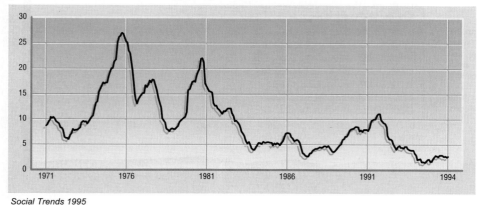

Social Trends 1995

1950

1995

"The pound in your pocket is now worth only 6 pence compared with how much it could buy at 1950 prices."

● **Interest rates:** The amount of money people have to spend will also depend in part on how much they borrow from banks and building societies. When interest rates are high, borrowing money becomes more expensive and people will tend to borrow less. An increase in interest rates will also make buying goods on hire purchase more expensive, and consumers will tend to buy less using this method (see 12.2).

Incomes, and therefore the purchasing power of consumers, are unequal. Some people have more money to spend than others. In general, firms will aim to produce goods and services for consumers who have enough money to buy them. People on low incomes may be unable to afford holidays overseas, new cars, video recorders, fashionable clothes, and holidays.

Confidence to spend

Consumer confidence has a large impact on the spending decisions of consumers. For example, if unemployment is rising, consumers may worry that they might lose their jobs in the future, and so may wish to cut their spending now and put more aside in savings. If, however, unemployment is falling, consumers may feel more confident and raise their spending in the belief that their jobs are safe.

Portfolio Activity 8.11

PC: Explain the causes of change in consumer demand for goods and services, Describe the effects of consumers on sales of goods and services

Range: Causes of change in consumer demand

Skills: Read and respond to written materials, Produce written material

1. What kinds of things might increase or reduce consumer confidence? (*Hint:* think about job security.)

2. Why might changes in consumer confidence affect how much people spend?

3. What kinds of spending does the article suggest have been cut because of a lack of confidence? Which industries will this affect?

4. What are the three main types of goods and services likely to gain from rising spending in the future, according to the graph?

Consumers delay home and holiday spending

Consumer confidence remained low last year in spite of the economy doing well, says a report published today. According to Mintel, the market research organization, spending on holidays, clothing, home improvements, and cars was postponed during the year. Mintel forecasts that in the next year or so, consumer confidence will improve and that this will lead to more spending on holidays, furniture, and mortgages. Other growth areas include stationery, garden products, books, and magazines.

Cuts in Value Added Tax will do most to boost consumer confidence, according to a survey of nearly 1,000 adults carried out for the report.

Financial Times 18.1.95

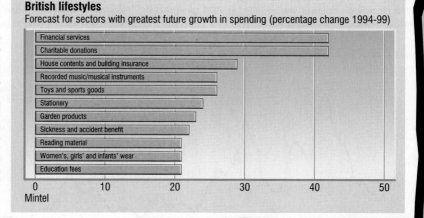

British lifestyles
Forecast for sectors with greatest future growth in spending (percentage change 1994-99)

Financial services
Charitable donations
House contents and building insurance
Recorded music/musical instruments
Toys and sports goods
Stationery
Garden products
Sickness and accident benefit
Reading material
Women's, girls' and infants' wear
Education fees

0   10   20   30   40   50
Mintel

Some people argue that the slump in house prices during the early 1990s reduced consumer confidence to spend. Retail sales fell over the same period. This is because people feel wealthier if the price of their property is increasing, and may spend more. They may also be willing to borrow more against the value of their houses in order to pay for home improvements, or other products for the home and garden.

Changing needs

All people have the same basic needs for food, water, and shelter. However, people also have other needs which will differ according to their particular lifestyle, health, and age. For example, an old person may need more medical attention and warmer clothes than a younger person. A disabled person may need a wheelchair and waist-level plug sockets and light switches fitted in their home.

Many people might argue they need a car to get to and from work each day because there is no regular bus or train service. Similarly, new parents will need baby clothes and nappies.

The most dramatic change in your needs will probably occur when you leave full-time education. If you have not already opened a bank account, it is likely you will need one so that you can receive your pay each month. You may need to buy overalls or a suit to wear to work. As you grow older, you may want to buy your own home and will need the services of a solicitor and building society to do so.

▼ Consumers have different needs.

Private sector businesses will only provide the goods and services we need if they can be produced at a profit (see 1.1). Some people cannot buy the goods and services they need because they cannot afford to pay for them. In some poor countries, many people cannot even afford to buy food.

In the UK, the government will often provide goods and services people need but cannot afford (see 1.4). For example, schools and hospitals are provided for people who cannot afford private education or healthcare. Benefits are paid to people who are disabled or out or work so that they can buy the basic items they need.

PC: Explain the causes of change in consumer demand for goods and services

Range: Causes of change in demand

Skills: Read and respond to written material

The table opposite shows projections for the UK population in different age groups.

1. According to the projections, what will happen to the UK population over time?

2. How are these changes likely to affect the needs of consumers in the UK?

3. Suggest how business organizations could use the information in the table to plan ahead.

▼ UK population, by age and gender

UK POPULATION, BY AGE AND GENDER

Percentages

	Under 16	16-39	40-64	65-79	80 and over	All ages (=100%) (millions)
Mid-year estimates						
1971	25.5	31.3	29.9	10.9	2.3	55.9
1981	22.3	34.9	27.8	12.2	2.8	56.4
1991	20.3	35.3	28.6	12.0	3.7	57.8
1993	20.6	34.9	28.8	11.9	3.9	58.2
Males	21.6	36.3	29.2	10.6	2.4	28.5
Females	19.6	33.5	28.4	13.1	5.4	29.7
Mid-year projections[1]						
2001	20.7	32.9	30.6	11.4	4.3	59.8
2011	19.2	30.0	34.1	11.9	4.7	61.3
2021	18.3	29.7	32.7	14.3	5.1	62.1
2031	18.2	28.4	30.5	16.3	6.6	62.2
2041	17.6	27.8	30.1	16.8	7.8	61.2
2051	17.6	28.0	30.3	14.9	9.2	59.6
Males	18.2	28.9	30.9	14.5	7.5	30.9
Females	17.0	27.2	29.7	15.2	10.9	30.1

1 1992-based projections
Social Trends 1995

Changing wants

In addition to income, one of the most important factors causing short- and long-term changes in demand for products is the changing wants of consumers. Our wants change much quicker than our needs. Our wants as consumers are also endless compared to our needs.

Most people do not have enough money to buy everything they want. When buying goods and services, they have to prioritize and make choices. In general, consumers will buy those products that give them the most satisfaction. Some of the main factors affecting consumer wants are:

● **Fashion and tastes:** Tastes and fashions can change rapidly. This is true of many products, not just clothes. Remember the shiny shellsuits that were fashionable in the late 1980s? Who would be brave enough to wear one now?

People in the UK now buy more wine than they ever did before, because they have acquired a taste for it from holidays abroad. We have also developed a taste for more healthy eating, and food manufacturers are now keen to advertise that their products are low in fat. Rabbit disappeared as a favoured meat many years ago, to be replaced by chicken.

▼ *Fashions and our wants for different clothes change rapidly.*

More people now want their own personal computer, mobile phone, and surround-sound TV; more people also want to eat out at restaurants, go abroad for their holidays, and use environmentally friendly products (see **Expanding markets** in Section 2.2).

● **Social and cultural factors:** The British spend more leisure time at home than other nationalities and are more willing to spend money on consumer electronics goods. This reflects, in part, cultural and social differences between consumers in Britain and consumers overseas.

More females are going to work now than ever before; women are also getting married later, and having fewer children. These important changes in UK society have affected the demand for many goods and services. Supermarkets and other shops have had to adapt by staying open later in the evening. Shops have also successfully campaigned to open on Sundays.

Cultural differences between people in different regions of the UK will also affect the regional pattern of demand. For example, did you know that men in the North and North West drink twice as much beer as men in East Anglia?

▼ *Good advertising can create wants and persuade consumers that the advertised product is better than the rest.*

Introducing a new Johnson's baby

At his tender age, only Johnson's Baby Powder
is pure enough to keep
Jack Walsh feeling comfortable with life.

● **Advertising:** Business organizations can influence the demand for their goods or services through advertising (see 9.1). Advertising not only tells a consumer that particular products exist, but can also create powerful images for products on posters, radio, and TV, to persuade people to buy them.

Advertising may try to prevent demand for an old product falling by telling consumers that it has been 'improved'. Alternatively, firms will often advertise their new products heavily to encourage people to believe that they need them. For example, until Sony invented the Walkman, most consumers had never thought of having portable personal music-players. However, strong advertising persuaded many people to buy them. Portable cassette, mini-disc, CD, and even television players are now a common sight.

A firm in competition with rival organizations to sell very similar products, such as washing powders and biscuits, will make great use of advertising to persuade consumers that their particular product is better than all the others. Here, advertising is used not only to create a want for their product, but also to attract customers away from rival firms.

● **Other factors:** A whole host of other factors can explain why our wants change over time. For example, changes in the seasons affect our demand for goods and services. We want Christmas trees and decorations in December, while in the summer we want T-shirts, ice creams, and holidays.

Section 8.5   The importance of customers

PC: Explain and give examples of the importance of customers to business organizations

Range: Importance of customers

Skills: Read and respond to written materials, Produce written material

Death of the corner shop

FOR 61 years, it has stood firm against the retailing revolution.

The corner shop of W English & Son survived by offering personal service, home deliveries, free credit, and fine foodstuffs from around the world.

Next week, however, this bastion of tradition will bow to so-called progress.

Bryan English will pull down the shutters at Chatsworth Stores for the last time after conceding defeat to the new supermarket 200 yards down the road.

He said yesterday: 'Shutting up the shop will be a sad day but it's inevitable, I'm afraid. We're catering to a dwindling generation of customers, and I am too old and set in my ways to adapt.'

Daily Mail 12.10.95

Read the articles above. Using the examples given, prepare a short summary to explain why customers are so important to business organizations.

£6.5 million Fashion Victim

Warmer winter weather has sent a chill through sales at one of Britain's biggest department store chains. Sales of winter clothes have fallen significantly. The 55-store House of Fraser chain suffered, because clothes account for 40% of all their sales. Profits fell £6.5 million to £28 million in the year to January.

Daily Mirror 21.4.95

We're still nutty for chocs after 90 years

Edward VIII was on the throne and Aston Villa won the FA cup. The AA also started motoring in 1905 and French fashion designer Christian Dior was born.

And George Cadbury Junior was starting another trend which celebrates its 90th anniversary this year. Dairy Milk has been Britain's most popular moulded chocolate bar ever since.

Sales of the pure CDM reached a tasty £103 million last year – nearly twice its nearest rival. On top of that, Cadbury's Whole Nut and Fruit & Nut, which use the same chocolate, ring up £83 million sales a year.

Daily Mirror 5.1.95

Customer focus

A consumer only becomes a **customer** of an organization once s/he has bought its product or used its services. Organizations, therefore, compete for the custom, or spending, of consumers. Those organizations that are best able to offer what consumers want are likely to win the most customers and the biggest share of their spending on a particular good or service.

Competition between organizations for customers can take many forms, for example:

- Offering lower prices than rivals
- Offering better-quality products
- Special offers
- Advertising

- Promoting a good image for the organization

- Offering good customer service, such as after-sales care and fast delivery

Organizations will constantly update their products, prices, promotions, and image in order to keep ahead of rival firms (see 9.1). All these measures will be designed to:

- Attract new customers

- Keep existing customers

- Increase their share of total consumer spending on particular goods and services (see 1.1)

More and more organizations are adopting a 'customer focus' (see 10.1). This means that they concentrate all their activities on winning and keeping customers, by finding out what consumers want and providing the products they want, in the amounts they want, when they want them, and at prices they are willing to pay.

Why are customers so important to a business?

BUSINESS ORGANIZATIONS NEED CUSTOMERS BECAUSE THEY:
1 PROVIDE INCOME
2 PROVIDE REPEAT BUSINESS
3 CONTRIBUTE TO PROFIT
4 ARE AN IMPORTANT SOURCE OF INFORMATION
5 ENSURE THE SURVIVAL OF THE BUSINESS

1. Customers provide income
Every firm needs a flow of income in order to buy machinery and materials, pay wages, rent, rates, and other business expenses, so that it can continue in production. Without a steady income a firm will not be able to pay its bills and may be forced to close down.

Customers provide firms with income, or revenue, by purchasing their goods and services. The amount of income a firm is able to earn will depend on the number of customers it has, and how much they spend. If enough customers buy enough of the product, there may be a surplus of income, or profit, left over after the firm has paid out all its costs. If consumers fail to purchase the product, the firm will make a loss.

In many cases, it may be easier to raise income by attracting new customers than by getting existing customers to spend more. For example, in 1993 the average UK household spent a total of £277 per week on all goods and services, of which around £50 was spent on food. It is unlikely that a supermarket will be able to persuade households to eat more food, but it may have more success in attracting customers away from rival stores.

2. Firms need the repeat business of customers

Many organizations are only able to earn regular income because of repeat business from their customers. For example, it would be of little use to a manufacturer of breakfast cereal if customers bought their product only once and then went off it. Unless there are repeat sales, the cereal manufacturer will not earn enough income to survive in business.

If customers are happy with the good or service they have purchased, they are more likely to buy the same product again, whether it is a packet of breakfast cereal or a make of car or television set. A happy customer is also likely to recommend products and organizations to family and friends to use. In this way, existing customers can help attract new ones.

The loyalty of the regular customer is, therefore, very important in business. Some firms even offer regular customers special privileges in order not to lose them, such as bonus offers, special discount cards, or exclusive shopping evenings (see 11.1).

3. Customers contribute to profit

Most private sector organizations and some public sector organizations, such as the Post Office, are run to make a profit. Profit is calculated as the difference between the total revenues and total costs of a business.

If customers are willing to pay more for a particular good or service than it cost to make, they will be providing the firm with a contribution to total profit. Thus, usually the more customers a business has, and the more it sells, the more profit it will make.

Profit is important in business because, as well as providing a return for the business owners, it provides funds for business expansion, or for investing in new, more efficient, machinery.

4. Customers provide a source of market research information

Firms can only survive by making what their customers want – and they will only know what customers want by asking them and by being in regular contact with them.

Finding out about consumer wants is called **market research** (see 11.2). Market research involves gathering information on customer wants from surveys and sales figures. Careful analysis of the results of surveys and sales figures can help a firm to develop products and promotions which will satisfy their wants, attract more customers, and increase the number of possible sales.

5. Customers ensure the survival of the business

Without customers an organization cannot survive in business. Customers provide income and profit for a business. Without this, there is no financial reason or incentive to be in business.

Different businesses can survive with different numbers of customers. A sole-trader decorating business may survive with steady work from, say, around 50-100 people per year. Others would be forced to close down long before customer numbers became so low.

▼ *The Sainsbury's Saver Card offers discounts for regular customers.*

Simply by looking at sales figures over time, a firm can discover important information about its customers. For example:

* What they want to buy
* What they do not want to buy
* Where they prefer to buy
* The product features they like
* The prices they are willing to pay
* The frequency of their purchases
* Their likes and dislikes
* How they respond to advertising and special promotions

Key wordsearch

There are 12 key words and terms from this chapter hidden in the
wordsearch below. Try to find them all and then write down
definitions and explanations of each one in your own words.

```
M  A  R  K  E  T  S  E  G  M  E  N  T  X  A  B
A  K  D  C  Y  I  F  O  N  K  S  R  P  Z  D  E
H  S  L  O  W  C  O  K  Y  Z  F  T  R  E  N  D
K  O  K  N  O  B  I  C  H  S  E  K  O  W  A  L
Y  G  R  S  M  I  T  N  H  O  D  T  D  I  M  C
S  N  T  U  B  S  Y  U  F  A  O  S  U  J  U  L
L  E  C  M  U  O  N  F  E  L  T  H  C  E  N  I
A  O  D  E  M  A  N  D  O  I  A  I  T  Z  E  N
D  S  O  R  D  I  T  Y  O  I  F  T  L  U  C  F
U  K  G  J  A  D  S  E  M  O  N  Z  I  L  U  E
A  R  K  A  N  Z  F  A  I  R  K  E  F  O  A  R
M  B  O  L  K  C  U  F  U  P  D  O  E  S  N  I
T  A  R  G  E  T  A  U  D  I  E  N  C  E  L  O
B  M  L  O  C  K  S  M  A  R  K  O  Y  P  O  R
R  A  C  Y  B  O  X  U  I  O  U  Z  C  Y  O  G
O  C  K  S  S  L  U  G  G  I  T  B  L  B  G  O
S  A  R  E  Y  O  C  U  S  T  O  M  E  R  Z  O
E  D  S  G  O  B  U  M  P  N  G  R  N  D  I  D
D  I  S  P  O  S  A  B  L  E  I  N  C  O  M  E
```

You must demonstrate that you are able to:

1. Describe the effect of consumers on sales of goods and services
2. Identify and explain the buying habits of consumers with different characteristics
3. Identify trends in consumer demand
4. Produce graphs to illustrate trends
5. Explain the causes of change in consumer demand for consumer goods and services
6. Explain and give examples of the importance of customers to business organizations

1 You and a number of business associates plan to open a new leisure centre. Which particular consumer characteristic is most likely to interest you in planning your business venture?

A lifestyle

B age

C gender

D ethnic origin

2 A chain of record shops is selling more and more CDs and fewer and fewer vinyl records. What is the main reason for this?

A more people own CD players than ever before

B vinyl records are cheaper than CDs

C CDs are dearer than vinyl records

D the demand for pop music is falling

3 A firm produces computer games. Which consumer characteristic will be important in targeting their advertising?

A region

B income

C gender

D age

4 Which of the following is most likely to cause an increase in the demand for motor cars?

A a rise in interest rates

B a rise in the price of petrol

C a rise in incomes

D a rise in car tax

5 Which of the following statements best describes personal disposable income?

A the amount of money a person earns

B the amount of money a person has left after paying for essential living expenses

C the amount of money a person has left after paying income tax and national insurance

D the amount of money a person spends

6 Which of the following is the most useful source of information for a firm trying to find out about trends in consumer demand?

A local newspapers

B published company reports

C government-published statistics in Social Trends

D national newspapers

7 If consumer confidence falls due to news reports about rising job losses, which of the following is most likely to happen?

A consumers will borrow more money

B people will buy more foreign holidays

C savings will rise and spending will fall

D savings will fall and spending will rise

Questions 8-10 share the following answer options:

The following factors may cause consumer demand for a particular product to change:

A an increase in health consciousness

B increased consumer concern for the environment

C an increase in the number of working women

D a rise in disposable income

Which of the above trends will be of the most interest to producers of the following products?

8 Motor cars

9 Aerosol sprays

10 Low-fat foodstuffs

Questions 11-13 share the following answer options:

A the increase in demand for chocolates before Easter

B the fall in demand for gas during summer months

C the rise in car ownership

D the fall in demand for cigarettes

Which of the above is an example of:

11 A long-term upward trend in consumer demand?

12 A short-term increase in consumer demand?

13 A short-term fall in consumer demand?

14 A fall in consumer demand for goods and services may be caused by all of the following except:

A an increase in the population

B a fall in consumer incomes

C a rise in unemployment

D a fall in consumer confidence

15 a. What is the difference between a consumer and a customer to a business?

b. Explain three reasons why customers are so important to business organizations.

c. Suggest three reasons why the number of customers buying goods from a business organization may fall.

16 a. Explain how consumers create demand and stimulate the supply of goods and services.

b. Suggest three reasons why the demand for personal computers has increased in recent years.

c. Give three examples of other products for which consumer demand has increased over the past five years or more.

d. How are changes in the seasons likely to affect the demand for some products?

17 a. Explain how consumer buying habits are likely to differ between consumers:

i of different ages

ii of different gender

iii of different socio-economic groups

b. Explain how the following may affect consumers' buying habits:

i rising price inflation

ii rising unemployment

assessment assignment

The following assignment meets all the evidence requirements needed to fulfil all the performance criteria in element 3.1. In addition it covers the following range points and core skills:

Range: Effect of consumers
Buying habits of consumers
Characteristics
Trends in consumer demand
Causes of change in consumer demand
Importance of customers

Skills: Communication
Produce written material
Use images
Application of number
Collect and record data
Interpret and present data
Information technology
Prepare information
Process information
Present information

Tasks

1. Choose one good and one service. For each product describe carefully in a written summary:

- How consumers create demand for these products

- How consumers have caused changes in the demand for them

- How consumers have stimulated producers to supply these products

2. Using a word processor, write a short summary of consumer buying habits, including:

- A description of how the buying habits of consumers with different characteristics have changed over the last 2-3 years

- Examples of changes in the type of goods and services different consumers buy, and their level and frequency of buying

- An explanation of why these changes in buying habits may have occurred

3. Look at the table below. It shows the trend increase in sales of bottled mineral water between 1984 and 1994.

Year	UK sales of bottled water, million litres
1984	70
1985	85
1986	115
1987	160
1988	230
1989	350
1990	420
1991	480
1992	520
1993	580
1994	690

Zenith International

a Input the data into a computer spreadsheet and produce a barchart or line graph of sales over time.

b Import your graph into a word processor to produce a 'consumer trends factsheet'. Your factsheet should contain:

- A description of the product range, including some examples of brand names and prices

- A graph of sales over time, including a line to show what you forecast will happen to sales over the next 2-3 years

- A description of the past trend in sales

- An explanation of all the possible causes of the change in consumer demand for the product

- Suggestions about how you think consumer demand for the product will change over the next 2-3 years

c Once you are satisfied with your factsheet, print out a hard copy. Do not forget to save your file on a floppy disk as well as the computer hard disk.

d Choose two more products for which you can obtain data on sales over time – for example, monthly data over 6-12 months, or annual data over 5-10 years. Some of the products and information in this chapter may help you to choose.

e Produce two more consumer trends factsheets for your chosen products. Follow the same format you used for your factsheet on bottled water sales (Tasks 3a-3c above).

3. A friend of yours is about to start up her own small shop selling pine furniture. You explain to her that as a business owner, her most important asset will be her customers. To support your argument, you offer to write her a short essay on the importance of customers:

- As a source of income

- For repeat custom

- To contribute to profit

- For business survival

To illustrate these points, use examples from other businesses, for example, reports in newspapers or on the TV, or from your own knowledge of other organizations.

4. Place your finished work in a file marked 'The Importance of Consumers and Customers in Business' and store it in your portfolio.

Social Trends

A very good source of information on consumer characteristics and trends in demand is *Social Trends*, published annually by the Government's Office of National Statistics. It contains a wealth of data on population, employment, expenditure, incomes, health, housing, leisure, crime, transport, and the environment in the UK today and in the past. Ask your tutor or local library for the latest copy.

Social Trends is also available on a CD-ROM and can be purchased from any HMSO bookshop (phone HMSO on 0171 873 0011).

chapter 9

chapter 9 Plan, Design, and Produce Promotional Material

THE END OF THE WORLD IS NIGH!

SO WHY NOT BUY **NEW**WIZZO SOAP POWDER BEFORE IT'S ALL OVER!

Key ideas

Promotions are the different ways in which firms communicate messages about their products to customers and persuade them to buy.

The main **purposes** of promotions are to **communicate messages to target audiences of consumers, create sales, influence the customer's perception** of the product or organization, and **provide information**.

Success in promotions requires firms to carefully **evaluate** the effectiveness of promotional materials in terms of how well they have communicated the message to the target audience, created sales, influenced customers' perceptions, and provided information.

Promotions may take the form of **advertisements** (including posters, radio, newspapers, magazines), **sponsorship,** and **competitions** as well as special offers in shops at the **point of sale**.

Some organizations may be tempted to make false claims about their products in order to create sales. In order to protect consumers, the government has passed a number of laws including the **Trade Descriptions Act, Sale of Goods Act,** and **Consumer Protection Act**. Organizations such as the **Trading Standards Office** and the **Advertising Standards Authority** exist in order to regulate business promotions.

Promotion is most likely to be effective if it is carefully planned. A **plan for promotion** should give details about the people required, the materials and equipment to be used, the expected costs of promotions, and the timescale in which things need to be done.

Good promotions involve the careful design and production of promotional materials to use in advertising, sponsorship, and competitions.

Section **9.1**

Promotions

What are promotions?

Marketing is all about finding out what consumers want (market research), developing the products they want at prices they are willing to pay, making sure the products are available when they want them in the places they want to buy them, and informing them about these products. This last function is called **promotion**. Promotion is usually a function of a marketing department in a business organization (see 4.2).

Almost every organization at some time or another will engage in promotional activities to let consumers know about the organization and the goods or services they provide. Small local businesses, large national and international firms, charities, government organizations, even your school or college – all use promotions to send messages to consumers.

Everywhere you look you will see promotions sending out messages to consumers: on posters, advertisements in newspapers and magazines, on leaflets, on television, even on footballers' shirts. Even if you close your eyes, promotional messages can still get to you over the TV or on the radio.

▼ *An informative promotion*

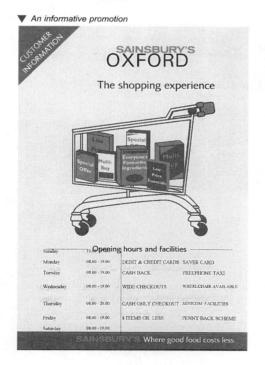

▼ *A persuasive promotion*

The messages conveyed by promotions can be informative or persuasive. **Informative messages** simply provide consumers with factual information about goods and services, such as weight, price, colours, or safety aspects. Examples of informative promotions will include restaurant menus, bus timetables, brochures on university courses. Charitable and government organizations tend to make the most use of promotions that give informative messages to consumers.

323

An organization that competes to supply a good or service for profit will often use promotions with **persuasive messages** in an attempt to make consumers believe their product is better than their rivals and is worth buying. Persuasive messages are designed to influence your behaviour and the behaviour of all other consumers. Political parties will also tend to use persuasive promotions to win votes at elections.

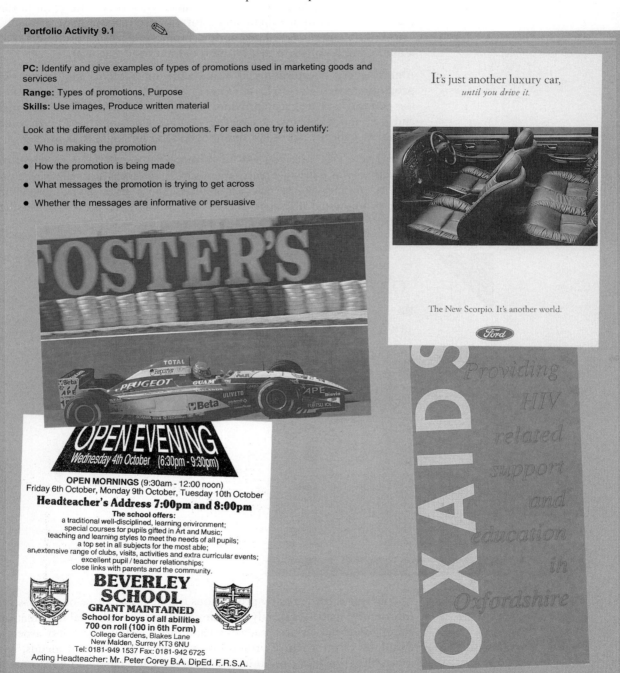

Portfolio Activity 9.1

PC: Identify and give examples of types of promotions used in marketing goods and services
Range: Types of promotions, Purpose
Skills: Use images, Produce written material

Look at the different examples of promotions. For each one try to identify:

• Who is making the promotion

• How the promotion is being made

• What messages the promotion is trying to get across

• Whether the messages are informative or persuasive

It's just another luxury car,
until you drive it.

The New Scorpio. It's another world.

Ford

OPEN EVENING
Wednesday 4th October (6:30pm - 9:30pm)
OPEN MORNINGS (9:30am - 12:00 noon)
Friday 6th October, Monday 9th October, Tuesday 10th October
Headteacher's Address 7:00pm and 8:00pm
The school offers:
a traditional well-disciplined, learning environment;
special courses for pupils gifted in Art and Music;
teaching and learning styles to meet the needs of all pupils;
a top set in all subjects for the most able;
an extensive range of clubs, visits, activities and extra curricular events;
excellent pupil / teacher relationships;
close links with parents and the community.

**BEVERLEY
SCHOOL
GRANT MAINTAINED**
School for boys of all abilities
700 on roll (100 in 6th Form)
College Gardens, Blakes Lane
New Malden, Surrey KT3 6NU
Tel: 0181-949 1537 Fax: 0181-942 6725
Acting Headteacher: Mr. Peter Corey B.A. DipEd. F.R.S.A.

OXAIDS
Providing HIV related support and education in Oxfordshire

The purpose of promotions

Each year business organizations spend many billions of pounds on promotions. We will now consider why so many firms are willing to spend so much on promotions.

Portfolio Activity 9.2

PC: Explain the purpose of the planned promotional materials

Range: Types of promotions, Purpose

Skills: Read and respond to written materials

Read the articles below. Identify in each case:

● The cost of the promotion

● The main purpose of the promotion

● Whether the promotion was successful

Heard the joke about the Lada advert?..they don't mention the car's name

IN AN ATTEMPT to polish up their corporate image, Lada Cars have come up with a novel strategy - their new advertising will not mention the word Lada.

A poster campaign which begins on April 1 emphasises the name of its most modern model, the Samara, rather than the brand, as part of a plan to reposition the sturdy but dated range of cars built in Togliatti, Russia.

Mr Gary Pepler, account director at the Leeds-based Brahm advertising agency which has devised the new campaign, said: "People have picked up the wrong perceptions about the cars.

"The current strategy is one of receding the brand of Lada and promoting the benefits of the individual models. We will be adding an emotive element to their reputation for value for money."

Daily Telegraph 30.3.94

Lloyds' creature comfort

PROFITS at Britain's Black Horse Bank have galloped up £107 million in six months - thanks to the help of a troll.

A series of TV ads tell tales of Lloyds' "legendary service", using such characters as the troll, a princess and a knight in shining armour.

Lloyds, which hopes the ads will help it ditch its stuffy image, made £605 million in the half year to July. The bank increased advertising spending by £10 million to £33 million.

Bosses at the bank - Britain's fourth-largest - claim more young customers have signed up since the ads started seven months ago.

"We've noticed a jump in the number of accounts opened by young people in the past four months," says a spokesman.

Daily Mirror 30.7.94

Promotions communicate a message to a target audience

We have already discovered that promotions are designed to send messages to people. If firms can identify the type of consumers who are most likely to buy their products, they can then design promotional materials that will appeal to them. That is, different promotional messages can be targeted at a different groups of consumers called **target audiences** (see 8.2). For example, the target audience for promotions of pop and rock magazines are primarily young people aged between 12 and 24. The target audience for promotions for baby foods and clothing are new parents and proud grandparents.

The type of message communicated will depend on the organization and the product being promoted. For example, government organizations will tend to be informative; banks will inform you about their range of services and try to persuade you that they offer good rates of interest on loans and savings and are financially secure; face-cream manufacturers will try to convince you that their products will give you healthy, younger-looking skin.

Messages that are designed to inform are generally obvious – for example, messages about train departure times, special offers, road safety, pop group tour dates, directions to superstores, etc.

Persuasive messages tend not to be so obvious. Many are subliminal, which means that they enter your thoughts subconsciously. For example, the imaginative use of colour, product names, packaging materials, logos, symbols, and music can all help to create persuasive images which stay in the mind. This can be done in a number of ways:

▼ Names for products are chosen carefully to give the right image.

- **The use of colour:** Women tend to prefer to buy products packaged in pastel colours, while men prefer to buy products packaged in darker colours. Bright colours are often used to attract children and teenagers. Dark, rich colours are often used to suggest elegance and high quality. For example, which television would you think was better quality – one that had a black casing, or one that was bright pink? By carefully choosing the colour of packaging, firms are sending a message to their customers about who should buy their products.

- **Product names:** The name of a product can also be chosen to communicate messages. For example, 'Comfort' fabric conditioner and 'Flash' liquid cleaner convey strong messages about the properties of these particular products. Similarly, many perfumes for women have been given names to make them sound romantic or sexy, such as 'Obsession', 'White Linen' and 'Beautiful'. These are called **brand names**.

- **Packaging:** Chocolates packed in a plain brown cardboard box are unlikely to attract much attention. Placing the same chocolates in a box with embossed gold lettering, tied up with ribbons, will suggest that the contents of the box are luxurious and exotic. Perfumes also tend to be sold in distinctive bottles and boxes to make them stand out from competing products.

▼ Perfumes in distinctive packaging can persuade consumers to buy.

- **Logos and symbols:** Organizations will also use logos, symbols, and distinctive product designs to promote awareness of the organization and its products. Every time a consumer sees the logo, symbol, or packaging they will recall past messages about the organization and the product. In this way, the logos and symbols become messages in themselves. For example, the 'St Michael' trademark on products sold in Marks & Spencer stores is recognized by many consumers as a symbol of quality. Under the Trademark Act, it is illegal to copy or use the logos or trademarks of other organizations or products.

- **Music:** Promotions on TV and radio advertisements may also use distinctive music. For example, in 1995 Levi jeans used a song called 'Tune in, Turn on, and Freak out' by a new group called Freak Power in an advert showing a man dressed as a woman riding in a New York taxi cab. The song went to number one in the record charts. Similarly, product elegance and quality may be suggested by using classical music to appeal to older people.

Most major film releases use pop records to help promote them to young people – the main cinema-going audience. For example,

'Everything I do, I do for you' sung by Bryan Adams from the film *Robin Hood, Prince of Thieves* stayed at number one for 13 weeks in the UK. More recently the film *Batman Forever* was promoted using songs by U2 and Seal.

Evaluating a promotion (1)

The success of a promotion in communicating a message to a particular audience can be measured by asking the following questions:

– Who was the audience for the promotion?

– Did the audience get the message? Has the firm checked this with customers?

– Were the messages appropriate? For example, were they too technical? Did they offend people?

– Which parts of the promotion were least successful and which were most successful?

– How could the promotion be altered to become more successful?

– Could the promotion have been made at a lower cost?

IBM shoots back up the list of most valuable brand names

IBM has reclaimed its third place in the list of most valuable brand names after slipping to 282nd position. Coca Cola holds off Marlboro as the world's most valuable brand for the second successive year, while Hewlett Packard has climbed five places to oust Budweiser from the number five spot, according to an annual survey. Coca Cola rises by $1.8 billion in value to $39 billion. Marlboro is worth $38.7 billion despite the aggressive battle in the cigarette market, followed by IBM at $17.1 billion, Motorola at $15.3 billion, and Hewlett Packard at $13.2 billion.

Europe's biggest brand is Nestlé's Nescafe coffee, the only brand in the top ten that is not American. The most valuable British brands are Johnnie Walker Black Label Whisky at number 47 and Guinness at number 55. The world's biggest brand is Microsoft.

Sunday Times 16.7.95

Portfolio Activity 9.3

PC: Identify and give examples of type of promotions used in marketing goods and services

Range: Types of promotions, Purpose

Skills: Use images, Produce written material

1. Choosing a name for a product is often as important as what is said about it in an advert, or its price and quality. What type of products are these brand names for? What message do they give the consumer about the product?

Aquafresh	Citrus Spring	Brillo
Black Magic	Parazone	Gold Blend
Imperial Leather	Flora	Crunchie
Pampers	Radox	Impulse

2. Some products have such well known trademarks or logos that it is possible to promote them without using word or pictures at all. How many of the following do you recognize? What products/organizations do they promote?

327

▼ Promotional images can influence consumers' perceptions of the lifestyle they can lead if they buy the product.

IF YOU'RE PARTIAL TO A 12 YEAR OLD MALT, A MATURE STILTON WITH VINTAGE PORT, OR SWISS CHOCOLATE TRUFFLES, YOU PROBABLY ENJOY IT ALREADY.

DOUWE EGBERTS

ENJOY A COFFEE TASTE THAT'S SERIO

More Affordable Than You Think

For those who want the best, there is little to compare with the high quality collection of Allibert Garden and Conservatory furniture. With twelve distinctive and elegant ranges from economy to de luxe to choose from, you can be sure there will be a style to complement your home whatever the size, shape or design of your garden - or pocket !

Write now for our FREE Full Colour Brochure and list of Appointed Stockists.

ALLiBERT
ALLIBERT GARDEN FURNITURE
FREEPOST WR 759   DROITWICH   WORCS WR9 7BR

Promotions are used to create sales

This is the main aim of most promotional activity. The whole point of creating awareness, interest, and desire is to persuade consumers to purchase. A promotion that just creates interest without converting this into sales is a failure. Sales may be achieved by promotions which convince consumers that the product is new, or that it is somehow better than competitors' products, or that the consumer will benefit from buying the product, either through the features of the product or by 'buying into' the image of that product.

Evaluating a promotion (2)

The effectiveness of a promotional strategy to create sales can be measured by asking the following questions:

– What increase in sales was expected as a result of the promotion?

– What increase in sales was experienced?

– Did sales increase only because of the promotion or would they have risen anyway? What evidence is there for this?

– What could have been done to increase sales more?

– What reasons did those consumers not buying the product give for their decision?

– Which aspects of the promotion could be changed to further raise sales?

McDonalds headquarters in the UK receives regular updates on the success of its promotions by computer modem link from all of its UK stores and so can monitor sales in each locality to see how consumers have responded to particular kinds of promotion. This gives almost immediate feedback to McDonalds on the effectiveness of promotional activities. The firm can then adjust its promotions to deliver whatever is the most effective message for increasing sales.

Promotions are used to influence customers' perceptions

Persuasive advertising is designed to persuade consumers to do things they might not otherwise do, in particular to buy a product that they might not otherwise buy. One way to do this is to change their attitudes, opinions, and perceptions of the organization and/or its product.

Consumers' perceptions of a product can be changed by creating a **brand image,** and using a distinctive brand name, logo, humorous catchphrase, or visual treatment to make it stand out from its competitors. It does not particularly matter whether the product really *is* different: what matters is whether or not customers *think* it is. For example, most soap and washing-up powders are quite similar except for their colouring and smell. Yet soap producers spend vast sums of money attempting to create brand images and make the products appear different so that they will appeal to particular kinds of consumers.

Brand imaging is successful because firms realize that consumers not only buy products, but also buy images associated with the ownership and use of those products. If consumers desire the lifestyle promoted by a product, they may believe that buying the product will give them the same lifestyle – even if only in a small way. For example, Bounty advertisements have shown young, attractive, and carefree people enjoying life on a tropical beach, while Volkswagen recently ran an advert showing typical VW drivers as being attractive and well-off. Some consumers will be influenced by this image, and may buy the product for the image as much as for the features of the product itself.

Promotions can also be used to create a better image for an organization – for example, one that is more caring towards the environment – or to make it more attractive to young people.

Evaluating a promotion (3)

The success of a promotion in influencing consumers' perceptions can be judged by asking the following questions:

– In what ways was it intended to influence consumers' perceptions of the product?

– What were consumers' views and perceptions of the product and/or organization *before* the promotion?

– What were customers' perceptions of the product/and or organization *after* the promotion?

– How successful was the promotion in achieving the desired change in perceptions?

– What could have been done better?

Portfolio Activity 9.4

PC: Identify and give examples of type of promotions used in marketing goods and services
Range: Types of promotions, Purpose
Skills: Read and respond to written materials

Slogans and catchphrases are used in a variety of promotions to send messages about products and organizations to consumers. What organizations or products use the following slogans in promotions? What messages do they convey about the product or organization? Try to think of at least 5 other slogans used in promotions.

- 'The listening bank'
- 'It's good to talk'
- 'Every little helps'
- 'Everything we do is driven by you'
- 'Helps you work, rest and play'
- 'It's you'
- 'Probably the best lager in the world'
- 'Pure genius'
- 'Your flexible friend'
- 'It is. Are you?'

Promotions are used to provide information

An important feature of promotion is to provide information about products, to let people know what is available, or give instructions.

In order to provide the information, the promotion must attract the attention of the consumer, and great skill is required in doing this. Images should be attractive and eye-catching, otherwise people may not bother to look at the promotion at all. Any written information must be big enough to read, accurate, and understandable.

Simple informative messages can often be promoted on television, especially if a strong image is needed. Examples include campaigns by the government to make children use the Green Cross Code and to make people aware of AIDS. Retail outlets will often promote information about opening times and dates for sales. Information may also be combined with persuasive messages in these promotions.

The effectiveness of promotions designed to inform can be judged by asking the following questions:

– Was all the information included?

– Was the information correct?

– Did people understand the information?

– Are people better informed now than before?

– How did consumers respond?

– How could the promotion be improved?

▼ *Some promotions are designed to provide information.*

Types of promotions

Organizations can choose from a variety of different ways to promote their goods and services. These include:

- Point of sale promotions

- Advertising

- Sponsorship

- Competitions

- Direct marketing

The choice of promotional method will depend on a number of factors, for example:

- **The size of the market:** Products and organizations that have small local markets will choose low-cost methods of local promotion, such as leafleting or adverts in local newspapers. Mass-produced items that are available nationally or even internationally can afford to be promoted through national TV, newspapers, and competitions offering fabulous prizes.

- **The type of product:** Highly specialized industrial products such as medical instruments, lasers, cranes, and weapons systems tend not to be promoted, except by publishing technical details in specialized journals and trade magazines. Consumer goods will be much more heavily promoted.

- **Cost:** Small businesses cannot afford to promote their products on national TV or newspapers, or run extravagant competitions. These methods will tend to be used by large organizations promoting mass-produced products to national markets.

Point of sale promotions

The **point of sale** is the shop or place where goods are actually sold. Promotions at the point of sale may include:

- Product display cabinets and stands
- Posters in shop windows and on walls
- In-store audio and video announcements, perhaps telling people about new products and special offers
- Free samples
- Food and drink tastings
- Illuminated signs and displays
- Working models
- Celebrity book and CD signings
- Cardboard cut-outs, for example of famous film stars or characters from cartoons and children's books

▼ *Some point of sale promotions*

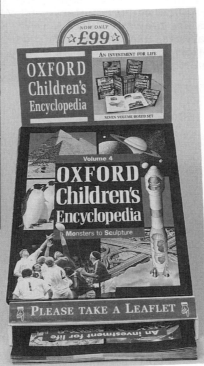

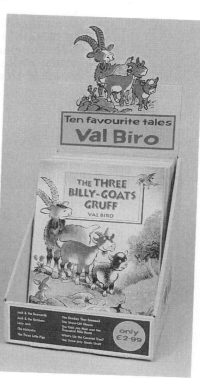

Retail outlets are even able to buy specially manufactured fragrances to release in different parts of the store. For example, perfumes can be sprayed around the cosmetics counter, the fragrance of coconut oils can be released near to suntan lotions to make people think of holidays, and the smell of freshly-baked bread can be wafted around food stores and in-store bakeries.

Point of sale promotions are designed to encourage people to buy when they are at the point of sale (or in the shop). They can be very effective. This is because the customer is in the shop with the product, and is likely to be carrying enough money either in cash or credit cards to be able to buy the product, if persuaded. Sales staff are also on hand to assist customers to choose products, and their role can be crucial. If they fail to provide accurate information, or are rude, or look scruffy, they may put the customer off making a purchase. Sales staff can also give out product leaflets and other promotional literature to passing customers.

Beware traps in store

Supermarkets are making life easier for parents by clearing sweets from checkout areas. They are bowing to pressure from mums and dads fed up with being pestered for crisps and chocolate bars by bored youngsters. A new survey by the 'Chuck The Sweets Off the Checkout' campaign shows that three-quarters of checkout counters in food stores are now sweet-free – but supermarkets use plenty of other promotion techniques in an attempt to make you buy.

For example, eye-catching displays at aisle ends can increase sales five fold. Essential items such as milk, tea, and cereals are spread around the store so you have to cover as much ground as possible. In an increasing number of stores more adult impulse buys such as magazines, video films, and cookery and slimming books are placed by checkouts. Stores consider everything that might lull you into spending more, from the placement of trolleys to the scents and sounds that waft through the store.

Daily Mirror 3.2.95

Portfolio Activity 9.5

PC: Identify and give examples of types of promotions used in marketing goods and services

Range: Types of promotions

Skills: Collect and record data, Use images

1. Visit the following types of business organization and investigate the use of point of sale promotions. Make a note of what you notice immediately you enter, as you walk through the building, and at the place you make a purchase.

- Bank
- Supermarket
- Department store
- Record shop
- Clothes shop
- Electrical goods superstore
- DIY superstore
- Leisure centre

2. Choose one organization you have visited and draw a map of the layout. Mark on it significant features such as aisles, counters, checkouts, etc, and indicate where you have noticed the point of sale promotions. These could be colour-coded. For example, blue dots could represent display stands, and red dots could be TVs playing promotional videos, and so on.

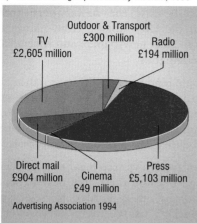
▼ *UK advertising expenditure by medium, 1993*

TV £2,605 million
Outdoor & Transport £300 million
Radio £194 million
Direct mail £904 million
Cinema £49 million
Press £5,103 million

Advertising Association 1994

Advertising

Advertising is a very powerful method of promotion. Organizations can choose from a variety of **advertising media** through which to promote their products and image. These include newspapers and magazines, TV, radio, the cinema, and posters. Adverts for products can also be placed on the packaging of other products, for example, on the back of matchboxes, on carrier bags and T-shirts, even on hot-air balloons.

Advertising is important because it can create a brand image for a product in the eyes of the consumer. For example, in the past Volvo always emphasized their image as a producer of safe family cars, targeting their advertising at people who might buy a family car, and who rate safety as an important feature. More recently they have found that their advertising actually encouraged people who prefer cars to have sporty features to choose other makes! Their latest advertising campaigns have therefore shown Volvo cars being used in dangerous situations by stuntmen. The purpose of this has been to use advertising to create a slightly different brand image involving excitement, danger, and speed.

Because advertising is so powerful, firms are willing to spend many billions of pounds each year producing and showing adverts to consumers. If successful, advertising can make a big difference to sales and profits.

It's good to spend a Bob or two on ads ...

IF YOUR phone bill is bigger than ever, here's a statistic that may help explain it.

British Telecom has spent a record £44.31 million on ads convincing us "It's Good To Talk".

The campaign puts the telecom giant at the top of the league of the country's biggest advertising spenders, according to a survey by the trade magazine Campaign. And the ads, starring Bob Hoskins, seem to be working a treat.

BT's profits have soared by almost £800 million to £2,756 million since the cockney actor began tiptoeing around living-rooms, urging us to pick up the dog-and-bone.

Its advertising budget is almost £34 million bigger than last year - putting it above McDonald's and Tesco in the big-spender stakes.

Daily Mirror 1.5.95

HOW THE PLUGGING PAID OFF

	1994 Ad spend	1993 Ad spend	Latest year Profit	Previous year Profit
BT	£44.31m	£10.66m	£2,756m	£1,972m
McDonald's*	£31.32m	£27.30m	£758m	£670m
Tesco(excl petrol)	£30.26m	£27.35m	£551m	£435m
Currys**	£27.15m	£19.86m		
Boots	£26.50m	£22.99m	£416m	£405m
Sainsbury	£25.88m	£24.74m	£738m	£733m
Comet	£24.11m	£23.99m		
Safeway(excl petrol)	£22.94m	£18.69m	£361m	£336m
B&Q	£21.12m	£22.32m	£83m	£82m
MFI	£20.81m	£20.22m	£88m	£15m
Woolworth	£20.62m	£19.81m	£51m	£75m
Texas Home Care	£19.12m	£24.47m	£8m	£8m
Franklin Mint Mail Order***	£18.75m	£12.46m		
Dixons	£18.07m	£14.77m	£165m loss	£16m loss
Sky TV	£17.73m	£13.00m	£93m	£76m loss
Peugeot 306****	£17.63m	£12.18m	£587m	£166m loss
Ford Fiesta	£16.49m	£5.55m	£3,291m	£1,988m
Peugeot 106	£16.00m	£12.11m		
Asda	£14.75m	£17.54m	£201m	£140m
Persil Power (Unilever)	£14.37m	£NA	●£2,383m	£1,927m

* US Company ** Currys is owned by Dixons whose figures included Curry's profits *** Private Company.
**** French Company. ● Profits are total of company.

▼ *Advertising to the advertisers*

If you thought the Government controlled consumer spending in the UK- THINK AGAIN

GOOD HOUSEKEEPING READERS CONTROL:-

£1 in every £8 of total household income
£1 in every £9 spent on cosmetics
£1 in every £10 spent on food
£1 in every £7 spent on holidays

HIGHEST CIRCULATION EVER

501,654

ABC Jan/June 1994

POWER BEYOND THE PAGE

THE NATIONAL MAGAZINE COMPANY LIMITED
National Magazine House, 72 Broadwick Street, London W1V 2BP. 071 439 5000
A Subsidiary of The Hearst Corporation Since 1910

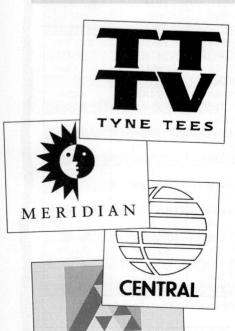

Newspapers and magazines

There are over 11,000 different newspapers and magazines available in the UK, ranging from national daily newspapers to free local newspapers and specialist magazines of limited circulation.

Different kinds of people tend to read different national newspapers, and so advertising can be targeted at different groups by finding out which papers they read. In 1994, 60% of all adults read a daily newspaper, and 38% of all males read either *The Sun* or *Daily Mirror*.

Most areas of the country receive free local newspapers paid for by advertising. Because these free newspapers are delivered to everyone, it is harder to select a particular target market using them. However, advertising in the local press is a lot cheaper than in the national papers.

Trade journals are magazines targeted at people working in specific trades or professions. There are also a wide variety of car buyers' guides, yachting, camera, video, and computing magazines published monthly and weekly.

Television

Television is an ideal means of advertising to reach mass markets using the benefits of movement and sound to promote a product.

There are an increasing number of commercial TV stations in the UK due to increasing sales of satellite and cable systems. Because their market is still relatively small, the cost of advertising on these channels tends to be much lower than on ITV and Channel 4, where a single showing of a 60-second peak-time advert could cost as much as £90,000 in 1994.

Different kinds of audience watch television at different times of the day. By choosing the time of day in which to advertise it is possible to target a particular group of consumers who might be interested in a particular product. For example, a toy manufacturer might choose to advertise on TV on Saturday mornings in the hope of reaching large audiences of young people. Different adverts can also be shown in different regions of the country.

Radio

There are many hundreds of local and national radio stations in the UK. Commercial stations are funded by sales revenues from advertising. Different kinds of radio station attract different kinds of listener (see 8.2). For example, Radio One tends to attract young people, while Radio Four attracts middle-aged and middle-income groups. Organizations can target their advertising by placing it on stations listened to by the kind of people most likely to buy their products.

▼ Posters can be an inexpensive way of grabbing the consumer's attention.

Local radio provides a relatively cheap and effective means of advertising for many medium and even smaller firms.

Cinema

In 1993 there were over 113 million cinema admissions in the UK – the highest number since 1978. Over 14 million people alone watched the film *Jurassic Park*. Because of the growth in cinema audiences, advertisers have begun to increase their use of cinema advertising and are designing adverts specially for cinema release. Adverts are also being included on video cassettes for rent or sale.

Posters

Large posters placed in highly visible sites can be a relatively cheap and effective means of grabbing people's attention as they pass by. Most major roads have billboards alongside them which can be used to show posters of pictures and slogans. Electronic billboards are also increasingly popular. These use changing neon displays to show different advertisements during the day.

Similarly, smaller posters can be placed on the side of buses and taxis, on railway stations, and in airports, where they can be seen by as many people as possible. Posters are also often placed on hoardings at sporting venues.

The main drawback of posters is that they cannot contain much information. Most people may only glance quickly at them as they walk or drive by.

▼ Choosing advertising media

Advertising media	Plus points	Minus points
National newspapers	Coverage is national Reader can refer back to advert Product information can be provided Many use colour Can be used for mail order replies	Use of colour limited Smaller adverts tend to get 'lost' among others Readers often ignore adverts
Regional /local newspapers	Adverts can be linked to local conditions Can be used for test marketing before national launch	Reproduction and layout can be poor Average cost per reader relatively high due to more limited circulation
Magazines	Can use colour Adverts can be linked with feature articles Adverts can be targeted in specialist magazines	Adverts must be submitted a long time before publication Competitors' products often advertised alongside
Radio	Can use sound and music Relatively cheap to produce Growing number of stations Audiences can be targeted	Non-visual Message usually short-lived Listeners may switch off or ignore adverts Reception may be poor
Television	Creative use of moving images, colour, and sound Can use visual endorsements by well known personalities Repeats reinforce message Growing number of channels	High production costs Peak time can be expensive Message short-lived Viewers may ignore or switch over during adverts
Cinema	Creative use of images, colour, and sound Adverts can be localized Adverts can be targeted at age groups for different films After decline during 1980s, audiences increasing again	Limited audiences compared to other media Audience restricted to mainly younger age groups Message may only be seen once due to infrequent visits to cinema
Posters	Good cheap visual stimulus Can be placed near to point of sale National campaigns possible	Only limited information possible Susceptible to vandalism and adverse weather

Portfolio Activity 9.6

PC: Explain the purpose of promotional materials
Range: Types of promotions, Purpose
Skills: Use images, Produce written material

Put your feet up in front of your television and watch some adverts.

1. Watch a sample of around 20 different adverts at different times of the day. Try to decide whether each advert :

● Is informative

● Is persuasive

● Makes meaningless statements

● Promotes a brand image

● Has a slogan or catchphrase

● Appears to suggest that buying the product will improve your quality of life

● Is sexist or racist in any way

Draw a table like the one started below. Mark each column with a tick if you think the heading applies to the advert you are watching:

2. Are any patterns evident from your completed table? Are most adverts on TV persuasive? Do most promote a brand image? etc.

3. Look through some newspapers and magazines. Select at least five adverts you like. For each one write down:

● What it is advertising

● Why it grabbed your attention

● What messages it contains

● What images it uses

● Which groups of consumers it is aimed at

Product advertised	Informative?	Persuasive?	Meaningless?	Brand image	Slogan	Quality of life	Sexist/racist
Washing powder		✔		✔		✔	✔

▼ *Sponsorship is an increasingly popular method of promotion.*

Sponsorship

Sponsorship by firms of high-profile sporting and cultural events, and of well known personalities, is becoming increasingly common. By paying to sponsor an event and have their name associated with it, firms hope that they will be able gain some of the positive image associated with the event, and also that people will see their name, logo, and advertising.

Lucozade was in the past seen as a drink to take when people were unwell, and it was heavily promoted with the slogan 'Lucozade aids recovery'. Today Lucozade has changed its image to being a lively and healthy drink for fit and competitive people. It has achieved this by heavy sponsorship of athletics events and by adverts featuring sporting personalities such as Daley Thompson and Linford Christie.

Drinks manufacturers are keen to sponsor sporting fixtures, because it helps them to project an image of fit people quenching their thirst after an event. Coca Cola has in the past sponsored the Olympics, and Carling Black Label has sponsored the English football Premier League.

Other firms such as sports clothing or equipment manufacturers may sponsor a 'personality' rather than an event, paying – say – a major tennis star or footballer to wear or use their products. In 1995, Wimbledon tennis champion Pete Sampras was sponsored by Nike. However, the choice of personality is important, because the wrong associations may put people off buying the product. For example, Pepsi Cola dropped its sponsorship of Michael Jackson after the singer was involved in allegations of drug addiction and child abuse.

Increasingly, business organizations are also paying to sponsor commercial TV programmes shown at peak viewing times. In return the organization is advertised before and after the programme, and during every commercial break. For example, can you think why the Midland Bank sponsored the comedy drama series *Moving*, about a firm of removal men? Or why the Commercial Union Insurance company sponsored *London's Burning*? It is also possible for firms to sponsor major films in order to get their products used in them.

The cost of sponsorship can be high, but the amount of publicity that firms receive as a result will often outstrip more expensive adverts on TV. Sports commentators may mention the name of the product or organization every time they discuss the event – for example, the Littlewood's Cup in football, the Nat West Trophy in cricket, and the Embassy Snooker finals.

In some cases sponsorship is the only promotional medium available to firms. For example, it is illegal for tobacco companies to advertise their products in the media, and so the only way they can persuade people to buy their products is to sponsor an event and hope that some of the glamour will rub off on them. Sponsorship is also used by small firms as a relatively cheap way of promoting their image to local people. For example, small firms can sponsor school fêtes, a bed in a local hospital, or a local charity. Zoos and animal sanctuaries have also been able to raise funds from sponsorship, by asking people and firms to sponsor their animals.

Portfolio Activity 9.7

PC: Identify and give examples of types of promotions used in marketing goods and services
Range: Types of promotions, Purpose
Skills: Use images, Produce written material

1. Try to find out the answers to the following questions:

- Who currently sponsors Liverpool football club?
- Who currently sponsors Manchester United football club?
- Who sponsored the last World Cup?
- Who will sponsor the next Olympics?
- Who sponsored the last UK tour by the Bon Jovi rock group?
- Who sponsored the last MTV video music awards?

2. Identify other examples of sponsorship locally, nationally, and internationally. Make a list of the organizations and products providing sponsorship, what or who they are sponsoring, and write down why you think they want to be associated with the event or person.

3. In groups, discuss and suggest organizations you think would find it useful to sponsor the following:

- Eric Cantona (footballer)
- Take That (pop group)
- Greenpeace (environmental pressure group)
- Breakfast television
- The Round the World Yacht race
- An opera or ballet production
- Your next school/college fête, sports day, or other event
- A TV quiz show that offers holidays as prizes
- The Natural History Museum in London

Write up a short summary of your discussions giving reasons for your choice of likely sponsors.

▼ *Lose some, lose some!*

Competitions

Another way of attracting consumers' interest in a product is to run a **competition**. Many competitions are linked to the purchase of a particular product. For example, you may have to collect three cereal packet tops to enter a competition advertised on the packet itself. In this way consumers are encouraged to buy more of the product.

However, running competitions for which no purchase is necessary can also be successful in attracting attention to products and generating sales. Competitions can appear as promotions in newspapers and magazines, on the radio or TV, or as leaflets handed out or posted through letterboxes. Charities will often use the sale of raffle tickets to raise money and awareness among the people who buy them.

The success of competitions in promoting products can vary considerably. The trick is not to make the competition so hard that consumers are put off, and to keep the rules simple so that everyone can understand them. Much also depends on the method used to promote the competition itself and the prize offered. The bigger the prize, the more people the competition will attract. The success of the National Lottery is based on the assumption that more people will buy tickets if there is a large first prize (even if there is only around a 14 million to 1 chance of winning it) than if there are more, smaller cash prizes which are easier to win.

▼ *Charity raffle tickets*

▼ *Camelot, the National Lottery organizers, expect to raise around £1 billion each year from the sale of instant tickets.*

Organizations that run competitions are legally required to publish the results, so that everyone who entered can see who the winner is. There must also be an accepted method of choosing an outright winner, for example, in the case of a tie-break.

Portfolio Activity 9.8

PC: Identify and give examples of types of promotions used in marketing goods and services

Range: Types of promotions

Skills: Collect and record data, Produce written material

1. Find five examples of competitions to cut out and save. For each competition write down:

- Where you found the competition, e.g. on a packet, in a newspaper, etc.

- The organization running it

- The products associated with it

- The prizes on offer

- What the competition involves

- The skills needed by the people who enter it

- Whether or not a purchase is necessary to enter

- Other conditions of entry, if any

- The main purpose of the competition

2. Investigate all the ways in which the National Lottery is promoted.

3. Suggest, in a short report, how you might devise and run a competition to raise funds for a new computer for your school/college. Your report should consider:

- The type of competition (e.g. raffle, lottery, quiz, treasure hunt, thinking up a slogan, etc.)

- The prizes you will offer and why

- How much you need to raise

- Conditions of entry

- How you will promote the competition

- How the winner(s) will be chosen

- How the winner(s) will be notified

Direct marketing

Promotion by **direct marketing** has grown rapidly in recent years. Methods of direct marketing include:

- **Home shopping** using the satellite TV channel QVC, where customers can see advertisements on TV and then telephone a number and order products with a credit card

- **Mail order advertisements** in newspapers and magazines, where consumers can cut out a coupon and order by posting it back to the manufacturer

- **Direct mail,** where manufacturers contact customers directly by post to advertise their products, and invite them to make a purchase by mail or telephone order

In the past, direct mail was often regarded as 'junk mail' because firms would send out identical letters to many thousands of homes. Today, firms build up a careful picture of consumer wants based on their past purchases and on the filling-in of product guarantee cards which ask a series of questions about tastes and buying habits. By storing this information on computer databases, firms can target mail at just those people likely to buy. Most word processors today have a mailmerge facility which enables a word processor to pick names and addresses off a database and then print out personalized letters with individual details. Modern computer technology has made this much easier, and even small firms can afford to send mailshots to many thousands of homes.

Hitting the target audience

Direct marketing's ever-closer targeting of individuals is one of the reasons why junk mail is less of a problem than it used to be: what might be junk to one person could be a welcome correspondence to another. The industry's improving reputation is also due to the fact that it appears to be sticking by and large to a system of self-regulation, says the Advertising Standards Authority. Rules which were introduced in 1992 require companies to make sure their information is up to date and consumers know why it is being collected.

Says the ASA: 'If a company intends to pass on information to anyone else or use it for a different purpose, consumers should be given an opportunity to say no. If a company decides to use information it already has for a different purpose, it must get permission first. Companies must comb their records for consumers who have stated that they do not want to receive mailings before sending them out. These rules also apply to press advertisements featuring response coupons.

Financial Times 15.9.94

Constraints on promotions

Because most firms are in business in order to make a profit, some may be tempted to mislead consumers in their promotions or make exaggerated claims about their products and those of competitors, in order to gain more sales. Because of this, the government has created laws to protect consumers, and organizations to enforce the law, such as local **Tradings Standards Offices**.

The advertising industry has its own watchdog, the **Advertising Standards Authority**, which attempts to encourage honesty in advertising and promotions. Some industries have also developed their own codes of practice for firms to follow. Examples include the **Federation of Master Builders** and **Association of British Travel Agents (ABTA)**. Consumers can appeal to these associations if they feel that a particular organization has broken the code of practice.

Legal constraints

The UK government has passed a number of laws designed to limit or constrain what firms can say or show to consumers in their promotions. The main laws are as follows:

- **Trade Descriptions Act 1968:** This is an important form of consumer protection, making it illegal to wrongly describe goods and services. The Act applies to spoken as well as written descriptions, and to descriptions implied in pictures. Under the Act, it is an offence to describe a sweater as 100% wool when it has only a 75% wool content, or to describe goods as being on sale at 'lower prices' if they have not been on sale at a higher price for at least 28 days previously. For example, if a hi-fi shop offered a stereo amplifier for sale at £90 in its January sales, claiming that they had been marked down from £150, when in fact they had been on sale a week earlier for £100 each, it would be committing an offence under the Act.

- **The Sale of Goods Act 1979:** This Act has three main parts:

  i Goods must be of 'merchantable quality'. This means goods must work properly, not be flawed in any way, and be of reasonable quality for the price charged. Defects are acceptable, however, if the consumer is made aware of them before buying – for example, if goods are advertised as 'seconds'.

  ii Goods must be fit for the purpose for which they were made, and this must be made known to the public by the seller. For example, if you asked a shop for a pair of trousers that could be machine-washed and would not have to be dry-cleaned, then the pair of trousers the shop sells you must be machine-washable.

  iii Goods must fit the description given of them. For example, if a box of matches is said to contain 250 matches, then it should not contain any less.

If any of these conditions are broken, the shopkeeper must refund the customer's money. The consumer could agree to take a replacement, but does not have to accept a credit note (see 12.3). Credit notes will allow the consumer to buy another good sometime in the future, up to the value of the one bought before, but only in the same shop. Notices saying 'no refunds' are illegal, and there is no legal obligation for the customer to produce a sales receipt. However, a consumer can be asked for proof of purchase, such as a cheque counterfoil or credit card copy (see 12.2).

Under the **Sale of Goods and Services Act 1982**, the law was extended to cover goods supplied as part of a service, on hire or in part exchange. For example, parts supplied in repairing a video recorder, a hire car, or a new vacuum cleaner part exchanged for an old one, all have to be of merchantable quality and fit for the purpose. Standards of service are also covered by the Act, which protects consumers from poor workmanship, long delays, and hidden costs.

● **Consumer Protection Act 1987:** This Act is mainly concerned with prices charged by businesses. Under the Act it is an offence to:

- mislead consumers about the true price they will pay for a good or service, by excluding any hidden extras, interest charges, and/or VAT

- make false statements about price reductions, for example, suggesting that the price of a product is 50% off the recommended price when it is not, or suggesting that the price is now £25 compared to a previous selling price of £50, when the good has only ever been sold at £30.

The law also makes it a criminal offence to sell goods that are unsafe in any way, or to possess unsafe goods which are intended for sale.

The above laws apply to England and Wales only. However, very similar laws apply in Scotland and Northern Ireland, although the names of their Acts and dates may vary.

Portfolio Activity 9.9

PC: Describe constraints on the content of promotional materials
Range: Constraints
Skills: Read and respond to written material

In groups, discuss which of the above consumer protection laws the following activities break:

● You buy a new dress which is described as 'machine washable' on the label. You wash it and it shrinks. The shop refuses to change it or give you a refund, arguing you washed it incorrectly.

● An advert on TV claims a glue can bond together two halves of a car so that it is roadworthy.

● A poster in the window of a DIY store advertises a foldaway garden patio set, showing a garden umbrella, table, and six chairs at the bargain price of £60. However, after you have bought the patio set and opened the box at home, you discover it does not include an umbrella and only has four chairs.

● A local hi-fi shop advertises a sale in which everything is '20% off'. Once inside you find that it is 20% off the manufacturer's recommended prices, and you know that few shops ever charge the full recommended price.

● A travel agent has advertised a bargain two-week holiday to Spain for £180. You phone the agent and book the holiday for two people using a credit card. A booking confirmation arrives in the post two days later with a credit card voucher for £440 which includes airport taxes, flight supplements, and an under-occupancy supplement, none of which was advertised or mentioned over the phone.

● The window of a shop selling pine furniture shows a poster stating 'everything half price'. In the shop you find out it applies to cash purchases only, and few prices appear very cheap anyway.

● You have bought a toy car for your young brother in a local toyshop. You asked the shopkeeper if it was safe for a child under five years old. He replied it was. After an hour playing with the car, your younger brother almost swallowed a small wheel that fell off the toy. The shopkeeper refuses to accept liability, arguing 'Of course it's not safe if the child pulls the wheels off'.

Standards and codes of practice

Standards in advertising and other promotions in the UK tend to be self-regulating. This means that organizations in the advertising industry will make sure that the adverts they make do not mislead or offend in any way, simply because any that do are unlikely to be accepted by newspapers, magazines, radios, TV stations, or on billboards.

There are two main industry watchdogs for promotions in the UK:

- The Advertising Standards Authority (ASA)
- Trading Standards Offices

The Advertising Standards Authority (ASA)

The ASA was set up in 1962 to monitor the standard of advertisements in the UK and to investigate complaints by members of the public. The ASA covers all advertisements in newspapers, magazines, posters, direct marketing, sales promotions, cinema, video cassettes, and teletext.

The ASA safeguards the consumer by ensuring that the rules contained in the British Code of Advertising Practice are followed by any organization that prepares and publishes advertisements. The code is voluntary, but most organizations follow it because the media will refuse to carry any advertisement which the ASA says breaks the code.

If an advertisement is found to be misleading or offensive, the ASA will act to have it changed or withdrawn. Failure to comply with an ASA ruling may lead to adverse publicity in the ASA's monthly report of judgements.

Before the last election, the *Today* newspaper used a poster saying 'Would Britain be better off with a hung Parliament?' The cartoon on the poster showed the leaders of the three main political parties with nooses around their necks. The advert was banned by the ASA as failing to meet the standards of the British Code of Advertising Practice. Similarly, a recent advert for clothes by Benetton showed a man dying of Aids which many people found offensive. The ASA required that the advertisements be dropped.

IF AN ADVERT IS WRONG, WHO PUTS IT RIGHT?

We do.
The Advertising Standards Authority ensures advertisements meet with the strict Code of Advertising Practice. So if you question an advertiser, they have to answer to us.

To find out more about the ASA, please write to Advertising Standards Authority, Dept. X, Brook House, Torrington Place, London WC1E 7HN.

ASA

This space is donated in the interests of high standards in advertisements

THE ESSENCE OF GOOD ADVERTISING

The British Code of Advertising Practice states all advertisements should be:

* Legal, decent, honest, and truthful
* Prepared with a sense of responsibility to the consumer and to society
* In line with the principles of fair competition generally accepted in business

No advertiser can make a claim about their product that cannot be proved.

The work of the ASA is financed by a levy of 0.1% on UK advertising expenditures. One criticism, therefore, of the ASA is that it is funded by the very people it is attempting to police, namely, the advertising industry.

The ASA does not regulate adverts on TV and the radio. The **Independent Television Commission (ITC)** polices advertisements appearing on television and cable. It has its own Code of Advertising Standards and Practice. Certain products and services, including cigarettes, spirits, private investigation agencies, and gambling, may not be advertised on TV. There are also strict rules about advertising aimed at children, and the use of child actors or models in adverts. Advertising on radio is controlled by the **Radio Authority**.

Trading Standards Offices

A **trading standards department** exists in all local authorities (see 1.4), except in Northern Ireland, where trading standards are the responsibility of the Department for Economic Development.

Local authority trading standards officers try to ensure that firms do not break consumer protection laws. They are also able to advise business owners on how to comply with the law, and consumers on their legal rights.

Trading standards officers make checks on business premises and will investigate complaints made by members of the public about particular businesses. For example, in a local food store officers may check:

- The accuracy of weighing and measuring equipment
- The accuracy of labels on products, including sell-by dates
- The standard of foods and other items on sale
- Licences to sell alcohol and offer credit
- Price lists
- Claims about price discounts and special offers
- Loading of delivery vans and lorries

Consumers can contact their local trading standards officer for advice. The officers usually recommend that an attempt is first made to settle disputes with the trader concerned. If this fails, trading standards officers will give advice on what to do next, and in some cases will even help people take businesses to court.

Portfolio Activity 9.10

PC: Describe constraints on the content of promotional materials
Range: Constraints
Skills: Read and respond to written material

The Advertising Standards Authority investigates around 8,000 complaints each year. Each month it publishes a case report giving details of complaints and any action taken by the ASA. Below is an example of one of the complaints they reported:

1. Suggest why the promotion might be described as misleading. Do you agree? Give your reasons.

2. Find out more about the Advertising Standards Authority – how it is able to help consumers like the one in the case below, and about any other complaints they have investigated. The ASA is located at Brook House, 2-16 Torrington Place, London, WC1E 7HN.

3. Collect information from your local tradings standards department on the help it can offer local businesses and consumers, and how it tries to enforce consumer protection laws.

4. Using a desktop publishing program, produce an attractive and easy-to-understand promotional leaflet for consumers about how trading standards departments and the Advertising Standards Authority can help them.

Dolphin Showers Ltd
t/a Dolphin Bathrooms
Bromwich Road
Worcester
Hereford & Worcester WR2 4BD

Agency:
BCMB Ltd

Press

Complaint from:
West Midlands

Complaint: Objection to a national press advertisement for a sale which, in a boxed-off section under the heading "The Dolphin Luxury Pack"", listed four bathroom products giving their normal prices. The total of these prices, £1550, had a line through it followed by "All this for only £250". A footnote in small type stated "Offers apply to minimum order of a fully fitted bathroom suite, comprising bath or shower cabinet plus wash basin and WC". The complainant considered the overall impression of the advertisement to be misleading. (BCSPP 4.5; 4.8; 5.4; 5.8)

Adjudication: Complaint upheld.
The advertisers stated that the items listed in the offer panel were clearly annotated as being additional to the main discount being advertised. The Authority considered that the footnote explaining the basis of the promotion was virtually illegible and noted that greater emphasis would be given to the restrictions of offers in future.

Section **9.3**

Planning and designing promotional material

Now that you know about promotions used by businesses to market their goods and services, it is a good idea to try to produce some promotional materials of your own – either to launch a new good or service, or to publicize an event. Your performance in this element will be judged in part by the promotional materials you produce. Details of this assignment are given at the end of this chapter.

It is not as easy as you might think to produce promotional materials which are effective in providing information to consumers, changing their perceptions, and persuading them to buy. Many organizations employ highly specialized marketing agencies to plan, design, produce, run, and evaluate their promotional campaigns. You will have to do all these things yourself. If you were in business and you did not get your promotions right, you could end up wasting a lot of money.

Planning your promotions

Careful planning of a promotional campaign is very important. Your plan should give details of:

● **Purpose:** What does the promotion aim to achieve – for example, raise consumer awareness of a new product? Create sales?

● **Types of promotion:** How are these aims likely to be achieved? What types of promotions will be used?

● **People:** Who will carry out the various tasks in the promotion? What skills will they need?

- **Resources:** What materials, equipment, and costs are required for each part of the promotion? How will these be obtained?
- **Timescales:** When will each part of the promotion be done?
- **Evaluation:** How will the success of the promotion be judged?

Purpose

In Section 9.1 we learned that there were four main reasons for promotions:

- To communicate a message to a target audience
- To create sales
- To influence customers' perceptions
- To provide information

In your plan you will need to specify exactly what the purposes of your promotional materials are to be. For example, if they are intended to create sales, then how many, and over what time period? For example, if you decide to promote a school/college disco, then state how many people your promotional materials are designed to attract, in advance ticket sales and on the night. Perhaps attendance at past discos has been low because students thought the light show and sound systems were not very good. How will your promotional materials try to change their views?

Promotional materials

In your plan, you will need to decide what type of promotional materials to use. You have three main choices:

- Advertisements (including leaflets)
- Sponsorship
- Competitions

The type and style of promotion you choose will depend on the purpose of your promotion. For example, a brochure about dental services is likely to be quite formal. On the other hand, a leaflet advertising a disco is likely to be far more imaginative, with eye-catching text, pictures, and colours. Your choice of promotional material will also be constrained by how much you afford.

'AIDA'

To be effective in achieving their purpose, it is important that your promotional materials:

- Attract the **ATTENTION** of the consumer by using colourful graphics, thought-provoking pictures, or eye-catching headlines
- Grab the **INTEREST** of consumers and make them want to find out more about the product. A good promotion will not only catch consumers' interest but provide further detail.

- Encourage the consumer to want or **DESIRE** the good or service
- Explain the **ACTION** needed to obtain the product – for example, where it is sold, where to send a mail order coupon, etc.

These steps in promotion, from attracting attention to creating the desire and action to buy a product, are known as **AIDA**.

Writing an advert: some useful hints

Skilled copywriting is crucial when promoting a good or service. The success or failure of an advertisement will depend on the words and phrases used.

* Advertisements must be clear, accurate and to the point – otherwise people are unlikely to read, watch or listen to them.

* Use bold headlines that grab the attention immediately. Look at newspapers and magazines to find examples.

* Be imaginative in your descriptions, and try and help consumers to picture the benefits of your product or service. For example, use words like 'economical' to describe the petrol consumption of a new car or the amount of electricity used by a washing machine or 'delicious' and 'mouthwatering' to describe a new food product, etc.

* Think up catchy rhymes and slogans consumers will remember, e.g. 'Don't book it. Thomas Cook it', 'Beanz Meanz Heinz', 'My mate Marmite', etc.

* Try to appeal to peoples' emotions and desires. For example, consider how charities appeal for donations by arousing pity and compassion, or how an advertisement for car alarms can appeal to people's need for security. Similarly, advertisements for suntan creams often show attractive tanned young men and women in exotic locations, because this is what many people want to be like.

* Try out your ideas on a small group of people from the intended audience for your advertisement before producing the final copy.

Advertisements

Advertisements usually combine written words and figures with pictures in an attractive and eye-catching way. Sound and moving images can be used in TV advertisements to great effect. The medium you choose will depend on the type of product you want to promote; whether the message is persuasive or informative, or both; the number of people you want the advert to reach; and the cost involved. In real life, making and showing a TV advert can cost many thousands of pounds. However, if you have access to a video camera, you could pretend to make a TV advert for a commercial television station.

When you prepare your own advertisement, you should always think about it from the consumer's point of view. Will it catch their eye and hold their interest? How much information do they need? Writing an advert for a newspaper or a script for a TV or radio advert is called **copywriting**. This is a very skilled task.

Large and many medium-sized firms will usually employ advertising agencies to create their advertising campaigns. Within an agency, a copywriter will write the text of the advert and a graphic artist will draw any illustrations and advise on the use of character fonts, colours, and layout. Finally, designers will design the whole advert before it goes into print or production as a TV commercial.

Sponsorship

Sponsorship is growing in popularity (see 9.1). You may find that many local businesses or even private individuals may be willing to sponsor your event because of the publicity it brings them. Another big advantage of getting sponsors is that money they provide can be used to develop better-quality promotional materials, such as leaflets, posters, and newspaper and TV adverts.

MANAGER
THE FRIENDLY BANK
23-25 BENEVOLENT STREET
CREDITSHIRE

Dear Sir
I am writing to ask you if
you would be willing to
sponsor the planting of a
tree in

Corporate sponsors

Corporate sponsors are businesses that are willing to give money in order to have their name and products associated with an event. This in turn can raise the profile of your event.

To obtain sponsorship for a local event, you should start by making a list of possible sponsors who may wish to be associated with it. For example, imagine that you wanted to plant some new trees in the school or college grounds. Top of your list of sponsors might be local DIY and garden centres, who might be willing to supply trees, topsoil, and garden tools instead of money. In return, you could offer to mark each tree with a plaque showing the name of the sponsor, and/or free adverts in your school or college magazine for a year. Other possible sponsors might include businesses owned by parents or school governors, suppliers of school equipment, and businesses you are familiar with through work experience. You might also get some free publicity from the local press or a local radio or cable TV station by inviting them along to see the managing director of your biggest corporate sponsor planting the first tree at a specially organized ceremony.

After you have made your list, you will need to write suitable personalized business letters to each potential sponsor (see 14.2). This should contain details on what you want them to contribute and how you will publicize their help. Be prepared for disappointments: firms receive many requests for sponsorship each year and cannot provide money, goods, or services for all of them.

Private sponsors

You may have collected individual sponsors in the past for charity events such as sponsored walks. You could collect individual sponsors for your event in much the same way. For example, individuals could be asked to pledge a fixed amount of money, or so many pounds or pence per mile of a sponsored walk, in order to raise money to buy new sports equipment for your school. It saves a great deal of time and effort if you can collect the money from your sponsors 'up front', rather than having to go round again to collect their money after the event.

Competitions

Competitions can take many forms: a quiz, raffle, lottery, or test of skill or endurance, e.g. a treasure hunt, or a public speaking or hamburger-eating contest. All will need to be carefully planned and designed.

For example, if people have to pay to enter the competition, you will need to estimate how many people will be willing to enter at different prices, how much you are likely to raise, and how much you can afford to spend on prizes to leave an acceptable profit. This can be difficult, because the bigger the prize, the more entrants you are likely to attract. It may be possible to combine a competition with sponsorship, by asking local businesses to contribute prizes. For example, a local off-licence may offer bottles of wine to give away as prizes; your local cinema may give away two free tickets to a film; a restaurant may be willing to provide a free meal, and so on. If you organize a special ceremony to present prizes, it may also attract local media attention, providing more free publicity for yourself and your sponsors.

Designing a competition – some useful hints

- Make sure that there will be a clear winner (or winners, if first, second, third, and runner-up prizes are offered). Consider what would happen if you had ten winners sharing a bottle of champagne! If a quiz ends in a draw, have some questions ready as tie-breakers to find an overall winner.

- Make the competition easy to judge. Judging a painting competition is difficult as judges' decisions may be questioned. Holding a raffle is more clear-cut.

- Do not make the competition too hard for people. Competitions which involve more luck than skill often attract more entrants. If

you hold a quiz, stick to relatively simple general knowledge questions.

- Check whether you need to obtain a licence from your local council to charge people for raffle tickets or entrance fees. Find out if any other legal restrictions apply.

- Advertisements and entry forms to promote your competition should be both persuasive and informative. People need to know exactly what they could win, how they can enter, and how winners will be selected and notified.

People

Promotions are usually produced by a team of people with different skills. Few firms could afford to employ a team of experts in advertising on a full-time basis. Instead, they tend to buy in advertising expertise from specialist advertising agencies. The role of an advertising agency is to create, develop, plan, and carry out promotional campaigns for their clients. To do this, they need the following skills:

- The ability to work in teams
- Creativity, and the ability to come up with attractive ideas and plans to promote products
- Presentation skills, to sell their ideas to clients
- Budgeting and financial skills, to keep accounts and control costs
- Writing skills, to produce scripts
- Graphic design and visualization skills to brief artists, designers, and photographers
- Technical skills, to use computer DTP, paint, drawing, and animation programs, and operate video cameras, sound equipment, etc.
- Negotiating skills, to negotiate with clients, sponsors, and to buy advertising space at the lowest cost
- Management skills, to see projects through to the finish

You will need to demonstrate similar skills to produce your own promotional materials.

Resources

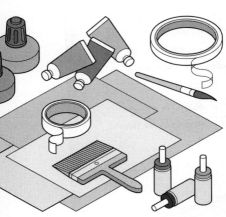

A wide range of materials can be used to produce promotional materials. For example:

- Paints – watercolours, acrylics, oils
- Inks in various colours
- Paper and card of different sizes, colours, and thickness
- Tracing paper
- Pens and pencils of different colours and thicknesses
- Masking tape
- Glue and adhesive tape

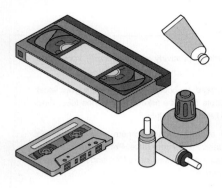

- Letraset transfers
- Acetate transparencies for overhead projectors
- Audiotapes
- Videotapes
- Photographic film

The materials you choose will depend on your skills as a graphic designer and artist, the type of promotional material you plan to use, and cost. It will also depend on access to different equipment. For example, to record a TV commercial you will at least need a video camera and videotape.

Graphic design — some useful tips

Good graphic design skills are very important in advertising. The success or failure of an advertisement will depend on the quality of layout, images, and presentation. Consider the advertisements below, designed to remind and persuade people to register to vote in local council elections. Which one has the most impact?

register to vote **X** now

by returning your ...cil

REGISTER TO VOTE NOW
by returning your registration form to the council
 X

- Vary the size, shape, and position of your headline until you agree on one that looks best. A headline does not always have to be across the top of a page.

- Vary the size and positioning of photographs and other illustrative materials in the advertisement. In many cases it looks better to position a photo, illustration, or logo off-centre and with one corner or edge dropping off the side of the advert.

- Use colours to evoke different moods and attract attention. For example, red is often associated with danger, black can be threatening and dramatic, green is used for many environmentally friendly products, while browns are often used on organic foods and raw cotton products. Bright colours can suggest fun and sunny days.

- BUT be careful not to choose colours that clash. For example, consider what a bright yellow headline on a bright blue background would look like!

- Do not try to be too fancy, and avoid clutter. For example, do not use too many different colours, typefaces, or elaborate borders.

- Experiment with different designs to see what they look like, and ask other people for their opinions.

Equipment

Graphic designers and artists work in studios. In a large studio you are likely to find some or all of the following equipment:

- Tools, such as knives and scissors

- Paintbrushes and airbrush equipment for painting

- Drawing boards and artists' easels

- High-quality photocopiers

- Film cameras, with different lenses and filters, to shoot photographs

- Video cameras to produce videos and a video recorder to play them

- Editing machines to edit video footage and audiotapes

- Tape recorders to record sound

- Computer hardware and software to produce graphics. (Animation and video editing are also possible using sophisticated computers. Most of the opening sequences and special effects in TV programmes and films are now produced using powerful image-editing and animation programs.)

- Laser printers for high-quality computer print-outs

- A flatbed document scanner and/or handheld scanner to convert photographs and other images into computer images which can then be used in desktop publishing and other graphics packages

Clearly, not all the above equipment will be available to you to produce your own promotional materials. However, you or your parents may own a number of the above items and machines, and your school or college may also have some. If you plan to use equipment belonging to other people – for example, a video camera to shoot your own TV commercial, or even an office photocopier – make sure you ask permission first.

If you decide to produce posters, leaflets, and/or newspaper adverts, a photocopier will be especially useful to you (see 14.3). Photocopiers can enlarge and reduce printed copy and can produce a large number of copies cheaply for distribution. If your school or college cannot provide one, there are specialist copy and design shops in most high streets who will print promotional materials relatively cheaply for you.

What is desktop publishing?

Modern office equipment and computing power mean that even the smallest business is able to generate professional-looking promotional materials. **Desktop publishing (DTP)** software allows the design of high-quality leaflets and posters at low cost. DTP can combine text with high-quality graphics, cartoons, and pictures. Most DTP programs also contain a wide variety of different fonts and special effects. Colour printers are now available for a few hundred pounds, so firms can produce high-quality graphics to improve their promotional materials.

Most DTP programs allow their user to:

- Design a variety of complex page layouts, using columns, boxes, diagrams, and pictures
- Use a wide variety of fonts, or typefaces, of different sizes and in different colours
- Import pre-drawn 'clip art' illustrations and computerized photographic images to include in documents
- Choose where to position text and artwork
- Enlarge, shrink, trim, squash, or elongate graphics
- Add borders and shading
- Store each design on disk

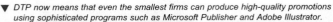
▼ *DTP now means that even the smallest firms can produce high-quality promotions using sophisticated programs such as Microsoft Publisher and Adobe Illustrator.*

Costs

Good managers will plan the costs of their promotions and carefully compare actual spending with the budget. Usually a budget will be drawn up for each aspect of the promotion, and expenditure planned week by week or month by month (see 13.1). Managers can control promotional costs by regularly comparing actual spending to the budgeted figure. If costs are lower than expected, they may be able to increase promotional effort. If costs are higher than expected, future promotions may have to be cut.

In exactly the same way, you will need to plan and manage the costs of your promotions. Some money for materials, such as paints and paper, may be made available from your tutor. However, if you need more – for example, if you want to have some leaflets printed professionally – you may need to think about raising some sponsorship money.

Details of the costs of your promotional campaign will need to be set out clearly in your plan. The costs should include those paid for by your school or college, parents, or guardians, and those you have paid for yourself. It would also be useful to attach a cost estimate to any materials and equipment provided free of charge. This is because in business you are unlikely to get these things free of charge and will have to buy or hire them yourself. The time you spend working on your promotions should also be costed at a realistic hourly rate.

Timescales

It is important to set realistic target dates for the completion of significant tasks in your plan for promotions. Five key stages can be identified in any promotional campaign:

- Information-gathering
- Planning
- Design
- Preparation and production
- Running the promotion
- Evaluation

If a date has already been agreed for the event or product launch you intend to promote, then it is useful to work backwards from this point in time. In this way you can see exactly when you need to start gathering information and planning the promotions. For example, if a school disco is planned for the first week in September, and you have calculated you need to spend a week on each key stage, then you must start gathering information in the last week of July at the latest.

Apart from the promotional period itself, the preparation and production stage will usually take the longest. You will need to gather the materials and equipment you need and then set about creating the posters, leaflets, magazine adverts, video films, or audiotapes you have designed.

The timescale for the release of promotional materials is critical. If you intend to grab people's attention and gain their interest, it is important not to do this too far ahead of your product launch or event, or people will lose interest. On the other hand, if the promotion starts too close to the date of the launch or event, there may not be enough time to create interest among consumers.

Evaluation

It is important to evaluate the success or failure of any promotional campaign (see 9.1). **Evaluation** takes place after the promotional campaign has finished and any post-event publicity has been arranged – for example, local newspaper coverage of a school fête or tree-planting ceremony, etc. Evaluation is critical if you want to learn how to improve future promotions.

The effectiveness of your promotional campaign will need to be judged against the aims and purposes set out in your promotional plan. Questions you should ask yourself include:

- Did the promotion communicate the intended message to your target audience?

- Did it create sales and, if so, how many?

- Did it influence customer perceptions in the intended way?

- Did it provide the information you wanted to communicate?

You can find the answers to some of these questions by asking members of your target audience and looking at sales revenues – for example, numbers of tickets sold for the school disco.

You should also consider whether you planned the promotion properly. For example, were all possible opportunities for publicity explored? How did the actual cost of the promotional campaign compare with your budget?

Key words

In your own words, write down explanations and definitions of the following key words and terms from this chapter:

Marketing	Promotions	Corporate sponsors	Competitions
Informative messages	Persuasive messages	Direct marketing	Consumer protection
Brand name	Trademark Act	Trade Descriptions Act	Sale of Goods Act
Brand image	Point of sale	Consumer Protection Act	Trading Standards Office
Advertisements	Sponsorship	Advertising Standards Authority	Planning promotions
		AIDA	Desktop publishing

You must demonstrate that you are able to:

1. Identify and give examples of types of promotions used in marketing goods and services

2. Describe constraints on the content of promotional materials

3. Plan to produce promotional materials to promote particular goods or services

4. Explain the purpose of the planned promotional materials

5. Design and produce promotional materials and use them to promote goods or services

6. Evaluate how successful the promotional materials were in achieving their stated purpose

1 A firm might sponsor a sporting event in order to:

A encourage competitors

B reduce prices

C promote their product

D reduce profit by spending more on advertising

2 A firm might use competitions in order to promote goods to:

A cut profits

B raise sales

C improve product quality

D lower sales

3 How could a new local bookshop best attract customers?

A advertise in a booksellers' trade magazine

B advertise in local papers

C rely on word of mouth

D raise prices

Questions 4-6 share the following answer options:

A Consumer Protection Act

B Trade Descriptions Act

C Sale of Goods and Services Act

D Trademark Act

Which of the above laws do the following promotions break?

4 An advertisement which claims a new skin cream will make people look 20 years younger

5 A leaflet that contains details about a competition to win a car. It shows a picture of a new Mercedes sports car but in reality the first prize is a Ford Fiesta.

6 A shop sign that reads '50% off all prices'. It does not say it applies to cash sales only.

7 The role of trading standards officers is to:

A ensure that advertisers keep to a voluntary code of advertising practice

B investigate consumer complaints about firms' behaviour

C prevent firms from being harmed by sharp practices by consumers

D ensure that firms charge reasonable prices

8 An advertisement must be 'legal, decent, honest, and truthful' in order to meet the requirements of:

A the trading standards department

B the local council

C the Advertising Standards Authority

D other firms who might be offended

Questions 9-11 share the following answer options:

A to communicate a message to an audience

B to create sales

C to provide information

D to influence customer perceptions

Which of the above do you think is the main purpose of the following promotional messages?

9 'A business that cares about the environment'

10 'Trains to Cambridge now run every half hour.'

11 'Special offer. Buy two, get one free.'

Questions 12-15 share the following answer options:

A Channel 4 television

B a local radio station

C a local newspaper

D posters

Which of the above ways to advertise would you recommend to the following firms?

12 A manufacturer of mass-produced biscuits

13 A small one-person garden-clearing business

14 A UK film distributor publicizing a new film release

Questions 15-17 share the following answer options:

A counting the number of people attending

B surveying people's awareness of a new product

C comparing the actual costs of the promotions to the budgeted costs

D comparing revenues before and after the promotional campaign

Which of the above ways would you use to evaluate the success of a promotional campaign to:

15 Create sales

16 Communicate a message to an audience

17 Provide information about the time and place of an event

18 a. Give three examples of point of sale promotions.

b. Suggest two purposes of point of sale promotions.

c. Explain two ways you could attempt to judge how effective point of sale promotions have been.

19 a. What is sponsorship? Give examples.

b. Suggest two advantages to a business from sponsoring a football team.

c. Suggest three ways a business could advertise a new mass-produced product. Explain the reasons for your recommendations.

d. Suggest three useful tips a business could follow when designing a leaflet.

assessment assignment

Assessment Assignment

The following assignment covers all the evidence requirements needed to fulfil all the performance criteria in element 3.2. In addition, it covers the following range points and core skills:

Range: Types of promotions
Constraints
Plan
Promotional materials
Purpose
Evaluate

Skills: **Communication**
Take part in discussions
Use images
Produce written material
Application of number
Collect and record data
Information technology
Process information
Present information

Tasks

1. **a** Look at the ways in which different goods and services are promoted in the media. Find three promotions for products that you especially like, or which you think are very effective. Investigate how these promotions are done, what message is being communicated, and how.

   b Using your research, use a word processor to prepare a report on three types of promotions. At least one of these should be a sponsorship scheme, and another an advertisement. Your report should:

   – Describe the product(s) being promoted in each case

   – Describe the content and messages of the promotion

   – Explain how consumer protection legislation, such as the Consumer Protection Act and the Advertising Standards Authority, might constrain how these promotions were carried out

2. The following task can be carried out as a class, in small groups, or on your own.

   a Think of something that you would like to promote. For example:

   ● An event designed to raise money for your school, college, or a charity

   ● A good or service you are supplying in a Young Enterprise or mini-enterprise project

   ● An event or product of a local business you are familiar with

   b Consider the types of promotions you will use to promote the product or event you have chosen. Who is your target audience and what messages do you want to give these consumers?

   c Prepare a detailed plan for your promotional campaign. This should cover:

   ● Details of the product or event you will promote

   ● The purpose(s) of your promotional materials

   ● The types of promotional materials you will use and why

   ● The people and/or skills you will need to produce your chosen promotional materials

   ● The materials and equipment you will use; how much they will cost, and how you will obtain them

   ● Deadlines and estimates of the amount of time you will need to complete the key tasks

   ● How you will evaluate your promotions, in terms of how well they achieve their purposes and the response of your target audience

d Prepare the promotional materials you have planned and designed for your chosen product or event. These might be an advertisement or an outline of a sponsorship scheme or competition. Your promotional materials could be in the form of a poster, leaflet, newspaper advertisement, video, or audiotape. You may be able to produce some of these promotions on a computer. However, do not forget there are certain legal constraints and standards you must be aware of when designing your promotions.

e Finally launch the promotional campaign for your chosen product or event.

3. After the promotional campaign has ended, evaluate its success in the ways you have suggested in your plan. These could include:

- Preparing a customer questionnaire
- Keeping a record of ticket sales for events
- Calculating sales revenues and profit
- Calculating the actual costs of the promotions and comparing them to budget

  Prepare a short summary of your findings using a word processor.

4. When you have completed all the above tasks satisfactorily, remember to file your work in a folder to be part of your portfolio. You should give your folder of work an appropriate name and file reference number.

chapter 10

chapter *10* *Providing Customer Service*

An organization will usually have two main groups of customers. **External customers** are the individuals and business customers who buy or use the goods and services provided by the organization. **Internal customers** are members of staff who rely on other members of staff to help them do their jobs properly.

A **paying customer** is a person or firm that buys a good or service. A **non-paying customer** is a person who does not pay directly for the provision of a good or service, for example, an NHS hospital patient, or a pensioner with a free bus pass.

All customers have **needs** which they expect business organizations to fulfil. These may include the need to make a purchase, obtain information about a product, obtain a refund or exchange a product, or to make a complaint. Successful firms are those which identify who their customers are and what their needs are quickly and accurately.

Some customers have **special needs**, such as people who are blind, deaf, physically or mentally handicapped, old, or with children.

Customers need to be able to rely on the personal honesty and integrity of the organizations and staff they deal with. That is, they expect organizations to maintain **ethical standards**.

Business organizations often have their own arrangements for dealing with **customer complaints**. Where these work well, customers are more likely to make repeat purchases. Where they do not work well, the customer may seek a solution through the law.

In order to meet the needs of internal and external customers, employees must communicate with the public and each other, face-to-face, on the telephone, and in writing. Typical written **communications with customer**s involve providing information on **products, prices, guarantees, statements of account,** and **safety procedures.** Whichever method of communication is chosen, it must meet customers' needs and be within the law.

A wide range of government **legislation** exists to protect customers when dealing with businesses. The main Acts are the **Trade Descriptions Act, Sale of Goods Act, Consumer Protection Act,** and **Health and Safety at Work Ac**t.

The Health and Safety at Work Act gives customers a legal right to compensation for any injury or financial loss caused by the sale of faulty goods, poor workmanship, or negligence by an organization.

Section **10.1**

Customer needs

A successful business is one that satisfies the wants of customers better than its rivals (see 1.1). Organizations that find out what their customers want and then provide those goods and services for them have a **customer focus**. A business that provides goods and services that customers do not want will fail.

Increasingly, businesses are becoming 'consumer led'. That is, they continually respond to the changing needs and wants of existing and potential customers. But before a firm can identify exactly what customers want, it needs to know who its customers are.

Every organization has two kinds of customer:

- **External customers**
- **Internal customers**

External customers

When you buy a hamburger from McDonalds or use the services provided by a Jobcentre you are an **external customer**. Similarly, when McDonalds buys meat and other products from its suppliers, it acts as an external customer of those organizations. Individuals and businesses who buy or use the goods and services of another organization are external customers of that organization. When they buy goods and services, as in the case of most private sector businesses, external customers are **paying customers**. Paying external customers are of clear importance to any organization that sells goods and services in order to make a profit (see 8.5).

Non-paying customers are those who do not pay directly for the use of a good or service provided by an organization. This will include people being treated in National Health Service hospitals, students attending state schools, pensioners using free bus passes, etc. In fact, the customers of most public sector organizations are non-paying, because many government services are provided free at the point of use (see 1.4). Some private sector organizations can encounter non-paying customers when payment is made by a third party – for example, when a customer of a garage has car repairs carried out which are paid for by another person's car insurance company.

Internal customers

Anyone who has been at work or on work experience knows that most people employed in an organization do not actually deal directly with external customers. Instead, most workers help each other in a firm, because they will tend to specialize in a narrow range of tasks (see 4.1). They may provide information for others, order materials or equipment for them, keep records of accounts, pay wages and salaries to them, maintain computers and equipment, provide secretarial and filing services, recruit staff, etc. In doing this work for each other, individual workers in an organization are customers for each others' services.

Increasingly, organizations are encouraging their employees to view each other as **internal customers**. Each employee has an obligation to provide a good level of service to other employees, who rely on them to do their own job to the best of their ability. For example, when a computer operator finds that his computer is not working, instead of being viewed as a nuisance by the computer maintenance department, that worker is seen as a valued customer, whose machine must be fixed as quickly as possible in order to keep standards of customer care as high as possible. However, achieving this new attitude takes a great deal of training and commitment on the part of staff at all levels in a business organization.

▼ Serving an external customer

▼ Serving an internal customer

Portfolio Activity 10.1

PC: Identify an organization's customers and its customer needs

Range: Customer needs

Skills: Read and respond to written material, Produce written material

Customer Service, who cares?

Once upon a time, in my granny's day, the customer was king (or queen) when she went shopping. Mr Adams the grocer knew her by name, he took enormous care to ensure that she got what she wanted and was happy to chat with her about life in general. She would never have thought of Mr Adams as an expert in customer service, and more than likely the idea of an expert in customer service had not been invented by that time. But the bottom line was that it was good customer care that kept her trotting down there every week with never a thought that the plums might be just as ripe, but cheaper across the road.

Somewhere in the 1970s this approach got lost in marketing and the desire for bigger businesses. When sales started to fall, price was the thing everyone immediately looked at, and the general feeling was that, if you cut your prices enough and then shouted loud enough, people would buy. The disadvantage of this is that it does not encourage customers to be loyal to your firm, and once prices are lower elsewhere, they will go there without a thought for you. But the good news is that attitudes have turned again towards customer service and this, added to new technology, is proving to be a very powerful force.

Depending on who you speak to, it costs four, five, or six times as much to attract a new customer as it does to keep an existing one. Customer care and customer service are where the smart money is going with a vengeance. One firm placing an important emphasis on customer service is communications company AT&T. Jean Wentzel, Customer Care Manager, says: 'We have identified precisely what customers want and have taken time to organize and supply exactly that. Customers will be able to contact us at one point of contact 24 hours a day, and the member of staff talking to that customer will be responsible for that customer's request from beginning to end. Customers will not need to ring different numbers to report faults, query their bills, or obtain information, and we will train our staff across this broad range of skills.'

Terry Wells, Customer Service Director at Sainsbury's says that 'Sainsbury's has been re-structured to ensure that everybody is focused on the customer, no matter what their actual job is. We have reorganized ourselves to recognize that people have internal customers too and they have to be viewed as such and treated with the same care. The benefits of this approach can be seen by comparing the situation four years ago when most new ideas would have been generated from Head Office and the stores would be instructed to carry them out. What happens now is that many good ideas are generated from action teams at individual stores, and these are often implemented both locally and nationally.'

London Evening Standard 11.7.95

1. What do you think is meant by 'customer service'?

2. Why does the article suggest that smaller firms in the past might have been better able to provide good customer care than some larger firms now?

3. Undertake a quick survey among people older than you. Find out their views on customer service in general. Do they think it has improved over time, stayed the same, or got worse? Find out the reasons for their views.

4. Why might it be better for firms to focus on keeping existing customers happy, rather than simply attracting new customers all the time?

5. Who does Sainsbury's say are its customers?

6. What are the key changes introduced in customer service by AT&T and Sainsbury? Why have these changes been introduced? How might they be better than previous arrangements?

Customer needs

Customers will contact a business organization for a variety of reasons. Whether they make contact in writing, on the telephone, or in person, customers will need one or more of the following from a business organization:

1. To obtain information

2. To make a purchase

3. To obtain a refund or exchange

4. To complain

In addition, there are those customers who may have special needs. For example, disabled people, people with sight or hearing difficulties, people with small children, and many more. All will need, and expect, to receive fair, honest, and efficient treatment.

Meeting the needs of customers in business is called **customer service.** Organizations that fail to meet the needs of their customers will lose them to those organizations that do. Staff training can help employees identify their customers and their needs, and to be more able to respond to those needs.

We will now look at customer needs in more detail.

1. The need for information

First impressions often last. In business, creating a poor first impression is likely to lose customers. A customer who contacts a business for the first time and is kept waiting and treated badly is unlikely to forget the experience. How sales staff greet people and deal with their enquiries is, therefore, of vital importance. In all cases, enquiries should be dealt with politely and quickly. This is true both for internal and external enquiries.

Usually the first reason for contact by a customer is to obtain information about the organization and the goods or services it provides. If the organization you work for is a small one, you may be able to answer all their enquiries. However, in much larger organizations you may have to pass on enquiries to other employees who specialize in the particular areas concerned. For example, suppose that you work in the accounts department of a large toy manufacturer that sells toys to large retail chains. You can help customers with queries about their accounts and methods of payment, but you are unlikely to be able to take orders or agree delivery dates. However, you should be able to tell the customer who to talk to instead, and provide them with a name, office address, and phone number.

What customers need to know
Customers may contact an organization to find out information on a variety of different matters:

- The name of a member of staff to contact
- Details about goods and services provided by the organization
- Latest prices
- Product features, including technical details
- How to place an order
- Delivery dates
- Discounts available
- Accepted methods of payment
- Credit facilities
- Product guarantees
- After-sales care, including refunds and repairs
- Product leaflets, brochures, and other sales literature available
- Company policy on giving refunds and making exchanges
- How to register a complaint
- Where to go for more information or advice

It is useful for an employee to know a little about all the different things customers are likely to ask about an organization and its range of products. Many firms run training courses for new staff to introduce them to all the areas of their business. This means they are prepared to deal with many of the more general enquiries from customers.

Even if an employee cannot answer an enquiry, s/he must still offer the customer help. This can be done by taking a note of their name, contact address, or phone number, and passing them on to another member of staff. An employee should never say they cannot help a customer, unless of course the customer has contacted the wrong organization in the first place.

It is also important to keep customers informed about any developments which may affect their enquiry. For example, you should always let the customer know when the item they want or have ordered is ready for collection, or when delivery can be made.

In many cases, customers who make general enquiries are satisfied simply to receive leaflets and brochures that provide them with basic facts about the organization and their products.

▼ *Answering enquiries*

✗ *wrong*

✓ *right*

2. The need to make a purchase

Most business organizations rely on external customers buying their goods and services in order to stay in operation and earn a profit. The same is true even of non-profit-making organizations such as charities and National Health Service hospitals. If a charity fails to attract donations, or if a hospital fails to attract patients sent to them by local doctors, then they face the risk of closing down.

Customers can make purchases by visiting an organization in person or by placing an order over the telephone or in writing (see 12.3). Individual customers make most of their purchases by visiting shops. Business customers are more likely to place orders for the products they want. In some cases they may even be visited by sales representatives from suppliers, who will take their orders.

Before making their purchase many customers will want some advice on product features and performance. It is, therefore, important that staff involved in sales know about the products they are selling. If staff in an organization are unable to provide advice, the customer may be put off making the purchase and take their custom elsewhere.

Some items require more **product knowledge** than others. For example, the most a customer may want to know about vegetables sold in a grocer's shop or supermarket is 'Are they fresh?' or 'How can I cook them?' However, a customer deciding between alternative video recorders may want to ask a number of technical questions about the quality of the picture and sound. For example, can it be used for video editing? How many channels can it store? How long can the timer be set for?

Technical experts with very specialized and detailed knowledge will be needed to explain about many industrial products such as weapon systems, medical instruments and drugs, and production machinery.

It is equally important that staff in service industries know about the services they provide to customers. For example, a person selling insurance needs to know about all the different the types of insurance

▼ *Lack of product knowledge can put off customers. But don't try to be too technical!*

AND THIS SIR IS THE OOGIMAFLIP OVERRIDE BUTTON ON THE THINGYMMBOB TO ALLOW THE WHATCHUMMACALLIT TO OPERATE IN QUARK MODE.

available, what they do and do not cover, premiums payable, etc. Similarly, a hairdresser could be asked to advise on styles, types of shampoos to use, hair colour, and perms.

Customers may also want advice and information on other matters relating to their purchase – for example, can the product be delivered? Is it guaranteed? What are the accepted methods of payment? What credit terms are available? The decision whether or not to buy will be based in part on these additional factors. For example, a shop that only accepts cash or cheques will not attract customers who want to pay by credit card. Similarly, a firm that does not provide a home delivery service for bulky items will lose customers to firms that do.

Portfolio Activity 10.2

PC: Identify an organization's customers and its customer needs
Range: Customer needs
Skills: Take part in discussions, Produce written material

In groups, discuss and list all the different things sales staff in the following organizations may need to know about in order to answer customer enquiries and provide advice:

- A shop selling mobile phones
- A DIY store
- A supermarket
- A bank
- A school
- A garden centre

---

3. The need for refunds or exchanges

All businesses should have an agreed policy on what staff should do if a customer wants to exchange goods they have purchased or obtain a refund. Such a policy is an important part of good customer service. If a customer feels that a firm has treated them unfairly by refusing to exchange goods or give them a refund on a faulty item, this can damage future sales and the long-term reputation of the business.

Whatever the refund or exchange policy, it must be in line with consumer laws such as the Trade Descriptions Act and Sale of Goods Act, which are designed to protect the customer (see 9.2). Customers who return faulty or sub-standard goods have a legal right to a refund: they do not have to accept an alternative product, credit note, or gift vouchers (even though shop staff sometimes try to persuade customers to do so).

Many large high street stores, including BHS and Mothercare, will exchange goods if the purchaser returns them, but will only give a refund if the customer has a receipt (see 12.3). Comet Warehouses will only exchange goods if they are returned within 14 days of purchase. Most retailers of computer software and computer games will not exchange any goods unless there is a genuine fault. This is because the customer may have made a copy of the computer software or infected it with a computer virus.

▼ *Many retail organizations set aside a small area staffed by experienced employees to deal with customers who want to return goods.*

A number of organizations have policies which offer consumers more than their legal minimum entitlement. For example, firms are not required by law to exchange goods simply because customers have changed their mind about what they want, but some firms may be willing to exchange goods in this situation, as long as they are still in their original packaging. They may even decide to do so if the customer does not have a receipt. These kinds of 'no quibble' exchange and refund policies mean that customers become more confident about buying goods, because they know they can take them back if necessary.

4. The need to complain

Even in the best-run organizations, customers will sometimes feel that they have been treated badly or unfairly. A complaint may be directed at a particular member of staff, a product that is faulty or sub-standard, or at the procedures used by an organization.

A good business will always listen to customer complaints and take them seriously. Firms can learn a great deal about how to improve their business by listening to customers who have a genuine grievance. Even if a customer is unhappy now, they are likely to be more satisfied in the long run if the firm has a well understood and clear policy of listening to customer complaints and taking corrective action.

Most large organizations have clear guidelines for staff to follow when dealing with, and monitoring, complaints. Consider the procedures used to deal with the following complaints.

Mr Smith telephones his telephone company to complain about being overcharged on his quarterly bill.

Telephone company records details of the customer and complaint in a paper or computer file.

Telephone company writes to Mr Smith the next day to acknowledge his complaint and to assure him that it will be investigated.

Telephone company investigates complaint. It finds that Mr Smith has been overcharged due to a computer error.

Telephone company writes to Mr Smith to apologize for the mistake and for any inconvenience it may have caused. A new bill for the correct amount is issued.

Telephone company contacts Mr Smith to ask him if he is satisfied with his new bill or if any further action is necessary.

Mrs Jones takes back the hairdryer she bought last week because it keeps overheating. She complains to the sales assistant who served her that the product is faulty.

The sales assistant apologizes and directs Mrs Jones to the Customer Help Desk.

A member of staff at the Customer Help Desk examines the hairdryer and apologizes for the inconvenience caused by the sale of the faulty item.

Mrs Jones says she would like a replacement.

The Customer Help Desk provides a new hairdryer. They test the replacement and check that Mrs Jones is satisfied.

The member of staff who dealt with Mrs Jones records details of the complaint and the action taken.

How to cope with unhappy customers: some golden rules

- Show concern for the customer's feelings – be sympathetic and listen

- Note down the important details

- Do not make excuses or try to cover up

- Never lose your temper – it will only infuriate the customer even more

- Always inform the customer clearly about how the complaint will be dealt with, how long it will take, and who should be contacted next

- Always show your customers you care

- If a customer is abusive or threatening, withdraw and seek assistance from senior staff or even the police

Portfolio Activity 10.3

PC: Identify and describe customer service in an organization, Describe procedures in one business organization for dealing with customer complaints

Range: Customer Service

Skills: Read and respond to written material, Collect and record data, Produce written material

1. Some firms like to sell things to consumers and then forget all about them after they have bought the product. Why might this strategy be damaging in the long run?

2. Why is a customer careline a good thing? Use examples from the article below.

3. How can setting up a customer careline be good for business? Explain your answer.

4. **a** Collect evidence on customer carelines from products and organizations you use. From the evidence you collect, do you think there are enough carelines?

b Choose one product or organization that does not offer a customer careline. Write a formal letter to the head office to suggest they introduce one and explain why it is in the interests of their business to do so.

5. Try to find out the procedures used for dealing with customer complaints in the following organizations:

- A bank
- A supermarket
- A large clothes store
- A car showroom
- A record shop
- A hospital
- Your school or college

Write up your findings in a short summary report.

Show your customers you care

What happens when a damaging rumour about your product goes around? Van den bergs, the margarine company discovered the answer when a false story about one of their margarines appeared on TV. Concerned customers had an immediate way of checking the story, by phoning a customer service telephone number which had for some time been a standard feature on Flora margarine packs. The telephone number was seen as an important factor in calming down customers' fears about the product. Telephone numbers on product packs, or at the point where services are delivered, are still quite rare in the UK. By contrast a recent L&R group survey found that 83% of branded goods carry a telephone number in the US, where carelines have been operating for some years. In France the figure is 30%, in Germany 15% but in the UK just 8%.

The benefits of a careline do not just become obvious in a crisis, or when dissatisfied customers need

to let off steam, says R Leiderman of L&R group. He sees direct telephone contact with customers as a valuable marketing tool, building customer loyalty and boosting consumer confidence.

Burger King displays its customer careline number on posters in its restaurants, and on takeaway bags and receipts. Comments from consumers have led to the introduction of a non-meat burger, and trials in the sales of sweatshirts and baseball caps. Before Burger King's careline was introduced, customer complaints were handled by letter in a 'very time-consuming, slow, and ineffective manner,' says Pauline Gallagher, the company's UK Customer Care Manager. Complaints were not noted down and customers' ideas for improvements were lost. 'Our customers were talking, giving us valuable information – but we were not listening,' she said. Now all information from calls is keyed into a computer and carefully studied.

Financial Times 13.1.94

Burger King's careline has led to innovations such as a breakfast menu.

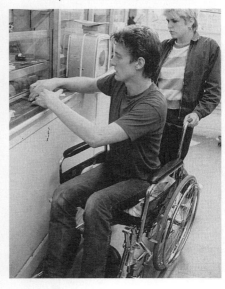
▼ *Organizations that do not provide for people with special needs will lose their custom.*

5. Customer with special needs

Some customers may have special needs which require particular attention by an organization. These include people who are:

- Blind or partially sighted
- Deaf
- Physically handicapped
- Mentally handicapped
- Elderly
- Foreign visitors
- With young children

There will also be people who need help in an emergency, for example, if they faint, are robbed, or taken ill. In these cases, assistance is required quickly. Staff may need to administer First Aid themselves or contact other staff members who can help. They will also need to be aware of procedures to evacuate customers from buildings during a fire or bomb scare.

Today, many organizations are keen to look after people with special needs. An organization that does not offer services for people with special needs will lose their custom to organizations that do. For example, disabled people can only shop where there is good access and facilities for wheelchairs. Even a single small step outside a shop can prevent disabled people from entering. It is just as easy in most cases to provide a wheelchair ramp as it is to provide a step. These customers may also need help to open doors, reach shelves, and carrying shopping.

Blind customers need to be able to take their guide dogs into shops with them. Because they will be unable to see the objects they want to buy, they will rely on staff with good product knowledge to provide clear descriptions. Some blind and partially sighted people may need staff to escort them around business premises, rather than simply giving them directions.

The mentally handicapped and foreign visitors may have difficulty expressing their needs and making themselves understood. Staff need to be patient and listen carefully and provide the help they need. Deaf people who can lipread will also need staff to speak slowly and clearly to them.

Elderly people are often confused by new technology and products, and take longer to make up their mind what to buy. Staff should never get impatient, and should be prepared to spend more time explaining product details, methods of payment, arrangements for delivery, and other features. Elderly people may also have difficulty with steps and doors, and may need help getting around a store and carrying their purchases.

Even families with young children have special needs and are more likely to visit stores where children are clearly welcomed and catered for. For example, IKEA stores have a supervised playroom and a cartoon cinema to entertain young children while their parents shop for furniture. This is good for parents, but it is also good business for IKEA.

Customers with special needs require more time, care, and attention than other customers. It is important to them that staff who give their time to help them do so willingly and treat them as individuals, rather than focusing on their particular disability or need.

Ethical standards

Business ethics are the values or standards of staff who work in an organization and which govern the way they deal with customers. Ethical standards can sometimes conflict with business targets. Some organizations may even deliberately mislead their customers in order to boost sales.

For example, in the early 1990s it was revealed that a large number of people had been misled by financial advisers who persuaded them to open pension schemes by exaggerating how much their pension contributions would be worth in the future. In the past, most financial advisers made their money from commission on sales of pensions, mortgages, and insurance. By misleading people about how much they would receive when they retired, financial advisers were able to sell more pension schemes and earn more commission. For this reason, some large pension and insurance companies no longer pay their staff on a commission basis to remove the temptation for them to behave in an unethical way.

Customers also have a right to **confidentiality** about their personal, financial, and medical details. Staff in organizations that have access to these details, such as banks, insurance companies, hospitals, schools, and many more, must be careful not to reveal details about customers to others. Written details on customers – for example, information on loan or credit card application forms – should be stored in files clearly marked 'confidential' (see 14.5).

Customers are unlikely to use an organization that behaves in an unethical way. A business that has a good reputation will attract more new customers and repeat sales. Therefore, it is in everybody's interests for firms to adopt ethical standards for their work. Customers need to be able to rely on the personal honesty and integrity of the organizations and the staff they deal with.

Portfolio Activity 10.4

PC: Identify an organization's customers and its customer needs, Identify and describe customer service in an organization

Range: Customer needs, Customer service

Skills: Produce written material, Collect and record data

1. Make a list of your main needs as a customer of each of the following organizations.:

● A fast food restaurant (e.g. Burger King or Pizza Hut)

● A hospital

● A railway station and train service

● Your school or college

● A leisure centre

● A holiday booking company

2. Choose one organization from the list and investigate how well staff are able to meet your needs as a customer. For example, visit a hamburger restaurant to buy a meal. Note your impressions of how quickly you were served, staff knowledge about products and prices, their friendliness, whether the staff and premises appeared clean and tidy, etc.

Write up your notes in a short report using a word processor.

Section **10.2** **Customer service**

PC: Identify and describe customer service in an organization

Range: Customer service

Skills: Produce written material, Collect and record data

1. What strikes you as unusual about the approach to customer care taken by Michael Pritchard?

2. Why does Mr Pritchard suggest that his approach is necessary to be able to compete with the big stores? What do they offer to attract customers?

3. How can firms find out about the needs of their customers? Undertake a survey of customer opinions on the levels of customer care provided by your school or college. Present the results of your findings to your course tutor.

Keeping the customer happy

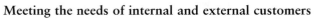

Among the features of the 'winning company' identified by management expert Tom Peters are a willingness to flatter its customers, an awareness of the importance of good customer service, and being able to respond to what the customer wants.

Customer service can start with the obvious. Michael Pritchard, owner and Managing Director of Spar Foodliner, a supermarket in South Wales, puts a great deal of effort into reducing the waiting time at his checkouts. Pritchard claims an average waiting time of 2.5 to 3 minutes and a maximum of five minutes, compared with the longer delays of his rivals. Staff are switched from refilling shelves to the checkouts when queues start to build up. Pritchard says he puts an emphasis on customer service because his is a small supermarket in competition with much larger stores owned by the big chains. Pritchard also runs a bus service to bring in customers who have no cars. The store is designed to allow wheelchair access, and the supermarket staff will make up orders

for disabled customers and accompany them around the aisles if necessary. Some other local stores positively discourage the handicapped, says Pritchard.

John Maddison, owner of a garden centre in Chester le Street, County Durham, says he insisted on an 'eyes up' policy in his business. Staff weeding beds or sweeping the floor were required to look up and greet customers. But ensuring that your staff make customers feel welcome is only the outward sign of an approach that must be grounded in a well thought out policy on customer care. This should start with research, or at least observation of what customers want. Maddison also practised 'management by drinking cups of coffee'. Selected customers would be offered a voucher guaranteeing a free cup of coffee in the garden centre's coffee bar. Maddison would then chat to them while they relaxed to find out about their needs and how well the garden centre met them.

Financial Times 19.10.93

Meeting the needs of internal and external customers

Most organizations have both internal and external customers (see 10.1). It is important that a firm identifies who its customer are, and their needs for help, information, advice, and assistance. Only then can it provide those services that will keep its customers happy. Internal customers need to be kept happy because these are the employees of the organization. Their commitment to the organization and their effort in achieving business targets will be lower if they are unhappy. External customers who buy products or use the services of an organization are the reason why the organization operates. If external customers are unhappy the organization will lose their custom and may be forced to close down.

We will now examine how one organization identifies its customers and provides services to meet their needs.

Case study: IKEA

IKEA is a Swedish company that provides furniture and many other items for the home, including lamps, rugs, and kitchen utensils.

IKEA has become popular because it offers good quality furniture at low prices. Many items of furniture are flat-packed, so that customers can take them away in their cars and assemble them at home.

The first IKEA store opened in the UK in 1987. There are now six large IKEA stores in the UK and plans are underway to open more.

External customers

IKEA's external customers are the private individuals and businesses that buy its products. Some may spend only a few pounds on small items such as lamps, picture frames, plates, cutlery, and plants. Others may spend many thousands of pounds on home and business furniture. All are equally important to IKEA. They want all their external customers to keep coming back to buy more – and to tell their friends and associates to shop at IKEA as well.

IKEA spends a large amount of money promoting the organization, its products, and its service features, producing free product catalogues and providing in-store facilities to attract new and repeat custom. In addition, prices published in the firm's catalogue remain fixed for 12 months, and purchases can be exchanged or refunded easily. Staff are trained in dealing with customers and providing detailed product information.

IKEA is particularly keen on its image as an organization that cares for the environment. Its free catalogues are printed on chlorine-free paper and contain 10-20% recycled fibres. Waste is recycled. Wood to produce furniture is only purchased from managed forests, and all staff take part in environmental training.

Because IKEA is keen to attract young families who are furnishing their new homes, their stores provide supervised playrooms and cartoon cinemas for young children so their parents can shop without hindrance.

Internal customers

Good customer service is not just for external customers. Many firms are adopting a system of management called **Total Quality Management (TQM)**, part of which involves all employees treating each other as valued customers.

It is estimated that up to one-third of the work done in UK firms is spent in correcting mistakes and poor quality work. The aim of TQM is to ensure that all work is done correctly and to the right standard at the first attempt, thereby saving a great deal of time and money. Achieving TQM calls for teamwork: staff at all levels need to be involved in problem-solving and decision-making to ensure that improvements are constantly made to products and procedures (see 4.4).

At IKEA, employees in each store rely on each other for help. For example, a sales assistant may need help from colleagues when his or her section is particularly busy. Similarly, warehouse staff rely on sales assistants to provide accurate printed details of the goods customers have ordered at help desks, so that they can be prepared for collection from the store.

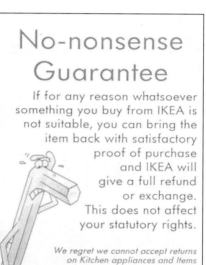

No-nonsense Guarantee

If for any reason whatsoever something you buy from IKEA is not suitable, you can bring the item back with satisfactory proof of purchase and IKEA will give a full refund or exchange. This does not affect your statutory rights.

We regret we cannot accept returns on Kitchen appliances and Items made to your special requirements such as Kitchen worktops and special delivery sofas.

The head office of IKEA in the UK is located in Wembley Park in London. UK stores are internal customers for head office functions such as:

- Advertising
- Printing price tags, leaflets, and brochures
- Restocking individual stores with items for sale
- Help with staff recruitment and information on employment law
- Planning special events, such as Christmas promotions and winter sales
- Store layout and design
- Installing and maintaining computer equipment
- Running staff training programmes – and much more...

Providing help or information for individuals
Thousands of people visit or contact IKEA stores each day. Some will simply want to browse and may not buy anything. Others may want advice on product ranges, prices, delivery services, methods of payment, etc. IKEA know that providing information, help, and advice whenever customers need it is vital to attract new customers and encourage repeat sales from existing ones.

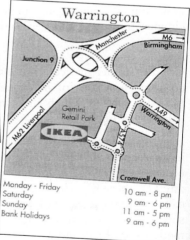

Welcome to IKEA.

IKEA STORE STAFF ARE MORE THAN HAPPY TO ADVISE YOU AND ANSWER YOUR QUESTIONS.
Sometimes it's hard to find just what you're looking for. Or perhaps you aren't even sure of exactly what you need?

In that case, don't hesitate to ask our store staff. They're there to assist you when you need help.

IKEA store staff are trained in their particular field to be able to offer you the very best advice.

And they are not happy until you are happy too with what you buy from IKEA.

Warrington

Monday - Friday   10 am - 8 pm
Saturday   9 am - 6 pm
Sunday   11 am - 5 pm
Bank Holidays   9 am - 6 pm

HOME INTERIOR CONSULTANTS AT IKEA
If you're about to furnish a whole room, or even your entire home, the Home Interior Service at IKEA will give you all the help and advice you need – free of charge. Just phone your nearest IKEA store to make an appointment with one of our Home Interior Consultants. You'll find the phone numbers on page 322.

One of our consultants will meet you at the store entrance and accompany you through the store, helping you select just the right kind of items from the IKEA range.

Special children's portions are always available in the IKEA Restaurant. They'll find our food delicious, you'll find our prices irresistable.

Only £1.95

To advertise their products and prices, IKEA produce thousands of free colour catalogues each year. Many are delivered to people's homes. Others are sent through the post on request, or can simply be picked up when visiting an IKEA store.

The product catalogue also contains maps to show people how to get to IKEA stores around the country. It tells readers about special events planned for the year ahead, such as the winter sale, as well as a number of related services available when people make their purchase, such as guarantees, methods of payment, the company policy on refunds, the children's playrooms, in-store restaurants, etc.

Staff employed by IKEA are trained in their particular field to be able to offer help and advice to customers. Help desks are located throughout the store. At each one, staff can use a computer terminal to find out from a database if items customers want are in stock at that particular store, or at other stores, or, if not, when they are expected in stock. Wide lifts and aisles in IKEA stores also make them accessible to people in wheelchairs.

Customers are also able to call a 24-hour telephone service to find out if the products they want are in stock. In many IKEA stores, they can arrange appointments to consult specialists in home interior design, as well as using a free kitchen design service.

Price tags on items on display in stores contain useful information for the customer, including sizes, materials, how to look after the product, as well as price. Each tag also gives the product name, and the aisle and section in the warehouse where the customer can find the item, which is flat-packed and ready to take home.

The IKEA Card,
more than just
an easier way to pay.

IKEA Card holders get even more out of IKEA. Not only can an IKEA Card be used to buy anything up to an agreed credit limit from IKEA stores throughout the UK; IKEA Card holders also enjoy a wide range of exclusive benefits and privileges too.

■ EXCLUSIVE OFFERS ■ ADVANCE CATALOGUE DETAILS ■ NO ANNUAL FEE
■ IKEA NEWS AND VIEWS NEWSLETTER
■ UP TO 55 DAYS INTEREST FREE CREDIT ON ALL PURCHASES

Simply complete the application form in this catalogue and return it to us freepost. Alternatively, hand in your completed application form at your local IKEA store. Subject to approval, you'll receive your card shortly afterwards, along with your Cardholders Welcome Pack. Full written quotation available on request. APR 26.8% variable, minimum monthly payments of either 5% or £5. (The interest rate is correct at time of going to press.)

Providing help or information for business organizations

Business customers are able to use the same services as individual customers at IKEA. To attract the business customer, IKEA offers a range of affordable office furniture and fixtures and fittings, such as lighting, filing boxes, and cabinets, all of which can be found in the IKEA catalogue. Staff in IKEA are also able to help design office layouts.

Small business owners and individuals may want to spread the cost of their purchases at IKEA, especially if they want to buy a lot of furniture and other items at once. To help them do this, IKEA have introduced their own credit card for customers to use in the store (see 12.2). Cardholders can pay off the amount they spend on their IKEA cards little by little each month, although interest charges are also payable. Businesses can also open special business accounts with IKEA. They are able to order items from stock and are given trade credit of up to 30 days to pay for them (see 12.2). They will receive regular statements of what they have bought and how much they owe.

IKEA is just one example of an organization providing good customer service to meet the needs of its external and internal customers. Most other respected organizations provide similar levels of customer service.

For example, staff employed in a bank will provide help and advice to both individual and business customers on their range of services, including opening accounts, issuing cheque books, changing foreign currency, selling shares in companies, providing mortgages for buying property, loans and overdraft facilities, and cashpoint machines. Different bank employees will be trained to specialize in providing different services.

In turn, bank staff will rely on each other for help. Head office staff will also provide services to individual banks such as staff recruitment and training, paying wages, bank refurbishments, computer installation and maintenance, specialist advice on how to deal with external customers with difficult enquiries, and the publishing of a range of leaflets and helpful brochures which are freely available to external customers.

Portfolio Activity 10.6

PC: Identify and describe customer service in an organization
Range: Customer service
Skills: Produce written material, Collect and record data

We have looked at how IKEA provides customer service to its customers. Now it is your turn to investigate customer service in an organization of your choice. For example, you may choose your school or college or work experience placement, or simply a store or chain where you regularly shop.

For your chosen organization try to identify:

- Its main external customer groups

- The needs of external customers
- Internal customers
- The needs of internal customers
- How it provides information and help to meet the needs – including any special needs – of external and internal customers
- Its policy on providing exchanges and refunds
- How it deals with customer complaints

Write up your findings in a short report, including a brief description of your chosen organization. Use a word processor to demonstrate core skills in information technology.

Section **10.3** **Business communications**

Good communication between an organization and its internal and external customers is vitally important to business success.

To an external customer, a member of staff *is* the organization they are dealing with. Because first impressions last, it is very important that the first communication between an organization and an external customer leaves a good impression.

Poor communications between members of staff within an organization will show up in lower output, sales and profits, and higher costs. Communications between staff need to be clear and understandable. Also, a member of staff should never talk down or be abusive to another employee: this will cause resentment and lead to poor staff relations.

Types of communications with customers

Business employees communicate with each other and with external customers using a wide variety of methods, for example:

● **Spoken communications** – face-to-face, or over the telephone

● **Written communications** – letters, memos, etc.

● **Customer/product information** – statements of account, price lists and catalogues, guarantees, safety notices, etc.

McDonalds staff told not to mince their words

McDonalds, the fast food chain, has found that its service with a smile is proving too much to chew on for the British stiff upper lip. The company which brought American 'Have a nice day' culture to nearly every high street in Britain has told its restaurant managers across the country to serve customers the way they like best. A senior spokesperson for McDonalds said a survey of staff and customers found that people had become unhappy with the 'robotic' service in McDonalds' restaurants.

She told *Personnel Management Plus* magazine: 'A lot of customers felt we were too machine-like. Customers wanted more warmth over the counter. It was only through our research that we discovered they thought we were a bit brash and a bit arrogant.' Staff were also uncomfortable and complained about having to say 'Thank you, please call again' to every customer.

McDonalds is now training its 500 managers to be more flexible to local needs. If thought fit by managers, McDonalds customers may be greeted in future by phrases such as 'Eh-up, chuck,' or 'Get that down your neck,' or 'Here's your Big Mac, whack'.

Financial Times 17.10.94

Oral (or spoken) communication

We all speak to people every day, so we should have good spoken skills. However, the kinds of formal spoken skills needed at work are different to those we may be used to. People sometimes find it difficult to speak to people who they have never met before, or people who are quite senior to them in age, experience, or position. These skills come with practice.

A person with good oral communication skills will:

● Have the confidence to talk to people they do not know

- Have a clear voice (regional accents are fine as long as people from other regions can understand them)
- Listen and not interrupt other people while they are talking
- Give the impression that they want to hear what the speaker is saying
- Not tap their fingers, look at the clock, or their watch
- Use the name of the person they are talking to, to make the listener feel recognized and important
- Not speak too quickly or too slowly
- Not use words that the listener does not know
- Not use slang words
- Not make the listener feel threatened or inferior
- Always give the other person, or listener, an opportunity to ask questions in order to clarify their own understanding
- Understand the messages people give with their body language
- Put people at their ease
- Use eye-contact when talking to someone face-to-face, but without staring

In business, it is very important to establish a good relationship with internal and external customers as quickly as possible and to find out what their needs are. External customers are more likely to buy products from firms where they feel that their needs have been listened to, and where the firm is genuinely trying to provide for their needs, rather than simply trying to persuade them to buy a product which may not be exactly what they want.

Face-to-face communication

This takes place when you meet a customer in person. You will be able to tell how the customer reacts to what you are saying by their body language.

Greeting the customer is very important. In large retail stores a few words of welcome and a smile will be enough, because many customers will be first-time visitors.

In organizations which supply goods and services by order, customers should be greeted with a handshake, especially the representatives of business customers. On first meeting you should give your own name and try and remember the name of the person you are meeting. Exchanging business cards will help. Regular customers should be greeted by name.

Some customers will tell you their needs – for example, to make a purchase or receive information – and ask how you intend to respond. Others may need to be asked some questions by you to find out their needs, particularly if they are not sure themselves. For example, customers browsing in a clothes shop may need help if they are unsure of the size or colour of item they want.

One chance to make a first impression

Because the way staff greet and say goodbye to customers is so important to the success of an organization, the retail subsidiary of a well known American film company provides the following guidelines to staff on acceptable greetings and goodbyes to use with customers:

In addition to the greeting, staff are encouraged to:

- Tell them some trivia about the organization
- Ask open-ended questions to establish customers' needs
- Incorporate product information
- Talk about current in-store promotions
- Acknowledge something special about the guest

'Good morning and welcome'
'Hi, how are you?'
'Hello'
'Hi, is this your first visit to the store?'
'Have fun.'
'Don't hesitate to ask if you need any help.'
'Hello, how are you today?'

'Goodbye'
'Goodbye, please call again.'
'Goodbye, have a great day.'
'Bye, safe journey.'
'Goodbye, hope to see you soon.'
'Goodbye and take care.'

Using the telephone

The telephone is an important piece of communications equipment in business. It allows an organization to talk to its customers and suppliers anywhere in the world. However, using the telephone in business requires skill.

Using a telephone in a business context is very different to using one to speak to family or friends. Even though the person you are talking to cannot see you, s/he will still be able to tell a great deal about what you are thinking from your tone of voice, the words you use, and from your breathing. The way you say things is as important as what you say.

Telephone courtesy: some golden rules

- Try to answer the phone in less than four rings.

- Be enthusiastic and friendly when you answer, and try to make callers feel welcome.

- Hold the transmitter directly in front of your mouth when speaking.

- State the name of your organization and department and offer your help.

- Be prepared to smile: people can often sense a smile in your tone of voice and will warm to this.

- Make sure the customer has plenty of opportunity to tell you what they want.

- Always double-check that you have recorded the important details correctly on paper.

- Before placing a caller on hold, ask their permission to do so.

- Make sure the caller is on hold before you discuss their enquiry with others.

- Do not keep callers on hold for too long.

- If you cannot provide an answer immediately, take down the caller's name and phone number, and follow up their call as soon as possible.

- Always be sure to let the caller or customer know what will happen next. For example, will you phone them back with information? If so, when?

- Always let the person who telephoned you end the conversation.

- At the end of the conversation, thank the caller for contacting your organization.

▼ *Communications in the future? But don't use one in the bathroom!*

With new technology, telephones in the near future will also have video screens and people will be able to see the person they are talking to, and respond to their facial expressions. This will mean that good communication skills will be even more important for business employees.

Portfolio Activity 10.7

PC: Demonstrate business communications which meet customer needs

Range: Business communications

Skills: Take part in discussions, Produce written material

In pairs, roleplay the following situations to examine how well you handle face-to-face and telephone communications with customers.

Face-to-face communications:

- A customer enters a large store and asks the sales assistant for directions to the electrical department.

- A customer asks the sales assistant to provide product details and give a demonstration of a video recorder (or other electrical good of your choice. It would be useful if you could demonstrate with an actual product).

- A customer returns an item of clothing and asks to make an exchange

Telephone communications:

(These are best carried out if you face away from each other, so that you cannot see the other person's facial reactions.)

- A customer telephones to order a product catalogue.

- A customer telephones to complain that the items they ordered have not yet been delivered.

- A customer telephones to ask if an item is in stock. This enquiry will take some time to check on the computer database.

Take it in turn to be the customer and the representative of the organization involved. Either take notes of your conversations or better still, make audio or video recordings.

After each conversation discuss and note how well you both thought the business representative responded to the customer. How could the responses be improved in each case?

Written communications

A variety of handwritten, typed, or word-processed business communications on paper are used by organizations to communicate with their external and internal customers. A poorly written communication will give a poor impression of the sender. In all cases, care and attention must be paid to spelling, grammar, punctuation, and layout.

Business letters

Most organizations will at some point communicate with their external customers and suppliers using business letters. Composing and writing business letters is a skilled task. Section 14.2 gives guidance on how to write business letters. You should look through this section before you read on.

▼ Figure 10.1: A business letter in response to a customer complaint

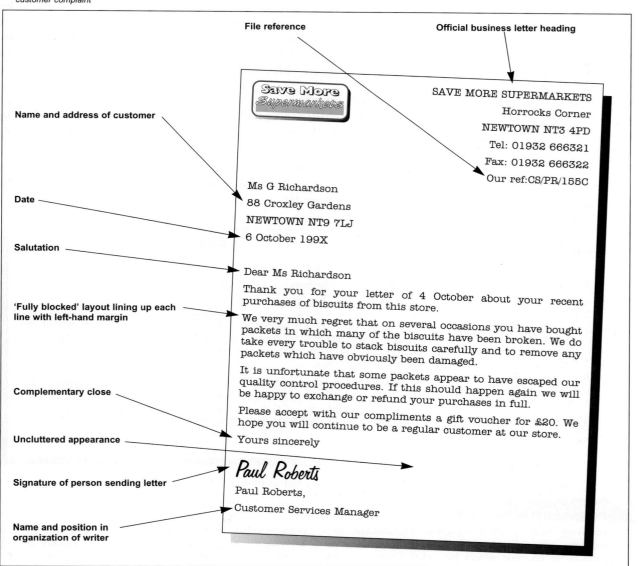

File reference

Official business letter heading

SAVE MORE SUPERMARKETS
Horrocks Corner
NEWTOWN NT3 4PD
Tel: 01932 666321
Fax: 01932 666322
Our ref:CS/PR/155C

Name and address of customer

Ms G Richardson
88 Croxley Gardens
NEWTOWN NT9 7LJ

Date

6 October 199X

Salutation

Dear Ms Richardson

Thank you for your letter of 4 October about your recent purchases of biscuits from this store.

'Fully blocked' layout lining up each line with left-hand margin

We very much regret that on several occasions you have bought packets in which many of the biscuits have been broken. We take every trouble to stack biscuits carefully and to remove any packets which have obviously been damaged.

It is unfortunate that some packets appear to have escaped our quality control procedures. If this should happen again we will be happy to exchange or refund your purchases in full.

Complementary close

Please accept with our compliments a gift voucher for £20. We hope you will continue to be a regular customer at our store.

Uncluttered appearance

Yours sincerely

Signature of person sending letter

Paul Roberts

Paul Roberts,

Name and position in organization of writer

Customer Services Manager

All business letters are similar in format. They are normally produced using a typewriter or word processor, and printed on headed notepaper giving details of the business name, address, and telephone number(s). They will be more formal than personal letters and will be signed by staff who have the necessary authority to send them.

Letters which start with 'Dear Sir' or 'Dear Madam' should close with 'Yours faithfully'. Letters that start with the person's surname, for example, 'Dear Mrs Smith', should close with 'Yours sincerely'.

Not all business letters are written from scratch. Most organizations have a range of standard responses to enquiries and complaints by customers. **Standard letters** are often stored on computer, with gaps left for the particular details of individual customers and their enquiries or complaints. Alternatively, details can be entered by hand.

Increasingly, organizations are promoting their goods and services by sending out personalized letters to thousands of customers. These letters are known as **circulars**. It is possible to print out thousands of letters, each one showing a different customer name and address, using a word processor equipped with a mailmerge facility (see 9.1).

Memoranda (memos)

Memos are written communications to internal customers. That is, memos are sent by members of staff within an organization to other members of staff.

A memo is less formal than a business letter and has no salutation or complementary close. It is also unlikely to be signed, although it may be initialled by the sender.

▼ Figure 10.2: An example of an internal memo

MEMO

TO: Karen Simons, Stockroom Supervisor

FROM: Paul Roberts, Customer Service Manager

DATE: 8 October 199X

I have received a number of complaints from customers about the sale of broken biscuits. It is likely that many more customers experience this problem when purchasing packets of biscuits from this store.

Please make sure all reasonable steps are taken to identify and remove packets which have been damaged internally before they are stacked on shelves. Regular checks of the stacking arrangements may also be necessary.

PR

Memos are considered in detail in Section 14.2.

Electronic communications

Increasingly firms are abandoning paper communications and introducing electronic communication, or E-mail, using computers linked to the telephone network (see 14.4). Workers using a computer network can type in a message and send it simultaneously to a large number of staff at various locations in the same building or anywhere else in the world. Firms will increasingly communicate electronically, with external and internal customers, using the Internet, or worldwide information superhighway.

Portfolio Activity 10.8

PC: Demonstrate business communications which meet customer needs

Range: Business communications

Skills: Produce written material, Present information

Imagine you are a senior manager of a large multiplex cinema with 10 screens, a number of bars and restaurants, and a disco.

You have received a letter dated 27 March 199X from Mrs G Hopkins of 14 Cedar Terrace, Newtown, NT6 7KY. In her letter she complains that her enjoyment of a recent evening film presentation was spoilt by noise vibration from the nearby disco.

1. Use a word processor to prepare and print a letter to send to Mrs Hopkins in response to her complaint. Your letter should contain the following details:

● A thank you for her recent letter

● An apology for any inconvenience caused

● The problem of noise vibration at Screen 8 is being investigated

● You will keep her informed of the outcome of the investigation

● You hope she will continue to use the cinema

● You enclose two free cinema tickets

2. Write a memo to the manager of the discothèque at the complex, with a copy for the on-site sound engineers. This should make the following points:

● Mrs Hopkins' letter is the fifth complaint received about noise disturbance from the disco

● Customer numbers at the cinema are down

● You would like a full investigation to be undertaken and a report on findings and possible solutions to be tabled at the next management meeting

● Date, time, and venue of the next management meeting

Customer and product information

A great deal of information needs to be communicated quickly and clearly to customers about the goods and services provided by organizations. Firms will often use the services of professional designers and printing firms to produce these communications, including leaflets and brochures. Many are in colour and serve two purposes: to be informative, and to persuade customers to buy.

In addition, organizations will provide information to customers via instruction manuals, price lists, guarantees, statements of account, and safety notices.

● **Product information:** Products are goods and services (see 2.2). Customers usually want to see and read about products at their leisure and compare details of different products before deciding what to buy or use. Most firms communicate information about their products to customers in carefully designed leaflets and brochures.

The more attractive a leaflet or brochure, the more likely it is to lead to a sale. Many products come with leaflets and booklets explaining how to assemble them, look after them, and/or use them safely. Instructions should always be clear and easy to understand.

● **Prices:** Customers will be particularly keen to compare the prices of different products before they decide to buy. For example, restaurants will display their prices on menus placed outside or in their window. Price lists will also be on display in many other shops and may be printed as advertisements in newspapers. Most stores, however, rely on printed price tags to give price information on individual items.

● **Statement of account:** Customers who buy products on credit from an organization are sent a **statement of account** at the end of each month. This gives a summary of the goods purchased by the customer since the last statement, the money the customer owes, any payments which have been received, and the total balance owed by the customer to the firm.

▼ *Product information is provided in brochures, leaflets, and user instructions.*

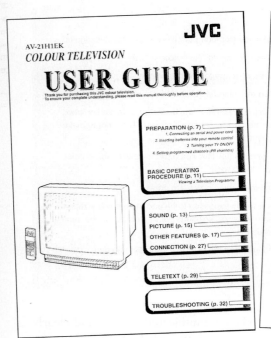

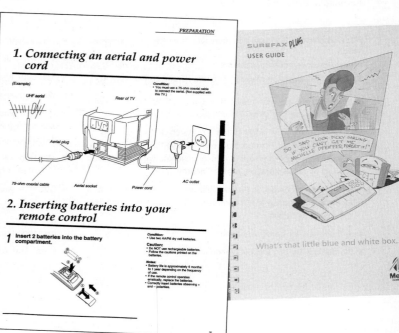

▼ *A customer guarantee certificate and registration card*

Statements of accounts are covered in detail in Section 12.3.

● **Guarantees:** Consumers are unlikely to buy expensive durable products, such as televisions and camcorders, unless they get a guarantee with them. If the product goes wrong, they want to know that they will be able to exchange it or get it repaired at little or no cost. Otherwise why take the risk of buying an expensive item?

Many durable products come with a one- or two-year parts and labour guarantee. Often a registration card is enclosed which the buyer is asked to complete. If the card is not returned, consumers are still entitled to their legal rights if they have a problem with the product.

Firms often use the warranty card as an opportunity to undertake market research, by including on it a number of questions which the buyer can fill in if they wish. The data received is then fed into a database and used to provide a customer list for further marketing and mailshots for future products.

A number of firms also offer consumers the opportunity to purchase an additional extended guarantee, usually up to five years, for a set fee.

● **Safety notices:** Some electrical and mechanical products can cause injury if used incorrectly. Some manufacturers therefore include safety notices with the user instructions for their goods. Customers also need to be advised about the use of certain chemicals and medicines they can buy.

▼ A saftey notice

Safety precautions

WARNING:
TO PREVENT FIRE OR SHOCK HAZARD, DO NOT EXPOSE THIS APPLIANCE TO RAIN OR MOISTURE.

CAUTION:
TO ENSURE PERSONAL SAFETY, OBSERVE THE FOLLOWING RULES REGARDING THE USE OF THIS UNIT.

- Operate only from the power source specified (AC 220–240 V, 50 Hz) on the unit.
- Avoid damaging the AC plug and power cord.
- Avoid improper installation and never position the unit where good ventilation is unattainable.
- Do not allow objects or liquid into the cabinet openings.
- In the event of a fault, unplug the unit and call a service technician. Do not attempt to repair it yourself or remove the rear cover.

* When you do not use this TV set for a long period of time, be sure to disconnect the power plug from the AC outlet.

WARNING:
DO NOT cut off the mains plug from this equipment...

Similarly, business premises can be dangerous places and must be carefully managed in order to protect staff and the public. There are a wide range of laws relating to health and safety, designed to protect customers and employees in the UK (see 10.4).

Firms communicate information on health and safety using a wide range of **safety notices**. For example, fire notices giving instructions on what to do in the event of a fire are usually displayed all around most business premises. 'No Smoking' signs are also widely used, as are a wide variety of other warning notices. The key issue with these kinds of notices is that they must be easily seen and clear to those reading them.

The **Safety Signs Regulations 1980** requires that all safety signs are made in either red, blue, yellow, or green, and that they are either rectangular, triangular, or circular. This helps people to recognize safety signs when they see them.

Sometimes firms put up signs saying that management bears no responsibility in the event of accidents. These signs have no legal effect. Firms are required by law to take steps to ensure the health and safety of their workforces, and the law holds them responsible for this, regardless of any disclaimer signs that may be put up.

Portfolio Activity 10.9

PC: Identify business communications which meet customer needs
Range: Business communications
Skills: Use images, Produce written material

1. Investigate and collect examples of how the following organizations communicate information on products and prices to customers:

- A holiday company
- A mail order organization
- A school or college
- A department store
- A leisure centre
- A video rental shop
- A DIY warehouse

In each case, suggest how the style of the different brochures, leaflets, and other literature you have collected reflects:

- The image of the organization
- The type of goods and services it provides
- The particular needs of customers

2. Collect examples of safety notices and signs used in the following organizations:

- A hospital
- A school or college
- A shop
- A manufacturing plant
- A DIY warehouse
- A local authority park
- A bus or train service

How effective do you think the notices and signs are in each case?

You may need to ask the permission of a manager in each of the above organizations to draw or take pictures of their notices and signs.

3. Design safety notices or signs for the following potential hazards:

- A kettle provided in the staff kitchen which spits out hot water and steam if it is over-filled
- A set of revolving doors to your business premises which can trap trailing clothing, bags, and children's fingers
- A set of sharp blades on a new lawnmower for sale

If possible, use a desktop publishing package to help produce your designs.

Section **10.4**

Legislation and the customer

A number of laws have been passed in the UK to protect customers from being exploited by unethical businesses. Three main Acts designed to do this are:

- **The Trade Descriptions Act**
- **The Sale of Goods Act**
- **The Consumer Protection Act**

Together, these laws protect customers from:

- Misleading product descriptions
- Misleading information about prices and special offers
- Poor workmanship and negligence
- Faulty, sub-standard, and dangerous goods
- Injuries and financial loss suffered as a result of business practices

A customer has a legal right to compensation for any of the above, if the organization that supplied them with the good or service is at fault. However, not all aspects of customer service are covered by legislation. For example, a customer cannot seek compensation simply because staff were impolite, or if the free product catalogue they wanted was unavailable.

Details of the above consumer protection Acts are provided in Section 9.2. You should re-read this section to refresh your memory.

Health and safety at work

The **Health and Safety at Work Act 1974** covers employees at work as well as customers visiting a firm (see 5.3).

Internal customers

Under the Act, every employer is required to prepare a written health and safety policy, and all employees must be informed of it. Management are responsible for carrying out the policy and should they fail to do so they can be taken to court. Firms are required to provide training, information, teaching, and supervision to ensure the health and safety at work of their staff. In turn, the law requires employees to take reasonable care of their safety while at work, and to follow the health and safety rules drawn up by employers.

Health and safety inspectors are employed by the government to back up the law and to ensure that it is carried out by firms. These inspectors have the power to enter workplaces in order to examine equipment, and take photographs and documents away for further examination, if required.

External customers

Health and safety legislation also covers external customers visiting business premises. A business can find itself liable under the law if:

- A customer is injured because s/he has been sold a faulty product

● A customer suffers financial loss or distress because of poor workmanship or professional negligence

● A customer is injured because of a lack of care by an employee or due to unsafe fittings or equipment

Businesses can protect themselves against paying out money to settle claims from injured customers by taking out appropriate insurance cover.

Business insurance

Firms are required by law to insure for public, product, and employer's liability.

● **Public liability insurance** covers firms against claims arising from injury to a customer caused by their business activities – for example, if a highly polished floor in a shop causes people to slip and hurt themselves. It also covers loss or damage to customers' property. This is an important safeguard for customers and for firms; without it, a claim for damages could easily bankrupt a business. The insurance is important for the public, because it guarantees them compensation if the firm is at fault.

● **Product liability insurance** provides cover against claims by customers for damages due to loss or injury caused by the use of goods or services they have been sold – for example, an electrical product which catches fire and causes damage due to an internal fault. This insurance also covers a business for the legal costs which might be incurred in defending itself against claims made against it by the public.

● **Employer's liability insurance** protects a business against claims for compensation from employees who have accidents at work.

Portfolio Activity 10.10

Pc: Identify relevant legislation to protect customers
Range: Business communications
Skills: Use images, Produce written material

1. Which laws, if any, have been broken in the following situations? What are the customer's legal rights? Who is at fault in each case?

● Your new coat is ripped on a sharp piece of metal sticking out from a shelving unit in a clothes shop.

● You have just bought three bottles of wine from a supermarket which you drop while struggling to open your car door.

● You have just bought three bottles of wine from a supermarket. The cashier placed them all in one carrier which split open, causing the bottles to smash to the ground in the car park.

● A hamburger meal which you bought from a takeaway was so hot that it burnt your mouth when you ate it.

● You have just bought a new pair of waterproof boots from a shoe shop. Unfortunately they are far from waterproof, as you discover during a heavy shower of rain.

● During the same rain storm, the conservatory a local firm of builders have just erected at the back of your house leaks water and ruins your new carpet.

● You trip and sprain your ankle on a loose paving stone in your local high street.

2. You have just bought a new video camcorder. When you get it home you find that it will not record any sound. You phone the shop you bought it from, only to be told that they cannot exchange it or provide a refund because it was on special offer, with 20% off the usual retail price. They are, however, willing to repair the camera for free, but only if you buy their 5-year warranty cover at a cost of £90.

From your knowledge of legislation to protect customers (see 9.2), write a letter of complaint to the organization, pointing out the legal rights you have in this case. (Make up a name and address for the shop.)

Key crossword

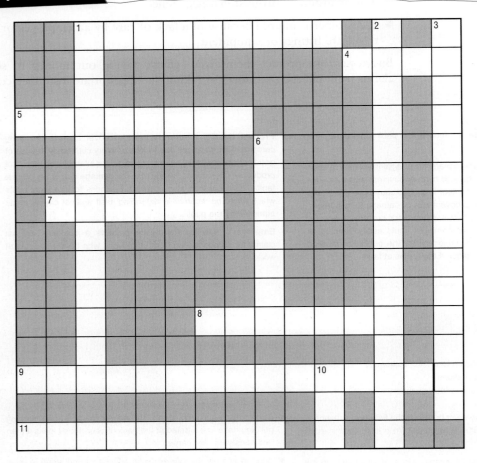

Across

1. A verbal or written protest by a customer to a business (9)

4. An internal business communication (4)

5. These customers are other workers inside an organization (8)

7. When an organization repays money to a customer who has returned an item (6)

8. A word describing individual and business customers who are otherwise unconnected with an organization (8)

9. A formal written communication sent by an organization (8,6)

11. A product warranty (9)

Down

1. An organization has this when it concentrates on the needs and wants of the people who buy or use its products (8,5)

2. Legislation concerning the welfare and well being of customers (6,3,6)

3. The term used to describe the giving and sending of verbal and written messages to customers (14)

6. These summarize information on the goods purchased from an organization by a customer, any payments which have been made, and the balance owed by the customer at the end of each month (7)

10. Short for a system of quality control in every aspect of business activity (1,1,1)

Test Questions and Assessment Assignment

You must demonstrate that you are able to:

1. Identify an organization's customers and its customer needs
2. Identify and describe customer service in an organization
3. Identify business communications which meet customer needs
4. Demonstrate business communications which meet customer needs

5. Describe procedures in one business organization for dealing with customer complaints
6. Identify relevant legislation to protect customers

Questions 1-3 share the answer options A to D below:
An organization has identified from a customer survey that it needs to make improvements in the following areas:

A providing customers with general product information

B providing refunds and exchanges

C providing after-sales care

D meeting customers' special needs

Which of the above could be improved by the following actions?

1 Setting up a customer help desk

2 Making sure sales staff are available at all times

3 Printing more information on price tags and providing product brochures

4 A customer returning a recently purchased, but faulty, electrical appliance will usually prefer:

A a refund

B a credit note

C repair

D more information on the product

5 The managing director of a high-speed train service has said that 'customer service' was the most important factor in the improved performance of the organization. To which of the following factors was he referring?

A an increase in the number of services per hour

B new, cleaner rolling stock

C a better and faster buffet service

D more attention to customer needs by staff before they board a train, during the journey, and when they depart

6 You work in the accounts office of a large department store. A telephone call from a customer of your organization comes through to you by mistake. You cannot answer the customer's enquiry about the range of products you have in stock. What is the best thing you can do?

A ask the caller to hold while you find someone who can help

B tell the caller s/he has got the wrong number

C take a note of the customer details and get an experienced salesperson to phone them back

D tell them you will send them some information leaflets

7 The manager of a DIY store finds that customers always want to ask questions about the best way to carry out building and decorating work. What would be the best way to meet their needs?

A set up an information desk

B give product demonstrations

C stock a series of books on DIY they can buy

D show in-store videos on DIY

8 Which of the following customer services would be found in a museum?

A after-sales service

B information desk

C goods exchange point

D refunds

9 The owner of a computer firm keeps a record of customer complaints about a product. This is useful, because it helps the firm to:

A keep prices low

B identify faults with the product

C monitor competitors' products

D keep records of sales

10 You buy a pair of boots labelled as having leather soles and uppers. When you get home you discover that the soles are in fact plastic. Which Act is the shoe shop breaking?

A Health and Safety at Work Act

B Consumer Protection Act

C Sale of Goods Act

D Trade Descriptions Act

11 If you buy a new CD player and it turns out not to work, which of the following is true:

A you are not entitled to a refund unless the shop says so.

B you must take vouchers to the same value if the shop says so.

C you must take a working CD if you are offered it.

D you are entitled to a refund if you want it.

12 What is the best way for a consumer electronics company to improve its levels of customer service?

   A to employ friendly staff

   B to spend more on advertising

   C to train staff in their products and enable them to give better after-sales service

   D to greet people at the entrance to the shops

13 The purpose of improving customer service is to:

   A be nice to customers

   B reduce theft

   C increase sales

   D increase costs

14 A company has recently trained all of its staff in customer care. This is most likely to lead to:

   A a fall in sales

   B more complaints about products sold by the organization

   C happier staff

   D fewer complaints about the organization

15 A shop is legally required to refund the price paid for a coat when:

   A the material does not match that stated on the label

   B the customer has changed their mind about the colour

   C it is an unwanted birthday present

   D it was bought in a sale and is now available at full price, enabling the customer to profit from a refund

16 A business is liable under health and safety law if:

   A a customer faints in the shop and is hurt falling over

   B a customer hurts himself after starting a fight with another member of the public

   C a customer receives an electric shock from the refrigerator at the food counter

   D a customer drops his purchases on his foot after leaving the store

17 All of the following are customer needs except:

   A the need to make a purchase

   B the need to obtain a refund

   C the need to make a complaint

   D the need to make commission on a sale

18 The difference between a business letter and a memo is:

   A a business letter is usually less formal than a memo

   B a memo ends with 'yours sincerely' or 'yours faithfully'

   C a business letter is designed for internal customers, while a memo is for external customers

   D a business letter is usually more formal than a memo

19 Which customers' needs are met when a firm replaces a product returned by a dissatisfied customer?

   A the need to make a purchase

   B the need to exchange goods

   C special needs

   D the need to obtain information

20 A bank has to let a customer know that they have approved a mortgage application. The bank manager writes a letter to the customer confirming repayment details. What is the advantage of sending the customer a letter?

   A it checks that the customer understands the mortgage details

   B it provides a record for future reference

   C it lets the customer discuss details with the bank manager

   D it is the most personal way to give the customer details

21 You are a floor manager in a large supermarket.

   a. Identify four main needs of the customers visiting your organization.

   b. Suggest how the supermarket could try to meet the special needs of different groups of customers.

   c. Suggest three ways your supermarket could provide customers with better product information.

   d. A customer comes up to you to complain that oranges are out of stock for the third week in a row. Explain how you would deal with the complaint and the face-to-face communication it involves.

22 Write a paragraph to show what you understand by the following terms:

   • customer service

   • internal customers

   • external customers

   • written communications with customers

   • customer needs for information

   • health and safety legislation

assessment assignment

The following assignment meets all the evidence requirements needed to fulfil all the performance criteria in element 3.3. In addition it covers the following range points and core skills:

Range: Customer needs
Customer service
Business communications
Legislation

Skills: Communication
Take part in discussions
Use images
Produce written material
Information technology
Present information

Tasks

1. a Choose an organization with which you are familiar. You will need to be able to talk to and question some of the staff.

b Prepare a list of questions to ask staff in your chosen organization. You are required to find out:

- The different groups of external customers they deal with (for example, businesses by industrial sector, size, etc., and individuals by age, gender, location, etc.)

- Their internal customers

- Their customer needs

- How customer complaints are recorded and dealt with

- Their exchange and refund policy

- Types of business communications with customers

c Arrange a visit to your chosen organization and get permission to ask different members of staff your questions.

d Obtain samples of written business communications used by the organization.

e Observe staff dealing with customers in your chosen organization. Take notes on the service they provide and whether you feel each customer is satisfied. Your notes should include at least one record of a face-to-face or telephone communication between a member of staff and a customer.

2. Using a word processor, prepare a report on customer services in your chosen organization from notes you made in Task 1. Your report should include:

- A title page

- A brief introduction to your chosen organization – name, location, size, business sector, etc.

- A description of its main external customers and their needs

- A description of internal customers and their needs

- A description of how staff deal with external and internal customers from your observation of them in action

- The procedure used to handle customer complaints. (If it does not have a formal procedure, then suggest steps they could take.)

- Business communications used by the firm, with a description of **one** oral communication, and an example of **at least one** written business communication used by the firm

- The exchanges and refund policy of the organization. (If it does not have one, suggest a policy that could be followed.)

3. This Task requires you to deal with customers. These can be customers you might deal with in the course of a Saturday or part-time job, or during a work placement. Or they could be customers at a school event that you are helping to run, such as an open evening, sports day, or disco.

Try to deal with a number of different situations as follows:

- a customer needing to make a purchase
- a customer requesting information
- a customer needing to obtain a refund
- a customer needing to exchange a good
- a customer needing to make a complaint
- a customer with special needs

In each case, you should greet the customer, find out what their needs are, make an attempt to meet these needs, and then finish the communication. Make notes on how you coped with each task. Make sure someone else – for example, another employee or your tutor – is able to witness your communications with customers and can provide written evidence that you carried them out satisfactorily.

chapter 11

chapter *11* *Present Proposals for Improvements to Customer Service*

Key ideas

Good **customer service** is important for organizations because it allows them to **gain and retain customers, to improve customer satisfaction, build customer loyalty**, and **enhance the image** of the organization.

Businesses can measure **customer satisfaction** by monitoring the **number of customers, the level of sales, the amount of feedback received from customers**, in terms of **repeat sales** and **complaints,** and by carrying out **market research**.

Market research involves finding out about consumer wants. Market research information can be collected in a variety of ways, including face-to-face interviews with existing and potential customers, telephone and postal surveys, consumer panels, test marketing a new product in one particular area, and from published sources in newspapers, magazines, and government statistical journals.

Businesses can improve their levels of customer service in a number of key areas, including **reliability, friendliness, the availability of goods and services, speed of delivery, access to buildings, care for the environment, customer safety,** and **policies for the exchange of goods and refunds**.

The importance of customer service

Think how you would feel in the following situation:

You go into a shop and are made to wait 15 minutes while a sales assistant has a chat with a friend on the telephone. Then, when the assistant serves you, s/he is offhand and unable to give you a demonstration of the product, or to tell you much about it. You notice that the till area is also very dirty.

When you get the product home, you find out that the item you have bought does not work properly, and that parts are missing. You take it back to the shop, but the staff do not seem to care and are reluctant to change it or refund your money.

The chances are that you will think twice about buying from the business again. Not only will you not buy again, you will also advise others not to buy. The firm will lose your repeat custom, and it will lose new customers as well, because it failed to provide you with the standard of customer service that you expected.

More and more firms today are understanding the need for good **customer service**, and what it means for sales and profits (see 10.1). The horror story given above is unlikely to happen, but even if just one part of it occurs, customers may go elsewhere. The simple rule in business is that good products do not sell themselves. Good products, with good customer service and marketing, sell products.

Features of good customer service

An organization that fails to provide good customer service could end up spending more effort dealing with complaints than selling goods and services. Its customers will be lost to organizations that *can* keep their customers happy.

Good customer service involves many aspects of the operation of a business organization. For example:

- **Staff:** should be
    - friendly and provide a prompt service
    - helpful and polite
    - clean and tidy
    - dressed smartly
    - knowledgeable about products, methods of payments, the layout of the business premises, etc.
- **Premises:** should be
    - clean, tidy, and well presented
    - equipped for people with special needs, e.g. ramps for people in wheelchairs and parents with prams and pushchairs
    - easy to find your way around
    - well sign-posted

- fitted with safety features, such as fire exits, wide doors, wide steps, handrails on stairs, emergency telephones in lifts, etc.

- **Products:** should be
  - reasonably priced
  - of good quality
  - safe
  - provided with clear instructions, if appropriate
  - guaranteed, if appropriate

- **After-sales care:** should aim to:
  - provide a prompt and reasonable repair service
  - deal with customer complaints quickly and sympathetically
  - exchange goods and provide refunds

- **Other services:**
  - customer orders should be fulfilled quickly
  - delivery services should be prompt and reliable
  - product catalogues, price lists, and information leaflets could be provided free of charge

Clearly not every organization will offer customers all the same features of customer service. For example, you would expect to find a customer toilet in a restaurant, but not in a record shop. Similarly, you would not expect car mechanics providing a service in a car repair centre to be smartly dressed or very clean. In fact you may be put off taking your car there if they were!

Portfolio Activity 11.1

PC: Identify improvements to customer service
Range: Improvements to customer service
Skills: Collect and record data, Produce written material

1. Using the checklist of good customer service features above, investigate customer service in a business organization of your choice. For example, this could be:

- A retail outlet, such as a shop, bank, sandwich bar, or hairdresser's

- A service provider, such as a window cleaner, car mechanic, painter and decorator, or bus and rail company

- An office, such as a Jobcentre, council office, or government department

- A factory

- A local hospital, school, or college

You may need to adapt the checklist to suit the particular activities of the organization you choose. For example, the product features above would not apply in a factory, hospital, or school.

In some cases you may have to ask permission to be on the organization's premises. In other cases, you will simply be just another member of the public looking around.

2. Write up your findings in a short report using a word processor. Your report should contain:

- An introduction describing your chosen organization, its name, and location

- Your impression of customer service in the organization, i.e. how well you think it lives up to the features of good customer service listed above

- What the organization could do to improve its customer service

The benefits of good customer service

Increasingly, business organizations are becoming **customer-focused**. This means that their goods and services are designed to meet the changing needs and wants of their customers (see 10.1). There are four main reasons for doing this:

1. To gain and retain customers

2. To improve customer satisfaction

3. To build customer loyalty

4. To improve the organization's image

1. To gain and retain customers

Most of the goods that we buy are offered by a wide range of businesses in competition with each other. In fact, the government encourages this by taking legal action against any firm that appears to be the only supplier of a good, if it can be proven that the firm takes advantage of its position against the consumer in a harmful way.

Businesses are in competition with each other for customers' money. However, many of the products offered for sale today are fairly similar, such as washing powders, soaps, margarines, even cars and televisions. Therefore, to make their business stand out from the crowd and appear to be better than the others, it pays a firm to provide a good customer service.

2. Improve customer satisfaction

If customers feel satisfied with their purchase and with the level of service provided, they are more likely to buy the same or other products from the organization again. If, however, premises appear dirty, staff are unhelpful, delivery is slow, and/or no after-sales care is provided, customers will be put off and take their custom elsewhere.

One of the benefits of advertising products is that advertisements not only make people want to buy, but they also help people who have already bought the product to feel good about their purchase (see 9.1). Advertising helps to confirm customers' faith in the correctness of their decision to buy and so encourages them to recommend the product to others and also to make repeat purchases.

3. To build customer loyalty

If customers can be encouraged to feel loyal to an organization and/or its product, they may stay with that firm and not buy from competitors. In fact, they may even be willing to pay a higher price for a product if they feel it is better than the rest. A firm that provides good customer service can make its customers become loyal, because they know they will always receive good and fair treatment.

Promotions can also encourage customer loyalty to particular products and organizations (see 9.1). Customers may be persuaded to make repeat purchases if they have to collect product labels or receipts to enter competitions. The same is true if they can build up 'loyalty bonuses', such as air miles which can be collected and converted into a airplane ticket, or points that give money off future purchases.

CLUBCARD

Good news.

If you are over 60 and shop at Tesco regularly, spending more than £5 but less than £10 each visit, you can still earn Clubcard points.

Not everyone can do all their Tesco shopping in one go. You may drop in several times and pick up a few items. To improve our service, we've come up with an exclusive benefit for Clubcard members who are over 60 and usually spend between £5 and £10 on each shopping trip.

From now on if you **spend more than £5 but less than £10 you will earn 1 Clubcard point** – so you can now enjoy all the benefits of Tesco Clubcard each time you shop.

▼ Good customer service can build customer loyalty.

Help with packing unpacking shopping & carry out services are available at this store. Please ask the cashier for help

Sainsbury's.

Everyones favourite ingredient

For example, Tesco introduced its Clubcard in early 1995. Every time a customer spends £5 in a Tesco store they are credited one point on their card. Every three months, their points are added up and converted into personalized vouchers which give them money off their future shopping bills in Tesco. Other supermarkets have since introduced similar schemes.

A great deal of advertising spending by firms is designed to create a **brand image**. This is an image which sets their product (or organization) apart from the others. For example, most brands of washing powder, soft drinks, and other goods you find in a supermarket are fairly similar to each other, and so firms attempt to make their products appear different by creating a distinctive image to go with each product. Customers are then able to recognize the brand as they shop and its advertised features, such as quality, value for money, performance, etc.

Similarly, most supermarkets offer very similar products and prices. If Sainsbury's are able to persuade shoppers that the level of service, care, and value for money they provide is better than say, Asda, then they can gain more customers and make sure they shop there every week.

395

Brand images are also created for many other goods and services, such as cars, banks, insurance services, and holidays. If a customer feels satisfied with the product or service they get, then they are likely to buy more of the same, for example, by taking an Airtours holiday each year, or replacing an old Rover car with a new one.

Portfolio Activity 11.2

PC: Explain the importance of customer service in business organizations

Range: Importance of customer service

Skills: Read and respond to written material

1. What was the purpose of the vouchers scheme launched by Boots?

2. How might the Boots vouchers plan have damaged the company's public image?

3. What evidence is there that it might be cheaper to keep existing customers loyal than to spend money on attracting new ones?

4. Conduct a survey of businesses that you know. Make a list of all of the customer loyalty schemes that they operate. How effective are they? Can you think of any others that could be introduced?

Rewards for the loyal shopper

Boots the Chemist was this week putting a brave face on what must be judged at the very least a public relations embarrassment. Its 'vouchers for sports equipment' scheme highlights some of the dangers in the current rush to create consumer loyalty schemes and reward regular spenders. Between September and November, Boots issued 36 million vouchers to customers – one for every £5 spent at its stores – which could be exchanged by schools for sports equipment. A total of 22,000 schools throughout the UK registered for the scheme, and started eyeing equipment in the Boots catalogue, for which they hoped parents would collect tokens.

Unfortunately the vouchers were worth so little individually that consumers threw them away, and when the required volume of vouchers failed to get through to schools there was a stream of complaints. Boots has recently announced that it will halve the number of vouchers needed for each piece of equipment. This is just one of the traps to be avoided by companies seeking to join the customer loyalty industry. Existing schemes range from Air Miles, now believed to be collected in one in ten households, to tie-ups between petrol stations and retailers. Premier points are, for example, collected at Mobil petrol stations and redeemed at Argos.

Many firms are now finding it cheaper to keep existing customers loyal rather than to advertise in order to recruit new customers. The longer the life' of a customer, the more the initial recruitment costs will be spread. If 80% of customers stay loyal each year, a firm's group of customers will need renewing once in every five years. But, by increasing the loyalty rate to 90%, the customer base will only need to be renewed once every 10 years. A recent study by the Cranfield School of Management, published this week, which looked at shopping centres across the UK, found that loyal shoppers spend up to four times more in their first-choice store than those who shop around.

---

4. Improving an organization's image

The products, activities, and general behaviour of a firm all combine over time to build an image in the public mind. If the general image of an organization is good, consumers will be more willing to buy from that firm. If the image of an organization is poor, consumers are less likely to try their product – even it is a very good one.

Providing a good customer service is one way a firm can enhance its image. If customers feel they have received good service from an organization and have been treated well, they are more likely to recommend that organization and/or its products to their friends.

However, the image of a organization can also be damaged very easily by bad publicity. For example, news items on television or in the press about customers taking companies to court; investigative reports on consumer affairs programmes such as *Watchdog*; or poor product test reports in magazines such as *Which?* – all these can seriously dent a company's image. In the summer of 1995, consumers in many countries stopped

▼ *An organization can improve its image and boost sales by providing good customer service.*

TESCO

TESCO

OPENING HOURS:
Monday-Wednesday 8.30am-8pm
Thursday 8.30am-9.00pm
Friday 8.30am-10pm
Saturday 8am-8pm
Sunday 10am-4pm*
*Beers, Wines and Spirits 12 noon – 2.55pm

Catch a FREE bus to Tesco New Malden.

buying Shell petrol when Greenpeace publicized the decision by Shell and the UK government to dump the old Brent Spar North Sea oil rig at sea.

For these reasons, large firms often employ public relations experts in order to create and manage their image. Honesty, reliability, professionalism, providing value for money, and caring for people and the environment are common themes in image creation.

For example, a recent advert by an oil company showed pictures of unspoilt landscape in the UK, and boasted that beneath the ground were miles of pipelines carrying oil. The advert promoted an image of the company as caring for the environment – so much so that it was prepared to go to great expense to restore the natural beauty of areas it had dug up to bury pipelines. The improved image of the organization was designed to make people feel better about buying petroleum products from the company, and so boost sales.

The importance of customer service in private sector organizations

The purpose of most private sector business activity is to make a profit by selling goods and services that consumers want and are willing and able to pay for (see 1.1). However, if consumers feel that the quality of good or service provided by one organization is not good enough, they may spend their money elsewhere. This loss of sales can lead to workers being made redundant and to eventual closure of the organization.

McDonalds is a good example of a private sector firm which prides itself on high standards of customer service. Before McDonalds opened in the mid-1970s, there were a large number of chip shops and other burger chains like Wimpy in most high streets. Today, McDonalds has taken a huge share of the fast food market, and large numbers of independent fast food retailers have been forced out as a result. One of the reasons for this is that McDonalds offers very fast service, good quality products, a clean, pleasant environment, and well trained staff. It is therefore a good example of the advantages of providing high standards of customer service.

The importance of customer service in public sector organizations

The public sector is made up of organizations that are accountable to central and local government (see 1.4). Most do not operate for profit. However, good customer service is as important in these organizations as it is in the private sector.

▼ *Good customer service has been a major factor in the success of McDonalds' fast food restaurants.*

Did you know? Nº1

TROPICAL RAINFORESTS
– The Facts

It has been said that McDonald's is involved with the destruction of rainforests of Central and South America in order to raise cattle for hamburgers.

LET'S PUT THE RECORD STRAIGHT. NOWHERE IN THE WORLD DOES McDONALD'S USE OF BEEF THREATEN OR REMOTELY INVOLVE THE TROPICAL RAINFORESTS.

In the UK McDonald's uses 100% EC produced beef, in Canada they use 100% Canadian beef, in the United States they use 100% US beef.

McDonald's restaurants in Central and South America (Argentina, Brazil, Costa Rica, Guatemala, Mexico, Panama and Venezuela) only use suppliers who document that their beef has come from long established cattle ranches—not rainforest land..

It is known that rainforest destruction threatens the well-being of the environment.

McDONALD'S HAS NO PART OF IT.

The Company will continue to monitor and adapt policies and practices as necessary to protect the global environment on which we all depend.

FACT SHEET

Produced by:
The Public Relations Department
McDonald's Restaurants Limited
11-59 High Road
East Finchley
London N2 8AW

THIS INFORMATION IS PRINTED ON RE-CYCLED PAPER.

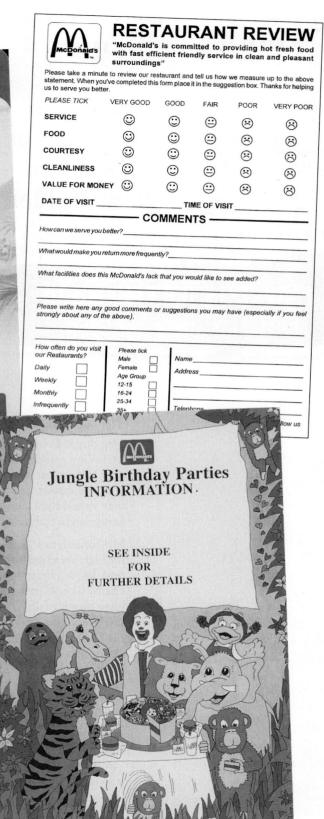

Most public sector organizations provide public services which are funded mainly from tax revenues raised from people and businesses in the UK. As taxpayers, we have a right to expect our money to be used to provide a good service. There is no reason why a public sector organization should provide a slow or inefficient service, whether it is maintaining street lamps and parks, providing healthcare and student grants, or any other important public function.

This is recognized by most public sector organizations in their published **charters**, which explain the standards of service they aim to provide to their clients. For example, the Inland Revenue has issued a Taxpayers' Charter, and every hospital will have a Patients' Charter.

Competition between different organizations occurs in the public sector as well as the private sector. For example, London Transport (LT) buses and underground services are in competition with overground rail and private bus operators, taxis, and even cycling. If LT provides a poor service, it will lose passengers to these other forms of transport.

▼ Figure 11.1: The Taxpayers' Charter

Inland Revenue

The Taxpayer's Charter

You are entitled to expect the Inland Revenue

To be fair
- by settling your tax affairs impartially
- by expecting you to pay only what is due under the law
- by treating everyone with equal fairness

To help you
- to get your tax affairs right
- to understand your rights and obligations
- by providing clear leaflets and forms
- by giving you information and assistance at our enquiry offices
- by being courteous at all times

To provide an efficient service
- by settling your tax affairs promptly and accurately
- by keeping your tax affairs strictly confidential
- by using the information you give us only as allowed by the law
- by keeping to a minimum your costs of complying with the law
- by keeping our costs down

To be accountable for what we do
- by setting standards for ourselves and publishing how well we live up to them

If you are not satisfied
- we will tell you exactly how to complain
- you can ask for your tax affairs to be looked at again
- you can appeal to an independent tribunal
- your MP can refer your complaint to the Ombudsman

In return, we need you
- to be honest
- to give us accurate information
- to pay your tax on time

Similarly, state schools and hospitals compete with other schools and hospitals in the public and private sector. If a school or hospital finds that pupil or patient numbers are declining, it will find it more difficult to raise money from central and local government funds, and may eventually be forced to cut staff, or even close.

Section **11.2**

How businesses monitor customer satisfaction

Customer service features are designed to keep customers satisfied and loyal to an organization and its products, in order to create new and repeat sales. Knowing just how satisfied customers are with the service they receive is, therefore, very important information to any organization.

Organizations can monitor customer satisfaction with their customer services in a variety of ways:

● **Monitoring the number of customers**

● **Tracking the level of sales**

● **Getting feedback from customers**

● **Market research**

Monitoring the numbers of customers

An easy way to measure customers' perceptions of service levels is simply to count the number of customers contacting or visiting a business over a period of time. If customers are not satisfied with the service they receive, this will be reflected in low and falling customer numbers.

For example, Figure 11.2 shows the number of cars entering the car park of a large supermarket in London at different times of the day. The information was collected by placing an electronic sensor on the entrance road to the store. Every time a car drove over the sensor, a signal was sent to a computer which then added up the number of vehicles in every 30-minute period. The information is useful because it not only tells the supermarket about the number of people wishing to use the store, but can help it to plan car parking space and opening times.

▼ *Figure 11.2: Incoming vehicle movements at a London supermarket*

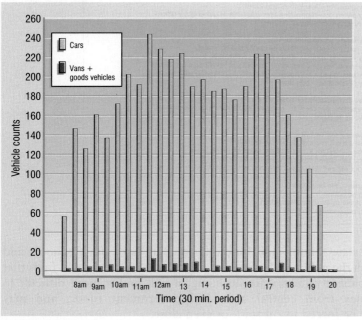

Transport Research Laboratory 1995

People may contact or visit a business to make an enquiry, order or buy a good or service, or to complain. Clearly, if a large proportion of the people contacting or visiting a firm wish to complain, this is a good indicator of a low level of customer service. If a large number of people enquire about products but do not buy them, this might also indicate that sales staff are providing poor levels of service and are putting people off. On the other hand, if a large proportion of enquiries are converted into sales, then this indicates that sales staff are providing a high level of customer service.

When monitoring numbers of customers it may be useful to sort them into categories, for example, age, gender, marital status, etc (see 8.2). A clothes store could monitor the number of people of different ages entering to browse. If they found that an increasing number of older people were visiting the store, they could then change their product lines away from young fashions.

It is also useful to monitor the time of day at which customers contact or visit an organization. Extra staff cover can then be provided at peak times. For example, a bus company could monitor the number of passengers boarding and getting off different buses at different stops. This information would help the company to plan new bus routes and service frequencies at different times of the day.

Retail surveillance cameras are being used more and more by large retail organizations to count the number of customers in their shops and stores. Filming customers also allows stores to pinpoint customer reaction to staff, layout, new products, prices, and promotions.

Monitoring the level of sales

If sales increase, this either means that existing customers are buying more, or that new customers are buying, or both. Rising sales provide a good indication that customers are happy with the service they are getting.

An important factor in obtaining a rising level of sales is the ability to persuade customers who enquire about products to buy them. This can be achieved by giving sales staff professional training in customer service techniques.

Sales may also increase due to special promotions or price reductions or display a seasonal pattern (see 8.3). For example, the sale of suntan lotions and ice cream rises during the summer. Toy purchases rise prior to Christmas. In fact, retail sales of all consumer goods and services peak in December every year. It is, therefore, important to compare sales in one period with the same period in the previous year to see if sales are higher or lower.

Sales values and volumes

An organization can monitor sales values and sales volumes or both. The **value** of sales is simply the total amount of revenue from sales of goods and/or services. The **volume** of sales is the number of goods sold or units of service provided – for example, the number of haircuts given, cars cleaned, or mortgages confirmed.

A firm that monitors sales value will have to adjust for the effects of price inflation to find out if customers really are buying more of their products (see 8.4).

For example, consider a customer who buys 10 bottles of French wine at £4 per bottle from an off licence every week. The total weekly spending of that customer in the off licence is £40 (i.e. 10 bottles x £4). Now suppose the off licence is forced to raise the price of French wine to £5 per bottle – an increase of 25%! From then on, the same customer buys only 9 bottles of French wine each week at a total cost of £45 (i.e. 9 x £5). If the off licence simply monitored sales revenues, it would appear that the value of sales from this customer had risen from £40 to £45.

However, if the off licence looked at sales volumes, they would discover that they were now selling one bottle of wine less than they did before.

Repeat sales

Finding out if the same customers are returning time after time to the same organization to buy goods and services can be difficult. For example, it is impossible to trace the sale of goods over the counter for cash unless customers are asked to give their names. This takes time, and some customers may not want to give details.

However, repeat purchases by customers who order and buy on credit are much easier to trace because their name and address are supplied with their payment details. These customers will include business customers placing orders with their suppliers, and individual customers who may telephone or post their orders through to mail order companies.

This form of monitoring is likely to increase with the introduction of 'home shopping' which will allow users to order goods and services direct by linking their personal computers to the telephone network via a modem. At the time of writing, the widespread use of 'home shopping' is still some years away, but pilot schemes have already started in some areas of the UK.

Some firms are also able to track repeat purchases by issuing membership cards to customers. Examples include Blockbuster Video, and 'loyalty bonus' cards like the Clubcard scheme introduced by Tesco. These cards contain details of the customer's name and address which can be read and stored by electronic tills.

▼ *Repeat sales can be monitored from customer orders, membership cards, and debit card sales.*

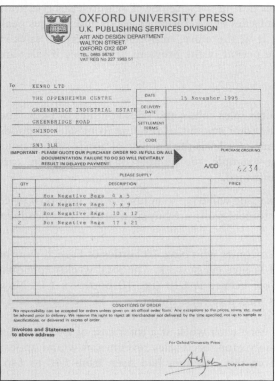

Monitoring feedback from customers

A very important way in which to judge customer satisfaction with customer service provision is to ask customers their opinion. This is called **feedback**.

Feedback can be informal, as when a customer simply thanks a member of staff for their help, or it can be obtained in a more formal way.

- **Immediate feedback** can be obtained simply by asking a customer if they are happy with the service. For example, an hotel receptionist may ask a guest if they are satisfied with their room, or a waiter can ask customers if they are enjoying their meal.

- **Questionnaires** can be filled in by customers while they are visiting and using an organization. Customers may be more frank about poor service when filling in a questionnaire than when confronted face-to-face by a member of staff.

▼ *A customer service questionnaire from Thomas Cook*

- **Consumer panels** are made up of members of the public who are paid to meet regularly with representatives of a firm to discuss levels of service, quality of products, and ideas for changes, etc. A number of large retail organizations use this method of obtaining feedback.

- **Covert customers:** These are 'undercover' customers. Many firms use their own staff to monitor levels of customer service by posing as customers in their stores. The managing director of McDonalds UK uses this technique in order to judge the quality of customer service in his stores, as do most brewery and hotel firms.

  Members of other organizations may also pose as customers in order to check on service levels in other businesses. For example, organizations that publish consumer guides, such as the *Good Pub Guide* or *Good Restaurant Guide*, will use this method. Similarly, representatives of the Consumers' Association, the publishers of *Which?* magazine, will also visit or telephone businesses posing as customers to judge service standards.

- **Customer complaints.** Clearly, complaints by customers are a key indicator of consumers satisfaction with service levels in a firm.

  Some complaints will be made in person to staff or business managers. Many more will be in the form of telephone calls and letters. In some serious cases, customers may also threaten legal action. It is, therefore, important for any business to record all complaints and deal with them sympathetically and quickly.

  If the same complaint is received from different customers time and time again, it could indicate a serious problem. Appropriate action will need to be taken by the organization if it wants to gain and retain customers.

  It is useful to look at both the total number of complaints and also changes in the numbers of complaints received over time. If complaints as a percentage of all enquiries are falling, this is a good sign. If they are rising as a percentage of all enquiries, then further investigation is clearly needed.

  A business may also keep a record of goods returned by customers. It is likely that a customer who has to return an item will be a dissatisfied customer: the risk is that they may not only cease using the company, but spread the word to other potential customers. Because of this, many organizations are willing to provide compensation, as well as immediate refunds or replacements. For example, a restaurant may provide a free bottle of wine or waive the cost of the meal if it was late being served.

Complaints in the public sector

Complaints against public sector organizations are usually dealt with by **consumer councils**. Members of each consumer council are chosen from the people and businesses who use its services. For example, the Post Office Users' National Council is made up of individual and business customers of the Post Office. The consumer councils' job is to receive and investigate customer complaints.

A number of industry 'watchdogs' have also been set up by the government to regulate service levels and prices in the privatized utilities, i.e. British Telecom, British Gas, the water companies, and the electricity supply companies (see 1.4).

Customers may also complain to the **Office of Fair Trading (OFT)** about illegal and unfair trading practices. The OFT is a government body that acts as a central collection point for all consumer problems.

PC: Identify how business organizations monitor customer satisfaction

Range: How businesses monitor customer satisfaction

Skills: Produce written material, Collect and record data

1. Using a computer spreadsheet, draw a barchart to show the number of people who have complained about rail services in the UK for each complaint category in 1994/95.

2. List the five most complained-about aspects of rail services in 1994/95.

3. Suggest practical ways rail companies might improve their service in the five areas you listed in Task 2 above.

4. What would be the purpose of the improvements you recommend?

Railways come under fire on three fronts

Complaints from rail passengers have reached an all-time high, with moans about train cancelations up by almost 25 per cent, a rail watchdog said yesterday.

Total complaints received by the Central Rail Users' Consultative Committee reached 10,166 in 1994-95– a rise of 2.4 per cent on the previous year.

Evidence of growing customer dissatisfaction came as both Labour and Liberal Democrates moved to deter would-be investors in the privatization of Rail Track, the company that owns Britain's rail network.

The Independent 11.8.95

WHAT RAIL PASSENGERS COMPLAIN ABOUT

Complaint Category	1994-95	1993-94	% change
Refunds and claims	1,525	1,261	+20.9
Punctuality	1,518	1,378	+10.2
Information at stations	1,145	1,031	+11.1
Fares and marketing policy	810	931	−13.0
Cancellations	751	605	+24.1
Suitability of timetable	693	1,127	−38.5
Station environment & facilities	628	680	−7.6
Staff conduct	482	494	−2.4
Correspondence delays	417	394	−2.4
On train environment & facilities	331	317	+4.4
Overcrowding	327	335	−2.4
Information on board train	215	145	+48.3
Connectional failures	189	167	+13.2
Passenger's Charter	184	249	−26.1
Telephone Enquiry Bureaux info	177	122	+45
Safety and security	125	80	+56.3
Reservations	119	78	+52.6
On-train catering	94	57	+64.9
Road-rail co-ordination	85	58	+46.6
Conveyance of cycles	30	183	−83.6
Smoking policy	30	35	−14.3
Miscellaneous	291	201	+44.8
Total	10,166	9,928	+2.4

Market research

Market research is all about finding out about consumers and what they want. It provides information to help answer many important business questions about product design, product prices, marketing, and customer service (see Figure 11.3). The purpose of market research in customer service is to find out what customers think about firms and their products, and also to identify strengths and weaknesses. An organization can then take action to improve areas of their service which customers suggest are weak.

▼ *Figure 11.3: The importance of market research*

Product design
What products do consumers want?

What particular features do consumers want a product to have?

What is the reaction of consumers to new products?

Product price
How much are consumers willing to pay?

How do people prefer to pay?

Place and method of sale
Where do consumers shop for the type of product?

What is the reaction of wholesalers and shops to new products?

Are customers satisfied with customer service?

Promotion
What is the reaction of consumers to new promotional ideas?

How effective have promotional campaigns been?

Market
What is the size of the market?

Is the market expanding or contracting?

What are the characteristics (age, sex, income, etc.) of potential customers?

Competition
Who are the competitors?

What are their strengths and weaknesses?

What is their market share?

What prices do they charge?

How do they promote their products?

Methods of collecting market research information

There are many sources of information and collection methods a firm can use to gather market research information. Often, carefully designed customer questionnaires are used to obtain peoples' views and opinions.

- **Face-to-face interviews** using a pre-designed questionnaire are a popular method. Interviews are cheap and allow the researcher to target particular kinds of people.

- **Telephone surveys** allow market researchers to target particular consumers by area. However, some potential consumers may be ex-directory or not on the telephone.

- **Postal surveys** involve sending out questionnaires for people to complete and return by post. However, many people simply throw them away.

Other methods include:

- **Consumer panels,** where firms invite groups of customers to give their views on products and monitor their buying habits over a period of time.

- **Observation:** Simply observing the behaviour of consumers and rival firms can generate a great deal of useful information – for example, monitoring TV and radio audiences for particular programmes, counting traffic on roads and at car parks, and examining the products and promotions of rival firms.

- **Test marketing** a new good or service in a small area to monitor consumer reaction and sales. This allows an organization to test consumer reaction before launching the product on a national or international market.

- **Studying published information.** Useful data can be found in newspapers and magazines, government statistical journals, and the annual reports of rival companies. Internal business records can also provide useful facts and figures – for example, details of production costs, consumer complaints, and sales over time.

Sampling

When carrying out market research interviews or surveys, it is usually impossible to ask everyone who might buy the product. Instead, firms ask just a small number of consumers, called a **sample**. As long as the sample of people chosen for research have similar buying habits and tastes to all the other consumers in the market, then the sample will give a good indication of what most consumers want.

For example, if the customers of a business are mainly male aged between 15 and 25, there is little point in questioning women or males aged from 25 upwards. However, it might be worth asking the views of males aged between 15 and 25 who do not buy from the firm, because this may lead to an understanding of why they go elsewhere, and what the business can do to stop this.

Market research, therefore, needs to be planned, designed, and carried out carefully. Businesses will often employ specialist market research organizations who are experienced in questionnaire design and sampling.

The rules of questionnaire design

Questionnaires are a very useful way of collecting information about consumers' buying habits and tastes. However, a poorly designed questionnaire will gather poor or inaccurate information. Consider the example opposite. See if you can spot what is wrong with it.

A market researcher would not learn very much from these questions because:

- Questions 1 and 2 are embarrassing and may put people off.

- People are unlikely to know the answer to Questions 4 or 5.

- Question 8 may force people to reply 'Yes'.

- Questions 3, 6, and 9 may produce so many different answers it may be difficult to make any sense of them.

- Many of the questions are pointless!

The DO's and DONT's of questionnaire design

The bad questionnaire opposite provides a number of clues to how questionnaires *should* be designed.

Questions should...

- Be easy for people to understand

- Be to the point

- Be designed to limit the number of meaningful responses. For example, in Question 9 respondents could be offered alternatives and asked to tick their choice, e.g.:

  a less than £2

  b £2-£3

  c more than £3

Questions should not...

- Be personal or embarrassing

- Force people to give the answer the researcher wants rather than one that is truthful

- Ask people to make calculations in their heads

Questionnaire

1. When did you last use a toilet?
2. How often do you use a toilet?
   a More than twice each day
   b Twice each day
   c Once each day
   d Less than once each day
3. What brand of toilet paper do you use?
4. How many sheets of paper does each toilet roll of your current brand have?
5. How much water do you use when you flush your toilet?

   50 litres   100 litres
   150 litres   more than 150 litres

6. Where do you buy toilet rolls?
7. Do you think the price and colour of toilet rolls are important?
   a Yes
   b No
8. You would be interested in a new toilet roll with a pleasant fragrance, wouldn't you?
   a Yes
   b No
9. How much would you pay for a pack of four scented toilet rolls?

Portfolio Activity 11.4

PC: Identify how business organizations monitor customer satisfaction

Range: How businesses monitor customer satisfaction

Skills: Read and respond to written material, Produce written material, Present information

1. Using a computer spreadsheet, draw a pie chart to show the proportions of different groups of people who choose to stay in hotels, according to the Novotel market research survey.

2. Draw a barchart to show what guests wanted, including those aspects of the hotel service that received a low score.

3. Suggest how this information could help Novotel plan the facilities they offer in their hotels and their promotional campaigns.

4. Using a word processor, prepare a questionnaire of no more than 10 questions, to ask hotel guests about their satisfaction with different aspects of hotel facilities and services.

5. a If possible, visit a local hotel and ask the manager's permission to interview a guest using your questionnaire. Wait in the lobby or outside the hotel and wait for a guest to leave the hotel building. Explain the purpose of your survey and ask them politely if they would answer your questions. Make a note of their answers.

b From the answers you obtain, evaluate:

i The guest's overall level of satisfaction with the service they received in the hotel

ii The design of your questions

Modern hotels show a clean pair of heels to tradition

When business travellers choose a hotel nowadays, cleanliness, comfort, convenience, and efficiency are the key considerations – ranking far above appearance and many of the traditional hospitality values. Even above price. Not so much a room with a view, as one with a clean bathroom, comfortable bed, desk, fax, and coffee-making machine close to the city centre. It is part of the 'office away from home' revolution that is also sweeping the hotel industry.

That is the evidence of a recent survey among guests by French hotels giant Novotel which runs 2,300 properties worldwide. It suggests a practical, no-nonsense approach to hotel stays, and gives a vote of confidence in the modern chains like Hilton, Novotel, and Holiday Inns that cut the individual frills in the interests of efficiency.

In the Novotel survey, more than 8 out of 10 guests when asked to identify what is important to them, emphasized cleanliness, comfort, and convenience. Other considerations, like helpful, friendly staff, efficiency, good car parking and flexible meal times, were rated highly by more than 7 out of 10. Image factors like a hotel's appearance, whether it is well known, has a good shop, a spacious lobby or is helpful with luggage were rated unimportant by Novotel's mainly business traveller customers. Price was only important to around half of all respondents.

WHO CHOOSES A HOTEL	
Business traveller	35%
Company travel dept	14%
Other company personnel	14%
Company visiting	10%
Secretary	6%
Travel agent	5%
Other	16%

WHAT GUESTS WANT	
Clean and tidy	89%
Comfortable	87%
Comfortable beds	83%
Convenient location	75%
Helpful staff	75%
Efficiency	73%
Flexible meal times	71%
Good car parking	71%
Well-trained staff	67%
Well-equipped rooms	65%

THE LOW SCORERS	
Different appearance	5%
Clinical appearance	6%
Innovative	8%
Well known	8%
Traditional	11%
Help with luggage	13%
Well-stocked shop	13%
Provisions for women*	13%
Spacious lobby	13%
Attractive building	14%

9% of men, 27% of women

London Evening Standard 8.2.95

Section **11.3** **Improvements to customer service**

In many organizations, customer surveys may reveal areas in which customer service needs to be improved. However, even if customer surveys suggest that customers are happy with the service they receive, improvements can and should still be made wherever possible. This is because:

- Not all customers will have participated in a survey of their opinions on service.

- Any organization that is in competition with other firms for customers must try to stay ahead of its rivals as they improve their services.

- Customers needs in terms of service are always changing. In general, customers are becoming more and more critical about the way they are treated by organizations.

Improvements to customer services can be made in many areas of a business. Key criteria for good customer service include:

- Reliability
- Friendliness
- Availability of goods and services
- Speed of delivery
- Exchanges and refunds
- Access to buildings
- Care for the environment
- Customer safety

We will now consider each of these key areas in detail.

Reliability

An organization that cannot be relied upon or trusted to provide goods or services that are of a high standard will fail to attract new customers or retain existing ones.

If you order a video recorder that is delivered late, does not work properly, and is not exchanged promptly, the chances are you will not buy from the same organization again. Similarly, if the bus or train service you use is continually late, overcrowded, and perhaps dirty, you will soon look around for alternative means of transport.

Reliability is important to both individual and business customers. Goods and services should be reliable, and standards of customer service should be high. Agreed delivery times should be met, repairs carried out quickly, and complaints dealt with efficiently and promptly.

It is not in the interests of a supplier to sell goods that are of poor quality or do not work properly. This will mean losing customers who may be important to the survival of the business. Business customers, especially, will rely on their suppliers to deliver quality materials and components on time, so that production is not held up.

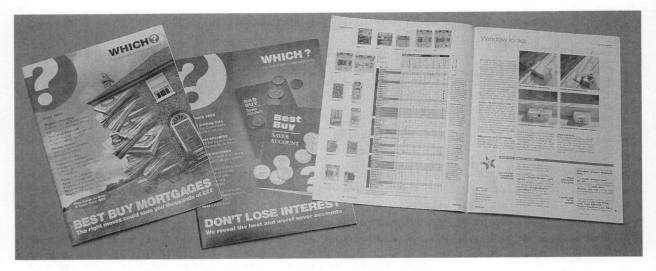

Improving reliability – some suggestions

When looking at improving reliability, it is important to look at both the product and the service given.

Improvements in customer service may be achieved by more staff training in different aspects of customer care. Treating your staff better is often the best way to get them to treat customers better.

Improvements in the quality of the product may be achieved by contacting suppliers and providing them with information on the problems and faults experienced by sales staff, as well as customers. The supplier may then look at redesigning the product to correct the fault.

Reliability is also important when buying a service. A decorator who drops paint on your carpet, a financial adviser who loses you money, or a garage that fails to repair your car properly or overcharges you, are not providing a reliable service.

Each month, the Consumers' Association magazine *Which?* publishes reports on the reliability and other features of different goods and services. Consumers can study these reports before deciding where and what to buy.

Portfolio Activity 11.5

PC: Identify improvements to customer service

Range: Improvements to customer service

Skills: Read and respond to written material, Produce written material

1. Why could the organizations featured in the article be described as 'unreliable'?

2. What could these organizations do to improve the reliability of their services?

TYRE FIRMS ARE PULLING A FAST ONE

MIRROR CONSUMER SPECIAL

DRIVERS risk getting dangerous advice on brakes and tyres at fast-fit centres, a damning report reveals today.

Six out of ten centres failed to spot all the brake defects on a car used in a secret survey.

And five out of six didn't look at the spare tyre, which had a deep cut capable of causing a blow-out at high-speed. The report in the consumer magazine Which?, follows a survey of 147 branches of Britain's eight leading fast-fit giants.

The eight firms involved in the ten-week survey were Halfords, Kwik-Fit, National Tyres and Autocare, Smiley Tyre and Exhaust Centrers, Charlie Browns, ATS and Hi-Q.

Halfords came top for both tyre AND brake advice. Charlie Browns were worst on tyres and often missed brake defects.

Daily Mirror 7.9.95

Friendliness

▼ Over-friendly

▼ Too abrupt

▼ Just right

Improving friendliness – some suggestions

Staff who deal with customers should be chosen carefully. People with cheerful personalities, and who are polite and helpful, can be identified at interview or during later job appraisals.

Specialist courses are also available to teach staff how to behave with customers in order to secure their purchase.

Friendliness is important to customers when making a purchase. They want to feel that their custom is valued, and that they are getting good advice and attention. Unfortunately, the trend towards bigger stores and quicker service has meant friendliness has been lost in some cases, and staff can seem abrupt because they are concentrating on speed of service.

Many stores are now retraining staff in how to be friendly towards their customers and serve them efficiently. Simple things like smiling and saying 'Hello' or 'Good morning', making eye-contact, saying 'Thank you' and 'Goodbye', can all help to make a good impression and encourage the customer to come back in future. However, staff who try to be too friendly can put off customers just as much as those who are too abrupt.

Customers can judge how friendly a sales assistant is by looking at his/her **body language**. The position of the body, the tilt of the head, whether or not eye-contact is made – all these give strong signals to the customer about what the salesperson is thinking.

Availability of goods and services

No organization can stock everything that customers want. Many specialize in providing a narrow range of goods and services. For example, an electrical shop will concentrate on the supply of home appliances, such as microwaves, video recorders, and washing machines. However, nothing is more frustrating than to find out that a store does not have the item that you want. It is even worse if you telephoned first and were told that the goods were in stock.

Many large stores now have computerized stock control systems linked to bar code readers at the till. The bar code readers scan every item leaving the shop and automatically update the central stock records, so that at any moment the computer has a complete record of what is available in the store. In the most advanced systems used by large supermarkets, the computer is set to automatically generate an order for new stock when stocks fall to a certain level.

For example, if it takes two days for a supermarket to receive a delivery of toilet rolls after placing an order, and the supermarket sells 2,500 toilet rolls every day, the supermarket knows it must place a new order when stocks are down to 5,000 rolls. By the time the existing stock has run out, a new delivery will have been received. By using new technology in this way, large stores are able to keep control of their stocks and avoid disappointing customers.

Sometimes consumers require a very wide range of goods and services. In this case it is important for an organization to operate a fast ordering and delivery service. However, it is pointless pretending to a consumer that a product can be obtained in a few days if it cannot.

Many mail order firms selling products like computer CDs and music and electronic equipment advertise a vast range of stock, most of which they do not actually hold. The reason for this is that it would simply be far too expensive for them to carry all the items that a customer might require. These firms trade in the hope that, if an item is ordered, they can get it quickly.

Improving the availability of goods and services – some suggestions

There is no point trying to stock everything customers want. First, it would tie too much money up in stocks, some of which may remain unsold. Secondly, storage would take up too much space.

Some firms may successfully expand into other products in an attempt to offer customers more choice. For example, many Esso petrol stations also offer on-site supermarkets, and Blockbuster Video rent and sell computer games, soft drinks, crisps, and sweets, as well as hiring videos. However, before a business makes this decision it will need to use market research to find out more about what their customers want.

If an ordering and delivery service is introduced, it is important that it is simple for customers to use, and that sales staff are honest about how long products will take to be delivered.

Speed of delivery

The time taken between a good or service being ordered and delivery is called the **delivery lead time**. There is increasing pressure on suppliers from their individual and business customers to reduce lead times. It is frustrating to wait a long time for something you have ordered to be delivered. A firm that is able to guarantee a short lead time between receiving an order and making delivery is likely to gain more customers than slower rivals.

Lead times will often depend on the type of good or service being supplied. For example, highly specialized items like hand-crafted furniture or industrial robots are likely to be made to order, and cannot simply be supplied from stock kept in a warehouse. Customers ordering a new Rolls Royce will have to wait around 2 years for it to be delivered!

Business customers will often rely on delivery lead times being as short as possible. This is because many now operate Just In Time systems, where materials needed for production are ordered and delivered 'just in time' for them to be used (see 4.2). In this way, firms can keep their stocks of raw materials and components to a minimum to reduce storage costs.

Improving the speed of delivery – some suggestions

A business should always be honest with customers about expected delivery times. If delivery is delayed, the customer should be contacted in good time and alternative arrangements made. It is very annoying to wait for a delivery that never arrives!

The speed of delivery often depends on the time it takes for the supplier to process an order. Taking orders and receiving payment confirmation by phone, fax, or over EDI computer links (see 12.2), can speed up the rate at which orders are turned around. Some organizations are even able to promise next-day delivery from their central warehouses, or a 24-hour emergency call-out service for service providers, such as car mechanics and plumbers, for an additional charge.

Delivery times may also be improved by changing the method used to deliver items – for example, using special delivery and courier services rather than first- or second-class post (see 14.4). Delivery by road may also be improved by planning in advance the best route to take. New technology such as routemaster programs can help drivers plan the most direct routes and warn them of any congestion along the way.

Exchanges or refunds

Before they make a purchase, customers want to know that if they change their mind, or if the good or service they buy is poor or faulty, they can exchange the item or obtain a refund without too much fuss. Many people may be put off buying a product if they cannot be guaranteed an exchange or refund if they are not entirely satisfied.

Many large organizations have a 'no quibble' policy on giving exchanges or refunds. This means they will replace or refund a purchase without asking why. However, this may often depend on the type of good or service sold. For example, how would you react to a customer who continued to return to your butcher's shop each week because they were not satisfied with the meat you sold them the previous week?

Policies on exchanges and refunds were discussed in Section 10.1. It would be useful to re-read this section now to refresh your memory.

Access to buildings

Most of us take access to buildings for granted. We have little difficulty in entering, moving around, and leaving shops, cinemas, pubs, and other places. However, elderly people, parents with prams and pushchairs, and people who are blind, deaf, or disabled can find it very difficult to gain access to buildings and transport. The provision of ramps, lifts, and clear signs would help these people enter and move around buildings more easily. These facilities are an important aspect of customer care, and by providing them, firms can attract a whole range of potential new customers.

Improving access to buildings – some suggestions

Many people still have problems gaining access to buildings and different modes of transport. An organization may improve the accessibility of their premises and services by providing the following features:

- Ramps for wheelchairs and pushchairs that are neither too steep or too long

- Installing automatic doors to replace old or heavy doors that may be difficult to open

- Providing wide lifts and toilets for people in wheelchairs

- Signposting the layout of facilities in business premises

- Installing voice synthesizers in lifts to give details of floor numbers and warnings to stand clear of the doors

- Providing staff to help customers pack and carry their shopping and open doors for them

Many of these features can be 'designed into' new premises with ease. However, it may be more difficult adding them to old buildings.

Portfolio Activity 11.6

PC: Identify improvements to customer service
Range: Improvements to customer service
Skills: Collect and record data, Produce written material

Investigate access in a business organization of your choice. How easy is it to find your way around? How easy would it be to gain access and move around the building if you were in a wheelchair? What features and facilities have been provided to improve access?

Write up your findings in a short report using a word processor. You may include photographs you have taken of some of the facilities provided on the premises, but remember to ask permission first.

Care for the environment

Care for the environment is an issue that is important to a growing number of people (see 8.3). Many firms have changed the ways in which they produce and promote their products due to pressure from customers and organizations such as Greenpeace and Friends of the Earth for them to take greater care of the environment, including rivers and seas, plants, animals, and the air we breathe.

Many organizations now publish environmental policies and targets and undertake regular **'green audits'**. These involve examining different aspects of their business operations to see how environmentally-friendly they are, and how they could be improved – for example, by recycling more waste, reducing the amount of paper used, and not using chemicals or products that have been tested on animals.

▼ *Showing customers that the organization cares for the environment has become an important element in customer service.*

..ENVIRONMENTAL INFORMATION.... ENVIRONMENTAL INFORMATION

EFS1

SAFEWAY
Safeway Stores plc
Corporate Affairs Dept.,
6 Millington Road,
Hayes,
Middlesex. UB3 4AY

SAFEWAY ENVIRONMENTAL POLICY

1. Safeway will operate in harmony with the global environment and promote environmental protection as part of its business activities.

2. Particular attention will be paid to the following areas:-

   a) Conservation of energy

   b) Sustainable use of raw materials

   c) Environmentally responsible waste management

   d) Progressive reduction of the company's environmental impact in all its premises, activities and developments

   e) Environmentally responsible marketing

   f) Compliance with the law and best available technology in environmental protection

   g) Effective environmental audit systems

   h) Staff training and recruitment to meet the environmental objectives.

Printed on recycled paper

SAINSBURY'S
Schoolbags

What is it?

It's a scheme that is about to set the nation shopping for some great causes. Simply by shopping at Sainsbury's, you have the opportunity to help the environment and a school, or schools, of your choice.

You will be able to save on waste and the amount of oil that's used in the production of carrier bags - by simply re-using them.

Here's how you do it...

Improving care for the environment – some suggestions

Customers are genuinely concerned about the environment and want firms to make significant improvements in the way they make their products. This can involve:

- Undertaking regular 'green audits'
- Recycling waste
- Conserving energy – for example, by turning off lights when not in use
- Using more recycled materials and biodegradable products
- Not testing chemicals and finished products such as cosmetics on animals
- Only buying wood from renewable forests
- Only buying products from suppliers who have a good environmental record

Organizations must also be aware of the environment in and around their premises. This should be kept clean and tidy and free from rubbish at all times.

Improving customer safety – some suggestions

Product safety is an important issue for people who design and manufacture goods. For example, paints, dyes, and materials should be non-toxic; sharp edges should be removed; electrical appliances should have cut-outs if they overheat, and be earthed so that they do not give electric shocks. Products that comply with quality and safety standards set by the British Standards Institution will be awarded a kitemark to prove they are safe.

Improvements to customer safety on business premises may be made by regularly checking on health and safety practices and taking action where necessary. Key questions to ask include:

- Are warning notices displayed in prominent places for fire and other hazards?
- Are the signs clear?
- Would staff be able to evacuate customers quickly?
- Are staff trained in safety and First Aid procedures?
- Are there First Aid kits nearby?
- Are there any obvious hazards like boxes or other obstacles blocking fire exits?
- Are fire exits open or locked?

Customer safety

Firms need to be aware of the safety of their customers when they visit their premises and when they purchase and use their products.

Firms are required by law to ensure customer safety at all times (see 10.4). The safety of visitors, workers, and customers on business premises is covered by the Health and Safety at Work Act. Product safety is covered by the Consumer Protection Act and the Sale of Goods Act.

It is not enough for an organization simply to warn customers about risks to their safety. For example, notices on fairground rides saying that 'riders ride at their own risk' have no meaning in law. If someone is injured while using the ride, the fairground is still liable. All firms are required to accept responsibility for the safety of their customers, and to abide by the legal health and safety regulations – whatever the signs may say.

Injuries suffered by customers on business premises or through using a product can mean bad publicity for the firm, and many customers may be put off using them again. The injured customer may also start legal action, which could cost the organization a lot of money. Good customer safety is, therefore, an important aspect of customer service.

Key words

In your own words, write down explanations and definitions of the following key words and terms from this chapter:

Customer service	Brand image	Consumer panel	Test marketing
Retail surveillance	Customer feedback	Sample	'Green audit'
Customer questionnaire	Market research		

You must demonstrate that you are able to:

1. Explain the importance of customer service in business organizations

2. Identify how business organizations monitor customer satisfaction

3. Identify improvements to customer services

4. Present proposals for improvements to customer services in one organization

1 One way customer service could be improved in an organization is by:

A cutting production costs

B more advertising

C offering a free phone information line

D producing more goods and services

2 Which of the following is unlikely to improve customer service in an organization?

A installing ramps for wheelchairs and prams

B reducing the range and amount of different goods held in stock

C reducing the lead time between receiving an order and making delivery

D introducing more recycling facilities

3 A failure by a business to consider the health and safety of customers could lead to:

A higher profits

B being taken to court and fined

C less training

D a better reputation

4 Firms often monitor customer complaints. The reason for doing this is to:

A identify problem customers and avoid them in future

B prepare for any legal problems likely to result from complaints

C identify areas where the firm can improve its customer service

D so it can say that it has a policy of monitoring customer complaints

Questions 5-7 share the following answer options:

A monitoring the number of customers

B tracking the level of sales

C getting feedback from customers

D market research

Which of the above methods of monitoring customer satisfaction would you advise the following organizations to use?

5 A manufacturer of chocolate bars

6 A local hospital

7 A tourist attraction, such as Stonehenge

Questions 8-10 share the following answer options:

A to gain and retain customers

B to increase customer satisfaction

C to make customers loyal

D to improve the image of an organization

Which of the above benefits of good customer service do you think each of the following business activities is chiefly designed to achieve?

8 A supermarket that introduces a free bus service for customers

9 A petrol station issuing membership cards to allow regular customers to receive discounts on petrol, or money-off vouchers for other products

10 A manufacturer refusing to buy chemicals that have been tested on animals

Questions 11-13 share the following answer options:

A the speed of delivery

B friendliness

C customer safety

D the availability of goods and services

The following are extracts from customer complaints received by different business organizations. Which of the above aspects of customer service do you think need to be improved in each case?

11 'I sustained severe bruising to my left leg after I slipped on your highly polished floor.'

12 'Your member of staff then told me I would have to wait to be served until after he had finished his conversation with his friend.'

417

13 'On the phone a member of your sales staff told me the item I wanted was in stock. An hour later I arrived at your shop, only to be told the item sold out some days ago.'

14 **a.** Suggest three reasons why good customer service is important in business organizations.

b. Write a short paragraph to show what you understand about the following aspects of customer service:

- speed of delivery
- reliability
- customer safety
- care for the environment

c. Suggest one way customer service could be improved in each of the areas listed above.

15 **a.** Explain three aspects of customer service that are likely to be most important in a shop that hires out power tools such as mechanical diggers, electric saws, and drills to members of the public.

b. Explain two ways the same organization could monitor whether or not its customers were happy with the service provided.

assessment assignment

Assessment Assignment

The following assignment meets all the evidence requirements needed to fulfil all the performance criteria in element 3.4. In addition it covers the following range points and core skills:

Range: Importance of customer service
How businesses monitor customer satisfaction
Improvements to customer service

Skills: **Communication**
Take part in discussions
Produce written material
Use images
Information technology
Process information
Present information

Tasks

The following tasks can be carried out in small groups or individually.

1. Investigate customer service in an organization of your choice.

   a Draw up a checklist of features of customer service you wish to investigate under each of the following headings:

   - Reliability
   - Friendliness
   - Availability of goods and services
   - Speed of delivery
   - Policies for exchanges and refunds
   - Access to buildings
   - Care for the environment
   - Customer safety

   b If possible, visit your chosen organization as an 'undercover customer'. Make notes of your first-hand experiences on all the different aspects of customer service you listed in Task 1a.

   c Arrange to visit the organization with the business owners or managers in order to investigate the provision of customer service. During your visit, ask if you can interview a senior manager in order to find out:

   i How customer satisfaction is monitored

   ii What improvements to customer service the organization has introduced over the last few years.

   d Use your notes and a word processor to write up the first part of a short report on your findings. This should include descriptions of:

   - The organization and its operations (see 1.1)
   - Customer services provided by the organization
   - How it monitors customer satisfaction

   You may also include evidence of customer satisfaction you have picked up from informal conversations with customers of the organization, and from your first-hand experience as an undercover customer.

2. **a** Prepare notes on:

   i How you think your chosen organization could improve its customer services in three of the key areas listed in Task 1a

   ii How the improvements to customer service you recommend could help to:

   - Attract more customers
   - Increase customer satisfaction
   - Secure customer loyalty
   - Enhance the image of the organization

   b Use your notes to complete the second part of the report you started in Task 1d. This should include your recommendations for customer service improvements and what you hope they will achieve.

3. Plan, make, and record a presentation to an invited audience on your proposals for improvements to customer services in your chosen business organization.

   a Plan your presentation. This should include:

- Writing a script or preparing notes
- Preparing overhead transparencies or posters to illustrate and give information about your proposals
- Preparing handouts containing brief details about the organization and your proposals

   b Deliver your presentation. This should include:

- An introduction to your chosen business organization
- Your observations on customer service provision in the organization
- A description of how the organization monitors customer satisfaction (if at all)
- Your proposals for improving customer services in three key areas
- The benefits you hope your proposals will bring the organization

   c If possible, arrange for your presentation to be recorded on audio or video tape.

Remember to store and file your finished work and notes appropriately in your portfolio.

chapter 12

Financial and Administrative Support

Unit Four

unit

4

chapter *12* *Financial Transactions and Documents*

BUT WE ORDERED A TANK FOR OUR FISH!

Key ideas

Financial transactions involve exchanging money for goods and services.

An **inward transaction** occurs when money is received by a business from its individual or business customers. An **outward transaction** occurs when a business pays money out to another person or business.

Outward transactions occur when **purchases** are made. These will involve payment for **materials** and **services**, such as insurance and power supplies, and **wages** to hire workers.

It is important for all firms to keep records of their transactions to **produce annual accounts** for business owners and for the tax authorities, to monitor business performance, and to reduce the risk of error, theft, or fraud, i.e. **ensure security**. Documents are needed by business organizations to record details of transactions relating to **purchases, sales, payments,** and **receipts**.

Purchase documents include **order forms, goods received notes,** and **purchase invoices**.

Sales documents include **orders received, delivery notes, sales invoices, credit** and **debit notes,** and **statements of account**.

Goods and services can be sold by **cash sale**, whereby goods and services are paid for immediately, or by **credit**. It is usual for businesses to allow their customers up to 30, 60, or even 90 days to pay for goods and services.

Payment for goods and services received can be made using **cash, cheques, credit** and **debit cards, BACS (Banking Automatic Clearing Service),** and **EDI (Electronic Data Interchange)**.

Receipts documents include **sales receipts, cheques, paying-in slips,** and **bank statements**.

Each year business organizations lose many millions of pounds due to fraud, theft, and criminal damage. **Security** is, therefore, very important to firms in helping to prevent fraud and theft, and ensuring high standards of honesty.

Businesses can reduce the risk of fraud and theft by introducing a range of security checks, including **authorization of orders, checking invoices** against orders and goods received notes, and **authorized cheque signatories**.

Section **12.1** ## What are financial transactions?

Trade takes place when producers supply their goods and services to consumers in return for money or other goods and services. A **financial transaction** takes place whenever a person or organization pays money to another person or organization for goods and services ordered or received.

Many millions of financial transactions take place every day all over the world. Whenever you buy an ice cream or a can of drink in a shop, you are making a financial transaction. You pay money to the shopkeeper to receive the ice cream or drink. When you travel on a bus or train, you pay money for a ticket which allows you to use the service.

Inward and outward transactions

Because most firms are not just producers, but also consumers of goods and services, they not only receive payments but also make payments to other people and organizations. That is, most firms will receive money and also pay money out. This means there are two types of financial transaction in business:

- **Inward transactions**
- **Outward transactions**

Inward and outward transactions

▼ Inward transactions

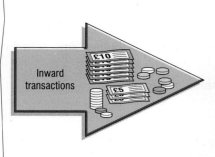

▼ Outward transactions

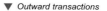

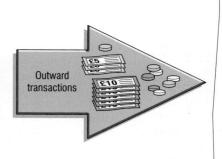

Inward transactions are payments of money received by a firm. For most business organizations inward transactions will include:

- Payments for goods and services sold to members of the public
- Payments for goods and services sold to other businesses
- Loans of money from banks and other lenders

Other organizations can receive inward transactions in other forms. For example, limited companies can receive money from the sale of shares; charities will receive donations; and the government receives money in the form of taxes (see 1.3–1.4).

Outward transactions are payments made by a firm to other firms or people. A firm will usually make payments for:

- Wages for the hire of workers
- Raw materials and component parts from suppliers
- Services, such as cleaning, maintenance, insurance, and advertising
- Fixed assets such as premises, machinery, vehicles, and other equipment
- Overheads such as telephone charges, stamps, stationary, rent and rates
- Loan repayments and interest charges
- Any Value Added Tax (VAT) collected on goods and services sold will also have to be returned to the government's Customs and Excise department

Recording transactions

Whenever a firm exchanges goods and services for money, it is important that it keeps detailed and accurate records. The types of information it will need to record include:

For inward transactions...

- Customer details, including name and address
- Type and amount of goods and services ordered or supplied
- Price of individual items and total price, including delivery, discounts, and VAT
- Payment details, including date, amount, and method

For outward transactions...

- Who money is being paid to, including name and account
- Type and amount of goods and services ordered or received
- Price of individual items and total price, including any delivery charges, discounts, and VAT
- Payment details, including date, amount, and method

It is essential for all organizations in business to record their transactions and to be able to retrieve them easily for the following reasons:

- **To record all purchases and sales:** Any business will need to keep track of total purchases and sales so that it can monitor that it is not spending more than it is earning. A firm that spends more than it earns in revenues from the sale of its goods and services will make a loss and could face closure. A business will also need to know how much money it owes to suppliers and how much is owed to it by customers paying by credit (see 12.2).

▼ With more ways for customers to pay for goods and services, opportunities for theft and fraud have increased.

- **To ensure security:** Records provide evidence that transactions have taken place. A firm will always be able to check payment demands from suppliers against records of goods and services received and payments made in the past. They will then be able to see whether they have overlooked settling their bill or if the supplier has made a mistake.

  A firm may also be vulnerable to theft or fraud if it does not keep accurate records. For example, if a firm did not keep records of how much cash was entering or leaving a till, a dishonest sales assistant might be tempted to take money without permission.

  Fraud is a sophisticated type of theft. Examples include people paying for goods using stolen credit cards, or employees paying out money to the bank account of a 'supplier' that does not exist, but to which they have access (see 12.4).

- **To monitor business performance:** Business owners and managers will want to receive up-to-date information on how well their business is doing in terms of output and sales, costs and revenues, profits or losses. A **profit** is made when revenues from the sale of goods and services are greater than business costs. An organization will make a **loss** if costs exceed revenues from sales. If sales revenues are exactly equal to costs, then profit is zero. This is known as **breaking even**.

  Financial information will allow business owners and managers to make decisions about the future performance of their organization. For example, if records show that monthly sales figures have been poor, managers may decide that they need to cut prices and mount a big advertising campaign to encourage more consumers to buy their products.

- **To produce accounts:** To help monitor business performance, organizations need to keep-up-to date accounts showing how much the business is spending, what it is spending money on, and how much it is earning from sales and any other sources of income. These records will also be needed by shareholders and government authorities such as the Inland Revenue (see below).

  Business accounts produced regularly for the use of business owners and managers are known as **internal accounts**. For example, separate accounts can be kept to provide up-to-date information on:

  - purchases, and how much is owed to individual suppliers

  - sales for cash and on credit, and how much is owed by individual customers

- VAT paid on purchases and VAT received from sales
- inflows and outflows of cash
- cash held on the premises
- deposits and withdrawals from the organization's bank account
- wages and salaries paid
- expenses, such as electricity, telephone, advertising, stationary, travel, etc.
- all incomes and expenditures

▼ Business organizations produce financial accounts for their own internal use and because the law requires them for tax purposes.

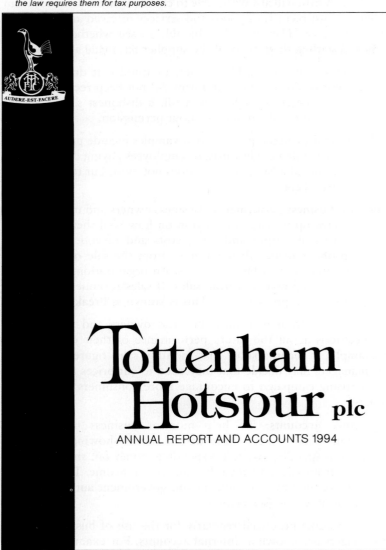

Tottenham Hotspur plc

ANNUAL REPORT AND ACCOUNTS 1994

At the end of each 12-month period, these accounts can be used to calculate the total value of assets, such as premises, machinery, and other equipment owned by a business. This is known as a **balance sheet**. Records can also be used to provide a summary of the total costs, revenues, and profit or loss for the year. This is known as a **profit and loss statement**. Business owners and managers will use these end-of-year accounts to judge business performance and make decisions on how it might be improved over the next 12 months.

● **To meet legal requirements:** The law requires that all business organizations produce annual accounts every 12 months so that the government's tax authorities can calculate how much tax each one must pay, if any.

Sole traders and partnerships may be liable for income tax on their earnings, while limited companies may have to pay corporation tax on their profits to the Inland Revenue. Any VAT collected on goods and services sold will have to be paid to the Customs and Excise department.

Private and public limited companies are also required to provide copies of their final year accounts to any person who wants them. These are called **external accounts**.

Internal and external business accounts are considered in more detail in section 13.1.

Income and expenditure accounts

Perhaps the simplest and most informative accounts a business can produce are those that list all money received and paid out each week or month.

Figure 12.1 shows a simple **income and expenditure account** for an imaginary business called Bestwick Auto Repairs for the month of June 1995. All sales revenues are recorded by showing the appropriate sales invoice number. It shows that during the month of June 1995 the income from the business was greater than the amount it spent on materials, parts, wages, and other equipment.

▼ *Figure 12.1: An example of a simple income and expenditure account*

BESTWICK AUTO REPAIRS

Date: June 1995

INCOME			EXPENDITURE		
Date	Description	£ amount	Date	Description	£ amount
1.6.95	Balance brought forward from May	+£320.00			
3.6.95	Ms C Biggs - accident repairs (invoice 256)	£175.55	2.6.95	Exhaust parts	£600.00
5.6.95	Mr G Lovett - 4 new tyres (invoice 257)	£240.95	6.6.95	Car paint supplies	£450.80
7.6.95	Mr B Hillyard - new windscreen (invoice 258)	£140.50	8.6.95	Rent	£600.00
12.6.95	Repairs to 4 Hertz rental cars (invoice 259)	£2,300.00	8.6.95	Tyres (x 100)	£230.00
15.6.95	Mr K Webster - fit new radiator (invoice 260)	£75.80	14.6.95	Business rates	£125.00
17.6.95	Mr R Vollo - full service (invoice 261)	£230.00	15.6.95	New welding equipment	£750.20
23.6.95	Ms M Lyes - accident repairs (invoice 262)	£560.20	16.6.95	Car parts	£4300.75
24.6.95	Mr N Hallett - wheel alignment (invoice 263)	£45.00	17.6.95	Engine oil (100 litres)	£60.00
30.6.95	Repairs to 7 Hertz rental cars (invoice 264)	£10,970.00	28.6.95	Wages	£3200.55
			29.6.95	Electricity	£220.70
31.6.95	**Total income**	**£15,058.00**	31.6.95	**Total expenditure**	**£10,538.00**
31.6.95	**Balance carried forward to July**	**+£4,520.00**			

Bestwick Auto Repairs has a surplus of income over expenditure at the end of June. This may not occur every month because some months are more expensive than others. That is, the flow of money into and out of a business is uneven over time. However, it provides a good indication that Bestwick Auto Repairs is performing well.

Because flows of money are uneven, it is important that Bestwick Auto Repairs saves a surplus in one month to cover another month in which total expenditure might exceed income, for example, due to a large quarterly telephone bill or annual insurance premium payment. However, if at the end of the year Bestwick Auto Repairs has received more income than it has spent during the year, it will have made a profit. Profit will be zero when income is equal to expenditure.

We will find out more about Bestwick Auto Repairs later in the chapter.

Portfolio Activity 12.3

Range: Records of transactions
Skills: Tackle problems

1. Below are jumbled records of purchases and sales made by two business organizations over the same period. Set out the information in two simple income and expenditure accounts and calculate whether at the end of the period they have made a profit, loss, or have broken even.

ALPHA Ltd: incomes (+) and expenditures (−)		The BETA partnership: incomes (+) and expenditures (−)	
Cheque received	+£340.00	Rent	−£550.00
Office stationary	−£125.50	Cash payment	+£475.20
Cash payment	+£57.50	Advertising	−£75.00
Materials	−£2,450.00	Cheque received	+£230.00
Rent	−£1,200.00	Office stationary	−£55.70
Invoice 125	+£500.00	Cash payment	+£47.00
Rates	−£160.00	Cheque received	+£128.00
Payment direct into bank account	+£2,500.95	Wages	−£3,250.00
Telephone	−£80.00	Cheque received	+£823.00
Postage	−£25.00	Electricity	−£145.00
Electricity	−£230.25	Cheque received	+£1,010.00
Cheque received	+£1,350.00	Rates	−£95.00
Gas	−£35.00	Cheque received	+£743.50
Wages	−£4,750.00	Materials	−£950.00
Direct debit payment	+£1,900.00	Cheque received	+£1,270.00
Cheque received	+£560.00	Insurance	−£125.00
Insurance	−£100.00	Telephone	−£65.00
Cheque received	+£760.75	Cheque received	+£499.00
Goods returned	−£500.00	Cash payment	+£85.00

Section **12.2**

Making a purchase

Every purchase made by a business or individual customer is a sale to the firm that receives money in payment. An outward transaction is a payment for goods and services. An inward transaction is a sale.

Payment is made once an **invoice** is issued following an order for goods and services. An invoice will contain details of goods and services supplied, how much is owed by the customer, and when payment is due (see 12.3).

Business to consumer sales

Organizations that sell goods and services to private individuals are suppliers in **consumer markets**. They will sell finished products which are for the immediate use, or consumption, of those who buy them. These include:

- Durable goods, e.g. video recorders, cars, jewellery, clothes
- Non-durable goods, e.g. washing powders, food and drink, paper
- Personal services, e.g. hairdressing, window cleaning, insurance

Business to business sales

However, not all organizations supply consumer goods and services. Many supply **industrial markets** in which the consumers are other business organizations. The goods and services supplied to business consumers are wanted because they will be used in the production of other goods and services. Raw materials, component parts, machinery, computer equipment, vehicles, stationary are just a few examples of unfinished and finished goods used by firms in producing, selling, and distributing their own goods and services. Specialist services such as advertising agencies, management training, maintenance, haulage, commercial insurance and banking, and many more, are also available to business customers.

Selling goods and services

In general, firms sell consumer and industrial goods and services in one of two main ways:

- **Cash sales** mean that goods and services are paid for immediately they are received, either by cash or by cheque. Most shops sell goods and services on this basis. When you buy a bar of chocolate or a CD, you will normally pay for it there and then.

- **Sales on credit** involve the customer 'buying now and paying later'. Sales on credit can take a number of forms.

  Trade credit is often given by suppliers to their regular business customers. They are allowed up to 30, 60, or even 90 days to pay in full for goods and services they have received.

  Credit sales are a popular method used by mail order firms. The customer is allowed to spread their payments for goods received over a number of weeks. A relatively low-price item, such as a pair of jeans,

▼ *Some consumer goods and services*

can usually be paid for in regular weekly amounts over 12-24 weeks, while a high-price item, such as a video recorder, can be paid for over 52 weeks, or sometimes even more. The customer owns the goods received after the first instalment has been paid.

Hire purchase (HP) also allows the customer to pay for the goods or services they have received in regular (monthly) instalments, often including an interest charge, with the repayments spread over anything from 6 months to a number of years. Unlike credit sales, an HP agreement will normally require the customer to pay a deposit of 10% or 20% of the total price immediately the goods or services are ordered or received. The goods do not become the property of the customer until the final payment has been made.

HP is a popular method of payment used by smaller firms to buy the machinery and other equipment they need. Many suppliers now offer interest-free HP to encourage customers to buy their goods and services.

People and organizations to whom goods or services have been sold on credit are known as **debtors**. The business organization that allows customers to pay on credit is known as their **creditor** until they pay for the goods and services they have received.

Allowing customers to pay on credit can encourage sales because they are able to spread their payments. This is an especially important advantage for individual and business customers who have limited incomes and/or savings. However, for the supplier there is always a risk that the customer may default - that is, not pay up. This will involve spending time and money chasing the debt in writing, and even legal action through a court if they still fail to pay.

Methods of payment

There are a number of ways an individual or business customer can choose to settle cash sales or payments for trade credit, credit sales, or hire purchase:

● **Cash:** Cash is generally thought of as notes and coins, and is the most popular method of payment. However, only smaller purchases tend to be made with cash. Around 90% of the total value of all payments today are made by other means. This is because cash can be awkward to handle, especially in large amounts, and is easily lost or stolen.

Many small businesses like to be paid in cash because there is little chance of it being traced if they do not declare it as income to the Inland Revenue for tax purposes. This is illegal. However, most large firms are unlikely to pay using notes and coins and prefer to receive payments by more secure methods.

▼ An example of a hire purchase payment for a television

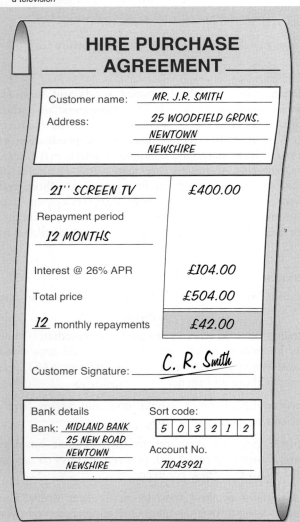

● **Cheques:** Most people and businesses have bank or building society accounts into which they can deposit money and from which they can make payments. Cheques are simply a way of transferring 'cash' from one account to another. Cheques avoid the inconvenience of cash and are more secure, provided they have been filled out properly and signed by the account holder. The name of the account holder will usually be printed on the cheque. We will look at cheques in more detail in section 13.3.

▼ *Most financial transactions today are made using cheques. In 1994 over £1,000 billion worth of cheques were cleared by UK banks.*

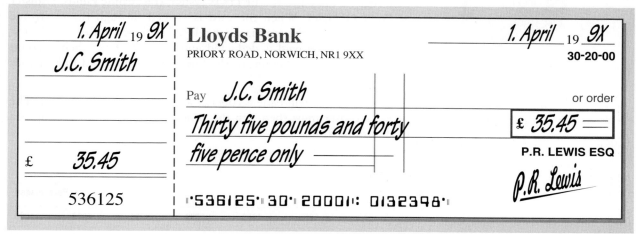

▼ *Figure 12.2: An example of how a cheque makes payment*

1 Customer pays £25 with cheque from the Lloyds' bank.

2 Shopkeeper 'pays' cheque into his/her account at the Midland bank.

3 Midland bank credits shopkeepers account with £25.

4 Midland bank contacts Lloyds bank.

5 Lloyds bank arranges transfer to Midland bank.

6 Llyods bank debits customer's account by £25.

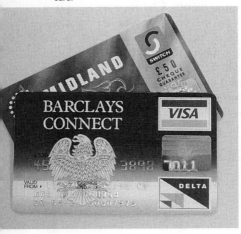

There are two debit cards available from UK banks: the CONNECT card and the SWITCH card.

- **Debit card:** Debit cards are a relatively new and easy method of paying for goods and services issued by banks to their account holders. Over half the adult population in the UK now hold a debit card.

  The debit card saves the customer the time and trouble of writing out a cheque. The advantage of debit card payment for the business making the sale is that the payment is transferred into their bank account immediately. Cheques have to be taken to their bank and may take several days before they are 'cleared' for payment by the customer's bank.

  To use a debit card, the shop or other supplier must have an electronic cash register linked to the **EFTPOS** system (**Electronic Funds Transfer at Point Of Sale**). When the card is swiped through the electronic register, details of the purchase are relayed to the card user's bank, and the amount to be paid is deducted automatically from their account and credited to the account of the business that has sold them goods or services.

  The cash register will issue a voucher as a record of the payment. The debit card user must then sign the voucher to show they have agreed to the transaction.

▼ The holding of plastic cards has increased over time

Plastic Cards[1]

Great Britain						Percentages
	1986	1989	1990	1991	1992	1993
ATM debit card	..	43	43	56	60	62
Debit card	..	30	40	45	51	52
Credit/charge card	33	37	39	39	38	38
Visa credit card	..	..	26	28	28	28
Mastercard	..	..	19	19	17	18
Retailer card	9	13	15	17	16	17
All plastic cards[2]	..	67	68	73	75	76

1 Percentage of persons aged 16 and over holding plastic cards
2 Includes cheque guarantee cards

Association for payment Clearing Services

- **Direct debit:** A person or firm can issue a written authority to their bank or building society to allow regular, or even irregular, transfers of agreed amounts of money from their account to the account of another person or firm to whom they owe money. The person or firm owed the money will arrange the necessary computer instructions on the amount and timing of the transfer from their customer's bank account.

  The direct debit system is particularly useful for credit card companies, and gas and electricity suppliers, who receive a large number of variable payments every month or quarter from their customers.

- **Standing order:** If payments for the same amount are regular, for example, monthly mortgage repayments to a building society, or payments for credit sales and hire purchase, a person or firm can instruct their bank or building society to make regular transfers to the account of the person or firm to whom they owe the money. This is known as a **standing order**.

● **Banking Automated Clearing Services (BACS)**: Paying by cheque and taking cash and cheques and other payments to and from banks can be time-consuming. In order to speed up standing order payments to regular suppliers, the major high street banks and building societies use a system known as **BACS (Banking Automated Clearing Service)**, which they jointly own. The system allows funds to be transferred between accounts electronically using computers.

A bank account holder wishing to make a regular payment completes a standing order form to tell their bank who they are to pay money to, how much should be paid, and how often. The bank will then input these instructions to a computer and the payments will be made automatically. Irregular payments by direct debit can also be made using BACS.

▼ Figure 12.3: How the Banking Automated Clearing Service works

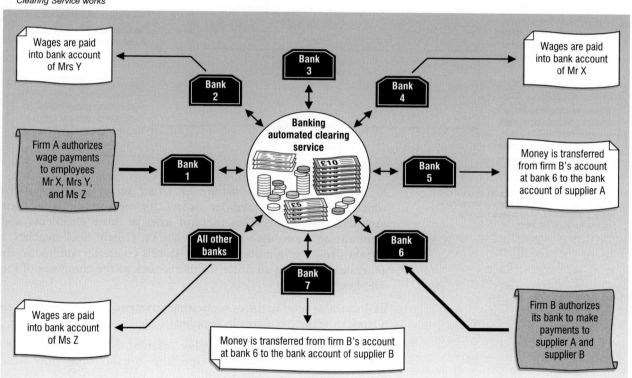

Today, most workers, especially those in medium-to-large organizations, are paid their wages directly into their bank or building society accounts through BACS.

● **Electronic Data Interchange (EDI)**: This system allows all the documents and payments involved in a sales transaction to be transmitted electronically using computers, rather than using fax or post. To do this, both the business customer and supplier must have computers connected to the telephone network by a modem.

▼ *Electronic Data Interchange reduces the need to record details of transactions by hand. Supermarket giant Tesco uses EDI to transmit almost all its orders and invoices.*

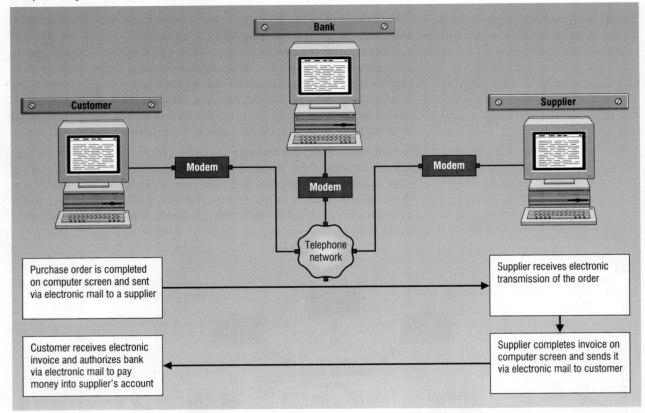

▼ *An increasing number of companies are offering credit cards to customers. Around 16 pence in every pound spent by consumers is now transferred by credit card.*

At present EDI is used mainly by larger retailing organizations which need to place regular orders for new stock with their suppliers. Barcode readers monitor sales at store checkouts and maintain an up-to-date record of stocks. When stock reaches a certain pre-set minimum level, the store's computer automatically generates and sends an order for more stock to the computer of the supplier.

EDI can also send invoices requesting payment, and instructions to a bank to make payments to suppliers

● **Credit card:** Instead of the supplier offering direct credit terms to their customers, a number of specialist organizations now issue cards that can be used to 'buy now, pay later.' Visa, Access, American Express, and Diners Club are examples of credit card companies who provide cards for general use. Many large retail organizations also offer their customers credit cards which can be used only in their stores. For example, Marks & Spencer and the Burton Group now operate credit card services.

With a credit card transaction, firms supply goods and services to the card holder but then have to wait for the credit card company to settle their bill. Suppliers need to send proof of the sale to the credit card company before they pay. The credit card company will then expect the card holder to pay them (by cheque or BACS), usually between 4-6 weeks after the sale was made (see Figure 12.4).

▼ *Figure 12.4: An example of how a credit card can be used to make a purchase*

1 **Customer pays £50 for goods with credit card.**

2 **Shopkeeper issues credit card invoice for £50.**

3 **Shopkeeper deposits invoice copy in his/her bank accont Bank.**

4 **Shopkeeper's bank arranges for invoices to be sent to credit card company.**

7 **Customer sends a cheque to his credit card company to settle his account balance.**

6 **Credit card company sends account statement to the customer listing all his purchases with his credit card.**

5 **Credit card company pays £50 to shopkeeper's bank.**

How credit card purchases are authorized

If a business is offered payment by credit card, they must check that the card is acceptable and gain necessary authorization. Most organizations today are able to do this electronically, but a number of smaller businesses still rely on manual methods.

Electronic methods

New technology means that businesses can get authorization from credit card companies much more easily than before:

- A sales assistant will swipe the card through a special terminal which then transmits the card details through to computers in the appropriate credit card company.

- The computers check that the card is not listed as stolen and checks that the card holder has not spent over his or her limit.

- A sales voucher with purchase and card details is then issued by the terminal. The card holder signs this and keeps the top copy as a proof of purchase

▼ *Printed electronically*

```
12:27                    13/08/9X
COMPLETED

B & Q PLC

NEW MALDEN
Till 8

02357423.6767  608658

VISA
No: 2033005731376667
Expiry date: 08/96
_____

THANK YOU
£25.95              Sign below


.........................................
```

How credit card purchases are authorized

Manual authorization

- First of all the business checks that the card is not a stolen one. This can be done by looking at up-to-date lists of stolen card numbers issued by the major credit card companies or by telephoning the appropriate credit card company. Using the telephone can be slow if the credit card company is busy.

- The business can also phone the credit card company to check that the customer has enough money left to spend on their card to pay for the goods or services. If they have, the credit card company will issue an authorization code to write on the sales

voucher. This code guarantees that the business will be paid by the credit card company.

- If the checks prove OK, then the business fills out a carbonated sales voucher. Card details are printed onto the voucher using a special hand-operated imprinting device. Purchase details are then written in before the customer signs it and receives the top copy as proof of purchase. The second copy is sent to the credit card company for payment, while the third and fourth copies are kept by the supplier.

▼ Completed by hand

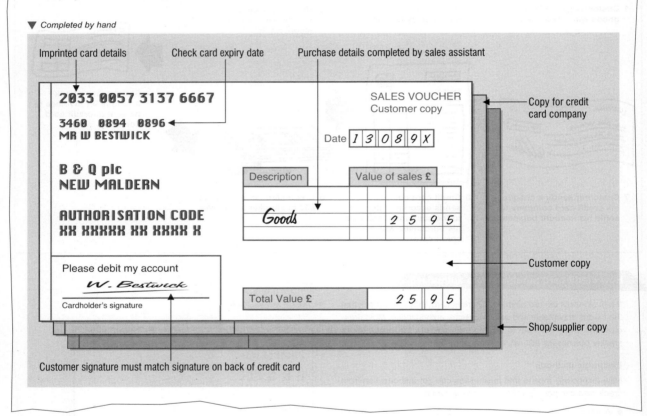

Imprinted card details

Check card expiry date

Purchase details completed by sales assistant

2033 0057 3137 6667

3460 0894 0896
MR W BESTWICK

B & Q plc
NEW MALDERN

AUTHORISATION CODE
XX XXXXX XX XXXX X

Please debit my account

W. Bestwick

Cardholder's signature

SALES VOUCHER
Customer copy

Date | 1 | 3 | 0 | 8 | 9 | X |

Description	Value of sales £				
Goods			2	5	9	5

Total Value £		2	5	9	5

Copy for credit card company

Customer copy

Shop/supplier copy

Customer signature must match signature on back of credit card

Section **12.3** **Using documents to record transactions**

PC: Explain why records of transactions are kept, Explain the importance of security and security checks for receipts and payments

Range: Records of Transactions, Documents, Importance of security

Skills: Read and respond to written material, Produce written material

This is the story of Billy Bestwick. He owns and runs a small car repair business. His office staff have run out of paper for the photocopier and printer on the computer. Read the story and then answer the questions.

1. Suggest reasons why business organizations like Billy's garage and Office Supplies Ltd should keep records of their financial transactions.

2. What information should Office Supplies Ltd record to make the process of selling their products easier, less wasteful, and more secure?

3. Suggest possible documents Office Supplies Ltd could use and issue to Billy to record the information they need.

Billy looks at the Office Supplies Ltd catalogue and calculates that it will cost him £70.50 to have 17 packets of white A4 size paper delivered. He phones Office Supplies Ltd to place his order for 17 packets of paper.

The sales assistant ot Office Supplies Ltd makes a written note of Billy's order but writes down 70 packets of paper by mistake.

The next day 70 packets of paper are loaded onto a van at Office Supplies Ltd and sent off to Billy's garage. The van driver has the piece of paper the assistant scribbled down Billy's order on but he cannot read the address properly. After several wrong turns the van driver manages to locate Billy's business and delivers the paper.

'But I only ordered 17 packets!' said Billy as the van driver unloads 70 packets of paper. The van driver apologises for the mistake and agrees to return the unwanted 53 packets to Office Supplies Ltd.

The next day Billy sends off his cheque for £70.50 to Office Supplies Ltd to pay for his 17 packets of paper.

When the cheque arrives at Office Supplies Ltd they can only find the scribbled note for an order for 70 packets of paper and write to Billy demanding payment of £250.

Billy receives the demand and phones up Office Supplies Ltd. He explains that he had only ordered 17 packets of paper and that the van driver had agreed to return the other 53 packets to Office Supplies Ltd.

Unfortunately, the storeman at Office Supplies Ltd had kept no record of stock going out or coming in. As neither Billy nor Office Supplies has any proof of delivery the company asks the van driver to confirm Billy's story. He does and so Office Supplies withdraws their demand.

But the crafty van driver had lied. He did not return the other 53 packets that Billy didn't want to Office Supplies Ltd. Instead he stole them and sold them for £50 to a friend.

'Phew! What a messy business' sighs Billy upon receiving an apology from Office Supplies Ltd. 'In future I think I'll buy my stationery from elsewhere.'

Types of documents

Recording information about transactions often requires a great deal of paperwork. To make the process less time-consuming, businesses have devised special documents to use. Invoices, order forms, purchase documents, bank paying-in slips, and receipts are just a few of the kinds of documents used to record transactions. Although the design of these documents may differ from business to business, the information each must contain will be the same.

The types of documents Billy Bestwick and Office Supplies should have used to make sure their transaction in Activity 12.5 went smoothly, and the order they should have used them in, are shown in Figure 12.5. The types and sequence of documents used are typical of any business transaction.

▼ Figure 12.5: Documents involved in a business transaction

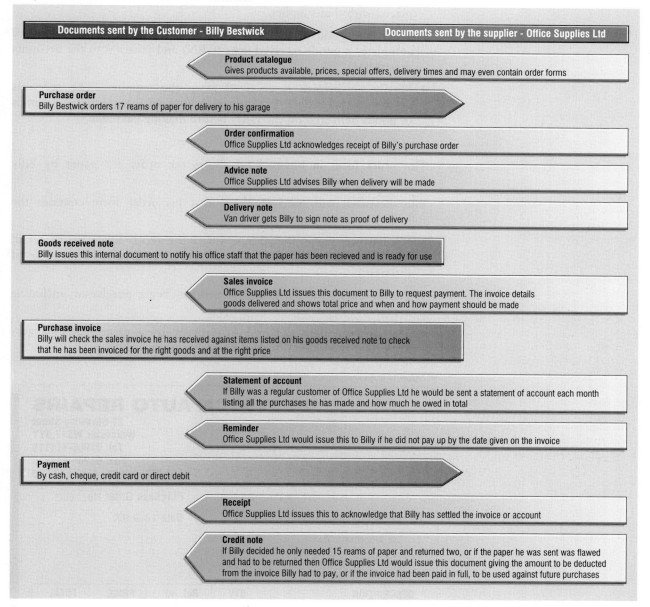

Documents sent by the Customer - Billy Bestwick	Documents sent by the supplier - Office Supplies Ltd

Product catalogue
Gives products available, prices, special offers, delivery times and may even contain order forms

Purchase order
Billy Bestwick orders 17 reams of paper for delivery to his garage

Order confirmation
Office Supplies Ltd acknowledges receipt of Billy's purchase order

Advice note
Office Supplies Ltd advises Billy when delivery will be made

Delivery note
Van driver gets Billy to sign note as proof of delivery

Goods received note
Billy issues this internal document to notify his office staff that the paper has been recieved and is ready for use

Sales invoice
Office Supplies Ltd issues this document to Billy to request payment. The invoice details goods delivered and shows total price and when and how payment should be made

Purchase invoice
Billy will check the sales invoice he has received against items listed on his goods received note to check that he has been invoiced for the right goods and at the right price

Statement of account
If Billy was a regular customer of Office Supplies Ltd he would be sent a statement of account each month listing all the purchases he has made and how much he owed in total

Reminder
Office Supplies Ltd would issue this to Billy if he did not pay up by the date given on the invoice

Payment
By cash, cheque, credit card or direct debit

Receipt
Office Supplies Ltd issues this to acknowledge that Billy has settled the invoice or account

Credit note
If Billy decided he only needed 15 reams of paper and returned two, or if the paper he was sent was flawed and had to be returned then Office Supplies Ltd would issue this document giving the amount to be deducted from the invoice Billy had to pay, or if the invoice had been paid in full, to be used against future purchases

Purchase documents

The job of the purchasing department in any business is to buy in services or materials of the right quality, in the right quantities, when the firm needs them, and at the lowest cost possible (see 4.2). Every pound saved by purchasing is an extra pound made in profits. Each of the different stages in the purchasing process requires different kinds of documentation.

1. The first stage in purchasing usually involves making enquiries with different suppliers to get a range of estimates or quotations, and choosing the best deal available.

2. Once the best supplier is identified, an **order form** is completed and placed with that supplier.

3. When the goods have been delivered, the person receiving them completes a **goods received note (GRN)** and passes it to the accounts department.

4. Finally an **invoice** is received from the supplier. The accounts department will check that information on the invoice matches details of goods delivered on the GRN before making payment.

The order form

The **order form in** Figure 12.6 shows the order for paper by Billy Bestwick.

Billy Bestwick will need to check that his order form contains the following information:

- His business name, the address where the goods are to be delivered, and the address to which the supplier should send the invoice (if different)

- Precise details of the goods or services being purchased, including make, model number, and unit price

- The delivery date required (if delivery by a certain date is very important this should be stated clearly on the order)

▼ Figure 12.6: An example of a Purchase order

BESTWICK AUTO REPAIRS

21 Shrawley Street
Worcester WS17 5YY
Tel: 01905-111119
Fax: 01905-111110
VAT Reg No. 4373 2437 18

Purchase Order No. 1853

To: Office Supplies Ltd

12 Woodland Way

Northwick NH4 3JX

Date 16.9.9X

DESCRIPTION	QTY	Ref. No	PRICE	TOTAL
A4 white photocopy paper	17	34/A	£3	£51

Deliver to above address a.s.a.p

Authorized by: *W. Bestwick*

for BESTWICK AUTO REPAIRS

- The signature of someone with the authority to approve the order. This is important, otherwise anyone in the firm could place an order for goods and services which might then be stolen without anyone knowing.

If Billy has a fax machine, he can send his order immediately to Office Supplies Ltd. Billy will also keep a copy of his order for his own records. This is so that he can check, at a later date, that the right goods have been delivered and that he has been invoiced to pay the right amount for the right goods.

Goods received note (GRN)

When Billy receives the goods he ordered from Office Supplies Ltd, he will complete a **goods received note (GRN)** for his records. The GRN records what has actually been delivered. This is important because goods might be damaged or missing, or the wrong goods may have been sent. Any deliveries should always be unpacked, counted, and carefully checked and recorded.

The person taking delivery of goods will not always be the same person who ordered them, and so completion of a GRN is vital in most organizations. The accounts department in any organization will need signed proof that goods have actually been received by their firm, in the form of a GRN, before it will authorize the payment of an invoice for them. The GRN can be checked against the original purchase order to make sure that nothing is being paid for that was not ordered or delivered. The firm will also check that the goods are not damaged or faulty or need to be replaced by the supplier.

▼ Figure 12.7: An example of a goods received note

BESTWICK AUTO REPAIRS
GOODS RECEIVED NOTE

Supplier:
Office Supplies Ltd
12 Woodland Way
Northwick NH4 3JX

GRN NO: 347
Date: 20.9.9X
Re; Delivery Note:
12/90120

ORDER NO.	QTY	DESCRIPTION	REF NO:
1853	17	A4 white copy paper 3 boxes x 5 reams plus 2 reams	34/A

Received by: *W. Bestwick*
for **BESTWICK AUTO REPAIRS**

441

Purchase invoice

After the paper has been delivered to Billy's garage, Office Supplies Ltd will request payment by sending him an **invoice**.

▼ *Figure 12.8: An Example of an Invoice*

INVOICE

Office Supplies Ltd

12 Woodland Way
Northwick NH4 3JX
Tel: 01604-65666
Fax: 01604-65660
VAT Reg No. 234 8999 16

To: Bestwick Auto Repairs

21 Shrawley Street

Worcester WS17 5YY

Date	Order No.	Account No.	Invoice No.
22.9.9X	1853	702300	25241

QTY	Description	Cat No.	Unit Price	Total
17	A4 white copy paper	34/A	£3	£51
1	Delivery		£9	£9

Sub-total	£60
Cash discount	–
Total (ex. VAT)	£60
VAT @ 17.5%	+£10.50
Total due	£70.50

Terms:
Cash discount of 2.5% only applies to orders over £100 if payment received within 10 working days

E & OE

Office Supplies Ltd will need to make sure that their invoice contains the following details:

- Their name and address as supplier
- The name and address of their customer
- The customer's account number (if applicable)
- An invoice reference number
- A full description of the goods supplied and their reference numbers
- The unit price of the goods
- A delivery charge, if any.

- Total price, including VAT and any deductions for any cash or trade discounts offered

- The date by which the invoice should be paid

An invoice is a legal document. Firms must keep all of their invoices in order to provide evidence of the amount they have spent on purchases both for VAT inspectors and for the Inland Revenue. VAT-registered businesses can claim back VAT money paid on purchases, and some may be tempted to claim they have purchased more than they really have. Similarly, a firm may be tempted to claim they spent more than they actually did in order to reduce the profit declared in their accounts, and so reduce the tax they have to pay. This is illegal, and business owners can be fined or imprisoned for misleading the tax authorities.

What else should be on an invoice?

- **Cash discounts:** In order to speed up the payment of invoices many suppliers offer a cash discount. This discount is a percentage of the goods total (usually around 2.5%) which the buyer can deduct if he or she pays immediately rather than waiting until the end of the period specified on the invoice. For example, if Billy Bestwick's order was worth £500, he would receive a cash discount of £12.50 (2.5%) if he paid the invoice within 10 days of receipt.

- **Trade discounts:** In addition to a discount for paying cash, some suppliers also give a discount for regular custom, called a **trade discount**. For example, most retailers will receive trade discount from their suppliers. The discount is deducted from the invoice total and will often vary with the quantity purchased. Bigger discounts tend to be given for bigger orders.

- **Invoice errors and omissions:** All invoices have the letters 'E & OE' printed on them. This stands for 'Errors and Omissions Excepted' which means that if the supplier has made any mistakes or left anything off the invoice, they have the right to correct the mistake later on and demand full payment.

Checking the invoice

All invoices received should be checked carefully before they are paid. Like any business, Billy Bestwick should check that:

- The invoice from Office Supplies Ltd has not been sent to him by mistake

- The order number quoted on it is the same as the number of his original purchase order

- The items listed match those listed on his goods received note

- The price given is the same as in the supplier's catalogue

- All calculations are correct

- It contains any discounts previously agreed with the supplier

If Billy is satisfied that the invoice is in order, he will pass it on to his accounts department for payment.

Payment, whether by cash, cheque, plastic card, or bank transfer, will usually require authorization by a designated member of staff. In Billy's small business this is likely to be Billy himself. In a large organization authorization is likely to be given by a senior manager in accounts. If payments could be made without authorization, some devious employees might write out cheques to themselves, or make payments into their own bank accounts without other people knowing.

Sales documents

The main objective of the sales department in any organization is to encourage sales and to record revenues accurately so that it can judge how well it is meeting its targets (see 4.2). In making sales, meeting customer orders quickly, and obtaining payments, a sales department will issue a variety of documents. The main ones are:

1. An **acknowledgement** to a customer that their order has been received. The supplier may also send an **advice note** to tell the customer when delivery will be made.

2. A **delivery note** containing a full description of goods delivered to the customer

3. A **sales invoice** requesting payment for goods delivered

4. If the total price on the invoice is wrong and the customer has been overcharged, the supplier may issue a **credit note.** If the customer has not been charged enough, a **debit note** will be issued.

5. If the customer makes regular purchases from the same supplier, they may have an account which they settle up each month. A **statement of account** is sent each month from the supplier to provide a record of purchases made and the total amount owed by the customer.

6. A **remittance advice note** will often be sent with an invoice or statement of account, summarizing how much is owed by the customer and when it should be paid.

Orders received

When a supplier receives an order, the sales department should check all the details to make sure that the information provided by the customer is complete and correct. For example:

● Has the customer given their full address?

● Does the description of goods ordered match the catalogue or reference number?

- Are there any special requirements? For example, morning delivery only?

- Does the customer qualify for any trade discounts?

The supplier should then check that it is able to meet the order and supply the goods in the right quantity, at the right price, and by the date requested in the order. The sales department may then send a written acknowledgement to the customer to confirm receipt of their order and give precise details of the delivery date and time.

If goods are to be in transit for some time, the sales department may also send an advice note to tell the customer that the goods are on their way. This will give details of the date the goods were despatched, and how they have been sent, for example, by parcel post or courier.

▼ Figure 12.9: An Example of a Delivery Note

Office Supplies Ltd

12 Woodland Way
Northwick NH4 3JX
Tel: 01604-65666
Fax: 01604-65660
VAT Reg No. 234 8999 16

Delivery Note No. 12/90120

Delivery address: Bestwick Auto Repairs

21 Shrawley Street

Worcester WS17 5YY

For delivery on: 20.9.9X

DATE	Order No	Account No.	Invoice No
19.9.9X	1853	702300	25241

QTY	Catalogue No.	Description
17	34/A	A4 white copy paper

Delivery by: Office Supplies Distribution Services Ltd
No. of items: 3 boxes + 2 individual reams
Goods received by: _W. Bestwick_ (signature)

W.Bestwick (please PRINT name)

Issued by: _D Martin_

D Martin
Sales Manager
for Office Supplies Ltd

Please retain this copy as proof of receipt

Delivery note

When goods are delivered by vehicle, either by the supplier or by an outside carrier such as TNT Express or DHL, the driver is given a **delivery note**. This gives a full description of the goods and states the number of packages being delivered. On receipt of the goods, the customer is able to check delivered items against those listed on the delivery note in order to identify any errors or damage. The delivery note is usually carbonated with two copies. It is signed by the customer and one copy is kept by the driver as proof that the goods were delivered as required.

Figure 12.9 shows the delivery note sent with the paper ordered by Billy Bestwick. Billy has signed the delivery note to provide the driver with proof that the goods have been delivered. Luckily he had time to check his order before signing the delivery note. If this was not possible Billy would have written 'goods received but not examined' on the bottom of the note.

Sales invoice

A sales invoice is issued by a supplier every time goods or services have been delivered without immediate payment. When payment is immediate, such as the purchase of food over a shop counter, no invoice will be issued to the customer.

You have already seen the invoice issued by Office Supplies Ltd to Bestwick Auto Repairs in Figure 12.8. The invoice issued by Office Supplies Ltd is a **sales invoice** to the company, containing details of how much Bestwick Auto Repairs owes them, and what for. For Billy Bestwick the very same invoice received from Office Supplies Ltd is a **purchase invoice** which he will have to pay.

Invoices are normally carbonated so that a number of copies of exactly the same invoice can be produced in one go. The customer will receive the top copy, while the other copies will be retained by various parts of the supplier's organization – the distribution department that sends out the order and the accounts department that receives payment.

Credit and debit notes

A **credit note,** often printed in red, is issued by a supplier to a customer if the total price on the invoice is too much. This may be because:

- The supplier has made a mistake and overcharged
- Goods were not delivered because they were lost or stolen in transit
- The customer has returned unsatisfactory or faulty goods

Figure 12.10 shows a credit note that might have been issued by Office Supplies Ltd to Bestwick Auto Repairs if Billy had returned one box containing 5 reams of A4 paper because it was pink and not white as ordered.

A **debit note** will be sent to a customer if the amount on their invoice is not enough - for example, if payment is late and is subject to a surcharge, or if equipment used to deliver goods was on loan but has not been returned.

▼ Figure 12.10: An Example of a Credit Note

▼ *Figure 12.10: An Example of a Credit Note*

Office Supplies Ltd

12 Woodland Way
Northwick NH4 3JX
Tel: 01604-65666
Fax: 01604-65660
VAT Reg No. 234 8999 16

To: Bestwick Auto Repairs	**CREDIT NOTE NO.**
21 Shrawley Street	CN123
Worcester WS17 5YY	

DATE	Reference Invoice No.	Customer Account No.
26.9.9X	25421	702300

QTY	Description	Cat No.	Unit Price	Total
5	A4 copy paper (pink)	34/A	£3	£15

Reason for credit:	Sub-total	£15
Paper returned — wrong colour	Cash discount	£0
	Total (ex. VAT)	£15
	VAT @ 17.5%	£2.63
	Total credit	£17.63

Statement of account

When a business organization regularly uses the same supplier, it is likely to receive a number of invoices each month. In this case, it is easier for the supplier to send out a **statement of account** summarizing all the purchases made by that customer each month, rather than to send out lots of individual invoices.

It is also more convenient for the customer to make one payment each month on the account balance outstanding, rather than have to make numerous payments to settle each separate invoice. Many firms prefer to pay on receipt of the monthly statement rather than on individual invoices. This is to the customer's advantage as it delays payment. An account statement shows the amount owed, or **balance outstanding**, at the beginning of the month, adding on any invoices for orders during that month and deducting any payments received. The balance left at the end of the month is the amount owed. The monthly statement is, therefore, a summary of transactions made during each month and a request for payment.

Imagine now that Billy Bestwick is a regular customer of Office Supplies Ltd. His account number is 702300. During the month of September 1995 he placed several orders for office stationary with the company. At the end of the month, Office Supplies Ltd issued the statement of the account in Figure 12.11 to Billy Bestwick. You will notice that included in the list of orders placed by Billy is the purchase order (No. 1853) for 17 reams of copy paper from Figure 12.6.

▼ *Figure 12.11: An Example of a Monthly Statement of Account*

<u>STATEMENT OF ACCOUNT</u>

Office Supplies Ltd

12 Woodland Way
Northwick NH4 3JX
Tel: 01604-65666
Fax: 01604-65660
VAT Reg No. 234 8999 16

Account No: 702300

Bestwick Auto Repairs

21 Shrawley Street

Worcester WS 17 5YY

Statement date: 30.9.9X

Date	Details	Debit	Credit	Balance
1.9.9X	Balance brought forward	£500		£500.00 Dr
8.9.9X	Goods(order 1854) Invoice No. 25289	£220		£720.00 Dr
22.9.9X	Goods(order 1853) Invoice No. 25241	£70.50		£790.50 Dr
25.9.9X	Payment-thank you		£800.00	£9.50 Cr
26.9.9X	Refund CN.123		£17.63	£27.13 Cr
29.9.9X	Goods(order 1856) Invoice No. 27763	£137.93		£110.80 Dr
	Balance now due			£110.80 Dr

Terms: Payment by 14.10.9X required

* Dr = debit / Cr = credit

Portfolio Activity 12.7

PC: Explain and give examples of purchases and purchase documents, Explain and give examples of sales and sales documents

Range: Purchase documents, Sales documents

Skills: Read and respond to written material, Tackle problems

1. Metal Mayhem Clothing designs and prints rock T-shirts and other clothing accessories. Based on the purchase order below from Metal Mayhem, design and complete a sales invoice from Polygon Textiles Ltd (preferably using a computer desktop publishing package). The invoice number is 5203. The VAT rate is 17.5%. Goods are subject to a 15% trade discount and a 2.5% cash discount if paid for within 10 days of the invoice date. Make sure these calculations are added to your invoice.

2. Make sure that you include the following information on your sales invoice and explain what is meant by each term:

   product code/catalogue number   unit price

   E & OE

   cash discount 10 days   Deliver to ...

   sub-total   VAT

3. Explain why the accounts department of Metal Mayhem Clothing will need to see a copy of a purchase order, purchase invoice, and goods received note for the same transaction before it pays for goods delivered.

Metal Mayhem *Clothing*

4 Rock Street
London W4
Tel: 0181-666-1234
Fax: 0181-666-4321
VAT Reg No. 1393 0774 5

Purchase Order No. 909867

To: Polygon Textiles Ltd

57 Factory Lane

Morden, Surrey

DATE	DESCRIPTION	QTY	CAT.No	PRICE	TOTAL
7.6.9X	XL T-shirts (black)	100	T570	£5	£500
	XL Long sleeved shirts (black)	50	T643	£8	£400
	Baseball caps	30	B750	£4	£120

Other charges	*Delivery*	£10
Deliver to above address	Sub-total	£1030.00
	VAT @ 17.5%	£180.25
	Total	£1210.25

Authorized by: *S. Tyler*

S Tyler
for **Metal Mayhem** *Clothing*

Remittance advice

When an invoice or statement of account is issued to a customer, it is also usual for the supplier to send a **remittance advice note** at the same time. This is a brief form which summarizes key information on an invoice or statement regarding the amount that needs to be paid, who it should be paid to, and when it should be paid, and including the appropriate reference number.

If payment is to be made by cheque sent through the post, the customer will simply return the remittance advice note with the cheque. This makes it easier for the supplier to match the payment, once it is received, with the right invoice or statement. If customers did not return remittance advice notes with their payments, the suppliers' accounts staff would have to spend a great deal of time and effort trying to match up many different cheques to invoices.

Figure 12.12 shows the remittance advice note sent by Office Supplies Ltd to Bestwick Auto Repairs. It summarizes the information required to settle the statement of account shown in Figure 12.12.

▼ *Figure 12.12: An example of a remittance advice note*

REMITTANCE ADVICE	**Date:** 30.9.199X
Customer name and address:	**Account No.:**
Bestwick Auto Repairs 21 Shrawley Street Worcester WS17 5YY	702300

Statement Date: 30.9.95

Amount owing: £116.80

Amount enclosed: ....

Cheque no: ....

Please return this slip together with your payment to:

Office Supplies Ltd
12 Woodland Way
Northwick NH4 3JX

All cheques should be made payable to Office Supplies Ltd.

Receipts documents (proof of purchase)

When you buy a good or service in a shop, you will receive a **receipt** as proof of purchase. Similarly, when an organization makes payment it will require proof that payment has been made for its own records and for the purpose of informing the tax authorities about its expenses.

A number of documents are available to act as proof that a transaction has taken place. These are:

- Sales receipts
- Cheques
- Paying-in slips
- Bank statements

Sales receipts

A sales receipt is usually issued when payment for goods or services received is immediate. It can take many forms, but will always include the following information:

● The name and address of the organization that made the sale

● The date the transaction took place

● A description of the goods or services purchased

● The cost of each item

● The total cost of all items

● The method of payment

Receipts can be produced electronically by tills and computers, or be handwritten on pre-printed forms. Each receipt will be numbered for ease of reference.

Figure 12.13 shows the electronic till receipt Billy Bestwick received when he went to buy a newspaper and a new book on classic cars from a WH Smith store during one lunchbreak. Figure 12.14 shows a handwritten receipt he received when he bought some old car parts from a scrap metal dealer.

▼ Figure 12.13: An example of a sales receipt

```
            WELCOME
              TO
          WH SMITH LTD
                            £
Newspaper                  0.40
Book                      22.50

Balance due               22.90

CASH                      30.00
CHANGE                     7.10

   5320  09  5 1314   11:03:05
          28SEPT9X

 THANK YOU FOR SHOPPING AT
        WH SMITH LTD
         WORCESTER
```

▼ Figure 12.14: A handwritten receipt

BROGAN SCRAP MERCHANTS

Receipt   **No.** 5387

Received from Mr W. Bestwick

the sum of £ forty five pounds and seventy   £ 45.70p
pence only

in payment for Ford Fiesta headlamp Units
and rear bumper

Received by: J.W.Sharman   **Date:** 28. Sept 199X
Sales Department

Portfolio Activity 12.8

PC: Explain and give examples of receipts documents
Range: Receipts documents
Skills: Produce written material

You work in the accounts section of Billy Bestwick's car repair business. Your computer usually prints out receipts for customers.

However, today the system is not working and you must design your own receipt. Mr S Moss has just paid £150 in cash to have a new exhaust fitted to his car. Produce a handwritten receipt for the customer.

Paying-in slip

To avoid keeping large amounts of money on business premises, takings should be banked regularly. Large organizations with large amounts of money may employ a specialist security company, like Securicor or Group 4, to take the money to the bank in an armoured van.

When a firm pays cash and cheques into a bank it will complete a **paying-in slip** (see Figure 12.15). On the back of the slip is space to list all the people and organizations that have paid by cheque, and the amount of each cheque. The total amount of cheques is then carried over to the front of the paying-in slip and added to the cash total. The amount of each note or coin paid into the bank should be listed separately, for example, '100 x £5 notes' and '300 x £1 coins'.

Figure 12.15 shows a paying in-slip completed by Billy Bestwick on 29 September. Billy has listed his takings in notes, coins, and cheques on the front of the document. Details of individual cheques are also listed on the back of the paying in-slip.

▼ *Figure 12.15: A completed paying-in slip*

Front

COUNTER CREDIT

Date 29.9.9X

Cashier's stamp and initials

Fee | Number of cheques 2

675-5

bank giro credit

Code No. 20-33-47

Bank Midland

Branch Worcester

Customer's Name Bestwick Auto Repairs

Account No. 9003476

Paid in by Billy Bestwick

Address ______ Ref. No. ______

PLEASE DO NOT WRITE OR MARK BELOW THIS LINE

	£	p
£50 Notes		
£20 Notes	40	—
£10 Notes	30	—
£5 Notes		
£1 Note/Coin	4	—
S. & I. Notes		
50p	—	50
20p		
Silver		
Bronze		
TOTAL CASH	74	50
CHEQUES, P.O.'s etc.	38	00
see over £	112	50

70

Back

Details of Cheques, P.O's etc.

£			brought forward £			brought forward £		
A.J. Smith	21	70						
P.D. Douglas	16	30						
Carried forward	38	00	Carried forward			Carried over £		

Paying-in slips are used to show the following information:

- The date money was paid into the account
- The bank (or building society) branch at which money was paid in
- The branch sort code (a bank identification number)

- The account holder's name
- The number of the account to be credited
- The amount to be credited
- The name and signature of the person paying in the money

The paying in-slip, along with cash and cheques, is handed to the bank cashier. The bank cashier will then check the totals on the slip against bags of cash and individual cheques. If they match, the cashier will stamp and initial both the slip and the counterfoil. The counterfoil acts as the customer's receipt. The paying-in slip counterfoil provides a means by which the business can check that the entries on its bank statement are correct.

Portfolio Activity 12.9

PC: Explain and give examples of receipt documents
Range: Receipt documents
Skills: Tackle problems

1. Obtain a blank paying-in slip from a local bank.

2. Billy Bestwick wants to pay some more takings into his bank. Use the paying-in slip to pay the following amounts into the Bestwick Auto Repairs bank account (make up a number for the account).

Cheques	Notes	Coins
£120.00	15×£50 = £750	243×£1 = £243
£64.25	8×£20 = £160	100×50p = £50
£400.00	35×£10 = £350	600×20p = £120
£37.50	6×£5 = £30	1,000×10p = £100
£145.47		600×5p = £30
£79.98		800×2p = £16
		1,200×1p = £12

A bank statement

A bank statement provides a monthly summary of receipts and payments made to and from a bank account. Building societies also provide their account holders with regular statements.

A bank statement can be checked by a business for any mistakes against documentary proof that the transactions have been made:

- **Credits** (deposits) can be checked against paying-in slip counterfoils and records of payments from customers
- **Debits** (withdrawals) can be checked against cheque 'stubs', counterfoils issued when debit cards were used, cash dispenser receipts, and direct debit and standing order agreements

The process of checking bank statements is known as **bank reconciliation.** Differences between the bank statement and a firm's records of transactions may arise due to:

- Clerical errors causing figures to be wrongly entered or not entered at all
- Payments being made into the bank which have not been entered in the firm's records
- Cheques being recorded in the firm's books before they have been cleared by the bank.
- Bank charges representing interest on loans or overdrafts and/or charges for other services (some current accounts also pay interest on credit balances).

▼ *Figure 12.16: An Example of a Bank Statement*

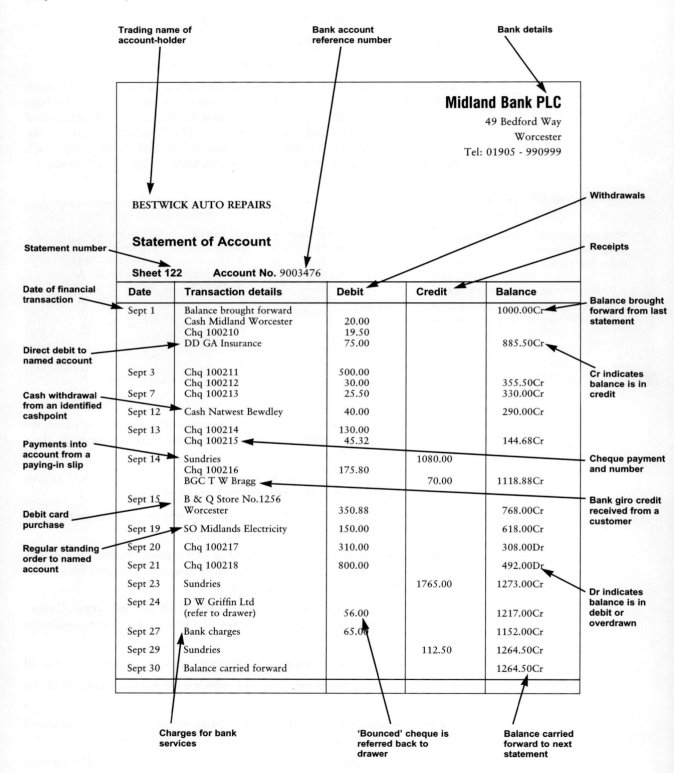

Trading name of account-holder

Bank account reference number

Bank details

Midland Bank PLC

49 Bedford Way
Worcester
Tel: 01905 - 990999

Withdrawals

BESTWICK AUTO REPAIRS

Statement of Account

Receipts

Statement number

Sheet 122   **Account No.** 9003476

Date of financial transaction

Date	Transaction details	Debit	Credit	Balance
Sept 1	Balance brought forward			1000.00Cr
	Cash Midland Worcester	20.00		
	Chq 100210	19.50		
	DD GA Insurance	75.00		885.50Cr
Sept 3	Chq 100211	500.00		
	Chq 100212	30.00		355.50Cr
Sept 7	Chq 100213	25.50		330.00Cr
Sept 12	Cash Natwest Bewdley	40.00		290.00Cr
Sept 13	Chq 100214	130.00		
	Chq 100215	45.32		144.68Cr
Sept 14	Sundries		1080.00	
	Chq 100216	175.80		
	BGC T W Bragg		70.00	1118.88Cr
Sept 15	B & Q Store No.1256 Worcester	350.88		768.00Cr
Sept 19	SO Midlands Electricity	150.00		618.00Cr
Sept 20	Chq 100217	310.00		308.00Dr
Sept 21	Chq 100218	800.00		492.00Dr
Sept 23	Sundries		1765.00	1273.00Cr
Sept 24	D W Griffin Ltd (refer to drawer)	56.00		1217.00Cr
Sept 27	Bank charges	65.00		1152.00Cr
Sept 29	Sundries		112.50	1264.50Cr
Sept 30	Balance carried forward			1264.50Cr

Balance brought forward from last statement

Direct debit to named account

Cr indicates balance is in credit

Cash withdrawal from an identified cashpoint

Payments into account from a paying-in slip

Cheque payment and number

Debit card purchase

Bank giro credit received from a customer

Regular standing order to named account

Dr indicates balance is in debit or overdrawn

Charges for bank services

'Bounced' cheque is referred back to drawer

Balance carried forward to next statement

Figure 12.15 shows the bank statement for the Bestwick Auto Repairs account at the Midland Bank in Worcester for the month of September 199X. Note the cheque for £800 paid to Office Supplies Ltd on 25.9.9X as shown in the Bestwick Auto Repairs customer account statement in Figure 12.11. Notes, coins and cheques deposited in the bank by Billy Bestwick using the paying in-slip in Figure 12.15 also appear on the statement on September. 29.

Portfolio Activity 12.10

PC: Explain and give examples of receipts documents
Range: Receipts documents
Skills: Tackle problems, Prepare information

1. Create a blank bank statement of your own using a computer word processing package.

2. Use the statement to record the following transactions made by a business account holder during one month. Entries should appear in date order.

3. Remember to calculate and show the 'balance carried forward' to the next statement.

Date	Details	Amount
1	Balance brought forward	£200.00
	Drawings:	
3	Cheque No. 10001	£20.50
5	Cheque No. 10002	£68.50
12	Cheque No. 10003	£10.99
14	Cheque No. 10004	£19.00
25	Cheque No. 10005	£30.70
9	Standing order to British Gas	£50.00
10	Cash dispenser withdrawal	£50.00
17	Cash dispenser withdrawal	£20.00
13	Standing order to Britannia Building Society	£100.00
14	SWITCH Tesco Superstore	£36.01
29	SWITCH Houghtons Garage	£15.75
21	Bank Charges	£5.25
	Receipts:	
2	Direct debit received from ABC Ltd	£30.00
9	Cheque No.4256 received	£16.30
17	Cheque No.6060 received	£10.00

Cheques

When payment is made by cheque there is no real need for a receipt to be issued by the person or organization receiving payment (see 12.2). Confirmation that payment has been made by cheque is shown on the bank statement of both the account holder who wrote the cheque and the account holder who received the cheque and paid it into his or her account.

Section 12.4 Security

PC: Explain the importance of security and security checks for receipts and payments

Range: Importance, Security checks

Skills: Use images, Produce written material

1. Suggest why maintaining security is so important to business organizations.

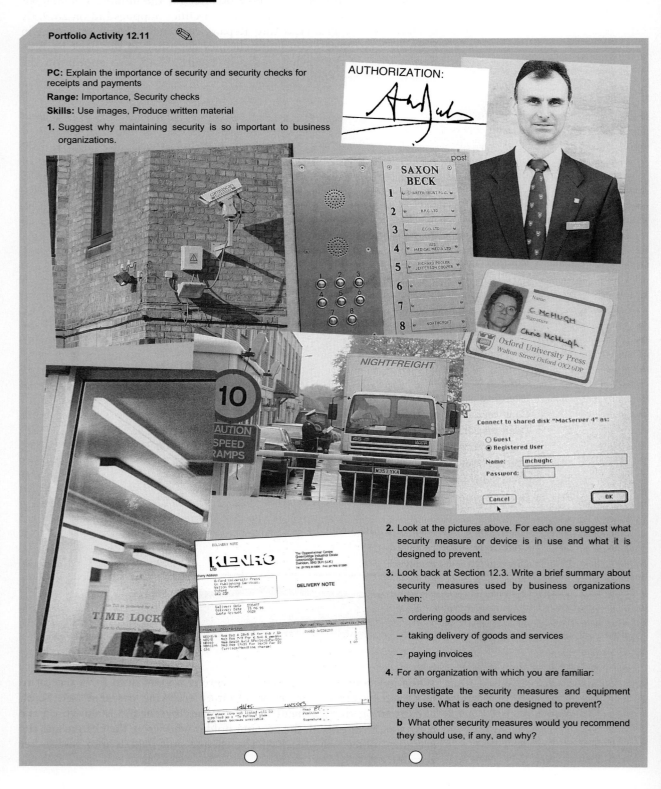

2. Look at the pictures above. For each one suggest what security measure or device is in use and what it is designed to prevent.

3. Look back at Section 12.3. Write a brief summary about security measures used by business organizations when:

   – ordering goods and services

   – taking delivery of goods and services

   – paying invoices

4. For an organization with which you are familiar:

   a Investigate the security measures and equipment they use. What is each one designed to prevent?

   b What other security measures would you recommend they should use, if any, and why?

Why is security important?

Each year UK business organizations lose billions of pounds due to theft, fraud, and criminal damage. These losses reduce company profits. Maintaining security is, therefore, extremely important in business.

Business organizations can insure themselves against theft and criminal damage. However, insurance premiums can be expensive and will tend to rise as crime increases and insurance companies are forced to pay out more in compensation.

A business may also attempt to protect itself from theft and damage by installing security equipment. However, this too can be expensive and will eat into profits.

In Great Britain the estimated cost of crime and crime prevention in shops and other retail outlets alone was £2 billion in 1992-93 (see Figure 12.17). External crime (comprising customer theft, burglary, and other crimes such as arson and robbery) accounted for just over half the total cost, with just over a quarter due to staff crime.

▼ Figure 12.17: Retail crime costs, 1992-93

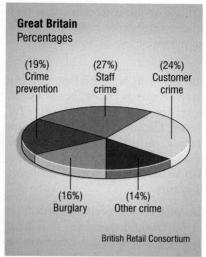

Great Britain
Percentages

(19%) Crime prevention
(27%) Staff crime
(24%) Customer crime
(16%) Burglary
(14%) Other crime

British Retail Consortium

Social Trends 1995

IT'S ALL AT THE CO-OP

Sex, cash, hols for bent bosses

Nights of torrid sex, flights to the Caribbean and slap-up meals were laid on for crooked bosses of the "caring, sharing" Co-op.

They revelled in champagne lifestyles in return for buying their greens from one supplier in a multi-million pound fruit and veg bribes scandal. Some executives were getting up to £300 a week in backhanders.

Daily Mirror 2.8.95

But the scam–thought to be one of Britain's biggest-ever High Street frauds–was finally exposed.

For the cost of the bribes led to huge debts for the supplier, self-made millionaire Gordon Faulkner.

And his Leamington-based firm went bust in 1992 owing £6million.

Fraud

Fraud is the term used to describe deliberate attempts to deceive people and organizations for financial gain. This will often take the form of recording false transactions or altering the accounts so that a firm is unaware that payments have been made. It can often take months to discover that an organization has been defrauded. The use of stolen or counterfeit cheques, credit and debit cards to make payment is also a form of fraud.

How to prevent fraud

To reduce the risk of fraud, most firms carefully record all their financial transactions and check their records thoroughly and regularly. Equipment is also available which can detect stolen plastic payment cards.

Measures used by business organizations to reduce and detect fraud include:

● **Keeping detailed and up-to-date records of all financial transactions.** If an organization keeps no records of goods and services received and money paid out, how will it ever be able to know and check if anything is missing?

- **Checking that all orders are authorized.** Orders for goods and services should be authorized by a member of staff whose job is to check that they are required by the business. Without proper safeguards some employees may be tempted to order items for their personal use or to sell them to other people.

  In a large organization all orders may be made by a central purchasing department after written and authorized requests have been made. Usually, different people within an organization will authorize orders for different items. The more money is involved, the more senior the person must be to authorize the order. For example, an office manager may be able to authorize an order for stationary, but an order for an entirely new computer network costing many thousands of pounds would probably have to be authorized by the board of directors.

- **Checking invoices against purchase orders and goods received notes.** You will remember from Section 12.3 that a purchase order gives details of goods required by a customer. When they are delivered an employee in the customer organization will normally complete a goods received note (GRN) which provides a record of the incoming goods.

  An invoice is sent by the supplier to the customer requesting payment for delivered items. However, the customer should not pay the invoice until the goods ordered have been received and checked to be satisfactory. This means that items charged for on the invoice must match the items ordered and received as recorded on the GRN, and at the prices agreed. Only then should the invoice be authorized and payment made.

  There are a number of reasons why invoices may differ from orders and GRNs. The most common ones are:

  - the invoice contains a mistake
  - the wrong goods were delivered and had to be returned
  - some goods were damaged and returned to the supplier
  - the customer is still awaiting delivery

  Regular customers will normally receive a statement of account listing all their purchases rather than individual invoices (see 12.3). Individual entries in the account must be checked against orders and GRNs before the account total can be accepted and payment authorized.

- **Making sure only authorized personnel approve payments.** Once an invoice or account statement has been authorized, the firm's accounts department will pay the supplier. Whatever the method of payment used (see 12.2), it is usual for a senior member of staff to provide authorization. If any employee was allowed to make payment, some might be tempted to make bogus payments into their own bank accounts or to fictitious companies.

  In some cases, particularly where large amounts of money are involved, two or more members of the same organization may be required to authorize payments and sign cheques. These are known as **company signatories.** The bank that holds the account of the organization will keep sample copies of their signatures so that it can check them against the signatures on cheques and orders to transfer funds out of the business account. Each signatory provides a check on the others and also protects individual signatories against allegations of fraud.

- **Internal audit.** This involves company accountants and independent auditors checking through financial documents and accounts to see that they are in order. If there are errors, omissions, or inconsistencies, these can be checked and the staff interviewed if fraud is suspected.

- **Checking bank notes and payment cards for counterfeits.** This is often done simply by holding notes up to the light, or under ultraviolet lights, to check for watermarks. However, counterfeit notes and plastic cards have become so sophisticated they can be very hard to detect.

Portfolio Activity 12.12

PC: Explain the importance of security and security checks for receipts and payments
Range: Importance, Security checks
Skills: Use images, Produce written material

Look at the order, goods received note, and invoice below.

Would you authorize the invoice for payment? If not, suggest why, and what further action you could take to clear up any errors or inconsistencies.

VISTECH LTD

Unit 4 Silvermead
Industrial Estate
Silvermead SM4 7JW
Tel: 015623-840704
Fax: 015623-840705
VAT Reg No. 5676 0234 60

Purchase Order No. 12345

To: Computer Warehouse

Unit 12 Hampwick Estate

Long Hampwick HP3 9KL

DESCRIPTION	QTY	REF. No	PRICE	TOTAL
Box of 10 3.5" high density computer disks	4	248/c	£10	£40
Cable trap anti-theft security devices	3	936/d	£20	£60

Authorized by: *R. U. Sure*
for VISTECH LTD

COMPUTER WAREHOUSE

INVOICE

Unit 12 Hampwick Estate
Long Hampwick HP3 9KL
Tel: 01312–777666
Fax: 01312–77766
VAT Reg No. 809 3333 12

To: Vistech Ltd.

Unit 4 Silvermead Industrial Estate

Silvermead SM4 7JW

Date	Order No.	Account No.	Invoice No.
4.3.96	12345	100700	10001

QTY	Description	Cat No.	Unit Price	Total
4	Diskettes	248/c	£11	£44
3	Cable-traps	936/d	£20	£60
1	Delivery		£30	£30
			Sub-total	£134
			Cash discount	–
			Total (ex. VAT)	£134
			VAT @ 17.5%	£23.45
			Total due	£157.45

Terms:
Cash discount of 5% only applies
to orders over £200 if payment
received within 10 working days

E & OE

GOODS RECEIVED NOTE

VISTECH LTD

Supplier:

Computer Warehouse

Unit 12 Hampwick Estate

Long Hampwick HP3 9KL

GRN NO: 2121

Date: 3.3.96

Re; Delivery Note:
05/09876

ORDER NO.	QTY	DESCRIPTION	REF NO:
12345	3 boxes 2 boxes	10 x 3.5" diskettes Cable trap anti-theft device kits	248/c 936/d

Received by: *R. U. Sure*

for VISTECH LTD

PSST. WANNA BUY A WATCH?

Theft

Theft refers to people stealing money or goods that do not belong to them. This can also include the theft of confidential business information, either from paper files or computer files.

People who steal from business organizations may be members of the public, customers of the organization, or even their own employees. Items stolen – either for the thief's own personal use or to sell for cash – can include cash, stock and equipment and the personal belongings of staff.

Whether the items stolen are worth a few pence or many thousands of pounds, theft is still unlawful. Many organizations are willing to overlook the fact that their employees use phones or photocopiers, or occasionally take home a pen and some paper for their own personal use. However, employees are trusted not to make excessive use of these perks. To do so is the same as stealing because it costs the organization money which lowers profits and reduces the amount available to buy new equipment and pay wages.

Security measures to prevent theft
The risk of theft can be reduced in a number of ways. Here are just a few simple rules:

- Keep cash holdings on business premises to a minimum. If cash is kept, always make sure it is locked away in a safe and that all cash inflows and outflows are carefully recorded.

- Empty cash registers in shops at regular intervals to keep cash holdings in tills to a minimum. This reduces the amount of money at risk from theft and/or pilfering by cash till operators.

- User IDs and passwords can restrict access to confidential information stored on computers (see 14.5).

- Important documents can be stored in secure cabinets and safes.

- Premises can be protected from unlawful entry by employing security guards, cameras and lights, always locking doors and windows, and restricting access to those who carry security cards or know the entry codes to sophisticated entry locks.

- Incoming and outgoing stock should be monitored closely and recorded. Stock should only be issued on the written approval of staff with the appropriate authority.

- Check with banks and credit card companies whether a customer who wants to pay on credit has any bad debts before allowing them to take delivery of goods or services.

Ensuring high standards of honesty

Most people are decent, honest, law-abiding citizens. They want crime reduced, and they want people who steal, defraud, and cause unlawful damage to be caught and punished. However, some people may be persuaded to become dishonest if they are presented with the opportunity to do so. They may also be tempted to be dishonest if their colleagues set a bad example. It is therefore important that firms maintain a high standard of honesty among their employees and customers.

To encourage honesty and reduce the opportunities for crime, firms will use a combination of rewards, punishments, and security measures. For example:

● Rewards can be offered to people who report and stop crime. For example, people are often given cash sums for reporting stolen or lost credit cards, or for information that leads to the recovery of stolen property or the apprehension of criminals.

● Special procedures can be used when recruiting new staff to check their honesty and good character - for example, asking their previous employers for references, making sure they live where they say they do, finding out whether they have any previous convictions.

● Employees who defraud or steal from an organization can be punished by dismissal, loss of pension rights, and criminal prosecution in law courts which could lead to a fine or imprisonment.

● Firms can take legal action against customers who are caught stealing from a business.

● A whole range of security devices and equipment can be used to prevent theft and fraud, such as burglar alarms, surveillance cameras, electronic tagging, security anchors, procedures to authorize orders and payments, and many more.

Key words

In your own words write explanations and definitions of the following key words and terms from this chapter:

Financial transaction	Inward transaction	Cheque	Debit card
Outward transaction	Overheads	Direct debit	Standing order
Fraud	Internal accounts	BACS	EDI
External accounts	Profit	Credit card	Purchase order
Loss	Break even	GRN	Invoice
Consumer market	Industrial market	Delivery note	Credit note
Cash sale	Trade credit	Debit note	Statement of account
Credit sale	Hire purchase	Remittance advice	Sales receipt
Debtor	Creditor	Paying-in slip	Bank statement
		Bank reconciliation	Company signatories

Test and Assignment

You must demonstrate that you are able to:

1. Explain financial transactions which take place regularly in an organization and explain why records of transactions are kept

2. Explain and give examples of purchases and purchase documents

3. Explain and give examples of sales and sales documents

4. Explain and give examples of payment methods and receipt documents

5. Explain the importance of security and security checks for receipts and payments

This unit is not examined externally. However, the following questions will help you test and revise your understanding of the range in element 4.1.

1 What is the main purpose of keeping records of financial transactions for business owners and managers?

A to provide information for lenders, for example, a bank

B to provide information for the government

C to provide information which will assist in monitoring and controlling the business

D to provide information to the registrar of companies

2 The person who signs a cheque to make payment is:

A the person who is paying the money

B the branch bank manager

C the person to whom the cheque is paid

D the person who pays the cheque in to the bank account

Questions 3-5 share the following answer options:

A checking invoices against goods received notes

B checking invoices against purchase orders

C requiring authorized personnel to sign orders

D installing surveillance cameras

Which of the above security measures could reduce the risk of the following situations occurring:

3 The theft of goods from delivery bays

4 Authorizing payment for goods not delivered

5 Employees making fraudulent payments to their own bank account

6 Which of the following would a firm send to a supplier requesting delivery of goods?

A statement of account

B purchase order

C goods received note

D invoice

Questions 7-9 share the following answer options:

A a sales invoice

B a delivery note

C a statement of account

D a sales receipt

Which of the above documents would be used to:

7 Provide proof that a purchase has been made?

8 Inform a customer of the value of goods supplied and terms of payment?

9 Request payment for goods delivered?

10 Which of the following is the more usual sequence in which firms will receive and send out documents for transactions?

A order, invoice, payment, delivery note

B order, delivery note, invoice, payment

C order, payment, invoice, delivery note

D order, payment, delivery note, invoice

11 a. What is a financial transaction?

b. Explain two reasons why businesses need to keep records of all their financial transactions.

c. What is the difference between an inward transaction and an outward transaction? Give two examples of each type of transaction.

12 a. Sports Fashions Ltd has just placed an order for trainers with a major sports shoe manufacturer. Suggest three ways Sports Fashions could pay for their order.

b. What is an invoice and what details should an invoice contain?

c. What is the difference between a delivery note and a goods received note?

d. Explain why it is important for Sports Fashions Ltd to check details on the invoice for their order with their goods received note.

assessment assignment

The following assignment meets the evidence requirements needed to
fulfil all the performance criteria in element 4.1. In addition it covers
the following range points and core skills:

Range: Financial transactions
Records of transactions
Purchases
Purchase documents
Sales transactions
Sales documents
Payment methods
Receipt documents
Importance of security
Security checks

Skills: **Communication**
Produce written material
Use images
Application of number
Collect and record data
Tackle problems
Information technology
Present information

Tasks

1. Mario D'Andrea owns and runs a hairdressing salon in Motspur Park, Surrey called Stefan Alexander (see 1.1). He records all his inward and outward financial transactions in an income and expenditure account for each week. This provides him with an up-to-date picture of how well his business is performing.

Over the last few weeks Mario has been very busy decorating his flat. He has not had time to complete his income and expenditure accounts as usual. All he has managed to do is to keep some notes in his diary on how much he has spent on the business and how much income it has earned. These are as follows:

WEEK 1

Monday
Remember to increase petty cash float to £3 per day from now on. Window cleaner calls for his usual £2.50 per week.

Tuesday
I had better visit the Capital Hair and Beauty wholesalers today to buy in some new stock of shampoos, hairspray, perm lotions, and hair tints. I will allow £200 for these purchases.

Wednesday
Quarterly telephone bill from Mercury Communications arrives. Thankfully we make few outgoing calls and the bill is only £23.40.

Thursday
More bills! Today our quarterly water meter bill for £1.78 is due.

Friday
Takings are good this week at £1,467.50. The self-employed stylist I employ is due £340 commission this week. I must also remember to pay my apprentice £50.

WEEK 2

Monday
Rent is due this week. Don't forget to write a cheque for £1,900 for this quarter.

Tuesday
Laundry bill for towels and aprons comes to £36 this week.

Window cleaner £2.50.

Wednesday
Send cheque to pay quarterly electricity bill for £178 today.

Thursday
Good news! I received a cheque for £105.20 today from the Inland Revenue for overpaid tax.

Friday
Takings down this week at £1,070.80. Stylists commission is only £180 this week. Wages for the apprentice are £50 as per usual.

WEEK 3

Monday
Monthly business rates of £245 are due this week.

Window cleaner £2.50.

Tuesday
Annual premium for public liability insurance is due next week. Remember to send off cheque for £680 by end of week.

Wednesday
Send cheque to pay £56 to Performing Rights Society for my annual licence to play the radio in the salon.

Thursday
Visited the wholesalers again to pick up some more stock. Bill came to £175.90.

Friday
Weekly takings are up again to £1,484.40. My stylist is due commission of £260 and the apprentice is due his usual £50.

1. a Enter details of Mario's business incomes and expenditures into a computer spreadsheet to produce three simple accounts with the following format:

> **STEFAN ALEXANDER**
> Income and expenditure account: WEEK _____
>
> **INCOME (£)**
> Sales revenues
>
> **EXPENDITURE (£)**
> Stock
> Services
> Water meter
> Business rates
> Electricity
> Telephone
> Insurance
> Premiums
> Wages
> Other
>
> Total expenditure
>
> Balance

b In which week was income **greater than** expenditure, income **equal to** expenditure, and income **less than** expenditure?

c Write a short note below the accounts to explain why the recording of financial information is essential, not just for Mario, but for all business organizations.

2. a Try to collect one example of each of the following financial documents from business organizations you are familiar with, including your school/college or work experience placement.

Purchase documents:

– Purchase order
– Purchase invoice received by a customer
– Credit note
– Goods received note

Sales documents:

– Order received by a supplier
– Sales invoice sent by a supplier
– Delivery note
– Statement of account
– Remittance advice

Receipts documents:

– Sales receipt
– Cheque
– Paying in-slip
– Bank statement

It may not be possible to obtain all the above documents from business organizations. Some may not keep old unwanted copies, while others may only provide 'sample' documents. In some cases your own personal transactions, or those of your family, will result in financial documents you can use. If you are really stuck, produce your own examples using a computer word processor or desktop publishing package.

b For each document listed above write a brief explanation of its purpose, i.e. what it is used for, and why it is needed.

c Choose four methods of making payment from the following list and write a detailed description of each one. You may use pictures and diagrams to illustrate your chosen method if appropriate.

Methods of payment

– Cash
– Cheque
– Banking Automated Clearing Services (BACS)
– Electronic Data Interchange (EDI)
– Credit card
– Debit card
– Trade credit
– Credit sale
– Hire Purchase

3. Choose a business organization, and list a number of security measures it could use to help prevent fraud and theft by staff, customers, and members of the public. Explain in writing why security is important to your chosen business organization.

4. When you have completed all the above tasks assemble the documents you have collected and your written notes into a folder to file in your portfolio. Mark your file 'Financial Transactions and Documents'. If your written work is also stored on computer, make sure you save a copy on a floppy disk to store in your file for back-up.

chapter 13 Financial Recording

Financial accounting is the recording and monitoring of financial information in business. Financial accounting is important for **security, to monitor income and expenditure, to keep customer and business accounts up to date, and to monitor business performance.**

Records of incomes and expenditures are entered in **ledger accounts**. These are **internal accounts** used by the business.

Financial summaries showing total profit and how much a business is worth are presented in the **final accounts** at the end of every accounting period.

The **balance sheet** shows the value of business assets and the source of funds used to buy assets. The **profit and loss statement** gives details of sales turnover, expenses, profit, and the use of profit. These are **external accounts** used by shareholders, potential lenders, and the tax authorities to assess the value and profitability of a business.

Financial plans for future spending, output, and sales are called **budgets**. Actual business performance can be compared to budget plans to judge how well a business is doing.

Businesses use a variety of financial documents to record purchases, sales, payments, and receipts. Information recorded on these documents is entered into the business accounts.

A customer will keep records of the following **purchase documents**: purchase orders, invoices, credit notes, and goods received notes.

A supplier will send and receive the following **sales documents**: orders received, delivery notes, sales invoices, statements of account, credit notes, and remittance advice notes.

Payments can be recorded on the following **payment documents**: **payslips, cheques,** and **petty cash vouchers**.

Receipt documents such as sales receipts, cheques, paying-in slips and bank statements provide proof that payments have been made.

Information technology is used by many modern business organizations to help record and monitor financial information. **Spreadsheets** can perform complex calculations on financial data and present information in graphs. **Accounting software** can be used to record and produce business accounts.

Section **13.1** **Financial accounting**

All businesses make financial plans and keep records of their incomes and spending in order to monitor how well or how badly they are performing over time. This is called **financial accounting**.

Financial information about businesses is contained in the following documents:

- Financial plans are set out in **budgets**

- Records of inward and outward financial transactions are entered into **ledger accounts**

- Financial summaries showing total profit and how much a business is worth are presented in the **final accounts**

- Simple **income and expenditure accounts** list all money received and paid out by a business

Large business organizations will often employ specialist personnel in their accounts departments to record financial transactions and to produce business accounts.

We will now consider how each of the different types of financial plans and accounts are prepared, and why they are so useful.

What is budgeting?

Each year business managers set targets for their firms to work towards. For example, a business might aim to expand production by 10%, increase market share by 5%, and/or raise profits by 20%.

▼ *Planning ahead is vital to the success of a business.*

NEW MACHINERY £15,000

MORE WORKERS £6,000 PER MONTH

MATERIALS £10 £10 £10 £10

Agreed business targets can effect future spending and revenues. For example, a firm that wants to increase production by 10% will need to buy more materials, use more power, and perhaps employ more workers and machinery. This means more money has to be spent. However, the firm will also have more goods or services to sell and so can earn more revenue.

Plans for spending and revenues linked to business targets are set out in a **budget**. A budget is simply a financial plan for the future prepared by business managers. Most budgets are for 12-months ahead but some budget plans are drawn up for longer periods. For example, research and development may involve spending large amounts of money over many years.

The preparation of budgets is known as **budgeting**. This is a very important task for any business. By planning ahead a firm can make sure it has enough money in the future, by retaining profits from previous years, or by arranging loans from banks and other lenders.

In the same way, the UK government prepares a budget at the end of every November for the whole economy. This is a statement of planned public spending and expected tax revenues for the coming financial year (see 1.4).

Preparing budgets

The preparation of budgets is an important aspect of business planning. Budgets will help an organization to:

- **Examine alternative courses of action.** For example, identifying the costs and benefits of using more workers to raise output, buying new machinery, moving to new premises, using different materials, introducing computerized accounting systems, etc.

- **Examine the impact of unforeseen changes on the business.** For example, what will be the effect of an increase in interest rates, rising prices, higher wage demands, falling consumer demand, etc.

- **Present information on incomes, expenditures, and expected profits** to potential lenders to raise finance.

- **Monitor business performance** by comparing actual results with plans

Drawing up a budget involves a number of steps. These are illustrated in Figure 13.1.

▼ *Figure 13.1: Preparing a budget*

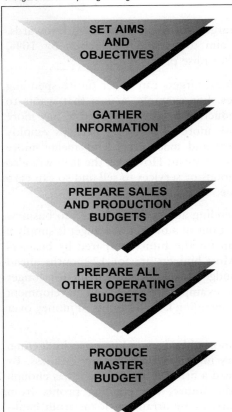

SET AIMS AND OBJECTIVES

GATHER INFORMATION

PREPARE SALES AND PRODUCTION BUDGETS

PREPARE ALL OTHER OPERATING BUDGETS

PRODUCE MASTER BUDGET

Stage 1: Decide upon a budget period. Most budgets are produced annually. It is usual for an annual budget to be broken down into plans for each quarter or month.

Stage 2: Agree business objectives and set targets. In a large organization individual targets will be agreed for each factory or office, or each department, area, or product. Targets should be realistic: a firm that sets out to increase market share by 50% in three months is unlikely ever to achieve its target.

Stage 3: Obtain information on which to base budgets. For example, past information on costs and revenues, or new information from market research and quotes from suppliers.

Stage 4: Based on targets agreed, the business must now prepare key operating budgets for sales and production:

- The **sales budget** shows planned revenues the firm hopes to achieve each month. This is calculated by multiplying predicted sales volumes by the product prices the firm hopes to achieve.

- The **production budget** shows the amount of materials, labour hours, and machine hours needed to meet sales targets.

Stage 5: Based on the sales and production budgets, the next step is to prepare operating budgets for:

- labour

- materials

- capital, i.e. assets such as premises, machinery, vehicles, and other equipment

- overheads, i.e. administration, telephone, postage, heating and lighting, etc.

- inflows of cash from sales and outflows of cash to pay bills

- and all other items that give rise to expenditure or revenues

Stage 6: Draw up the master budget. This is a summary of all the incomes and expenditures identified in the operating budgets. It also shows expected profit.

Figure 13.2 shows a simple master budget prepared for a manufacturer of luxury chocolate bars for the first six months of the year (cash inflows and outflows are not shown). The target is to expand output by 20% by June. To do this, the owners have calculated they will need to expand the premises, buy new machinery, and take on extra staff. There will also be a need for more materials, power, and administration, etc. The simple master budget in Figure 13.2 lists all the revenues and costs expected from the business expansion. At the end of six months, the owners calculate that their plans will have resulted in an accumulated surplus revenue of £354,150. If at the end of the six-month period they find they have failed to achieve this, they can start to investigate why and make sure they do not make the same mistakes again. For example, they may have underestimated the cost of buying the extra machinery they needed, or overestimated the strength of consumer demand.

▼ Figure 13.2: An example of a master budget

	January	February	March	April	May	June
Output	100,000	100,000	105,000	110,000	115,000	120,000
Materials	£1,000	£1,000	£1,050	£1,100	£1,150	£1,200
Wages	£30,000	£32,000	£34,000	£35,000	£35,000	£35,000
Capital (premises, machinery, etc.)	–	–	£42,000	£28,000	£7,500	
Overheads	£7,000	£7,000	£7,300	£7,500	£7,500	£7,500
All other costs	£2,000	£2,000	£2,000	£2,000	£2,100	£2,200
Total expenditure	**£40,000**	**£42,000**	**£86,350**	**£73,600**	**£53,250**	**£45,900**
Unit price	£0.90	£1.10	£1.10	£1.25	£1.00	£1.00
Sales volumes	90,000	95,000	110,000	135,000	110,000	110,000
Sales revenues	**£81,000**	**£104,500**	**£121,000**	**£168,750**	**£110,000**	**£110,000**
Surplus(+)/Deficit (–)	**+£41,000**	**+£62,500**	**+£34,650**	**+£95,150**	**+£56,750**	**+£64,100**
Cumulative surplus/deficit	**+£41,000**	**+£103,500**	**+£138,150**	**+£233,300**	**+£290,050**	**+£354,150**

Monitoring budgets

If a business is to be successful it must always be aware of how well it is performing and its financial position. This can be done by comparing actual results with budget plans. **Budgetary control** is the process of setting targets, preparing budget plans, monitoring those plans, and then investigating why actual results may differ from what had been planned for.

A business that is **underperforming** is one that has not achieved its targets. Output and revenues may be lower than expected, and/or costs higher. In this case the financial position of the business will be getting worse because spending and revenues are not going according to plan. The firm may even run out of cash to pay its bills.

For example, consider the firm producing chocolate bars. In Figure 13.3 the managers of the business have plotted figures on sales from the master budget in Figure 13.2, against actual sales. Clearly, sales have not performed as well as planned, especially during April when sales are expected to be higher over the Easter period. Knowing this, managers may decide to cut product prices and/or launch a new advertising campaign in an attempt to raise sales of their chocolate bars. In addition, cutting the number of people employed and introducing new equipment could reduce costs so that profit targets are met.

Figure 13.3: Sales of chocolate bars, January-June

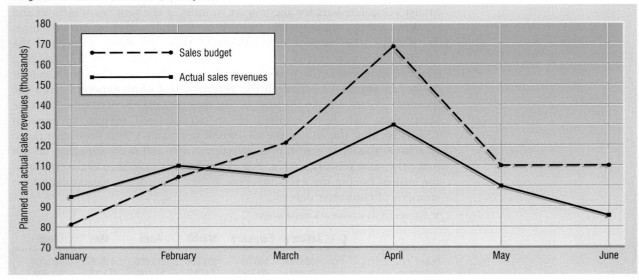

A business that is **overperforming** is one that has achieved more than it had planned. Output and revenues will be more than expected, and/or spending less than had been budgeted for. The financial position of the business will be improving.

Portfolio Activity 13.1

PC: Explain why financial information must be recorded
Range: Financial information
Skills: Interpret and present data, Produce written material

The production budget for the first six months of the new tax year for a firm that assembles television sets is shown in the table opposite. The production budget gives details of planned outputs each month and the amount of materials, labour, and machine hours needed to produce the planned output. The production of each TV requires the following inputs:

– 2 units of materials

– 30 minutes of labour time

– 45 minutes of machine time

The next stage will be to work out how much the inputs of materials, labour, and machines will cost.

The table also shows what was actually produced each month. As you can see, things did not quite go according to plan.

1. Suggest what information the production budget may have been based on.

2. Calculate the difference between actual output and planned output each month. Is the firm under- or overperforming?

Month	Planned output (TVs)	Planned materials hours	Planned labour hours	Planned machine hours	Actual output
April	1,000	2,000	500	750	800
May	1,000	2,000	500	750	910
June	1,200	2,400	600	900	1,150
July	1,500	3,000	750	1,125	1,400
August	1,500	3,000	750	1,125	1,700
September	1,300	2,600	650	975	1,500

3. Explain what might have caused the large differences between planned and actual output.

4. Why is this information useful to business managers?

5. Suggest how the following events could affect the difference between planned and actual output in a firm:

● suppliers fail to deliver materials on time

● a strike by workers

● a power failure

● workers agree to work more overtime

● a flu outbreak among workers

Ledger accounts

Most business organizations enter details of their financial transactions into **ledger accounts**. These are internal accounts used by business managers. The main ledger accounts are:

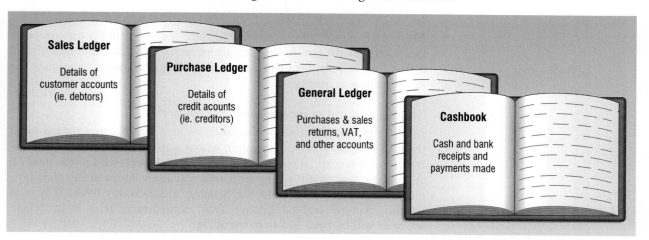

Sales Ledger

Details of customer accounts (ie. debtors)

Purchase Ledger

Details of credit acounts (ie. creditors)

General Ledger

Purchases & sales returns, VAT, and other accounts

Cashbook

Cash and bank receipts and payments made

The ledger accounts provide details of:

Sales ledger:

- How much has been sold

- The value of sales

- How much money is owed by customers (known as **debtors**)

Purchase ledger:

- How much has been purchased

- The cost of purchases

- How much money is owed to suppliers (known as **creditors**)

General ledger:

- All purchases and sales

- Money spent buying assets, such as premises, machinery, vehicles, fixtures and fittings

- The cost of wages

- The amount and cost of materials purchased

- VAT receipts and payments

- Loan repayments

- Money paid out for overheads, such as rent, rates, telephone, stationary, advertising, heating and lighting, and other expenses

Cashbook:

- Cash held on premises

- Cash held in a bank or building society account

- Deposits and withdrawals of cash from the account

- Cash received and why it has been received

- Cash paid out and why it has been paid out

- The difference between cash-in and cash-out

Most large organizations today keep their ledger accounts on computer (see 13.4). At the end of the accounting period an accountant employed by the firm will use the information in the ledger accounts to prepare the final business accounts.

Keeping a record of incomes and expenditures

In order to complete business accounts a firm must keep a record of all the money it has received (income), who it was from, and what it was for. It must also record all money paid out (expenditure), who it was paid to, and what it was paid for. These records will allow a firm to calculate how much money is available to the firm on a day-to-day basis. If it is in surplus, income will be greater than expenditure. If it is in deficit, incomes will be been less than spending.

However, simply deducting spending from incomes every month does not tell us how much profit the business has earned. This is because incomes and expenditures can occur at different times. For example, sales revenues may be received every day of the week, but wages will only be paid once a month. Similarly, electricity and phone bills tend to be paid quarterly. Clearly, those months in which electricity bills are paid will show a smaller surplus, or even a deficit, over previous months. However, this does not mean the firm is not earning an overall profit over time.

▼ Figure 13.4: Incomes and expenditures in a typical private sector business

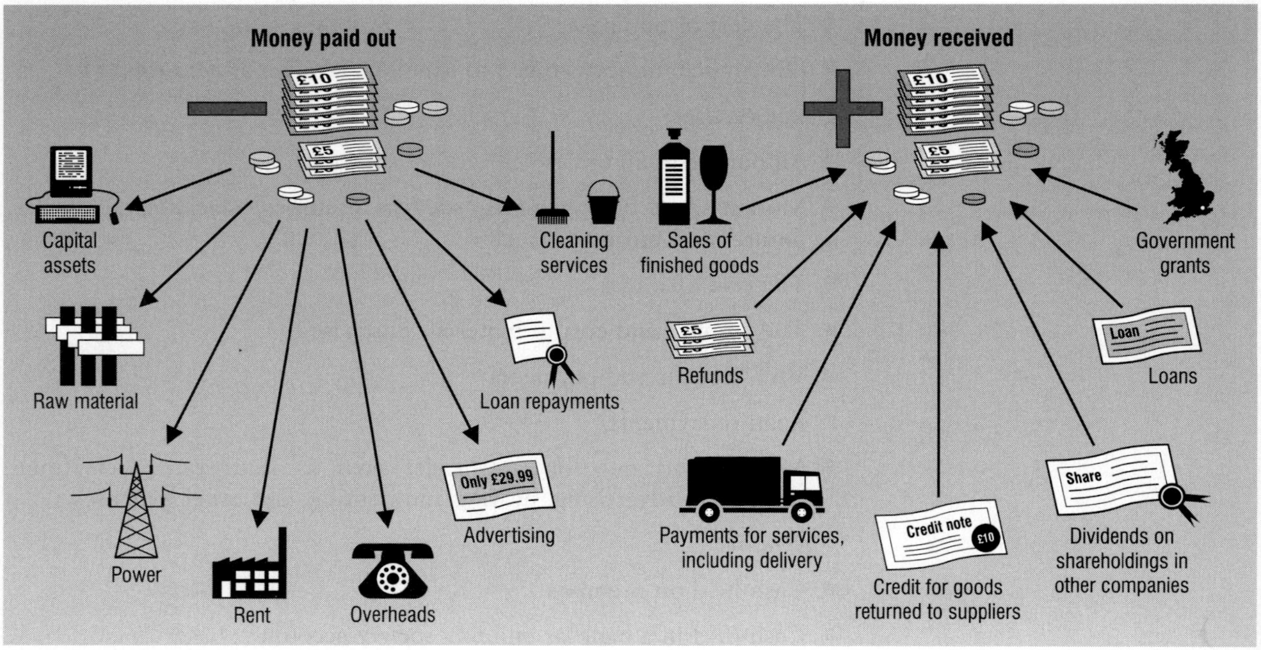

Portfolio Activity 13.2

PC: Record income and expenditure over time periods

Range: Financial information

Skills: Interpret and present data

A friend of yours has just set up his own painting and decorating business. He has asked you to draw up and complete a simple business account summarizing all the incomes and expenditures he has received and made during his first month in business.

You start by collecting together documents recording all payments made and received. These are listed. You will need to sort them into incomes and expenditures (with sub-headings such as tools, paints, petrol, loan repayments, miscellaneous, etc.) before entering their details into an account. Use a computer spreadsheet to help you.

What is the balance on the income and expenditure account at the end of the month?

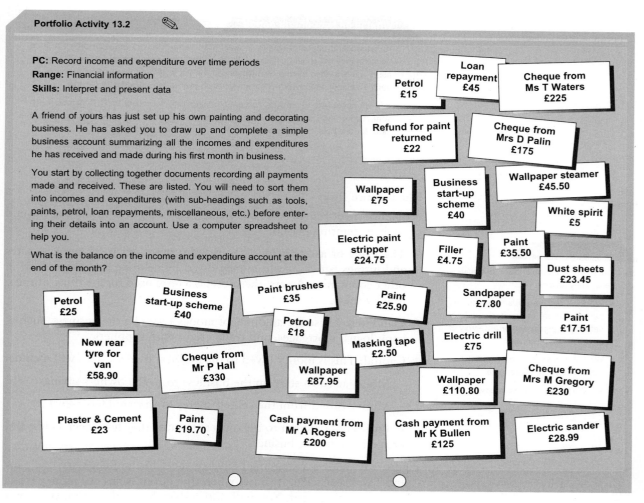

Petrol £15

Loan repayment £45

Cheque from Ms T Waters £225

Refund for paint returned £22

Cheque from Mrs D Palin £175

Wallpaper £75

Business start-up scheme £40

Wallpaper steamer £45.50

White spirit £5

Electric paint stripper £24.75

Filler £4.75

Paint £35.50

Dust sheets £23.45

Petrol £25

Business start-up scheme £40

Paint brushes £35

Paint £25.90

Sandpaper £7.80

Paint £17.51

Petrol £18

Masking tape £2.50

Electric drill £75

New rear tyre for van £58.90

Cheque from Mr P Hall £330

Wallpaper £87.95

Wallpaper £110.80

Cheque from Mrs M Gregory £230

Plaster & Cement £23

Paint £19.70

Cash payment from Mr A Rogers £200

Cash payment from Mr K Bullen £125

Electric sander £28.99

Final accounts

The final accounts of an organization are drawn up at the end of each accounting period and are primarily for external use. They summarize financial information about a business which can be used by other people and organizations outside the business. The main final accounts are:

- **The balance sheet**

- **The profit and loss statement**

All businesses have to produce accounts each year so that their tax liability can be assessed. Sole traders and partnerships will be assessed for income tax, which is paid twice a year. Private and public limited companies will be assessed for corporation tax payable on profits (see 1.3).

Limited companies are required by law to prepare final accounts at the end of each accounting period and to have them checked and approved by an independent **auditor**. Copies of the approved accounts must then be sent to the government's Registrar of Companies (see 1.3). Public limited companies must make their annual accounts available to anyone who asks to see them.

The balance sheet

A **balance sheet** provides the following details about a business at the end of each accounting period:

- **The value of assets held:** This includes premises, machinery, fixtures and fittings, stocks, cash, money owed by debtors, and shares held in other companies. **Assets**, therefore, is a term used for anything of value to a business.

- **Liabilities:** These are amounts of money owed by the business, such as bank loans, mortgages, and trade credit with suppliers

- **Capital:** This is money owed to the business owners. This will include:

  - Money used to start up the business from the owners savings

  - Money raised from the sale of shares to shareholders (see 1.3)

  - Profits not paid out to the owners because they have been held back, or retained, by the business

Figure 13.5 shows a simplified balance sheet for an imaginary company called TW Plastics Plc. It shows where the business has got money from, and how it has used it. You will notice that the total amount of money used by the business to buy assets is equal to the total amount of money owed by the business to its owners and providers of finance.

What are stocks?

Stocks are a valuable asset to a business. They include:

- Stocks of raw materials or component parts which are to be used at a later date in the production or assembly of other goods or services

- Work in progress – i.e. semi-finished goods not yet ready for sale

- Finished goods that are ready for sale

▼ Figure 13.5: A simple balance sheet

TW Plastics Plc

Balance sheet for the year ended 31.12.95

Capital and liabilities	£	Assets	£
Shareholders' funds	110,000	Premises	130,000
Retained profits	60,000	Machinery	40,000
		Vehicle stock	25,000
Bank loan	45,000	Fixtures and fittings	15,500
Creditors	12,000	Stocks	10,000
		Debtors	4,000
		Cash	2,500
	227,000		227,000

To be correct, a balance sheet must always balance. That is:

Assets = Liabilities + Capital

This means that all the money raised by a business from owners, loans and/or suppliers, will be invested in assets.

The profit and loss statement

With the exception of charities, the main objective of most private sector organizations is to make a profit (see 1.1). A profit is made when total income over an accounting period exceeds total expenditures or costs. A loss occurs when costs are greater than incomes. A business can either make a profit, loss, or break even when revenues are exactly equal to costs.

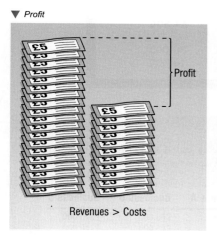

▼ Profit

Revenues > Costs

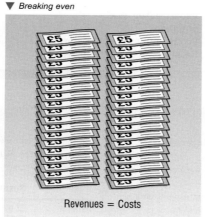

▼ Breaking even

Revenues = Costs

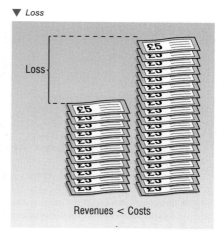

▼ Loss

Revenues < Costs

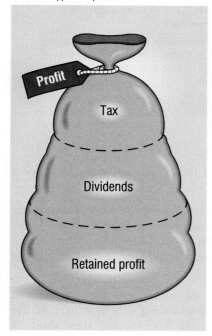

▼ What happens to profit?

A **profit and loss statement** shows how much profit or loss an organization has made at the end of an accounting period. It shows:

- **Turnover** = total sales revenue

- **Gross profit** = the difference between turnover and the cost of producing all the goods or services sold (known as the **cost of sales**)

- **Net (or operating) profit** = gross profit less all other overhead expenses, such as rent, rates, administration, advertising, telephone, etc.

- **Profit before tax** = net profit plus any other income, less any interest paid on loans

- **Profit after tax** = profit less corporation tax

If a profit is made after tax at the end of an accounting period, some is likely to be paid out to the business owners either in the form of drawings, or, in the case of limited companies, as dividends on shares. The remainder of the profit after tax may be retained by the business as savings or used to buy more assets, such as bigger premises or machinery. These asset purchases will be added to the balance sheet.

Figure 13.6 shows the profit and loss statement for TW Plastics Plc for the 12-month accounting period ending 31.12.95.

▼ Figure 13.6: An example of a profit and loss statement

TW Plastics Plc

Profit and Loss Account for the year ended 31.12.1995

	£
Turnover	**210,000**
Less cost of sales	70,000
Gross profit	**140,000**
less expenses	60,000
Net profit	**80,000**
add other income	2,000
less interest payable	4,000
Profit before tax	**78,000**
less corporation tax	23,500
Profit after tax	**54,500**
of which:	
Profit paid to shareholders	35,000
Retained profit for the year	19,500

Portfolio Activity 13.3

PC.: Record income and expenditure over time periods

Range: Financial information

Skills: Collect and record data, Produce written material, Tackle problems

1. Investigate and report on how incomes and expenditures are likely to differ between the following organizations:

- A charity

- A bank

- A supermarket

- A local council

2. In your report show some worked examples of how to calculate gross and net profit at the end of an accounting period using the following information:

	Business A	Business B	Business C
Turnover	£2 million	£60,000	£220,000
Cost of sales	£750,000	£45,000	£140,000
Overheads	£350,000	£17,000	£80,000

3. Which of the businesses in Task 2 has made an operating profit, an operating loss, or broken even?

4. Suppose Business B finds that it has lost records of equipment purchases worth a total of £5,000. Explain how this is likely to affect the calculation of profit/loss for the purpose of tax assessment.

Section **13.2**

Recording financial information

Business organizations keep records of their financial transactions for a number of reasons:

- **To monitor incomes and expenditures:** A firm will need to know exactly how much it is spending and how much it is earning from day to day. This is so it knows how much money is available to spend on wages, materials, and all the other items it needs to carry on making and selling its products.

Actual incomes and expenditures each month can be compared to budget plans. If a business is underperforming and in danger of not meeting agreed targets, managers can take action they think is appropriate to make it perform better.

Portfolio Activity 13.4

PC: Explain why financial information must be recorded
Range: Recorded
Skills: Produce written material, Use images

1. Look at the illustrations below. What do they suggest about the need for business organizations to keep accurate records of their incomes and expenditures. Are there any other reasons you can think of?

2. Investigate why a business organization of your choice keeps records of financial transactions.

● **To keep customer accounts up to date:** Allowing business customers to pay for goods or services up to 90 days later is a way of attracting their custom. However, it also means that the business that has supplied the goods or services on credit must keep an accurate record of who owes them money and when payment is due. Without these records, it will not be able to identify customers who fail to pay.

Regular customers will receive regular statements of the goods and services they have bought on credit from a supplier (see 12.3). An account statement will show all the purchases made by the customer including any returns and the total amount, or balance, that needs to be paid to clear the account.

If accurate records are not kept, customer accounts will not be up to date and will show the wrong amount. If it shows too much the customer may get angry and take their business elsewhere. If the account balance is too low, then the revenues of the supplier will be lower than they should be.

● **To monitor business performance:** The final accounts of a business provide a record of how well a business has performed over the last accounting period in terms of sales, costs, and profits. These figures can be compared to those from earlier periods to see if business performance has improved, stayed about the same, or deteriorated.

The performance of a business can also be compared to that of competing firms in order to judge whether or not it is doing better than its rivals. For example, Figure 13.7 shows how pre-tax profits have changed over time in some well known supermarket chains. From the chart it is clear that Sainsbury's out-performed its main rivals over the period 1984-1993.

▼ *Figure 13.7: Pre-tax profits of selected supermarket chains*

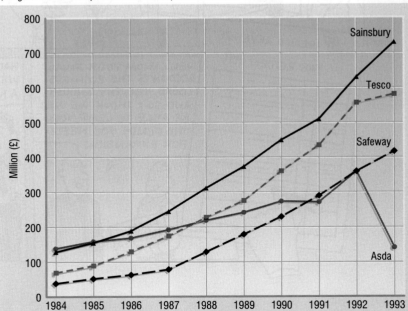

- **To keep business accounts up to date:** Business owners and managers need up-to-date financial information in order to monitor the performance of their business and take decisions that could help to improve it. Business accounts are their main source of information for this.

- **For security:** Unless a business has accurate and up-to-date records of its financial transactions, it could be vulnerable to fraud, theft, and false claims (see 12.4).

- **To secure and maintain finance:** All businesses need money to buy or hire assets, such as premises and machinery, and to pay everyday bills. Many businesses borrow money from banks and building societies. However, these organizations will not lend money to a business that does not display sound financial management. They will want evidence from business accounts that the firm earns enough money to be able to repay a loan.

- **To calculate how much tax to pay:** All firms must provide annual accounts for taxation and VAT purposes. The tax authorities will often need proof of business expenditures. If a business has failed to keep records of all the items it has spent money on, and how much they cost, it will be unable to deduct these from its income. The end-of-year profit will appear bigger than it actually is, and the organization will consequently pay more tax than it should.

How do firms record financial information?

In Chapter 12 we learnt that business organizations must complete a number of different financial documents to record sales and purchases of goods and services. These documents must be completed fully, accurately, and neatly if they are to provide a record of flows of money and products that can be entered into business accounts (see 13.1).

We will now look at how financial documents for purchases, sales, and receipts are completed and checked. You should also refer back to Section 12.3 to examine each document in detail. (Section 13.3 considers financial documents used to record payments made by a business.)

Purchase document checklists

Section 12.3 described the following documents used to make and record purchases:

- Purchase order
- Purchase invoice
- Goods received note
- Credit note

Some golden rules for completing financial documents

1. Check that all the information needed has been provided

A document that has not been filled in with all the necessary information will not do the job it is designed to do. For example, a cheque without a signature cannot make payment; a purchase order without a delivery address will not be able to order goods; a delivery note that does not list what has been delivered provides no record of delivery; an invoice that does not include the delivery charge will not get paid in full – and so on.

Most documents are pre-printed with clear spaces and headings where information is needed, so as to reduce the risk of missing out vital information.

2. Make sure that the information provided is accurate

Consider what would happen if someone wrote down the wrong house number on a delivery note, added up an invoice incorrectly, or ordered the wrong quantity of goods. Correcting mistakes can waste a lot of time and money.

Often, documents are designed to reduce the risk of errors by asking for the same information twice. For example, a cheque needs to be completed with the amount to be paid in both words and figures. Order forms have spaces to write a description of the goods wanted and their catalogue or reference number.

3. Always write neatly

If you do not write neatly on a document, other people may not be able to read it. Some people may take a guess but may not get it right.

4. If you make a mistake on a document, tear it up and start a new one

Never send out a document which is illegible or which has mistakes scribbled or blotted out. Wherever possible, use a typewriter or a word processor. These are neater than handwriting – but remember that mistakes can still occur. Always double-check the information you provide on every document you complete.

Purchase order

This is a written or electronic request for goods to be delivered by a supplier (see Figure 12.6). The employee placing an order should:

- Obtain the necessary authorization for the purchase
- Check the name and address of their supplier
- Check that the supplier has the items in stock, or agree a future delivery date
- Check catalogue numbers and prices
- Use the next order form in number sequence
- Complete the order form and obtain an authorizing signature

Purchase invoice

A supplier will send an invoice to a customer to request payment for goods delivered (see Figure 12.8). The customer should always check:

- Invoices received from suppliers against goods or services ordered

That the correct prices have been charged

The total price on the invoice to see if it has been added up correctly, includes VAT and all other charges, plus any discounts for bulk purchases, cash, or early payment

Goods received note (GRN)

An employee of the customer organization will complete a GRN when goods are delivered from a supplier (see Figure 12.7). The GRN should note:

The date and time of delivery

Items that were actually received (which may not necessarily be those ordered)

Any visible damage to goods delivered

Sometimes a delivery may contain items from several orders, or only part of an order. In all cases the GRN should be checked against the original purchase orders.

Credit note

A credit note is issued by a supplier if a customer has been overcharged on an invoice – for example, if goods have been returned or the invoice contained an error (see Figure 12.12). The customer should check:

That the credit note contains the same information as the purchase invoice. For example, if VAT was charged on goods delivered, then VAT must also be added to the amount on the credit note.

That any items returned to the supplier are listed

That the prices of individual items returned to the supplier are the same as on the invoice

That any error on the invoice is corrected in full by the credit note

---

Portfolio Activity 13.5

PC: Complete purchase and sales documents clearly and correctly and calculate totals

Range: Purchase documents

Skills: Produce written material, Interpret and present data

Stoneshire County Council has ordered some computer equipment from Computech Ltd, a leading supplier of computer equipment and accessories. Carefully check the purchase order and invoice involved in the transaction. Have they been completed correctly? Is any information missing?

1. Ask your tutor if you can make a photocopy of the order and the invoice in this activity.

2. Mark on each copy where mistakes may have been made and information is missing.

3. Wherever possible, write down what the correct information should be on both documents.

STONESHIRE COUNTY COUNCIL
County Hall, Milton Barnet
STONESHIRE

Tel: 0171-123-6789
Fax: 0171-123-6780

VAT Reg 129 8093 14
Purchase Order No. 0001
Date: 15th April 199X

To: Computech Ltd
Unit 19-22
Moleville Industrial Estate
STONESHIRE ST17 5MW

DESCRIPTION	QTY	Ref.No	PRICE	TOTAL
Microsoft Word 6.0	2		£230.00	£560.00
Dataflex desktop modem	3	76/M	£164.00	£392.00
Panasonic KX-P4440 laser printer	1	49/PT	£339.00	£339.00

Authorized by: *H. B. Simpson*

for STONESHIRE COUNTY COUNCIL.

Computech Ltd
Unit 19 – 22, Moleville Industrial Estate
Tel: 01237-4095, Fax: 01237-4096
VAT Reg No. 707 3434 11

To: Bestwick Auto Repairs
21 Shrawley Street
Worcester WS17 5YY

INVOICE

Your Order No.	Invoice No.	Date
	77771	22 April 199X

QTY	Description	Cat No.	Unit Price	Total
2	Wordperfect 6.0	33/S	£213.00	£526.00
4	Dataflex modems	76/M	£164.00	£656.00
1	Panasonic KX–P4440 laser printer	49/PT	£339.00	£339.00
		Sub-total		£1521.00
		Discount 10%		£76.05
		Total (ex. VAT)		£1444.95
		VAT @ 17.5%		
		Total due		£1697.81

Terms:

E & OE

Sales document checklist

Section 12.3 described the following documents that a supplier would need to complete or check when making a sale:

- Orders received
- Sales invoices
- Delivery notes
- Credit notes
- Statements of account

Orders received

Once a purchase order is received from a customer (see Figure 12.6), the supplier should check: ·

- That the order is complete and understandable
- That descriptions of items on order match the catalogue or reference numbers
- That prices given are up to date
- That the goods are in stock
- When delivery can be made

Sales invoice

Once goods have been delivered, the supplier will issue an invoice to the customer (see Figure 12.8). This must show:

- An invoice reference number
- Catalogue numbers and a description of items supplied
- The quantity of individual items supplied
- The unit price of each item
- The total price of each group of items (unit price x quantity)
- The total price of all goods supplied
- Delivery charges
- Any discounts for trade, bulk purchase, or payment in cash
- A calculation for VAT
- The total amount due for payment (i.e. price of goods plus delivery charges, less any discounts, plus VAT)

Invoice example

Buildit Brick Merchants Ltd has supplied 1,000 bricks to Smith and Son Builders at a total price of £1,081. This was calculated on an invoice as follows:

	Price per brick	£1.00
(A)	Total price of 1,000 bricks (1,000 x £1)	£1,000.00
(B)	Deduct trade discount of 5% (i.e. 0.05 x £1,000)	£50.00
(C)	Deduct cash discount of 5% (i.e. 0.05 x £950)	£47.50
(D)	Add delivery charge	£17.50
(E)	Calculate VAT payable at 17.5% (i.e. 0.175 of A - B - C + D)	£161.00
(F)	Calculate total amount due for payment (A - B - C + D + E)	£1,081.00

Delivery note

A supplier should make out a delivery note at the same time an invoice for an order is prepared (see figure 12.9). In this way items arranged for delivery should correspond to those charged for. The delivery note should contain:

- A delivery address

- A description of items delivered and catalogue numbers

- The quantity of items delivered

- The number of boxes the items are packed in

On delivery a representative of the customer organization must sign the delivery note to prove that the items have been received.

Sales credit note

If an invoice contains an error or goods delivered are returned, the supplier must complete a credit note to send to the customer (see Figure 12.10). This will show the amount the customer needs to deduct from the invoice when making payment.

Statement of account

Regular customers will usually receive their account statements at the end of each month (see Figure 12.11). Before sending them out, the supplier should check that each statement contains:

- The name and address of the customer

- The customer's account number

- The balance carried forward from their last account statement

- The month of the statement

- A record of all the transactions made with the customer in that month, including invoices, credit notes, and payments received

- The balance on the account after each transaction

- The balance owed by the customer at the end of the month after adjusting for all the transactions entered into the account

Remittance advice

A supplier will send this document to a customer with an invoice or statement of account (see Figure 12.12). It shows how much the customer owes the supplier. The customer is asked to return the remittance advice note with payment so that the supplier knows who has paid what and why. The supplier must therefore check:

- That the invoice total or account balance matches the amount on the remittance advice

- That the customer and payment matches the name and amount on the remittance advice once the payment has been received.

▼ A statement of account

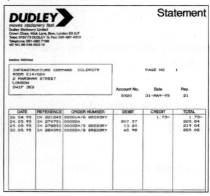

▼ A remittance advice

484

Portfolio Activity 13.6

PC: Complete purchase and sales documents clearly and correctly and calculate totals
Range: Purchase documents
Skills: Produce written material, Interpret and present data

1. Obtain a photocopy of the following blank documents provided at the end of this chapter:

- Invoice
- Remittance advice
- Statement of account
- Credit note

   Alternatively produce your own versions on a word processor using the line draw function, or a desktop publishing package.

2. You work in the accounts department of Computech Ltd. TW Plastics Plc has ordered some boxes of computer disks. Make out an invoice in full for:

- 20 boxes of disks at £10 per box (catalogue number 10/DS)
- Less a trade discount of 5%
- Plus a delivery charge of £10
- Plus VAT at 17.5%

   The invoice should be dated 3 April 199X and given the invoice number 37892.

3. Prepare a statement of account for TW Plastics Plc using the following information for April 199X. Their account number is 654/02345 and the statement should be dated for the last working day of April.

Day

1 Balance of £2,300 brought forward from previous month

3 Invoice (number 37892) for 20 boxes of diskettes plus delivery charge – total amount on invoice £235.00

4 Payment received for £2,300

9 Issue credit note (CN/256) for £300 for goods returned

17 Invoice (number 37953) for 3 laptop computers plus delivery – total amount on invoice £4,277

23 Invoice (number 37959) for 2 laserjet computer printers plus delivery – total amount on invoice £1,293

Do not forget to show the outstanding balance at the end of the month.

4. Complete a remittance advice to include with the statement of account you produced in Task 3.

5. On receipt of their account statement TW Plastics Plc telephone you to point out that invoice 37892 contained an error. Only 10 boxes of computer disks were ordered and delivered. You check your own records and confirm this error. You must now issue TW Plastics Plc with a credit note for the following refunds:

- 10 boxes of disks at £10 per box
- Less trade discount of 5%
- Plus VAT at 17.5%

   Number the credit note CN/26

6. Check and file all the documents you have completed.

Receipt documents checklist

Section 12.3 described four documents that are used to record the receipt of money or goods:

- Sales receipt
- Cheque
- Paying-in slip
- Bank statement

Sales receipt

This provides proof of purchase and can either be handwritten or issued by a till or computer (see Figures 12.13 and 12.14). In all cases a receipt should record:

- The date of the sale
- The items purchased
- The price of individual items

▼ Sales receipt

```
          The Reject Shop Plc
            62-63 East Street
        Brighton East Sussex BN1 1HQ
        R.JS HOMESHOP LTD. THE REJECT SHOP
VAT NO:239 6745 23          DOC'MNT 2482
BR:1002/04 06 AUG 95               12:58 1
- - - - - - - - - - - - - - - - - - - - -
CHINA
3                  VTI              3.99
CHINA
3                  VTI              2.99
- - - - - - - - - - - - - - - - - - - - -
ITEMS 2            TOTAL            6.98
                   VAT INC          1.04
             PAID BY VISA

    YOU WERE SERVED BY: ASSISTANT 1
      THANK YOU FOR SHOPPING AT
            The Reject Shop

    MADE TO ORDER SOFAS AVAILABLE.
```

- The total price of all items purchased
- VAT charged if any
- Where they were purchased
- The method of payment

Cheques received

Most payments by customers to their suppliers are by cheque (see 13.3). Some cheques will have been printed electronically. Most will have been handwritten. It is important to examine each cheque received in payment to make sure that:

- It is dated for less than six months ago
- The name of the payee is correct
- The amount written in words matches the amount in numbers
- It has been signed
- Any alterations have been initialled by the signatory
- The payment can be matched to sales invoices and/or statement of accounts sent out using the remittance advice

If the customer presents a cheque in person, as is often the case in a shop, the sales assistant will also need to:

- Ask for the customer's cheque guarantee card
- Check that the signature on the card matches the signature on the cheque
- Check that the card was issued by the same bank or building society that issued the cheque
- Write on the back of the cheque the serial number and expiry date of the cheque guarantee card

Paying-in slip

A paying-in slip will be completed by an employee of an organization when paying cash and cheques received into a bank account (see Figure 12.15). A bank will only accept the paying-in slip and deposit if:

- The total amount on the paying-in slip matches the total value of cash and cheques presented
- Notes and coins are sorted into different denominations
- The values of notes and coins in different denominations are noted separately
- The value of each individual cheque is noted on the back of the slip
- The total value of cheques presented is the sum of the value of individual cheques
- It is signed
- It contains the name and number of the account into which the money is to be paid

▼ Paying in slip

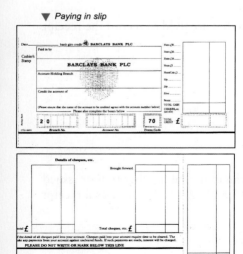

Bank statement

A business organization will use a bank or building society account to make payments to their suppliers and deposit takings from their customers. These transactions will be itemized on a bank statement received each month (see Figure 12.16). It is important for an organization to check:

- That their name and account number are correct
- All deposits against paying-in slips
- All withdrawals including against records of payments made by cheque, BACS, and EDI (see 12.2).
- That the account balance is correct

Portfolio Activity 13.7

PC: Complete purchase, sales and receipt documents clearly and correctly and calculate totals

Range: Receipt documents

Skills: Produce written material, Use images, Present information

1. Mrs Anne Parkin will be calling in person to Computech Ltd on 14 April 199X to collect goods she has ordered. The total price of her items is £150 plus VAT. You have been asked to serve her. Payment is in cash. Write out a receipt for this money on a photocopy of the blank receipt document at the end of this chapter.

2. The accounts department at Computech Ltd has asked you to take some cash and cheques to the bank as follows:

CASH		CHEQUES
3 x £50 notes	13 x 20p coins	£127.89 from F Howard & Sons
5 x £20 notes	13 x 10p coins	£56.50 from Mr G Paul
9 x £10 notes	30 x 5p coins	£495.99 from KLX Ltd
12 x £5 notes	9 x 2p coins	
19 x £1 coins		
54 x 1p coins		
7 x 50p coins		

Complete a paying-in slip for this money dated 26 April 199X. Use a photocopy of the blank paying-in slip at the end of this chapter.

3. Computech Ltd receives a bank statement on the 25th day of each month. Opposite is the bank statement they have received for the period 26 March-25 April 199X.

The accounts department has noted that the following cheques and direct debits were authorized to be paid from the account between 26th and 30th April:

- Direct debit of £156.04 to Stoneshire County Council
- Cheque for £1,900.40 to Sony Corporation
- Cheque for £3,785 to Compaq

In addition, the following deposits were made into the account between 26th-30th April:

- The amount you paid into the bank in Task 2 above
- £2,969

How much money was in the Computech bank account on 30th April?

STONESHIRE COUNTY BANK Plc

49 High Street
Northbrook
STONESHIRE ST7 5BX

COMPUTECH Ltd
Statement of Account

Sheet 354   Account No 3455435   Date: 26 April 199X

Date	Transaction details	Debit	Credit	Balance
May 26	Balance brought forward			5,000.00Cr
May 29	Cash Stoneshire N'brook	120.00		
May 30	Chq 31110	4,299.50		
	DD Stoneshire Insurance	875.00		294.45 Dr
Apr 5	Chq 31111	1,500.00		
	Chq 31112	2,330.70		4,125.25 Dr
Apr 9	Chq 31113	425.25		4,550.45 Dr
Apr 12	Sundries		8,950.00	4,399.55 Cr
	Chq 31114	4,175.80		223.75 Cr
	Sundries		14,938.90	1,5162.65 Cr
Apr 14	SO British Gas Plc	150.00		1,5012.65 Cr
Apr 17	Chq 31115	7,310.65		7,702.00 Cr
Apr 21	Chq 31116	4,867.00		2,835.00 Dr
Apr 23	Sundries		5,765.55	
	Bank charges	75.00		8,525.55 Cr
Apr 24	Sundries		9,237.89	17,763.44 Cr
Apr 25	Balance carried forward			17,763.44 Cr

Section **13.3**

Completing payment documents

Business organizations will often use different pre-printed documents to record details of different types of payments. The main ones are:

- Pay slips to pay wages to employees
- Cheques to pay bills
- Petty cash vouchers to pay for small items

Pay slips

Details of wages paid to employees are recorded on a **pay slip** or **pay advice note**. It is a legal requirement for an employer to provide each employee with a pay slip each time they are paid their wages or salary (see 5.3). Pay is normally in arrears, which means an employee will be paid at the end of each week or month worked.

▼ *Figure 13.8: A typical pay slip*

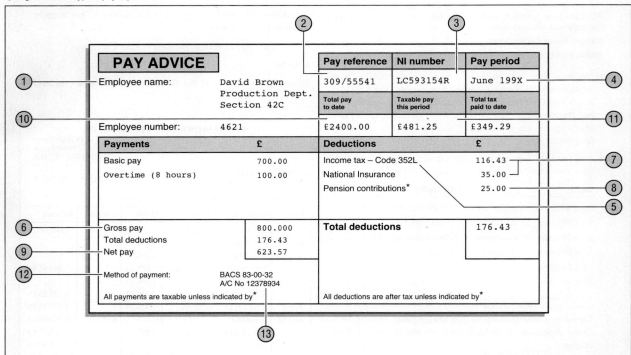

Key

1 Name of employee
2 Employee's pay reference number
3 Employee's national insurance number
4 Pay period
5 Tax code – indicates amount of income you are allowed to earn each year that is not taxable
6 Gross pay – total pay before any deductions are made
7 Amount of income tax and national insurance contributions deducted

8 Other deductions, e.g. pension contributions, season ticket loans, 'give as you earn' donations to charities, etc.
9 Net pay – amount of money actually received by employee after deductions
10 Total pay up to and including the current pay period
11 Amount of pay this period on which income tax will be levied
12 Method of payment
13 Details of employee's bank and account number if payment is direct into their bank account

A pay slip informs an employee how much they are being paid. It is a confidential document and will normally be sealed in an envelope, or 'pay packet', before it is given or sent to the employee. Some workers may be paid by cash or cheque enclosed in their pay packet. However, most people today are paid directly into their bank or building society account via BACS (Banking Automated Clearing Service – see 12.2).

Not all pay slips look the same, but they will show the same information. Figure 13.8 shows a typical pay slip.

Understanding your pay slip

It is important that you know how your pay is calculated before and after any deductions are made so that you are able to check for any errors. The important things to look at are:

- **Gross pay:** This is how much you are paid, including any overtime, bonuses and/or commission, before any deductions are made.

  If you are paid a salary, it is normal to divide your gross annual salary into twelve equal monthly payments. For example, if your gross annual salary is £24,000, your gross monthly pay will be £2,000.

  If you are paid an hourly wage rate, your gross pay will be calculated by multiplying the number of hours you have worked in a week or month by that wage rate. Hours worked over and above your normal hours may be paid at an overtime rate of 1.5 times the hourly wage rate, or in some cases even at 'double time.'

  For example, imagine that you are paid weekly and that your wage rate is £5 per hour. Over the last week you worked 40 hours plus 5 additional hours at 'time and a half.' We can therefore work out your gross pay for that week as follows:

  40 hours × £5.00 = £200.00

  5 hours × £7.50 = £37.50

  Gross pay = £237.50

- **Taxable income:** The Inland Revenue collects income tax from people's earnings for the government (see 1.4). The amount of income tax a person has to pay will largely depend on how much they earn in each **tax year**. A tax year runs from the 6th April each year to 5th April in the following year.

  Everybody is allowed to earn a certain amount of income each tax year before paying income tax. This is called a **personal allowance**, and will vary according to age and marital status. Any income over and above the allowance is subject to income tax. **Taxable income** is therefore calculated by deducting an employee's personal allowance from their gross pay.

  Employees who do not earn as much as their personal allowance each year will pay no income tax. This might apply to students and workers with Saturday or part-time jobs.

- **Income tax:** Income tax is deducted from your earnings by your employer, who then sends it to the Inland Revenue. This is known as **PAYE** (the **Pay As You Earn** system).

Each year the Inland Revenue notifies taxpayers of their PAYE tax code number. Your **tax code** will tell you what your personal allowance is. Your employer will also be informed of your tax code in order to calculate your taxable income and how much tax you must pay.

A tax code consists of a three-digit number followed by a letter. For example, if your tax code was 352L in the tax year 1995-96, it meant that you had a single person's allowance of £3,525. That is, you could earn up to £3,525 in 1995-96 without having to pay tax.

Your personal allowance for each tax year will usually be spread evenly over 12 months. If, however, you are new to a job and do not have a tax code, you will be placed on an **emergency tax** coding. This means you will have to pay tax on everything you earn until your tax allowance has been worked out and a tax code issued. If at the end of a tax year you have paid too much tax, you will receive a **tax rebate**.

- **National insurance contributions (NICs):** These are also deducted from your earnings by your employer, depending on how much you earn each week or month. In the tax year 1995-96 an employee earning less than £59 each week paid no NICs. People earning over £59 each week would have to pay between 3% and 10.2% (on earnings in excess of £205 per week) of their gross pay in NICs.

  Every employee is identified by a unique national insurance number allocated to them by the Department of Social Security (DSS).

- **Other deductions:** These can include repayments of season ticket loans, donations to charity, and pension contributions. Some firms operate payroll giving schemes. These allow employees to make tax-free donations from their gross pay to charity.

- **Net pay:** This is the amount of pay you will actually receive after all deductions have been made.

The role of the wages department

It is usually the job of trained personnel in the wages department of a business organization to work out how much each employee is paid, how much tax and national insurance contributions need to be deducted, and issue pay slips. Today, most organizations use computers to make these calculations and to print out pay slips using payroll software.

At the end of every tax year, the wages department will also complete a **P60 form** for each employee. This gives details of total pay received, the total amount of income tax and NICs paid, and any statutory sick pay or maternity pay received. Each employee will receive a copy of their P60 at the end of each tax year.

Cheques

Most business debts are settled by cheque. Except when made payable to 'cash,' a cheque is simply a way of arranging a transfer of money between two bank (or building society) accounts.

Portfolio Activity 13.8

PC: Complete payments and receipt documents clearly and correctly and calculate totals
Range: Payment documents
Skills: Use images, Tackle problems

1. Look at the pay slip below for Susan Smith for the first month of the new tax year, then answer the following questions:

a What is Susan's gross annual salary?

b By what method is Susan paid each month?

c What is her tax code for?

d Why does her taxable pay differ from her gross pay?

2. Angus Young is a security guard at Computech Ltd. He is paid on an hourly basis at the following wage rates:

Standard	£8 per hour
Saturday working	1.5 x standard rate
Sunday working	2 x standard rate

a Last week was the first week of the new tax year. During that week Angus worked his usual 40 hours, plus 5 hours on Saturday and 2 on Sunday. Calculate his gross pay for the week.

b The following deductions were made from Angus's gross pay:

Income tax	£78 (based on taxable pay of £340)
NIC	£30
Pension contributions	£34
Payroll giving	£10

What was his net pay that week?

c Obtain a photocopy of the blank pay slip provided at the end of this chapter. Use the information provided in the questions above to complete the pay slip for Angus. His pay reference number is 127/18623, his NI number is WD405637A, and his tax code is 352L.

PAY ADVICE

Employee name:	Susan Smith Sales Department Room 14/03	Pay reference	NI number	Pay period
		402/188133	WL533214C	01APR95 – 30APR95
		Total pay to date	**Taxable pay this period**	**Total tax paid to date**
Employee number:	1331865	£2814.50	£2478.53	£674.12

Payments	£	Deductions	£
Basic pay	2666.50	Income tax – Code 352L	674.12
London weighting allowance	148.00	National Insurance	140.75
		Pension contributions*	42.22
		Season ticket loan repayment	90.00
Gross pay	2814.50	**Total deductions**	947.09
Total deductions	947.09		
Net pay	1867.41		

Method of payment: BACS 32-47-25
A/C No 32051273

All payments are taxable unless indicated by*

All deductions are after tax unless indicated by*

The person or organization that writes out a cheque is known as the **drawer**. The amount of money written on the cheque will be withdrawn from their bank account. The person or firm named on the cheque to receive payment is known as the **payee**. Both the drawer and the payee will receive confirmation that the transaction has taken place on their monthly bank statements (see 12.3).

All cheques pass through what is known as the **clearing system** which transfers funds between banks and building societies. A cheque will only be cleared for payment once the bank is satisfied that it has been completed correctly, that the signature on it has not been forged, and that the drawer has enough money in the account to pay it. This process takes about three working days.

Completing a cheque

A cheque is simply a pre-printed form that has to be completed accurately and with enough information to allow a bank or building society to transfer money between the drawer's account and the payee's. A cheque book is provided by a bank (or building society) when a current account is opened.

Every cheque has the following information printed on it:

- The name of the account holder
- The name and address of the bank at which the account is held
- A bank sort code (every bank has a unique identification number)
- The number of the account
- An individual serial number

The bank sort code, account number, and cheque number are also usually printed in a format that can be read by a computer.

The person who completes a cheque must, therefore, provide the following information:

- The name of the person or organization to be paid
- How much they are to be paid
- The date the cheque was written
- A signature to authorize the payment

▼ Figure 13.9: An example of a correctly completed cheque

It is usual to write out the sum to be paid in figures as well as in words on a cheque, so as to make sure the precise amount cannot be mistaken. The drawer must also sign each cheque with his or her usual signature.

In most organizations cheques can only be signed by authorized staff, usually in the accounts department. When a cheque is for a lot of money, two signatories may be required, with at least one at a senior managerial level (see 12.4).

Types of cheques

Cheques can be either open or crossed.

- A **crossed** cheque has two parallel lines across it. This tells a bank that it must be paid into the payee's account regardless of who presents the cheque for payment. This makes the cheque of no use to anyone stealing it. For additional security the words 'A/C payee' are often written or printed between the two vertical lines to make sure that the cheque can only be paid into the payee's account.

- An **open** cheque, which does not have the two lines, can be cashed over a bank counter by whoever presents it.

A cheque is valid only if:

- It is written in ink or printed

- It is signed by the name of the account holder, or, in the case of a business, by an authorized representative

- The amount in words is the same as the amount in numbers

- The cheque is made payable to someone or to the bearer (the person holding the cheque)

- The cheque is dated and is not more than six months old

What is a cheque guarantee card?

Cheque guarantee cards are issued by banks and building societies to their reliable account holders. They can be used to guarantee that the cheque will be honoured (i.e. paid) even if the person who wrote it does not have enough money in their account. However, a cheque will only be guaranteed:

- Up to a maximum of either £50 or £100, depending on the amount printed on the cheque guarantee card

- If the card serial number is copied onto the back of the cheque

- If the name and signature on the cheque match those on the cheque card

Businesses only usually insist on noting the cheque card number on the back of a cheque when a customer pays for goods or services received in person. Clearly this cannot be done if a cheque is sent through the post in payment for goods delivered, which is usually the case.

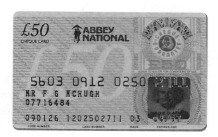

Portfolio Activity 13.9

PC: Complete payments and receipt documents clearly and correctly and calculate totals

Range: Payment documents

Skills: Use images, Tackle problems

1. You work in the accounts department of Computech Ltd. You have just received the cheque opposite from a customer. Has it been completed correctly? Are you willing to accept it in payment for goods or services Computech has supplied? Explain your answer and mark any errors and omissions on a photocopy of the cheque.

2. Imagine you are the company signatory for cheques up to a value of £5,000. Write out three cheques for the following payments to suppliers from Computech Ltd.

- £575.50 to Opus Technology Ltd

- £2,030 to TDK Electronics Corp.

- £134.37 to British Telecommunications Plc

Use photocopies of the blank cheques provided at the end of this chapter.

Petty cash vouchers

All businesses keep a certain amount of cash on their premises in order to make small and often unexpected payments. This is known as **petty cash**. In a large organization each department will be allocated an amount of petty cash to use. The amount of money held in petty cash is often called the **petty cash float**. The size of the float will vary between organizations depending on their size and the type of purchases they allow from petty cash.

▼ *What petty cash is used for:*

Petty cash is usually locked away in a cash box, and a receipt must be obtained for any payment made from it. A petty cash voucher will be issued every time petty cash is needed (see figure 13.10). The expenditure will usually have to be approved first by an employee in authority. There is normally an upper limit to how much can be spent at one time from petty cash. If the purchase exceeds this limit it will need to be ordered and paid for by cheque or via BACS by the accounts department.

▼ *Figure 13.10: A petty cash voucher*

Petty Cash Voucher   No. _____ *35* _____
Date: _____ *8.9.9X* _____

Purpose	Total inc. VAT	VAT excl. VAT	NET
4 marker pens	£4.70	70	£4.00
Jar of coffee	£3.55	–	–
1 pint of milk	£0.50	–	–
	£8.75	70p	

Signature: _*J Watts*_   Approvedby: _*S Hinkley*_
Name: _*J Watts*_
Department: _*Marketing*_   All receipts and invoices must be attached

The petty cash voucher is rather like an IOU which shows how much money has to be repaid to the petty cash float. In all cases, a receipt for goods or services purchased with petty cash should be pinned to the petty cash voucher and stored safely. In this way all money taken from petty cash can be accounted for. If an organization is able to reclaim VAT paid on items purchased, then the amount of VAT paid should also be shown on the petty cash voucher.

The job of petty cashier

It is the job of petty cashier to:

- Ensure the security of petty cash

- Obtain authorization to use petty cash for small purchases

- Record spending in a petty cash book

- Issue petty cash vouchers

- Obtain copies of receipts

- Check that any purchases made are authorized

- Keep a record of how much is left in the petty cash float

- Restore the **imprest** at regular intervals, for example, at the end of each week or month. This is the amount needed to restore petty cash to the full amount allocated to the float.

Portfolio Activity 13.10

PC: Complete payments and receipt documents clearly and correctly and calculate totals
Range: Payment documents
Skills: Use images, Tackle problems

In addition to your normal duties you have been asked to be the petty cashier for the sales department in Computech Ltd. The sales department is allocated a petty cash float of £80 each week.

1. During your first week as petty cashier you are asked to issue and sign the following petty cash vouchers, starting with number 154. (Use photocopies of the blank petty cash voucher provided at the end of this chapter, or draw your own using a computer).

- Taxi fare £5.60

- Tea bags £1.60

- Coffee £3.40

- Sales management training video £16 plus £2.80 VAT

- Sandwiches £12, orange juice £1.75 and mineral water £2.50, for a business meeting

Ask a friend or your tutor to authorize the vouchers and check that the they have been completed correctly.

2. What amount is left in petty cash after each of the vouchers has been paid out?

3. How much will you need to restore the float at the end of the week?

Section **13.4** # Information technology and financial accounting

Using information technology

Throughout this chapter and in Chapter 12 you have learnt how to record details of business transactions and to complete financial documents accurately. You will also know from these chapters how important it is to record financial information in business.

However, recording transactions and filling out documents by hand can be very time-consuming and errors are easily made. To save time and improve accuracy, most modern business organizations use computers to help them record financial information, complete documents, and produce their internal and external accounts.

Computer software refers to predesigned packages or programs which give instructions to a computer to process text and numbers. Today, a vast array of software is available to businesses to help them record and monitor financial information.

Two of the most useful types of computer program a business can use for financial accounting are:

- **Accounting software**

- **Spreadsheets**

Most programs are 'user friendly,' meaning that it is relatively easy for a person to learn how to use them in a few days. However, the old saying 'rubbish in, rubbish out' will always apply to the use of computers. Computers will only use information and follow instructions given to them. If you type in the wrong figures or wrong instructions to a computer, you will get a wrong answer. The computer is useful only because it can perform often complex calculations in a fraction of the time it takes to use a calculator, or to do so by hand. It is therefore important that a person using a spreadsheet or accounting software knows about financial transactions and how to record them accurately.

Accounting software

What can accounting software do? There are many different programs available to businesses to help them record financial transactions and produce their accounts. For example, the advertisement opposite shows an accounting program called 'Quickbooks'.

Accounting software for computers is often designed with the small business in mind, because these organizations are unlikely to be able to afford to employ accountants on a full-time basis to produce their accounts.

Good accounting software will enable the user to:

- Record all cash sales and sales on credit
- Set up a database of customer names, addresses, telephone, fax and E-mail numbers, and details of how much discount each one is allowed
- Record how much is owed by different customers and when payment is due
- Produce invoices, remittance advice notes, credit notes, and statements of account to send to customers
- Record all purchases from cash and on credit
- Set up a database of suppliers' names, addresses, telephone numbers, etc.
- Record how much is owed to different suppliers and when payment is due
- Enter details of cash inflows and outflows
- Record deposits to, and withdrawals and payments from, a bank account
- Calculate total sales and purchases per period of time
- Prepare an audit showing every transaction made
- Produce ledger accounts (for materials, sales, purchases, VAT, cash, capital, assets, overheads, etc.) and the general ledger
- Produce income and expenditure accounts
- Produce VAT returns showing VAT received on sales and paid out on purchases
- Produce balance sheets
- Produce profit and loss statements
- Combine the accounting software with payroll software to calculate wages and print pay slips automatically
- Keep records of incoming and outgoing stocks. Some programs can also link to stock control software to recognize when stocks are running low and automatically complete purchase orders to send via EDI
- Export accounts to word processors and desktop publishing packages to produce published annual reports and accounts

At the end of each month the software will tell the user to run a function to generate the end-of-month accounts. This will automatically print out a copy of the accounts for the last month, and carry forward the balances on each account (sales, purchases, VAT, overheads, capital, assets, cash, etc.) into the next month.

Spreadsheets

A spreadsheet is a powerful program that can perform complex calculations and present data on a variety of graphs. A spreadsheet is, therefore, a very useful tool for recording, storing, and monitoring financial information.

On the computer screen a spreadsheet looks rather like a large sheet of paper ruled off into rows and columns. Columns are identified by letters – A, B, C... Y, Z, AA, AB, etc. Rows are identified by numbers – 1, 2, 3, etc. Each box formed by the intersection of rows and columns is called a **cell**. Cells are identified by a column letter and a row number, e.g. A1, D57, X230, etc. Text, numbers, or mathematical formulae can be typed, or entered, into any cell.

Figure 13.11 below shows how a spreadsheet looks on screen. The columns B to F have been given headings in row 1 for each month in a sales budget. Row headings for product price, sales volume, and revenues have been typed in cells in column A, which has been expanded in width to accommodate them. Cells in row 6 contain mathematical formulae to calculate sales revenues from figures entered into cells for product price and sales volumes. These cells will show the results of the calculations but will not show the formulae. However, by placing the cursor on one of these cells the formulae will be usually displayed at the top of the screen off the main spreadsheet.

For example, cell B6 contains the formulae B2*B4. This tells the spreadsheet to multiply the figure entered into cell B2 for price by the figure in cell B4 for sales. Similarly formulae entered into cells in row 8 tell the computer to calculate the percentage change in revenue each month and those in row 10 to keep a running total of sales revenues from month 1. The spreadsheet will recalculate these cells automatically every time a new figure is entered into other cells.

▼ Figure 13.11: An example of a spreadsheet in use

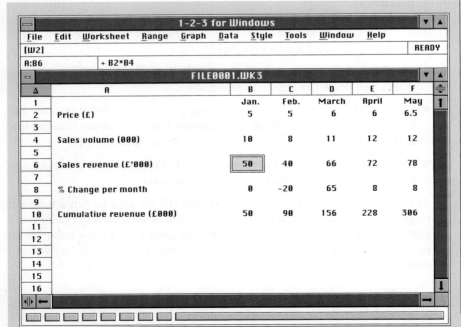

Common spreadsheet functions

A good spreadsheet will allow the user to:

- Insert and delete rows and columns
- Protect specific cells and formulae from erasure
- Expand column widths
- Store and search for data in a database
- Choose the number of decimal places
- Import data from other programs and files
- Copy cells
- Export data to other programs
- Move cells
- Produce and display graphs
- Perform statistical analysis
- Print out specified cell ranges and graphs
- Perform financial analysis
- Perform 'what if' analysis
- Perform mathematical calculations

and much, much more...

'What if' analysis

Spreadsheets are particularly useful for preparing financial plans or budgets (see 13.1) and testing the impact of possible changes that may occur in the future. This is called **'what if' analysis**. For example, you may want to test the impact of an increase in wages or raw material prices on your production budget – or the impact of increasing spending on advertising or lowering product prices on costs, sales revenues, and profits. A spreadsheet can perform these calculations in a matter of seconds. It can also display the results on a variety of different graphs, such as barcharts, pie charts, and line graphs.

Portfolio Activity 13.11

PC: Identify and give examples of information technology which businesses use to record and monitor financial information

Range: Information technology

Skills: Collect and record data, Produce written material

New accounting software and spreadsheet programs are becoming available all the time. Every new product tries to outperform rival software in terms of number of functions, speed, accuracy, presentation, price, and a host of other factors.

1. Below is a list of some well-known business software that were on sale in 1995. For each program try to find out:

- If it is still available

- If it has been updated

- Whether it is spreadsheet or accounting software

- What it can do

- How much it costs

- Who supplies it

2. From your research try to add at least five programs to the list.

3. Write up your findings in a short report.

4. Find out as much information as you can about one spreadsheet program of your choice. Use the information to create an appealing and informative advert for the product.

Useful sources of information to help you complete all the tasks in this activity will include:

- Computer magazines, such as *Personal Computer World* and *PC Plus*

- Office staff who use computers in business organizations

- Computer shops

- Software suppliers and manufacturers

Quattro Pro Version 6.0

It's the perfect way to make numbers count. This powerful spreadsheet has interactive

Quattro Pro

Quattro Pro 6.0

The Perfect Way to Make Numbers Count

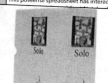

Pegasus Solo

Fully integrated accounting software, ideally suited to the small business.

Pegasus Solo is ideally suited for every small business, incorporating Sales, Purchase and Nominal ledgers along with invoicing and stock control, allowing you to keep track of customer's and supplier's transactions. Produce statements and debtors' reports, as well as handling all of your VAT requirements.

PEG001 Pegasus Solo (DOS) **£67²⁰**

Pegasus Solo Payroll

Fully-integrated accounting software for small businesses, covering all aspects of NIC and PAYE.

Pegasus Solo Payroll is ideally suited for every small business. It is a perfect companion for all accounts packages or can be used standalone. It also fits neatly into Pegasus Accounts Solo.

This great, comprehensive package combines ease-of-use with a frien... interface.

PEG002 Pegasus Solo Payroll (DOS) .... £

SAGE

SAGE STERLING for DOS

Accountant	£160
Accountant Plus	£242
Financial Controller	£319
Financial Controller LAN	£506
Payroll II	£129

STERLING + 2 for Windows

Accountant +2	£1
Accountant Plus +2	£2
Financial Controller + 2	£3
Financial Controller + 2 LAN	£5
Payroll for Windows	£1
Instant Accounting for Windows	
Instant Payroll for Windows	

Microsoft Excel for Windows 95.

The spreadsheet for anyone who needs a spreadsheet with flexibility. Microsoft Excel for the Windows 95 operating system was designed based on your needs and requests. Whether you're working on a simple summary, charting sales trends, or performing advanced analysis, Microsoft Excel helps you work the way you want to get your job done easily.

Microsoft Excel

Lotus 1-2-3 for Windows

Lotus 1-2-3 Release 5 for Windows (RRP £ 365 +VAT) multi-dimentional spreadsheet is one of the most flexible applications available and will enable you to do virtually anything with numerical information. Lotus 1-2-3 is the world's most widely used spreadsheet and includes database functions as well as a wide range of scientific and financial ones. Its' macro language will enable you to automate operations when performing complicated calculations and it can generate charts or graphs automatically, simply by highlighting an area of data.

Lotus 1·2·3₅

Key wordsearch

Hidden in the box of jumbled letters below are some key words and terms from this chapter.
Use the definitions below to help you find them.

S	P	R	E	A	D	S	H	E	E	T	G	E	J	V	X
P	D	T	U	D	M	B	W	L	Z	L	U	R	C	L	B
G	F	H	X	A	U	D	I	T	O	R	B	C	I	T	A
H	N	O	C	S	T	L	N	O	G	P	T	U	L	I	L
W	E	C	L	S	G	H	P	A	Y	S	L	I	P	E	A
E	T	K	K	E	W	O	F	Q	L	R	I	N	S	L	N
G	P	C	M	T	V	P	Y	R	M	S	H	V	R	P	C
O	R	U	Y	S	C	R	E	D	I	T	N	O	T	E	E
P	O	O	G	Q	D	Z	R	U	D	Y	O	I	A	N	S
Q	F	N	S	B	U	D	G	E	T	U	L	C	R	L	H
A	I	J	I	S	O	F	S	I	C	J	F	E	K	D	E
R	T	L	A	M	P	E	T	T	Y	C	A	S	H	I	E
X	Z	S	Q	B	G	R	D	A	G	A	K	T	E	K	T
F	U	Z	P	X	L	I	O	R	D	E	R	N	N	U	L
C	H	E	Q	U	E	C	L	F	W	R	L	B	A	G	J
T	O	X	I	S	J	A	U	U	I	A	J	I	W	Y	L
C	A	S	H	B	O	O	K	C	J	T	B	T	G	R	N

Key words

Definitions

- Computer program that can be used to perform complex calculations on financial data and present it graphically
- Specialist who is able to check the accuracy of business accounts
- Short for 'goods received note'
- Request sent by a customer to a supplier to deliver goods
- Request for payment sent by a supplier to a customer
- Things of value to an organization, including premises, machinery, stocks, cash, and money held in bank accounts
- Financial plan drawn up by a business
- Internal business accounts used to record items of expenditure and revenues

- Account used to record inflows and outflows of cash
- Difference between turnover and the cost of producing all the goods or services sold
- Gross profit less all other overhead expenses
- Cash held on premises to pay for small purchases
- External business account that shows the value of business assets equal to liabilities and capital
- Document that records the payment of wages, before and after tax, to an employee
- Most popular method of making and recording payments – a written instruction from an account holder to his or her bank or building society to transfer money to the account of another person or organization

Test and assignment

You must demonstrate that you are able to:

1. Complete purchase and sales documents clearly and correctly, and calculate totals

2. Complete payment and receipts documents clearly and correctly, and calculate totals

3. Record income and expenditure over time periods

4. Explain why financial information must be recorded

5. Identify and give examples of information technology which businesses use to record and monitor financial information

---

This unit is not examined externally. However, the following questions will help you test and revise your understanding of the range in element 4.2.

1 A budget is:

A a record of actual spending

B a record of incomes received

C a financial plan

D an external business account

2 The following are all examples of payment documents used in business, except:

A remittance advice

B pay slip

C cheque

D petty cash voucher

3 A cheque should NOT be accepted in payment if:

A it has been signed

B the amount in words is not the same as the amount in writing

C it is less than six months old

D it is crossed

4 Which of the following is an external account produced by a company?

A ledger account

B income and expenditure account

C cash book

D profit and loss statement

5 A business will prepare a budget for all of the following reasons, except:

A to calculate future financial needs

B to examine alternative courses of action

C to present information on total profit to the tax authorities

D to monitor actual business performance

Questions 6-8 share the following answer options:

A profit and loss statement

B balance sheet

C income and expenditure account

D sales ledger

Which of the above accounts will show:

6 The value of assets held by a business at the end of an accounting period?

7 All money received and paid out by a business per period of time?

8 Turnover, expenses, and profit at the end of an accounting period?

9 a. What is a spreadsheet?

b. Give an example of a well-known spreadsheet program used in business.

c. List at least five functions that can be performed by a spreadsheet.

d. Explain how accounting software can help a business to record and monitor financial information.

10 Give four reasons why it is so important for business organizations to record financial information.

11 Suggest three checks you could make before accepting a cheque in payment for goods delivered.

12 a. What is a pay slip?

b. List at least five things that would be recorded on a pay slip.

c. Explain the difference between gross pay, taxable pay, and net pay.

Assessment Assignment

The following assignment meets the evidence requirements needed to fulfil all the performance criteria in element 4.2. In addition it covers the following range points and core skills:

Range: Purchase documents
Sales documents
Payment documents
Receipt documents
Time periods
Financial information
Recorded
Information technology

Skills: Communication
Produce written material
Use images
Read and respond to written material
Application of number
Tackle problems
Information technology
Present information
Evaluate the use of IT

Blank documents are provided at the end of this chapter for you to photocopy and use to complete the tasks in this assignment.

Your role

You are a new accounts management trainee in Computech Ltd, a medium-sized organization that supplies computer hardware, software, and other accessories.

As part of your training, you are to spend some time in the purchasing, sales, wages, and accounts departments. You will be expected to learn how to complete and check various financial documents, and produce an income and expenditure account. We will assume that you begin this training on 1 February. (Of course, in reality you can complete this assignment at any time.)

Throughout your training you keep a diary noting the important tasks you have been asked to do. Complete these tasks in date order and, for each one, make a note of whether they have involved expenditure or income, the amount of money involved, and what it was for.

Forward planner

Week 1 (1-5 February):

Working in purchasing department. Report to Joseph Perry, Purchasing Manager, Room C5/14.

Week 2 (8-12 February):

Working in sales department. Report to Ms Rowan Monks, Sales Manager, Room S4/3.

Week 3 (15-19 February):

Working in wages department. Report to Cathy Gregg, Department Manager, Room C4/9.

Week 4 (22-27 February):

Working in accounts department. Report to Nick Page, Accounts Manager, Room N7/12.

Week 5 (2-6 March):

Second week in accounts department.

assessment assignment

February 199X

1 Monday

Report to room C5/14 at 9.30 am. Joe Perry introduced me to other staff and then explained how to complete purchase orders and goods received notes.

Task 1

Last week a plumber was called in to repair a leaking radiator in the purchasing department. An invoice has arrived for this from WJ Griffiths. Because it is for less than £25, Joe has told me to pay it from petty cash once I have checked that the invoice is correct. I have to **complete a petty cash voucher for the amount of the invoice.** Mr Griffiths has said he will call in for the money tomorrow.

2 Tuesday

Task 2

Joe gave me the attached memo from the marketing department. They want to order some new equipment for their offices. I have to fill out an **order form** in accordance with their instructions. The order number is 12/9251.

MEMO

14 The Avenue
Northbrook
STONESHIRE ST5 9KY

Computech Ltd
Purchasing Dept.
Unit 19-22
Moleville Industrial Estate
Stoneshire ST17 5MW

VAT Reg 905 5683 23

INVOICE

No. 247   **Date:** 26 January 199X

	£
Repair leak in heating system	
Parts (rubber washers)	1.50
Labour	18.00
Sub-total	19.50
Plus VAT	3.41
Total	22.91
E & OE	

---

3 Wednesday

Gary Preston phoned from marketing department to ask if 200 red pens could be added to his order. Their catalogue number is 67/P and they are priced at £1 each.

ORDER

To: Purchasing Department   **Date:** 1.2.199X

From: G Preston, Marketing Manager   **Ref:** CP/JP

Subject: Request for office equipment

Please order the following items from Office Supplies Ltd, 12 Woodland Way, Northwick, NH4 3JX:

Description	Catalogue number	Unit price
120 reams of A4 white copy paper	34/a	£3.00
60 x 50ml bottles of white correction fluid	12/t	£1.50
300 A3 buff envelopes	14/e	£0.30

G.P.

Task 3

I explained that the previous order had already been sent to Office Supplies but that I would **fill out another purchase order** for the pens and send it immediately.

Meet Bill at cinema at 8 pm.

4 Thursday

A delivery arrives from Office Supplies Ltd. Joe has asked me to go to the loading bay to check in the goods received and sign the delivery note.

Task 4

I accept the delivery. It consists of 24 boxes of white A4 paper with 5 reams in each box, one box of A3-size buff-coloured envelopes, and 60 bottles of correction fluid packed into 6 small boxes. On closer inspection, I noticed that 2 of the boxes contained blue correction fluid. These must be returned. In the meantime I must **fill out a goods received note** (number GRN3047) for the delivery.

5 Friday

Task 5

Another delivery arrives from Office Supplies Ltd. It is the red pens from order number 12/9252 and consists of 2 boxes each containing 100 red pens. I must **complete a goods received note** (GRN3048) accordingly.

Meet 6 pm at Flicker and Firkin for a drink after work with Joe, Mary, and Paul from purchasing.

February 199X

8 Monday

Report to sales department, room S4/3 at 9.30 am. Rowan Monks introduced me to the staff 'team' and then showed me how to prepare delivery notes, invoices, credit notes, and remittance advice notes. Copies of all these documents must be sent to accounts who are responsible for receiving and making payments.

Task 6

After lunch Rowan gave me a customer order from Bloomin Marvellous Garden Centre. Product catalogue numbers and prices quoted on the order are correct. The goods ordered are due to be delivered tomorrow morning. **I must complete a delivery note, sales invoice, and remittance advice for the order.** The customer qualifies for a 5% trade discount. Delivery costs £10.

The next delivery note number in sequence is DN/7783 and the invoice number will be 45635.

ORDER No: 7773	**Bloomin Marvellous** *Garden Centre*

Bloomin Marvellous *Garden Centre*

Date: 4.2.9X

Cedar Gates Drive
Little Barnworth
STONESHIRE ST12 3XX
Tel: 01233 1112
Fax: 01233 1113
VAT Reg 4373 2437 18

Supplier:
Computech Ltd
Unit 19-22
Moleville Industrial Estate
STONESHIRE ST17 5MW

Description	Qty	Ref No	Price	Total
Canon B200s Fax machine	1	93/F	£439.00	£439.00
Faxroll thermal rolls (100mm x 25mm)	12	40/F	£5.80	£69.60

Delivery A.S.A.P

Authorized by: *A. J Bloomin*
for **Bloomin Marvellous** *Garden Centre*

9 Tuesday

Rowan has told me that a customer, Mr B Jones, faxed an urgent order for computer equipment through yesterday from his home at 75 Longton Lane, Moleville, Stoneshire. He will be calling in person to Computech at about 11 am today to collect his order for:

   1 x Toshiba CD400A CD-ROM drive at £344 plus VAT

Task 7

i   Make out a sales invoice for Mr Jones' order.

ii   Serve Mr Jones at the trade counter. He wants to pay **in cash. Make out a handwritten receipt** for this money.

10 Wednesday

Task 8

Complete a delivery note, sales invoice, and remittance advice for the order from Books Galore Ltd. The order has been checked. No errors have been made and the goods are in stock. Delivery will be tomorrow. Books Galore Ltd is a valued customer and has negotiated a 10% trade discount on all orders placed with Computech.

Books Galore Ltd

14 The Quadrant, Milltown
STONESHIRE ST8 6HY
Tel: 01239 9090 Fax: 01239 9099
VAT Reg 872 2095 19

Purchase Order No: 896   Date: 8.2.9X
To: Computech Ltd
      Unit 19-22
      Moleville Industrial Estate
      Stoneshire ST17 5MW

Description	Qty	Ref No	Price	Total
NEC Versa M/100 notebook PC	2	37/NB	£4,100.00	£8,200.00

Delivery ASAP
Authorized by: *P. S. Galore*
for **Books Galore Ltd**

11 Thursday

Rowan explained that a customer phoned in last week to complain that the Hewlett Packard 4L laserjet printer they had bought just before Christmas last year did not work any more. Because the printer was still under guarantee, a replacement was sent out immediately.

A sales invoice (number 45599) had been issued for the full amount of the replacement printer. Details on the invoice were as follows:

Customer name: JP Gilmott and Partners (Solicitors)

Address: 57 The High Street, Northbrook, Stoneshire

Product code: 76/PT

Price: £440 plus VAT. No delivery charge

Unless the faulty printer is returned within 28 days the invoice must be paid in full. If it is returned the customer pays nothing for the replacement.

Task 9

The loading bay has advised me that the faulty printer has now been returned. I must now **issue a credit note (CR/322) to JP Gilmott and Partners for the full amount on invoice number 45599.**

12 Friday

My last day in sales. Rowan asks me to file all the documents I have received and issued this week and to make sure that the accounts department has copies.

Meet Bill, Alison and Penny outside Blue Hawaii at 9 pm. Don't forget Bill's CD.

15 Monday

Report to wages department at the agreed time. Cathy Gregg showed me around the offices and explained my job for the week. As well as filling in pay slips I will be the petty cashier for the week. The weekly float is £120.

Cathy explained that this week will be busy for the department. Wages are due to be paid to staff at the end of next week and all the pay slips must be ready by then.

Computech employs 42 staff. Cathy tells me that the monthly wage bill for February will be £24,000, not counting the salary of the managing director.

16 Tuesday

Task 10

Cathy asks me to **complete a pay slip** for one of the part-time cleaners who is leaving at the end of this week. Her name is Annie Beardshaw. She is paid £5 per hour and always works 20 hours each week. Her tax code is 352L and her national insurance number is SM335778D.

The following deductions must be made from her gross pay:

Income tax: £6.40

NICs: £5.30

Her taxable income to date has been £1,507.

17 Wednesday

Task 11

Today I have to **fill out a pay slip for the managing director of the company**, Mr James Franklin. I had better make sure I do it correctly! He is paid a gross salary of £35,040 per year in twelve equal monthly payments. His tax code is 352L and his NI number is WL582536B. His taxable pay to date is £27,255.

The following deductions must be made from his gross salary this month:

Income tax: £650

NICs: £110

Season ticket loan: £90

Payroll giving to WSPA: £30

18 Thursday

Task 12

i   Cathy had to go to a meeting yesterday in London. Her train ticket cost her £23. **I must write out a petty cash voucher for the train fare** and give her £23 from petty cash. The number of this first voucher is 37.

ii   I go shopping for some tea, coffee, and biscuits for the wage department offices. These items cost me £6.50 at a nearby supermarket. **I must write out a petty cash voucher for the tea, coffee and biscuits.**

19 Friday

Task 13

i   I have to **complete four more petty cash vouchers for the following items:**

Milk bill: £12.75

Postage stamps: £5

Taxi fare: £4.50

Petrol: £25 items

ii   I must now **calculate how much has been paid out from petty cash this week and the amount remaining in the float.**

Don't forget to video 'Roseanne' on Channel 4 tonight at 10 pm.

February 199X

22 Monday

Task 14

My first day in accounts. Met Accounts Manager Nick Page to discuss my job for the week. He has suggested that I start by checking the details on some incoming cheques in payment for goods delivered.

Any cheques that have not been completed correctly must be referred back to the customer. **Make a note of any errors or omissions on these cheques.**

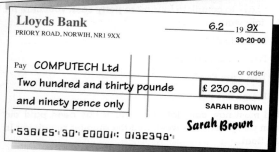

23 Tuesday

An invoice and credit note were received last week from Office Supplies Ltd. They refer to the purchase order (number 12/9251) that I sent them on my second day in the purchasing department. Nick has asked me to settle the invoice, less the amount on the credit note.

Office Supplies Ltd

12 Woodland Way
Northwick NH4 3JX
Tel: 01604-65666
Fax: 01604-65660
VAT Reg No. 234 8999 16

To: Computech Ltd
Unit 19-22
Moleville Industrial Estate
STONESHIRE ST17 5MW

INVOICE

Your Order No	Invoice No	Date
12/9251	22956	11.2.9X

Qty	Description	Cat No	Unit Price	Total
120	A4 white copy paper	34/a	£3.00	£360.00
60	Correction fluid 50ml	12/t	£1.50	£90.00
300	A3 envelopes	14/e	0.30	£90.00
	Delivery		£10.00	£10.00

Terms of payment: 30 days

Sub-total	£550.00
Discount 10%	£55.00
Total(ex VAT)	£495.00
VAT @ 17.5%	£86.63
Total due	£581.63

E & OE

Office Supplies Ltd

12 Woodland Way
Northwick NH4 3JX
Tel: 01604-65666
Fax: 01604-65660
VAT Reg No. 234 8999 16

To: Computech Ltd
Unit 19-22
Moleville Industrial Estate
STONESHIRE ST17 5MW

Credit Note No.
CN/9173

Your Order No	Invoice No	Date
12/9251	22956	15.2.9X

Qty	Description	Cat No	Unit Price	Total
20	Correction Fluid	24/t	£1.50	£30.00

Reason for credit:

Goods returned. Wrong colour delivered

Sub-total	£30.00
Discount 10%	£3.00
Total(ex VAT)	£27.00
VAT @ 17.5%	£4.73
Total due	£31.73

Task 15

I must **check the invoice and credit note against the purchase order and GRN3048** I completed when the goods were delivered. Copies of these are on file.

If the invoice and credit note are correct I must write out a cheque for the difference to send to Office Supplies Ltd.

24 Wednesday

Task 16

Having checked through a number of invoices received Nick Page asks me to **write out some more cheques to the following suppliers:**

- £295 to British Telecommunications Plc for the phone bill
- £276 to Stoneweb Plc for electricity
- £35 to Moleville Newsagents for newspaper and magazine deliveries
- £5,830 to Microsoft Corporation for software supplies (stock)
- £7,340 to Dan Technology Plc for equipment supplies (stock)
- £500 to IPC Magazines for colour advert in computer magazine

25 Thursday

Nick explained that Computech employ Securicor to make regular trips to the bank to deposit cash and cheques received. This is to keep the amount of money kept on the premises to a minimum in case of fire or theft.

The notes and coins have already been sorted into separate piles and sealed in bags ready for collection by Securicor.

Task 17

i Nick has given me a table listing the number of notes and coins of different values. I must **complete column 3 of the table and calculate the total amount of cash received.**

In addition to the cheques I accepted on 22 February in Task 14, the following cheques have also been received and accepted:

£678.90 from TW Plastics Ltd

£1,799 from Music Maker Instruments

£45.99 from SG Worth and Partners

£597.30 from Daniel Gee and Sons

ii Fill in a paying-in slip with details of all the notes, coins, and cheques to be paid into the bank.

Notes and coins	Number	Amount £:p
£50	8	
£20	13	
£10	17	
£5	28	
£1	63	
50p	25	
20p	18	
10p	37	
5p	22	
2p	22	
1p	26	

Total cash: £ _____

26 Friday

Statements of account for regular customers are prepared today to send out next week. These statements will list all the transactions between each customer and Computech during February.

Nick has asked me to make sure the sales department has provided us with copies of all the invoices and credit notes they sent out.

 ✓ Done

Task 18

Prepare a statement of account for Books Galore Ltd. Their account number is 547/2459. At the beginning of February they owed Computech £269.

In addition to the invoice for goods I sent them on 10 February while I was working in sales, the following transactions with Books Galore Ltd were also made during February:

February 2nd: Invoice no. 45360 for goods – £597.90

February 17th: Invoice no. 45371 for goods – £147.80

February 24th: Credit note CR/331 for goods returned – £48.85

Don't forget to show the closing balance on their account at the end of February, and to **attach a remittance advice** to the account statement.

March 199X

2 Monday

My second week in accounts. Nick Page wants me to complete a number of important tasks during this week.

Nick has started to gather information from all the departments in Computech to produce an income and expenditure account for February. All he needs to complete it are records of the incomes and expenditures from all the tasks I have completed.

Task 19

It will be my job today to **complete the income and expenditure account started for February**. I must fill in the blanks, and add the various incomes and expenditures resulting from Tasks 1-18 to the other figures.

Computech Ltd
INCOME AND EXPENDITURE: FEBRUARY 199X

	£
Income from sales	
Cash	10,438.00
Credit	52,970.00
Total income	
Expenditure	
Stock	15,940.60
Rent	1,200.00
Rates	347.85
Electricity	
Telephone	
Stationary	
Advertising	
Newspapers/Magazines	
Travel	
Petty cash	294.45
Wages and salaries	24,000.00
Total expenditure	
Balance on account	

Task 20

Remember to file all completed documents from Tasks 1-19 in a file marked 'Financial documents and records' and store in my portfolio.

3 Tuesday

Nick wants to improve the efficiency of recording and monitoring financial information in the accounts department. He has asked me to use the rest of the week to investigate computer software that may be able to help.

Task 21

I am to **prepare a list, using a word processor, of possible software programs, their main features, prices, and suppliers. It would also be useful to compile advertisements for each of the software products on the list. The list and advertisements can then be placed neatly in a file headed 'Computer software to record and monitor financial information'.**

Nick has suggested I will be able to obtain information from a variety of sources including:

- Computer magazines, e.g. Personal Computer World, PC Magazine, Practical PC, PC Plus, CD-ROM magazine
- Local computer shops and showrooms
- Local suppliers of computer software
- Software manufacturers

Blank financial documents

The following documents can be photocopied for use in element 4.2:

Purchase order

Computech Ltd
Unit 19 – 22, Moleville Industrial Estate
Stoneshire ST17 5MW
Tel: 01237-4095, Fax: 01237-4096
VAT Reg No. 707 3434 11

To: _____

_____

_____

Purchase Order No.

Date: _____

DESCRIPTION	QTY	Cat No.	PRICE	TOTAL

Authorised by: _____

For Computech Ltd

Sales invoice

Computech Ltd
Unit 19 – 22, Moleville Industrial Estate
Stoneshire ST17 5MW
Tel: 01237-4095, Fax: 01237-4096
VAT Reg No. 707 3434 11

To: _____

_____

_____

INVOICE

Your Order No.	Invoice No.	Date

QTY	Description	Cat No.	Unit Price	Total

Terms:

_____

_____

_____

E & OE

Sub-total	
Discount ___ %	
Total (ex. VAT)	
VAT @ 17.5%	
Total due	

Goods received note

Computech Ltd
GOODS RECEIVED NOTE

Supplier:

GRN No: _____

Date: _____

Re; Delivery Note:

_____

Order No.	QTY	DESCRIPTION	TOTAL

Received by: _____

For Computech Ltd

Credit note

Computech Ltd
Unit 19 – 22, Moleville Industrial Estate
Stoneshire ST17 5MW
Tel: 01237-4095, Fax: 01237-4096
VAT Reg No. 707 3434 11

To: _____

CREDIT NOTE NO.

Your Order No.	Invoice No.	Date

QTY	Description	Cat No.	Unit Price	Total
			Sub-total	
			Discount ____%	
Reason for credit:			Total (ex. VAT)	
_____			VAT	
_____			**Total credit**	

Remittance advice

REMITTANCE ADVICE

Date:

Customer name and address

Account No.

Statement Date:

Amount owing:

Amount enclosed ....

Cheque no. ....

Please return this slip together with your payment to;

Computech Ltd
Unit 19 – 22,
Moleville Industrial Estate
Stoneshire ST17 5MW

All cheques should be made payable to **Computech Ltd**

Delivery note

DELIVERY NOTE NO: _____

Computech Ltd
Unit 19 – 22, Moleville Industrial Estate
Stoneshire ST17 5MW
Tel: 01237-4095, Fax: 01237-4096
VAT Reg No. 707 3434 11

Delivery address: _____

For delivery on: _____

Your Order No.	Invoice No.	Date

QTY	Catalogue No.	Description

Delivery by: _____
No. of items: _____
Goods received by: _____ (signature)
_____ (please PRINT name)

Issued by: ....
  Sales Dept.
  Computech Ltd
Please retain this copy as proof of receipt

Receipt

Computech Ltd
Unit 19 – 22, Moleville Industrial Estate
Stoneshire ST17 5MW
Tel: 01237-4095, Fax: 01237-4096
VAT Reg No. 707 3434 11

No: _____

Received from _____

the sum of £ _____

_____   £: _____

in payment for _____

_____

Received by: _____   Date: _____

Sales Department
Computech Ltd

Paying-in slip

Front

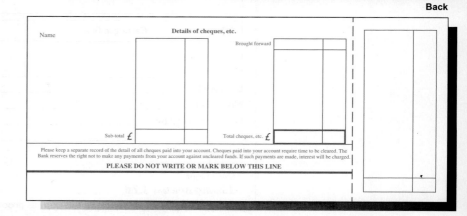

Back

Pay slip

PAY ADVICE		Pay reference	NI number	Pay period
Employee name:				
		Total pay to date	Taxable pay this period	Total tax paid to date
Employee number:				

Payments	£	Deductions	£

Gross pay
Total deductions
Net pay

Total deductions

Method of payment:

All payments are taxable unless indicated by*

All deductions are after tax unless indicated by*

Statement of account

STATEMENT OF ACCOUNT

Computech Ltd

Unit 19 – 22, Moleville Industrial Estate
Stoneshire ST17 5MW
Tel: 01237-4095, Fax: 01237-4096
VAT Reg No. 707 3434 11

Account No: _____
Customer name: _____
Customer address: _____

Statement Date: _____

Date	Details	Debit	Credit	Balance
			Balance now due	

Terms: Payment by _____ required

Cheques

Lloyds Bank

HIGH STREET, NORTHBROOK, ST5 4KZ

19 _____

30-20-00

Pay

or order

£

On behalf of Computech Ltd

⑆536125⑆30⑈20001⑆ 0132398⑆

Lloyds Bank

HIGH STREET, NORTHBROOK, ST5 4KZ

19 _____

30-20-00

Pay

or order

£

On behalf of Computech Ltd

⑆536125⑆30⑈20001⑆ 0132398⑆

Petty cash voucher

PETTY CASH VOUCHER

No: _____

Date _____

Purpose	Total incl. VAT	VAT	NET excl. VAT

Signature: _____

Approved by: _____

Name: _____

All receipts and invoices must be attached

Department: _____

chapter 14 Producing, Evaluating, and Storing Business Documents

Key ideas

Businesses need to communicate with their customers and with other business organizations. Employees in a business will also need to communicate with each other.

Business organizations use a variety of documents for routine communications with customers, other businesses, and employees. The main ones are **letters, memos, invitations** and **notices**.

Business documents can be **handwritten**, **typed**, or printed out from a computer **word processor**. Computer printers can print multiple copies of the same document. A **photocopier** can also be used to reproduce business documents.

When choosing the best way to produce a document, the key points to consider are speed, cost, and how easy it is to make changes. Memos and other short messages can be handwritten relatively quickly, but mistakes cannot easily be corrected. Most formal business letters are best typed or word-processed. Making changes to documents produced with a word processor is easy.

No matter how a document is produced, it should conform to an accepted business **style** and **layout**, and be free from errors of spelling and grammar.

Business documents can be sent to customers and other business organizations in a variety of ways. Most letters and other documents are sent by first- or second-class **post**, but if a business wants to guarantee delivery the next day a **special delivery** service will be needed.

There are a number of postal services available to business, including airmail, registered and recorded delivery, freepost, and business reply service.

Increasingly, businesses are sending documents by **electronic transmission** using **fax** machines and computers connected to phonelines. **Electronic mail (E-mail)** involves transmitting computer files without the need for paper copies.

When choosing how to send a document the key factors are how much it weighs, cost, and how urgently it is needed.

Files are devices for storing documents for easy reference. Documents can be stored in paper-based files or on computer.

Because of the risk of computer failure or theft, it is important to keep **back-up** copies of all the files stored on a computer hard disk.

A **filing system** is a method used to sort and arrange documents into files. All filing systems will involve grouping and sorting documents into some kind of order, so that people can find and retrieve them easily.

Files can be arranged **alphabetically**, by **subject**, and/or by **number**. Papers kept on file will normally be arranged in **date order**. Carefully indexed filing systems are needed so that people can find and retrieve documents easily.

Section **14.1** # Business communications

Communication is the process by which information is passed from one person or organization to another.

When we talk to each other or write letters and notes to other people, we are communicating information to them. Communication is very important in business. A business that fails to communicate the right messages at the right time to customers, other businesses, and employees will not be successful.

Portfolio Activity 14.1

PC: Explain the purpose of routine business documents

Range: Purpose

Skills: Read and respond to written material, Collect and record data, Produce written material

1. The following situations arise from day to day in many business organizations. All of them will involve communication. In each case write down:

- Who the communication is with

- Why you need to communicate with them

- What message you need to communicate

- What is the best way of getting the message to them

> **i** A customer has written to your company asking for information about your products. How would you reply?

> **ii** You take an important phone call for a work colleague who is out of the office. You do not know if your colleague will be back before you leave for a meeting. How would you make sure your colleague gets the phone message?

> **iii** Some new fire fighting equipment has been installed in your office. How would you make sure people know how to use it in an emergency?

> **iv** You have to cancel a meeting with other staff in your department at short notice. How would you make sure they know it has been cancelled, and let them know about alternative arrangements?

2. Investigate the purpose and methods of written communications in a business organization of your choice:

- Why do they need to send and retrieve information?

- Who do they send to, and retrieve information from?

- What types of information do they send and retrieve?

- What documents does the business use to record, send, and retrieve information?

Collect examples of business documents used by the organization (Remember to ask the business owner's or manager's permission to use them).

Write up your findings in a short report using a word processor. Include, if possible, examples of business documents you have collected.

> **v** A customer has written in to complain about late delivery of goods ordered from your company. How would you reply?

> **vi** An employee is consistently late for work and has ignored all verbal warnings. How would you tell them that if they do not start on time in future they are likely to get the sack?

> **vii** The goods inward department has taken delivery of the office equipment you ordered. How could they notify you?

There are a number of reasons why businesses need written communications:

- **To communicate with customers:** The main purpose of any commercial business is to sell goods and/or services to customers. A business that fails to communicate the right information at the right time to customers is in danger of losing them to rival firms.

  Sometimes a business may write to potential customers advertising its new goods or services. However, it is often the customer who first contacts a business – for example, to find out about products and prices. Some may write to complain about a product, while others may write to say how pleased they are with the product. In all cases a business should reply quickly to customers with the information they want. For example, in the case of a complaint, the firm should send a letter of apology and offer either a refund or a replacement.

- **To communicate with other businesses:** A business will need to make regular contact with other business organizations if they are customers or suppliers.

  A business will have dealings with many different suppliers. Banks, insurance companies, employment agencies, solicitors, accountants, advertising agencies – are all suppliers of business services. Others will provide materials, component parts, fuel, machinery, and other equipment. As a customer of these organizations, a business may write to make enquiries, complain, or thank them for their services.

  A business will also need to communicate with government organizations such as the Inland Revenue, Customs and Excise department, Health and Safety Executive, Environment Agency, etc.

- **To communicate with colleagues:** Everyone in a business works as part of a team to achieve the firm's objectives (see 1.1). Communication between work colleagues is therefore very important. For example, managers will need to communicate business objectives to the workforce, negotiate wages, and inform them of changes to working practices. More informally, employees may need to take phone messages for colleagues, or arrange business and social meetings.

▼ All businesses need to communicate with customers, other organizations, and employees on a daily basis.

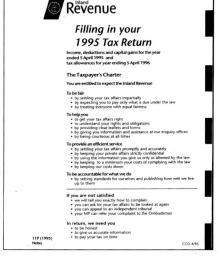

517

Section **14.2**

Routine business documents

The safest way to make sure that the right information reaches the right people is to write it down. Unless details of conversations, phone calls or meetings are written down, information passed between the people who are talking may be forgotten or misunderstood.

People in business organizations use a variety of documents to communicate with other people and firms. The main routine non-financial business documents are:

- Business letters
- Memos
- Invitations
- Notices
- Messages

Copies of the most important documents can be placed on file in case they are needed again.

Business letters

By far the most important means of sending information to customers and other business organizations is by a formal **business letter**. It is very important that business letters are well presented and accurate.

Business letters can be used for many different purposes. Below are just a few examples:

- Arranging and confirming meetings
- Asking job applicants to attend interviews
- Offering jobs to successful applicants
- Providing details of prices or cost estimates for work
- Making complaints to suppliers about poor delivery times or faulty goods
- Asking banks to check the creditworthiness of a customer
- Advertising details of new goods or services to customers
- Making enquiries or seeking information and help from other organizations
- Recording the main points of business conversations
- Writing to members of parliament on matters of concern
- Notifying employees that they are no longer required
- Responding to customer enquiries and complaints

How to write a business letter

The layout and style of business letters will vary greatly between organizations. However, there are some golden rules all organizations need to follow. If a business letter is to be effective and get its message across, it must be well presented, to the point, tactful, accurate, and addressed correctly.

Spelling and grammar in a business letter must also be correct. Poor spelling, bad grammar, and any other errors can give a poor impression. Careful preparation, drafting out the letter first, and getting the agreement of others in your organization, perhaps a manager, are very important before sending out a business letter.

Most business organizations use headed notepaper for their letters. This will usually show the name of the organization, address, phone numbers, and, if available, fax and E-mail numbers (see 14.3). The notepaper may also show the organization's logo and the names of business owners or company directors.

Figure 14.1 presents an example of a business letter from Pantera Computing Limited, a provider of computer training courses, in response to an enquiry by a potential customer.

▼ Figure 14.1: An example of a business letter

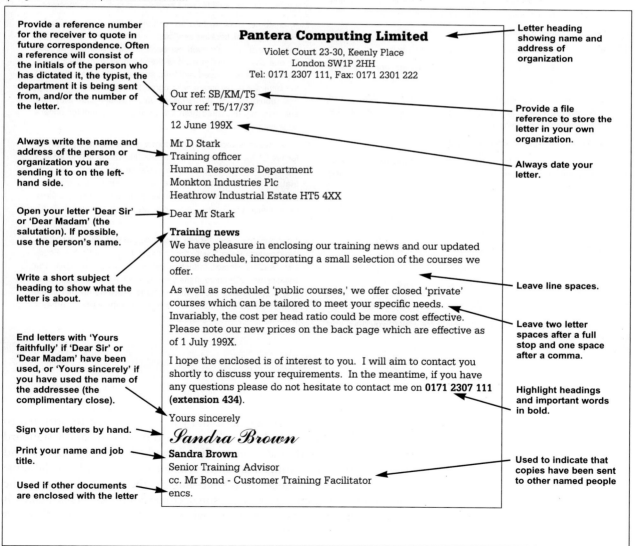

Provide a reference number for the receiver to quote in future correspondence. Often a reference will consist of the initials of the person who has dictated it, the typist, the department it is being sent from, and/or the number of the letter.

Always write the name and address of the person or organization you are sending it to on the left-hand side.

Open your letter 'Dear Sir' or 'Dear Madam' (the salutation). If possible, use the person's name.

Write a short subject heading to show what the letter is about.

End letters with 'Yours faithfully' if 'Dear Sir' or 'Dear Madam' have been used, or 'Yours sincerely' if you have used the name of the addressee (the complimentary close).

Sign your letters by hand.

Print your name and job title.

Used if other documents are enclosed with the letter

Pantera Computing Limited

Violet Court 23-30, Keenly Place
London SW1P 2HH
Tel: 0171 2307 111, Fax: 0171 2301 222

Our ref: SB/KM/T5
Your ref: T5/17/37

12 June 199X

Mr D Stark
Training officer
Human Resources Department
Monkton Industries Plc
Heathrow Industrial Estate HT5 4XX

Dear Mr Stark

Training news
We have pleasure in enclosing our training news and our updated course schedule, incorporating a small selection of the courses we offer.

As well as scheduled 'public courses,' we offer closed 'private' courses which can be tailored to meet your specific needs. Invariably, the cost per head ratio could be more cost effective. Please note our new prices on the back page which are effective as of 1 July 199X.

I hope the enclosed is of interest to you. I will aim to contact you shortly to discuss your requirements. In the meantime, if you have any questions please do not hesitate to contact me on **0171 2307 111 (extension 434)**.

Yours sincerely

Sandra Brown
Sandra Brown
Senior Training Advisor
cc. Mr Bond - Customer Training Facilitator
encs.

Letter heading showing name and address of organization

Provide a file reference to store the letter in your own organization.

Always date your letter.

Leave line spaces.

Leave two letter spaces after a full stop and one space after a comma.

Highlight headings and important words in bold.

Used to indicate that copies have been sent to other named people

Most business letters are typed on one side of an A4 sheet of headed or plain paper. The style used is what is known as **fully blocked, open punctuation**. This means that all words including addresses, dates, and titles start at the left margin. No line indents are used. With modern word processors the text can be justified against both the left and right margins. This means words on each line start and end in the same place – at the margins.

Portfolio Activity 14.2

PC: Evaluate each business document produced, Produce draft and final versions of business documents

Range: Business documents, Evaluate

Skills: Produce written material, Present information

Preparing business letters to customers and other external organizations is a very important task. Letters must always be clear and to the point, courteous, accurate, have a pleasing layout, and contain no spelling errors, abbreviations, jargon, or slang.

When preparing a letter:

● Check that you have all the information you need.

● Decide on a suitable reference, heading, opening, and conclusion.

● If the subject matter is confidential, add the word 'CONFIDENTIAL' at the very top of the letter and on the envelope that contains it.

● Always prepare the letter in draft first.

● If you are replying to a letter (or fax) you have received, start your letter with '*Thank you for your letter/fax of (date) concerning (subject) ...*'

● If the letter follows a telephone conversation with the addressee, then start your letter with '*Following our recent telephone conversation regarding (subject) ...*'

● Conclude your letter appropriately. For example:

　– '*I look forward to hearing from you...*'

　– '*I hope this information will be helpful to you...*'

　– '*Please let me know if I can be of any further assistance...*'

　– '*Please do not hesitate to contact me should you have any further queries...*'

● Read through your draft letter to check spelling, grammar, accuracy, and tone. Make sure you have not used jargon, and that no important information has been omitted.

Imagine now that you work for a large bank. You have received three written communications to which you must reply in the form of a business letter. Using the guidelines above, prepare draft letters first, and ask your tutor and fellow students for comments, before producing final versions for your portfolio using a word processor.

1. A customer has written to complain that she has been overcharged for banking services. She has had to pay £25 for being overdrawn, although her bank account was only in debit for one day, and the amount of the overdraft was only £15.75. Because she is a valued customer and has held an account with the bank for many years, you agree to refund her the money. You apologize for the charges and explain that they are automatically deducted from the account by computer once a negative balance is recognized.

2. You have received an enquiry from a student currently studying for his GNVQ business qualifications. He would like to know if the bank can offer him a work experience placement. You reply that the bank is unable to offer any further work experience places this year, but that you will keep his letter on file if a place becomes available next year. You also wish him luck with his studies.

3. Your bank manager, Sheila Jones, has asked you to arrange a meeting with Peter Smith, the financial director of Fretton Foods Ltd, Unit 75, Hogton Industrial Estate, Hogton, HT5 7DB. The meeting will take place at the bank at 10.00 am in ten days' time, and a car parking space will be made available for him at the rear of the building. Mr Smith is to contact the bank if he has a problem with these arrangements.

Standard business letters

Business letters which are standard and routine are often pre-printed to save time and money. Modern computer word processors allow standard letters to be stored and 'personalized' with individual names and addresses prior to printing. This allows the business to send out the same letter to a large number of people but at the same time give the impression that each one is a personal correspondence. This makes it much less likely that the person receiving the letter will simply throw it away without reading it.

▼ An advertisement for services and a request for payment – two examples of the type of standard business letters used by firms

QUANTIME

Quantime Ltd

Maygrove House
67 Maygrove Road
London NW6 2EG

Tel: 071-625 7222
Fax: 071-624 5297

June 1995

Dear Client,

Because the world's best survey software deserves the best support

It is in our interest as much as yours that you should use our software to the best of its capabilities. Therefore, I am happy to enclose a leaflet giving full details of the Quantime Support Service, which is available to all Quantime's clients.

The leaflet gives the contact numbers and opening hours of the three international service centers and details the various support methods offered. I hope you will find it informative and useful. I am also enclosing a label for you to attach to your computer or telephone, thus ensuring the Quantime Support Service contact numbers are always close at hand!

Please do not hesitate to contact me should you have any further questions about the Quantime Support Service, or any of the other services mentioned in the brochure. Further copies of the brochure or label are available via your Account Manager.

Yours sincerely,

Madeleine Ashbery

Madeleine Ashbery
Support Director

Badger Builders Ltd
Unit 49A
Marsh Lane Industrial Estate
Marsham
Newshire
Tel: 01334–5073
Fax: 01334–5077

Our Ref: 4703/ACC/AM/RAD

7 June 1995

Radcliffe Ltd
14 Brambledown Road
Watford
Hertfordshire

Dear Sirs

OVERDUE PAYMENT FOR BUILDING SERVICES

We are again contacting you about your cheque number 207893 for £750.75 which was returned to us because of insufficient funds. We wrote to you once before about this matter, but you have not responded.

Within 10 working days from the date of this letter, we expect to receive payment in full. If you are unable to send payment for the entire amount, please call me to explain the circumstances and work out a payment solution.

You have been a good customer and we don't want to lose you. Please respond today.

Yours faithfully

A Morrison

A Morrison
Accounts Representative

P.S. If your remittance is already in the post, please accept our thanks and disregard this notice.

Business memos

Businesses often use **memos**, or **memoranda**, for short important messages when there is no time for a formal letter. Memos are generally for internal use only, and are often handwritten on small pieces of paper which are sometimes pre-printed with the word 'Memo' at the top of each sheet.

Memos can be used for a variety of internal messages. For example:

● Making a specific request or query

● Providing information

● Notifying people of a change of date, time, or venue for a meeting

● Notifying people who are arranging a meeting that you are not able to attend

● Arranging more informal meetings – for example, a lunch

● Notifying people that a letter or parcel has arrived for them

Figure 14.2 shows an example of a memo cancelling a business meeting.

▼ *Figure 14.2: An example of a memo*

MEMO

To: All senior managers
From: A Bowmer MD

Date: 12.2.96
Ref: AB/CG

Subject: Meeting on 15.2.96

Meeting cancelled. Rescheduled to 23.29.96 at 2 pm. Venue unchanged.

Please phone Clare Biggs (x6783) to confirm attendance.

Apologies for inconvenience.

AB

Most business organizations use pre-printed memo forms. The layout and content of these forms will vary between organizations, but will usually contain the following headings:

To – the name of the person(s) the memo is intended for

From – the name of the person sending the memo

Date – the date the memo was prepared

Ref: – a filing reference

Like business letters, memos should also have a clear subject heading, so that people immediately know what the communication is about.

The word 'urgent' may also be added to the memo if it is very important and needs to be read quickly. It is usual to finish a memo by writing or typing your initials. Memos are never signed in full.

Portfolio Activity 14.3

PC: Produce draft and final versions of business documents
Range: Business documents
Skills: Produce written material, Take part in discussions

1. In groups, prepare memos for the following messages. These can be handwritten, typed, or produced using a word processor. (You can make up names, and other details, for the people and business organizations involved in each case.)

- The managing director has had to rearrange the date and time of the next board meeting.

- Your line manager asks for sales figures for the last quarter.

- You provide your line manager with the latest sales figures as requested.

- The goods inward department notifies you that the new computer equipment you ordered has arrived and is ready to collect.

- You notify the sales and marketing department that a new photocopier has been installed for their use on Floor 3 near the lifts.

2. Swap the memos you have produced between fellow students in your group. Discuss each one in terms of:

- Spelling and grammar

- Style and layout

- Whether the message is clear

3. From your discussions in Task 2, compile a list of 'do's and don'ts' for memo-writing.

Invitations

Business invitations are personalized requests for people to attend special business functions.

Businesses will often entertain their important customers and suppliers at special functions. These can be exhibitions of the products sold by that business, or parties to celebrate Christmas or important anniversaries, such as '50 years in business'. Some businesses may also invite guests along to important sporting and social events, such as the Epsom Derby or Henley Regatta. Record companies may hold parties to launch new pop groups and their records.

Business functions or parties are intended to create a good image for the organization, and good relations with customers and suppliers. They are an important part of the overall marketing strategy of the organization to promote itself and its products. It is, therefore, important that the invitation gives a good impression. Many will be printed in colour on card and have eye-catching designs. Details about time, date, venue, and the need to reply, i.e. RSVP, must be clear. (RSVP stands for 'Répondez s'il vous plaît', meaning 'please reply' in French.)

Notices

Business letters, memos, and invitations are personal communications which are only meant to be read by the people they are sent to. Notices, however, are meant to be read by everyone – or at least, those interested in the messages they contain. Examples include bus timetables provided at bus stops, or health and safety regulations in factories. Notices will contain largely factual information and can therefore serve many purposes.

▼ *Notices can contain important information.*

THE LEIGH CITY TECHNOLOGY COLLEGE

IN CASE OF FIRE:

1. IF YOU FIND A FIRE, RAISE THE ALARM IMMEDIATELY BY PRESSING THE NEAREST ALARM, OR BY SHOUTING 'FIRE'.
THEN EVACUATE THE ROOM, FOLLOWING THE PROCEDURES BELOW.

2. WHEN THE FIRE ALARM SOUNDS, EVERYONE SHOULD LEAVE THE BUILDING, IMMEDIATELY, BY THE NEAREST ROUTE.

3. STUDENTS SHOULD FILE OUT OF THE ROOM IN SILENCE, LEAVING ALL BOOKS AND BAGS BEHIND. ON THE TEACHER'S INSTRUCTION, STUDENTS SHOULD PROCEED, IN PAIRS, TOWARDS THE NEAREST FIRE EXIT.

4. ENSURE THAT THE DOOR OF THE CLASSROOM IS CLOSED.

5. WALK BRISKLY, AND IN SILENCE, KEEPING TO THE RIGHT SIDE OF THE CORRIDOR OR STAIRS.

6. ONCE OUTSIDE, PROCEED TO THE NEAREST ASSEMBLY POINT, WHERE STUDENTS SHOULD LINE UP IN SINGLE FILE, IN REGISTER ORDER, AND WAIT IN SILENCE WHILE THE TEACHER CHECKS THAT ALL ARE PRESENT.

7. ASSEMBLY POINTS:

   EAST CAMPUS -   YRS. 7, 8 AND 9 ON THE COURT BEHIND TECHNOLOGY

                   YRS. 10, 11 AND 12 ON THE COURT BEHIND THE SPORTS HALL

   WEST CAMPUS -   ALL YEARS ON THE NETBALL COURTS BEHIND THE GYM

8. STUDENTS MAY NOT BE DISMISSED TO RETURN TO THEIR CLASSROOMS UNTIL THE SENIOR MEMBER OF STAFF IS SATISFIED THAT ALL ARE PRESENT, AND THAT THE FIRE DRILL HAS BEEN CARRIED OUT AS QUICKLY, EFFICIENTLY AND SAFELY AS POSSIBLE.

9. STAFF SHOULD USE THEIR MARK BOOKS TO CHECK ATTENDANCE. OFFICE STAFF WILL BRING OUT THE VISITORS' BOOK AND THE SIGNING OUT BOOK SO THAT ABSENCES CAN BE CHECKED.

THE DEPARTMENT OF TRANSPORT

DEPARTMENTAL NOTICE

DN 15/95   11 August 1995

ANNUAL LEAVE: DELEGATION TO LINE MANAGERS

1. This Notice concerns staff in **CTG, DVLA, TRL and VCA**. The arrangements for those staff in other groups are unaffected.

2. The Department's annual leave arrangements are set out in Section 503 of the new Staff Handbook. This reflects that all line managers are responsible for considering applications for annual leave from members of their staff.

3. With effect from **1 September** line managers in **CTG, DVLA, TRL and VCA** will assume additional responsibilities including:

- calculating annual leave entitlements for their staff;

- considering requests to anticipate or carry-over annual leave;- deciding applications for compensation in lieu of untaken annual leave; and authorising deductions from pay where a member of staff who is leaving the Department has taken leave in excess of their entitlement.

Detailed guidance for these line managers is included in Section 503 Annex C of the Staff Handbook. (Line managers in CTG may also refer to the "Line Manager's Guide" (which will be published shortly).

ENQUIRIES

4. Enquiries about this Notice should be addressed to Neil Stoker, PMT 3A, 4/15, Great Minster House. Tel. 0171 (GTN) 271 5676.

RICHARD BIRD
Director of Personnel

If notices are to attract people's attention they must be placed somewhere they can be seen easily. They should also be short, to the point, and easily understandable to all the different people who might read them. Attractive layout will catch the attention of people passing by. They will also usually be dated so that people will know if the information contained in the notice is new or old.

Sometimes businesses will place notices in newspapers to reach a wide audience. For example, notices may be used to advertise the sale of shares in a public limited company, or to recall faulty electrical goods, or to notify local residents that planning permission has been granted to develop an area of land.

Portfolio Activity 14.4

PC: Explain the purpose of routine business documents, Produce draft and final versions of business documents
Range: Business documents
Skills: Collect and record data

1. Draw a table like the one below with enough rows for at least ten business notices.

Examples of business notices

Place	Information	Intended audience
Bus timetable	Bus departure times	Customers/passengers
Factory floor	Safety procedures	Employees

2. Identify at least ten different notices used by different business organizations in your local area. For each one write down in your table where you would expect to find them, the messages or information they contain, and who they are intended for. The table already contains two examples of business notices to help you.

3. Design an invitation using a word processor or desktop publishing program to invite an important business customer to a party to celebrate your firm's 25th year in business. Make up your own business name and details of the date, time, and venue for the celebration.

▼ Figure 14.3: A pre-printed telephone message form

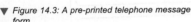

Post-it™ Telephone Message Pad 7660

To _____
Date _____ Time _____

WHILE YOU WERE OUT

M _____
of _____
Phone No. _____

TELEPHONED	PLEASE CALL
WAS IN TO SEE YOU	WILL CALL BACK
WANTS TO SEE YOU	**URGENT**
RETURNED YOUR CALL	

Message _____
_____
_____
_____

FT-5001-6785-1   Operator _____

Messages

People working in busy organizations will often need to take messages for their colleagues or even to remind themselves to do things. Messages can be personal – for example, to tell someone that his wife rang while he was out of the office – or work-related.

Messages may be written down following:

- A phone call
- A conversation with a work colleague
- A conversation with a supplier or customer

Messages will usually be jotted down on a pad or Post-it note, which can then be stuck in a position where the person is most likely to see it, for example, on their computer screen. If you cannot give them the message in person, it is often useful to contact them later to make sure that the message has been received and understood.

In all cases, a message should be simple, clear and to the point, accurate, and marked 'urgent' if necessary. The date and time the message was taken should also be recorded.

It is vitally important that the person receiving the message is able to understand it and has all the information he or she needs. You may need to question the person leaving the message. For example, you might ask them what their full name is, what the message concerns, and where can they be contacted. A good way to check that you have written down the right message is to read it back to the caller.

To help people take accurate messages over the phone, business organizations often provide their staff with pre-printed message forms (see Figure 14.3).

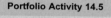

Portfolio Activity 14.5

PC: Produce draft and final versions of business documents

Range: Business documents

Skills: Produce written material

Use an enlarged photocopy of Figure 14.3 to take a message from the following phone call received for an absent work colleague. What other information would have been helpful for the caller to provide, and how would you obtain it?

> Hello. This is Key Motors. I am trying to contact Richard Sambora. He asked us to prepare an estimate for repair to accident damage to his car. We want to know if he would like us to go ahead and carry out the repairs based on our estimate. If he could let us know by 3 pm today we can get the parts ordered for delivery tomorrow, otherwise it will take another day to get them. Could you ask him to give me a ring on 0181 901 0001? Thank you.

Evaluating business documents

If a business document is to do the job it is intended to do, it must be produced with care. In a business environment, it will not always be possible for someone to check the documents you have written, so you will have to learn to evaluate them yourself.

You can evaluate a document in terms of its:

- **Appearance** – style and format

- **Language** – spelling, grammar and tone

Simply by looking at other business documents you receive at work you can learn a lot about the do's and don't's of producing business documents.

Appearance

This is simply what the document looks like. Is it pleasing to look at? Is it neat or scrappy-looking? Is it too cluttered with text, or clear and easy to read? In all cases, documents should be well presented. Every business will have its own business style for documents. This will include the type of paper they are written on, which may be thick, display a company logo, be embossed, and/or coloured. Thick embossed paper with an eye-catching logo can promote a good image for the business.

Style also includes the way documents are addressed. For example, some business organizations may insist that internal documents always show the first name as well as the surname of the people to whom they are sent; that they are listed in terms of their seniority if there is more than one addressee on the same document; that information such as the date and a file reference is positioned in a certain way – and so on.

Format refers to the layout of a document. This will include paper size, margins, line spacings, the use of headings, block paragraphs, size and type of characters, and so on. Clearly, style and format are closely related. For example, a business letter which filled the page with a mixture of fancy typefaces would not only demonstrate a poor layout but also a lack of style.

Many business organizations have set rules on style and format that all employees must follow when preparing business documents. This is called their **house style**.

Language

Language refers to how the document is worded. Does it make sense? Are words spelt correctly? Is it grammatically correct? Are sentences and/or paragraphs too long? Are commas and full stops used in the right places? Is the tone appropriate? For example, in response to a customer complaint, is the letter apologetic or aggressive?

Grammatical errors and spelling mistakes are unprofessional and can create a bad image for a business, and for individual members of staff.

Portfolio Activity 14.6

PC: Evaluate each business document produced, Produce draft and final versions of business documents
Range: Business documents, Evaluate
Skills: Collect and record data, Produce written material

1. Obtain some examples of standard and non-standard letters used by business organizations.

2. Evaluate each of the letters you have collected in Task 1 in terms of the following criteria:

● Whether it is clear and to the point

● Spelling and grammar

● Tact and courtesy

● Style and layout

3. Prepare a draft standard letter using a word processor. The letter should explain the facilities and courses available in the Business Studies department of your school/college.

4. Save and print a copy of your draft letter from Task 3. Check your draft using grammar and spelling functions on your word processor, if available. Also read through and check your draft letter yourself before carrying out any necessary redrafting. Save the final version of your letter and print a copy for your portfolio.

Section **14.3** **Methods of processing documents**

There are a number of different ways business documents can be prepared and printed. These are:

- Writing by hand
- Typing
- Word processing
- Printing
- Photocopying

Writing documents by hand

Before the invention of typewriters and word processors, all correspondence had to be written by hand. Many letters are still handwritten today, especially if the message is short and simple, because handwriting is a relatively quick and easy method. It also makes a message more personal.

It is also common for draft documents to be handwritten before they are typed or word-processed. Often one person will prepare the draft and another person will type it out or input it to a computer – for example, a manager drafting out a business letter for his or her secretary to produce and send out. Preparing a draft beforehand allows any changes to be made before the final version is produced.

If final versions of documents such as business letters are to be handwritten, then the writer should bear in mind:

- Not everyone can write neatly
- Mistakes cannot easily be corrected

▼ Two handwritten memos

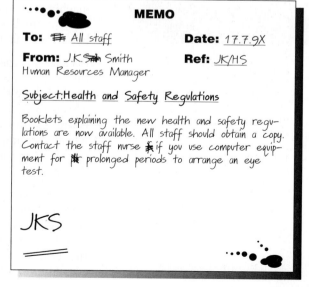

Right

Wrong

- Tippex or correction fluid to correct mistakes can look messy and unprofessional
- It is time-consuming to write out the document again once a mistake has been made
- A photocopier will be needed to make copies

For these reasons most business organizations prefer to use typewritten or word-processed documents.

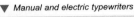

▼ Manual and electric typewriters

Using a typewriter

A typewriter is a machine that prints raised letters, symbols, and numbers on to one sheet of paper at a time. A photocopier will be needed if exact copies are to be made of a typed document, unless it is typed out in full over and over again.

On an old-fashioned manual typewriter, the raised characters are on the end of a series of metal levers connected by small springs to appropriate keys on the keyboard. When a key is pressed hard, the lever lifts up and punches the character onto the paper through a ribbon impregnated with ink. The paper is then moved along for the next character. The typist will have to choose when to end a line and use a mechanical arm on the machine to move the paper up and back to the left-hand margin to start the next line. Not surprisingly, using manual typewriters is slow and requires good layout skills. Mistakes cannot be corrected easily without either rubbing the ink off the paper or using correction fluid before back-spacing and retyping.

Nowadays, most typewriters are either electrically operated or electronic. These machines require less effort to operate. The paper will also be realigned automatically once you have reached the end of a line.

Electronic typewriters are now the most common form of typewriter in general use today, and they are available with a range of functions. Most will have microchips similar to those in computers. This allows the machine to remember what you have typed into the keyboard and display it on a small screen. This facility allows the user to correct mistakes before the machine types it all out in one go.

Because all typewriters rely on raised characters being printed onto paper through an inked ribbon, the choice of typeface and character size is limited, unless you continually swap one set of characters for another. This is relatively easy to do on an electric or electronic typewriter which is fitted with single elements – a small metal 'golf ball' or a plastic 'daisy wheel' – containing all the characters. However, if you wanted to change the character set in a manual typewriter, you would have to replace all the levers!

Because electronic machines have fewer moving parts than manual and electric typewriters they tend to be more reliable and less expensive to repair. However, electronic typewriters can be quite expensive to buy and the user may need training. Firms should, therefore, look carefully at the cost of buying a typewriter compared to the cost of buying a computer and word-processing program.

▼ *Using a computer word processing program*

Word processing (WP)

Many people now have access to a personal computer in their place of work. Special programs can be loaded on to computers to provide word processing functions. The cost of buying and repairing a computer can be quite expensive compared to typewriters. However, because they are so much faster than typewriters, have so many more functions, and produce better-quality documents, it is a cost that most business organizations are willing to pay.

Word processors can be used for producing all types of business documents, but are mainly used for writing letters, reports, and notices. Like typewriters, a word processor still requires the writer to type in words and figures using a keyboard. However, computers and WP programs have many advantages over typewriters.

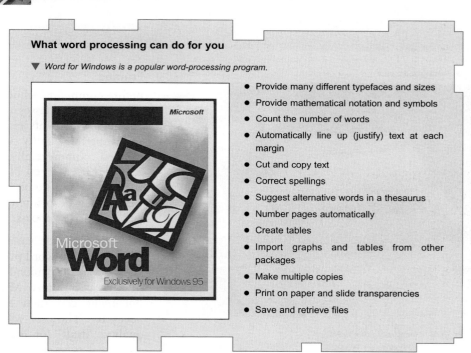

What word processing can do for you

▼ *Word for Windows is a popular word-processing program.*

- Provide many different typefaces and sizes
- Provide mathematical notation and symbols
- Count the number of words
- Automatically line up (justify) text at each margin
- Cut and copy text
- Correct spellings
- Suggest alternative words in a thesaurus
- Number pages automatically
- Create tables
- Import graphs and tables from other packages
- Make multiple copies
- Print on paper and slide transparencies
- Save and retrieve files

The latest versions of word processing programs such as Word for Windows and WordPerfect are very like **desktop publishing (DTP)** programs (see 9.2). DTP allows users to design complex page layouts using columns, boxes, diagrams, and pictures in the same way as a newspaper or magazine. Using programs such as Aldus Pagemaker, Ami Pro, and Microsoft Publisher, even the smallest businesses can produce high-quality business documents and other publicity and marketing materials.

Voice recognition software is likely to revolutionize the way in which people use computers over the next few years. Computers will be able to recognize spoken words and commands so that people can write messages without having to use a keyboard to input letters and numbers.

▼ *Printing in the past*

Printing

Before computer technology became miniaturized and affordable, businesses that needed multiple copies of business documents either had to use a photocopier or, if better quality was required, to have copies printed commercially. Traditionally, this would require raised metal blocks to be produced for each letter, line, and number. Typeset blocks of each page would then be printed on to paper. This was a slow and expensive process.

Nowadays a wide variety of business documents can be input into a word processing or desktop publishing package and downloaded directly to a printer linked to the computer. Multiple copies of the same document can then be printed out, in colour if necessary. The user will often have a choice of print quality: 'draft' for draft documents, 'letter quality', and 'near-typeset quality' for reports and published documents.

▼ *Printing today using computers*

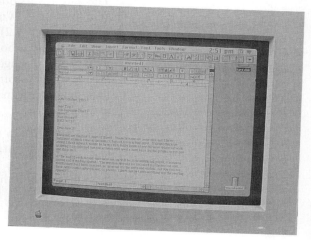

Modern printers linked to computers can be used to print out multiple copies of the same document to send to different people and to place on file.

If a business letter is sent to a great number of people, it can be very time-consuming for the person sending it to sign each copy individually. However, in the same way that photographs can be scanned and turned into digital images, it is possible to scan in the signature of a person sending a letter. The computerized image of the signature can then be incorporated at the end of a word-processed business letter. Every time the letter is printed out it will contain the signature of the writer.

Types of computer printer

There are many different types of computer printer offering different speeds and quality of printing. The most common types are:

Dot matrix printers

These are similar in principle to a typewriter. They produce an image by striking the paper through a ribbon. The print head consists of a number of very small pins. As the print head moves across the page, one or more pins strike the ribbon and produce dots on the paper in the shape of letters, numbers, or symbols. The more pins in the head, the better quality the print. However, these machines are quite slow, cannot produce complex graphics, and quality tends to be inferior.

Inkjet printers

These produce characters by spraying minute jets of ink at the paper in the shape of letters, numbers, and symbols. They are very quiet and can produce very high-quality black and white or coloured text and graphics.

Laser printers

These have become increasingly popular as prices have fallen. They produce fast and very high-quality text and graphics, and are virtually silent in operation. Prices for black and white printers were as low as £300 in early 1996, similar to good-quality inkjet printers. However, colour laser printers remain very expensive.

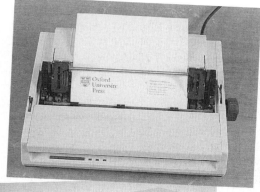

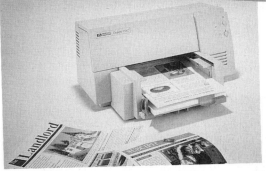

Photocopying

A business can use a photocopying machine to make multiple copies of the same document.

A **photocopier** will produce an exact replica of printed or handwritten text, diagrams, and pictures on a sheet of paper. The quality of many machines today makes it difficult to tell the original document from the copy. Some of the more expensive machines can also reproduce colours.

PC: Compare the methods of processing business documents
Range: Methods of processing, Compare
Skills: Collect and record data, Produce written material, Present information

Does your school/college, or a local business you know, have a photocopier? What make is it? What can it do? How easy is it to use? What costs are involved (e.g. paper, toner, maintenance)?

1. Write a short pamphlet advertising a photocopier in use in your school/ college or in an organization of your choice. Arrange the text on both sides of an A4 sheet of paper using a word processor or desktop publishing package. The pamphlet should explain what a photocopier is and what your chosen machine is able to do.

2. Once you have checked your pamphlet, print one copy. Insert any drawings or photographs you have made of the photocopier into your pamphlet.

3. Now make three double-sided photocopies of your finished pamphlet using the photocopier you are advertising.

▼ Desk top photocopier

▼ Large computer-controlled photocopier

Most large modern photocopy machines are computerized and have several useful functions. For example:

- Detailed user requirements can be programmed into the machine
- Automatic paper feed
- Many different sizes of paper can be used. Some photocopiers can even reproduce very large maps.
- Documents and images can be enlarged and reduced.
- Copies can be printed on both sides of the paper.
- Pages can be arranged in order in different trays to make the multiple copying of large reports easier (this is called **collation**).
- Contrast and brightness can be adjusted.
- Reports can be bound or even stapled together.

Because the price of equipment has fallen due to advances in technology, most small businesses can afford to buy, or lease, their own small photocopier. It may not have many of the functions of a larger machine, but it may still work out cheaper than taking original documents to be photocopied at specialist printing shops such as Prontoprint.

PC: Compare the methods of processing business documents, Evaluate each business document produced
Range: Methods of processing, Compare, Evaluate
Skills: Collect and record data, Produce written material, Present information

1. Collect examples of business documents, including letters, memos, invitations, and notices, that have been handwritten, typed, and produced using a word processor linked to a printer.

2. In small groups, gather together the business documents you collected in Task 1. Now compare the handwritten, typed, and word-processed documents you have collected in terms of:

● The quality of their appearance

● Legibility

● Cost and length of time to produce

● How easy it is to make changes

● Methods and ease of storage

3. Your group has been asked by a medium-sized local business to advise the owners on what methods they should use to produce different business documents. From your discussions in Task 2, write a short report making recommendations on how best to produce, copy, and store business letters, memos, invitations, and notices.

Section **14.4**   **Sending documents**

Ways to send business documents

There are many different ways a business can choose to send documents today. These are:

● By post

● By special delivery

● By electronic transmission (e.g. E-mail, fax, and telex)

Most large businesses will use all these methods. Smaller businesses may not have their own telex, fax machine, or a computer that can send and receive electronic mail. However, some shops and post offices can provide fax and E-mail services at a small cost.

Postal services

For many years now the main method of sending letters, reports, and other documents to people and organizations in different places has been by post.

Postal services in and from the UK are mainly provided by the Royal Mail division of the Post Office. A wide variety of services are available, including many specifically designed for use by business.

First- and second-class delivery
There are two main ways of sending letters and other documents through the post. **First-class mail** aims to deliver letters the day after they have been posted. **Second-class mail** aims to deliver by the third working day after posting.

▼ *Rates for letters (1995)*

Letter services
Rates for Letters
Royal Mail aims to deliver (Monday to Saturday) First Class letters the day after collection and Second Class letters by the third working day after collection, but actual service depends on the time of posting and the destination of the letter. Please refer to your local Customer Service Centre for details of the services provided in your area.

Weight not over	First Class	Second Class	Weight not over	First Class	Second Class
60g	25p	19p	500g	£1.25	98p
100g	38p	29p	600g	£1.55	£1.20
150g	47p	36p	700g	£1.90	£1.40
200g	57p	43p	750g	£2.05	£1.45
250g	67p	52p	800g	£2.15	Not
300g	77p	61p	900g	£2.35	admissible
350g	88p	70p	1000g	£2.50	over 750g
400g	£1.00	79p	Each extra 250g		
450g	£1.13	89p	or part thereof 65p		

▼ *Registered and recorded delivery are reliable methods of sending documents through the post.*

PARCEL ✦ FORCE

GUARANTEED ON-TIME DELIVERY

Prices effective from 3 April 1995

A quick guide to the UK's most reliable parcel services

In 1995, the cost of first-class mail within the UK started from 25 pence, and second-class from 19 pence for letters and packages weighing less than 60 grammes. Higher charges applied for letters weighing more than 60 grammes and for letters being sent overseas. Postage stamps to the required value can be bought from Post Offices and some shops. These are stuck to letters to show that the mail delivery service has been pre-paid for.

Recorded and registered delivery
Sometimes it is necessary to have proof that an item you have posted – for example, an urgent or confidential document – has been delivered to the right address. **Recorded delivery** provides this by requiring items to be signed for on delivery.

Registered delivery is a fast, reliable service which guarantees next-day delivery to most UK destinations. A signature is collected as proof of delivery, and compensation is paid for any loss or damage to letters and small packages up to a specified maximum.

The cost of both registered delivery and recorded delivery services is additional to the cost of first-class postage.

Airmail
The Royal Mail offers two types of airmail. Delivery by standard airmail usually takes 3-4 days inside Europe, and 4-7 days elsewhere in the world. Airmail labels must be stuck on all letters and small packets or alternatively you may write 'Par Avion – By Airmail' on them. Special lightweight paper to keep down the cost of postage is available to write letters on. A **Swiftair** express service is also available which is faster than ordinary airmail.

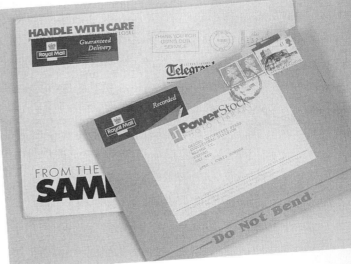

▼ *Special delivery services are available from the Royal Mail and a growing number of private sector couriers.*

Parcel delivery

Sometimes bulky documents have to be sent through the post. The Royal Mail **Parcelforce** service reaches over 230 countries and territories. For the economy service, you should allow from 10 working days for your parcel to reach a destination in Europe, and a minimum of 20 working days to the rest of the world. The cost of the service increases the more your package weighs. The **Red Star** service operated by the railways provides a fast station-to-station parcel delivery service at home and abroad. **City Link** also operates in conjunction with Railtrack to provide a fast door-to-door parcel collection and delivery service to and from any address in the UK.

Special delivery

Special delivery services are available at a price for letters, packets, and large parcels. These services make special arrangements to guarantee express delivery usually by the next working day to most UK destinations and countries nearby. Guaranteed express deliveries to other countries may take more than a day.

There are a growing number of private courier firms in the UK, such DHL, TNT, and Courier Systems who are willing to guarantee a delivery time for deliveries anywhere in the world.

Reply services for businesses

The Post Office provides a number of services to business to encourage people to reply to the letters and other mail they receive.

Business reply service

A business organization may send documents, such as mail order advertisements or questionnaires, to potential customers to fill in and return. To encourage them to reply, the business may enclose a **business reply envelope** for free postage.

Business reply service envelopes show a licence number and a class of postage. The business will pay the cost of postage on every reply received.

Freepost

Some business organizations may also operate a service that allows people to write to them without having to pay postage. All they have to do is include the word 'FREEPOST' in the address on the envelope. The business organization will then pay the cost of second-class post for every Freepost letter they receive.

▼ *A business reply service envelope*

BUSINESS REPLY SERVICE
LICENCE NO. HA4294

Merloni Domestic Appliances Limited,
Merloni House,
3 Cowley business Park,
High Street, Cowley,
UXBRIDGE,
Middlesex
UB8 2BR

Electronic transmission

Imagine that the New York office of your organization has asked you to prepare a report on UK sales figures for the last three months. You prepare the report containing text, tables, and graphs using desktop publishing software. The New York office wants a **hard copy** (i.e. paper copy) of the report and a copy of the computer file. You store the computer file on a floppy disk, print out the report, and send both by special delivery to New York. However, there is a much easier and quicker way of doing this without the need to send paper or disks over long distances.

Electronic mail (E-mail) is an increasingly popular means of sending information and business documents without the need to send paper. Computers linked to the telephone network can send and receive computer files containing business documents to and from other computers all over the world. E-mail can be sent via computers either within the same organization or between different organizations.

To send E-mail, all you have to do is to call up a file on your computer or input a letter or message. You then type in the E-mail 'mailbox'

▼ Figure 14.4: How electronic mail works

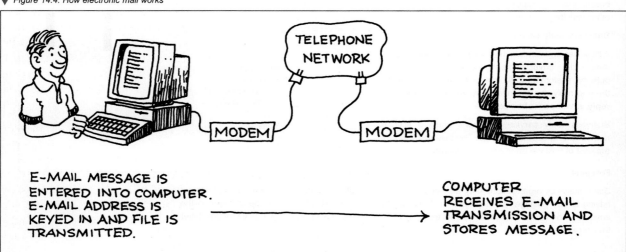

536

address of the computer terminal of the person or organization you are sending it to. An E-mail address code is very similar to a phone number except that it will consist of letters and symbols as well as numbers. For example, 'bigbreakfast@planet24.co.uk' is the well known E-mail address of Channel 4's Big Breakfast TV studios.

Once the E-mail address has been entered, the computer will transmit the document over the phoneline to the other computer, often in just a matter of seconds, even for large amounts of information. The cost of sending the document is charged for in the same way as an ordinary phone call and often costs only a few pence, although the cost will be higher for international transmissions.

A computer at the E-mail address will receive the transmission. The person or organization to whom the computer belongs can then save their file onto their own hard disk or floppy disks, and print out the document.

The advantage of E-mail is that a large number of people at different E-mail addresses can be sent the same message at the same time. Once sent, the message will wait in an electronic mailbox in a computer for the user to access it.

Why E-mail?

- It saves stationery and paper costs
- It allows workers to tele-work from home
- Transmission is rapid
- It reduces the need to talk over the phone and cuts bills
- It can be integrated with other systems, for example, the Internet
- Incoming and outgoing messages can be held in a 'mailbox'
- The time and date of incoming messages are automatically recorded
- Addresses can be stored and recalled
- It has a multiple addressing facility
- Messages can be printed out

The information superhighway

You have probably heard of the Internet. This is a worldwide network of computers linked via telephone lines, often called the 'information superhighway'. Information is free on the Internet – only the use of the telephone is charged for. 'Surfing' the net refers to browsing through all the information it has to offer.

Many companies are now linked via the Internet system, and sending E-mail has become even easier. Commercial uses of the Internet are also increasing as businesses are finding it a useful means of contacting customers and advertising their products.

Facsimile transmissions (FAX)

Fax machines are small desktop machines connected to a telephone line. To operate the fax, the user types in the fax number of the recipient of the message. The sender's fax then rings the receiver's fax and establishes contact (this may be heard as a series of screeching tones). Once contact is made, documents placed in the sender's fax machine are read through one page at a time and the details are sent via the phonelines to print out as an exact copy at the receiver's fax machine.

Fax machines are a useful way of sending pictures, drawings, and many other very urgent documents. Sometimes fax machines may be engaged with other incoming messages or documents, although modern machines often have automatic re-dial facilities. The quality of the printout from a fax machine may also be poor on occasions. You will know yourself from talking on the phone to your friends that phonelines are not always very clear. For the fax machine, this means that transmissions may be faulty. Because of this, it is often better to write or type information you intend to send by fax using larger letter and number sizes.

▼ Fax machines are found in most modern business organizations.

A fax machine is an essential piece of modern business equipment. Prices started at around £199 in 1995 – an affordable amount even for the smallest of businesses. Using a fax is also relatively inexpensive. For most modern machines it will take about one minute to fax ten A4 pages – the cost of a one-minute phone call plus some electricity to power the machine. Larger documents sent by fax and international faxes will clearly be more expensive.

Portfolio Activity 14.11

PC: Identify and evaluate ways to send business documents
Range: Ways to send, Evaluate
Skills: Collect and record data, Produce written material

The business organization you work for has asked you to send out the following documents. They have asked you to find out the easiest, quickest, and cheapest method of doing so in each case. Security is also a consideration for some documents.

- A confidential UK marketing report (weight 10 kilograms). Full colour printed version to be sent to senior managers in Japanese headquarters.

- Letter of complaint to a regular local computer maintenance company for failing to respond to calls for repairs within 2 working days as agreed

- Purchase order for urgent office supplies to office supplies company 100 miles away

- An urgent message for a work colleague to return a call to an important business customer

- A set of presentation slides which are urgently required in the London office for a presentation to government ministers the next day

- Details for customers and employees about refurbishments taking place in four weeks' time in a large department store

- A request for business clients to attend an open evening at an organization, including buffet and refreshments

- Urgent notice of the cancellation of an internal business meeting

Write up your recommendations of the best method(s) of sending each document in a short report.

Choosing the best way to send a business document

There is no 'right' way to send business documents. Each organization must choose a method that best suits their needs. The choice will largely depend on the answers to the following questions:

- **How much does it cost?** Second-class post is clearly one of the cheapest methods of sending mail. But it is rather slow.

- **How urgent is it?** If a document is needed urgently, first-class post offers a better option than second-class. However, there is no guarantee it will arrive the next day. Special delivery is more expensive but can guarantee a delivery time.

● **How bulky is it?** The more a document weighs, the more it will cost to send. Very bulky parcels will need to be sent by a parcel delivery service. Many will guarantee a delivery time for a price.

● **Does the business have access to new technology?** Fax and E-mail are quick and cheap methods of sending documents over long distances. However, both require relatively expensive equipment and phoneline connections. Not all firms have this equipment.

● **How secure is it?** Although it happens very rarely, letters and parcels can be tampered with or lost in the post. Even E-mail may be intercepted by hackers who are able to break into computer files via the phoneline. If documents are confidential it is sensible to send them by registered or recorded delivery.

Section **14.5** **Storing and retrieving documents**

Portfolio Activity 14.12

PC: Identify and evaluate ways to store business documents
Range: Ways to store, Reference, Evaluate
Skills: Collect and record data, Produce written material, Process information

1. Suggest why the following organizations might want to keep documents:

● A doctor's surgery

● A large supermarket

● A toy manufacturer

● A farm

● A clothing shop

● Your school/college

Use a word processor to write up your suggestions

2. Design filing systems that could be used to store important

documents in the organizations listed in task 1. You will need to design your systems so that people who are not familiar with them will be able to find the documents they want quickly and easily.

3. Separate the information you have written on each organization in Tasks 1 and 2 into six individual files to store on a computer floppy disk.

4. Print out your written work in each file and a list of the files you have saved. Attach your floppy disk of files to your printed sheets for inclusion in your portfolio.

Business organizations send and receive a lot of important documents and other information by post, electronic mail, fax, and other methods. It is sensible to keep some of this information in case it is needed again in the future. For example, business letters dealing with customer complaints need to be kept in case similar complaints arise at a later date. Old sales figures may be needed to make comparisons with more recent data. Financial documents on sales and purchases will be needed for tax purposes. What would happen if an employee was taken seriously ill but no records were kept of his or her address or next of kin?

Staff turnover also means that different people could take over responsibility for a number of jobs in the future. They will not know what has gone on in the past if no records have been kept. For example, imagine how difficult it would be for a new member of staff to take over the job of dealing with customer enquiries if the previous person did not keep copies of all the letters s/he had received and written in reply.

What is a filing system?

Business documents that have been stored may one day be needed again. That is why it is important that a business has a quick and easy way of finding them – and why documents need to be filed away in a logical order.

Filing is the storing of correspondence, records, and other documents in business. **Files** are simply devices for storing documents arranged for reference. Files can be:

- Paper-based
- Held on computer

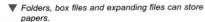

▼ *Folders, box files and expanding files can store papers.*

A **filing system** in a business is the method used to sort and arrange documents into files and store them physically. Every business organization will have its own filing system to suit its particular needs. But all filing systems will involve grouping and sorting documents into some kind of order. A good filing system must be:

- Simple and easy to use
- Safe and secure, to protect important and confidential information from fire and theft
- Suitable for the type of material it contains
- Easily accessible to the people who need to use it
- Consistent, to avoid confusion over where documents should be stored

In addition, a good filing system should have a mechanism for recording what files have been borrowed and who has borrowed them, so that it is possible to trace a file that has not been returned, or that someone else wants to use.

Paper-based filing systems

These rely on different types of filing equipment to hold documents, plans, and other types of material. Papers can be stored in ring binders or card or plastic folders. Box files and expanding files can hold even more papers.

▼ *Lateral filing*

Most files are stored in **filing cabinets**. Filing cabinets contain files in drawers. It is usual to find **suspension files**, which are a continuous chain of cardboard pockets, hung vertically from runners fitted inside cabinet drawers. Files can then be suspended in these pockets. This makes access to each file easier than piling up the files one on top of another.

Filing cabinets can be locked to store confidential files containing important papers. However, cabinets can take up a lot of space and are very heavy to move, especially once they have been filled with files.

Alternatively, files can be arranged on shelves in tall cabinets similar to bookcases. This is called **lateral filing** and is a useful way to store box files.

▲ *Suspension filing*

The main drawback of a paper-based filing system is that it takes up a lot of space. Files are also easily destroyed by fire, although increasingly filing cabinets nowadays can be fireproof, waterproof, and able to withstand being dropped out of a window should anyone attempt to smash them open. Old unwanted files should, however, be destroyed so that they do not take up valuable space.

Another drawback of a paper-based system is that only one person at a time is able to use a file. If documents have been misfiled, it can also take a long time to find them.

Storing documents on computers

Computers provide a fast and easy way of storing large amounts of information. Documents produced on a word processing or desktop publishing program can be saved as separate files. In most programs the user will be able to type in the filename they want to use.

Records can also be stored on a computer **database**. For example, a database might be used to store market research survey data, or names, addresses, and telephone numbers of business clients and customers. The computer can then be used to sort the data into alphabetical order, and/or group it under different headings. For example, peoples' names and addresses could be sorted by postcode into different geographical areas. A computer search function can then be used to find names and numbers stored in the database.

Data on computer can be stored either temporarily or permanently. Information stored temporarily in the computer's **working memory** (or **RAM**) will be lost when the computer is switched off. The more memory a computer has, the more it can store in temporary files. Even the cheapest new personal computers now have around 8 megabytes of memory (8Mb RAM), while top business machines can have 64 megabytes or more.

▼ *Computer files can be stored on floppy disks*

▼ *and CD–ROMs*

▼ *Computer files can be stored on a hard disk inside a computer*

Permanent storage mediums allow computer files to be called up and worked on whenever they are needed:

● **Floppy disks** are portable and available in two sizes: 3.5 inches, and the now obsolete 5.25 inches. Simple commands typed in at the computer keyboard tell the computer to save files to a floppy disk. Disks should be clearly labelled so that you know what is stored on each one.

● **CD-ROMs (Compact Disc – Read Only Memory)** are similar to audio compact discs except that they store much more information than just music. Many newspaper archives, encyclopaedias, and atlases are now available on CD-ROM.

● **Hard disks** are fixed within the computer. Entry-level computers usually provide around 500Mb of disk storage capacity – enough to hold a small library full of information. Some desktop business machines, especially those at the centre of a network, may have up to 3.5 gigabytes of capacity.

The advantages and disadvantages of storing files on computer
The advantages of storing files on computers are:

● A firm can save a great deal of floorspace, and therefore rent, by doing away with filing cabinets and storing business documents on computer instead.

● Files can be retrieved and restored to the computer screen in a matter of seconds. There is no need to go to filing cabinets and spend time searching for the document you want.

● Different people can work on the same files at the same time, if computers are networked or file copies are available on floppy disks. If there is only one paper file, photocopies will have to be made of documents if more than one person wants to use them.

However, relying on computer files to store documents also has disadvantages. These are:

● Computer hard disks can be corrupted by viruses or inexperienced users.

● Computer hackers from outside an organization may 'break into' confidential files stored on computer via phonelines.

● Computers can break down and files may be lost.

● Computers cannot be used during power failures.

Computer security
Computer files need to be protected for a number of reasons:

● They can be accidentally overwritten

● They can be accessed by unauthorized users

● Computer hardware and disks can be stolen

● Computers can be destroyed by fire or water-damaged

- Computers can be corrupted by viruses. These are unwanted programs that can wipe out files if copied onto hard disks by mistake from an 'infected' floppy disk.

Many of the security threats associated with computers can be overcome by taking simple precautions:

- Floppy disks can be 'write protected' simply by sliding a small plastic clip on the disk casing into the appropriate position. This stops any more files being added to the disk and so prevents anyone else from accidentally overwriting files or deleting them.

- Access to computer files can be restricted by using a user identification (user ID) and password system. Authorized users can be given user IDs which the computer is able to recognize. They can also type in a password which enables the computer to double-check that the person logging on is authorized to do so.

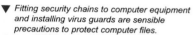

▼ Fitting security chains to computer equipment and installing virus guards are sensible precautions to protect computer files.

- Important files can be saved on both hard disks and floppy disks, and/or recordable CDs (CD-Rs). This means that you have **back-up files** in case anything goes wrong with one set of files, or if your computer or disks are stolen.

- Security chains or anchoring devices can be fitted to computer equipment to prevent it from being moved easily. Also, use electronic security tags or ultra-violet marker pens to mark equipment so that it can be identified easily if it turns up again.

- Floppy disks and CD-Rs containing important files can be stored securely at different locations in fireproof boxes or safes.

- 'Virus guard' programs can be installed which detect unwanted programs and destroy them.

- Most modern organizations also keep both paper and computer files of important documents in case one is lost, destroyed, or stolen.

Arranging filing systems and references

The way in which files and papers are arranged in a filing system is very important. The main ways of arranging files and the documents they contain are:

- By subject
- By number
- By date
- Alphabetically

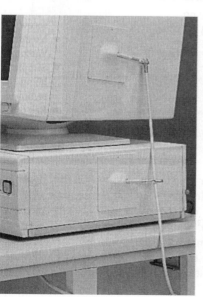

Arranging in subject order

Because there are so many different things a business organization has to deal with, it is sensible to group documents and other information together in files according to the main subject areas they cover. For example, subjects might include human resources, finance, sales, computing, insurance, and purchasing.

▼ *Files can be arranged under different subject headings.*

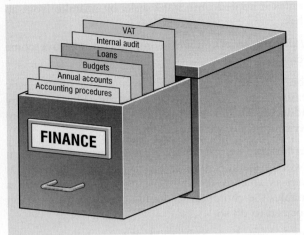

Even within each subject area, there will be many documents and other information covering a host of different topics. For example, within the main subject of human resources there will be documents on employee records, accommodation requirements, sick leave records, training, and pay. It would not be sensible to place all these different documents on the same files. Imagine how difficult it would be to find records on the sick leave of a particular employee if these had simply been filed together with hundreds of other documents on pay, accommodation, and training.

Instead, files can be created for each sub-topic. For example, under the subject heading of 'finance', individual files can be opened to store documents on accounting procedures, budgets, loan agreements, internal audit, VAT, and many other topics.

Arranging by number

Files stored under each subject heading could be numbered for easy reference. For example:

So that people know in which file to store a business document, the person writing a document will often quote the appropriate file reference on their document (see Figure 14.1). For example, a letter sent by a firm to the Customs and Excise department about VAT receipts could show the file reference number AC 3/4/2. Clearly, it is much easier to refer to file numbers on business documents than to keep writing down the full name of the file.

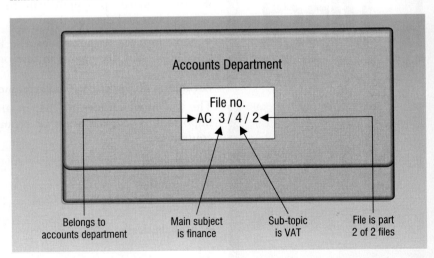

Numbering files also makes it easier to store information on them on a computer database. For example, file details such as name, date opened, whether they have now been closed or destroyed, and details of where they are kept, can be stored under each file number. The computer database will be able to sort files into reference number order. Users can then use the computer to type in the number (or name) of a file they need to retrieve, and call up information on what it contains and where to find it.

Individual documents may also be arranged in number order on files. For example, an estate agent could create separate files for each road in an area, and arrange them in alphabetical order, from, say, 'Acacia Avenue' to 'Zenith Street'. Information on houses and flats in each road can then be put on file in number order. In this way it is easy to look up details about the property at, for example, number 56 Letsby Avenue.

Arranging in date order

Most individual papers on file will be arranged in date, or **chronological**, order, so that the most recent papers are on the top of the file. This is because it makes sense to place documents on file as they are produced or received by an organization. Arranging documents on files in this way is particularly useful if you want to find old documents and know roughly when they were sent or received. As individual files become full they can be closed and filed away in an archive, or even destroyed if the documents they contain are very out of date and are not needed any more.

Arranging alphabetically

It is usual to list subjects and files in alphabetical order. This makes it easier to find documents if you know the first letter of the subject they deal with. In the case of paper-based filing systems, individual filing cabinets can be marked with the first letters of files they contain. For example, a filing cabinet marked 'A-D' could contain files on subjects from 'Administration' to 'Distribution'.

Files stored under each heading can also be arranged in alphabetical order. So, for example, all correspondence with 'Business Customers' could be stored on files arranged in alphabetical order, using the first letter of each business name. Finding records on organizations such as Marks & Spencer Plc, Marshall Food Group Ltd, Mitsushita Electric Industrial Co Ltd, and Mobil Corporation will be easy – they will all be stored under 'M' and in the alphabetical order of letters that follow 'M'.

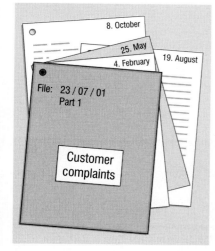

▼ Papers can be filed in date order.

8. October

25. May

19. August

4. February

File: 23 / 07 / 01
Part 1

Customer complaints

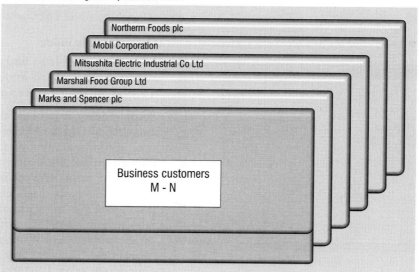

▼ Files can be arranged in alphabetical order.

Northerm Foods plc

Mobil Corporation

Mitsushita Electric Industrial Co Ltd

Marshall Food Group Ltd

Marks and Spencer plc

Business customers
M - N

In the same way, information on people – for example, customers or employees – can be stored alphabetically under their surnames, as they appear in telephone directories. If two people have the same surname, then they will be arranged in order of the first letter(s) of their christian names or initials. For example, files on the following people with the surname Smith would be arranged as follows:

1 Smith, DA

2 Smith, Daphne

3 Smith, Derek G

4 Smith, Francis

5 Smith, FW

6 Smith, SL

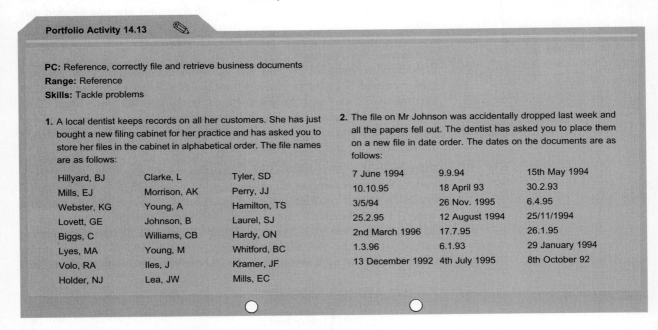

Portfolio Activity 14.13

PC: Reference, correctly file and retrieve business documents
Range: Reference
Skills: Tackle problems

1. A local dentist keeps records on all her customers. She has just bought a new filing cabinet for her practice and has asked you to store her files in the cabinet in alphabetical order. The file names are as follows:

Hillyard, BJ	Clarke, L	Tyler, SD
Mills, EJ	Morrison, AK	Perry, JJ
Webster, KG	Young, A	Hamilton, TS
Lovett, GE	Johnson, B	Laurel, SJ
Biggs, C	Williams, CB	Hardy, ON
Lyes, MA	Young, M	Whitford, BC
Volo, RA	Iles, J	Kramer, JF
Holder, NJ	Lea, JW	Mills, EC

2. The file on Mr Johnson was accidentally dropped last week and all the papers fell out. The dentist has asked you to place them on a new file in date order. The dates on the documents are as follows:

7 June 1994	9.9.94	15th May 1994
10.10.95	18 April 93	30.2.93
3/5/94	26 Nov. 1995	6.4.95
25.2.95	12 August 1994	25/11/1994
2nd March 1996	17.7.95	26.1.95
1.3.96	6.1.93	29 January 1994
13 December 1992	4th July 1995	8th October 92

▼ Electronic card files can now be set up and stored on many computers.

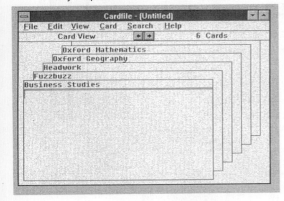

Creating a file index

In order to be able to find and retrieve documents from a filing system, users need to know how the filing system is arranged. This can be done by preparing an **index**.

Some indexes may contain all the information you need – for example, an index of business names, addresses, and telephone, fax, and E-mail numbers. Other indexes will only contain enough information for the user to find what they want elsewhere, rather like the index in a book. For example, a good index will contain brief details of what is on each file and where it is stored. An index can also be useful for cross-referencing, if relevant information on the same or similar topics is placed in different files. For example, under the index reference for 'marketing', a user may also be advised to look at files containing related papers on 'advertising budgets', 'pricing strategies', and 'product development'.

One of the easiest way to set up an index is to use a **card file**. One card can be completed for each file in the system. It can show the number, name, and location of the file in the filing system. All the cards can then be sorted by file number or by subject.

A card file index is also useful for keeping track of which files have been borrowed, the date they were taken, and who borrowed them. Every time a file is borrowed, the card for that file can be used to note who has taken it and when.

An example of a filing system

Let us now look at a real example of a paper-based filing system used by the London Traffic Assessment Division in the Department of Transport. This division is responsible for running computer simulation models of London transport networks, undertaking research into transport, and providing advice to government policy makers.

Themes

The first step in creating the filing system was to identify major subject headings, or **themes**. Each theme was then given a number. The 9 themes were:

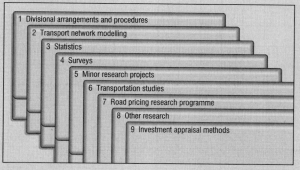

1 Divisional arrangements and procedures
2 Transport network modelling
3 Statistics
4 Surveys
5 Minor research projects
6 Transportation studies
7 Road pricing research programme
8 Other research
9 Investment appraisal methods

Sub-themes

The next stage in setting up the filing system was to identify a number of **sub-themes** within each main subject area. For example, the following sub-themes were created within theme 1 (Divisional arrangements and procedures):

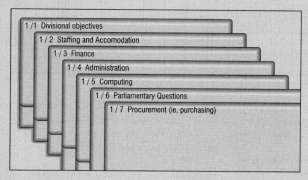

1 / 1 Divisional objectives
1 / 2 Staffing and Accomodation
1 / 3 Finance
1 / 4 Administration
1 / 5 Computing
1 / 6 Parliamentary Questions
1 / 7 Procurement (ie. purchasing)

Sub-themes can be identified by their numbers. For example, 1/4 tells us that the main theme is Divisional arrangements and procedures, and the sub-theme is Administration. Similarly, files with numbers starting with 4/4 would tell us that they contained documents and information on Surveys, and in this case the sub-theme would be surveys of land use.

Files

The next stage was to create individually numbered files to store documents on specialized topics within each sub-theme. For example, within sub-theme 1/1 the following files exist:

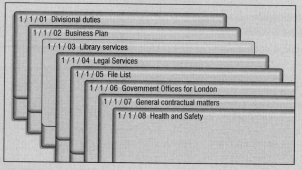

1 / 1 / 01 Divisional duties
1 / 1 / 02 Business Plan
1 / 1 / 03 Library services
1 / 1 / 04 Legal Services
1 / 1 / 05 File List
1 / 1 / 06 Government Offices for London
1 / 1 / 07 General contractual matters
1 / 1 / 08 Health and Safety

Storing documents on file

Documents are stored on individual files in date order, with the most recent documents on top.

Preparing a file list

To allow everyone who works in the London Traffic Assessment division to retrieve information stored in files, a file list was prepared listing all the files under each theme, their file numbers, the number of the filing cabinets in which they are stored, and the numbers of rooms in which filing cabinets are located. So, for example, it was possible to use the file list to locate file number 2/2/08, in cabinet 4 in room 14/02.

Computer files

All the staff employed in the division produce their own documents using word processors. They save the documents they have produced either on the hard disk of their personal computer or on floppy disk, so that they can retrieve documents easily if required and make changes to them.

Computer files will often be stored in subject order in directories created on computer hard disks. The computers can then sort files that have been saved either by date or alphabetically by filename.

In 1995, there were over 200 files stored in cabinets in the offices of employees who worked in the London Traffic Assessment Division – just some of the many thousands of paper and computer files stored in the entire Department of Transport. That is the equivalent of an awful lot of trees!

Portfolio Activity 14.14

PC: Reference, correctly file and retrieve business documents
Range: Ways to store, Reference, Evaluate
Skills: Collect and record data, Produce written material

1. Investigate the filing system used in your school/college.

2. Produce a notice to be pinned up in your school/college office to explain how to use the filing system. This should include examples of how the system can be used to find the following files:

- Smith, AJ (a student)
- Sports Department budget

(It does not matter that these files might not actually exist. It is how the filing system *might* be used to find them that is important.)

Remember that your notice should be clear and easy to understand, free of errors, and have a pleasing layout.

3. Write up your evaluation of the school/college filing system in terms of:

- How easy it is to store documents correctly
- How easy it is find and retrieve documents
- How secure documents are

Key crossword

Clues across

1. A paperless way of sending information over phonelines between two computers (10,4).

6. A device for holding papers arranged for reference (4).

8. The abbreviation for a computer program which can be used to write and arrange text and pictures like a newspaper (1,1,1).

9. The abbreviation for computer programs which are used to type and layout business documents (1,1).

11. The disk inside your computer that sounds like it might feel (4).

12. A method of posting letters quickly to other countries (7).

16. A teleprinting device which can send and receive typed messages over phonelines (5)

17. The name given to a copy of a file on a computer disk which should be made in case of fire damage, corruption, or theft of the original (4,2).

19. A method of sending letters with a guaranteed time of arrival at the mailing address (7,8).

Clues down

2. A fast, high-quality printer for computers (5,7).

3. Documents containing factual information, usually pinned up where everyone can see them (7).

4. The long name for a memo (10).

5. A formal written request to attend a business function (10).

7. Important business documents used to write to customers and other organizations (7).

10. A machine that is able to make exact copies of documents (11).

13. A paper copy of a document sent over a phone line by a machine (3).

14. A small computer disk which can be used to store files (6).

15. You will need one of these to post a letter (5).

18. Abbreviation for those compact disks which can be used to record files from computer (1,1,1)

You must demonstrate that you are able to:

1. Explain the purpose of routine business documents

2. Produce draft and final versions of business documents

3. Evaluate each business document produced

4. Compare the methods of processing business documents

5. Reference, correctly file, and retrieve business documents

6. Identify and evaluate ways to send and ways to store business documents

This unit is not examined externally. However, the following questions will help you test and revise your understanding of the range in element 4.3.

Questions 1-3 share the following answer options:

A to communicate with customers

B to communicate with other businesses

C to communicate with colleagues

D to keep records

Which of the above purposes will the following business documents serve?

1 Writing a memo to remind managers within a business that the time and venue of a meeting have been changed

2 Producing a standard letter to advertise the services of a new business

3 Writing a letter to a supplier to confirm arrangements for deliveries

Questions 4-6 share the following answer options:

A standard business letter

B invitation

C memo

D personal business letter

Which of the above business documents would you use in the following situations?

4 To reply to a customer who has complained about receiving the wrong order

5 To attach an urgent request for photocopying to a business report

6 To ask important customers to attend a Christmas party

Questions 7-9 share the following answer options:

A E-mail

B special delivery

C fax

D second-class post

Which of the above ways to send documents would best suit the following requirements?

7 Sending out 5,000 standard business letters to potential customers

8 A word-processed document containing written text and tables of figures that is needed urgently in the Northern Ireland office of an organization based in London

9 Sending 10 copies of a printed report to the German headquarters of an organization, to arrive before an important business meeting tomorrow

10 Handwritten business messages have the following advantages except:

A they are personalized

B errors cannot be corrected easily

C short messages can be written quickly

D they do not require electronic equipment

11 Sending documents by E-mail has all of the following advantages except:

A it saves stationery and paper costs

B transmission is rapid

C the cost of sending documents is relatively cheap

D you need a personal computer linked to the telephone network

Questions 12-14 share the following answer options:

A by subject

B by date

C by number

D alphabetically

Which of the above methods of filing documents are best used for the following:

12 A pile of letters of enquiry from potential customers that have yet to be replied to

13 Details of houses and flats in different roads that are for sale in an estate agents

14 Reports on the performance of different departments in a business organization

The following assignment meets the evidence requirements needed to fulfill all the performance criteria in element 4.3. In addition it covers the following range points and core skills:

Range: Purpose
Business documents
Evaluate documents
Compare
Reference
Ways to send
Ways to store
Evaluate ways to send and store

Skills: Communication
Produce written material
Use images
Application of number
Collect and record data
Information technology
Prepare information
Process information
Present information

Tasks

1. You work in a firm that specializes in carpet and upholstery cleaning services. You are asked to produce draft and final versions of the following documents (the names, addresses, and other details of people and organizations can be made up):

- A business letter replying to a customer complaint about the service they received that shrunk their expensive Chinese rug.

- A memo to senior managers notifying them that a meeting has had to be cancelled at short notice. They will be advised of a new date, time, and venue for the meeting soon.

- An invitation to local business owners to attend an evening presentation on the services provided by your organization. The presentation will be followed by light refreshments.

- A notice advising employees of Christmas leave arrangements

- A message of a telephone call for your absent colleague. The call is from a customer who would like to know if she can change the time of her appointment next week to clean her hall carpet from 10 am to 2 pm in the afternoon.

You may use different methods to produce the above documents in draft form.

2. Before you produce final versions of the documents in Task 1, in small groups, check the spelling, grammar and intended layout of all your documents. Produce a short note to explain what you liked/disliked and what was right/wrong for each draft document.

3. Now produce final versions of your own draft documents. You can use the same or different methods to produce them. Take photocopies, or print multiple copies of your final documents to provide to members of your small group. They will do the same. Together, evaluate each document in terms of quality of appearance, style, and layout. Check spelling and grammar again, in case you did not spot all the mistakes in your drafts. Write up your evaluations in a short note.

4. Collect together your own draft and final documents, and your written notes, to include in your portfolio.

To complete the following Tasks 5-8, you will need to choose an organization to investigate. This could be your school or college, work experience placement, or your employer.

5. Investigate the following methods used to produce and copy business documents:

- Handwriting
- Typing
- Word processing
- Printing
- Photocopying
- Obtain examples of documents produced by each method.

6. From your investigations in Task 5, prepare a summary to compare the methods of producing the business documents you have collected in terms of:

- Quality of production and readability
- Time taken to produce documents
- Cost of each method (in terms of staff time, paper costs, number of machines needed, power consumption, etc.)
- Ease of making changes
- Ease of storage

7. Investigate the filing system used in your organization. What methods are used to store and reference documents?

8. Use the filing system in the organization over a number of weeks. Provide a record that shows clearly how you have referenced, filed, and retrieved at least 36 different documents and 6 files.

Alternatively, organize a filing system for all the work you have stored in your portfolio. Decide on appropriate subject headings for files and an appropriate referencing system. For example, one subject could be 'Business documents'. This could be divided into 'Financial documents' and 'Non-financial documents'. Business letters could then be referenced and stored under 1/2/1 to denote the subject, part, and sub-section. Then make a record to show clearly how you have referenced, filed, and retrieved at least 36 documents from your portfolio from at least 6 files.

Appendix ☛

Index

Where more than one page reference is shown for a particular subject, pages containing main text and definitions are in bold if appropriate.